Communications
in Computer and Information Science 1066

Commenced Publication in 2007
Founding and Former Series Editors:
Phoebe Chen, Alfredo Cuzzocrea, Xiaoyong Du, Orhun Kara, Ting Liu,
Krishna M. Sivalingam, Dominik Ślęzak, Takashi Washio, and Xiaokang Yang

Editorial Board Members

More information about this series at http://www.springer.com/series/7899

Anirban Sengupta · Sudeb Dasgupta ·
Virendra Singh · Rohit Sharma ·
Santosh Kumar Vishvakarma (Eds.)

VLSI Design and Test

23rd International Symposium, VDAT 2019
Indore, India, July 4–6, 2019
Revised Selected Papers

Editors
Anirban Sengupta, FIET, FBCS
Computer Science and Engineering
Indian Institute of Technology Indore
Indore, India

Virendra Singh
Department of Electrical Engineering
Indian Institute of Technology Bombay
Mumbai, India

Santosh Kumar Vishvakarma
Electrical Engineering
Indian Institute of Technology Indore
Indore, India

Sudeb Dasgupta
Department of Electronics
and Communication Engineering
Indian Institute of Technology Roorkee
Roorkee, India

Rohit Sharma
Department of Electrical Engineering
Indian Institute of Technology Ropar
Rupnagar, India

ISSN 1865-0929   ISSN 1865-0937 (electronic)
Communications in Computer and Information Science
ISBN 978-981-32-9766-1   ISBN 978-981-32-9767-8 (eBook)
https://doi.org/10.1007/978-981-32-9767-8

This Springer imprint is published by the registered company Springer Nature Singapore Pte Ltd.
The registered company address is: 152 Beach Road, #21-01/04 Gateway East, Singapore 189721, Singapore

Preface

This book presents the state of the art developments on advances in VLSI for IoT and consumer electronics. The book is comprised of several important contributions by leading experts in the field. The chapters presented in this book, as contributions, are part of the 23rd International Symposium on VLSI Design and Test (VDAT 2019), held during July 4–6, 2019, in Indore, India. The contributions were rigorously peer reviewed by a team of leading experts from industry and academia. VDAT 2019 was spearheaded by the following international leaders: general chairs, Dr. Anirban Sengupta, *FIET, FBCS* (IIT Indore) and Dr. Santosh Kumar Vishvakarma (IIT Indore).

Each chapter of this book, adopted from VDAT 2019 proceedings, has been peer-reviewed by at least 2 reviewers (single-blind) in terms of novelty, technical correctness, impact of contribution, and advancement to the state of the art. There were 199 submissions in total for VDAT 2019 from around the world and there were 63 accepted papers under oral and poster category. Each of the accepted conference papers have been lucidly presented as a book chapter in these proceedings. The collection of these important contributions are grouped into six categories:

- Analog and Mixed Signal Design
- Computing Architecture and Security
- Hardware Design and Optimization
- Low Power VLSI and Memory Design
- Device Modeling
- Hardware Implementation

The Technical Program Committee of VDAT 2019, who performed the review process, comprised of more than 80 experts nationally and internationally. The authors who contributed to this book spanned across several countries ranging from India, USA, Austria, Germany, Italy, Sweden, UK, etc. This truly reflects the international nature of the contributions compiled under this book.

We sincerely hope that you will enjoy the contributions of the book and that it will serve as a great reading for experts, students, practitioners, designers, researchers, and academics. We, the editors, would like to thank all the contributing authors, reviewers, and other supporting members for their help.

July 2019

Anirban Sengupta
Sudeb Dasgupta
Virendra Singh
Rohit Sharma
Santosh Kumar Vishvakarma

Organization

Steering Committee

V. Agrawal	Auburn University, USA
Jaswinder Ahuja	Cadence Noida, India
A. Bharadwaj	IISc Bangalore, India
Santanu Chaudhury	IIT Jodhpur, India
Satya Gupta	SenZopt Bangalore, India
Manoj S. Gaur	IIT Jammu, India
M. Huebner	BTU, Germany
Milos Krstic	IHP, Germany
Roy P. Paily	IIT Guwahati, India
Niranjan Pol	Seagate Pune, India
V. Ramgopal Rao	IIT Delhi, India
Anirban Sengupta	IIT Indore, India
Surindra Singh	SCL Mohali, India
Sunita Verma	MeitY New Delhi, India

Program Committee

Satyadev Ahlawat	IIT Bombay, India
Sk Subidh Ali	IIT Bhilai, India
Naushad Alam	Aligarh Muslim University, India
Ansuman Banerjee	Indian Statistical Institute, India
Kunal Banerjee	Intel, India
Gaurab Banerjee	IISc Bangalore, India
Lava Bhargava	MNIT, India
Sitangshu Bhattacharya	IIIT Allahabad, India
Fabrizio Bonani	Politecnico di Torino, Italy
Dharmendar Boolchandani	MNIT, India
Susanta Chakraborty	IIEST Shibpur, India
Rajat Subhra Chakraborty	IIT Kharagpur, India
Anjan Chakravorty	IIT Madras, India
Rajeevan Chandel	NIT Hamirpur, India
Shouri Chatterjee	IIT Delhi, India
Shaileshsingh Chouhan	Aalto University, Finland
Bishnu Prasad Das	IIT Roorkee, India
Sudeep Dasgupta	IIT Roorkee, India
Masahiro Fujita	The University of Tokyo, Japan
Chandan Giri	IIEST Shibpur, India
Neeraj Goel	IIT Ropar, India
Simona Donati Guerrieri	Politecnico di Torino, Dipartimento di Elettronica, Italy

Prasanta Guha	IIT Kharagpur, India
Vinayak Hande	IIT Ropar, India
Ramrakesh Jangir	Government Polytechnic Narwana, India
John Jose	IIT Guwahati, India
Hemangee Kapoor	IIT Guwahati, India
Sougata Kar	NIT Rourkela, India
Chandan Karfa	IIT Guwahati, India
Abhijit Karmakar	CSIR-CEERI Pilani, India
Baljit Kaur	NIT Delhi, India
Brajesh Kumar Kaushik	IIT Roorkee, India
Subhadip Kundu	Synopsys, India
Kusum Lata	LNMIIT Jaipur, India
Trupti Lenka	NIT Silchar, India
Manoj Kumar Majumder	International Institute of Information Technology, Naya Raipur, India
Shubhankar Majumdar	NIT Meghalaya, India
Sushanta Mandal	Centurion University of Technology and Management, India
Anzhela Matrosova	Tomsk State University, Russia
Usha Mehta	Nirma University Ahmedabad, India
Nihar Mohapatra	IIT Gandhinagar, India
Arijit Mondal	IIT Patna, India
Subhankar Mukherjee	Cadence Noida, India
Madhu Mutyam	IIT Madras, India
Ashutosh Nandi	IIT Roorkee, India
Sergei Ostanin	Tomsk State University, Russia
Pankaj Kumar Pal	NIT Uttarakhand, India
Ajit Panda	NIST Berhampur, India
Preeti Ranjan Panda	IIT Delhi, India
Brajesh Pandey	IIT Bombay, India
Soumya Pandit	University of Calcutta, India
Gayadhar Pradhan	IIT Patna, India
Hafizur Rahaman	IIEST Shibpur, India
Balwinder Raj	NIT Jalandhar, India
Ashwani Rana	NIT Hamirpur, India
Surendra Rathod	IIT Roorkee, India
Karun Rawat	IIT Roorkee, India
Sudip Roy	IIT Roorkee, India
Debasri Saha	University of Calcutta, India
Mounita Saha	IIT Kharagpur, India
Vineet Sahula	Malaviya National Institute of Technology Jaipur, India
Arnab Sarkar	IIT Guwahati, India
Biplab Sarkar	IIT Roorkee, India
Pallabi Sarkar	VIT University, India
Manoj Saxena	Deen Dayal Upadhyaya College and University of Delhi, India

Contents

Computing Architecture and Security

Hardware Design and Optimization

Low Power VLSI and Memory Design

Device Modelling

Hardware Implementation

Analog and Mixed Signal Design

Automations and Methodologies for Efficient and Quality Conscious Analog Layout Implementation

Varun Kumar Dwivedi$^{(\boxtimes)}$, Madhvi Sharma, and Chandaka Venu

STMicroelectronics Pvt. Ltd., Noida, India
{varun.dwivedi,madhvi.sharma}@st.com

Abstract. Though there has been spectacular development of EDA tools for digital circuit implementations and validations, analog and custom circuit implementation have been slow in catching up. There are some layout design requirements unique to Analog layout such as Tiling, Fringe capacitance usage, and Dummy devices insertion for matching. Validation of Analog layout before BE delivery is another area which requires many additional checks owing to unique Analog nature such as Extended Pin, SRD, LFD, PERC, voltage marker check etc. Efforts have been put to automate some design and verifications tasks which took considerable manual effort and consumed more EDA license resources. This paper presents such automations and flow development which has resulted in productivity enhancement and ensures better quality layout deliverables. Paper presents conventional methods and practices, the proposed scripts and methodologies and gains thereof.

Keywords: Matching · Tilling · Fringe cap · Analog layout implementation · Physical design validation · Current mirror · Differential amplifier caliber · PERL and shell languages

1 Introduction

With the increasing number of applications demanding Voltage Regulators, Temperature and Voltage sensors, PLL etc. there is a growing need for different analog IPs to be developed to address different aspects of specifications. These include requirements like high performance, high density, low power etc. This requires a number of analog IPs to be delivered for a particular technology node, which are optimized and tuned for different end applications. So, to take advantage of the latest technology shrink, it is very important that the cycle time of the overall IPs generation process is reduced as far as possible. One of the major bottlenecks in this process is the layout generation phase which traditionally involves manual efforts Shrinking technologies and complex Design Rules have further increased the time cycle for layout development. It has also increased the license cost for layout development tools such as Cadence Interactive license, DRC/LVS licenses. In order to bring down the layout generation cycle time and cost, the paper presents four different methodologies addressing different aspects of

© Springer Nature Singapore Pte Ltd. 2019
A. Sengupta et al. (Eds.): VDAT 2019, CCIS 1066, pp. 3–13, 2019.
https://doi.org/10.1007/978-981-32-9767-8_1

analog layout development. Automations are done using combinations of Cadence SKILL [1], Mentor Caliber [2], and PERL [3] and Shell [4] languages.

Significant automation exists for the development of the custom analog layout however in validation part flow is not as matured to reduce the cycle time. Sections 2 and 3 present a Combined Validation Check Solution to address validation need of Analog Layouts.

Sections 4, 5 and 6 present the automations to address three unique requirements of Analog layout development.

2 Layout Verification: Existing Method

At nanometer nodes, design signoff is no longer just DRC and LVS as shown in Fig. 1. These basic components of physical verification are being augmented by an expansive set of yield analysis and critical feature identification capabilities, as well as layout enhancements, and printability and performance validation like (SRD, BE Lithography Hot-Spot & P&R Auto-Correction), Embedded metrology (FE + BE), Redundant VIA, IP (density) Check, PERC checks. It has now become mandatory to have essential techniques for circuit verification strategies and tools to effectively and efficiently address the reliability and functional yield challenges of today's advanced and complex IC designs.

Tech	DRC	LVS	SRD	LFD BE	LFD FE	VIA R	IP den.	PERC GDS	PERC CDL
90nm	√	√	X	X	X	X	X	X	X
65nm	√	√	X	X	X	X	X	√	√
40nm	√	√	X	X	X	X	X	√	√
28nm	√	√	√	√	√	√	√	√	√

Fig. 1. Validations across the technology

License management is a very critical aspect especially for layout verifications like DRC/LVS/DFM/SRD and many other Signoff/quality checks due to limited number of licenses. In interactive mode each task occupies one caliber interactive license resulting in long waiting time due to limited availability. As number of sign off checks is large, as shown in Fig. 2, this can result in loss of time in license queues.

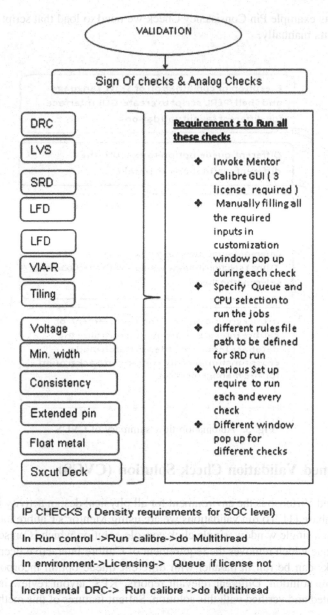

Fig. 2. Steps involved to run a single validation DRC

To run each validation it requires number of inputs. For example to run DRC we need to specify large number of inputs as shown in Fig. 3. Similar inputs are required to run LVS, SRD, Tiling, via redundancy. To run analog design specific checks like extended pin, SXcut Deck, Minimum metal width, floating metal check we have to load deck path manually and then need to specify inputs as shown in Fig. 2. To run various scripts example Pin Consistency Check we need to load that script and provide multiple inputs manually.

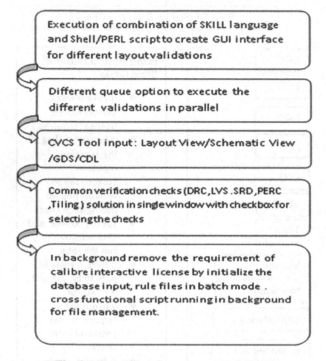

Fig. 3. Automation flow summary of CVCS

3 Combined Validation Check Solution (CVCS)

Cadence based Virtuoso is the environment for all physical design activity it can handle CDSOA database [1]. To run validations we are using Mentor's Calibre tool [2]. So we came up with a single window, single click console solution which is presented here as a first technique which removes the requirement of Calibre interactive license. Also, all signoff checks can be run in parallel with different queue option incorporated in this single window solution. Different relevant reports, KPS, layout review inputs can be easily generated and verified with this solution. Salient features of this methodology are (Fig. 4):

- Reduced run time of all checks (no need of caliber Interactive license)
- Single window as well as single click solution for all signoff checks (Run DRC, LVS, PERC, GDS, perc CDL, SRD, Voltage marker, Extended pin tiling, Via redundancy, LIBBE, consistency check, bulk check)
- Automation of BE delivery signoff checks
- Can be used to get results of DRC/LVS/PLS/SRD/VIAREDUNDANCY PERCCDL/ PERCGDS/TILING for sub blocks

- Reduces number of inputs
- All checks run on Parallel queues to shorten time
- Single GDS/CDL extraction for all checks
- Dump all reports in single directory
- Checks for latest DK from upt and flash if different from .ucdprod

Fig. 4. Combine validation check solution

4 Analog Tiling Generator

In advanced technology node IC designs, dummy geometric shapes density fill structures are required to maintain layer planarity at the time of chemical mechanical polishing (CMP) process. For mixed-signal physical designs, these flows have been seen to have concerns as necessity to maintain symmetric, ordered, non- floating dummy filling for critical analog section. As in case of sensors sub block ADC and PLL sub block VCO it is mandatory to fill these structure manually. Tiling may result in parasitic capacitances which can have undesired effects in high accuracy analog IPs. CAD layers are put in the critical areas of such IPs. Designer put these structure meeting all the requirement and tie these structure to required potential according to design requirement. But it is very tedious and time consuming process. Some time there is probability of design left with floating structure then we run one deck to ensure non floating dummies.

4.1 Proposed Solution

The Smart density fill tool functionality is Controllable, uniform & symmetric. Tool is written in skill language. We can fill density in specific area according to design requirement. Single click solution has been proposed as second technique here for calculating and generating these dummy tiling. Salient features are (Fig. 5):

- Metal dummy for all the FE and BE layer
- Uniform controllable dummy filling
- No floating Dummy (Connect all the dummy together as much as possible)
- Minimum and maximum density control
- Density gradient control
- Fill geometrical transforms including mirroring
- Consider sign off checks specially DRC

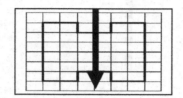

Fig. 5. Half symmetric & uniform

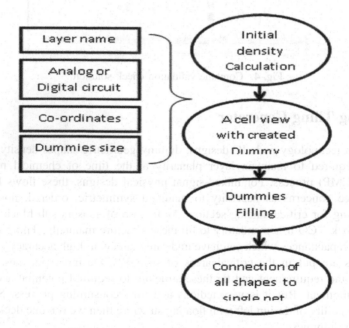

Fig. 6. Key steps of flow of uniform tiling

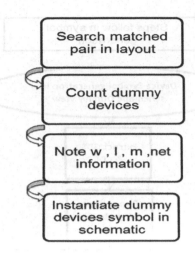

Fig. 7. Manual steps is dummy device symbol insertion

Key step of flow is explained in Fig. 6. It require BE FE information, coordinates, dummies size as input and generate tiles accordingly.

5 Dummy Devices Symbol Creation for Lvs Cleaning

Analog layout often requires dummy devices on the sides of matched devices to reduce the well proximity effect, corner effect and for stress reduction [5]. Dummy device information needs to be put in schematic once layout of that particular circuit is done because of following reasons:

- In advanced technology nodes if floating dummy devices are present in layout in critical areas then it can affect the circuit performance. All dummy devices present in layout must present in schematic with appropriate potential to ensure that there are no surprises in post layout simulations.
- Insertion of Dummy device in schematic for LVS cleaning
- Visibility to designer for available dummy devices for usage in future

Adding dummy devices manually in schematic for sign off LVS can be very cumbersome and time consuming process. Multiple loops are often required between schematic and layout designer to clean the LVS. Conventional Manual flow is shown in Fig. 7. A script to automate the dummy insertion in schematic has been developed. The algorithm is shown in Fig. 8. Schematic is updated by inserting dummy devices as indicated in Fig. 9.

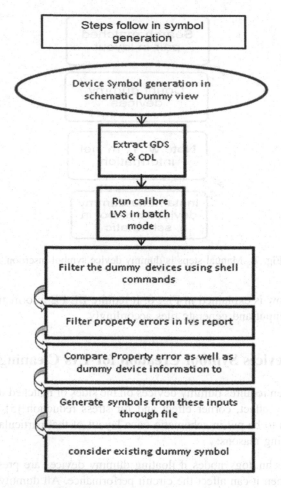

Fig. 8. Steps involve in dummy device symbol generation flow

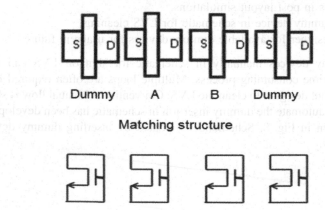

Fig. 9. Dummy in matching structure, and symbols the script generate in schematic

6 Fringe Cap Pcell

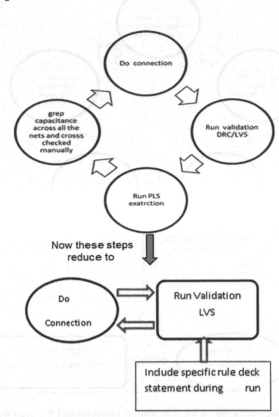

Fig. 10. Fringe capacitance validation conventional v/s proposed methodology

Capacitors are frequently used in ADC/DAC based IPs in large numbers and in complex interconnections. Metal fringe capacitors are often used to implement the capacitors because of their better matching and linearity [7, 8]. In many technologies fringe capacitors are not offered as device thus making correct layout implementation a time consuming process. Many ad-hoc procedures are adopted for LVS cleaning such as placing small resistances in schematic and layout at capacitor nodes which is a very cumbersome process. Correctness of implementation can only be guaranteed after exhaustive post layout simulations which may be very late in product cycle. Analog circuits comprise metal fringe capacitors in critical section. These capacitors consist of metal stripes and have good matching. The critical requirement is in analog circuits where mismatch of the order of 0.05% is desired (ADC capacitor bank). In some processes, there is a thin dielectric between two metal layer and a specific material is used as dielectric to increase the capacitance density to around 1fF/µm2. In Design Kit (DK) technology library we have these capacitors accessible but to accomplish high quality we customized them according to our requirements i.e. symmetric, mirrored,

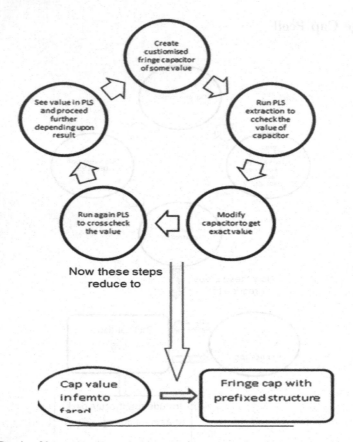

Fig. 11. Precise fringe capacitance implementation conventional v/s proposed methodology

effective, high quality, area, metals used, coupling effects and many more. But problem occurs in validation of these modified capacitors.

- It does not catch any open in between metal rails of the capacitor can only capture during post layout parasitic extraction.
- There is also probability of getting cross connection between two fringe capacitors between two nets which can also capture during post layout parasitic extraction.

P-cell based custom fringe structure is proposed as forth technique to assist in glitch free and simple layout implementation in presence of fringe capacitors. Comparison of steps involves in design of customized fringe capacitors with and without the proposed methodology is shown in Figs. 10 and 11.

7 Conclusion

Validation is a key step in physical design process that directly affects the cost, quality, yield, performance of those circuits in as we are moving to lower node the number of checks is increasing already discussed in paper. CVCS methodology leads to cost saving as well as improve quality. Its implementation has resulted in Zero caliber interactive license usage in Analog team. Any time at least #3 licenses were used earlier leading to a saving of 30K dollars. The solution has also been adapted for other design teams such as SRAM which should enable further license cost saving. Automatic tiling generation for critical analog section results in achieving high performance along with half day saving of manual effort every time such layout is done. Dummy symbol generation results in saving 2 man days of efforts for analog IP's such as thermal sensor, regulator & PLL. Fringe Capacitor methodology has resulted in easier LVS cleaning resulting in #2 man days effort saving and also ensure Zero surprise during Post layout simulations.

References

1. Smith, T.F., Waterman, M.S.: Identification of Common Molecular Subsequences. J. Cadence online support. http://www.cadenceonlinesupport
2. Calibre yield Enhancer Mentor Graphics. www.mentor.com/products/ic_nanometer.../calibre-yieldenhancer
3. Perl Monks. www.perlmonks.com
4. Unix & Linux Stack Exchange. unix.stackexchange.com/
5. Hastings, A.: The Art of Analog Layout, 2nd edn. (2006)
6. SVRF - Mentor Graphics. www.mentor.com/.../svrf-aea5db04-3174-4fcc-8887-0f833e78cabc
7. Design and Optimization of Metal-Metal Comb-Capacitors - OEA. www.oea.com/assets/files/Optimiz_Metal.pdf
8. High-Resolution 12-Bit Segmented Capacitor DAC in Successive. waset.org/.../high-resolution-12-bit-segmented-capacitor-dac-in-successive

A 2.4 GHz High Efficiency Capacitive Cross Coupled Common Gate Class-E Differential Power Amplifier

Archana Sunitha[(⊠)] and Bhaskar Manickam

NIT Tiruchirappalli, Tiruchirappalli, TamilNadu, India
archa.vrindavan@gmail.com

Abstract. In this paper, a fully integrated, differential, common gate class-E power amplifier with capacitive cross-coupling is proposed for wireless applications at 2.4 GHz. Capacitive cross-coupled (CCC) common gate structure enhances the power added efficiency (PAE) and reduces the total harmonic distortion (THD) of the circuit. The power amplifier, implemented in UMC 180 nm technology, is designed without series harmonic rejection tanks and uses dc feed inductor. Post-layout simulations with corner analysis are performed in Cadence Virtuoso tool. The power amplifier achieves a maximum PAE of 52%, output power of 18 dBm and third harmonic distortion of −25 dBm for 1.8 V supply.

Keywords: Class-E power amplifier · Common gate · Capacitive cross coupled

1 Introduction

Future wireless applications demand low power and cost-effective fully integrated system-on-chip transmitters as well as receivers. At 2.4 GHz Industrial, Scientific and Medical (ISM) band, wireless application include ZigBee, WLAN and wireless sensor networks etc. At the transmitter side, power amplifier is the main block that consumes high power and area. Technology scaling aids in reducing the total chip area. In addition, optimization of the power amplifier in terms of power added efficiency and area could improve the overall performance of the transmitter. A high PAE indicates higher output power, lower power dissipation and better reliability. Switching power amplifiers have higher PAE compared to linear power amplifiers since the switching transistors are operated as a switches [1], when the modulation is digital. Hence class-E PAs can however be used in transmitters that use digital modulation techniques [2]. Class-E power amplifier is a switching mode amplifier. It can be of RF Choke or DC feed inductance type [3]. In RF choke type, the inductors are bulky, hence it is difficult for integration. DC feed inductance type uses small inductors between power supply and switching transistor. This reduces chip area consumed and lowers power dissipation.

The output of the power amplifier can be increased by using a cascode topology since a higher supply voltage can be chosen. Cascode topology also provides good

© Springer Nature Singapore Pte Ltd. 2019
A. Sengupta et al. (Eds.): VDAT 2019, CCIS 1066, pp. 14–22, 2019.
https://doi.org/10.1007/978-981-32-9767-8_2

isolation between the input and output. A differential architecture provides higher output power and is less sensitive to common mode noise fluctuations, hence better resistance to noise. It removes even harmonics and provides better reduction in THD. A 5.7 GHz differential class-E power amplifier in [4] uses complementary CMOS cross coupled technology to realize an LC tank oscillator. It has lower phase noise, better THD and a PAE of 42%. In [5], cross coupling neutralization has been employed to the differential power amplifier at 2.4 GHz to achieve a PAE of 43.6%. The differential class-E amplifier at 2.43 GHz in [6] has its series harmonic rejection tanks eliminated for improving the PAE and achieves a high PAE of 48%.

A capacitive cross coupling common gate architecture which lowers power consumption as well as THD is used in the proposed 2.4 GHz class-E power amplifier to achieve high PAE. The power amplifier is of cascode differential structure. Common gate amplifier provides better bandwidth, linearity and stability, while capacitive cross coupling is used to enhance the output power and lower the dc power consumed. A dc feed inductor is used in the circuit and the series tanks are eliminated for optimum chip area consumption. In Sect. 2, the circuit design is described. Section 3 gives the post layout results of the proposed power amplifier and also includes discussions on the results. Section 4 concludes the paper.

2 Circuit Design

A typical dc feed inductance class-E power amplifier is shown in Fig. 1.

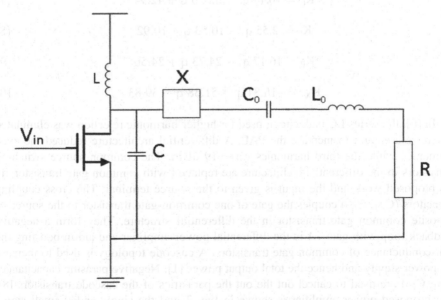

Fig. 1. Circuit diagram of dc feed inductance class-E power amplifier

L is the dc feed inductor and C is the shunt capacitor. L_1 and C_1 forms the series harmonic rejection circuit and used for filtering the higher harmonics. R is the output resistance of the power amplifier. The power amplifier can be designed using the following equations given in [7]

$$K_L = \omega L/R \tag{1}$$

$$K_C = \omega C R \tag{2}$$

$$K_P = P_{out}R/V_{dd}^2 \tag{3}$$

$$K_X = X/R \tag{4}$$

$$\omega = 2\pi f \tag{5}$$

where P_{out} is the output power, f is the operating frequency and V_{dd} is the supply voltage. The design set K_L, K_C, K_P and K_X defined above are also related to the term q given by

$$q = 1/\omega\sqrt{LC} \tag{6}$$

The design equations for $1.65 < q < 1.95$ are useful for designing integrated power amplifiers with high PAE and small size. The design set for this range of q is given as

$$K_L = 16.17\,q^2 - 52.26\,q + 42.94 \tag{7}$$

$$K_C = 2.55\,q^2 - 10.53\,q + 10.92 \tag{8}$$

$$K_P = 16.17\,q^2 - 24.73\,q + 24.56 \tag{9}$$

$$K_X = -16.84\,q^2 + 51.38\,q - 39.83 \tag{10}$$

In [6], the series LC tank circuit used for higher harmonic rejection was eliminated to reduce area and to increase the PAE. A differential architecture reduced the even harmonics while the third harmonics was -19 dBm. The common source switching transistors in the differential architecture are replaced with common gate transistors in the proposed work and the input is given to the source terminal. The cross coupling capacitors (C_{C1}, C_{C2}) couples the gate of one common-gate transistor to the source of opposite common gate transistor in the differential structure. They form a negative feedback loop with gain $-A$ in the differential power amplifier and aid in boosting the transconductance of common gate transistors. A cascode topology is used to increase the power supply and hence the total output power [1]. Negative parasitic capacitances (C_{P1}, C_{P2}) are used to cancel out the out the parasitics of the cascode transistors [8]. The proposed power amplifier is shown in Fig. 2 and the single ended small signal model is shown in Fig. 3. G_m is the transconductance of the common gate transistor with capacitive cross coupling and g_m is the transconductance of the cascode amplifier. By application of the capacitive cross coupling to the common gate transistors, the input impedance, transconductance G_m and noise figure (NF) is given as [9]

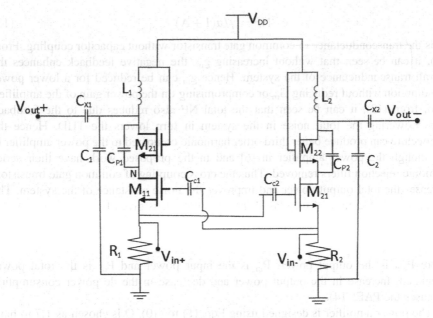

Fig. 2. Proposed differential class-E power amplifier

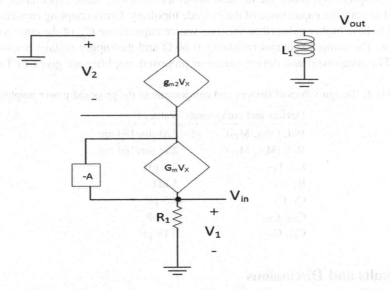

Fig. 3. Single ended small signal circuit model of proposed power amplifier

$$Z_{in} = 1/g_m(1 + A) \qquad (11)$$

$$G_m = g_m(1 + A)/2 \qquad (12)$$

$$NF = \gamma/\alpha(1 + A) \tag{13}$$

g_m is the transconductance of common gate transistor without capacitor coupling. From (12), it can be seen that without increasing g_m, the negative feedback enhances the overall transconductance of the system. Hence g_m can be reduced for a lower power consumption without reducing G_m or compromising on the power gain of the amplifier. Also, from (12), it can be seen that the total NF also reduces due to the feedback loop. Lowering the total noise in the system in turn lowers the THD. Hence the architecture can produce better third order harmonic compared to the power amplifier in [6], though the power amplifier in [6] and in the proposed work have their series harmonic rejection filters removed. Thus the cross coupling of common gate transistors increases the total output power and improves the noise resistance of the system. The power added efficiency of the class-E power amplifier is given by

$$PAE = (P_{out} - P_{in})/P_{dc} \times 100\% \tag{14}$$

where P_{out} is the output power, P_{in} is the input power and P_{dc} is the total power consumed. Increase in the output power and decrease in the dc power consumption increases the PAE (14).

The power amplifier is designed using Eqs. (1) to (10). Q is chosen as 1.7 to have higher PAE and from Eqs. (6)–(9), K_L, K_C, K_P and K_X are 1.15, 0.36, 0.26 and -1.6722 respectively. Since the dc feed inductors are used, shunt capacitance can be included as parasitic capacitance of the cascode topology. Cross coupling capacitors are selected to have higher values than the gate-source capacitance C_{gs} of the common gate transistor. The computed output resistance is 60 Ω and the supply voltage is chosen as 1.8 V. The component and device values of proposed amplifier are given in Table 1.

Table 1. Design values of devices and components in the proposed power amplifier

Devices and components	Values
W/L (M_{11}, M_{12})	320 µm/180 nm
W/L (M_{21}, M_{22})	250 µm/180 nm
L_{01}, L_{02}	2.8 pH
R_1, R_2	5 kΩ
C_1, C_2	0.5 pF
C_{X1}, C_{X2}	1.1 pF
C_{P1}, C_{P2}	0.18 pF

3   Results and Discussions

The class-E power amplifier has been designed and implemented in UMC 180 nm.

MM/RF technology using cadence virtuoso simulation tool. The layout of the proposed amplifier is shown in Fig. 4. The total area of the proposed amplifier is 0.65 mm^2. Post layout simulations along with corner analysis has been carried out on the layout of the amplifier. The variation of PAE, Drain Efficiency (DE) and output power with input power and V_{dd} are shown in Figs. 5 and 6. The obtained maximum

PAE and output power are 52% and 18 dBm. The variation of PAE and output power for with input power for fast-fast (FF), slow-slow (SS) and typical-typical (TT) corners are shown in Figs. 7 and 8. Common gate configurations are more resistant to process variations and this feature can be observed in Figs. 7 and 8. The variation of stability factor with frequency is shown in Fig. 9 and the proposed PA is stable at 2.4 GHz. In Table 2, the proposed power amplifier is compared to other state of the art differential class-E amplifies reported in literature using FoM1 and FoM2 reported in [6]

$$FoM1 = PAE \times f[Hz]^{0.25} \quad (15)$$

$$FoM2 = PAE \times f[Hz]^{0.25}/chip\ size[mm^2] \quad (16)$$

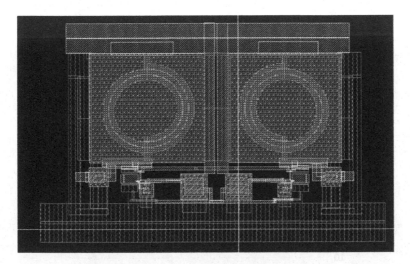

Fig. 4. Layout of proposed class-E power amplifier

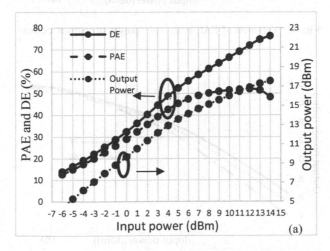

Fig. 5. Variation of PAE, DE and output power with input power

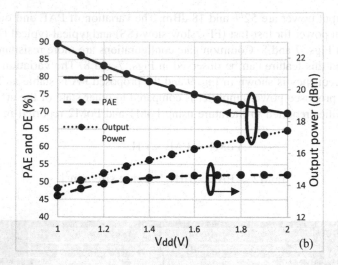

Fig. 6. Variation of PAE, DE and output power with V_{dd}

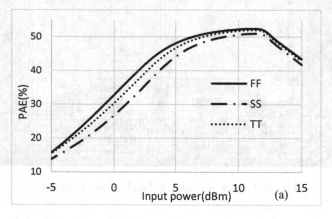

Fig. 7. Variation of PAE with input power at various corners

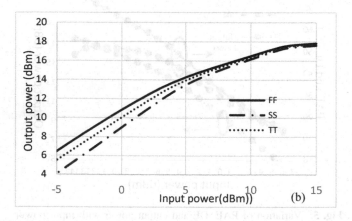

Fig. 8. Variation of output power with input power at various corners

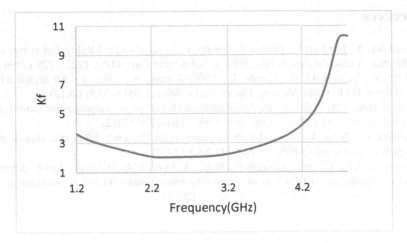

Fig. 9. Variation of stability factor with frequency

Table 2. Performance comparison of proposed power amplifier with those reported in literature

Reference	[6]	[10]	[5]*	[4]	[11]	This work+
Frequency (GHz)	2.3	2.45	2.4	2.4	5.7	2.4
Voltage (V)	2.4	2.4	1.8	1	1.8	1.8
Technology (nm)	90	180	180	130	180	180
Max output (dBm)	28.7	20	35.6	22.83	25	18
Max PAE (%)	48	43.6	43.6	31.13	42.6	52
Area (mm²)	1.2	2.24	-	-	-	0.65
FoM1	105.1	97	96.5	68.9	117	115
FoM2	87.5	44.2	-	-	-	177

*Pre layout result, +Post layout result

From Table 2, it can be seen that the proposed power amplifier has very high PAE compared to other state of the art differential power amplifiers. The area is also very small compared to other differential power amplifiers. It can be inferred from Table 2 that the proposed power amplifier has the highest FoM2, while FoM1 is higher than most other power amplifiers listed in Table 2. Also, the proposed power amplifier has a higher third order rejection of −25 dBm, compared to the −19 dBm rejection reported in [6].

4 Conclusion

A novel common-gate differential class-E power amplifier with capacitive cross coupling has been proposed at 2.4 GHz to improve the power added efficiency and reduce the area consumed. The power amplifier, implemented in UMC 180 nm technology has a high PAE and low area. The performance parameters of the amplifier are suitable for wireless applications at 2.4 GHz ISM band.

References

1. Mazzanti, A., Larcher, L., Brams, R., Svelto, F.: Analysis of reliability and power added efficiency in cascode class-E PAs. IEEE J. Solid-State Circ. **41**(5), 1222–1229 (2006)
2. Alavi, M., Staszewski, R., Vreede, L., Visweswaram, A., Long, J.: All digital RF I/Q modulator. IEEE Trans. Microw. Theory Techn. **60**(11), 3513–3526 (2012)
3. Tan, J., Heng, C.H., Lian, Y.: Design of efficient class-E power amplifiers for short-distance communication. IEEE Trans. Circ. Syst. I **59**, 2210–2220 (2012)
4. Heydari, P., Zhang, Y.: A novel high frequency high efficiency differential class-E power amplifier in 0.18 μm CMOS. In: ISPLED 2003 (2003)
5. Ghorbani, A.R., Ghaznavi-Ghoushchi, M.B.: A 35.6 dB 43.3% PAE class-E differential power amplifier in 2.4 GHz with cross coupling neutralization for IoT applications. In: 24th Iranian Conference on Electrical Engineering (2016)
6. Whei, M.D., Kalim, D., Erguvan, D., Chang, S.F., Negra, R.: Investigation of wideband load transformation networks for class-E switching mode power amplifiers. IEEE Trans. Microw. Theory Techn. **60**(6), 1916–1927 (2012)
7. Acar, M., Annemma, A.J., Nauta, B.: Analytical design equations for class-E power amplifiers. IEEE Trans. Circ. Syst. I **54**(12), 2706–2717 (2007)
8. Song, Y., Lee, S., Cho, E., Lee, J., Nam, S.: A CMOS class-E power amplifier with voltage stress relief and enhanced efficiency. IEEE Trans. Microw. Theory Techn. **58**(2), 310–317 (2010)
9. Sanghyun, W., Wooyun, K., Chang-Ho, L., Hyoungsoo, K., Laskar, J.: A wideband lo power CMOS LNA with positive-negative feedback for noise, gain and linearity optimization. IEEE Trans. Microw. Theory Techn. **60**(10), 3169–3178 (2012)
10. Li, Z., et al.: A 2.45 GHz +20 dBm fast switching class-E power amplifier with 43% PAE and 18-dB wide power range in 0.18 μm CMOS. IEEE Trans. Circ. Syst. II Express Briefs **59**(4), 224–228 (2012)
11. Issa, A.H., Ghayyib, S.M., Izzulddin, A.S.: Towards a fully integrated 2.4 GHz differential pair class-E power amplifier using on-chip RF power transformers for Bluetooth systems. AEUE-Int. J. Electron. Commun. **69**(1), 182–187 (2015)

A 1.25–20 GHz Wide Tuning Range Frequency Synthesis for 40-Gb/s SerDes Application

Javed S. Gaggatur$^{(\boxtimes)}$ ⓘ and Abhishek Chaturvedi

High Speed Circuits Design Group, Terminus Circuits Pvt Ltd,
Bengaluru 560094, Karnataka, India
{gsjaved,abhishek}@terminuscircuits.com

Abstract. A high-frequency high performance frequency synthesizer designed for 40-Gb/s SerDes is presented. In this work, a 20 GHz frequency is generated using a 10 GHz phase locked loop (PLL) that improves its power and area efficiency. The fundamental 10 GHz signal, its sufficiently strong second harmonic at 20 GHz, the divided outputs at 5/2.5/1.25 GHz are generated simultaneously using an integer-N PLL and a mixer-based frequency doubler. The proposed mixer uses an inductorless fully-differential active-inductor topology to reduce the area with marginal tradeoff in phase noise. The frequency synthesizer was designed and implemented in CMOS 55-nm technology. The doubler is integrated with a 10 GHz LC-VCO based PLL having an active area of $390 \times 520\,\mu m^2$ (without pads), with a phase noise of $-115\,dBc/Hz$ at 10 MHz offset frequency and consumes 40.08 mW power from 1.2 V power supply, one of the lowest among the reported literature. The mixer has a maximum conversion gain (CG) of 5.46 dB, 1-dB compression point (P_{-1dB}) of $-2.5\,dBm$ and an input-referred third-order intercept point (IIP3) of $-3.2\,dBm$. The proposed inductorless mixer-based doubler occupies an active area of $55 \times 35\,\mu m^2$ and it adds $< 1.5\,dB$ phase noise at 20 GHz. The frequency synthesizer was used in a Serializer of the 40-Gb/s SerDes transmitter which is critical in back-haul communication for IoT and cyber physical systems.

1 Introduction

The rapid development of communication equipment, high-speed computers, consumer electronics (3C) and the network of wired and wireless connected devices, the amount of data generated, transformed and processed every hour keeps on increasing dramatically. The requirement of high-speed transformation requires the shift from parallel interface to a serial one in all applications. The high performance clocks with low jitter become necessary for wireline communication. In a Serializer/Deserializer (SerDes), the phase locked loop (PLL) provides clock to synchronize the transmitter (Tx) and serve as a reference for the clock and data recovery (CDR) in the receiver (Rx). The communication bandwidth, from baseband to the clock frequency, is wider than the conventional

© Springer Nature Singapore Pte Ltd. 2019
A. Sengupta et al. (Eds.): VDAT 2019, CCIS 1066, pp. 23–35, 2019.
https://doi.org/10.1007/978-981-32-9767-8_3

wireless communication. The SerDes PLL does not have narrow-band filters in Rx and is sensitive to spur and out-of-band noise. The CDR in Rx can track low frequency jitter with the integration range of the random jitter is from the bandwidth of CDR to infinite (Fig. 1).

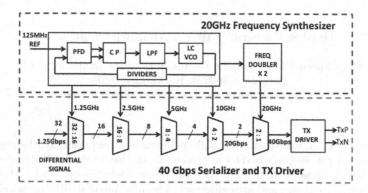

Fig. 1. Block diagram of the 40 Gbps SerDes transmitter and the 1.25–20 GHz frequency synthesis.

Several frequency synthesizer architectures for low phase noise have been reported [8–10] and the high-frequency dividers are the key design challenges. The primary difficulty of 20 GHz oscillators is the parasitic capacitance (C_{par}) of active devices that take up a large share of the relatively small tank capacitance, limiting the frequency tuning range (TR). Secondly, to achieve a tuning range >15%, the poor Q-factor of the tuning capacitance dominates the Q-factor of the 10 GHz resonator, thus limiting the achievable phase noise (PN). The 20 GHz frequency multiplier much achieve large locking range to ensure sufficient overlap with the oscillator TR under PVT variations. However, there is a strong trade-off between the locking range and the power consumption. A 20 GHz frequency generation technique based on a 10 GHz oscillator and an implicit frequency doubler is proposed in this work. Frequency doublers have been reported [7] which use on-chip inductors for frequency selective amplification and low phase noise, but having a drawback of increased overall area. To overcome this challenge, a Gilbert-mixer based inductorless frequency doubler has been proposed.

This paper is organized as follows. In Sect. 2, the overall architecture and description of each building block of the PLL and the proposed inductorless mixer-based doubler are given in detail. Section 3 describes the 40-Gb/s transmitter and its building blocks. Section 4 presents the results and Sect. 5 concludes the paper.

2 Wide Tuning Range 20 GHz Frequency Synthesis

Frequency doubler circuits at microwave and millimeter-waves can be categorized in two main groups: (1) mixer based, (2) device nonlinearity based. The principles of operation and the limits in CMOS technology are discussed in this section.

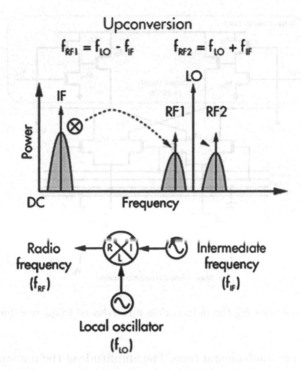

Fig. 2. Conceptual diagram of upward frequency translation using a Gilbert cell mixer.

Upward or downward frequency translation requires the use of a local oscillator (LO) input signal, intermediate-frequency (IF) input/output signal and an RF input/output signal. Figure 2 illustrates the concepts of frequency translation using an up-conversion mixer where the output frequency (f_{RF}) > input frequency (f_{IF}, f_{LO}). In the specific condition of mixing, when the RF and LO ports of a Gilbert-mixer are driven by the same input signal, the output component generated is twice the input frequency. The main merit of this solution is the broad frequency range of operation. As a drawback, a large DC offset appears at the desired double frequency signal output. It may saturate the mixer limiting the conversion gain. In order to suppress the fundamental component, fully balanced mixer topologies are employed, with the drawback of large capacitance at the input ports. Maximum operation frequency is also limited by the parasitic capacitance at the sources of the switching quad [7].

2.1 Proposed Frequency Doubler

Figure 3 shows the simplified schematic of the proposed inductorless mixer-based frequency doubler. If a MOS transistor is driven into compression, the drain current contains the harmonic components of the input signal. A resonant active load selects the desired frequency (e.g., 2nd harmonic for frequency doublers)

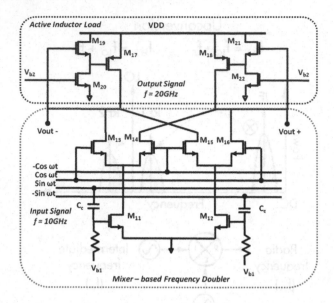

Fig. 3. Schematic showing the inductorless mixer-based frequency doubler design

and suppresses the fundamental tone. The amplitude of the fundamental is nevertheless much larger than its harmonics and achieving adequate suppression by means of integrated LC filters, showing a moderate quality factor, is troublesome [1]. An active inductor was used to achieve a high quality factor in place of an integrated L for the mixer, though a spiral inductor was used as the LC tank in the VCO.

In Fig. 3, the active inductor, formed by M17-M19 and M20-M22 transistor group, is added to resonate with the parasitic capacitance and increase the swing, and hence increase the conversion gain and lower the noise figure of mixer. The 10 GHz LO with four phases (cosωt, -cosωt, sinωt and -sinωt) (0°, 90°, 180° and 270°) is injected to the gate of M13-M16, and as a result, twice the LO frequency appears at the drain of M17-M18 using current doubling. Current doubling causes the frequency to be doubled. The active inductor enables to have an enhanced tuning range of the mixer using the transistor M20 and M22. The above techniques enable the design of a wideband μ-wave/mm-wave mixer with a larger bandwidth and higher conversion gain while consuming lower power consumption compared to similar topologies reported in the literature.

2.2   10 GHz PLL Design

The 10 GHz PLL consists of a phase-frequency detector (PFD), a current-steering charge pump, a 2nd-order on-chip low pass filter, an LC-VCO with a tuning range of 9.92-to-11.8 GHz, followed by a cascade of 3 divide-by-2 CML dividers (divide-by-8) and a divide-by-10 digital divider, having a total divide

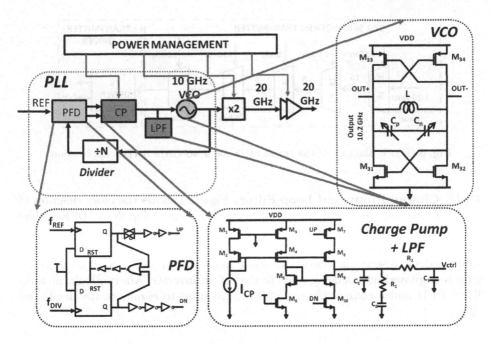

Fig. 4. Block diagram of the PLL Architecture using frequency multiplier. The block diagram contains the PLL, the frequency doubler and the power management circuit [5].

ratio of (N=) 80. This divide ratio enables synthesis of the tones at 10-/5-/2.5-GHz with input reference frequency of (f_{REF}=) 125 MHz. The proposed 20 GHz frequency synthesizer mainly consists of a 10 GHz PLL, a frequency doubler and a buffer. The block diagram of proposed 20 GHz synthesizer with the schematic description of the critical blocks of the PLL is depicted in Fig. 4.

Voltage Controlled Oscillator. The VCO is realized as cross-coupled LC VCO with buffers. The cross coupled nMOS transistors act as negative resistance to compensate the losses of the LC tank. The LC tank is built by spiral inductor together with MOS varactors. The spiral inductors are generally designed to be high Q, by reducing the losses caused by the parasitic series resistance, featuring frequency dependence due to skin effect, and the parasitic shunt capacitance to the substrate. In order to achieve high Q, the inductors are shaped to be octagonal and symmetrical structure and implemented with the top-metal layer (Al) in the process. The simulated inductance (using EM simulation tool, EMX from Integrand Software) of the inductor is 100 pH and the Q is around 15 at the operating frequency of 10 GHz. The output buffer of the VCO is a single-stage source follower amplifier, which features high input impedance to minimize the loading of the VCO core and low output impedance to permit the impedance matching to 50-Ω load.

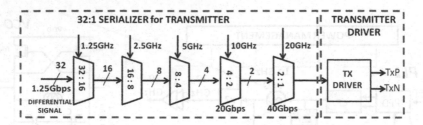

Fig. 5. Block diagram of the transmitter for a 40-Gb/s SerDes application.

PFD, Charge Pump and Loop Filter. Figure 4 shows the block diagram of the PLL wherein the PFD is realized using dynamic D flip-flops (DFFs). The reset path in the PFD is designed to effectively eliminate the dead-zone problem caused by the required time of turning on the charge pump. In order to compensate the delay discrepancy between output signals of UP and DN, a transmission gate is employed with a delay equal to that of an inverter. Alternatively, an auxiliary PFD and a coarse charge pump can be used to eliminate the dead-zone [2–4].

Divide-by-N. The divider for the PLL are implemented using both current mode logic (CML) and CMOS based dividers. The CML dividers are used in the initial divide-by-2 blocks to allow for the high frequency divisions while the subsequent dividers are digital CMOS based. These dividers provide the clocks from 1.25 GHz to 5 GHz which are used to drive the serializer of the 40-Gb/s transmitter, as described in the following section.

3   40-Gb/s Transmitter for SerDes

A transmitter in a multi-standard SerDes is required to support a wide range of swing and feed-forward equalization levels in a power efficient manner. Figure 5 shows the block diagram of the transmitter of the 40-Gb/s SerDes. The transmitter contains three main sections: (a) a serializer, to convert the 32-bit parallel data to serial data, (b) the pre-driver and the driver, to support the wide range of swing and feed-forward equalization levels and (c) a programmable termination resistance to take care of process variation as well as adjustment for impedance matching with the channel (board/cable).

The 20 GHz frequency synthesizer (Fig. 4) is used to clock the various blocks of the serializer as shown in Fig. 5.

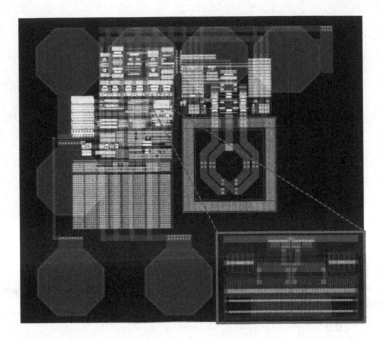

Fig. 6. Layout screenshot of the implemented 10 GHz PLL with a LC-VCO and the proposed inductorless mixer-based frequency multiplier shown inset. The area of the layout is 0.39 mm × 0.52 mm. The screenshot shows the bumps used for flip-chip [5]

4   RC Extraction Results

The transmitter for the 40-Gb/s SerDes is implemented in 55-nm CMOS technology. The oscillator, the mixer and the output driver need special care in layout. The dense interconnects of the power mesh and the capacitor banks around the core transistors may contribute to extra parasitic capacitance and undesired magnetic coupling. The layout routing should be optimized for undesired coupling between the capacitor banks as it is sensitive to layout asymmetry and interconnect parasitics. Layout screenshots of the mixer and the 10 GHz PLL with the integrated mixer are shown in Fig. 6.

4.1   PLL and Doubler

Figures 7 and 8 show the frequency spectrum of the output of the PLL with the center frequency $f_0 = 10$ GHz and the frequency doubler having an output at $2f_0 = 20$ GHz, respectively. In Fig. 7, the spurs are due to the effect of the 125 MHz input reference frequency and the nearest spur is 44 dB lower than the output power of the desired tone. The spurs from the PLL output are suppressed in the mixer output as shown in Fig. 8.

The phase noise around the 20 GHz doubler output is known to degrade due to the nonlinearity in the mixer [1,4,7]. Figure 9 shows the phase noise of the

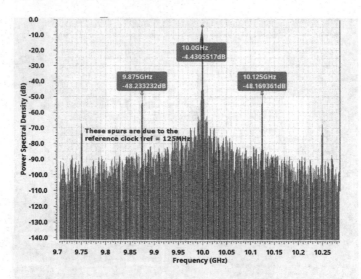

Fig. 7. Power spectral density of PLL output at 10 GHz showing the nearest spur being 44 dB lower than the 10 GHz tone.

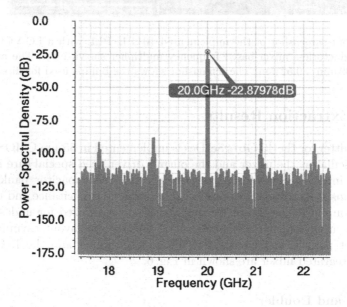

Fig. 8. Power spectral density of frequency doubler output at 20 GHz.

10 GHz PLL output and the 20 GHz output from the frequency doubler. The frequency doubler adds < 1.5 dB phase noise into the existing PLL noise at 20 GHz at a frequency offset of 1 MHz.

The mixer saturation characteristics are shown in Fig. 10 where the output power begins saturation P_{-1dB} at −2.5 dB. The linearity performance is mea-

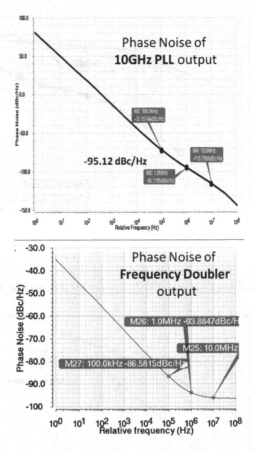

Fig. 9. The simulated phase noise of the 10 GHz PLL output and the 20 GHz doubler output. The phase noise added by the doubler to the existing PLL noise at 10 GHz is less than 1.5 dB @ 20 GHz at 1 MHz frequency offset. [5]

sured via a two tone test. With two RF signals of equal amplitude at 10.01 and 10.11 GHz along with LO input at −5 dBm, the third-order intermodulation (IM$_3$) distortions are positioned at 18.82 GHz and 20.14 GHz, and the second-order intermodulation (IM$_2$) distortion is at 20.1 GHz. The extrapolated plot of the input-referred third-order intercept (IIP$_3$) is observed to intersect at −3.2 dBm as shown in Fig. 11.

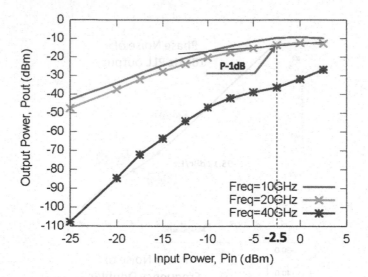

Fig. 10. Compression point P_{-1dB} at 20 GHz for the mixer

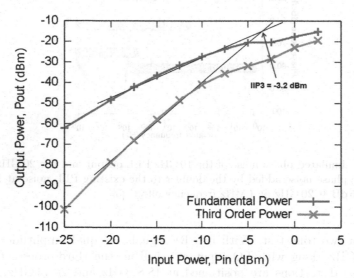

Fig. 11. Simulated linearity of the mixer indicated by IIP3 with a frequency spacing of 100 MHz.

4.2   40 Gbps Transmitter for SerDes

Figure 12 depicts the simulation results, an eye diagram of the output data equalized by the FFE equalizing -18 dB RLGC channel. Table 2 shows the eye opening in terms of the eye width and height for two rates of 20-Gb/s and 40-Gb/s.

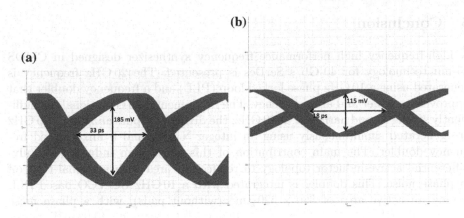

Fig. 12. Eye diagrams of the transmitter outputs for a high speed input data along with the eye width (EW) and eye height (EH): (a) 20-Gb/s and (b) 40-Gb/s.

Table 1. Summary of 20 GHz output oscillator systems

		This work	[9] ISSCC '11	[8] ASSCC '10	[10] RFIC '14	[6] JSSCC '14
Technology		55 nm	45 nm	65 nm	65 nm	65 nm
Type		Frequency doubling	LC-VCO	LC-VCO	LC-VCO	LC-VCO
VDD (V)		1.2	1.1	1.2	1.2	1.2
P_{DC} (mW)	Osc.	6.36	-	-	-	-
	Divider	28.8	-	-	-	-
	PLL	36.72	32.3	65.5	20.2	148
	Mixer	3.36	-	-	-	-
Center frequency (GHz)		20.1	24.8	20.16	20.16	42
Tuning range (GHz)		19.84–23.6 (18.8%)	- (25%)	17.9–21.2 (16.5%)	NA	21–48 -
Phase noise (dBc/Hz)	1 MHz	−93.88	-	−106	-	−108
	10 MHz	−115.73	−121 @23.3 GHz	-	−115	-
Area	Mixer (μm^2)	55 × 35	-	-	-	-
	PLL (mm^2)	0.39 × 0.52	0.48 × 0.29	-	-	2.1
Normalized area	$\frac{Area}{Technology}$	1	1.432	-	-	0.9

Table 2. Summary of the transmitter data rates

Data rate	Eye diagrams	Eye width	Eye height	UI
20-Gb/s	Fig. 12(a)	33 ps	185 mV	50 ps
40-Gb/s	Fig. 12(b)	18 ps	115 mV	25 ps

5   Conclusion

A high-frequency high performance frequency synthesizer designed in CMOS 55-nm technology for 40-Gb/s SerDes is presented. The 20 GHz frequency is generated using a 10 GHz phase locked loop (PLL) and a frequency doubler that improves its power and area efficiency. The fundamental 10 GHz signal, its sufficiently strong second harmonic at 20 GHz, the divided outputs at 5/2.5/1.25 GHz are generated simultaneously using an integer-N PLL and a mixer-based frequency doubler. The main contribution of this work is an inductorless fully-differential active-inductor topology to reduce the area with marginal tradeoff in phase noise. This doubler is integrated with a 10 GHz LC-VCO based PLL having an active area of $390 \times 520\,\mu m^2$ (without pads), with a phase noise of $-115\,dBc/Hz$ at 10 MHz offset frequency and consumes 40.08 mW power from 1.2 V power supply, one of the lowest among the reported literature. The mixer has a maximum conversion gain (CG) of 5.46 dB, 1-dB compression point (P_{-1dB}) of $-2.5\,dBm$ and an input-referred third-order intercept point (IIP3) of $-3.2\,dBm$. The proposed inductorless mixer-based doubler occupies an active area of $55 \times 35\,\mu m^2$ and it adds $< 1.5\,dB$ phase noise at 20 GHz. The frequency synthesizer, having a low phase noise and wide bandwidth, was used in a Serializer of the 40-Gb/s SerDes transmitter which is critical for back-haul communication systems.

Acknowledgement. The authors would like to thank the members of high speed circuits design group for the technical discussions and Terminus Circuits Pvt Ltd for the CAD tool support.

References

1. El-Nozahi, M., Sanchez-Sinencio, E., Entesari, K.: A 20–32-GHz wideband mixer with 12-GHz IF bandwidth in 0.18-μm SiGe process. IEEE Trans. Microwave Theory Tech. **58**(11), 2731–2740 (2010). https://doi.org/10.1109/TMTT.2010.2077572
2. Gaggatur, J.S., Banerjee, G.: Noise analysis in ring oscillator-based capacitance sensor interface. In: 2016 IEEE 59th International Midwest Symposium on Circuits and Systems (MWSCAS), pp. 1–4, October 2016. https://doi.org/10.1109/MWSCAS.2016.7870078
3. Gaggatur, J.S., Dixena, P.K., Banerjee, G.: A 3.2 mW 0.13μm high sensitivity frequency-domain CMOS capacitance interface. In: 2016 IEEE International Symposium on Circuits and Systems (ISCAS), pp. 1070–1073, May 2016. https://doi.org/10.1109/ISCAS.2016.7527429
4. Gaggatur, J.S., Khatri, V., Raja, I., Lenka, M.K., Banerjee, G.: Differential multiphase DLL for reconfigurable radio frequency synthesizer. In: 2014 IEEE International Conference on Electronics, Computing and Communication Technologies (CONECCT), pp. 1–5, January 2014. https://doi.org/10.1109/CONECCT.2014.6740334
5. Gaggatur, J., Deshmukh, P.: A low power, high conversion gain CMOS inductorless frequency doubler for 1.25–20 GHz frequency synthesis in mm-wave receivers. In: Proceedings of the IEEE IMaRC 2018, Kolkata, India, November 2018

6. Li, A., Zheng, S., Yin, J., Luo, X., Luong, H.C.: A 21–48 GHz subharmonic injection-locked fractional-n frequency synthesizer for multiband point-to-point backhaul communications. IEEE J. Solid-State Circ. **49**(8), 1785–1799 (2014). https://doi.org/10.1109/JSSC.2014.2320952
7. Monaco, E., Pozzoni, M., Svelto, F., Mazzanti, A.: Injection-locked CMOS frequency doublers for μ-wave and mm-wave applications. IEEE J. Solid-State Circ. **45**(8), 1565–1574 (2010). https://doi.org/10.1109/JSSC.2010.2049780
8. Musa, A., Murakami, R., Sato, T., Chiavipas, W., Okada, K., Matsuzawa, A.: A 58–63.6 GHz quadrature PLL frequency synthesizer in 65 nm CMOS. In: 2010 IEEE Asian Solid-State Circuits Conference, pp. 1–4, November 2010. https://doi.org/10.1109/ASSCC.2010.5716587
9. Osorio, J.F., Vaucher, C.S., Huff, B., vd Heijden, E., de Graauw, A.: A 21.7-to-27.8 GHz 2.6-degrees-rms 40mW frequency synthesizer in 45nm CMOS for mm-wave communication applications. In: 2011 IEEE International Solid-State Circuits Conference, pp. 278–280, February 2011. https://doi.org/10.1109/ISSCC.2011.5746317
10. Siriburanon, T., et al.: A 60-GHz sub-sampling frequency synthesizer using subharmonic injection-locked quadrature oscillators. In: 2014 IEEE Radio Frequency Integrated Circuits Symposium, pp. 105–108, June 2014. https://doi.org/10.1109/RFIC.2014.6851670

Analyzing Design Parameters of Nano-Magnetic Technology Based Converter Circuit

Bandan Kumar Bhoi[1], Neeraj Kumar Misa[2]([✉]),
Shailesh Singh Chouhan[3], and Sarthak Acharya[3]

[1] Department of Electronics and Telecommunication,
Veer Surendra Sai University of Technology, Burla 768018, India
[2] Department of Electronics and Communication Engineering,
Bharat Institute of Engineering and Technology, Hyderabad 501510, India
neeraj.mishra3@gmail.com, neerajmisra@ieee.org
[3] Embedded Internet Systems Lab, Department of Computer Science,
Electrical and Space Engineering, Luleå University of Technology,
Luleå, Sweden

Abstract. Digital circuits need improvement in computation speed, reducing circuit complexity and power consumption. Emerging Technology NML can be such an architecture at nano-scale and thus emerges as a viable alternative for the digital CMOS VLSI. This technology has the capability to compute the logic as well as storage into the same device, which points out that it great potential for emerging technology. Since Nano-magnetic, technology fast approaches its minimal feature size, high device density and operate at room temperature. NML based circuits synthesis has to opt for novel half subtraction and Binary-to-Gray architecture for achieving minimal complexity and high-speed performance. This manuscript pro-poses area efficient binary half-subtraction and Binary-to-Gray converter architecture. Circuits' synthesize are performed by MagCAD tool and simulate by Modelsim simulator. The circuit's performance are estimated over other existing designs. The proposed converter consume 73.73%, and 94.49% less area than the converter designed using QCA and CMOS technique respectively. This is a significant contribution to this paper. Simulation results of converter show that the critical path delay falls within 0.15 μs.

Keywords: Nano-magnetic logic · Binary-to-gray converter ·
Magnetic anisotropy · Minority voter · Perpendicular nano-magnetic logic

1 Introduction

Very Large Scale Integration (VLSI) circuits based on complementary metal oxide semiconductor (CMOS) may scale down to the nano-meter range. CMOS computing is reaching its downscaling but beyond its certain disadvantage such as leakage cur-rent, short channel effect and lithography cost [1].

No academic titles or descriptions of academic positions should be included in the addresses. The affiliations should consist of the author's institution, town/city, and country.

© Springer Nature Singapore Pte Ltd. 2019
A. Sengupta et al. (Eds.): VDAT 2019, CCIS 1066, pp. 36–46, 2019.
https://doi.org/10.1007/978-981-32-9767-8_4

Miniaturization towards high computation in VLSI is a challenging factor for new generation product. The essence of the nonmagnetic technology must be approachable to the emerging technology designers. Minimal feature size and high device density, especially in digital circuits, where the main factor in circuit synthesizes [2]. The state-of-art technology was strained towards high-density and small size. Emerging design tools were popularized towards achieving these aims [3]. A nano-magnetic tool developed by ToPoliNano (TOrinoPOLLItecnico Nanotechnology) is MagCAD [4]. Nano-magnetic logic (NML) is further separated into two parts based on magnetic anisotropy. These parts are perpendicular NML (pNML) and in-plane NML (iNML). The primary advantage of NML technology has no standby power consumption, no leakage power consumption and operate at room temperature [5]. When the magnetic orientation of the nano-magnets are in-plane; it is referred to as iNML and when the orientation is perpendicular to the plane then it is referred to as pNML. Perpendicular NML (pNML) here is one of the most efficient implementations of the NML technology this is because of its less area occupation and reduced power consumption over iNML [6].

In this article, we implement nonmagnetic-based half subtraction and Binary-to-Gray converter architecture. In a data communication system, Binary-to-Gray code competes a significant role in error correction. Fast computation and high density in digital design of VLSI approaching its certain limitation, emerging technology in the digital design of code converter circuit are mandated for fast computation speed and high-density. Thus, to improve performance in parametric analysis such as bounded box area, critical delay and latency of code converter in NML to enhance the performance. In NML, we use minority voter (i.e. the minority gate) to reduce the circuit complexity. Logic verification of these designs can be tested easily when Verilog code is produced from MagCAD tool. The functionality of the designs is checked using Modelsim simulator. This article main contributions as:

- We implement typical NML based half adder and code converter.
- We have expressed all the proposed designs equation in minority voter form then go for the synthesis in MagCAD tool.
- We simulate proposed designs by exhaustive testing and compare with the truth table.
- Bounded box area, latency and critical delay of combinational designs are measured experimentally.
- Proposed designs enjoy the aspect of less Bounded box area, latency and critical delay.

2 Theoretical Description of p-NML

NML is an emerging magnetic coupled Nano-electronics that is made of magnet cell. The basic functional units in pNML are minority voter and the inverters [7]. Fundamental pNML units are depicted in Fig. 1. In Fig. 1a logic inverter is presented, where the input magnet is adjoining the output magnet. The output type magnet structure is depicted in Fig. 1b, denoted as an artificial nucleation centre. Whenever an odd i.e., minimum one and maximum five number of inputs are provided around it, the total structure leads to a minority voter [8]. Similarly, there are various magnetic elements in pNML executing various functions. The architecture is depicted in Fig. 1c named as the normal magnet, which is a fundamental part of this emerging technology. It is mainly used to route signals. Figure 1d represents the architecture of a corner type mag-net that is also a basic magnet but with 90^0 rotation. Figure 1e, via type magnet, is depicted, which is used to associate to the nucleation centre situated in another plane. In Fig. 1f, T-connection type magnet presents, which is utilized to divide the input into two distinct directions. The cross-connection type magnet depicted in Fig. 1g is also a magnet that divides the input into three distinct directions.

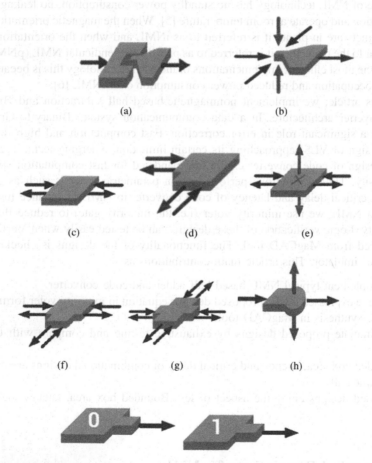

Fig. 1. Fundamental pNML units (a) Logic inverter (b) Nucleation centre (c) Domain wall magnet (d) Corner based magnet (e) Via based magnet (f) T type connection (g) X type connection (h) Pad based magnet (i) Fixed logic '0' Magnet (j) Fixed logic '1' magnet.

In Fig. 1h, pad magnet is depicted, which is primary utilize as the ending of the magnetic wire. Its output can only be a nucleation centre. We also require definitely fixed inputs to carryout different logic functions based on pNML, architecture is depicted in Fig. 1i, j are the constant '0' and constant '1' input of the magnets, respectively.

For the formation of NML circuits, fundamental gates are utilized, which are minority gate, as depicted in Fig. 2. Three inputs are set to some logic level then the output is decided by the number of minority logic value. The output of a minority gate will be equivalent to the minority of its inputs. A mathematical expression is expressed as $Y = M(A, B, C) = \bar{A}\bar{B} + \bar{B}\bar{C} + \bar{A}\bar{C}$.

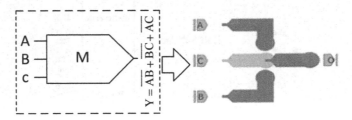

Fig. 2. Minority gate (a) Symbol (b) NML 3-D design.

3 Related Work

Several code converters have been proposed in the available literature. Most of the converters design use CMOS or QCA Technology [9–17]. In order to improve the computation speed and high device density, the recent advance technique may be required [8]. Moving away from the QCA and CMOS designs towards the NML based designs give enough opportunity to saving area, critical delay and latency for the nano-electronics application. Recently, many design cases of QCA and CMOS have been reported [9–12]. Islam et al. proposed a 3-bit Binary-to-Gray converter in CMOS Technology [9]. Microwind tool is used for prototype layout design and the layout provides a optimize area of 44.2 µm2. Das et al., proposed a Binary-to-Gray converter in QCA Technology [10]. The reported area is 92,664 µm2 and robust architecture is achieved with coplanar crossing technique. The major drawback of the existing designs in [13–17] is the relatively higher magnitude of the area. As the size of the input increase, the device density also increases. We propose nano-magnetic based designs that have the same functionality as that of existing designs available in literature and better parameter as area and latency than existing designs. Discussion of the proposed work in the domain of nano-magnetic based code converter is elaborated in the next section.

4 Proposed Work

In this paper, we have further explored digital circuit architectures based on pNML technology. We have designed a half subtraction and a 3-bit Binary-to-Gray convert-er. In pNML technology, all the layout designs start with a nucleation centre i.e. the initial input is given to the nucleation centre.

4.1 Half Subtraction Design in pNML

Half subtraction is a digital electronic circuit that performs two binary digit sub-traction. Here in this work the layout of a Half subtraction using the pNML technology has been proposed. In this circuit, binary numbers i.e. 0 or 1 is used for subtraction.

There are two inputs namely A and B, and the resultant terms are Difference and Borrow, which is shown in Fig. 3a.

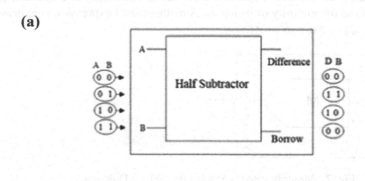

(a)

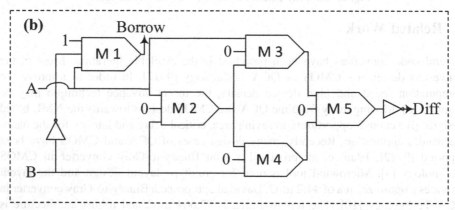

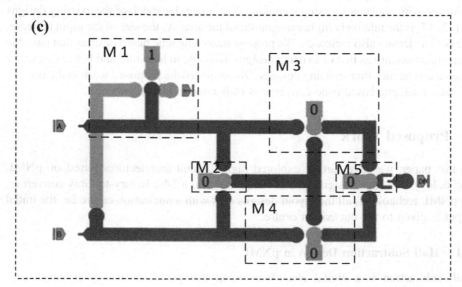

Fig. 3. Half subtraction (a) block diagram (b) pNML schematic (c) 3-D pNML layout.

The half subtraction block diagram is represented in Fig. 3a, while the pNML schematic and 3-D pNML layout are illustrated in Fig. 3b and c, respectively. The output equations are derived in the below. The simulation results are presented in Fig. 4 with all the possible combination of inputs.

$$\text{Borrow} = \text{M1}\,(1, \overline{B}, A) = 0 + B\overline{A} + 0 = \overline{AB}$$

$$\text{Difference} = \overline{\text{M5}\,(\text{M3}(A, 0, \text{M2}\,(A, 0, B)), 0, \text{M4}\,(\text{M2}(A, 0, B), 0, B))}$$

$$= \overline{(\text{M5}(\text{M3}(A, 0, \overline{AB}), 0, \text{M4}\,(\overline{AB}, 0, B))}$$

$$= \overline{\text{M5}\,(\overline{A.\overline{AB}}, 0, \overline{\overline{AB}.B})} = A\overline{B} + \overline{A}B$$

The proposed design is a 3-D circuit because the magnetic wires are in different layers. According to the nano-magnetic phenomenon an input in a particular layer is propagated in its inverted form in another layer i.e. we can get the invert of input by just changing the layer. Here both the inputs A and B are given to the circuit in layer '0' initially. To get the Borrow output, the input A is applied to the minority voter directly in layer '0' but the input B is applied in layer '1' so as to provide its inverted form without using an inverter circuit. Then a fixed '1' input is given to the other in-put terminal of the minority voter. The basic concept of perpendicular Nano-magnetic logic states that if any of the inputs of a minority voter is being logic '0' then it will function as a NOR gate. Hence the minority voter produces the required output Borrow. To get the output Difference, it requires four numbers of minority voters along with an inverter which in term forms an Ex-OR gate.

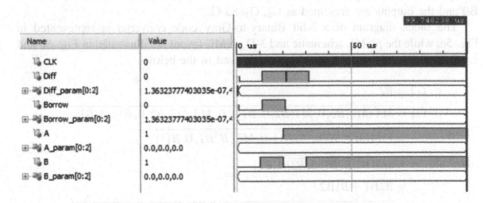

Fig. 4. Simulation result of the pNML layout of half subtraction

4.2 Computational Based Analyzing Design Parameters of Half Subtraction

In this section, the analyzing design parameters on the pNML have investigated. The following effects will be studied: bounded box area, critical path and latency. The above Fig. 4 shows the simulation result of the proposed layout of the Half sub-traction. The result clearly shows that the proposed design successfully satisfies the truth table of the Half subtraction. The total design occupies a bounding box area of 2.4336 μm² and it uses only five numbers of minority voters and one inverter to implement the whole circuit. The circuit shows a critical path delay of 0.15 μs. It also exhibits different latencies for different input combinations which are shown in Table 1.

Table 1. Performance table of 2-bit Half subtraction

3-D half subtraction				
Bounding box area = 2.4336 μm²				
Critical path = $1.5E^{-7}$ s				
Inputs		Outputs		Latency (in sec)
A	B	Difference	Borrow	
0	0	0	0	$0.88E^{-6}$
0	1	1	1	$0.79E^{-6}$
1	0	1	0	$0.89E^{-6}$
1	1	0	0	$0.99E^{-6}$

4.3   Binary to Gray Code Converter Design in p-NML

Binary-to-Gray converter is a digital electronic circuit that performs Binary-to-gray code conversion. Here in this work the layout of a 3-bit Binary-to-Gray converter using the pNML technology has been proposed. In this circuit, a 3-bit binary number is given as input, while the output is a 3-bit Gray code. The inputs used are namely B2, B1 and B0 and the outputs are presented as G_2, G_1 and G_0.

The block diagram of a 3-bit Binary-to-Gray code converter is represented in Fig. 5a, while the pNML schematic and 3-D pNML layout are illustrated in Fig. 5b and c, respectively. The output equations are derived in the below

$$G2 = B2$$

$$G1 = \overline{M4\left(M2(B2, 0, M1(B2, 0, B1)), 0, M3(M3(B2, 0, B1), 0, B1)\right)}$$

$$= \overline{(M4(M2(B2, 0, \overline{B2B1}), 0, M3\left(\overline{B2B1}, 0, B1\right))}$$

$$= \overline{M5(\overline{B2.\overline{B2B1}}, 0, \overline{B2B1}.B1)}$$

$$= \overline{B2}B1 + \overline{B1}B2$$

$$G0 = \overline{M8(M6(B1, 0, M5(B1, 0, B0)), 0, M7(M8(B1, 0, B0), 0, B0))}$$

$$= \overline{(M8(M6(B1, 0, \overline{B1B0}), 0, M7(\overline{B1B0}, 0, B0))}$$

$$= \overline{M8(\overline{B1.\overline{B1B0}}, 0, \overline{B1B0}.B0)}$$

$$= \overline{B1}B0 + \overline{B0}B1$$

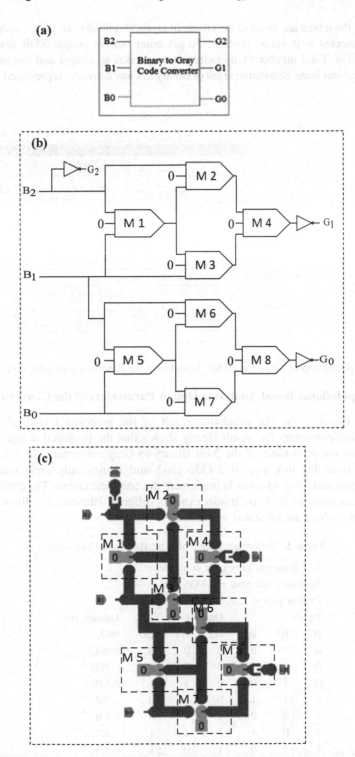

Fig. 5. Three-bit Binary-to-Gray code converter (a) block diagram (b) pNML schematic (c) 3-D pNML layout.

Here all the inputs are given to the circuit in layer '0' initially. To get G_2 output, B_2 is directly connected to it via an inverter. To get other outputs simple XOR operation is performed. The Total number of minority voters needed was eight and the number of inverters used was three. Simulation result of Binary to Gray converter is presented in Fig. 6.

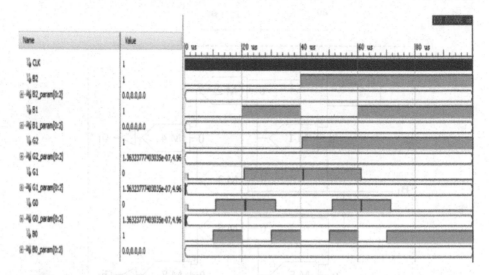

Fig. 6. Simulation result of the pNML layout of 3-bit Binary to gray code converter.

4.4   Computational-Based Analyzing Design Parameters of the Converter

The above Fig. 6 shows the simulation result of the proposed layout of the 3-bit Binary-to-gray-converter. The result clearly shows that the proposed design successfully satisfies the truth table of the 3-bit Binary-to-Gray converter. The total design occupies a bounding box area of 2.4336 µm2 and it uses only eight numbers of minority voters and three inverters to implement the complete circuit. The circuit shows a critical path delay of 0.15 µs. It also exhibits different latencies for different input combinations, which are tabulated in Table 2.

Table 2. Performance table of 3-bit Binary-to-Gray code.

3-D Binary to gray code converter						
Bounding box area = 2.4336 µm^2						
Critical path = 1.5E^{-7} s						
Inputs			Outputs			Latency (in sec)
B2	B1	B0	G2	G1	G0	
0	0	0	0	0	0	0.88E^{-6}
0	0	1	0	0	1	0.79E^{-6}
0	1	0	0	1	1	0.89E^{-6}
0	1	1	0	1	0	0.99E^{-6}
1	0	0	1	1	0	0.83E^{-6}
1	0	1	1	1	1	0.92E^{-6}
1	1	0	1	0	1	0.82E^{-6}
1	1	1	1	0	0	0.89E^{-6}

5 Analyzing Parameters

Post-synthesis design parameter analysis such as area are tabulated in Table 3. The proposed designs are synthesized in NML tool using physical model parameters with the default library setting. Bounding Box area saving achieved for the Binary-to-Gray converter are evaluated based on NML tool. In the proposed designs, using the NML based Verilog library the NML layout is converted to its equivalent hardware description language (HDL). The design is synthesized in NML tool and simulation are taken from ModelSim simulation. The area result shows the benefit of the novel designs in comparison with the existing design. The design consumes 94.49%, and 73.73% less area than the code converter designed using existing in [9, 10].

Table 3. Synthesis analyzing parameters of various Binary-to-Gray converters

Parameter	Existing CMOS technology in area (μm^2) [9]	Existing QCA technology in area (μm^2) [10]	Proposed NML technology in area (μm^2)
Area (μm^2)	44.2	9.2664	2.4336
% improvement	94.49	73.73	-

6 Conclusion

In this manuscript, we proposed area efficient half subtraction and Binary-to-Gray converter based on NML technology. The new half subtraction and Binary-to-Gray converter consume minimal area compared to other published designs in literature. For the first design in literature, half subtraction and Binary-to-Gray converter are utilized in nano-magnetic technology. The simulation results based on Verilog code generated from NML tool ensure the accurate synthesis of the proposed layout. Less critical delay of the designs, which may show the efficient design synthesis method-ology. This design has presented layout of the proposed design in NML can be com-mitted higher order building block to synthesize high-density circuit in the future. The customary minimal bounded area of nano-magnetic designs makes allowance for a high density of higher order designs, which may further improve the synthesis cost.

References

1. Misra, N.K., Sen, B., Wairya, S., Bhoi, B.: Testable novel parity-preserving reversible gate and low-ost quantum decoder design in 1D molecular-QCA. J. Circ. Syst. Comput. **26**(09), 1750145 (2017)
2. Pala, D., et al.: Logic-in-memory architecture made real. In: 2015 IEEE International Symposium on Circuits and Systems (ISCAS), pp. 1542–1545. IEEE, May 2015
3. Cofano, M., et al.: Logic-in-memory: a nano magnet logic implementation. In: 2015 IEEE Computer Society Annual Symposium on VLSI, pp. 286–291. IEEE, July 2015

4. Riente, F., Turvani, G., Vacca, M., Roch, M.R., Zamboni, M., Graziano, M.: Topo-linano: a cad tool for nano magnetic logic. IEEE Trans. Comput. Aided Des. Integr. Circ. Syst. **36**(7), 1061–1074 (2017)

5. Cairo, F., et al.: Out-of-plane NML modeling and architectural exploration. In: 2015 IEEE 15th International Conference on Nanotechnology (IEEE-NANO), pp. 1037–1040. IEEE, July 2015

6. Breitkreutz, S., Eichwald, I., Ziemys, G., Schmitt-Landsiedel, D., Becherer, M.: Influence of the domain wall nucleation time on the reliability of perpendicular nanomagnetic logic. In: 14th IEEE International Conference on Nanotechnology, pp. 104–107. IEEE, August 2014

7. Breitkreutz, S., et al.: Experimental demonstration of a 1-bit full adder in perpendicular nano-magnetic logic. IEEE Trans. Magn. **49**(7), 4464–4467 (2013)

8. Bhoi, B.K., Misra, N.K., Pradhan, M.: Design of magnetic dipole based 3D integration nano-circuits for future electronics application. Int. J. Nano Dimension **9**(4), 374–385 (2018)

9. Islam, S., Abdullah-al-Shafi, M., Bahar, A.N.: Implementation of binary to gray code converters in quantum dot cellular automata. J. Today's Ideas - Tomorrow's Technol. **3**, 145–160 (2015)

10. Das, J.C., De, D.: Reversible binary to grey and grey to binary code converter using QCA. IETE J. Res. **61**(3), 223–229 (2015)

11. Iqbal, J., Khanday, F.A., Shah, N.A.: Efficient quantum dot cellular automata (QCA) implementation of code converters. Commun. Inf. Sci. Manag. Eng. **3**(10), 504 (2013)

12. Mukherjee, C., Panda, S., Mukhopadhyay, A.K., Maji, B.: Towards modular binary to gray converter design using LTEx module of quantum-dot cellular automata. Microsyst. Technol. **25**, 1–8 (2018)

13. Misra, N.K., Sen, B., Wairya, S.: Towards designing efficient reversible binary code converters and a dual-rail checker for emerging nanocircuits. J. Comput. Electron. **16**(2), 442–458 (2017)

14. Misra, N.K., Wairya, S., Singh, V.K.: Optimized approach for reversible code converters using quantum dot cellular automata. In: Das, S., Pal, T., Kar, S., Satapathy, S.C., Mandal, J. K. (eds.) Proceedings of the 4th International Conference on Frontiers in Intelligent Computing: Theory and Applications (FICTA) 2015. AISC, vol. 404, pp. 367–378. Springer, New Delhi (2016). https://doi.org/10.1007/978-81-322-2695-6_31

15. Misra, N.K., Sen, B., Wairya, S., Bhoi, B.: A novel parity preserving reversible binary-to-BCD code converter with testability of building blocks in quantum circuit. In: Bhateja, V., Tavares, J.M.R.S., Rani, B.P., Prasad, V.K., Raju, K.S. (eds.) Proceedings of the Second International Conference on Computational Intelligence and Informatics. AISC, vol. 712, pp. 383–393. Springer, Singapore (2018). https://doi.org/10.1007/978-981-10-8228-3_35

16. Karkaj, E.T., Heikalabad, S.R.: Binary to gray and gray to binary converter in quantum-dot cellular automata. Optik **130**, 981–989 (2017)

17. Abdullah-Al-Shafi, M., Bahar, A.N.: Novel binary to gray code converters in QCA with power dissipation analysis. Int. J. Multimedia Ubiquit. Eng. **11**(8), 379–396 (2017)

Design of Current Mode Sigmoid Function and Hyperbolic Tangent Function

Debanjana Datta[✉] [ID], Sweta Agarwal, Vikash Kumar, Mayank Raj, Baidyanath Ray, and Ayan Banerjee

IIEST, Shibpur, Howrah 711103, West Bengal, India
debanjanadatta2014@gmail.com

Abstract. In this paper, two design procedures for sigmoid function using exponential function have been proposed implementing division operation and feedback methodology. Hyperbolic tangent function has also been synthesized using the later. All the proposed circuits along with their building blocks have been implemented using current mode device Operational Transconductance Amplifier (OTA). Sensitivities of the circuit and process parameters on the output have been calculated. Performances of all synthesized circuits have been verified with SPICE simulation, establishing the effectiveness of the proposed methodology.

Keywords: Operational Transconductance Amplifier (OTA) · Sigmoid · Hyperbolic · Synthesis

1 Introduction

Sigmoid functions, having wide application in communication, signal processing, Artificial Neural Networks (ANN) [2–10], image analysis and statistics, have been implemented using numerous methods in literature in digital and analog domain. The analog realizations are faster and power efficient compared to the digital realizations [8,10] with a prominent area saving, but suffers from lack of precision and vulnerability to circuit mismatch and variations. Among the wide variety of sigmoid functions, the logistic function [3–7] (commonly referred as sigmoid function) and hyperbolic tangent function [10–12], are mostly used as the activation function in artificial neurons. Their differentiable nature makes them compatible with back propagation algorithm. Both functions have similar S-shaped curve but their output range is different.

Due to the difficulties involved in the exponentiation and division required for both sigmoid and hyperbolic tangent functions, researchers applied different approximation methods instead of direct hardware implementation. One such approximation method for sigmoid function approximation is centered recursive interpolation (CRI) as reported in [5,6]. Taylor series have been used in [7] to approximate sigmoid function and has been implemented using transistors operating in both triode and saturation regions. Authors in [3] proposed

© Springer Nature Singapore Pte Ltd. 2019
A. Sengupta et al. (Eds.): VDAT 2019, CCIS 1066, pp. 47–60, 2019.
https://doi.org/10.1007/978-981-32-9767-8_5

a neural network-like sigmoid function calculator where a function is approximated by training a neural network. An adaptive sigmoidal activation function is proposed in [9] for the hidden layers' node in an artificial neural network. Hyperbolic functions have been realized in [11,12] using BJTs or OTAs. Bhanja et al. [1] proposed a realization of logarithmic function for any arbitrary input signal along with implementing exponential and hyperbolic functions using the proposed logarithmic circuit. The approximation methods suffer from approximation errors while direct implementation has the drawback of requiring excess hardware.

In that context, we have proposed two systematic procedure, using divider and using feedback, for synthesizing sigmoid function directly considering exponential function as its input. Hyperbolic tangent function has also been realized using the proposed synthesis methodology. Current mode device, OTA has been used for implementing the proposed circuits and has been introduced in the next section.

2   OTA Basics

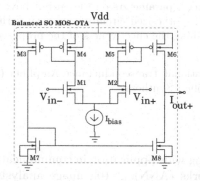

Fig. 1. Schematic of balanced differential OTA

OTA [13] is an excellent differential voltage controlled current source to design high frequency analog systems. Because of its structural simplicity and convenient controllability, OTA is chosen to implement the proposed methodology. OTA is composed of an input differential pair, a transconductance control unit and output current mirror. Figure 1 depicts a single-output balanced differential MOS-OTA. Output current of a OTA is $\pm I_{out} = \pm(V_{in+} - V_{in-}) \cdot g_m$, where, V_{in+} and V_{in-} are the input signals applied at the non-inverting and inverting input terminals and g_m is its transconductance that is controlled by the bias current, I_b as shown in Fig. 1. This OTA provides a good linear range for efficient analog circuit design. g_m of the OTA can be varied from $5\,\mu S$ to $400\,\mu S$. In the subsequent discussion, notation g_{mi} and I_{bi} are used to denote the transconductance and bias current of OTAi respectively, where i = 1, 2, 3, ...

In the next section, synthesis methodology for sigmoid function is presented.

3   Synthesis of Sigmoid Function

A sigmoid function [2] is a bounded, differentiable, real, nonlinear function that is defined for all real input values and has a non-negative derivative at each point. It is represented by mathematical functions having a characteristic "S"-shaped curve or sigmoid curve, often referring to the special case of the logistic function defined by,

$$Sig(x) = \frac{1}{1 + e^{-x}} = \frac{e^x}{e^x + 1} \tag{1}$$

Sigmoid functions have return value monotonically increasing most often from 0 to 1 or alternatively from -1 to 1, depending on convention. The reason for popularity of sigmoid function as activation function in neural networks is because the sigmoid function satisfies a property between the derivative and itself (ref. Eq. (2)) such that it is computationally easy to perform.

$$\frac{d}{dx} Sig(x) = Sig(x)(1 - Sig(x)) \tag{2}$$

Sigmoid curves are also common in statistics as cumulative distribution function. In this paper sigmoid function, i.e, Eq. (1) has been implemented using two methods.

1. Division Method

Equation (1) can be expressed in the terms of its numerator and denominator polynomials as,

$$Sig(x) = \frac{e^x}{e^x + 1} = \frac{N_{sig}(x)}{D_{sig}(x)} \tag{3}$$

where numerator polynomial, $N_{sig}(x) = e^x$ and denominator polynomial, $D_{sig}(x) = e^x + 1$. Therefore, sigmoid function can be realized using a divider with e^x and $e^x + 1$ as its dividend and divisor inputs respectively.

2. Feedback Method

In general any function of the form $\frac{f_1(x)}{g_1(x)}$ is implemented by dividing $f_1(x)$ by $g_1(x)$. Here, it is shown that it is possible to realize equation of the same form by a model given in Eq. (4).

$$y(t) = Sig(x) = \frac{e^x}{1 + e^x}$$
$$= e^x - e^x.y(t) \tag{4}$$

Equation (4) is demonstrated by the block diagram of Fig. 5, explained in Sect. 3.3.

In both the methods, represented by Eqs. (3) and (4), the basic building block for synthesizing a sigmoid function is the exponential function, whose OTA based realization has been illustrated next.

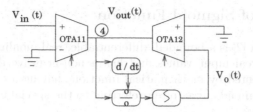

Fig. 2. OTA based exponential function generator

3.1 OTA Based Realization of Exponential Function

Figure 2 depicts the OTA-based block for generating the exponential function, as presented in [1], which consists of a differentiator block, a divider block, an integrator and two OTAs. These sub-blocks are exhibited in Fig. 3. Uniformity has been maintained in numbering the active and passive components in all the figures of this paper.

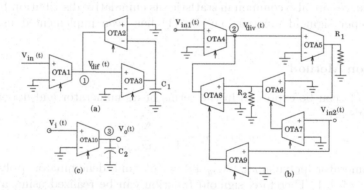

Fig. 3. OTA based (a) differentiator (b) divider and (c) integrator

Output of the differentiator block $V_{dif}(t)$ at node 1 of Fig. 3(a) is given by,

$$V_{dif}(t) = \frac{g_{m1}C_1}{g_{m2}g_{m3}} \frac{d}{dt}[V_{in}(t)] = k_{dif} \cdot \frac{d}{dt}[V_{in}(t)] \qquad (5)$$

where, $k_{dif} = \frac{g_{m1}C_1}{g_{m2}g_{m3}}$ = coefficient of the differentiator block and $V_{in}(t)$ is the input of the same.

Figure 3(b) shows the divider block with output $V_{div}(t)$ at node 2 expressed as,

$$V_{div}(t) = \frac{g_{m4}}{\alpha^2\gamma\beta\sqrt{g_{m7}g_{m9}}.R_2R_1g_{m5}} \cdot \frac{V_{in1}(t)}{V_{in2}(t)} = k_{div} \cdot \frac{V_{in1}(t)}{V_{in2}(t)} \qquad (6)$$

where, $k_{div} = \frac{g_{m4}}{\alpha^2\gamma\beta\sqrt{g_{m7}g_{m9}}.R_2R_1g_{m5}}$ = coefficient of the divider block. $V_{in1}(t)$ and $V_{in2}(t)$ are the dividend and divisor inputs respectively, of the divider block. Here

OTA, operating above threshold has been considered, for which transconductance g_m is expressed as, $g_m = \alpha\sqrt{\gamma\beta I_b}$, where α is the gain of the attenuation stage, γ is the body effect coefficient and β is a physical constant that is related to the differential pair's geometry and the doping concentration.

Output of the integrator $V_o(t)$ at node 3 of Fig. 3(c) can be written as,

$$V_o(t) = \frac{g_{m10}}{C_2} \int V_i(t)dt = k_{int}.\int V_i(t)dt \qquad (7)$$

where, $k_{int} = \frac{g_{m10}}{C_2}$ and $V_i(t)$ are the coefficient and input of the integrator respectively.

When the outputs of the sub-blocks of Fig. 3(a), (b) and (c) are applied in Fig. 2, $V_{in}(t)$ of differentiator and $V_{in2}(t)$ of divider are provided same inputs, output of the differentiator is connected to $V_{in1}(t)$ of divider and output of divider is used as input of integrator, thereby generating

$$V_o(t) = k_{int}.k_{div} \int \frac{V_{dif}(t)}{V_{in}(t)}dt = k_{ln}.ln[V_{in}(t)] \qquad (8)$$

where, $k_{ln} = k_{int}.k_{div}.k_{dif}$ with k_{int}, k_{div} and k_{dif} being the coefficients of integrator, divider and differentiator block respectively.

Applying KCL at node 4 of Fig. 2 we get,

$$V_{in}(t).g_{m11} - V_o(t).g_{m12} = 0 \qquad (9)$$

Using the value of $V_o(t)$ from Eq. (8), output of Fig. 2, $V_{out}(t)$ can be expressed as,

$$V_{out}(t) = e^{V_{in}(t).\frac{g_{m11}}{k_{ln}.g_{m12}}} = e^{V_{in}(t).k_{exp}} \qquad (10)$$

where, $k_{exp} = \frac{g_{m11}}{k_{ln}.g_{m12}}$ is the coefficient of the exponent. Therefore, OTA-based block of Fig. 2 generates an exponential function and has been used for realizing sigmoid function in the next section.

3.2   Realization of Sigmoid Function Using Division Method

In this method, as defined by Eq. (3), exponential block of Fig. 2 has been used to generate $e^{V_{in}(t).k_{exp}}$ and $(1 + e^{V_{in}(t).k_{exp}})$ and provide it to the two inputs of the divider block (ref. Fig. 3(b)) as depicted in Fig. 4.

With the help of Eqs. (6) and (10), output of Fig. 4 can be written as,

$$y(t) = \frac{g_{m13}}{\alpha^2\gamma\beta\sqrt{g_{m15}g_{m14}}.R_3R_4R_5g_{m16}g_{m19}}.\frac{e^{V_{in}(t).k_{exp}}}{1 + e^{V_{in}(t).k_{exp}}} \qquad (11)$$

which is the characteristic equation of sigmoid function with, $k_{exp} = \frac{g_{m11}}{k_{ln}.g_{m12}}$, as defined in section III-A. Feedback method for realizing sigmoid function is demonstrated next.

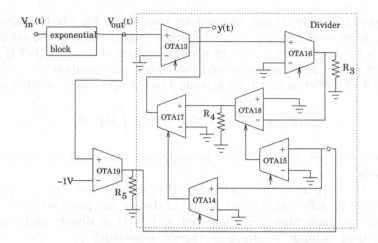

Fig. 4. Sigmoid function using exponential block and divider

3.3   Realization of Sigmoid Function Using Feedback Method

Figure 5 realizes sigmoid function using feedback method, as defined by Eq. (4). The exponential block of Fig. 2 has been used here to provide one input to OTA16, which gets the other input by feeding back its output to OTA14.

OTA13, OTA14 and OTA15 multiplies $V_{out} = e^{V_{in}(t).k_{exp}}$ with y(t). The result is subtracted from V_{out} by OTA16, thereby generating output y(t).

Applying KCL at node 5 and assuming $I_{b14} = I_{b15}$ we get,

$$I_{b14} = I_{b15} = \frac{V_{out}(t)g_{m13}}{2} \tag{12}$$

Voltages at node 6 ($V_6(t)$) and node 7 ($V_7(t)$) can be written as,

$$V_6(t) = R_3 g_{m14} y(t) \tag{13}$$

$$V_7(t) = R_4 g_{m15}.V_6(t)$$

$$= R_4 g_{m15} R_3 g_{m14}.y(t) \tag{14}$$

where, $g_{m14} = \alpha\sqrt{\gamma\beta I_{b14}}$ and $g_{m15} = \alpha\sqrt{\gamma\beta I_{b15}}$. Replacing the values of g_{m14}, g_{m15} and using Eqs. (12), (14) can be re-written as,

$$V_7(t) = \alpha^2 \gamma\beta R_3 R_4.\frac{V_{out}(t)g_{m13}}{2}.y(t) \tag{15}$$

Applying KCL at node 8 we get,

$$(V_{out}(t) - V_7(t))g_{m16} = \frac{y(t)}{R_5} \tag{16}$$

Putting the values of $V_7(t)$ from Eq. (15) and $V_{out}(t)$ from Eq. (10) in Eq. (16), output of Fig. 5 can be expressed as,

$$y(t) = \frac{R_5 g_{m16}.e^{V_{in}(t).k_{exp}}}{1 + \alpha^2\gamma\beta R_3 R_4 R_5.\frac{g_{m13}}{2}g_{m16}.e^{V_{in}(t).k_{exp}}} \tag{17}$$

which resembles the defining equation of sigmoid function given in Eq. (1). Here, $k_{exp} = \frac{g_{m11}}{k_{ln} \cdot g_{m12}}$, as defined in section III-A. Therefore, Fig. 5 can realize sigmoid function following the synthesis of Eq. (4).

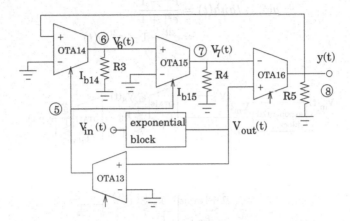

Fig. 5. Sigmoid function using exponential block with feedback

3.4   Comparison of Division Method and Feedback Method

Comparing the two methodologies for sigmoid function, discussed so far, it can be concluded that, feedback method can implement sigmoid function using 16 OTAs, 5 resistors and 2 capacitors while division method requires 19 OTAs, 5 resistors and 2 capacitors to implement the same. Therefore, feedback method is advantageous among the two in terms of hardware utilization.

It is to be noted that, hardware requirement can further be reduced if the circuits of Figs. 4 and 5 are provided with ramp function (t) or parabolic function ($\frac{1}{t}$) as inputs, as demonstrated in [1]. In the next section, hyperbolic tangent function has been synthesized using the feedback method.

4   Synthesis of Hyperbolic Tangent Function

Hyperbolic tangent function [12] is defined as the ratio between the hyperbolic sine and hyperbolic cosine functions and expressed as,

$$tanh(t) = \frac{e^t - e^{-t}}{e^t + e^{-t}} = \frac{e^{2t} - 1}{e^{2t} + 1} \tag{18}$$

In multi-layer neural networks, the tanh function is preferred compared to the sigmoid function because it gives better training performance. Several authors in literature have proposed different methods for generating hyperbolic tangent function [11,12]. Bhanja et al. in [1] used four exponential blocks with divider for generating $tanh(t)$ in a procedure similar to the division method given in Eq. (3). Feedback method, stated in Eq. (4), can be used to synthesize $tanh(t)$, if Eq. (18) is re-arranged as,

$$y(t) = tanh(t) = \frac{e^{2t} - 1}{e^{2t} + 1}$$
$$= e^{2t} - 1 - e^{2t}.y(t) \tag{19}$$

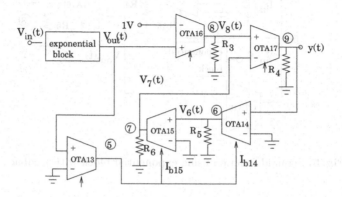

Fig. 6. Hyperbolic tangent function using exponential block and feedback

Figure 6 depicts the OTA realization of the above synthesis (Eq. (19)). OTA13, OTA14 and OTA15 multiplies $V_{out} = e^{V_{in}(t).k_{exp}}$ with y(t). OTA16 subtracts 1 from V_{out}. The output of OTA15 is subtracted from the output of OTA16 using OTA17 to produce final output y(t), complying with the synthesis of Eq. (19). Applying KCL at node 5 and assuming $I_{b15} = I_{b14}$ we get,

$$I_{b15} = I_{b14} = \frac{V_{out}(t)g_{m13}}{2} \tag{20}$$

Voltages at node 6 ($V_6(t)$) and 7 ($V_7(t)$) can be written as,

$$V_6(t) = y(t)g_{m14}R_5 \quad and \quad V_7(t) = V_6(t)g_{m15}R_6 \tag{21}$$

where, $g_{m14} = \alpha\sqrt{\gamma\beta I_{b14}}$ and $g_{m15} = \alpha\sqrt{\gamma\beta I_{b15}}$. Replacing the values of g_{m14} and g_{m15} and using Eq. (20), voltage at node 7 can be re-written as,

$$V_7(t) = R_5 R_6 \alpha^2 \gamma\beta \frac{V_{out}(t)g_{m13}}{2}.y(t) \tag{22}$$

Applying KCL at node 8, voltage $V_8(t)$ is expressed as,

$$V_8(t) = g_{m16}R_3.(V_{out}(t) - 1) \tag{23}$$

Application of KCL at node 9 and replacement of values from Eqs. (22) and (23) gives,

$$\frac{y(t)}{R_4} = (V_8(t) - V_7(t))g_{m17}$$

$$y(t) = \frac{g_{m16}g_{m17}R_4R_3(V_{out}(t) - 1)}{1 + R_4R_5R_6\alpha^2\gamma\beta g_{m17}\frac{g_{m13}}{2}V_{out}(t)} \tag{24}$$

Using the value of $V_{out}(t)$ from Eq. (10), output of Fig. 6 can be re-written as,

$$y(t) = \frac{g_{m16}g_{m17}R_4R_3(e^{V_{in}(t).k_{exp}} - 1)}{1 + R_4R_5R_6\alpha^2\gamma\beta g_{m17}\frac{g_{m13}}{2}.e^{V_{in}(t).k_{exp}}} \tag{25}$$

where, $k_{exp} = \frac{g_{m11}}{k_{ln}.g_{m12}}$ as defined in section III-A. By adjusting the values of the parameters g_{m11}, g_{m12} and k_{ln} so that, $\frac{g_{m11}}{k_{ln}.g_{m12}} = 2$, hyperbolic tangent function of Eq. (19) can be realized using Eq. (25).

Figure 6 can produce hyperbolic tangent function using one exponential block, 5 OTAs and 4 resistors. By applying ramp function (t) or parabolic function ($\frac{1}{t}$) to the input of Fig. 6, hardware utilization can be reduced further, as demonstrated in [1].

5   Sensitivity Analysis

Tolerances associated with the component values make the actual circuit response deviate from the ideal response. The classical sensitivity function [1] is defined as,

$$S_x^y = \lim_{\triangle x \to 0} \frac{\triangle y/y}{\triangle x/x}, \quad S_x^y = \frac{dy}{dx}.\frac{x}{y} \tag{26}$$

where 'x' denotes the value of a component (resistor, capacitor etc.) whereas 'y' is the circuit parameter of interest. Thus, the value of S_x^y is used to determine per unit change in 'y' due to a given per unit change in 'x'. The sensitivity of process parameters and circuit parameters on the gain has been discussed here. Gain (G_1) of the circuit of Fig. 4 is given by,

$$G_1 = \frac{g_{m13}}{\alpha^2\gamma\beta\sqrt{g_{m15}g_{m14}}.R_3R_4R_5g_{m16}g_{m19}} \tag{27}$$

Therefore, G_1 depends on the circuit parameters g_{mi}, i = 13, 14, 15, 16, 19, R_3, R_4, R_5 and process parameters α, β, γ. Sensitivity of G_1 to the circuit parameters are given by,

$$S_{g_{m13}}^{G_1} = 1, \quad S_{g_{m14}}^{G_1} = S_{g_{m15}}^{G_1} = -\frac{1}{2}$$

$$S_{g_{m16}}^{G_1} = S_{g_{m19}}^{G_1} = S_{R_3}^{G_1} = S_{R_4}^{G_1} = S_{R_5}^{G_1} = -1 \tag{28}$$

Equation (28) demonstrates that, gain of the circuit G_1 changes with circuit parameter variation. For example, 1% increase in g_{m16} results in 1% decrease in G_1. Sensitivity of G_1 to the process parameters are,

$$S_{\alpha}^{G_1} = -2, \quad S_{\gamma}^{G_1} = S_{\beta}^{G_1} = -1 \tag{29}$$

which indicates that, a 1% increase in α, γ and β cause G_1 to decrease by 2%, 1% and 1% respectively.

Similarly, sensitivities of circuit parameters and process parameters on the gain G_2 of the circuit of Fig. 5 are given by,

$$S_{g_{m16}}^{G_2} = S_{R_5}^{G_2} = \frac{1}{1 + \alpha^2 \gamma \beta R_3 R_4 R_5 . \frac{g_{m13}}{2} g_{m16}}$$

$$S_{g_{m13}}^{G_2} = S_{R_3}^{G_2} = S_{R_4}^{G_2} = S_{\gamma}^{G_2} = S_{\beta}^{G_2} = \frac{1}{2} S_{\alpha}^{G_2}$$

$$= -\frac{\alpha^2 \gamma \beta R_3 R_4 R_5 . \frac{g_{m13}}{2} g_{m16}}{1 + \alpha^2 \gamma \beta R_3 R_4 R_5 . \frac{g_{m13}}{2} g_{m16}} \tag{30}$$

All the sensitivities are lower than unity if $\alpha^2 \gamma \beta R_3 R_4 R_5 . \frac{g_{m13}}{2} g_{m16} \geq 1$. Sensitivities of circuit parameters and process parameters on the gain G_3 of the circuit of Fig. 6 have also been calculated as given below.

$$S_{R_3}^{G_3} = S_{g_{m16}}^{G_3} = 1$$

$$S_{R_4}^{G_3} = S_{g_{m17}}^{G_3} = \frac{1}{1 + R_4 R_5 R_6 \alpha^2 \gamma \beta g_{m17} \frac{g_{m13}}{2}}$$

$$S_{g_{m13}}^{G_3} = S_{R_5}^{G_3} = S_{R_6}^{G_3} = S_{\gamma}^{G_3} = S_{\beta}^{G_3} = \frac{1}{2} S_{\alpha}^{G_3}$$

$$= -\frac{R_4 R_5 R_6 \alpha^2 \gamma \beta g_{m17} \frac{g_{m13}}{2}}{1 + R_4 R_5 R_6 \alpha^2 \gamma \beta g_{m17} \frac{g_{m13}}{2}} \tag{31}$$

All the sensitivities, except $S_{R_3}^{G_3}$ and $S_{g_{m16}}^{G_3}$, are lower than unity if $R_4 R_5 R_6 \alpha^2 \gamma \beta g_{m17} \frac{g_{m13}}{2} \geq 1$. Therefore, it can be concluded that sensitivities of circuit parameters and process parameters on the output is minimized as well as can be controlled, if feedback method is implemented. Sensitivities related to the parameters included in the exponential function realization had been elaborated in [1].

6   Simulation Result

Performances of all the circuits have been verified through SPICE simulation with $0.13\,\mu$ MOSIS BSIM3V3 model. For simulation of all the circuits, OTA of Fig. 1 has been used in ± 1.2V supply environment with $W/L = 0.18\mu/0.15\mu$ (for pmos), $W/L = 0.15\mu/0.13\mu$ (for nmos). The linear range and frequency response of the OTA is shown in Fig. 7(a) and (b) respectively.

Figure 8(a) and (b) depict the responses of the proposed sigmoid circuits using division method (ref. Fig. 4) and feedback method (ref. Fig. 5) respectively while Fig. 8(c) shows the simulated output of $tanh(t)$ function generated by Fig. 6. Values of all g_{mi} lie between $20\,\mu$S and $400\,\mu$S. All resistors and capacitors are considered to have equal values of $10\,$K and $5\,$pF respectively. The simulation

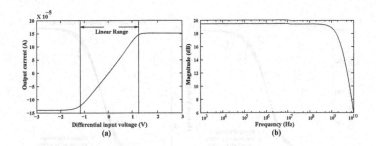

Fig. 7. (a) Linearity and (b) Frequency response of OTA of Fig. 1

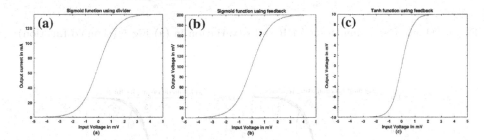

Fig. 8. Simulation results of the proposed circuits: (a) Output of Fig. 4, (b) Output of Fig. 5, (c) Output of Fig. 6

results prove the capability of the proposed circuits of producing sigmoid function and hyperbolic tangent function. For further analysis, the circuits using feedback method have been considered only due to its advantages.

Figure 9(a) and (b) reflect the effects of circuit parameter variation (values of R and C) on the outputs of Figs. 5 and 6 respectively. For ±10% change of R and C values from their nominal values the maximum deviation in output is ±0.65% for the sigmoid output (Fig. 5) and ±3.45% for the $tanh(t)$ output (Fig. 6). Impact of process parameter variation on the circuits under observation is depicted in Fig. 10. For ±10% deviation of W, L and t_{ox} from their nominal values causes the sigmoid output (Fig. 5) and $tanh(t)$ output (Fig. 6) to shift by maximum of ±0.37% and ±4.09% respectively. Dependence of sigmoid and $tanh(t)$ output on temperature is given in Fig. 11. Test has been performed at T = 0 °C, 27 °C and 50 °C. Figure 11(a) shows that the maximum deviation is 5% from the nominal value measured at T = 27 °C, for the circuit of Fig. 5. A larger temperature dependence can be seen for Fig. 6, where the maximum change from the nominal value (27 °C) is 10%. The maximum output noise in $9.2\,\mu V/\sqrt{Hz}$ for the sigmoid output and $0.15\,\mu V/\sqrt{Hz}$ for the $tanh(t)$ output. Total harmonic distortion is < 3% for both the outputs of Figs. 5 and 6 considering sinusoidal input. The corner analysis confirms minimum variation in gain response at slow-slow (SS) and fast-fast (FF) corners compared to typical-typical (TT) corner.

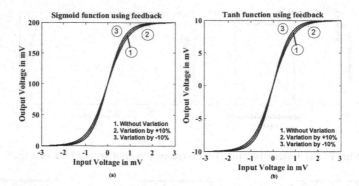

Fig. 9. Monte Carlo simulation for R and C variation in (a) Fig. 5 (sigmoid function) (b) Fig. 6 ($tanh(t)$ function)

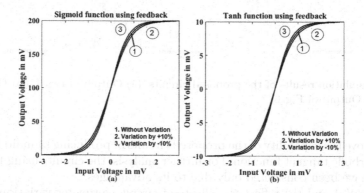

Fig. 10. Monte Carlo simulation for process variation in (a) Fig. 5 (sigmoid function) (b) Fig. 6 ($tanh(t)$ function)

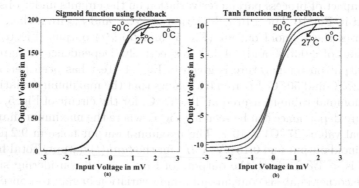

Fig. 11. Temperature dependence of the output of (a) Fig. 5 (sigmoid function) (b) Fig. 6 ($tanh(t)$ function)

7 Comparison of Previous Results

The aim of this work is to generate sigmoid and hyperbolic tangent function directly by hardware implementation without any approximation process for any arbitrary input. The exponential function generation block, used for providing input to the proposed circuits, can accept any arbitrary input. Gain and sensitivity to circuit and process parameters can be controlled by adjusting the g_m of the OTAs. Sensitivities of circuits synthesized using feedback method are less than unity due to the presence of feedback. The grounded capacitors and resistors, used in the design are suitable for optimized chip area.

The researchers [2–7] concentrated on various approximation methods for sigmoid function approximation considering the hardship of exponentiation and division. But approximation methods suffer from inaccuracy and in some cases from hardware overhead. Authors in [2] and [4] reported approximation errors along with requirement of excess hardware for fitting. The approximation error is minimized to a great extent in [5] but with limited application. It is to be noted that approximation methods are more suitable from digital platforms as digital multipliers require excess hardware. The architecture of sigmoid function calculator proposed in [3] used memory and digital gates to provide a maximum of 92.29% accuracy. Use of LUT based implementation processes increases memory requirement. Moreover analog sigmoid implementations consume less power compared to the FPGA implementations [8,10]. Direct implementation of hyperbolic tangent function has been presented in [1] requiring 4 exponential blocks, 6 OTAs and 3 resistors while the proposed $tanh(t)$ circuit of Fig. 6 realizes the same using single exponential blocks, 5 OTAs and 4 resistors.

Hardware requirement can be reduced further if ramp or parabolic function is considered as the input of the exponential block. Ability of controlling the properties of the generated sigmoid function through OTA bias currents, enables the generated circuits to be used in communication systems where adaptive function generation is required. The proposed $tanh(t)$ circuit is most suitable to be used in the companding process required in designing log-domain filters.

8 Conclusion

Two design procedures for sigmoid function realization using exponential function have been reported in this paper, among which the feedback method comes out to be the superior in terms of performance. Hyperbolic tangent function has also been synthesized using the feedback method. The feedback method shows lower sensitivities and minimum hardware overhead. Effectiveness of using the proposed circuits is adaptive systems and log-domains filters needs further intervention.

References

1. Bhanja, M., Ray, B.N.: OTA-based logarithmic circuit for arbitrary input signal and its application. IEEE Trans. Very Large Scale Integr. (VLSI) Syst. **24**(2), 638–649 (2016). https://doi.org/10.1109/TVLSI.2015.2406953

2. Zhang, M., Vassiliadis, S., Delgado-Frias, J.G.: Sigmoid generators for neural computing using piecewise approximations. IEEE Trans. Comput. **45**(9), 1045–1049 (1996). https://doi.org/10.1109/12.537127
3. Tsai, C.-H., Chih, Y.-T., Wong, W.H., Lee, C.-Y.: A hardware-efficient sigmoid function with adjustable precision for a neural network system. IEEE Trans. Circ. Syst. II Exp. Briefs **62**(11), 1073–1077 (2015). https://doi.org/10.1109/TCSII. 2015.2456531
4. Yamanashi, Y., Umeda, K., Yoshikawa, N.: Pseudo sigmoid function generator for a superconductive neural network. IEEE Trans. Appl. Supercond. **23**(3) (2013). https://doi.org/10.1109/TASC.2012.2228531
5. Basterretxea, K., Tarela, J.M., Del Campo, I.: Approximation of sigmoid function and the derivative for hardware implementation of aftificial neurons. IEE Proc.-Circ. Devices Syst. **151**(1), 18–24 (2004). https://doi.org/10.1049/ip-cds:20030607
6. Basterretxea, K., Tarela, J.M., Campo, I.D., Bosque, G.: An experimental study on nonlinear function computation for neural/fuzzy hardware design. IEEE Trans. Neural Netw. **18**(1), 266–283 (2007). https://doi.org/10.1109/TNN.2006.884680
7. Khodabandehloo, G., Mirhassani, M., Ahmadi, M.: Analog implementation of a novel resistive-type sigmoidal neuron. IEEE Trans. Very Large Scale Integr. (VLSI) Syst. **20**(4), 750–754 (2012). https://doi.org/10.1109/TVLSI.2011.2109404
8. Pan, S.P., Li, Z., Huang, Y.J., Lin, W.C.: FPGA realization of activation function for neural network. In: 2018 7th International Symposium on Next Generation Electronics (ISNE), pp. 1–2. IEEE (2018). https://doi.org/10.1109/ISNE. 2018.8394695
9. Sharma, S.K., Chandra, P.: An adaptive sigmoidal activation function cascading neural networks. In: Corchado, E., Snášel, V., Sedano, J., Hassanien, A.E., Calvo, J.L., Ślęzak, D. (eds.) SOCO 2011. Advances in Intelligent and Soft Computing, vol. 87. Springer, Heidelberg (2011). https://doi.org/10.1007/978-3-642-19644-7_12
10. Zhang, L.: Implementation of fixed-point neuron models with threshold, ramp and sigmoid activation functions. In 4th International Conference on Mechanics and Mechatronics Research (ICMMR 2017). IOP Conference Series: Materials Science and Engineering, vol. 224, p. 012054 (2017). https://doi.org/10.1088/1757-899X/224/1/012054
11. Zamanlooy, B., Mirhassani, M.: Efficient VLSI implementation of neural networks with hyperbolic tangent activation function. IEEE Trans. Very Large Scale Integr. (VLSI) Syst. **22**(1), 39–48 (2014). https://doi.org/10.1109/TVLSI.2012.2232321
12. Robles, M.C., Serrano, L.: A novel CMOS current-mode fully differential tanh (x) implementation. In: IEEE International Symposium on Circuits and Systems 2008, pp. 2158–2161 (2008). https://doi.org/10.1109/ISCAS.2008.4541878
13. Sanchez-Sinencio, E., Silva-Martinez, J.: CMOS transconductance amplifiers, architectures and active filters: a tutorial. IEE Proc. Circ. Devices Syst. **147**(1), 3–12 (2000). https://doi.org/10.1049/ip-cds:20000055

Flexible Adaptive FIR Filter Designs Using LMS Algorithm

M. Mohamed Asan Basiri$^{(\boxtimes)}$

Department of Electronics and Communication Engineering, IIITDM,
Kurnool 518007, India
asanbasiri@gmail.com

Abstract. This paper proposes the least mean square (LMS) algorithm based versatile, vector, and fault tolerant adaptive finite impulse response (FIR) filter designs. Here, the M-taps versatile design is to perform the filter operation with the number of filter co-efficients varied from 2 to M. The M-taps vector design is to perform $\lfloor \frac{M}{L} \rfloor$ numbers of L-taps filter operations in parallel, where $M \geq L$. The fault tolerant M-taps filter is to perform the $(M-N)$-taps fault free filter operation under the N numbers of faulty filter kernels, where $(M-N) \geq 2$. All the existing and proposed designs are implemented with 45 nm CMOS technology. The proposed 16-taps vector adaptive filter design achieves 93% of improvement in throughput as compared with the distributed arithmetic based design.

Keywords: Adaptive filter · FIR filter · LMS algorithm

1 Introduction

In the present advancement of technology, adaptive filters play a major role in echo cancellation, noise cancellation, channel equalization, beam forming, and identifying the unknown system. Here, the filter co-efficients (or filter taps) are adaptively varied with respect to the desired response of the system. The most widely used adaptive filter algorithms are LMS, normalized LMS, and delayed LMS. Figure 1 shows the LMS algorithm based adaptive FIR filter with 4-taps, where $x[n]$, $y[n]$, $d[n]$, and $e[n]$ are the input, output, desired, and error signal sample values respectively. The filter co-efficients are $h[3]$, $h[2]$, $h[1]$, and $h[0]$. The filter co-efficients will be updated until the convergence stops at $e[n] = 0$. Here, the width of input and filter co-efficients is n-bits. The adder width is equal to $(2n + log_2 M)$-bits, where M is the filter length ($M = 4$). In Fig. 1, two portions are involved. They are 4-taps FIR filter and LMS algorithm. The dotted box represents the 4-taps FIR filter and the rest represents the LMS algorithm. The M-taps FIR filter equation is shown in (1).

$$y[n] = \sum_{k=0}^{M-1} x[k].h[n-k];$$ (1)

© Springer Nature Singapore Pte Ltd. 2019
A. Sengupta et al. (Eds.): VDAT 2019, CCIS 1066, pp. 61–71, 2019.
https://doi.org/10.1007/978-981-32-9767-8_6

According to the steepest descent LMS algorithm, the weight updation and error calculation of the adaptive filter are shown in (2) and (3) respectively.

$$h^{new} = h^{old} + \mu.e[n].x[n] \qquad (2)$$

$$e[n] = y[n] - d[n] \qquad (3)$$

The order of the adaptive filter is crucial during the operations. If the filter is too short, then the output will be degraded. If the filter is too long, then convergence will be slow. In the filters with fixed number of co-efficients, the registers are loaded with zero co-efficients that causes some unnecessary calculations. Similarly, the mean square error of the adaptive filter will be increased if the filter length is undermodeled. To resolve these issues, the number of co-efficients needs to be varied with respect to the requirement. In the recent signal processing architectures, versatile and vector hardware implementations are inevitable. In the versatile implementations, the same architecture is to perform multiple modes. For example, the adaptive filter length (or number of filter co-efficients or number of filter taps or filter order) is varied in the run time with respect to the requirement [1–4]. In the vector implementations [5,6], multiple similar operations are performed in parallel to improve the throughput. Also, the fault tolerant digital circuit [7] is one of the emerging techniques in the recent VLSI design technologies. Here, the function of faulty hardware modules is done with fault free redundant hardware unit [8]. In all the aforementioned techniques, the hardware flexibility is the key factor. The flexibility is directly proportional to the area and power dissipation. Our proposed designs use the versatility, vector, and fault tolerant hardware implementations. The following literature shows the various adaptive filter hardware implementations.

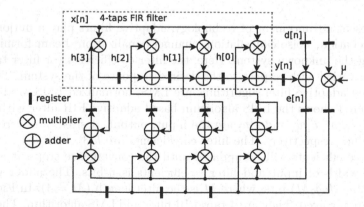

Fig. 1. LMS algorithm based adaptive FIR filter with 4-taps.

1.1 Related Work

In [11–13], systolic array of processing elements (PEs) are involved in the adaptive filter design, where each PE is made up of few multipliers and adders. The output from each PE is sent to the next/previous immediate PEs to perform the filter operation. In [14], the partial products from the multipliers of the FIR filter are added using a pipelined tree of adders instead the multiplier followed by an adder as shown in the Fig. 1. In [15], the multiplied outputs from all the filter taps are added using the tree of adders, where the adaptive filter structure is reconfigurable to perform LMS and DLMS. In [16], few extra registers are used in between each multiplier and adder of the DLMS based adaptive filter structure to reduce the critical path. In [17], distributed arithmetic based adaptive FIR filter is shown, where the cycles to complete the operation is greater than all the other existing designs due to bit serial arithmetic. In all these existing designs, the filter order cannot be changed in the hardware during the run time, multiple filter operations (vector operations) cannot be performed in parallel, and the fault tolerance ability is absent. These three drawbacks give the motivation to our proposed techniques.

1.2 Contribution of This Paper

This paper proposes the LMS algorithm based versatile, vector, and fault tolerant adaptive FIR filter designs. Here, the M-taps versatile design is to perform the filter operation with the number of filter co-efficients varied from 2 to M. The M-taps vector design is to perform $\lfloor \frac{M}{L} \rfloor$ numbers of L-taps filter operations in parallel, where $M \geq L$. The fault tolerant M-taps filter is to perform the $(M - N)$-taps fault free filter operation under the N numbers of faulty filter kernels, where $(M - N) \geq 2$. All the existing and proposed designs are implemented with 45 nm CMOS technology.

The rest of the paper is organized as follows. Section 2 explains the proposed flexible architectures of the adaptive FIR filter. Design modeling, implementation, and results are stated in Sect. 3, followed by a conclusion in Sect. 4.

2 Proposed Flexible Architectures of LMS Algorithm Based Adaptive FIR Filter

The multiplier followed by an adder in Fig. 1 is replaced by fused multiply add (FMA) [9] in our proposed designs as shown in Figs. 3 and 4. The FMA is to compute multiplication followed by the addition (Example: $(A \times B) + C$), whose circuit depth is equal to the multiplier. Figure 2 shows the fixed point FMA architecture, where the 8×8-bits multiplication result is added with 16-bits third operand (C). The Wallace structure is to add eight partial products along with C. In a $n \times n$-bits FMA using Wallace structure, the number of inputs at 1st level of the carry save adder (CSA) tree is $(n + 1)$. The number of outputs at each level of CSA is $(\frac{2}{3})$ of the previous level. Therefore, the number of outputs at 1st, 2nd, 3rd, and last level of the CSA tree are $\frac{2}{3}.(n+1)$, $\frac{4}{9}.(n+1)$, $\frac{8}{27}.(n+1)$, 2 respectively. The last level of the CSA tree (l) and n have the relationship as $(\frac{2}{3})^{l}.(n+1) = 2$. Therefore the height of the CSA tree would be $l = -1.71 + 1.71log_2(n+1)$. The carry look ahead adder (CLA) is to add the sum and carry from the CSA at the last level.

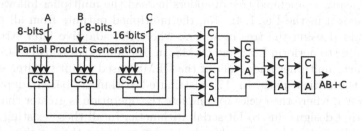

Fig. 2. Fixed point FMA is to add 8×8-bits multiplication result with 16-bits third operand.

Figure 3(a) shows the LMS algorithm based proposed versatile adaptive FIR filter with 4-taps. Here, the operations with 4-taps, 3-taps, and 2-taps are done with respect to the corresponding assignments of resets (R1, R0, and R). The register output is zero if the reset is one. The proposed M-taps versatile adaptive FIR filter equation is shown in (4), where the operations are done with respect to the number of filter taps varied from 2 to M.

$$y[n] = \sum_{k=0}^{L-1} x[k].h[n-k]; \ 2 \le L \le M \tag{4}$$

The number of FMAs, multipliers, adders, and registers in M-taps proposed versatile design are $(2M-1)$, 2, 1, and $(3M+3)$ respectively. The circuit depth of the proposed versatile design is equal to $T(FMA)$, where the circuit depth of FMA is $T(FMA)$.

Figure 3(b) shows the LMS algorithm based proposed vector adaptive FIR filter with 6-taps. Here, the control lines $s[0]$ and $s[1]$ are to perform the operation with various filter lengths such as 6-taps, 4-taps, and 2-taps. Few 2-to-1 multiplexers (MUXes) are used to incorporate the vector operations. The maximum number of parallel operations with 2-taps performed in the proposed vector design is $\lfloor \frac{M}{2} \rfloor$. The number of parallel L-taps filter operations using the proposed M-taps vector design is $\lfloor \frac{M}{L} \rfloor$, where $M \ge L$. The FIR filter equation, error calculation, and LMS algorithm for the proposed M-taps vector adaptive filter are shown in (5), (6), and (7) respectively, where the term **parallel** represents that the filter operations with respect to i varied from 0 to $\lfloor \frac{M}{L} \rfloor$ are done in parallel.

$$y_i[n] = \sum_{k=0}^{L-1} x_i[k].h_i[n-k]; \ \textbf{parallel} \ i = 0 \ to \ \lfloor \frac{M}{L} \rfloor \tag{5}$$

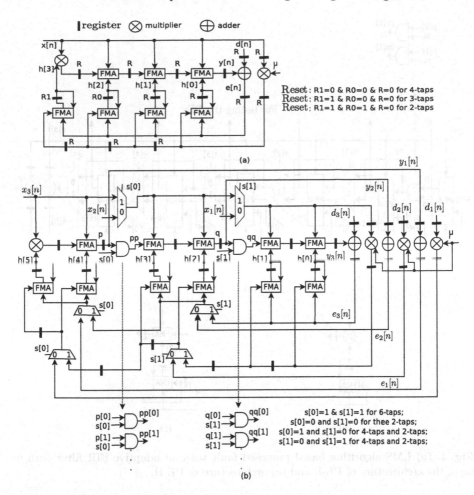

Fig. 3. LMS algorithm based proposed (a) versatile adaptive FIR filter with 4-taps and (b) vector adaptive FIR filter with 6-taps.

$$e_i[n] = d_i[n] - y_i[n]; \textbf{ parallel } i = 0 \ to \ \lfloor \frac{M}{L} \rfloor \tag{6}$$

$$h_i^{new}[n] = h_i^{old}[n] + \mu.e_i[n].x_i[n]; \textbf{ parallel } i = 0 \ to \ \lfloor \frac{M}{L} \rfloor \tag{7}$$

The number of FMAs, multipliers, adders, multiplexers, and registers in M-taps proposed vector design are $(2M - 1)$, $(\frac{M}{2} + 1)$, $\frac{M}{2}$, $3(\frac{M}{2} - 1)$, and $(5M - 1)$ respectively. The circuit depth of the proposed vector design is equal to $T(FMA) + (\frac{M}{2} - 1)T_{MUX}^{2-to-1}$, where T_{MUX}^{2-to-1} is the circuit depth of 2-to-1 multiplexer. Since the 6-taps filter is shown in Fig. 3(b), the maximum possible number of filter operations is 3. During the mode $s[1 : 0] = 01$ or 10, two filter operations (with 2-taps and 4-taps) can be done in parallel. The operation of Fig. 3(b) is shown in Table 1.

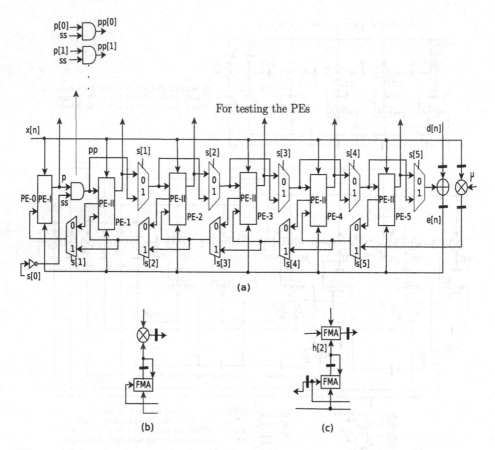

Fig. 4. (a) LMS algorithm based proposed fault tolerant adaptive FIR filter with 6-taps, (b) architecture of PE-I, and (c) architecture of PE-II.

Figure 4(a) shows the LMS algorithm based proposed fault tolerant adaptive FIR filter with 6-taps, which consists of the processing elements PE-I and PE-II as shown in Fig. 4(b) and (c) respectively. In the proposed M-taps fault tolerant adaptive FIR filter, $(M - N)$-taps fault free filter operation can be done under N faulty filter kernels, where $(M - N) \geq 2$. In Fig. 4(a), the filter kernels are represented as PE-0, PE-1, PE-2, PE-3, PE-4, and PE-5. If N numbers of PEs are faulty, then the $(6 - N)$ numbers of fault free PEs are able to do the $(6 - N)$-taps filter operation using the 6-bits control line $s[5 : 0]$, where $(6 - N) \geq 2$. Initially, the particular PE will be tested, then that PE will be avoided during the operation if a fault occurs. For example, the following steps show the fault testing and fault tolerance behaviour of the proposed filter as shown in Fig. 4(a) under the assumption of faulty PE-2, where the other PEs are assumed as fault free.

Table 1. Operation of the proposed 6-taps vector adaptive FIR filter as shown in Fig. 3(b).

$s[1:0]$	Filter taps	Input	Desired output	Filter output	Error signal	Filter length
00	$h[5],h[4]$	$x_3[n]$	$d_1[n]$	$y_1[n]$	$e_1[n]$	2
	$h[3],h[2]$	$x_2[n]$	$d_2[n]$	$y_2[n]$	$e_2[n]$	2
	$h[1],h[0]$	$x_1[n]$	$d_3[n]$	$y_3[n]$	$e_3[n]$	2
01	$h[5],h[4],h[3],h[2]$	$x_3[n]$	$d_2[n]$	$y_2[n]$	$e_2[n]$	4
	$h[1],h[0]$	$x_1[n]$	$d_3[n]$	$y_3[n]$	$e_3[n]$	2
10	$h[5],h[4]$	$x_3[n]$	$d_1[n]$	$y_1[n]$	$e_1[n]$	2
	$h[3],h[1],h[1],h[0]$	$x_2[n]$	$d_3[n]$	$y_3[n]$	$e_3[n]$	4
11	$h[5],h[4],h[3],$ $h[2],h[1],h[0]$	$x_3[n]$	$d_3[n]$	$y_3[n]$	$e_3[n]$	6

- Testing: Assign $s[5:0] = 6'b111111$ and find out the output of all the PEs. Let's assume the output of PE-0, PE-1, PE-2, PE-3, PE-4, and PE-5 are o_0, o_1, o_2, o_3, o_4, and o_5 respectively. Since PE-2 is faulty filter kernel, $o_2 \neq o_1$ and $o_0 = o_1 = o_3 = o_4 = o_5$.
- Fault tolerance by avoiding the PE-2: Assign $s[1:0] = 2'b00$, $s[2] = 1$, and $s[5:3] = 3'b000$. Now, fault free 5-taps filter operation can be performed.

Similarly, the following steps show the fault testing and fault tolerance behaviour of the proposed filter as shown in Fig. 4(a) under the assumption of faulty PE-2 and PE-4, where the other PEs are assumed as fault free.

- Testing: Assign $s[5:0] = 6'b111111$ and find out the output of all the PEs. Since PE-2 and PE-4 are faulty filter kernels, $o_2 \neq o_1$, $o_4 \neq o_1$, and $o_0 = o_1 = o_3 = o_5$.
- Fault tolerance by avoiding the PE-2 and PE-4: Assign $s[1:0] = 2'b00$, $s[2] = 1'b1$, $s[3] = 1'b0$, $s[4] = 1'b1$, and $s[5] = 1'b0$. Now, fault free 4-taps filter operation can be performed.

In the same way, the fault free filter operations with filter length varied from 2 to 6 can be performed using our proposed fault tolerant design as shown in Fig. 4(a) if the number of faulty filter kernels varied from 4 to 0 respectively. The number of FMAs, multipliers, adders, 2-to-1 multiplexers, and registers in M-taps proposed fault tolerant design are $(2M-1)$, 2, 1, $2(M-1)$, and $(3M+3)$ respectively. The circuit depth of the proposed fault tolerant design is equal to $T(FMA) + (M-1)T_{MUX}^{2-to-1}$.

3 Design Modeling, Implementations, and Results

All the existing and proposed designs are modelled in Verilog HDL. These Verilog HDL models are simulated, verified, and synthesised using Cadence Simvision/Genus/Innovus ASIC design tool (version 15.20). All the proposed designs

Table 2. Theoretical analysis of the LMS algorithm based various M-taps adaptive FIR filter designs.

	# multipliers	# FMAs	# adders	# registers	# 2-to-1 MUXes
[10]	$2M$	0	$2M+1$	$3M+1$	0
TF-FPDLMS [11]	$2M+1$	0	$2M+1$	$23M$	0
Architecture-II [12]	$2M+1$	0	$2M+1$	$4M+2$	M
Systolic [13]	$3M$	0	$2M$	$5M$	0
Using tree of adders [14]	0	0	$10M+2$	$>2M+14$	0
Configurable LMS/DLMS [15]	$2M+1$	0	$N+2^{log_2 N}$	$2M+4$	0
DF-RDLMS [16]	$2M+1$	0	$2M+1$	$8N-1$	0
Distributed arithmetic [17]	0	0	$>M$	$>M$	4
Proposed versatile (Fig. 3(a))	2	$2M-1$	1	$3M+3$	0
Proposed vector (Fig. 3(b))	$\frac{M}{2}+1$	$2M-1$	$\frac{M}{2}$	$5M-1$	$3(\frac{M}{2}-1)$
Proposed fault tolerant (Fig. 4(a))	2	$2M-1$	1	$3M+3$	$2(M-1)$

	Critial path depth	Possible filter length for operation	Max. # operations in parallel
[10]	$T(MUL)$	M	1
TF-FPDLMS [11]	$T(MUL)$	M	1
Architecture-II [12]	$T(MUL)$	M	1
Systolic [13]	$2T(MUL)+T(ADD)$	M	1
Using tree of adders [14]	$T(ADD)$	M	1
Configurable LMS/DLMS [15]	$(log_2 N)T(ADD)$	M	1
DF-RDLMS [16]	$T(MUL)$	M	1
Distributed arithmetic [17]	$2T_{MUX}^{2-to-1}+2T(ADD)$ $+T(Look\text{-}up\text{-}table)$	M	1
Proposed versatile (Fig. 3(a))	$T(FMA)$	$2, 3, 4,...M$	1
Proposed vector (Fig. 3(b))	$T(FMA)+(\frac{M}{2}-1)T_{MUX}^{2-to-1}$	$2, 4, 6, ...M$	$\frac{M}{2}$
Proposed fault tolerant (Fig. 4(a))	$T(FMA)+(M-1)T_{MUX}^{2-to-1}$	$2, 3, 4,...M$	1

are implemented with 45 nm CMOS technology, where the operating voltage is 0.9v. The actual implementations (CMOS library or FPGA) used in the reference papers for all the existing techniques are different. In this manuscript, the existing techniques are implemented as per the reference papers using one particular 45 nm library. Therefore, the comparisons of our proposed techniques with various existing techniques are valid. At the end of the physical design (after the .*gds* file generation), we have done all the physical verifications (DRC, LRC, Antenna check, and LVS check) followed by post layout simulation (gate level simulation) using the netlist generated from the physical design. In all our implementations, $Ip\_asserted\_probability$ and $Ip\_asserted\_toggle\_count$ are taken as 0.5 and 0.02 respectively. $Ip\_asserted\_probability$ is the probability for the net to be one (high). For example, the tool considers all nets in the design to be at logic level 1 for total of 50% of the simulation time, then the probability is 0.5. $Ip\_asserted\_toggle\_count$ is the toggle count per toggle rate unit. For

Table 3. Performance analysis of the LMS algorithm based various 16-taps adaptive FIR filter designs with 45 nm CMOS technology.

	Critical path delay (ps)	Frequency (MHz)	Total cell area (μm^2)	Switching power (nw)
[10]	0603.9	1655.9	62355.5	4230.0
TF-FPDLMS [11]	0603.9	1655.9	98542.1	6908.7
Architecture-II [12]	0603.9	1655.9	70556.4	4568.9
Systolic [13]	1467.8	0681.3	92506.9	6030.4
Using tree of adders [14]	0321.7	3108.4	56672.1	3890.2
Configurable LMS/DLMS [15]	1287.9	0776.5	65888.9	4330.2
DF-RDLMS [16]	0603.9	1655.9	98099.6	6340.6
Distributed arithmetic [17]	1117.5	0894.8	48901.3	3471.2
Proposed versatile (Fig. 3(a))	0603.2	1657.8	75690.5	4789.9
Proposed vector (Fig. 3(b))	0641.3	1559.3	86899.8	5568.9
Proposed fault tolerant (Fig. 4(a))	0689.4	1450.5	79034.6	5102.4

	Leakage power (nw)	Energy per operation (fJ)	Throughput ($\frac{Operations}{ps}$)
[10]	0669.9	02.95	$\frac{1}{0603.9}=01655.9$
TF-FPDLMS [11]	1502.5	05.10	$\frac{1}{0603.9}=01655.9$
Architecture-II [12]	0780.4	03.20	$\frac{1}{0603.9}=01655.9$
Systolic [13]	1202.2	10.61	$\frac{1}{1467.8}=00681.3$
Using tree of adders [14]	0601.1	01.44	$\frac{1}{0321.7}=03108.4$
Configurable LMS/DLMS [15]	0702.2	06.48	$\frac{1}{1287.9}=00776.5$
DF-RDLMS [16]	1309.8	04.62	$\frac{1}{0603.9}=01655.9$
Distributed arithmetic [17]	0542.1	04.48	$\frac{1}{1117.5}=0894.8$
Proposed versatile (Fig. 3(a))	0840.5	03.39	$\frac{1}{0603.2}=01657.8$
Proposed vector (Fig. 3(b))	1099.8	04.27	$\frac{8}{0611.3}=12474.4$
Proposed fault tolerant (Fig. 4(a))	0950.5	04.17	$\frac{1}{0689.4}=01450.5$

example, considering a signal toggling 2 times in 100 ns, then the toggle rate is $2/100 = 0.02$.

Table 2 shows the theoretical analysis of the LMS algorithm based various M-taps adaptive FIR filter designs. Table 3 shows the performance analysis of the LMS algorithm based various 16-taps adaptive FIR filter designs with 45 nm CMOS technology. Since the circuit depth of the multiplier is equal to the FMA, the critical path delay of [10], TF-FPDLMS [11], Architecture-II [12], DF-RDLMS [16], and proposed versatile designs are more similar. In the proposed vector and fault tolerant designs, the critical path includes an FMA and few 2-to-1 multiplexers. Therefore, the critical path delay of these proposed designs is greater than proposed versatile design. Similarly, the critical path of [14] includes an adder rather than a multiplier, so the critical path delay of [14] is less than all the other designs. The number of 2-to-1 multiplexers in the critical path of the proposed fault tolerant design is greater than the proposed vector design. Therefore, the critical path delay of proposed fault tolerant design is greater than the proposed vector design. Since multiple similar filter operations can be done in parallel, throughput of the proposed vector design is much greater than others.

The proposed 16-taps vector adaptive filter design achieves 93% of improvement in throughput as compared with distributed arithmetic based design [17].

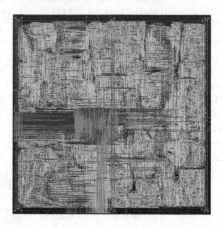

Fig. 5. Chip layout diagram for the LMS algorithm based proposed vector 16-taps adaptive FIR filter with a core area as $102235.06\,\mu m^2$, die space around core as $15\,\mu m$, and total chip area as $122325.06\,\mu m^2$ using 45-nm CMOS technology.

Due to more 2-to-1 multiplexers, the area and power dissipation of the proposed vector and fault tolerant designs are greater than the proposed versatile design. Since the bit serial arithmetic is used in [17], area and power dissipations are much less than other designs, where the bit parallel arithmetic is used. Due to the flexibility in the hardware of our proposed designs, the area and power dissipations are greater than many of the existing designs as shown in Table 3. Figure 5 shows the chip layout diagram of the LMS algorithm based proposed vector 16-taps adaptive FIR filter, where the aspect ratio and core utilization are 1 and 85% respectively. Therefore, the core area in the layout is $\frac{86899.8}{0.85} = 102235.06\,\mu m^2$.

4   Conclusion

This paper proposes the LMS algorithm based versatile, vector, and fault tolerant adaptive FIR filter designs. Here, the M-taps versatile design is to perform the filter operation with the number of filter co-efficients varied from 2 to M. The M-taps vector design is to perform $\lfloor \frac{M}{L} \rfloor$ numbers of L-taps filter operations in parallel, where $M \geq L$. The fault tolerant M-taps filter is to perform the $(M - N)$-taps fault free filter operation under the N numbers of faulty filter kernels, where $(M - N) \geq 2$. All the existing and proposed designs are implemented with 45 nm CMOS technology. The proposed 16-taps vector adaptive filter design achieves 93% of improvement in throughput as compared with the distributed arithmetic based design [17].

References

1. Schuldt, C., Lindstrom, F., Li, H., Claesson, I.: Adaptive filter length selection for acoustic echo cancellation. Sig. Process. **89**(6), 1185–1194 (2009)
2. Gu, Y., Tang, K., Cui, H., Wen, D.: Convergence analysis of a deficient-length LMS filter and optimal-length sequence to model exponential decay impulse response. IEEE Signal Process. Lett. **10**(1), 4–7 (2003)
3. Gu, Y., Tang, K., Cui, H.: LMS algorithm with gradient descent filter length. IEEE Signal Process. Lett. **11**(3), 305–307 (2004)
4. Gong, Y., Cowan, C.F.N.: A novel variable tap-length algorithm for linear adaptive filters. In: IEEE International Conference on Acoustics, Speech, and Signal Processing, pp. ii–825 (2004)
5. Gerlach, L., Paya-Vaya, G., Blume, H.: An area efficient real- and complex-valued multiply-accumulate SIMD unit for digital signal processors. In: IEEE Workshop on Signal Processing Systems (SiPS), pp. 1–6 (2015)
6. Robelly, J.P., Cichon, G., Seidel, H., Fettweis, G.: Implementation of recursive digital filters into vector SIMD DSP architectures. In: IEEE International Conference on Acoustics, Speech, and Signal Processing, pp. 1–4 (2004)
7. Jenkins, W.K., Schnaufer, B.A.: Fault tolerant adaptive filters based on the block LMS algorithm. In: IEEE International Symposium on Circuits and Systems, pp. 862–865 (1993)
8. Lee, C.-Y., Meher, P.K.: Fault tolerant dual basis multiplier over $GF(2^m)$. In: IEEE Circuits and Systems International Conference on Testing and Diagnosis, pp. 1–4 (2009)
9. Basiri M, M.A., Sk, N.M.: An efficient hardware based higher radix floating point MAC design. ACM Trans. Des. Autom. Electron. Syst. (TODAES) **20**(1), 15:1–15:25 (2014)
10. Mandal, A., Mishra, R., Kaushik, B.K., Rizvi, N.Z.: Design of LMS adaptive radar detector for non-homogeneous interferences. IETE Tech. Rev. **33**(3), 269–279 (2015)
11. Ting, L.-K., Woods, R., Cowan, C.F.N.: Virtex FPGA implementation of a pipelined adaptive LMS predictor for electronic support measures receivers. IEEE Trans. Very Large Scale Integr. (VLSI) Syst. **13**(1), 86–95 (2005)
12. Santha, K.R., Vaidehi, V.: Design of efficient architectures for 1-D and 2-D DLMS adaptive filters. Integr. VLSI J. **40**(3), 209–225 (2007)
13. Kim, H., Soeleman, H., Roy, K.: Ultra-low power DLMS adaptive filter for hearing aid applications. IEEE Trans. Very Large Scale Integr. (VLSI) Syst. **11**(6), 1058–1067 (2003)
14. Meher, P.K., Park, S.Y.: Area-delay-power efficient fixed-point LMS adaptive filter with low adaptation-delay. IEEE Trans. Very Large Scale Integr. (VLSI) Syst. **22**(2), 362–371 (2014)
15. Rocher, R., Herve, N., Menard, D., Sentieys, O.: Fixed-point configurable hardware components for adaptive filters. IEURASIP J. Embed. Syst. 1–13 (2006). https://link.springer.com/article/10.1155/ES/2006/23197
16. Goel, P., Chandra, M.: VLSI implementations of retimed high speed adaptive filter structures for speech enhancement. Microsyst. Technol. **24**(12), 4799–4806 (2018)
17. Khan, M.T., Ahamed, S.R.: A new high performance VLSI architecture for LMS adaptive filter using distributed arithmetic. In: IEEE Computer Society Annual Symposium on VLSI (ISVLSI), pp. 219–224 (2017)

An Efficient Test and Fault Tolerance Technique for Paper-Based DMFB

Chandan Das[1] (ID), Sarit Chakraborty[2(✉)] (ID), and Susanta Chakraborty[3] (ID)

[1] Department of AEIE, Dr. B. C. Roy Engineering College, Durgapur, India
chandan.das@bcrec.ac.in
[2] Department of CSE, Government College of Engineering and Leather Technology, Kolkata, India
sarit.iiest@gmail.com
[3] Department of CST, Indian Institute of Engineering Science and Technology, Shibpur, India
susanta.chak@gmail.com, sc@cs.iiests.sc.in

Abstract. Recent advancement on **P**aper-based **D**igital Microfluidic **B**iochip (PB-DMFB) creates a new opportunity for low cost diagnostic tests and treatment compared to conventional DMFB. Such DMF chips require new test models and methodologies for testing and fault diagnosis due to its inherent physical structure which is different from traditional DMFBs or 'Lab-on-a-Chip'(LoC)s. The elementary fluidic operations like droplet transportation, mixing, splitting, incubation and detection are executed on the paper-based microfluidic arrays. However the reliability of those basic fluidic operations can be ensured by functional testing of such chips. In this work a new method is proposed to diagnose various types of faults on a PB-DMFB. Routing based new diagnosis model is proposed where different types of single as well as multiple-site faults on the routing path are considered. We have also considered single site and dual site faults in different mixing modules on such chips and proposed solutions for tackling such mixing-faults to accomplish the entire bio-assay on a Paper-based DMF chip. We are able to find alternate routing path for all such faults occurred and viability of the proposed method is ensured through experimental result which are quite encouraging and significant.

Keywords: Digital microfluidics · Biochips · Paper-based · Open-fault · Short-fault

1 Introduction

DIGITAL MICROFLUIDICS (DMF) technology is based upon micro/nano-scaled manipulation of discrete droplets of bio samples and reagents. Typical DMF operations include transportation, storage (incubation), mixing, reaction, detection and analysis of unit sized ($10^{-6}/10^{-9}$ltr.) droplets of discrete fluids on a 2-dimension electrodes grid [5,6,14]. Traditional Digital Microfluidic

© Springer Nature Singapore Pte Ltd. 2019
A. Sengupta et al. (Eds.): VDAT 2019, CCIS 1066, pp. 72–86, 2019.
https://doi.org/10.1007/978-981-32-9767-8_7

Biochips(DMFB's) come with high manufacturing cost, as a result, the cost becomes a limiting factor for the DMF based test and applications. Recently, paper-based microfluidics has emerged as a simple, scalable, and cost-effective solution for microfluidic operations compared to traditional DMFB [4], especially for point-of-care diagnostics. Inkjet printing technology is used to draw the electrodes on a cell instead of conventional lithography. The benefits of paper-based devices include lower demand for expensive equipment, stability of reagents and samples, and ease of mixture and disposal for microfluidic biochips. On the other hand, due to the passive nature, the relative low sensitivity of previous paper-based microfluidic devices makes it hard to control some part of multi-step assays with high precision. To deal with the problem, the Paper-Based Digital Microfluidic (PB-DMF) technology employs active DMF to achieve high precision control of multi-step operations on inkjet paper [4].

PB-DMFB chips can carry out reagent transport and mixing by electro wetting. Discrete droplets are transported as per pre-programmed paths (trajectories) through the electrodes printed on a low-cost paper [8]. The fabrication process of an active microfluidic paper chip is discussed in [8]. First, the designs in personal computers with inkjet-printing of the patterned electrodes are printed in printers [9]. Second, it provides surface coating with dielectric and oil films. The next step is to actuate reagent drops on the paper chips in the integrated power system as illustrated in Fig. 1.

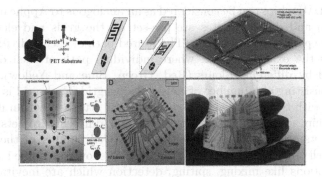

Fig. 1. Fabrication process of generating paper based-DMF chip [8]

Like silicon chips (used in traditional DMFB), paper-based DMF chips are also susceptible to physical defects and droplet manipulation may not be carried out correctly. Therefore, PB-DMF chips are also needed to be tested before they are actually used just like conventional DMF chips. Several test methodology for traditional DMFB's has been developed [1], and many optimized test schemes have been proposed till date [11,12,17,18]. But the mentioned DMF testing methods in [11,12,17,18], however, may not be directly applicable to PB-DMF chips for several reasons. First, since PB-DMF biochips are disposable, each chip is designed for a specific purpose in contrast to traditional DMFB's which are manufactured for general purpose applications and need to be fully programmable. Secondly, both electrodes and conducting wires for control signals in PB-DMFB's are fabricated through inkjet printing on a low-cost single paper layer at the same time. For traditional DMFB, routing of the control signals is usually carried out in separate routing layers. For these reasons, testing and diagnosis method for PB-DMFB's can be very different from traditional DMF chips, which is not much explored area in the field of DMF based research till date. In [10], Ho et al. proposed a test mechanism fo PB-DMF chips But no mixing operations are considered on the paper grid during the functional testing of the chip and practically no bio-assays could have been completed without performing any mixing operations of sample and reagent droplets. So tackling and tolerating the faults in specific cell locations of mixing module on such chips are essential for chip performance and error free results of the assay.

In this paper, we have discussed how to carry out routing based testing and diagnosis in Paper-based DMF chips. We categorizes different types of faults which may occur on a PB-DMFB grid and how to tolerate such faults for accomplishing a specific bio-protocol, for which the paper-chip is manufactured. Also the faults in dedicated mixing-module cell locations are considered and tackled.

2   Preliminaries

2.1   Droplet Operations on PB-DMFB Chips

Paper based DMF chips can be considered as an analogous to Application specific IC's (ASIC's) and droplet routes are pre-set on the grids and electrodes are printed on the paper accordingly [8]. The routed path of each individual droplet are shown in the example Fig. 2, where individual path of each droplets are demonstrated by different colours (Red, Green, Blue and Yellow). Each PB-DMF chip consisting of a number of cells called as grid. Each grid is active high or active low with the help of an electrode which is attached within it. A typical PB-DMFB chip and the projected paths of four different droplets are shown in Fig. 2 and its corresponding activation path (Cell number of the grid) with respect to each time stamp t where $1 \leq t \leq 7$ is shown in Table 1. Also other droplet operations like mixing, spiting, detection which are inevitable part of any bio-assays, needs to be performed on a PB-DMFB.

Table 1. Trajectories of four droplets

Droplet	Time							
	t_0	t_1	t_2	t_3	t_4	t_5	t_6	t_7
Red	1	2	3	4	5	6	12	18
Blue	11	17	16	15	14	20	26	25
Green	31	32	33	34	35	36	30	30
Yellow	13	14	20	26	27	28	28	28

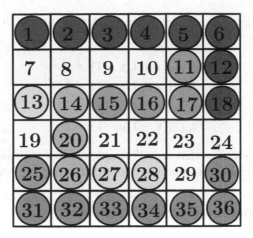

Fig. 2. Droplet routes on a 6×6 PB-DMFB chip (Color figure online)

2.2   Routing Constraints in PB-DMFB

Different constraints are framed for efficient routing, cross-contamination avoidance on standard DMFB platform [16], which are valid for PB-DMF chips also. At any time instant a droplet can occupy a single cell position on the chip until and unless fault occurs. Initially at $t = 0$ all droplet are at their source location, then $dp(i, s_{ix}, s_{iy}, t) = 1$ Where 'i' represents iteration number, 'S_{ix}', 'S_{iy}' is X and Y-coordinate value of the droplet at $t = i$.

Fluidic constraint is used to avoid any undesirable mixing of droplets from different nets during their transportation and it can further be divided into two types.

Static fluidic constraint [7] states that the minimum spacing between any two droplets is one cell at any instant of time t such that for any two droplets d_i and d_j the distance magnitude among X and Y coordinate values among them has to be greater or equal to 2.

$$|X_{i,t} - X_{j,t}| \geq 2 \quad and \quad |Y_{i,t} - Y_{j,t}| \geq 2 \tag{1}$$

The dynamic fluidic constraints [7] are same as static constraints but here two droplets defer by one timestamp and the following condition has to be satisfied. That is X and Y coordinate distance magnitude for droplets $d_i = (X_i, Y_i)$ and $d_j = (X_j, Y_j)$ from time instant t to t + 1 has to be greater or equal to 2.

$$|X_{i,t+1} - X_{j,t}| \geq 2 \quad or \quad |Y_{i,t+1} - Y_{j,t}| \geq 2 \tag{2}$$

$$|X_{i,t} - X_{j,t+1}| \geq 2 \quad or \quad |Y_{i,t} - Y_{j,t+1}| \geq 2 \tag{3}$$

In Digital microfluidic chips droplet cannot move diagonally due to its physical design constraint. It has to move either horizontally or vertically only at any particular instant. For any droplet $d_{i,t}(x,y)$ at time instant 't' following moves are not permissible: [2]

$$d_{i,t+1}(x+1, y+1) \neq 1 \tag{4}$$
$$d_{i,t+1}(x+1, y-1) \neq 1 \tag{5}$$
$$d_{i,t+1}(x-1, y+1) \neq 1 \tag{6}$$
$$d_{i,t+1}(x-1, y-1) \neq 1 \tag{7}$$

where, $d_{i,t}(x,y) = 1$ signifies that any i^{th} droplet at any time instant 't' can hold a cell on DMFB, which is positioned at co-ordinate value of (x, y) on the chip.

3   Problem Formulation

Paper-Based DMF chips are the low-cost alternative for conventional DMFB. Since PB-DMF chips are easy to design and manufacture at minimum cost, an array of electrodes with fully programmable routes are not desirable on such chips. They are designed for a specific bio-assay, with predefined and fixed droplet paths to be followed. So the best way to test a PB-DMF is simply to carry out the intended operations with test droplets. In other words, the correctness of the chip functionality can be ensured with a complete functional test. If, for every specified path in the chip, a test droplet can be moved (routed) from its source to the sink within the given time period, the chip is functionally correct. The function of a PB-DMF chip may be affected by open and short faults on the electrodes and wires. Unlike conventional DMFB it is susceptible to more number of short faults between its adjacent cells as single-layer (1-dimension) architecture is used on a coated paper. If an electrode on the droplet trajectory is affected by open fault, it will not be able to move a test droplet through the faulty electrode and droplet will not arrive at the sink reservoir within a threshold time.

An example problem of the droplet movement is illustrated in below Fig. 3 and its corresponding activation sequence is given in Table 2. Assume that a droplet is dispensed from the dispenser (source) at time-step 0 (t_0) and its coordinate position is (1,1). Starting from (1,1) cell on the grid, the droplet should be moved till the sink in ten time units (t_1 to t_{10}), as shown in Fig. 3. The droplet can be routed using three control pins indicated by red, blue and green colour in our example problem as minimum three control pins are required to satisfy the blockage window constraint for a PB-DMFB [10]. The wires connecting these control pins to their respective electrodes are shown by the respective colours.

In our problem formulation each control pins can control 3 number of printed electrodes on the chip. When an electrode is applied with signal "1", a droplet at an adjacent electrode will be moved to this electrode. We have considered electrode open and short faults [3,13,15] on the all cell positions of the droplet routes. We have also considered single or dual-site faults which may present in different mixing modules of the paper grid in this work.

The following faults on PB-DMF chip are considered in our work.

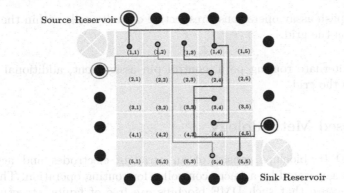

Fig. 3. A Paper-based DMF chip diagram of size 5×5 along with respective coordinate positions and Control Pins (Color figure online)

Table 2. Routing activation sequence/droplet path

Time	Activation sequence			Present location	Next location	Output
	Red	Green	Blue			
t_0	0	0	0	**Source**	(1,1)	0
t_1	1	0	0	(1,1)	(1,2)	0
t_2	0	1	0	(1,2)	(1,3)	0
t_3	0	0	1	(1,3)	(1,4)	0
t_4	1	0	0	(1,4)	(2,4)	0
t_5	0	1	0	(2,4)	(3,4)	0
t_6	0	0	1	(3,4)	(4,4)	0
t_7	1	0	0	(4,4)	(5,4)	0
t_8	0	1	0	(5,4)	(5,5)	0
t_9	0	0	1	(5,5)	**Sink**	0
t_{10}	0	0	0	**Sink**	-	1

Case 1: A single fault is assumed in the faulty chip.
Case 2: Multiple Fault sites may present on the routing path of the chip /grid (combination of open and short faults)
Case 3: Faults in the cells occupied by Mixing Modules

The problem is formulated as follows

Given: An input array of $n \times n$ electrodes, and T droplet trajectories (path).

Objectives:

1. Achieving high diagnosability rate
2. Requiring the minimum number of extra electrodes for recovery
3. Minimum number of control pins

4. To accomplish assay operations irrespective of faulty cells within the Mixing modules on the grid.

Outputs: Alternate routing path, control pin assignment, additional printed electrodes on the grid.

4 Proposed Methodology

Traditional DMF biochips consist of an array of electrodes and activation sequences are generated by a micro controller for routing operation. Therefore, in order to ensure that such DMF biochips are free of faults, structural test [11,12,17,18] methods have been developed to ensure that test droplets can be routed to all electrodes. Parallel test routes can be designed for the testing and diagnosis of DMF chips. Alternatively, biochips can be verified by functional testing [19] that applies test procedures to check whether groups of cells can be used to perform certain operations (e.g., droplet mixing and splitting). Therefore, the corresponding droplet movements are tested on the target cluster of cells with the help of CCD camera or other detection mechanisms like LED's. We can ensure the correctness of the chip function with a complete functional test. If, for every specified path in a chip, a test droplet can be moved from its source to the sink within the given time period, the chip is functionally correct.

We have diagnosed and tolerate the faulty electrodes and shown the alternative paths such that every opened electrode (single fault) and one or more pairs of shorted electrodes (multiple faults) can be bypassed. For each electrode in a PB-DMF chip, there are two to four vertically and horizontally adjacent electrodes. Therefore, in additional to the two adjacent electrodes that are also part of the droplet path, there are up to two spare locations that could be used to construct alternative routes. For that purpose, the arrangements of the additional control pins are given and shown by pink color in Fig. 4.

The solution of the example problem on a 5×5 grid is illustrated in Fig. 4. Assume that a droplet is created at the source and it can be moved to the sink in ten time units (t_0 to t_{10}). The droplet can be routed with the help of three (at minimum) or more number of control pins. We have used three pins only as indicated by Red, Green, and Blue in Fig. 4. The wires connecting these control pins to their respective electrodes are also shown by the same colors. The respective electrodes of the routing path are mapped as nodes of a graph G, where G = N_1, N_2, N_3, N_4, N_5 .... N_9 as shown in Table 3. In our example all the control pins (Red, Green, Blue) can activate three electrodes each. When an electrode is applied with signal "1", a droplet at an adjacent electrode will be moved to this electrode.

The proposed algorithm named Alternate Path Assignment Algorithm (APAA) is given in Fig. 5. The alternate route path is found for each faults occurred in the droplet route. Single site fault (Line: 6–9) as well as multi-site faults/short-faults (Line: 11–15) are considered by our method. The detailed

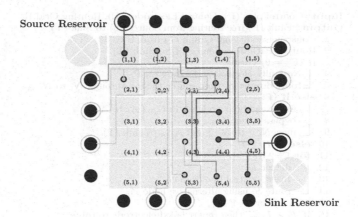

Fig. 4. Solution path and electrodes arrangements on a 5×5 PB-DMF chip (Color figure online)

Table 3. Mapping between nodes (N_i) and Electrodes(E)

Node	N_1	N_2	N_3	N_4	N_5	N_6	N_7	N_8	N_9
Electrode	(1,1)	(1,2)	(1,3)	(1,4)	(2,4)	(3,4)	(4,4)	(5,4)	(5,5)

Table 4. Mapping between additional nodes (A_i) and printed electrodes on the grid

Node	A_1	A_2	A_3	A_4	A_5	A_6	A_7	A_8	A_9	A_{10}
Electrode	(2,1)	(2,2)	(2,3)	(3,3)	(4,3)	(5,4)	(1,5)	(2,5)	(3,5)	(4,5)

analysis of fault diagnosis on the basis of functional testing and how to recover from such faults with additional control pins are explained in the following subsections.

4.1 Traceability of Alternate Routing Path

In our proposed technique (APAA) functional testing is done through droplet routing. Traceability of alternate path depends on various factors like chip size, fault site location on the chip and the routing algorithm used for droplet transportation. We have considered the droplet path as a linear directed Graph (G), where each node $N_i \in G$ has a degree of 2 in fault-free scenario. Degree of node is given by

$$N_i = 1(in\_degree) + 1(out\_degree) = 2 \tag{8}$$

In case of a faulty electrode (node) in G, the alternate path can be obtained via G_A and the connecting nodes of G with G_A will have increased degree by at least 1 i.e. at least one alternate route path needs to exist. In our example problem droplet path consisting of nine electrodes, as indicated by the black color

Input: Control pins (P), Control Electrodes (E), Routing Grid R
Output: Fault (F) free routing from Source (S) to Sink (T).
1. Construct additional Graph G_A from S to T.
2. Routing Path from Source (S) to Sink (T).
3. **if** (F== 0) **then**
4. | No faulty electrodes (E) exist on P;
5. └ route droplet S_i from source to sink through N_1 to N_{max}
6. **else if** (F==1);
7. | find Neighbour node set in G_A $\{A_1$ to $A_n\}$
8. | bypass N_i via G_A;
9. └ moveN_{i-1} to N_{i+n} and N_{i+n} to sink (T)
10. **else if** $F > 1$;
11. **for** F=2 to F=$|F_{threshold}|$;
12. | detect F_n
13. | Insert control line from G_A
14. └ route S_i using alternative node A_n
15. Set counter F=F+1;
16. **if** $F \geq F_{max.}$ then report failed electrode to route.

Fig. 5. Alternate Path Assignment Algorithm (APAA)

nodes labelled from N_1, N_2 .... $N_9 \in$ G, which is a liner array of electrodes
as shown in Fig. 6. An edge between two nodes of G implies the corresponding
electrodes are adjacent. Solid lines indicate the droplet path, while the dashed
lines demonstrate the alternative paths between droplet source and sink. The
alternative paths can be used to construct fault tolerant routing paths for the
target droplet path. We form an additional graph G_A consists of two bi-partite
sub graphs G_2 and G_3 signifying alternate path's electrodes A_n where $G_2 = A_1$,
A_2, A_3, A_4, A_5, A_6 and $G_3 = A_7$, A_8, A_9, A_{10}. The corresponding additional
pin assignments and cell numbers on the grid are shown in Fig. 4 and in Table 4
respectively.

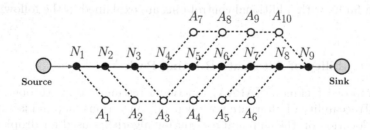

Fig. 6. Alternate Path (electrode) arrangements on a PB-DMF chip

In ideal scenario if no electrode faults occurred at any of the nodes, the
droplet will take the path P_1 where P_1: Source (S)→N_1→N_2→ .... N_{i-1}→
N_i → Sink (T); $\forall N_i \in$ G; where $1 \leq i \leq 9$ and $F == 0$.
    The alternative path for the droplet movements are shown with the help of
additional nodes given in G_A in Fig. 6, if node N_2 is incurred with open fault

then the alternative electrode A_1, A_2, A_3 are of help and droplet gets bypass from N_1 to N_5 and degree of these two joining nodes will be increased at least by 1 to check weather any alternate path exists on not. Similarly, if there is any open fault in node N_3 or N_4 additional electrodes A_1, A_2, A_3 are used to bypass the droplet to node N_5. In case of any open faults in N_5, N_6, N_7 or N_8 then A_7 to A_{10} would be used to move the corresponding droplet from N_4 to N_9. Analysis of different faults are given in detail in the following sub sections.

4.2 Analysis of Single Fault (Open Faults) on the Routing Path

An electrode open fault means that a droplet cannot be moved to or from the given electrode because of the open circuit between the faulty electrode and the voltage source. We have considered single open faults in each node given in Fig. 6 (except node N_1 and N_9), which are assumed to be non-faulty. We are able to find the alternate route path for each cases (Path: P_2–P_8) shown below and corresponding electrode arrangements (E) on the paper based DMF chip and control pin configuration are also shown in Fig. 4.

The path details for P_2 to P_8 are shown below:

P_2: Source $\to N_1 \to A_1 \to A_2 \to A_3 \to N_5 \to N_6 \to N_7 \to N_8 \to N_9 \to$ Sink (for node N_2)
P_3: Source $\to N_1 \to N_2 \to A_2 \to A_3 \to N_5 \to N_6 \to N_7 \to N_8 \to N_9 \to$ Sink (for node N_3)
P_4: Source $\to N_1 \to N_2 \to N_3 \to A_3 \to N_5 \to A_6 \to N_7 \to N_8 \to N_9 \to$ Sink (for node N_4)
P_5: Source $\to N_1 \to N_2 \to N_3 \to N_4 \to A_7 \to A_8 \to A_9 \to A_{10} \to N_9 \to$ Sink (for node N_5)
P_6: Source $\to N_1 \to N_2 \to N_3 \to N_4 \to N_5 \to A_8 \to A_9 \to A_{10} \to N_9 \to$ Sink (for node N_6)
P_7: Source $\to N_1 \to N_2 \to N_3 \to N_4 \to N_5 \to N_6 \to A_9 \to A_{10} \to N_9 \to$ Sink (for node N_7)
P_8: Source $\to N_1 \to N_2 \to N_3 \to N_4 \to N_5 \to N_6 \to N_7 \to A_{10} \to N_9 \to$ Sink (for node N_8)

4.3 Analysis of Short Faults on the Routing Path of PB-DMFB

If two adjacent electrodes on the droplet trajectory (P) are shorted, droplet will be stuck between the two electrodes. For example, if electrodes N_4, N_5 at grid locations $(1, 4)$ and $(2, 4)$ are shorted, the test droplet will be stuck between them at time instant t_4 and t_5. Electrode at $(2, 3)$ will be activated next at time t_4. Another type of short fault occurs when an electrode on the trajectory is shorted with an adjacent electrode that is not on the droplet trajectory. For example if $(1, 4)$ and $(1, 5)$ or $(2, 4)$ and $(2, 5)$ are shorted, then by activating additional electrodes at A_3, A_4, A_5 we are able to tolerate the faults and alternate path can be found. But in case of $(1, 3)$ and $(2, 3)$ are shorted, by activating electrode A_2 at location $(2, 2)$ won't able to pass the test droplet further and the test droplet will not reach the sink reservoir. So as per our arrangements of using minimum number of additional electrodes (A) we are able to tackle all the short-faults lying on the right-upper hand side of the grid. The following examples (P_9 to P_{12}) demonstrates some possible short-faults (only single pair of adjacent electrodes are shorted at any instant of time) and its respective alternate paths traced.

P_9: Source $\to N_1 \to A_1 \to A_2 \to$ $A_3 \to N_5 \to N_6 \to N_7 \to N_8 \to$ $N_9 \to$ Sink
 (for node N_2 and N_3 short)

P_{10}: Source $\to N_1 \to A_1 \to A_2 \to A_3 \to N_5 \to N_6 \to N_7 \to$ $N_8 \to$ $N_9 \to$ Sink
 (for node $N3$ and N_4 short)

P_{11}: Source $\to N_1 \to N_2 \to N_3 \to A_3 \to A_4 \to A_6 \to N_7 \to N_8 \to$ $N_9 \to$ Sink
 (for node N_4 and N_5 short)

P_{12}: Source $\to N_1 \to N_2 \to N_3 \to N_4 \to A_7 \to A_8 \to A_9 \to A_{10} \to$ $N_9 \to$ Sink
 (for node N_5 and N_6 or N_6 and N_7 or N_7 and N_8 short)

4.4   Analysis of Random Multiple Faults

Here we have considered multiple faults (open or short) on the chip. It may be possible more than two electrodes are simultaneously open on a random basis on the entire droplet route path or there may be more than two adjacent electrodes get shorted or any other combination of open and short faults may occur at same time instant. We have analysed such random multiple faults also and able to find the alternate paths with minimum control pins and minimum number of additional printed electrodes. Some of the case analysis for random multi faults and their respective alternate paths are given below as P_{13} to P_{16}.

P_{13}: Source $\to N_1 \to A_1 \to A_2 \to A_3 \to N_5 \to N_6 \to N_7 \to N_8 \to$ $N_9 \to$ Sink
 (for node N_2 open and N_3–N_4 short)

P_{14}: Source $\to N_1 \to N_2 \to A_2 \to A_3 \to A_4 \to N_6 \to N_7 \to N_8 \to$ $N_9 \to$ Sink
 (for node N_3 open and N_4–N_5 short)

P_{15}: Source $\to N_1 \to N_2 \to N_3 \to N_4 \to A_7 \to A_8 \to A_9 \to$ $A_{10} \to$ $N_9 \to$ Sink
 (for node N_5–N_6 short and N_7–N_8 short)

P_{16}: Source $\to N_1 \to A_1 \to A_2 \to A_3 \to N_5 \to N_6 \to N_7 \to A_{10} \to$ $N_9 \to$ Sink
 (for node N_2 and N_8)

4.5   Analysis of Mixing Module Induced Faults (MMIF) in PB-DMFB

We have also considered single or multiple site faults (Open/Short faults) in a mixer unit of the PB-DMFB. As mixing of sample and reagent droplets are one of the most essential operations without whom no bioassay could have been completed. So any faults in a mixing module (cell locations) can have most adverse effects on the assay outcome. It may results in incomplete assay operations and leads to erroneous assay outcome which is undesirable for any real time health critical diagnostics. So considering this aspect we can also tackled such Mixing Module Induced Faults (MMIF) on a PB-DMFB grid.

There are some standard mixing modules available in DMFB library which spreads over 1×4, 2×2, 2×3 or 2×4 number of cell locations surrounded by padding cells on all sides of the modules for avoiding cross contamination. But as PB-DMF chips are intended for one specific bioassay, we can avoid the concept of padding cells and include them into the mixing module if needed and accordingly place additional electrodes on those cells in case of faults within the mixing units.

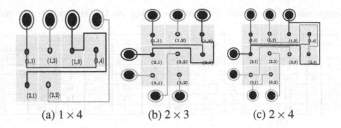

(a) 1 × 4   (b) 2 × 3   (c) 2 × 4

Fig. 7. Different types of mixing module and their corresponding alternative arrangements

From Fig. 7a instead of 1×4 mixing module an alternative 2×2 mixing module can be formed to overcome any kind of short or open fault in cell locations (1, 3) and (1, 4) within the module. If (1, 3) or (1, 4) cell which is connected by blue and red electrode pin respectively are associated with any kind of fault, corresponding (2, 1) and (2, 2) cells can be made active and mixing operation can be performed. Similarly in Fig. 7b an 2 × 3 mixing module is replaced with help of (3, 1) and (3, 2) cells in case of faults in (1, 3) and (2, 3) cells. Similarly with the use of two extra control pin and one extra electrode can convert the 2 × 4 mixing modules into a 2 × 3 module as in Fig. 7c. Thus faults (open/short) in one side of the mixing module can be tackled with proper additional pin assignments.

5   Experimental Results

In order to validate the effectiveness of the proposed design-for-diagnosis and fault-tolerance method, the example problem given in Fig. 4 and other benchmark assays are synthesized. The results are summarized in Fig. 8 and in Table 5 for single and multiple faults respectively. In these tables, Columns 2 to 6 give the chip size, the initial number of control pins, and the numbers of electrodes, sources, and sinks in each assay design. Additional printed electrodes and control pins needed for diagnosis and fault tolerance are listed in Columns 7 and 8 respectively. Columns 9 and 10 signify the number of open faults and diagnosable open faults, while Columns 11 and 12 are the numbers of short faults and diagnosable short faults for Fig. 8.

The last column gives the diagnosis rate, which indicates the percentage of diagnosable faults vs. all faults. For single faults more than 80% fault tolerance rate is achieved for all the assays. In Table 5 we have categorize multiple-faults into different combinations and tested. However exhaustive set of multiple-faults are not considered in this work rather a subset of all possible multiple-faults are taken. Maximum 4 number of open faults are considered at any time instant and 5 number of short-faults are considered for all the assays except Protein-2. Around 80% of such multiple-faults are tolerated for our example problem

Table 5. Diagnosis rate for multiple faults exiting on the droplet route using APAA

Bio-Assay	Chip Statistics					Overhead		Multiple Faults						Avg. Dia.
								Open		Short		Open-Short combined		
	Size	Pin	Electrode	Source	Sink	Electrode	Pins	# Fault	# Diag.	# Fault	# Diag.	# Fault	# Diag.	Rate
Our Example	5x5	3	8	1	1	10	7	4	4	6	4	6	5	93.7 %
amino-acid-1	6x8	8	20	4	2	12	7	8	6	10	8	10	8	85.7 %
amino-acid-2	8x8	10	24	4	2	12	12	12	10	12	10	10	7	79.4 %
protein-1	13x13	7	34	2	2	30	12	20	14	20	18	20	12	73.3 %
protein-2	13x13	23	49	2	2	45	20	20	15	20	17	20	10	70 %

and for amino-acid-I and amino-acid-II benchmarks. For Protein-1 and Protein-2 bio-assays, the average rate of fault tolerance is more than 70% as shown in Table 5. We have also considered different types of faults within the mixing module regions of the chip and the detailed results are given in Table 6.

Table 6. Diagnosis rate for mixing module induced faults

Mixing module statistic			Overhead		Open fault		Short fault		Avg. diagnosis rate
Size	Pin	Electrode	Pins	Electrode	# Fault	# Diag.	# Fault	# Diag.	
1×4	3	4	1	2	4	2	3	2	57.1%
2×2	4	4	1	2	4	2	4	2	50%
2×3	4	6	2	2	6	4	7	4	61%
2×4	6	8	2	2	8	4	10	6	55%

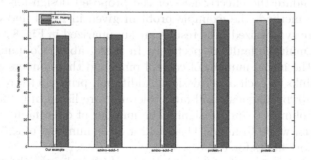

Fig. 8. Comparison between Li et al. [10] and our method

For such faults also we are able to achieve at least $\geq 50\%$ diagnosis rate for all the mixing-modules considered and are able to tolerate such MMIF faults by finding alternate mixing cells. Thus the overall results are quite significant and encouraging for smooth functionality of a paper-based chip.

6 Conclusion

Paper-based DMF chips are not reconfigurable and work as ASIC to perform a particular assay. But low manufacturing cost and highly disposable nature of such chips make it more popular than conventional DMFBs. In this work routing based fault testing (open and short faults) and diagnosis methodologies are proposed for such chips. Single site as well as multiple site fault diagnosis and tolerating such faults by finding alternate paths on the chip are discussed. Also a new approach given to overcome faults in mixing module induced cells (MMIF) and converting the dimension of mixing modules by appropriate pin assignment is proposed, which is first of its kind. Hence, the bio-assay can be continued irrespective of faults in mixing cells. Most of the faults (Approximately more than 90%) which is occurred during droplet routing is diagnosed and tackled by our method by finding alternate paths. However, a few locations on the paper grid are pre-assumed to be fault-free for simplicity and a subset of multiple-faults on the droplet route path is considered in this work. Thus 100% fault free chips covering all possible cell locations of faults for a paper-based platform can be targeted as future scope of this work.

References

1. Chakrabarty, K.: Design automation and test solutions for digital microfluidic biochips. IEEE Trans. Circ. Syst. I Regul. Pap. **57**(1), 4–17 (2010). http://doi. acm.org/10.1109/TCSI.2009.2038976
2. Chakraborty, S., Chakraborty, S., Das, C., Dasgupta, P.: Efficient two phase heuristic routing technique for digital microfluidic biochip. IET Comput. Digit. Tech. **10**(5), 233–242 (2016). http://doi.acm.org/10.1049/iet-cdt.2015.0161
3. Datta, S., Joshi, B., Ravindran, A., Mukherjee, A.: Efficient parallel testing and diagnosis of digital microfluidic biochips. J. Emerg. Technol. Comput. Syst. **5**(2), 10:1–10:17 (2009). http://doi.acm.org/10.1145/1543438.1543443
4. Fobel, R., Kirby, A.E., Ng, A.H.C., Farnood, R.R., Wheeler, A.R.: Paper microfluidics goes digital. Adv. Mater. **26**(18), 2838–2843 (2014). http://dx.doi.org/10. 1002/adma.201305168
5. Ho, T.Y., Zeng, J., Chakrabarty, K.: Digital microfluidic biochips: a vision for functional diversity and more than moore. In: Proceedings of the International Conference on Computer-Aided Design, ICCAD 2010, pp. 578–585. IEEE Press, Piscataway (2010). http://dl.acm.org/citation.cfm?id=2133429.2133551
6. Huang, T.W., Ho, T.Y., Chakrabarty, K.: Reliability-oriented broadcast electrode-addressing for pin-constrained digital microfluidic biochips. In: 2011 IEEE/ACM International Conference on Computer-Aided Design (ICCAD), pp. 448–455, November 2011. http://doi.acm.org/10.1109/ICCAD.2011.6105367
7. Huang, T.W., Lin, C.H., Ho, T.Y.: A contamination aware droplet routing algorithm for digital microfluidic biochips. In: 2009 IEEE/ACM International Conference on Computer-Aided Design - Digest of Technical Papers, pp. 151–156, November 2009
8. Ko, H., et al.: Active digital microfluidic paper chips with inkjet-printed patterned electrodes. Adv. Mater. **26**(15), 2335–2340 (2014). http://dx.doi.org/10. 1002/adma.201305014

9. Li, J., Wang, S., Li, K.S., Ho, T.: Congestion and timing-driven droplet routing for pin-constrained paper-based microfluidic biochips. In: 2016 21st Asia and South Pacific Design Automation Conference (ASP-DAC), pp. 593–598, January 2016. http://dx.doi.org/10.1109/ASPDAC.2016.7428076

10. Li, J.D., Wang, S.J., Li, K.S.M., Ho, T.Y.: Test and diagnosis of paper-based microfluidic biochips. In: 2016 IEEE 34th VLSI Test Symposium (VTS), pp. 1–6, April 2016. http://dx.doi.org/10.1109/VTS.2016.7477273

11. Li, Z., Dinh, T.A., Ho, T.Y., Chakrabarty, K.: Reliability-driven pipelined scan-like testing of digital microfluidic biochips. In: 2014 IEEE 23rd Asian Test Symposium, pp. 57–62, November 2014. http://doi.acm.org/10.1109/ATS.2014.22

12. Paşaniuc, B., Garfinkel, R., Măndoiu, I., Zelikovsky, A.: Optimal testing of digital microfluidic biochips. INFORMS J. Comput. **23**(4), 518–529 (2011). http://doi.acm.org/10.1287/ijoc.1100.0422

13. Srinivasan, V., Pamula, V.K., Fair, R.B.: An integrated digital microfluidic lab-on-a-chip for clinical diagnostics on human physiological fluids. Lab Chip **4**, 310–315 (2004). http://dx.doi.org/10.1039/B403341H

14. Su, F., Chakrabarty, K., Fair, R.B.: Microfluidics-based biochips: technology issues, implementation platforms, and design-automation challenges. IEEE Trans. Comput.-Aided Des. Integr. Circ. Syst. **25**(2), 211–223 (2006). http://doi.acm.org/10.1109/TCAD.2005.855956

15. Su, F., Hwang, W., Mukherjee, A., Chakrabarty, K.: Testing and diagnosis of realistic defects in digital microfluidic biochips. In: Tehranipoor, M. (ed.) Emerging Nanotechnologies. Frontiers in Electronic Testing, vol. 37, pp. 287–312. Springer, Boston (2008). https://doi.org/10.1007/978-0-387-74747-7_11

16. Su, F., Hwang, W., Chakrabarty, K.: Droplet routing in the synthesis of digital microfluidic biochips. In: Proceedings of the Design Automation Test in Europe Conference, vol. 1, pp. 1–6 (2006)

17. Su, F., Ozev, S., Chakrabarty, K.: Concurrent testing of digital microfluidics-based biochips. ACM Trans. Des. Autom. Electron. Syst. **11**(2), 442–464 (2006). http://doi.acm.org/10.1145/1142155.1142164

18. Xu, T., Chakrabarty, K.: Parallel scan-like test and multiple-defect diagnosis for digital microfluidic biochips. IEEE Trans. Biomed. Circ. Syst. **1**(2), 148–158 (2007). http://doi.acm.org/10.1109/TBCAS.2007.909025

19. Xu, T., Chakrabarty, K.: Functional testing of digital microfluidic biochips. In: 2007 IEEE International Test Conference, pp. 1–10, October 2007. http://doi.acm.org/10.1109/TEST.2007.4437614

A Generalized Technique of Automated Pin Sharing on Hexagonal Electrode Based Digital Microfluidic Biochip Along with Its Design Methodology

Amartya Dutta[1($\boxtimes$)], Riya Majumder[2], Debasis Dhal[3], and Rajat Kumar Pal[3]

[1] Department of Computer Science and Engineering,
B. P. Poddar Institute of Management and Technology, Kolkata, India
dutta.kultu@gmail.com
[2] Department of Computer Science and Engineering,
Supreme Knowledge Foundation Group of Institutions, Chandannagar,
West Bengal, India
riyamanai@gmail.com
[3] Department of Computer Science and Engineering, University of Calcutta,
Acharya Prafulla Chandra Roy Shiksha Prangan, JD-2, Sector-III, Salt Lake,
Kolkata 700106, India
{debasisdhal06,pal.rajatk}@gmail.com

Abstract. Digital based microfluidic biochip appeals to the notion of micro-fluidic technology, with a wide variety of applications in electronics, biology, chemistry, environmental science, etc. Such a composite system replaces the conventional laboratory experiments by handling liquids as discrete with nanolitre or microliter volumes and providing reconfigurable and scalable devices following the electrowetting on dielectric (EWOD) principle. In this paper, we have focused on a new application area of digital microfluidic biochip technology with regular hexagonal electrode instead of conventional square electrodes. The structural and behavioural facets of the proposed hexagonal electrode digital microfluidic biochip (HDMFB) are discussed regarding its associated methodology in comparison with the existing square electrodes. Additionally, care is taken about the key challenges to influence the multiplexed bioassay operation, control pin assignment for safe droplet routing and mixing operation. An algorithm is proposed here to control the whole HDMFB array with minimum pin sharing. Finally, a scheduled bioassay is performed on the HDMFB and the result is compared with the existing one.

Keywords: Bioassay operation · Droplet routing · Hexagonal cluster · Lab-on-a-chip (LoC) · Mixing operation

1 Introduction

Presently, digital microfluidic biochips (DMFB) bring much more observations to the field of biomedical and biochemical experiments and testing. These microfluidic based biochips surround biology with electronics and as a consequence of it a

© Springer Nature Singapore Pte Ltd. 2019
A. Sengupta et al. (Eds.): VDAT 2019, CCIS 1066, pp. 87–101, 2019.
https://doi.org/10.1007/978-981-32-9767-8_8

bio-micro-electro-mechanical system [1] is formed. DMFBs are addressed as lab-on-a-chip (LoC) [2, 3], because the whole lab equipment can be replaced with this kind of tiny chip. Following the electrowetting on dielectric (EWOD) principle [3], digital micro-fluidic system manipulates different liquid samples and reagents as discrete droplets in a digital manner throughout the chip. This promising craze establishes a novel approach that offers highly scalable system architecture by introducing a two-dimensional (2D) digital microfluidic array of uniform basic unit cells, controls the nanolitre or microliter volume of droplets and yields high speed in droplet routing (near about 25 cm/sec), ensures energy efficiency (as less power is needed), near about 100% utilization of samples, and less error in testing outcomes [4]. Various enzymatic analysis, DNA detection, analysis and amplification, protein and glucose analysis, immunoassays, different toxicity observation, and a number of biomedical testing [2, 3] can be carried out with the help of DMFB. Although the basic cells like standard square electrodes are much more familiar [5], the new representation for DMFBs with two-dimensional equilateral triangular electrode array [6, 7] and closed packing representation of two-dimensional regular hexagonal shaped electrode array [3] are also realizable.

A geometrical shift from conventional square electrode array to regular hexagonal shaped cell array maintaining all the constraints and the performance of fundamental modular operations like the droplet transportation, mixing, and other design issues on microfluidic systems are addressed in this paper for the betterment of this kind of emerging system [3–5]. This proposed regular hexagonal 2D electrode array is designated as hexagonal electrode digital microfluidic biochip (HDMFB). Here in our proposed model we have mentioned the fabrication of hexagonal electrode array, different routing constraints like fluidic constraint and electrode constraint, mixing operation, and devised an effective control pin assignment algorithm to perform the multiplexed bioassay operations.

1.1 Design Specification of DMFB Using Hexagonal Electrodes

As the system integration and complexity of the chip increase day by day, biochip designers are seeking for new design technology along with different design tools. Though it is true that the traditional microfluidic biochip with square electrodes is more progressive and favoured layout in the DMFB area, but it has some restrictions due to its shape. In square electrode array an electrode has four direct adjacent neighbours, contributing droplet motion in only four available directions. In addition, due to its geometrical alignment on chip, droplet movements always follow the Manhattan distance [2].

It is expected that the DMFB with hexagonal shaped cells effectively improves the droplet transportation because of the six direct adjacent neighbours of an interior cell. In the hexagonal array six-sided shapes fit together perfectly where every point on the perimeter of an electrode is of equidistant from the centre of the cell and offers a compact closed packing design [3, 8] as a whole.

This section focuses on the initial geometrical measurements of a hexagonal shaped cell while maintaining some design constraints with respect to that of a square cell. By simultaneous activation and deactivation of adjacent electrodes, droplet advances through the whole chip floor. To secure the constant requirement of voltage for droplet motion, while switching the design issues from the square cell to HDMFB, let us consider two assumptions while investigating the new design technique; the volume of the droplet on the hexagonal electrode is kept same as on the square electrode, and the expanded/overlapped portion of the droplet on the activated adjacent electrode remains unchanged as it is kept on its square counterpart. In Fig. 1(a), a droplet is taken on an activated hexagonal electrode with side y. As the side of a hexagon is same as the droplet's radius, we have $y = 0.58a$ [9], where a is the side of a square electrode. Area of the hexagonal cell is $A_{\text{hexagon}} = 0.87a^2$ [9]. So, the hexagonal cell is smaller than a square cell in terms of area while maintaining all the above assumptions.

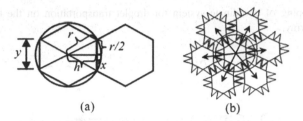

(a)   (b)

Fig. 1. (a) Top view of droplet with radius r is placed on a charged regular hexagonal shaped electrode with side y. x is the portion of the droplet outside the electrode and it is estimated along the radius of the droplet. (b) Top view of a cluster of seven regular hexagonal electrodes.

Figure 1(b) shows the placement of a droplet on a charged hexagonal cell; here possible traces of movement of the droplet are also indicated by arrows. The saw tooth maintains the connectivity between adjacent electrodes as the droplet overlaps, though a gap is there in between each pair of adjacent electrodes that controls the leakage.

1.2 Fluidic Constraints for Droplet Routing

This new configuration helps to make a droplet flexible to move into six possible directions. As a result, a droplet can route in both ways, horizontally and diagonally addressing the betterment in droplet routing time. To avoid unintentional droplet splitting, merging, interference, and contamination, fluidic constraints must be maintained during routing of a droplet [7]. Fluidic constraints introduce the concept that a safe separation between two droplets must be maintained during droplet routing. These constraints are of two types: static and dynamic.

Static Fluidic Constraints
If there are two droplets D_i and D_j kept at time instant t at positions (X_i, Y_i) and (X_j, Y_j), respectively, then for avoidance of unintended mixing, the secure gap between them is at least two electrodes, i.e. $|X_i(t) - X_j(t)| \geq 2, |Y_i(t) - Y_j(t)| \geq 2$, and $(|X_i(t) - X_j(t)| \geq 1$ && $|Y_i(t) - Y_j(t)| \geq 1)$. While transporting to the next adjacent cell at time instant $t + 1$, the inequality can be expressed as $|X_i(t + 1) - X_j(t + 1)| \geq 2, |Y_i(t + 1) - Y_j(t + 1)| \geq 2$, and $(|X_i(t + 1) - X_j(t + 1)| \geq 1$ && $|Y_i(t + 1) - Y_j(t + 1)| \geq 1)$.

Dynamic Fluidic Constraints
Here one droplet is moving while the other is kept static. Let D_i changes its position when time t changes to $t + 1$ and droplet D_j is static. Hence, the fluidic constraints

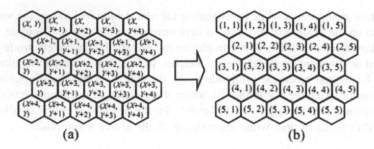

Fig. 2. The mapping of coordinate system for droplet transportation on the two-dimensional hexagonal chip array.

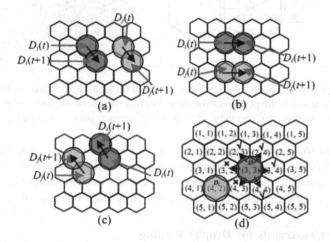

Fig. 3. Illustration of fluidic constraints, where the black arrow is used to indicate the direction of movements. (a) Static fluidic constraint is encountered for a pair of droplets keeping their relative positions along (a) horizontal, (b) vertical, and (c) diagonal directions. (d) Allowable and restricted motions of droplet D_i in satisfying the dynamic fluidic constraint. '$\sqrt{}$' denotes permissible movement and '$\times$' is used for restriction.

become $|X_i(t + 1) - X_j(t)| \geq 2$, $|Y_i(t + 1) - Y_j(t)| \geq 2$, and $(|X_i(t + 1) - X_j(t)| \geq 1$ && $|Y_i(t + 1) - Y_j(t)| \geq 1)$. Similarly, if D_i is made static and D_j is moving then $|X_i(t) - X_j(t + 1)| \geq 2$, $|Y_i(t) - Y_j(t + 1)| \geq 2$, $(|X_i(t) - X_j(t + 1)| \geq 1$ && $|Y_i(t) - Y_j(t + 1)| \geq 1)$.

Figure 2(a) specifies the coordinate system that is assumed for carrying out microfluidic operations, and its mapping to 2D array is shown in Fig. 2(b), where the marking (i, j) on any hexagonal cell describes the coordinate of the cell, i and j being the row number and column number of a cell, respectively. In Fig. 3(a)–(c), static fluidic constraints are followed by droplets D_i and D_j at their initial (at time t) and final (at time $t + 1$) positions. There must be one electrode gap between D_i and D_j. During an assay operation, no droplet should occupy the region of another droplet's cluster. In Fig. 3(d) two droplets D_i and D_j are placed at coordinate positions (3, 3) and (4, 2), respectively. Now, D_i can move safely to its four adjacent cells, viz. (2, 3), (2, 4), (3, 4), and (4, 4). However, if D_i wants to move toward either cell (3, 2) or cell (4, 3), then interference may arise between droplets D_i and D_j causing unwanted droplet mixing. This phenomenon clearly states that in every cluster there must be only one single droplet other than the mixing operation; thus, dynamic fluidic constraints are maintained. Again, the mixing operation is the most dominant and time-consuming part in any bio-assay schedule, the timing constraint reveals that the routing time in any assay operation should not overreach 10% of the total assay execution time.

2   Our Contribution

2.1   On Chip Pin Sharing Method

In this section, we focus on the utilization of independent pin constrained chip design problem for two-dimensional HDMFB. As six possible directions are open for a droplet to walk that gives the belief that any central cell has six direct adjacent neighbours. Thus, we can pick the number 7 as the minimum number of control pins. Figure 4 describes a 5×5 2D array with arbitrary pin assignment. Let droplets D_i and D_j have initial positions (2, 1) on control pin 6 and (1, 3) on control pin 3, respectively. Now if we activate the cell at position (1, 1) and the cell at location (2, 1) is deactivated, then droplet D_i is supposed to move to its new position at (1, 1). However, incidentally droplet D_j has to spread automatically to its adjacent cell at position (2, 3) on pin number 1 (as both the pins 3 and 1 are activated now). Similarly, suppose another droplet D_k has to move to position (3, 2), and for this pin 5 is activated (and pin 4 is deactivated). Then confusion arises for droplet D_k about its appropriate movement (as position (4, 4) also contains a control pin 5, which is activated too).

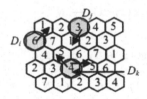

Fig. 4.   Unintentional droplet movement and splitting due to randomized pin sharing.

The above indicated problem can be removed by an organized pin planning technique. Finding a least number of control pins to supervise droplet routing without any unintended mixing or splitting on a 2D hexagonal electrode array is imaginable to formulate popular graph colouring problem. As the droplet can advance in six possible sides, a minimum of seven control pins are needed to avoid unwanted droplet intervention. From designers' points of view, pin reuse or pin planning means the control pin assignment to each cell of the whole chip to conquer these types of constraints. Here a cluster is constructed with seven cells and each cluster looks like 'honeycomb' of size $N_C = 7$, where N_C is the number of cells in a cluster and the pin reuse factor in each cluster is 1/7. Now, a new pin assignment algorithm in the 2D hexagonal electrode array is discussed with explanation, and this is called after Cluster Based Pin Sharing (CBPS), which can be deemed as a modified version of the BSA-7 algorithm [9].

Algorithm: Cluster Based Pin Sharing (CBPS)
Input: A 2D regular hexagonal chip array.
Output: Assignment of control pin throughout the chip array so that no droplet trespassing occurs.
1: To begin with, select a cluster, C on the 2D hexagonal array. Then assign the central electrode in C with control pin number, $N = 1$.
2: Starting from this assigned cell, proceed linearly to all six directions through the sides of the central electrode in C and cover i number of cells.
2.1: Take 60° clockwise turn (or 60° counter-clockwise turn) and move j number of cells through the sides.
2.2: Assign the same control pin number, $N = 1$ to each of these cells in a respective new cluster.
3: Repeat Steps 1 and 2 until all 1's are assigned to its intended positions.
4: Select any cluster centre with $N = 1$, and invoke function CB_PS (r, c, MZ).

CB_PS (r, c, MZ)

```
1 set_value(r, c) ← N
2 N ← 1
3 set_zone1(UZ) ← MZ - 1
4 set_zone2(LZ) ← MZ + 1
5 If UZ ∈ Z₁, then
6         r ← r - 1
7         i ← 1
8         While (i ≤ 2)
9                 Nᵢ ← set_value(r, i)
10                N ← N + 1
11                set_value(r, i) ← N
12                i++
13        End While
14        N_MZR ← set_value(r + 1, c + 1)
15        N ← N + 1
16        set_value(r + 1, c + 1) ← N
17 End If
18 If LZ ∈ Z₃, then
19        r ← r + 1
20        j ← 2
21        While (j ≥ 1)
22                Nⱼ ← set_value(r, j)
23                N ← N + 1
24                set_value(r, j) ← N
25                j--
26        End While
27        N_MZL ← set_value(r - 1, c - 1)
28        N ← N + 1
29        set_value(r - 1, c - 1) ← N
30 End If
```

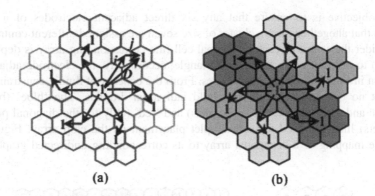

(a)   (b)

Fig. 5. Pin assignment in 2D hexagonal array having the shifting parameters, $i = 2$ and $j = 1$. (a) Seven clusters with control pin 1 in each cluster centre by taking 60° clockwise turn. (b) Seven clusters with control pin 1 in each cluster centre by taking 60° counter-clockwise turn.

Figure 5(a) reveals how control pin 1 is assigned to each cluster centre satisfying algorithm CBPS. We first label the centre of the middle cluster with pin number 1. Now starting from this electrode, six possible paths are traced out. After crossing two cells in any direction, we take a 60° clockwise turn (or a 60° counter clockwise turn, which is shown in Fig. 5(b)) and move one cell straight. This cell is marked with pin number 1, i.e. it is also controlled by control pin 1. Here in case of HDMFB, the cluster size is $N_C = 7$, and the shifting parameters are assumed as $i = 2$ and $j = 1$.

A cluster can be viewed in the form as shown in the Fig. 6. The cluster centre is marked as $N = 1$; then it can be subdivided into three zones, like Upper Zone (*UZ*), Middle Zone (*MZ*), and Lower Zone (*LZ*). The coordinate system for each cluster is also shown in the figure, where r and c are the allied row value and column value of the cluster sharing cells, respectively.

1 Upper Zone (*UZ*) Z_1

2 Middle Zone (*MZ*) Z_2

3 Lower Zone (*LZ*) Z_3

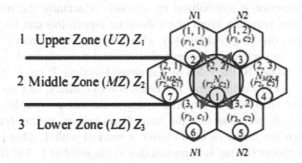

Fig. 6. Hexagonal cluster that narrates algorithm CBPS. The cluster is subdivided into three zones, upper, middle, and lower. Cluster centre is marked as $N = 1$, and the cell position in the cluster is denoted by (r, c), where r and c reveal the row and column values, respectively.

Our objective is to ensure that any six direct adjacent electrodes of a central electrode that altogether form a cluster of size seven are assigned different control pins. We consider the centre of each hexagonal cell (the corresponding array is depicted in Fig. 7(a)) to a vertex of an equilateral triangle; accordingly, the electrode adjacencies are shown in Fig. 7(b) using 'black' lines. From the concept of fluidic constraints, it is clear that no two adjacent cells can hold individual droplets. The 'blue' (both for horizontal and vertical positions of droplets) and 'red' (only for the diagonal positions of droplets) lines are used for safe droplet placement on the chip array. Figure 7(b) shows the mapping of a hexagonal array to its corresponding undirected graph.

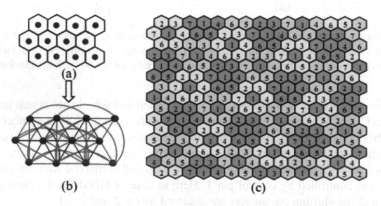

Fig. 7. (a) A 3 × 4 hexagonal electrode array. (b) Graphical representation of the array. Black, blue, and red lines represent electrode adjacency; adjacency of droplets in horizontal and vertical positions, droplet adjacency in diagonal positions, respectively. (c) Full addressable control pin assignment in a 15 × 15 hexagonal electrode array. (Color figure online)

The minimum number of pins required to control the movement of droplet without any droplet interference is symbolized by k which is actually the number of independent control pins required. From graph theoretic aspect, this can be visualized as a well-known graph colouring problem [2], where the chromatic number of a graph is same as the minimum number of independent control pins required, i.e. in graph G, $\chi(G) = k$. For an HDMFB, the value of k is never less than 7, i.e. $k \geq 7$.

Essentially, a 2D hexagonal array is a collection of clusters, and the assignment of control pins to the electrodes is required in the sense that no droplet interference is occurred. First of all, we subdivide the array into clusters, as has been depicted in Fig. 7(c), and then the centre of each cluster is marked with 1. This process is continued so that no cluster sharing is happened due to pin number 1. The first pin number 1 is assigned to any electrode on the chip. Then, according to algorithm CBPS, we move straight i (= 2) number cells in a direction and take a counter-clockwise (or clockwise) 60° turn and move j (= 1) number of cells and mark the cell as pin number 1. We follow the function CB_PS to assign pin numbers to all the remaining cells.

Thus, using the Cluster Based Pin Sharing (CBPS) algorithm on a 15 × 15 2D hexagonal array, the chip can be handled by seven control pins without any interference of droplet, as shown in Fig. 7(c).

3 Mixing Operations

Inside of the electrode array virtual modules are formed by a group of adjacent electrodes, as shown in Fig. 8. To achieve a desired level of mixing, necessary phase changes of a droplet are shown in this figure. Mixing operation is not confined to a certain area; it can be executed anywhere on the microfluidic array, and that is the reason for claiming that mixing is a reconfigurable operation [10].

From the existing works, it is found that the harmonic motion of droplets developed two types of flow among a set of electrodes. One is forward flow, and another is backward flow. Forward flow is countered by a backward flow [10, 11]. The presence of reverse flow prevents mixing from completing faster. The bidirectional effects in droplet motion can be reduced by creating the circular motion of droplet in the virtual module [7]. In the previous work [7, 10, 11], it is also claimed that the forward flow, i.e. 0° movement yields the best outcome for mixing rather than circular flow, i.e. 90° movement. Hence, in a mixer module as the forward movement increases the betterment is possible in terms of mixing. According to the existing experimental results, it has been observed that the completion time of mixing operation is reduced if 0° movement is increased [10].

However, another type of droplet movement is taken into consideration when the droplet is moved in a zigzag way among a set of hexagonal electrodes [7]. The droplet can move through the hexagonal electrode with phase change of 0° and 60° both, as has been shown in the Fig. 8(b). Four types of droplet movement are addressed depending upon the phase difference between two consecutive movements of a droplet. The movements are classified as forward movement (M_f), zigzag movement (M_z), orthogonal movement (M_o), and backward movement (M_b) [7], [10] for the phase changes of 0°, 60°, 90°, and 180°, respectively.

The following declaration '$M_b < M_o < M_f$' is precisely true towards the contribution of the mixing completion time as active mixing is proportional to the rate of diffusion [10, 12]. A relationship can be built up from this conclusion that the rate of diffusion (D) is inversely proportional to the value of phase change ($\emptyset$) of a (mixed) droplet, i.e. $D \propto 1/\emptyset$. To eliminate the negative influence on the quality of mixing, a good mixer should avoid the backward movement and at the same time 0° movement is allowed more as it is the most effective movement type in terms of mixing rather than 90°. An intermediate stage between this forward motion (0°) and the orthogonal motion (90°) is the zigzag motion that means 60° phase change is there throughout a mixing zone in HDMFB. Hence, the above declaration can be modified into the following: '$M_b < M_o < M_z < M_f$' [7, 10]. It can be stated from the previous information that the total mixing completion time is decreased as 60° movement of droplet is available in HDMFB in place of 90° movement as it is available in square electrode arrays.

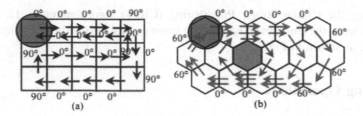

Fig. 8. Phase change of a droplet traced on (a) a 3×5 square mixer zone, and (b) a 3×5 hexagonal mixer zone.

Since mixing is one of the most significant concerns to perform a complete bioassay operation and almost the leading performance to analysis the assay, so the reduction in the mixing completion time will affect exceptionally to the total assay operation in terms of time. Now we are going to calculate the required mixing time in a 3×5 hexagonal mixer (mixing cover up with 15 hexagonal electrodes only) as shown in Fig. 8(b), which is one of the essential components of our multiplexed bioassay.

3.1   Calculation of Mixing Time of the Mixer Module

Let p be the percentage of mixing over one electrode. The percentage of mixing for the forward movement over one electrode (p_0^1) is 0.29 [10] and the percentage of mixing when forward movement is continued for two electrodes (p_0^2) is 0.58 [10]. Therefore, the total percentage of mixing becomes $0.29 + 0.58 = 0.87$, when a droplet covers two consecutive electrodes in forward direction [10]. In this way, it is found that the percentage of mixing due to three such consecutive phase changes of $0°$ is 1.74 [10] and that due to four consecutive phase changes of $0°$ is 2.9 [10]. Let p_{60} be the percentage of mixing over one electrode due to $60°$ phase change. The percentage of mixing for the $60°$ phase shift over one electrode (p_{60}^1) is 0.2 approximately [7]. These values of the mixing percentage for $60°$ phase shift due to covering the number of two, three, four, and five electrodes are 0.4, 0.8, 1.2, and 1.8, respectively [7].

Thus, the total mixing percentage for the 3×5 hexagonal mixer module (covering 15 electrodes), $\text{MP}_\text{H} = \sum(p_0^4, p_{60}^3, p_0^3, p_{60}^3, p_0^2, p_{60}^3, p_0^2, p_{60}^3, p_0^1, p_{60}^5, p_0^2) = \sum(2.9, 0.8,$ 1.74, 0.8, 0.87, 0.8, 0.87, 0.8, 0.29, 1.8, 0.87) = 12.54. Finally, the total completion time of the mixing operation in the hexagonal mixer zone of size 3×5, $\text{T}_{\text{H}(3 \times 5)} = (\text{T}_{\text{S}(3 \times 5)} \times \text{R}_{\text{H}(3 \times 5)})/\text{R}_{\text{S}(3 \times 5)} = 0.47$ s [7, 9], where, $\text{T}_{\text{S}(3 \times 5)}$ is the total mixing completion time for the existing 3×5 square mixer, and $\text{R}_{\text{H}(3 \times 5)}$ and $\text{R}_{\text{S}(3 \times 5)}$ are the total number of rounds required to complete the mixing 100% for hexagonal and square mixer module of size 3×5, respectively. By the way, $\text{R}_\text{H} = 100 /\text{MP}_\text{H}$ [10]. The total time elapsed in the mixing operation for the existing 3×5 square mixer is T_S $(3 \times 5) = 0.65$ s [9, 10], as shown in Fig. 8(a). From the above calculations, it is clear that the mixing time is reduced in the case of hexagonal mixer modules.

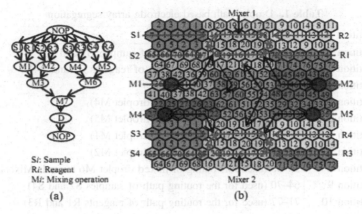

Fig. 9. (a) Sequence graph representation for a multiplexed bioassay. S1, S2, S3, S4 are the samples, R1, R2, R3, R4 are the reagents, M1, M2, M3, M4, M5, M6, M7 are the mixing operations, D is the detection operation, and NOP means 'no operation' (starting and ending positions of the sequence graph). (b) A 15 × 15 hexagonal cell array is taken to perform a multiplexed bioassay experiment. Here, S and R indicate the sample and reagent reservoirs, respectively, and D denotes the detection site. In this figure, two mixer zones are formed by 3 × 5 hexagonal array each. The droplet trace is shown by arrows.

4   Experimental Results

To compare the scheduling span in terms of time based on colorimetric enzymatic reactions, we consider a multiplexed bioassay operation composed of glucose and lactate assay [2]. Here, the whole bioassay operation is represented by a sequence graph as shown in the Fig. 9(a). In this graph, each node V represents an operation and an edge $e(i, j)$ denotes that the output of operation Oi is the input of operation Oj. In this way the operations are categorized as follows: O1, O2, O3, O4, O5, O6, O7, O8 are the dispensing operations (dispensing of samples S1, S2, S3, S4 and reagents R1, R2, R3, R4) that are termed as I1, I2, I3, I4, I5, I6, I7, and I8, respectively. Similarly, O5, O6, O7, O8, O9, O10, and O11 are the mixing operations, named M1, M2, M3, M4, M5, M6, and M7, respectively, and O12 is the detection operation, namely D.

The executable steps of the aforesaid sequence graph are described in Table 2. To carry out the scheduled steps properly, the 15 × 15 2D regular hexagonal electrode array is partitioned into eleven regions using the concept of time division pin sharing (TDPS) [2]. Due to the relevance of TDPS method, at a time eleven droplets can be routed over the whole array without any contamination. The total assay performance is governed by 77 pins. The specific scenario of the HDMFB after the TDPS is shown in the Fig. 9(b). The partitions and the associated control pins are illustrated by a chart, which is given in Table 1. Particularly, it is mentioned that to complete the assay operation successfully, not only the pin reuse concept is taken care of, rather the fluidic constraints and the electrode constraints are also maintained carefully.

Table 1. Droplet path based electrode array segregation

Partition name	Used control pins
Partition 1	1–7 (used for the routing path of samples S1 and S3)
Partition 2	8–14 (used for the routing path of reagents R2 and R4)
Partition 3	15–21 (used for the mixer zone)
Partition 4	22–28 (used for storing mixed droplet M4)
Partition 5	29–35 (used for storing mixed droplet M5)
Partition 6	36–42 (used for storing mixed droplet M1)
Partition 7	43–49 (used for storing mixed droplet M2)
Partition 8	50–56 (used for routing of mixed droplet M6 towards Mixer1)
Partition 9	64–70 (used for the routing path of samples S2 and S4)
Partition 10	71–77 (used for the routing path of reagents R1 and R3)
Partition 11	57–63 (used for detection area)

In order to assess the impact of the new design approach we schedule a bioassay operation in Table 2, where the elapsed time during each operation is measured in sec and the assay operation is simulated on both 15×15 2D square electrode array and 15×15 2D regular hexagonal electrode array. Different configurable reservoirs (sample and reagent), mixer, and detection zones are implanted on the said HDMFB array, as shown in Fig. 9(b). The details of the control pins used for different steps of the whole assay are listed in Table 3. The total assay completion time can be calculated by adding the droplet mixing time, the routing time, and the detection time (tentatively). The total routing time is equal to the time taken by the droplets to route from the reservoir ports to the mixer region plus the time taken by the mixed droplet from the mixer region to the detection port, and finally thrown away from the array. In this experiment, the droplet speed is assumed to be 25 cm/sec [4] and the required time to move from an electrode to its adjacent one is 0.01 s [9, 10]. The total elapsed times (measured in sec) in both the scenarios (a 15×15 2D square electrode array and a 15×15 2D hexagonal electrode array) are also estimated.

Table 2. An assay schedule plan for a fully addressable hexagonal chip array

Step number	Time elapsed (in s)	Actions taken
Step 1	0.06	S1-R1 and S3-R3 start routing towards mixer zone Mixer1 and Mixer2, respectively
Step 2	0.47	Mixing starts at Mixer1 and Mixer2 and getting mixed
Step 3	0.06	Mixed droplets due to S1-R1 and S3-R3 are stored at mixing positions M1 and M4, respectively
Step 4	0.06	S2-R2 and S4-R4 start routing towards mixer zone Mixer1 and Mixer2, respectively
Step 5	0.47	Mixing starts at Mixer1 and Mixer2 and getting mixed

(continued)

Table 2. (*continued*)

Step number	Time elapsed (in s)	Actions taken
Step 6	0.07	Mixed droplet due to S2-R2 and S4-R4 are stored at mixing positions M2 and M5, respectively
Step 7	0.07	Droplets at M1 and M2 start routing towards Mixer1 and droplets at M4 and M5 start routing towards Mixer2 in parallel
Step 8	0.47	Mixing starts at Mixer1 and Mixer2 and getting mixed
Step 9	0.07	After completion of mixing at Mixer2, the mixed droplet M6 (due to mixing of M4 and M5) is started to go at Mixer1
Step 10	0.47	Mixing starts at Mixer1 and M6 getting mixed with M3 (mixed droplet due to mixing of M1 and M2)
Step 11	0.84	Mixed droplet M7 due to mixing of M6 and M3 starts routing towards the detection zone D and get detected

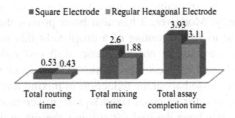

Fig. 10. The performance variation of the assumed assay using square DMFB and HDMFB.

Here, the proposed new algorithm is verified on a system having a 2.40 GHz Intel Core i5 CPU with 4 GB RAM under JAVA platform and the machine is running under 64-bit Windows operating system. The overall routing performance of the assay operation, its mixing time, and the total assay execution time of conventional square DMFB and HDMFB are apparent from Fig. 10. From this figure, it is quite evident that the potency of this closed packed design of HDMFB is superior to the standard square electrode array.

Table 3. Catalogue of activated control pins under the execution operation

Scheduling steps	Activated control pins
Step 1	7, 1, 4, 6, 5 and 74, 71, 77, 73, 72
Step 2	15–21
Step 3	20, 16, 39, 40, 41, 39 and 16, 18, 27, 24, 23, 26
Step 4	65, 66, 70, 64, 67 and 12, 13, 11, 8, 14
Step 5	15–21
Step 6	21, 20, 44, 43, 46, 48, 47 and 18, 21, 34, 33, 30, 31

(*continued*)

Table 3. (*continued*)

Scheduling steps	Activated control pins
Step 7	39, 41, 40, 39, 16, 20 and 47, 48, 46, 43, 44, 20, 21, and 26, 23, 24, 27, 18, 16 and 31, 30, 33, 34, 21, 18
Step 8	15–21
Step 9	16, 50, 52, 54, 50, 51, 15
Step 10	15–21
Step 11	17, 62, 59, 57

5 Conclusions

Shifting to 2D regular hexagonal electrode array apart from square electrode array, we have developed a better alternative in the DMFB scheme over the traditional one. Avoidance of droplet interference is an important factor for droplet movement; here we have maintained the fluidic constraints and pin constraints for droplet routing over the hexagonal electrode array. Moreover, it has also been proved that the 'mixer performance' is improved due to zigzag routing of a droplet. In this work, we have shown that the droplet can move with an oblique phase shift (60°) along with a forward movement (0°) on the hexagonal electrodes, which definitely increased the quality of mixing. We have also discussed about the reduction in mixing time for a specific mixer module with respect to that for an equal sized square mixer module. In this work, a well-planned algorithm has been devised for solving the pin assignment problem. In hexagonal electrode array, the total number of control pins is minimally increased. As the time reduction is probable, caused by droplet route flexibility and mixer operation so the total time to synthesize the bioassay is effectively decreased. The generalized technique for optimized routing on the array and the creation of mixer library could be assumed as the tasks for future researchers.

References

1. Su, F., Chakrabarty, K., Fair, R.B.: Microfluidics-based biochips: technology issues, implementation platforms, and design-automation challenges. IEEE Trans. Comput. Aided Des. Integr. Circuits Syst. **25**(2), 211–223 (2006)
2. Xu, T., Chakrabarty, K.: Digital Microfluidic Biochips: Design Automation and Optimization. CRC Press, Boca Raton (2010)
3. Su, F., Chakrabarty, K.: Digital Microfluidic Biochips: Synthesis, Testing, and Reconfiguration Techniques. CRC Press, Boca Raton (2006)
4. Fair, R.B.: Digital microfluidics: is a true lab-on-a-chip possible? Microfluid. Nanofluid. **3**(3), 245–281 (2007)
5. Chakrabarty, K., Fair, R.B., Zeng, J.: Design tools for digital microfluidic biochips: toward functional diversification and more than moore. IEEE Trans. Comput. Aided Des. Integr. Circuits Syst. **29**(7), 1001–1017 (2010)

6. Schneider, L., Keszocze, O., Stoppe, J., Drechsler, R.: Effects of cell shapes on the routability of digital microfluidic biochips. In: Proceedings of International Conference on Design, Automation and Test in Europe (DATE), pp. 1631–1634 (2017)
7. Datta, P., Dutta, A., Majumder, R., Chakraborty, A., Dhal, D., Pal, R.K.: Enhancement of mixing operation through new movement strategies in digital microfluidic biochip. In: Devices for Integrated Circuit (DevIC), pp. 611–614 (2017)
8. Su, F., Chakrabarty, K., Pamula, V.K.: Yield enhancement of digital microfluidics-based biochips using space redundancy and local reconfiguration. In: Proceedings of International Conference on Design, Automation and Test in Europe (DATE), vol. 2, pp. 1196–1201 (2005)
9. Dutta, A., Majumder, R., Dhal, D., Pal, R.K.: Structural and behavioural facets of digital microfluidic biochips with hexagonal-electrode-based array. In: 32nd International Conference on VLSI Design and 18th International Conference on Embedded Systems, pp. 239–244 (2019)
10. Maftei, E., Pop, P., Madsen, J.: Droplet-aware module-based synthesis for fault-tolerant digital microfluidic biochips. In: Design, Test, Integration and Packaging of MEMS/MOEMS (DTIP), pp. 47–52 (2012)
11. Chakrabarty, K.: Design automation and test solutions for digital microfluidic biochips. IEEE Trans. Circuits Syst. I 57(1), 4–17 (2010)
12. Chang, H.-C., Yeo, L.Y.: Electrokinetically Driven Microfluidics and Nanofluidics. Cambridge University Press, New York (2010)

A Space Efficient Greedy Droplet Routing for Digital Microfluidics Biochip

Jyotiranjan Swain$^{(\boxtimes)}$, Kolluri Rajesh, and Sumanta Pyne

Department of Computer Science and Engineering, National Institute of Technology,
Rourkela 769008, Odisha, India
jrswain85@gmail.com, kollurirajesh556@gmail.com, sumantapyne@gmail.com

Abstract. Digital microfluidics biochip (DMFB) is capable of automating biochemical reactions or assays. It has three phases namely scheduling, planning and routing. Scheduling deals with when operation has to be executed, planning handles where to execute the operation and routing specifies how to perform the operation. The input to the biochip is an DAG of the biochemical reaction to be performed. A node in the DAG is an operation like mix, split, dilute etc, and the edges represents the inter-operational dependencies. Here we propose a new space efficient, greedy routing algorithm, based on rectangle overlapping. It combines both exploration and compaction in an iteration. The space requirement is reduced by storing routes in terms of L-lines in a new triplet format. Simulation result shows improvement of execution time and space consumption by 21.3% & 35.01% respectively.

Keywords: DMFB · Droplet routing · Greedy · Rectangle overlapping

1 Introduction

Microfluidics deals with design and analysis of Microelectromechanical systems (MEMS) that works with nano or pico liter fluid droplets [8]. The droplets are moved through a network of microchannels having diameter less than 1 mm [3]. Microfluidics devices or Lab-on-chip or Biochip is used extensively in medical diagnostics, DNA sequencing, cellular research, drug discovery, protein synthesis etc [4,6,9,10,13]. Biochip are capable of automating bio-chemical reactions or assays i.e. programmable chemistry e.g. the instructor can specify the assay to be performed to the chip, the chemical reaction is executed and analyzed by the Biochip and the result is shown instantaneously [5,14]. There are many pros of Biochip over traditional bio-laboratory i.e. precision analysis, portability, contamination free, fast and accurate result [6,15,22]. The first generation of Biochip is based on the continuous flow of fluids through micro-channels using micro-pumps. These devices suffers from the limitations like, inflexibility (can only execute specific assay) and contamination i.e. fluids sticking to the walls of the micro channel. The second generation Biochip is based on the principle of electro-wetting i.e. moving droplets by application of electric field. These

A. Sengupta et al. (Eds.): VDAT 2019, CCIS 1066, pp. 102–114, 2019.
https://doi.org/10.1007/978-981-32-9767-8_9

devices able to generate discrete droplets and the individual droplets can be transported by switching ON/OFF the electrodes beneath the cells [3]. Due to the similarity in working method of Biochip and binary digital system, it is called digital microfluidics system or digital microfluidics Biochip (DMFB) [13]. DMFB systems have three phases i.e. scheduling, placement and routing. The scheduling phase assigns execution time steps to operation like mixing. In placement, various modules are optimally placed over the biochip to have optimal execution time. The goal of routing, is to execute the operation. The tasks include specifying the routes to be followed by droplets to reach from source to their destination, while making sure no two droplets becomes adjacent. Droplet routing has two phases i.e. exploration and compaction. In exploration phase, path for individual droplets are found, then all the routes are mapped to generate the parallel movement sequence. In this work, we apply divide and conquer approach i.e. We consider a route as a collection of sub-routes, after finding optimal sub-routes we combine all these routes to get the final route. So instead of finding the whole path, we explore partial routes for all the droplets and then perform compaction. In order to get an optimal route we reduced the routing problem into an optimization problem. We defined a new heuristics called "intersection points" so selection of better routes. This paper is organized as follows Sect. 2 describes the DMFB system, Sect. 3 gives a brief summary about various routing methods till date. Proposed method is elaborated in Sect. 4 and Simulation and analysis is done in Sect. 4. The article ends with Conclusion and future work.

2   Digital Microfluidics System

Digital microfluidics System consists of three parts i.e. Biochip, micro-controller and a PC [13,21]. The assays are stored as directed acyclic graphs (DAG). Every node in DAG is a biochemical operation like mixing or splitting etc. The edges connecting the nodes are the inter-dependency among the operations [9,12]. The assays are stored in the PC. Initially, the user selects which assay to be performed, then the PC controller generates corresponding activation sequence for the micro-controller. The micro-controller on receiving this activation sequence sends signals to the biochip for activation of the electrodes at the specified instance of time. The droplets are generated from the fluid reservoirs around the chip's periphery and the biochemical reactions or assays are performed in biochip [13,14]. The Biochip contains two glass plates placed over each other with some space in between. Both plates are painted with hydrophobic material, to prevent sticking fluids to the plates. The top plate has a single ground electrode while the bottom plate have many small equal sized control electrodes placed at uniform space between each other. The droplets reside on cells and moved to other cells by activating the electrodes beneath the adjacent cells [3,6,10]. The DMFB works in following way, first DAG of the assay to be performed is selected. In scheduling, all the nodes in the DAG i.e. operations are assigned a start and end time. In placement, these operations are allocated the needed modules to execute the operations. Finally droplet routing is done to execute all operations in their allocated modules at the assigned time period by moving the droplet throughout the Biochip.

2.1 Droplet Routing

A Biochip is modelled as a two dimensional grid of cells [4]. There are three types of cells i.e. free cells (can be occupied by any droplet), occupied cell (cells that are already occupied by a droplet) and blockages (cells that can't be occupied by droplets). Let us consider a $m \times n$ Biochip with b blockages. Two autonomous droplets D_i and D_j are at cell (X_i^t, Y_i^t) and (X_j^t, Y_j^t) respectively during time period t. The goal is to move both droplets from their initial cells to their final cell or module to perform the operation. Mathematically, the droplet routing problem is described as

Input: A set of n droplets droplets $D = \{ D_0, D_1, ..., D_{n-1} \}$, where each droplet D_i has a source and target cell, A $m \times n$ Biochip G (C,B), C is the set of cells and B is the set of blockages.

Output: A set of paths $P = \{P_0, P_1 ..., P_{n-1}\}$, where P_i is the route for the droplet D_i.

Constraint: Fluidics constraints is to be maintained at every instant of time t.

Static [3,6,9,15]: $|X_i^t - X_j^t| \geq 2$ OR $|Y_i^t - Y_j^t| \geq 2$.
Dynamic [3,6,9,15]: $|X_i^{t+1} - X_j^t| \geq 2$ OR $|Y_i^{t+1} - Y_j^t| \geq 2$
     OR $|X_i^t - X_j^{t+1}| \geq 2$ OR $|Y_i^t - Y_j^{t+1}| \geq 2$.

3 Related Works

Droplet routing has two stages i.e. path exploration and compaction. In path exploration, multiple number of paths are discovered for every droplet. Out of all routes, one is selected based on a defined heuristics. After completion of exploration, compaction is performed. The aim of compaction is to generate a parallel movement sequence for droplets. Two methodologies are employed in compaction i.e. sequential and parallel. In sequential approach routes are mapped one after another, while in parallel method, all routes are mapped simultaneously by examining each cell in every route in a time step. Researchers have proposed many droplet routing methods which can be classified into three groups i.e. VLSI routing, Graph routing and Network flow. In VLSI routing based methods, Su et al. [3] use random route selection and mapping, Xu et al. [4] apply clique partition, Yuh et al. [8] adopt a progressive Integer linear programming (ILP) for droplet routing. VLSI routing based methods, tries to find disjoint path only i.e. the cells belong to the route of a droplet can't be used by others. DMFB allows a cell to be used by multiple droplets but not at same time interval. Hence these methods can improved by relaxing the disjoint criteria. In network flow based solutions, the droplets are modeled as flows and biochip's architecture is assumed to fixed. Many approaches like vertex coloring by Akella et al. [11], a variation of Open Shortest path First protocol by Griffith et al. [9] has been applied. Cho et al. [6] introduced bypassibity and concession zone, while Grissom et al. [14] apply restriction on rate of injection of droplet and flow directions constraint to solve routing problem. These method don't allow flexible movement of droplets leading to low efficiency. In graph based routing, there are two phases In exploration phase, the routes are discovered and in compaction phase, the routes are mapped so that all the droplets can move simultenously. For exploration phase Zhao et al. [7] apply modified Lee algorithm Singha et al. [16] proposed a method based Carrier Sense Multiple Access with collison detection (CSMA/CD), Pan et al. [17] use a dependency graph along with graph coloring, Bhattacharya et al. [18] apply modified Hadlock's algorithm and Roy et al. [15] use Soukup's algorithm, line probing [19], clustering [20] in exploration phase. In compaction phase stalls and detouring is used for solving deadlock. These methods are fast but have high memory requirement. Other methods includes a priority A* search method by Bohringer [1], integer linear programming by Peng et al. [2], motion vector analysis by Huang et al. [10], Ant colony optimization by Pan et al [21] and Gentic algorithm by Juarez et al. [22] produce optimal solution but the execution time is high.

4   Proposed Method

All routing procedures described above, the whole route for the first droplet is searched, and the cells in this route are reserved. Then, the second droplet's route is find out and so on. Once the routes for all droplet is explored, parallel movement plan is generated by mapping the routes. When the number of droplets becomes high, finding disjoint paths becomes difficult, leading to failure in exploration of path. This is due to the reservation of cells. To solve this, we use divide and conquer strategy, i.e. dividing a large route into smaller sub-routes. Then these sub-routes are mapped to generate the parallel movement sequence. This process is repeated until the all the droplets are routed. The idea is to reduce the number of blockages. As we are dealing with a smaller route in every iteration, and after the parallel movement sequence is generated, the cells are freed to be used by any other droplet, leading to less blockages improving probability of successful compaction. The biochip is a rectilinear grid in which diagonal movement is prohibited and droplets can only move into cells present in left, right, top or bottom. This results in two isomorphic routes i.e. equal cost and mirror to each other for every droplet. If we connect these two routes, it forms a rectangle. Hence, for n droplets, n rectangle are created in every iteration. Next we try to remove two edges from every rectangle to generate the final route between source and destination. So there are n rectangles with 4n edges and goal is to remove 2n edges. Hence reducing the droplet routing to an edge optimization problem. To solve this, we propose a greedy method i.e. we select the best route in every iteration (local maxima) and assume that it will leads to final optimal value (global maxima) or near to it.

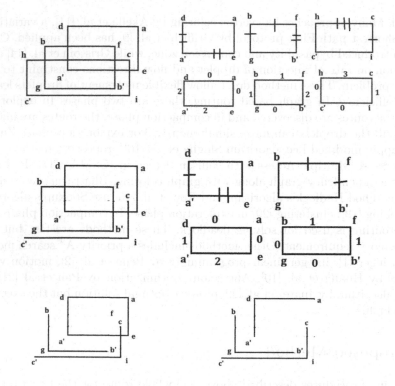

Fig. 1. Path optimization in rectangle overlapping

Let us consider a biochip, without any blockages. There are three droplets D_1, D_2 and D_3 currently present at cells a, b and c and desired to move to cell a', b' and c'. We have two routes for every droplet forming a rectangle and in total three rectangles ada'e, bfb'g and chc'i as shown in Fig. 1a. First we draw each rectangle and count the number of intersection points in it (Fig. 1b). In this case all the rectangles have 4 intersection points. We randomly select one rectangle i.e. chc'i. In this rectangle our goal is to connect a and a' with least number of intersection points. So out of two routes cic' is selected and chc' is removed from the graph resulting the graph presented in Fig. 1c. Next rectangles ada'e and bfb'g are considered and the number of intersection point present are 3 and 2 respectively (Fig. 1d). So the rectangle bfb'g is selected and bgb' is selected and bfb' is removed from the graph. The resulting graph is illustrated in Fig. 1e. Finally, the rectangle ada'e is considered, and ada' is selected and aea' is eliminated. Hence the final route connecting a and a', b and b' and c and c' is shown in Fig. 1f. In compaction phase, in time step 1, the first cell of each route is checked to see are they violating fluidic constraint. If not then, the second cells of each route is considered in the second iteration. If the fluidic constraint are not satisfied then the droplets are in deadlock. To break the deadlock, stalling and detour is used to break the deadlock. This procedure is repeated until all cells in every routed is mapped for a parallel movement sequence.

4.1 Algorithm

We have two phases, i.e. route exploration and compaction. In exploration phase we draw a rectangle for every droplet. First we draw a L-line begins by moving in X direction then Y direction and stops after a single turn. Then we draw another L - line by moving in Y direction first then in X direction. If they meet, rectangle is generated. Then the rectangles are optimized by removing 2 sequential edges so that corners of the rectangle i.e. source and destinations remain connected. But in most cases these two L-lines don't intersect, so we select the best L line among the two lines. Here, the criteria of selection is the longest L - line. There are cases in which only a single L-line is drawn, in such cases the L line is selected. We repeat this until all droplets are routed to their destination.

Algorithm 1. Path Exploration Phase

Data: A grid of n unit cells and a set of blockages and A set of droplets D   {
$D_0, D_1, ..., D_{n-1}$}. Each D_i have a source cell S_i and destination cell T_i .
Result: A set of L-lines L = {$L_0, L_1, L_2, ... L_{n-1}$ }

1   for $j = 0$ *to* $n - 1$ do
2 | Draw Rectangle R_j for D_j
3 | Sort Rectangles based on number of intersection points
4   end
5   while *L is not empty* do
6 | if *r_j have 2 intersecting L - lines* then
7 | | Select L-line with minimum number intersection points
8 | else
9 | | if *r_j have 2 non-intersecting L - lines* then
10 | | | Select L-line with minimum number intersection points
11 | | else
12 | | | Select L- line
13 | | end
14 | end
15 end

In compaction phase, parallel movement sequence is generated in round robin fashion. For every iteration, we have a single L -line for every droplet. We check i^{th} cell of every L-line in i^{th} iteration. If two cells becomes adjacent, then droplet occurs. The deadlock is solved by using stalling and detouring. If deadlock can't be solved, then routing is failed.

5   Simulation and Analysis

We have implemented proposed algorithm in UCR microfluidics static Simulator. We performed our experimentations on a 64 - bit Windows 10 machine having 8 GB RAM and Intel core i7 processor operating at 3.4 GHz. Three well

Algorithm 2. Compaction Phase

Data: A set of routes rectangles L = {$L_0,L_1,L_2, ... L_{n-1}$ } obtained from Path
exploration phase, n is the max length of a route in R
Result: Parallel movement sequence

```
1  for  i = 0 to n − 1 do
2  │    Check the i^{th} cell of every route in L
3  │    if two cells are not adjacent then
4  │    │    move to next route in L
5  │    else
6  │    │    if two cells are adjacent then
7  │    │    │    use stall or detour
8  │    │    else
9  │    │    │    Deadlock can't be solved and routing is failed
10 │    │    end
11 │    end
12 end
```

known routers i.e. Cho Router [6], Roy Router [15] and Grissom router [13] are
selected for their efficiency and performance. For performance analysis traditional benchmarks like PCR, In vitro and Protein based are chosen. The size
of the grid is taken to be 21 × 21. Two types of architecture are considered i.e.
virtual topology [9,14] where movement paths are fixed and free topology [6,15]
with no such constraint used. In scheduling phase, path scheduler [14] is selected.
In planning phase Path binder and Krammer placer are used for virtual and free
topology respectively. The operating frequency is set at 100 Hz. The routing time
is measured in milli-seconds.

Table 1. Simulation result: latest arrival time

Benchmark	Nodes		Cho [6]		Roy [15]		Grissom [14]		Proposed	
	Total	Non I/O	Virtual	Free	Virtual	Free	Virtual	Free	Virtual	Free
PCR	16	7	67	86	61	83	70	Failed	67	87
In Vitro 1	20	8	83	132	79	132	97	205	87	143
In Vitro 2	30	12	130	257	142	241	153	312	145	239
In Vitro 3	45	18	Failed	273	Failed	279	293	Failed	263	287
In Vitro 4	60	24	251	373	215	369	301	Failed	209	351
In Vitro 5	80	33	315	493	317	512	369	Failed	314	497
Protein 1	118	62	Failed	Failed	820	Failed	1021	Failed	793	873
Protein Split 1	28	14	173	319	171	315	218	378	179	321
Protein Split 2	58	30	379	521	412	602	493	Failed	398	597
Protein Split 3	118	62	Failed	Failed	715	Failed	1031	Failed	689	979
Protein Split 4	238	126	Failed	Failed	1505	2104	2213	Failed	1417	1437
Protein Split 5	478	254	Failed	3752	4017	4217	4348	Failed	3647	3748

5.1   Runtime

The execution of various benchmark and their latest arrival time is listed in Table 1. In case of Free Topology, Grissom router failed for most benchmarks as it was defined for virtual topology only. Cho router able to run most benchmarks and gives best performance for Protein Split1 benchmark. Roy router able to run all benchmark except Protein1 and ProteinSplit 3. Roy router's performance degrades as the size of benchmark increases. Our algorithm able to run all the benchmarks and as the size of the benchmarks increases, its latest arrival time improves, this is due to reserving the cells that are explored in a particular iteration i.e. not reserving all the cells in route. This reduces blockages leading to success in finding route. For smaller assays, the number of iteration is more in many cases when compared to other routers. To measure improvement in runtime, we consider each benchmark separately, we find the maximum time taken among the routers and then normalize it to the time taken by the current router. In case of a failed case, the routing time is taken as 0. The formula used for normalization is defined below

$$Improvement(in~\%) = \frac{time~taken~by~the~current~router}{maximum~time~taken~among~the~routers} \times 100$$

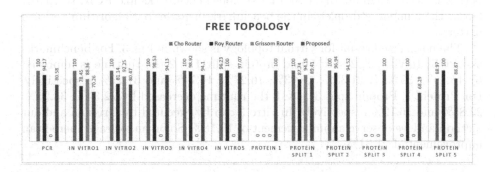

Fig. 2. Comparison of latest arrival time in virtual topology

The normalized result for free topology is presented in Fig. 2. For PCR, Grissom router fails so have a value of 0, Cho router takes maximum time hence it has a value of 100. Roy router has 94.17 and our proposed method has 80.58. This implies an improvement of 19.42%. In case of In vitro 1, In vitro 2 and protein split 1 runtime improved by 29.74%, 19.53% and 11.59% respectively. In vitro 3, 4 and 5 and Protein split 5, Grissom router fails to route and runtime is reduced by 5.87%, 5.9%, 3 % and 39.18% respectively. Our proposed method is able to run both Protein 1 and Protein split 3 while other routers have failed. Protein split 4 is successfully executed by roy router and our method with an improvement of 31.71%. So on an average there is an improvement of 13.83%.

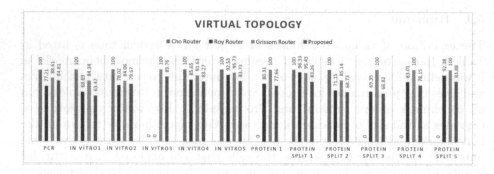

Fig. 3. Comparison of latest arrival time in free topology

In case of virtual topology, Cho router [6] could not execute many benchmarks e.g. In Vitro 3, Protein Split 3,4 & 5. This is due to the unable to find concession zone as the number of droplets increases. Roy router [15] gives best result for small benchmarks, but performance degrades as the size of the benchmarks increases. But it failed to run In vitro 3 benchmark. Grissom router [14] able to run all the benchmarks as it is a deadlock free protocol. The proposed algorithm performs better than Grissom router for all benchmarks. Roy router performs better than our algorithm for smaller benchmarks like PCR, In vitro1, but as the number of droplets in the benchmark increases our algorithm perform better.

The normalized result for virtual topology is shown in Fig. 3. For benchmarks like PCR, In vitro 1, 2, 4 & 5 and protein split 1 & 2 the runtime is improved by 15.19%, 36.53%, 21.33%, 16.73%, 16.27%, 16.74% and 31.27% respectively. For Protein 1, Protein split 3, 4 & 5 the runtime decreased by 22.34%, 33.28%, 22.85% and 16.12% respectively. In vitro 3 can by executed by Grissom and our method and we observe an improvement of 19.18%. So on an average there is an improvement of 21.31%.

5.2   Space Requirement

We use a triplet entry <S, M, E> to represent a L - line. Where S, M and E represents the start, middle and end node of a L - line. Cho router [6], Roy router [20] and Grissom router [14]routes are represented individual cells. For measuring the memory requirement, we recorded number of entries for each routes for every benchmark. The data collected is presented in Table 2.

In free topology, benchmarks like Invitro 1 & 2 and protein split 1 are successfully executed by all four routers. Roy router and proposed router able to execute Protein split 4 only. Only proposed router is able to execute Protein 1 and Protein split 2. Roy router have minimum number of entries for PCR and in vitro 1 benchmark, while proposed router have minimum number of entries in all other benchmarks. To perform comparative analyze we first normalize the data by using following formula.

$$Improvement(in~\%) = \frac{Number~of~entries~in~the~current~router}{maximum~number~of~entries~among~the~routers} \times 100$$

Table 2. Space requirement in number of entries

Benchmark	Nodes		Cho Router [2008]		Roy Router [2016]		Grissom Router [2015]		Proposed	
	Total	Non I/O	Virtual	Free	Virtual	Free	Virtual	Free	Virtual	Free
PCR	16	7	375	363	295	279	320	Failed	297	293
In Vitro 1	20	8	457	473	338	320	357	379	323	347
In Vitro 2	30	12	517	561	423	415	419	409	353	372
In Vitro 3	45	18	Failed	725	Failed	503	459	Failed	371	398
In Vitro 4	60	24	831	879	623	659	673	Failed	470	481
In Vitro 5	80	33	977	1023	727	783	731	Failed	543	559
Protein 1	118	62	Failed	Failed	1109	Failed	1157	Failed	784	797
Protein Split 1	28	14	498	517	415	431	417	398	343	361
Protein Split 2	58	30	803	843	593	601	557	Failed	419	432
Protein Split 3	118	62	Failed	Failed	1171	Failed	1217	Failed	811	802
Protein Split 4	238	126	Failed	Failed	2237	2287	2259	Failed	1593	1617
Protein Split 5	478	254	Failed	6752	5138	5217	5167	Failed	4021	4107

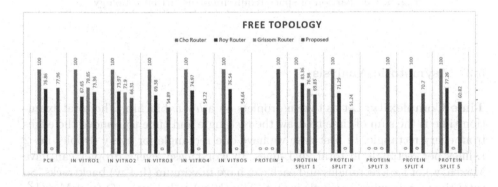

Fig. 4. Comparison of space requirement in free topology

The normalized data for free topology is presented in Fig. 4. For benchmarks In Vitro 1 & 2 and Protein split 1 the number of entries reduced by 26.64%, 33.69% and 30.17% respectively. For PCR, In vitro 3, 4 & 5, Protein split 2 & 5 the memory requirement is reduced by 22.04%, 45.11%, 45.28%, 48.76% and 39.18%. Roy router and proposed router able to run Protein split 3 with an improvement of 29.3%. Only our proposed router able to run protein split 3 benchmark hence have a value of 100. So on an average 35.01% reduction on memory requirement.

In virtual topology, benchmarks PCR, In vitro 1, 2, 4 & 5, Protein split 1 & 2 Cho router have highest number of entries while proposed router have minimum number of entries. Cho router failed for In vitro 3, Protein 1, Protein split 3, 4 & 5. In these benchmarks, Grissom router have largest number of entries while prosed method have lowest. Only Grissom router and proposed router able to execute In vitro 2 benchmark and proposed method have optimum number of entries.

The normalized data for virtual topology is presented in Fig. 5. The number of entries is reduced for the benchmarks PCR, In vitro 1, 2, 3, 4 & 5, Protein 1, Protein split 1, 2, 3, 4 & 5 are 20.8%, 32%, 31.73%, 19.18%, 44.44%, 44.43%, 32.24%, 32.13%, 47.82%, 33.36%, 29.49% & 22.11% respectively. On an average the 32.47%. As the size of the benchmark increases the number of entries reduced.

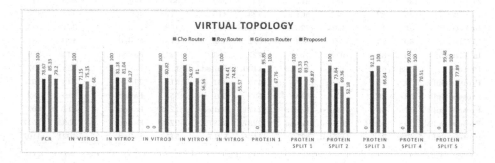

Fig. 5. Comparison of space requirement in virtual topology

5.3   Asymptotic Analysis

Time Complexity: Let us take n droplets on a $h \times w$ biochip. The total execution time is the sum of time to draw the rectangle and time to remove the edges from every rectangle. In best case we have one rectangle for every droplet i.e. 2 L-lines per rectangle in total 2n L-lines. In worst case, every droplet can have Max(h, w) of 1×1 rectangles and each can have maximum (h + w) backtracks. So total time for drawing rectangle is O(n×Max(h, w) ×(h + w)) = O (n × Max(h^2, m^2)) = O(n^3). To remove edges from rectangle, we have to check all the cells in an line to find the number of intersection points i.e. 2(h + w) + a + b. (a and b are constants for selection and deleting edges. In total = n × (2(h + w) + a + b) = O (n^2). So total runtime is O(n^3) + O (n^2) = O(n^3).

Space Complexity: To reduce memory requirement Depth First Search (DFS) is used. Line probing methods stores the routes as collection of lines i.e. (initial cell, final cell). In our method, L - shape lines are stored as (initial cell, middle cell, final cell). So for a rectangle, we need 2 entries in total six Co-ordinates. But in a line searching algorithm, we need to store 4 lines i.e. 8 entries. So the space complexity is O(L) where L is the number of L segments. Experimental result shows it requires 30% less memory.

6 Conclusion and Future Work

Digital microfluidics Biochip (DMFB) is capable of automating biochemical synthesis. It is used extensively in DNA research, medical diagnostics, environmental monitoring applications. Routing is an important phase of synthesis, the goal is to move the droplets to the destination cells from their sources, such that they don't become adjacent to each other. Here, we transformed routing problem to an edge removal optimization problem and use a greedy approach to select routes. In our proposed method, we first find partial routes for each droplet, then we perform compaction on these routes. This procedure is continued until all the droplets reach their destination. We implement our proposed method in UCR microfluidics static simulator. All the benchmarks are executed in both virtual and free topology. It also gives best performance for dense benchmarks and near optimal result for smaller benchmarks. We observed 21.3% and 35.01% improvement in latest arrival time and memory requirement compared with other routing methods. In future, we plan to improve the routing algorithm, by defining a better heuristics, then we will work on scheduling and planning phases.

References

1. Bohringer, K.F.: Modeling and controlling parallel tasks in droplet based microfluidic systems. IEEE Trans. Comput. Aided Des. Integr. Circuits Syst. **25**(2), 334–344 (2004)
2. Peng, J., Akella, S.: Coordinating multiple robots with kinodynamic constraints along specified paths. Int. J. Robot. Res. **24**(4), 295–310 (2005)
3. Su, F., Hwang, W.L., Chakrabarty, K.: Droplet routing in the synthesis of digital microfluidic biochips. In: Proceedings of the Design Automation & Test in Europe Conference, vol. 1, pp. 1–6 (2006)
4. Xu, T., Chakrabarty, K.: A cross-referencing-based droplet manipulation method for high-throughput and pin-constrained digital microfluidic arrays. In: Proceedings of Design Automation and Test in Europe, pp. 552–557, April 2007
5. Yuh, P.H., Yang, C.L., Chang, Y.-W.: BioRoute: a networkflow based routing algorithm for digital microfluidic biochips. In: Proceeding of IEEE/ACM Computer-Aided Design, ICCAD 2007, San Jose, CA, USA, 4–8 November 2007 (2007)
6. Cho, M., Pan, D.Z.: A high-performance droplet routing algorithm for digital microfluidic biochips. IEEE Trans. Comput.-Aided Des. Integr. Circuits Syst. **27**(10), 1714–1724 (2008)
7. Zhao, Y., Chakrabarty, K.: Cross-contamination avoidance for droplet routing in digital microfluidic biochips. In: Proceeding of conference on Design, automation and test in Europe, DATE 2009, Nice, France, 20–24 April 2009, pp. 1290–1295 (2009)
8. Yuh, P.-H., Sapatnekar, S., Yang, C.-L., Chang, Y.-W.: A progressive ILP based routing algorithm for cross referencing biochips. In: Proceedings of Design Automation Conference, pp. 284–289, June 2008
9. Griffith, E., Akella, S.: Coordinating multiple droplets in planar array digital microfluidics systems. In: Workshop on the Algorithmic Foundations of Robotics (2004)

10. Huang, T., Ho, T.: A fast routability- and performance-driven droplet routing algorithm for digital microfluidic biochips. In: Proceedings of IEEE ICCD, Lake Tahoe, CA, pp. 445–450 (2009)
11. Akella, S., Griffith, E.J., Goldberg, M.K.: Performance characterization of a reconfigurable planar-array digital microfluidic system. IEEE Trans. Comput.-Aided Des. Integr. Circuits Syst. **25**, 340–352 (2006)
12. Griffith, E., Akella, S.: Coordinating multiple droplets in planar array digital microfluidics systems. Int. J. Robot. Res. **24**(11), 933–949 (2005)
13. Grissom, D., Brisk, P.: A high-performance online assay interpreter for digital microfluidic biochips. In: Proceeding of 22nd Great Lake Symposium on VLSI, (GLS-VLSI), Salt Lake City, UT, USA, 3–4 May 2012, pp. 103–106 (2012)
14. Grissom, D., Brisk, P.: Fast online synthesis of digital microfluidic biochips. IEEE Trans. Comput.-Aided Design Integr. Circuits Syst. (TCAD) **33**(3), 356–369 (2014)
15. Roy, P., Rahaman, H., Dasgupta, P.: A novel droplet routing algorithm for digital microfluidic biochips. In: Proceedings of the 20th Symposium on Great Lakes Symposium on VLSI, GLSVLSI 2010, Rhode Island, USA, 16–18 May 2010, pp. 441–446 (2010)
16. Singha, K., Samanta, T., Rahaman, H., Dasguptay, P.: Method of droplet routing in digital microfluidic biochip. In: Proceeeding of 2010 IEEE/ASME International Conference on Mechatronics and Embedded Systems and Applications, (MESA), QingDao, China, China, 15–17 July 2010 (2010)
17. Bhattacharya, R., Roy, P., Rahaman, H.: Homogeneous droplet routing in DMFB: an enhanced technique for high performance bioassay implementation. Integr. VLSI J. **60**, 74–91 (2018)
18. Pan, I., Samanta, T.: Weighted optimization of various parameters for droplet routing in digital microfluidic biochips. In: Thampi, S., Abraham, A., Pal, S., Rodriguez, J. (eds.) Recent Advances in Intelligent Informatics. Advances in Intelligent Systems and Computing, vol. 235, pp. 131–139. Springer, Cham (2014). https://doi.org/10.1007/978-3-319-01778-5_14
19. Roy, P., Bhattacharya, R., Rahaman, H., Dasgupta, P.: A best path selection based parallel router for DMFBs. In: IEEE International Symposium on Electronic Design, ISED 2011, Kochi, India, pp. 176–181 (2011)
20. Roy, P., Rahaman, H.: Parthasarathi dasgupta,"two-level clustering-based techniques for intelligent droplet routing in digital microfluidic biochips". Integration **45**(3), 316–330 (2012)
21. Pan, I., Dasgupta, P., Rahaman, H., Samanta, T.: Ant colony optimization based droplet routing technique in digital microfluidic biochip. In: International Symposium on Electronic System Design, pp. 223–229 (2011)
22. Juarez, J., Brizuela, C.A., Martínez-Pérez, I.M.: An evolutionary multi-objective optimization algorithm for the routing of droplets in digital microfluidic biochips. Inf. Sci. **429**, 130–146 (2018)

Design of 635 MHz Bandpass Filter Using High-Q Floating Active Inductor

Aditya Kumar Hota[✉] and Kabiraj Sethi

Veer Surendra Sai University of Technology, Burla, Odisha, India
{akhota_etc,ksethi_etc}@vssut.ac.in

Abstract. This paper presents the design of a bandpass filter using a CMOS floating active inductor with a quality factor of 14.7. By tuning the biasing current in the circuit we can tune the quality factor and the resonant frequency of the floating active inductor as well as bandpass filter. The power consumption of the bandpass filter is 3.72 mW with a supply voltage of 1.8 V. The 1 dB compression point and IIP3 are 26.3 dBm and 27.6 dBm respectively. The centre frequency of the filter is 635 MHz with a bandwidth of 8 MHz which can be used in the broadcasting applications. The noise figure of the filter is 0.16 dB. The filter is designed in UMC 180 nm mixed mode CMOS process.

Keywords: Cross coupled structure · Floating active inductor (FAI) · Quality factor (Q) · Radio frequency integrated circuit (RFIC)

1 Introduction

Inductors, both passive and active, play very important role in radio frequency Integrated Circuits (RFICs) used for systems like low noise amplifier (LNA), oscillators, filters, phase shifters etc. The on-chip passive inductors suffer from issues like tunability, area and cost. So, active inductors (AIs) replace them, though not completely, on RFICs in-spite of their inherent limitations like higher power consumption, non-linearity and noisiness. Many authors have proposed several design methodologies for AIs (both single ended and floating) [1–10]. They adopt different methods to improve the quality factor (Q) by incorporating local feedback, cascode structures and negative impedance circuit. AI behaves as a resonator since it is associated with the inherent parasitic resistance and capacitance [11]. For this behaviour, they are used in the design of bandpass filters (BPFs). A BPF for IF-Receiver architecture is proposed in [12] whereas [13] uses a voltage differentiating transconductance amplifier for high frequency BPF design. For multi band, multimode applications BPF using inductorless bi-quads is proposed [14] and [15] uses the varactors in the design of AI to tune the parasitic capacitances of the BPF. In this paper we have designed a high-Q FAI using transistors-only and it is used to design a RF BPF.

Supported by VSSUT, Odisha.

2 Design of Floating Active Inductor

The single ended AI [16] has a cross couples structure which provides a negative
impedance to compensate the parasitic series and parallel resistive losses in the
circuit, as such increasing the Q value. Here, the AI uses a single current source
to define the currents in all transistors. We have proposed an FAI based on this
design as shown in Fig. 1.

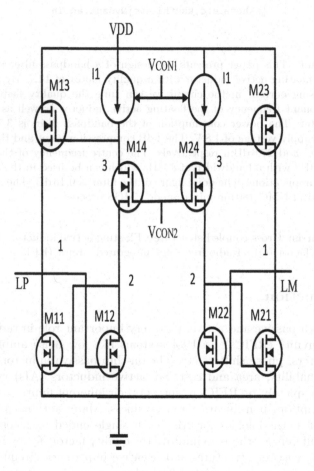

Fig. 1. Proposed FAI

Figure 2 shows the equivalent circuit of proposed FAI which includes the
negative resistance (RNIC).

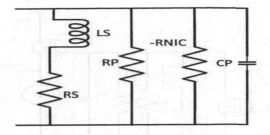

Fig. 2. Equivalent circuit of FAI

From the small signal analysis the input impedance of the AI [16] is found to be

$$Z_{in} = \frac{S(C_{gs3} + C_{gs4})}{S^2 C_{gs2}(C_{gs3} + C_{gs4}) + SC_{gs2}g_{m4} + g_{m2}(g_{m4} - g_{m3})} \tag{1}$$

From the above transfer function the different parameters extracted as

$$\omega_0^2 = \frac{g_{m2}(g_{m4} - g_{m3})}{C_{gs2}(C_{gs3} + C_{gs4})} \tag{2}$$

$$Q = \frac{\omega_0(C_{gs3} + C_{gs4})}{g_{m3}} \tag{3}$$

$$L_S = \frac{C_{gs3}}{g_{m2}g_{m3}} \tag{4}$$

Generally, for a FAI the inductance value is twice that of a single ended AI [11]. Hence the inductance of the proposed FAI found to be $\frac{2C_{gs3}}{g_{m2}g_{m3}}$.

3   Design of Bandpass Filter

The characteristics of input impedance Z_{in} of the FAI resembles the characteristics of a bandpass filter, around the resonant frequency. Hence we suggest a bandpass filter using the proposed FAI as shown in the Fig. 3, which enhances the Q value of the filter. The input transistor M_{in}, supplies the required current to the FAI by converting the input voltage to current. A source follower transistor M_{out}, prevent the loading effect on the Q and ω_0 of the FAI. The additional parasitic capacitance and resistance arising due to the input and output transistors M_{in} and M_{out}, are added to the capacitance C_p and resistance R_P of the FAI. Thus the new values of Q and ω_0 of the FAI become that of the bandpass filter. The complete RF BPF is shown in Fig. 4. Here MB1, MB2 and MIB constitute the differential input section where as MOUT1, MOUT2 and IB constitute the differential output section and the rest of the circuit represents the FAI.

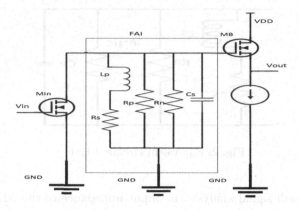

Fig. 3. Bandpass filter design using the FAI

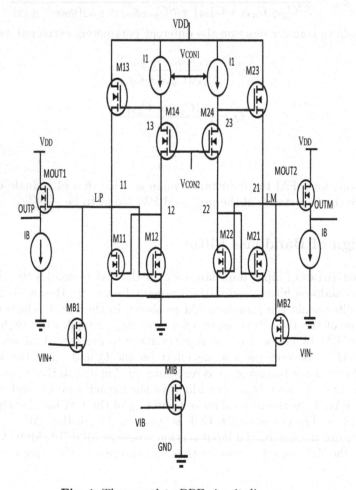

Fig. 4. The complete BPF circuit diagram

4   Results and Discussion

The proposed FAI and bandpass filter are designed in Cadence (IC6.1.6) using UMC 0.18 μm CMOS mixed mode process (1Poly 6Metal). The BPF comprises of MOSFET only without any passive elements. All the simulations are done in Spectre RF simulator. The design specifications of the BPF are mentioned in Table 1. The length of all the transistors are 180 nm.

Table 1. Transistors specification used in the design

Transistor	M1	M2	M3	M4	MIB
Width (W) (μm)	4.5	9	4.5	2.7	0.7

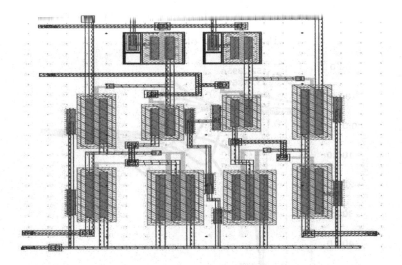

Fig. 5. Layout of the FAI

Figure 5 shows the layout of the FAI having an area of $18.2 \times 22.6 \,\mu m^2$ while Fig. 6 shows the layout of the total BPF occupying an area of $21.5 \times 23.82 \,\mu m^2$.

From Fig. 7 it is found that the inductance value of FAI is constant near upto the resonant frequency for all the tuning ranges. The simulated inductance value ranges from 27 nH tp 3.6 μH with the control voltage variation VCON1 from 760 mV to 940 mV and VCON2 from 1.2 v to 1.45 V. But practically on-chip inductance values above few hundreds of nH is not achievable. The self resonating frequency of the FAI ranges from 400 MHz to 5.76 GHz.

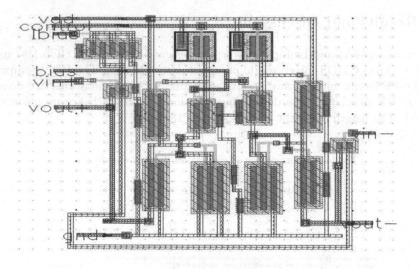

Fig. 6. Layout of the BPF

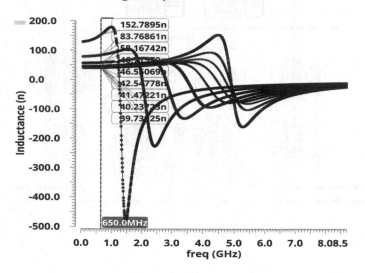

Fig. 7. Plot of frequency vs inductance of the FAI

The maximum Q value obtained from the simulation is 10K at 1.62 GHz as per Fig. 8 which is again practically not achievable. Here we have set the values of VCON1 as 937 mV and VCON2 as 1.3 v for a inductance value of 46.5 nH and Quality factor 14.7 to design the BPF for a centre frequency of 635 MHz.

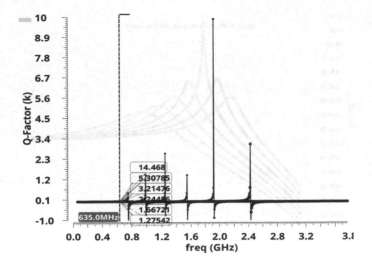

Fig. 8. Plot of frequency vs Q of the FAI

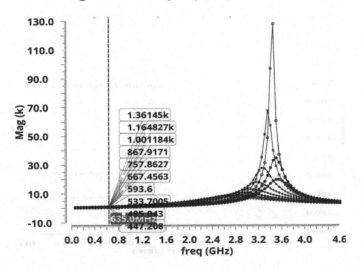

Fig. 9. Plot of frequency vs magnitude of input impedance of the FAI

The input impedance is also varies between 0.47 KΩ to 127 KΩ for higher frequencies as shown in Fig. 9. The FAI behaves as an inductor upto the resonant frequency and after that it become capacitive. At resonance the impedance is vary high which indicates the high Q value of the FAI. Figure 10 shows the frequency response of the BPF for different tuning voltages. For centre frequency of 635 MHz the mid band gain is 1dB with a bandwidth of 8 MHz. Hence it can be used in narrowband applications.

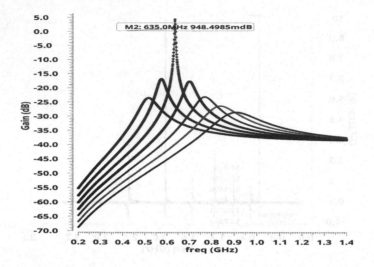

Fig. 10. Frequency response of the BPF

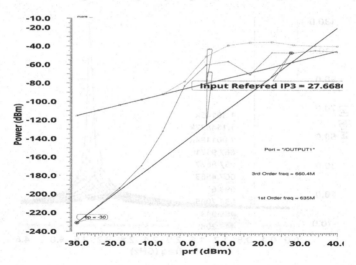

Fig. 11. IIP3 of the BPF

The linearity of the bandpass filter is verified from IIP3 and the 1dB compression point for a load of 500 Ω with a source resistance of 50 Ω. Figures 11 and 12 show the IIP3 and the 1 dB compression point as 27.6 dBm and 26.3 dBm respectively. As they lie within 10 dBm range, it seems that the proposed design is tolerable enough in linearity point of view.

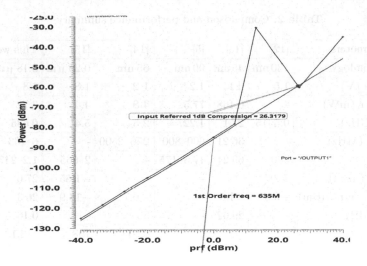

Fig. 12. 1 dB compression point of the BPF

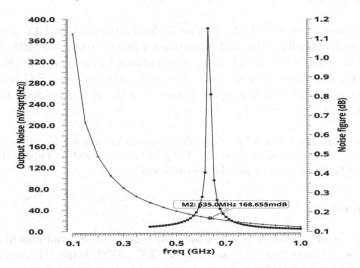

Fig. 13. Output noise and noise figure of the BPF

As the whole design is comprising of transistors only, it is obvious that the circuit generates some amount of intrinsic noise. From the noise analysis in Fig. 13, the output noise is found to be 370 nV/√Hz which is tolerable and the noise figure (NF) is 0.16 db at 635 MHz frequency.

The performance of the proposed work is summarized and compared with the state of the art methods as in Table 2.

Table 2. Comparison and performance summary

Parameters	[12]	[13]	[5]	[14]	[15]	This work
Technology	130 nm	45 nm	90 nm	65 nm	0.25 μm	0.18 μm
VDD (V)	1.5	±1	1.2	1.2	1.8	1.8
Power (mW)	-	0.168	77.5	4.8	4.4	3.72
ω_0 (GHz)	0.5–15	2.51	1.227	2.5	5.4	0.635
B.W (MHz)	-	36.21	600–800	250–2500	-	6–163
Q	300	69.21	17.5–175	-	2–665	1.2–247
IIP3 (dBm)	7.2	-	-	-	−1.65	27.6
1dB comp (dBm)	−0.38	−1.5		−6.7	−13.9	26.3
NF (dB)	-	29.62	-	30	-	0.16
Area (μm^2)	-	-		0.011	798	512.13

5 Conclusion

A RF bandpass filter with high Q value is designed using an FAI. The centre frequency is around 635 MHz and the tuning range is from 435 MHz–900 MHz which can be used in the broadcasting applications in the range of 400 MHz to 900 MHz. The linearity of the designed filter using the proposed FAI is better in comparison to others. But due to the presence of the active inductor the Noise performance is poor.

Acknowledgement. I thank Mr. Suvendu Narayan Mishra for his support in this research work. I am also thankful to the TEQUIP cell of VSSUT, Odisha, Burla for the provided facilities to carry out the research work.

References

1. Arif, M., et al.: Advances in active inductor based CMOS band-pass filter. Analog Integr. Circuits Signal Process. **89**, 727–737 (2018). https://doi.org/10.2174/1876402910666180524121649
2. Momen, H.G., et al.: Low-loss active inductor with independently adjustable self-resonance frequency and quality factor parameters. Integr. VLSI J. **58**, 22–26 (2017). https://doi.org/10.1016/j.vlsi.2016.12.014
3. Ghasemzadeh, H., et al.: Design of a new low loss fully CMOS tunable floating active inductor. Analog Integr. Circuits Signal Process. **89**(3), 727–737 (2016). https://doi.org/10.1007/s10470-016-0784-3
4. Bhuiyan, M.A.S., et al.: Active inductor based fully integrated CMOS transmit/receive switch for 2.4 GHz RF transceiver. Ann. Brazilian Acad. Sci. **88**, 1089–1098 (2016)
5. Ren, S., Benedik, C.: International journal of electronics and communications (AEÜ) RF CMOS active inductor band pass filter with post fabrication calibration. AEUE - Int. J. Electron. Commun. **67**(12), 1058–1067 (2013). https://doi.org/10.1016/j.aeue.2013.06.008

6. Chen, S.-W., et al.: Tunable active bandpass filter design. Electron. Lett. **47**(18), 1019 (2011). https://doi.org/10.1049/el.2011.1401

7. Reja, M.M., et al.: A wide frequency range CMOS active inductor for UWB bandpass filters. In: Midwest Symposium on Circuits and Systems, pp. 1055–1058 (2009). https://doi.org/10.1109/MWSCAS.2009.5235983

8. Wu, Y.W.Y., et al.: RF bandpass filter design based on CMOS active inductors. IEEE Trans. Circuits Syst. II Analog Digit. Signal Process. **50**(12), 942–949 (2003). https://doi.org/10.1109/TCSII.2003.820235

9. Chang, Y., et al.: The design and analysis of a RF CMOS bandpass filter. In: IEEE International Symposium on Circuits and Systems, Geneva, Switzerland, pp. 625–628 (2002). https://doi.org/10.1109/iscas.2000.856406

10. Akbari-Dilmaghani, R., et al.: A high Q RF CMOS differential active inductor. In: IEEE International Conference on Electronics Circuits and Systems, pp. 157–160 (1998). https://doi.org/10.1109/icecs.1998.813957

11. Yuan, F.: CMOS Active Inductors and Transformers. Springer, Boston (2008). https://doi.org/10.1007/978-0-387-76479-5

12. Sachan, D.: A high-Q floating active inductor using 130 nm BiCMOS technology and its application in IF band pass filter. Analog Integr. Circuits Signal Process. **96**(3), 385–393 (2018). https://doi.org/10.1007/s10470-018-1196-3

13. Kumar, V., et al.: A 2.5 GHz low power, high-Q, reliable design of active bandpass filter. IEEE Trans. Device Mater. Reliab. **17**(1), 229–244 (2017)

14. Wang, Y., et al.: Cost-efficient CMOS RF tunable bandpass filter with active inductor-less biquads. In: IEEE International Symposium on Circuits and Systems, Seoul, South Korea, pp. 2139–2142. IEEE (2012)

15. Xiao, H., Schaumann, R.: A 5.4-GHz high-Q tunable active-inductor bandpass filter in standard digital CMOS technology. Analog Integr. Circuits Signal Process. **51**(1), 1–9 (2007). https://doi.org/10.1007/s10470-007-9040-1

16. Reja, M., Filanovsky, M.: Wide tunable CMOS active inductor. Electron. Lett. **57**(6), 982–984 (2008). https://doi.org/10.1049/el:20081375

Design and Physical Implementation of Mixed Signal Elapsed Time Counter in 0.18 μm CMOS Technology

Saroja V. Siddamal$^{(\boxtimes)}$ ⓘ, Suhas B. Shirol, Shraddha Hiremath, and Nalini C. Iyer

KLE Technological University, Hubbali, India
{sarojavs, suhasshirol, shraddha, nalinic}@kletech.ac.in

Abstract. The paper reports the development of low power elapsed time counter that tracks a real time and elapsed time. The mixed signal ASIC is implemented in UMC 0.18 μm CMOS mixed signal technology, 3.3 V/1.8 V. This operates at two frequencies 2 MHz and 32.768 kHz. The ultra low power oscillator designed consumes current of 250 nA with minimum frequency variation for all process voltage temperature conditions. The oscillator is simulated using spectra simulator and designed using cadence virtuoso. The area consumed is 0.003064 mm^2. The counters count at real time of 1 s. This is achieved by frequency divider which scales down 32.768 kHz to 1 Hz. The entire ASIC is designed using cadence innovus. The die size is 697.5 μm × 697.5 μm. The ASIC is taped out to Taiwan at mini@sic runway for fabrication.

Keywords: Elapsed time counter · Application specific integrated circuit · Mixed signal technology · Ultra low power oscillator · Ultra voltage lockout

1 Introduction

Elapsed time counter monitors, records, and displays the passage time. They are deployed in applications, where this is an important operational parameter and documentation of the running time of powered equipment, is required. The most common type of elapsed time indicator is the hour meter. Hour meters are prominent in industrial vehicles and other equipment outfitted with engines or motors, and sometimes in medical and recreational machinery. Such ETIs measure the total operational time of the monitored machinery, including idle and standby time, and enables estimates of wear and tear of the equipment. Modes of operation often include a countdown, count-up, alarm and memory [1]. The products of Maxim Integrated include DS1682 which is a Total-Elapsed-Time Recorder [2] with Alarm. A internal RC time base oscillator is present in DS1682. DS1682 requires no backup power source as it uses EEPROM technology to maintain data in case there is no power. The EVENT pin records the total event time elapsed from the time the IS was reset to '0'. The user can program the ALARM for particular set of time. When this set time matches with accumulated time the user is alerted. The DS1682 monitors the total time the device is in operation [2]. Similar to other products, DS1318E+ is a parallel-interface elapsed time counter. It has 44bit

© Springer Nature Singapore Pte Ltd. 2019
A. Sengupta et al. (Eds.): VDAT 2019, CCIS 1066, pp. 126–140, 2019.
https://doi.org/10.1007/978-981-32-9767-8_11

counter which records the time for which a device operates. The counter clock has a frequency of 4.096 kHz providing a resolution of 244 s. A maximum count for over 136 years is obtained. It has an inbuilt circuit for power sensing which detects a power failure and switches to the backup power supply so the count is maintained. It has an option for an external event timer. The control input present in the IC manages the counter's operation. This can be used in power meters and servers [3]. The DS1602 is a real-time clock/elapsed time counter [4]. It has two counters which count in seconds with battery power and supply power. Using a software algorithm, the time of day, week, month and year is obtained. The amount of time that V_{CC} power is applied is recorded by the V_{CC} powered counter. It can be used in applications in which we need to know the operational time of the device, in which it is used. It can be used to record the real-time events [4]. Oscillators are an integral part of many electronic systems [13]. Oscillators find application as clock generation in microprocessors, carrier synthesis in cellular telephones etc. [14]. Design of robust and high performance still remains as challenge [5].

The proposed oscillator design is used in the elapsed time counter product which used to count seconds when power supply is applied [6]. Typically, an external crystal is used for clock generation, which becomes an input to the counter which continuously keeps the track of time. Increasing demand for on-chip devices motivates to design an on-chip oscillator as a replacement of external crystal to reduce bill of material cost. Therefore the user has an option to switch between the external crystal and the on-chip clock. The variation in oscillator frequency should be as minimal as possible for all Process Voltage Temperature (PVT) conditions. Since the oscillator has to run on the battery supply, it has to consume very less current for longer battery life.

The rest of the paper is organized as follows. Section 2 discusses the front end design of the mixed signal elapsed time counter. It explains the design of individual blocks and the results. Features of the ASIC are described in Sect. 3. Back end implementation is described in Sect. 4. Section 5 pays a path to conclusion.

2   Proposed Front End ASIC

The diagram of the proposed Elapsed Time Counter (ETC) is as shown in Fig. 1. The mixed signal ETC consists of 2, 32 bit counters, one operating at battery VBAT voltage of 1.8 V and another at VCC of 1.8 V. The ASIC operates at two frequencies, 1 Hz for counting the real and elapsed time, 2 MHz to communicate with external devices. The ASIC named as NKETC2019 is designed to count seconds with VCC power. The real time counter counts under battery power VBAT. The NKETC2019 finds its application in determining the operational time of the equipments. The ASIC has an internal RTC ultra low power oscillator, oscillating at 32.768 kHz. A 1 Byte protocol register selects trim bits of oscillator, functions to clear the counter and selects read/write functions.

2.1   Serial Port

To and from communication in this ASIC is done using serial port. This is a 3 wire port which is activated by driving 'RST' to low state. With 'RST' at low state protocol register is loaded with 8 bits of information. On the rising edge of 2 MHz clock signal the 8bits are serially fed.

The NKETC2019 operates at V_{CC} and V_{BAT} power. When $V_{CC} < V_{BAT}$ the ASIC operates on V_{BAT} power. During this time the serial port is disabled to save battery capacity. The V_{CC} controlled active counter is gated by power good signal and generated 1 Hz clock signal as shown in Fig. 1.

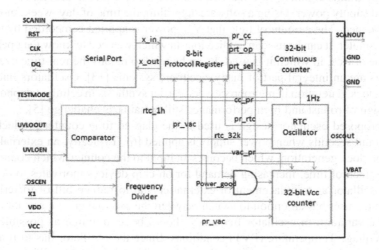

Fig. 1. Block diagram of NKETC2019

2.2   Serial Port

To and from communication in this ASIC is done using serial port. This is a 3 wire port which is activated by driving 'RST' to low state. With 'RST' at low state protocol register is loaded with 8 bits of information. On the rising edge of 2 MHz clock signal the 8 bits are serially fed. The NKETC2019 operates at V_{CC} and V_{BAT} power. When $V_{CC} < V_{BAT}$ the ASIC operates on V_{BAT} power. During this time the serial port is disabled to save battery capacity. The V_{CC} controlled active counter is gated by power good signal and generated 1 Hz clock signal as shown in Fig. 1.

2.3   Protocol Register

This is 8 bit register which decides what action is to be performed. Figure 2 shows the protocol bit definitions. For ex. if the 7th bit is high this selects 32 bit V_{BAT} counter for operation. The 0th bit selects read or write operation.

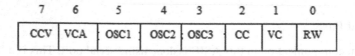

7	6	5	4	3	2	1	0
CCV	VCA	OSC1	OSC2	OSC3	CC	VC	RW

Fig. 2. Protocol register

Bits 5, 4, 3 are used to trim the frequency of on chip oscillator. A value of '100'will give accurate oscillating frequency of 32.768 kHz at 25 °C. Increasing the binary value towards 7 will make this oscillator frequency higher. For proper operation all the 8 bits of protocol register needs to be sent.

2.4 Read/Write Data Transfer

NKETC2019 operates on two frequencies, 2 MHz external clock to communicate to external devices and 1 Hz clock derived from 32.768 kHz for counting. Every new data is entered into the counter when $\overline{RST}$ is transitioned to high and on the rising edge 32 clock cycles as shown in Fig. 3.

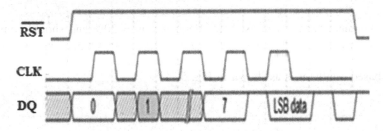

Fig. 3. Timing diagram for read data transfer

2.5 Oscillator

A CMOS current starved inverter based oscillator is designed to drive counter in the ASIC. The oscillator runs at battery supply of 1.8 V. The design requirements of this oscillator are

1. There should be minimum frequency variations for all process voltage temperature conditions.
2. The oscillator should consume very less power.
3. Oscillator frequency should be close to 32.768 kHz.

The proposed design comprises of process and temperature compensated biasing circuit, chain of current starved inverters and output buffers [16] as shown in Fig. 4.

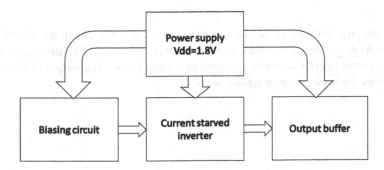

Fig. 4. Proposed block diagram of oscillator

Design Specifications: Table 1 shows the designed specification the oscillator is designed.

Table 1. Oscillator specifications [16]

Parameter	Min	Typ	Max	Unit
Frequency	22.937	32.768	42.598	kHz
Duty cycle	40	50	60	%
Supply current	-	200	350	nA
Supply power	1.6	1.8	1.9	V
Temperature range	0	27	125	°C

The maximum variation in oscillator frequency is ± 30% and should consume a current less than 250 nA from the battery, for variations in temperature ranging from 0 °C to 125 °C, at different process corners. The proposed schematic of current starved inverter based oscillator is as shown in Fig. 5.

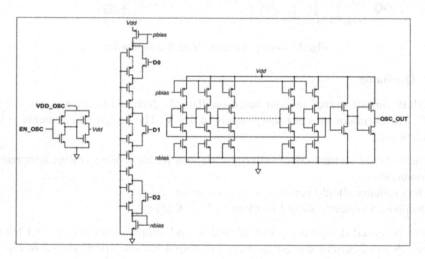

Fig. 5. Proposed schematic diagram of oscillator [16]

The starving MOSFETs of the current starved inverter chain are biased using biasing voltage generated through current in the biasing circuit. The design consists of nineteen current starved inverters cascaded in a closed loop. The output of the inverter chain drives the buffer to give square wave.

2.5.1   Results of Oscillator

The design is simulated using spectra simulator and post layout simulation results, after parasitic extraction is summarized. At power supply of 1.8 V, various process corners, with trim bits as '000', temperature variation of 0° to 125 °C the oscillator frequencies obtained are as shown in Fig. 6.

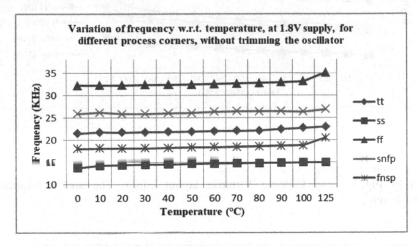

Fig. 6. Oscillator frequencies for trim bits '000'

At power supply of 1.8 V with trim bit combinations the frequency variation is as shown in Table 2.

Table 2. Frequency variation for trim bit combinations

Sl.no	Process corner	Trim bits 543	Frequency variations (in %)
1	tt	1 0 0	−3.35% to +1.65%
2	ss	1 1 0	−6.71% to +1.59%
3	ff	0 0 0	−2.04% to +5.77%
4	snfp	0 1 0	−0.12% to +3.39%
5	fnsp	1 0 1	−2.07% to +4.00%

With temperature variation from 0 °C to 125 °C at trim bit combinations the current is less then 250 nA as shown in Fig. 7.

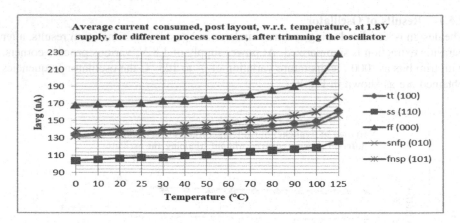

Fig. 7. Current drawn from battery at varying temperature

The oscillator design is implemented in UMC 0.18 μm CMOS technology as shown in Fig. 8 using Cadence Virtuoso layout editor. The area consumed is 0.003064 mm².

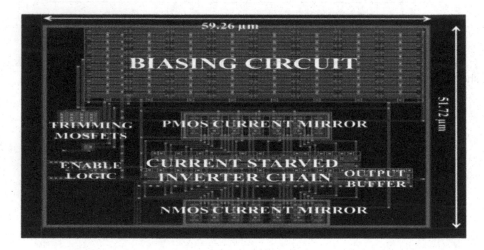

Fig. 8. Layout of oscillator

2.6 Under Voltage Lockout(UVLO)

In the design of mixed signal ASIC, NKTC2019 an active counter is used which counts when system power is active. UVLO is used to detect this active power. The block diagram of UVLO is shown in Fig. 9. Operational amplifier based comparator is selected for this application. This circuit detects when input logic power drops below a specified threshold voltage (V_{TP}) and toggles Power Good signal. Based on Power Good signal, the device will shift to battery backup state.

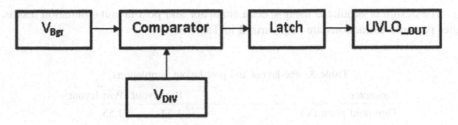

Fig. 9. Block diagram of UVLO.

This circuit contains internal reference which can work properly till supply voltage of 1.5 V (or low). Using this reference, threshold point for comparator can be set. There are primarily three blocks in the design.

They are

1. Bandgap Reference
2. Current Reference
3. Comparator

Bandgap Reference is designed to provide a reference Voltage and checked across Process Voltage Temperature (PVT). Current reference is used to provide constant current across PVT to bias the comparator. Comparator compares supply voltage to reference voltage and gives a binary output depending on the comparison. Seven pack opamp is used as comparator in open loop operation. The two inputs to the UVLO are Bandgap Reference voltage (VBgr) and power supply (Vdiv) which is divided according to Bandgap Reference design using voltage divider. As the power supply goes down the Vref is constant but Vdiv decreases linearly and at desired threshold point (1.55 V) switching happens. Figure 10 shows the switching of UVLO at different process corners.

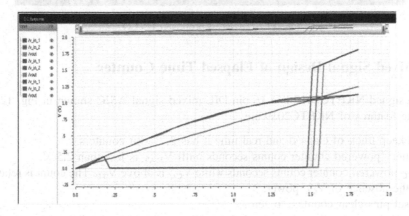

Fig. 10. Switching of UVLO

The design is simulated using spectra simulator and post layout simulation results, after parasitic extractions are summarized in Table 3.

Table 3. Pre-layout and post-layout simulations

Parameter	Pre layout	Post layout
Threshold point (V)	1.54	1.55
BGR output (V)	1.11	1.09
Current reference output Iref (uA)	1	0.9
Temperature coefficient for BGR (ppm/°C)	174	140
Temperature coefficient for Iref (ppm/°C)	80	50

The UVLO design is implemented in UMC 180 nm CMOS technology as shown in Fig. 11 using Cadence Virtuoso layout editor. The area consumed is 10.4 mm^2.

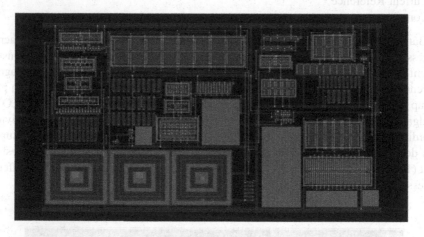

Fig. 11. Layout of proposed UVLO.

3   Mixed Signal Design of Elapsed Time Counter

The designed NKETC2019 is a 16 pin DIL mixed signal ASIC shown in Fig. 12. The features of NKETC2019 are

- To keep track of elapsed and real time it has 2, 32 bit counters.
- Battery powered counter counts seconds until V_{BAT} is less than 2.5 V.
- V_{CC} powered counter counts seconds while V_{CC} is above V_{TP}. The count is retained in the absence of V_{CC} power.
- Reset pins clear counters to zero.
- Read/write operations, counter clear, oscillator trimming are defined by one byte protocol.

- Operating temperature range of 0 °C to 125 °C.
- 16 pin DIL.
- Maximum current drain of 250 nA.

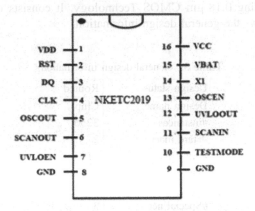

Fig. 12. 16 pin DIL of NKETC2019

Table 4 shows the pin description of the designed ASIC.

Table 4. Pin description of NKETC2019

Port	Description
VDD	It is 3.3 V power supply provided for the IO pins
RST	During read or a write operation the RST pin should be made high
DQ	It is bidirectional data pin
CLK	2 MHz signal, used for data movement on the serial interface
OSCOUT	32.768 kHz internal oscillator output to test the functioning of internal oscillator
SCANOUT	Test output to check ASIC in Test mode
UVLOEN	Comparator enable
GND	Ground
GND	Ground
TESTMODE	When '1' the ASIC is in test mode and '0' the ASIC is in Function mode
SCANIN	Test mode Input
UVLOOUT	Comparator test
OSCEN	Internal oscillator enable pin
X1	Crystal Input. 32.768 kHz quartz crystal
V_{BAT}	Battery input 1.8 V. Battery voltage must be held between 1.5 V and 2.3 V for proper operation
V_{CC}	V_{CC} is the 1.8 V power supply provided to core

4   Back-End Implementation NKETC2019

The physical implementation was done using cadence innovus. The NKETC2019 is a relatively small design consisting of approximately 3000 Standard Cell Instances. The chip is designed using 0.18 μm CMOS Technology. It consists of 6 metal routing layers. Table 5 shows the general design information.

Table 5. General design information

Design status	Routed
Design name	Chip
#instances	3250
#Hard macro	2
#Std cells	3193
#Pad	55
#Net	1210
#Special net	3
#IO pins	11
Average pins per net	3.608

The following steps were considered in the physical design.

4.1   Floor Planning

Cadence innovus tool is used for placement and routing. Here the placement of blocks and macros is done. *Minimum Chip area is achieved bu proper placing of various blocks, I/O pins and Pads.*

4.2   Power Planning

Power planning is a process of creating a power grid network to distribute power to each part of design. It involves creation of power and ground rails for standard cell rows, power rings around the macros and core, and power stripes across the whole chip to ensure power/ground connectivity to each part of chip.

4.3   Routing

Routing involves creation of physical connections for all design objects (cells, Macros and pins/pads). It is a process of creating an electrical connection using metal layers and vias in layout based on logical connectivity (design netlist). It determines actual path of interconnections. It involves interconnection between standard cell and macro pins, pins on the boundary and pads at chip boundary. Figure 13 shows the process of floor planning, power planning and routing.

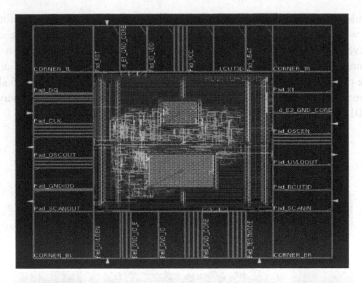

Fig. 13. Floor-planning, power-planning and routing of NKETC2019

The area coverage information is shown in Fig. 14.

Total area of Standard cells	92337.840 μm²
Total area of Standard cells (Subtracting Physical Cells)	30273.062 μm²
Total area of Macros	13874.063 μm²
Total area of Pad cells	312400.342 μm²
Total area of Core	114203.442 μm²
Total area of Chip	486506.250 μm²
Effective Utilization	0.99818
Number of Cell Rows	66

Fig. 14. Area coverage of NKETC2019

4.4 Timing Report

The timing analysis is done using Tempus tool. The ASIC communicates with external devices with 2 MHz frequency. The design meets the timing requirements

Physical Verification

The Calibre tool by Mentor Graphics is used to do physical verification the run-set like the Layout Versus Schematic (LVS), the Design Rule Check (DRC), Parasitic and the

Antenna rules provided by foundry are added to the Calibre tool. The Calibre tool is integrated with Cadence Virtuoso tool. The design has passed all the above checks.In order to evaluate the proposed design techniques, a ASIC is designed in 0.18-μm mixed-signal CMOS technology with the power supplies of 1.8 V (core) and 3.3 V (I/Os). The proposed design consumes area of 486506.250 μm². The Fig. 15 shows the GSD II streamed out file sent to UMC foundry Taiwan for mini@sic runway on 29th October 2018. Figure 16 shows the 16 pin DIL NKETC2019.

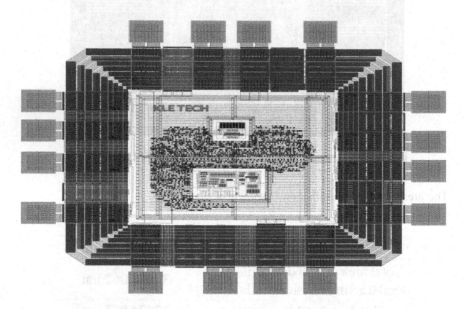

Fig. 15. Signed off GDSII of NKETC2019

Fig. 16. 16 pin NKETC2019

5 Conclusion

This paper presents the design and development of Elapsed Time Counter which tracks real time and elapsed time. The mixed signal ETC is implemented in 0.18 μm, 1.8 V mixed signal CMOS technology. The design has the ultra low power oscillator designed which consumes current of 250 nA with minimum frequency variation for all Process Voltage Temperature conditions. The entire ASIC is designed in using cadence innovus. The die size of the chip is 697.5 μm × 697.5 μm. This is sent for fabrication to UMC foundry Taiwan for mini@sic runset on 29th October 2018.

Acknowledgment. The authors would like to thank Dr. Anand Bariya, VP SiFive, for his valuable discussion on the mixed signal ASIC flow, and Shri Shripad Annigari for his valuable discussion on circuits. This work is supported under 'IRP' scheme by the KLE Technological University.

References

1. Kalra, P.K., Mudenagudi, U., Banerjee, S.: Space-time super-resolution using graph-cut optimization. IEEE Trans. Pattern Anal. Mach. Intell. **33**(5), 995–1008 (2011)
2. https://datasheets.maximintegrated.com/en/ds/DS1682.pdf
3. http://www.newark.com/maxim-integrated-products/ds1318e/elapsed-time-counter-binary
4. https://datasheets.maximintegrated.com/en/ds/DS1602.pdf
5. Razavi, B.: Design of analog CMOS integrated circuits (2005)
6. DS1602 elapsed time counter. https://datasheets.maximintegrated.com/en/ds/DS1602.pdf
7. Mahato, A.K.: Ultra low frequency CMOS ring oscillator design. In: Recent Advances in Engineering and Computational Sciences (RAECS). IEEE (2014)
8. Suman, S., Bhardwaj, M., Singh, B.: An improved performance ring oscillator design. In: 2012 Second International Conference on Advanced Computing & Communication Technologies (ACCT), pp. 236–239. IEEE (2012)
9. Keshri, P., Deka, B.: CMOS thyristor based low frequency ring oscillator. Indian Institute of Technology, Kanpur (2007)
10. Somvanshi, S., Kasavajjala, S.: A low power sub-1 V CMOS voltage reference. EEE Dept, BITS-Pilani, Rajasthan, India and Stanford University, USA (2008)
11. Choi, M., Lee, I., Jang, T.-K., Blaauw, D., Sylvester, D.: A 23pw, 780 ppm/oC resistor-less current reference using subthreshold MOSFETs. In: ESSCIRC 2014-40th European Solid State Circuits Conference (ESSCIRC), pp. 119–122. IEEE (2014)
12. Choi, M., Bang, S., Jang, T.-K., Blaauw, D., Sylvester, D.: A 99 nW 70.4 Khz resistive frequency locking on-chip oscillator with 27.4 ppm/oC temperature stability. In: 2015 Symposium on VLSI Circuits (VLSI Circuits), pp. C238–C239. IEEE (2015)
13. Li, W.-J.: A current compensated reference oscillator. In: 2009 International Symposium on VLSI Design Automation and Test, April 2009
14. Deva Priya, M., Valarmathi, M.L., Jaya Bharathi, K., Sundarameena, V.: QP - ALAH: QoS provisioned - application layer auxiliary handover in IEEE 802.16e networks. In: Unnikrishnan, S., Surve, S., Bhoir, D. (eds.) ICAC3 2013. CCIS, vol. 361, pp. 366–380. Springer, Heidelberg (2013). https://doi.org/10.1007/978-3-642-36321-4_34

15. Filanovsky, I., Baltes, H.: CMOS schmitt trigger design. IEEE Trans. Circuits Syst. I: Fundam. Theory Appl. **41**(1), 46–49 (1994)
16. Kalburgi, S., Gupta, D., Holi, S., Saroja, V.S.: Ultra low power low frequency on-chip oscillator for elapsed time counter. In: 32nd International Conference on VLSI Design and 2019 18th International Conference on Embedded Systems (VLSID), pp. 251–256. IEEE (2019). https://doi.org/10.1109/vlsid.2019.00062

Clock Pulse Based Foreground Calibration of a Sub-Radix-2 Successive Approximation Register ADC

M. Mahendra Reddy$^{(\boxtimes)}$ (iD) and Sounak Roy (iD)

Department of Electronics and Communication,
Indian Institute of Information Technology, Guwahati 781015, India
mhreddyktp@gmail.com, rajroy04@gmail.com

Abstract. This paper proposes a foreground calibration algorithm of a Successive-Approximation-Register (SAR) ADC using pulsed injection at the analog front-end. Unlike pseudo-random noise injection based calibration, this algorithm uses the clock signal to provide an offset injection at the DAC sub-circuit of the SAR ADC. The DAC portion of the SAR ADC presented in this paper follows sub-radix-2 based architecture. Such architecture produces non-linearity at the ADC output due to obvious result of capacitor mismatch. Non-linearity removal is ensured by extracting the coefficients of the ADC output code. Coefficients are calculated by post processing the ADC output code at the digital calibration block. For calibration, two sets of ADC output codes are collected, at two clock phases. In one clock phases ADC output codes are collected with an incremental offset added and at the other clock phase, same offset value gets subtracted. These collected data are then passed through an LMS algorithm to determine the coefficients. In this paper, behavioral simulation result of a 10-bit SAR ADC shows that after coefficient determination and output code correction, SNDR, SFDR and ENOB improves from 25.85 dB, 34.63 dB and 4.13 bits respectively to 60.60 dB, 78.78 dB and 9.77 bits respectively.

Keywords: Capacitor mismatch · Foreground calibration · SARADC · Sub-radix-2

1 Introduction

For low sampling speed and high resolution applications, SAR-ADCs provide impressive figure-of-merit (FoM) [1–3] as its construction require very nominal power budget. A typical SAR-ADC contains a comparator and a digital back-end to perform the binary search algorithm. Figure 1 shows a typical charge redistribution [4,5] capacitor-array based analog front end of a SAR ADC. CMOS dynamic comparators typically consumes power in the order of few tens of microwatts. Digital back-end of a SAR ADC contains register circuits and combinatorial circuits. Both power budget and die area budget of such blocks are very nominal.

© Springer Nature Singapore Pte Ltd. 2019
A. Sengupta et al. (Eds.): VDAT 2019, CCIS 1066, pp. 141–149, 2019.
https://doi.org/10.1007/978-981-32-9767-8_12

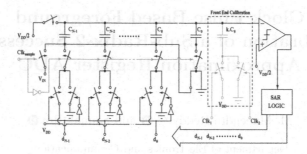

Fig. 1. Charge redistribution successive approximation architecture

The circuit shown in Fig. 1 follows typical binary weighted SAR algorithm to perform the conversion. In binary weighted DAC part of the SAR-ADC, each higher-rank capacitor is equal to the sum of all the lower-rank capacitors which enables the binary search in SAR-ADC. The converter resolves digital bits in N clock cycles. As the resolution of a SAR-ADC increases, capacitor sizes of the higher rank capacitors increases exponentially. Such high value capacitors creates challenge in proper layout of a prototype and also limits the sampling speed of the ADC. Hence faster and compact design demands smaller size capacitors. Reduction of capacitor sizes, however, are prone to mismatch. This mismatch leads to ADC output static non-linearity. To remove such non-linearities, proper coefficients of the ADC output codes are extracted using several calibration algorithms [6–8]. In this paper, one such extraction algorithm has been proposed. To design the calibration algorithm, a sub-radix-2 type [8,9] capacitor array of the DAC has been chosen for obvious advantages.

1.1 Sub-Radix-2 Capacitor Array

Sub-radix-2 type capacitor array has two main advantages in designing an effi-cient SAR-ADC. **First**, compared to radix-2 or super-radix-2 design, sub-radix-2 design requires smaller size higher rank capacitors, which enables reduction of die area and enhances sampling speed. **Second**, a sub-radix-2 design provides calibrability of the SAR-ADC, by providing missing digital codes rather than missing levels. Using digital calibration, which post processes the ADC output code, non-linearity arising due to missing levels can not be corrected. But, with higher rank capacitors defined as

$$\sum_{j=0}^{i-1} C_j + C_0 - C_i > 0, \tag{1}$$

in sub-radix-2 based architecture, missing codes can be corrected using calibra-tion. For a charge redistribution DAC, if C_i/C_0 is considered as α, and variation found in the fabricated capacitor value is considered as σ, from [], to satisfy the sub-radix-2 condition,

$$\frac{2-\alpha}{\alpha-1} - 1.65\sigma_{C0}\frac{\alpha}{\sqrt{\alpha^2-1}} \geq 0 \tag{2}$$

Using Eq. (3), Table 1 shows some typical values of α, for some given values of σ. For a given σ and α, number of capacitors needed to resolve the input signal to its desired resolution are also listed.

Table 1. Tradeoffs between, σ, number of capacitors N_c and α of a 10-bit SARADC

ENOB	σ	N_c	α
10	0.05	12	1.865
10	0.1	12	1.815
10	0.15	13	1.765
10	0.2	13	1.7

2 Proposed Calibration Algorithm

Figure 3 shows the block diagram of the proposed calibration algorithm. At the analog front end of the SAR-ADC, a small analog signal of value ΔV_a is added to and subtracted from the input analog signal V_{IN} and N_F number of the SAR-ADC output are collected. Addition and subtraction of ΔV_a occurs when Clk_1 and Clk_2 are high, respectively. This small analog signal is added to the analog front end using a capacitor $k \times C_0$, as shown in Fig. 1. As shown in Fig. 2, frequency of Clk_1 and Clk_2 are half of Clk_{sample}. Phases of the signals Clk_1 and Clk_2 are such that if at i_{th} Clk_{sample} Clk_1 is high, at $(i+1)_{st}$ Clk_{sample} Clk_2 is high. In this manner, from N_F samples, two memories, Mem A and Mem B collect $N_F/2$ samples each. In this way, D+ and D− are collected at alternate clock pulses, where $D+ = [d_{N-1}^+, d_{N-2}^+...d_0^+]$ is the digital equivalent of $V_{IN} + \Delta V_a$ and $D- = [d_{N-1}^-, d_{N-2}^-...d_0^-]$ is the digital equivalent of $V_{IN} - \Delta V_a$.

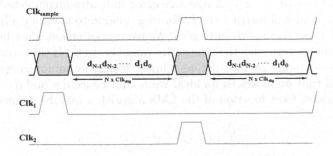

Fig. 2. Clock waveforms used in the proposed algorithm

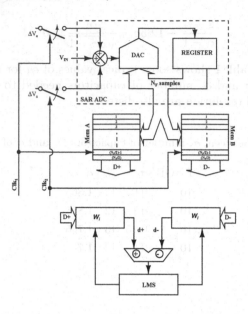

Fig. 3. Block diagram of the proposed algorithm

To form the proper digital output code of the SAR-ADC is passed through a weighing block w_i, which is defined by,

$$d+ = w_{N-1}d_{N-1}^+ + w_{N-2}d_{N-2}^+ + ... + w_0 d_0^+$$
$$d- = w_{N-1}d_{N-1}^- + w_{N-2}d_{N-2}^- + ... + w_0 d_0^-$$

(3)

According to linear and superposition property of the SAR-ADC, offset ΔV_a added to analog input V_{IN} can be precisely removed in the digital domain owing to the linearity of the ADC. In ideal case, $(d+) - (d-) = 2\delta v$, where δv is digitized value of ΔV_a. This suggests that the difference between $(d+) - (d-)$ and $2\delta v$ can serve as the error to be minimized to obtain the optimal weights $[w_{N-1}, w_{N-2}, .., w_0]$. The coded digital outputs, d+ and d- are then subtracted and fed to LMS block, for extracting the coefficients W_is, in order to minimize the error of $(d+) - (d-) - 2\delta v$. A non-zero error indicates incomplete learning of all bit weights and will instruct the calibration engine to continue adjusting the weights until this error is driven to zero. Above measurement must be repeated for various input levels, such that the entire range is swept. If the error is defined as $\epsilon = [(d) + -(d-) - 2\delta v]$ for different input levels, by minimizing this error, it is expected that δv moves to its ideal value and hence d+ and d- also reach their ideal values. Cost function of the LMS algorithm may be defined as,

$$err = \frac{\sum_{j=1}^{N}(d+(j) - d-(j) - 2\delta v)^2}{N_F}$$

(4)

The LMS update equations of this procedure for coefficient extraction can be written as

$$w_i[k+1] = w_i[k] - \mu \frac{d(err)}{dw_i}; \quad i = 1, ...N. \tag{5}$$

in practice, the mismatch between ΔV_a and δv also need to be identified, and it is given by

$$\delta v[k+1] = \delta v[k] - \mu \frac{d(err)}{d\delta_v} \tag{6}$$

3 Simulation Results

Behavioural simulation of a 10-bit SAR-ADC has been presented here to verify the calibration algorithm. In order to model the capacitor mismatch, a capacitor ratio error of 15% has been considered. With these conditions, at first a simulation has been performed at an over-sampling ratio of $(4096/19)$. An input signal of dynamic range 1.8 V and offset voltage value of $\Delta V_a = 0.02$ V has been provided at the input. This value amounts to only 1.1% of the dynamic range. Digital equivalent of this value is 12.5 LSB. It is found that for an injection offset of 12.5 LSB, the scaling factor k as shown in Fig. 1 is $k = 25$. Among the resulting 4096 samples, 2048 samples have been collected with Clk_1 signal high and other 2048 samples during Clk_2 high. Figure 4 shows the dynamic performance of the SAR-ADC, before and after calibration.

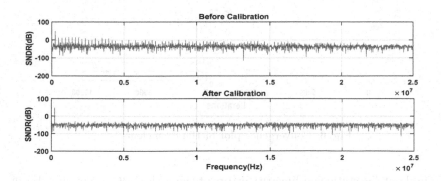

Fig. 4. Dynamic performance of the ADC at over-sampling ratio of $(4096/19)$

Next, similar simulation has been performed at near Nyquist rate with an over-sampling ratio of 4096/2047. Figure 5 shows the dynamic performance of the SAR-ADC, before and after calibration.

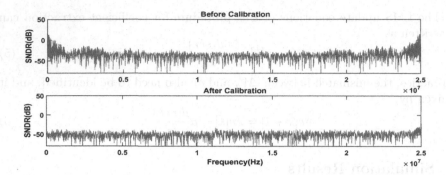

Fig. 5. Dynamic performance of the ADC at over-sampling ratio of (4096/2047)

For the above simulation, convergence of the coefficients are plotted in Fig. 5. As shown in Table 1, as 13 capacitors are needed to resolve an input signal to all 1024 code levels, 13 coefficients are to be extracted. To extract the coefficients w_i, 10000 iterations have been performed (Fig. 6).

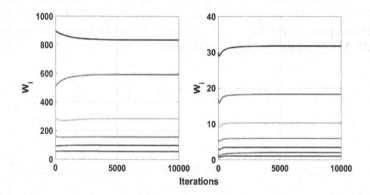

Fig. 6. Convergence plot of the coefficients

To find out the static non-linearity errors of the SAR-ADC, input signal over-sampling ratio of (8192/511) has been considered. Figure 7 shows the differential non-linearity (DNL) plot of the ADC. After calibration, DNL improves from $-1\ LSB < DNL < 2.87\ LSB$ to $-1\ LSB < DNL < 0.56\ LSB$. Integral non-linearity (INL) plot of the SAR-ADC is plotted in Fig. 8. After calibration, INL improves from $-43.5\ LSB < INL < 39.8\ LSB$ to $-0.98\ LSB < DNL < 1.61\ LSB$.

Table 2 summarizes a few dynamic performance simulations, before and after calibration.

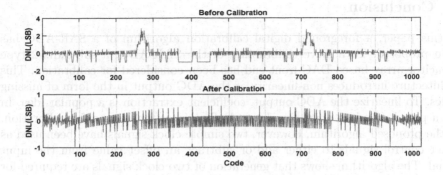

Fig. 7. Static performance: DNL plot

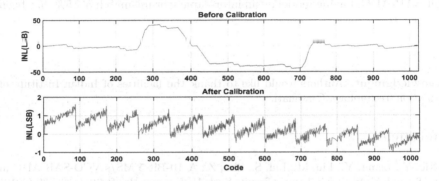

Fig. 8. Static performance: INL plot

Table 2. Dynamic performance, BC: Before Calibration, AC: After Calibration

Approximate Oversampling Ratio	SFDR BC (dB)	SFDR AC (dB)	SNDR BC (dB)	SNDR AC (dB)	ENOB BC (bits)	ENOB AC (bits)
(4096/19)	34.63	78.63	25.85	60.62	4.13	9.77
(4096/511)	34.63	78.57	25.85	60.61	4.13	9.77
(4096/2047)	34.6	78.78	25.85	60.60	4.13	9.77

Table 3. Comparison table

Reference	Over-sampling ratio	SNDR BC (dB)	SNDR AC (dB)	No. of bits (bits)	ENOB (bits)
[10]	≈ 100	47.23	60.76	10	9.8
[11]	-	57.2	72.2	12	11.7
Proposed	$\frac{4096}{2047}$	25.85	60.60	10	9.77

4 Conclusion

In this paper, a foreground digital calibration algorithm of a SAR-ADC has been proposed. To achieve calibrability of the SAR-ADC, a sub-radix-2 type capacitor array based DAC front end has been considered for calibration. This architecture introduces non-linearity at the ADC output in the form of missing codes. To linearize the ADC output, coefficient extraction is a popular idea. In [9], a pseudo-random noise signal based offset injection is used for calibration. In the proposed algorithm, however, two simple clock signals have been used as select control signals to either add or subtract an offset value from the input signal. The algorithm shows that generation of two clock signals are required for calibration, which are of half the frequency of the sampling clock. Generating such clock signals pose no challenge as far as circuit development is concerned. A 10-bit SAR-ADC, having modelled an inter-capacitor mismatch of 15%, has been simulated to verify the calibration algorithm. Algorithm successfully extracts the coefficients which improves the ENOB from 4.13 bits to 9.77 bits. Table 3 compares the proposed work with a few published material.

Acknowledgment. Authors would like to thank the facilities of Indian Institute of Information Technology, Guwahati.

References

1. Xie, Y., Liang, Y., Liu, M., Liu, S., Zhu, Z.: A 10-Bit 5 MS/s VCO-SAR ADC in 0.18-μm CMOS. IEEE Trans. Circuits Syst. II: Express Briefs **66**(1), 26–30 (2019)
2. Zhu, Z.-M., Liang, Y.-H.: A 0.6-V 38-nW 9.4-ENOB 20-kS/s SAR ADC in 0.18 μm-CMOS for medical implant devices. IEEE Trans. Circuits Syst. I Reg. Pap. **62**(9), 2167–2176 (2015)
3. Liu, C.-C., Kuo, C.-H., Lin, Y.-Z.: A 10 bit 320 MS/s low-cost SAR ADC for IEEE 802.11ac applications in 20 nm CMOS. IEEE J. Solid-State Circuits **50**(11), 2645–2654 (2015)
4. McCreary, J.L., Gray, P.R.: All-MOS charge redistribution analog-to-digital conversion techniques. IEEE J. Solid-State Circuits **10**(6), 371–379 (1975)
5. Suarez, R.E., Gray, P.R., Hodges, D.A.: All-MOS charge-redistribution analog-to-digital conversion techniques. II. IEEE J. Solid-State Circuits **10**(6), 379–385 (1975)
6. Liu, W., et al.: A 12b 22.5/45 MS/s 3.0mW 0.059 mm² CMOS SAR ADC achieving over 90dB SFDR. In: 2010 IEEE International Solid-State Circuits Conference - (ISSCC), pp. 380–381 (2010)
7. Chang, A.H., Lee, H.-S., Boning, D.: A 12b 50MS/s 2.1mW SAR ADC with redundancy and digital background calibration. In: Proceedings of the ESSCIRC (ESSCIRC) (2013)
8. Liu, W., Chiu, Y.: An equalization-based adaptive digital background calibration technique for successive approximation analog-to-digital converters. In: 2007 7th International Conference on ASIC, Guilin, pp. 289–292 (2007)
9. Liu, W., Huang, P., Chiu, Y.: A 12-bit, 45-MS/s, 3-mW redundant successive-approximation-register analog-to-digital converter with digital calibration. IEEE J. Solid-State Circuits **46**(11), 2661–2672 (2011)

10. Li, W., Wang, T., Temes, G.C.: Digital foreground calibration methods for SAR ADCs. In: IEEE International Symposium on Circuits and Systems (2012)
11. Ling, D., et al.: A digital background calibration technique for successive approximation register analog to digital converter. J. Comput. Commun. **1**, 30–36 (2013)

Approximate Computing Based Adder Design for DWT Application

Moumita Acharya[1], Samik Basu[1(✉)], Biranchi Narayan Behera[2],
and Amlan Chakrabarti[3]

[1] Institute of Radio Physics and Electronics, University of Calcutta,
92, A.P.C. Road, Kolkata 700009, India
moumita.vlsi@gmail.com, samikbasu2010@gmail.com
[2] Electronics and Tele-Communication Engineering Department,
C.V.Raman Collage of Engineering, Bhubaneswar 752054, India
er.biranchibehera@gmail.com
[3] A.K Choudhury School of Information Technology, University of Calcutta, 92,
A.P.C. Road, Kolkata 700009, India
achakral2@yahoo.com

Abstract. Approximate computing is gaining popularity in hardware design of different application circuits. The bit-width reduction in approximate computing reduces the power requirement and chip area though it introduces error in the processed output. In this paper, we have proposed approximate computing based various designs of approximation of mirror adder (MA) circuit, which can be used to implement discrete wavelet transform (DWT) hardware for various image processing applications. We have also used voltage-scaling approach in our design, which reduces the power requirement appreciably. We have studied four levels of approximation of mirror adder and among them the fourth level of approximation is tested and justified for the design application. The goodness of our design is well justified as it shows marginal reduction in signal to noise ratio with a good reduction of layout area and power. We have used 180 nm technology node in our proposed ASIC design.

Keywords: Approximate computing · Adder · Voltage scaling · DWT · Image compression

1 Introduction

Image and video processing is an important tool to develop a multimedia application based on digital signal processing blocks and the final output is either an image or a video for human perception. The constrained impression of human vision enables the yield of these algorithms to be numerically estimated as opposed to precise. This relaxation allows the uses of some approximation in the algorithms. Image and video processing through approximate algorithms is a lossy type compression technology where the techniques are used to reduce data size for storing, handling and transmitting content thus achieving a low power design. In multidimensional signal processing, wavelet transformation is widely accepted [1] for time-frequency transformation of

© Springer Nature Singapore Pte Ltd. 2019
A. Sengupta et al. (Eds.): VDAT 2019, CCIS 1066, pp. 150–163, 2019.
https://doi.org/10.1007/978-981-32-9767-8_13

image as an alternative of Fourier Transformation (FT), DCT, and DFT. The approximate technique in wavelet transform application is a new approach to extract the redundant data from the image and for that the area saving and power consumption efficiency as well as the fault tolerance nature leads to better performance with some allowable loss of accuracy. In nano-scale CMOS technology power dissipation becomes a sensitive issue by considering the approximate computing plays an important role to trade off between speed and power consumption rate [2].

There are some related works on image and video processing through approximate computing for low power design. Some approximate adder architectures exhibit the convenience of the approximations for digital signal processing through DCT and infinite impulse response filter with specific quality constraints [3, 4]. The authors in [2] have nicely described the design philosophy, approach, and motivation for approximate computing. We can find different types of approximation approaches applied for adder and multiplier to reduce the power consumption with moderate accuracy [5, 6]. The approach on 32-bit approximate adder was designed which has low power consumption and significantly reduction of area [7]. Another approximate computing technique was proposed by XOR/XNOR based adders, which evaluates energy consumption, delay, area, and power delay product [8]. The authors in [9] have used a technique of dynamic bit-width adaptation scheme in DCT applications for efficient trade-off between image quality and computation energy. In [10, 11], a low power CMOS circuit is designed using the voltage scaling technique to reduce the power consumption. A fault tolerant technique and their execution on approximate computing are discussed in [12, 13].

The authors in [1] have used a technique of bit width reduction through approximation by using wavelet transformation technique. Our proposed methodology is an extension of the same, where we use some conventional methods for reducing the complexity of adder in ASIC level and evaluate the area and power consumption individually. The uniqueness of our work is that we have developed new approximation logic through voltage scaling techniques for DWT of image data, which promises a considerable reduction in power and chip area.

The reminder of the paper is organized as follows. In Sect. 2 we proposed and discussed different trade off levels of full adder (FA) unit. In Sect. 3 we demonstrate about the image compression by different trade off levels of FA for bit width reduction and the efficient use of approximate adder in Discrete Wavelet Transform (DWT) architecture. Section 4 contains the Result and discussion. Finally conclusion is drawn in Sect. 5.

2 Approximate Adder

In Digital signal processing system, approximations of the adder circuit introduce a new concept to save area and power dissipation with moderate accuracy [7]. To reduce area and power consumption generally, two types of methodologies are involved by approximation process; one is the modification of a logic circuit in different approximate levels to reduce area and the second one is voltage scaling technique for CMOS circuit to save power. In approximate computing, the logic complexity is reduced at transistor level by eliminating some transistor from conventional adder design [8].

2.1   Modifications of MA Cells in Different Approximation Level with Layout

The mirror adder is extensively used as a low cost implementation of the full adder; we exploit it as our basic building block for proposing the distinctive approximation of full adder cell. Elimination of series connected transistors reduce the αC term (switched capacitance) in the dynamic power expression $P_{dynamic} = CV_{dd}^2 f$, where α is the average number of switching transistors per unit time and C is the load capacitance being charged/discharged. Ejection of the series connected transistors also conduct faster charging/discharging of node capacitances. The process exhibits area reduction and low power dissipation.

Traditional MA (MA): Figure 1 represents the transistor level schematic diagram of the traditional Mirror Adder (MA) that is designed with 24 transistors. The process of the design is not based on complementary CMOS logic technique. So it is easy to design the different level of approximation by eliminating the transistor.

Approximation 1 (AMA1): Here, the approximation circuit is designed with 16 transistors as shown in Fig. 2. The transistors are designed with the input combination of A, B and C_{in} that does not result in short circuit or open circuit in the approximate design. For the simplification of the design, some minimal errors should be introduced in the FA truth table. In this design, there is one error in the C_{out} and two errors in the Sum as shown in Table 1. In the Table 1, green color represents a match with real output.

Approximation 2 (AMA2): Here, the approximation circuit is designed with 14 transistors as shown in the Fig. 3. As per the truth table of FA, Sum = Cout1' for six out of eight cases, except for A = 0, B = 0, Cin = 0 and A = 1, B = 1, Cin = 1. Here Cout' is computed in the first stage, so to set sum = Cout' a buffer stage is introduced Cout'. Due to that the total capacitance at the sum node would be a combination of four source-drain diffusion and two gate capacitances. That design leads to delay penalty in case of cascading of multi-bit approximate adder. Here C_{out} is correct for all the cases and sum has only 2 errors as shown in Table 1.

Approximation 3 (AMA3): In approximation 3 the schematic is an approach of a combination of approximation 1 and 2 as shown in the Fig. 4. One error is introduced in the C_{out} and 3 errors in the Sum as shown in Table 1.

Approximation 4 (AMA4): As per the FA truth table C_{out} = A and separately C_{out} = B for six out of eight cases. Since A and B are interchangeable, we consider C_{out} = A. So for the proposed design an inverter is used with input A to calculate C_{out}' and Sum is calculated as approximation1. Here approximation circuit is designed with 11 transistors as shown in the Fig. 5. Here C_{out} owns 2 errors and Sum owns 3 errors as shown in Table 1. In all the approximations, C_{out} is calculated by using an inverter with C_{out}' as the input.

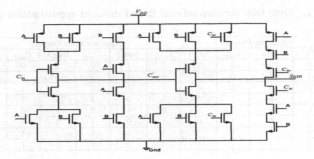

Fig. 1. Schematic diagram of conventional MA

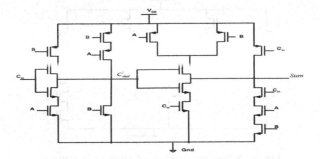

Fig. 2. Schematic diagram of approximation 1

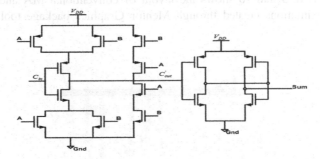

Fig. 3. Schematic diagram of approximation 2

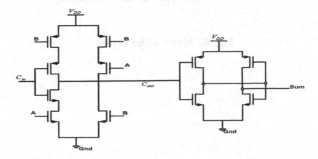

Fig. 4. Schematic diagram of approximation 3

Table 1. Truth table for conventional fa and different approximation cells

Input			Accurate Outputs		Approximation Outputs							
A	B	C_{in}	Sum	C_{out}	Sum1	C_{out1}	Sum2	C_{out2}	Sum3	C_{out3}	Sum4	C_{out4}
0	0	0	0	0	0	0	1	0	1	0	0	0
0	0	1	1	0	1	0	1	0	1	0	1	0
0	1	0	1	0	0	1	1	0	0	1	0	0
0	1	1	0	1	0	1	0	1	0	1	1	0
1	0	0	1	0	0	0	1	0	1	0	0	1
1	0	1	0	1	0	1	0	1	0	1	0	1
1	1	0	0	1	0	1	0	1	0	1	0	1
1	1	1	1	1	1	1	0	1	0	1	1	1

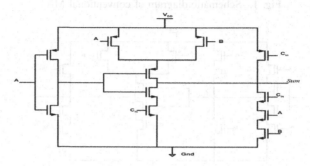

Fig. 5. Schematic diagram of approximation 4

Figures 6, 7, 8, 9 and 10 shows the layout of conventional MA and that of the different approximations created through Mentor Graphics package tool of 180 nm technology.

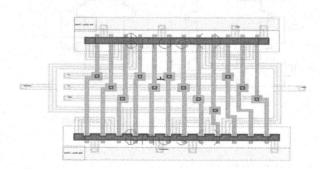

Fig. 6. Mirror adder layout

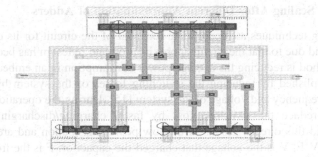

Fig. 7. Trade off level 1 layout

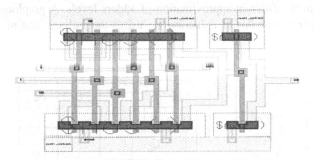

Fig. 8. Trade off level 2 layout

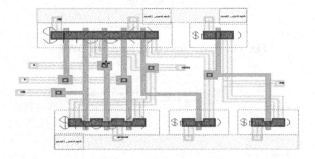

Fig. 9. Trade off level 3 layout

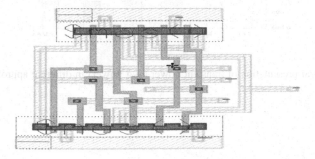

Fig. 10. Trade off level 4 layout

2.2   Voltage Scaling After Different Approximation of Adders

Voltage scaling techniques are appropriate for most of the circuit for its error tolerant applications and due to that the circuit approximation and redesign has been advocated [11]. This method is reducing the average power consumption in an embedded system. This is accomplished by reducing the switching losses of the system by selectively reducing the frequency and voltage of the system [15]. During the operation of the MA cells, it will reduce the switching loss by faster charging/discharging of switch capacitance and this directly results in the low power dissipation and area reduction. Power = $1/2CV^2F$; V is the voltage that charged the capacitor; F is the frequency that the voltage is switched across the capacitor. Power goes up by the square of the voltage and linearly with switching frequency. So reducing the supply voltage adds up to power savings in the different approximation of adders levels. A graphical view of the DC power and transient Power reduction by using the voltage scaling technique is shown in the Figs. 12 and 13.

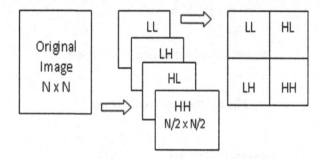

Fig. 11. Image processing based on DWT

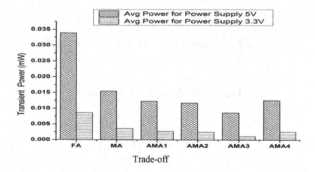

Fig. 12. Graphical presentation of transient power (avg power) in different approximation level

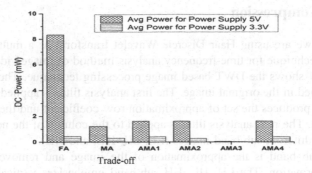

Fig. 13. Graphical presentation of DC power (avg power) in different approximation level

From the graph it is observed that if we scale down the power supply voltage at 3.3 V, the average transient power and the average DC power for the trade off level 3 is lowest as compared to the other trade off levels. The result for trade on level 4 is also significant. So for error tolerant application the use of trade off level 3 and 4 can be considered.

2.3 Power Dissipation of Different Approximation Adders

A CMOS device is low static power consumption device. During the time of switching at a high frequency, the overall power consumption becomes a factor of dynamic power consumption. Dynamic power consumption will increase due to charging and is charging of capacitance output load. The dynamic power reduction is possible by reducing supply voltage, operation frequency, and the capacitance. In recent years the principles for power dissipation through voltage scaling becomes a prime choice. Power dissipation increases the performance and reliability of the design and as well as reduce the cost.

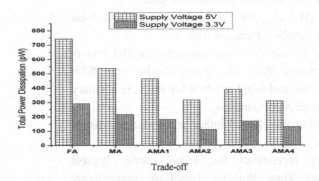

Fig. 14. Graphical representation of total power dissipation in different approximation level

In our work, we are applying the voltage scaling technology for different 4 bit approximate parallel adders to calculate the total power dissipation for the designs. A graphical view of the power dissipation is shown in Fig. 14. From the graphical view it is very easy to conclude that the lowest power will be dissipated for the trade off level 4 with the voltage scaling of 3.3 V.

3 Image Compression

In this paper, we are using Haar Discrete Wavelet transform as a multi-scale image compression technique for time-frequency analysis method of image/video processing [10]. Figure 11 shows the DWT based image processing technique. The two analysis filters are applied in the original image. The first analysis filter is applied to the row of the image and produces the set of approximation row coefficient and the set of details row coefficient. The next analysis filter is applied to the column of the new image and produces four different sub-band images (LL, LH, HL, and HH).

The LL sub band is the approximation of the image and removes of all high frequency information. The LH, HL, HH sub-band emphasizes vertical edges, horizontal edges, and diagonal edges of the image respectively.

In this section, we are introducing different approximation of FA cells and set up the approximated results in the truth table of an FA. Due to the human imperceptibility and robustness the bit width reduction of the image can be tolerable up to some rejection level by applying approximate FA cells. For image here we are applying the

---

Algorithm1: Bit width reduction of gray scale image by using approximate parallel adder through Discrete Haar Wavelet Transformation (DHWT).

Input: Input grayscale image f(i) having a resolution of 256x256.

Output: Final image Z(i).

1. Level 1 2D DHWT is applied on the image, which produces four different sub band images cA_1, cH_1, cV_1, cD_1.

2. Here we are applying the approximate adder circuit on the cH_1, cV_1, cD_1 sub band images.

3. Each cH_1, cV_1, Cd_1 is then converted into 8-bit binary numbers representation.

4. Apply all the 4bit approximation parallel adders one after another and clipping the bit from 8-bit binary no. and adapt it into 4-bit equivalent binary no. image representation.

5. Rescaling the clipped image as coefficient matrix cH2, cV2, cD2.

6. Lastly, reconstruct the image using Inverse Discrete Haar Wavelet Transform respectively (IDHWT) and compute PSNR.

7. Compute the power dissipation.

Restore: Final image Z(i).

---

different approximation cells of parallel adder on the details coefficients of the Discrete Haar Wavelet Transformation (DHWT) for bit width reduction and also retain the output quality of the image. The peak signal-to-noise ratio (PSNR) is a measure to compare the image compression quality.

cA_1, cH_1, cV_1, cD_1 denotes approximation, horizontal, Vertical, and diagonal coefficient respectively PSNR means Peak signal to noise ratio. Figure 16 shows the output image quality for the different approximation levels. Figure 15 shows the complete design flow of the proposed algorithm.

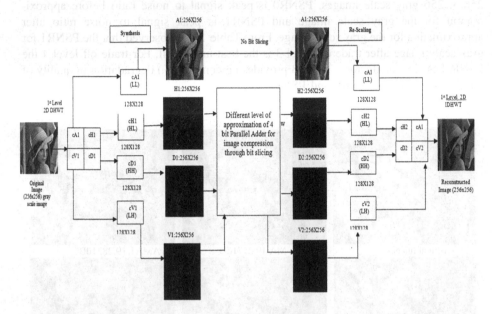

Fig. 15. Design flow

4 Result and Discussion

4.1 PSNR Calculation

The peak signal-to-noise ratio (PSNR) is an approximation to human perception of reconstruction quality. The PSNR is computed between the reconstructed images and is compared with the original image. PSNR defined as the Mean Squared Error (MSE) of two $m \times n$ size images f and z; where f is original image and z is the reconstructed image.

$$MSE = \frac{1}{mn} \sum_{i=0}^{m-1} \sum_{j=0}^{n-1} [f(i,j) - z(i,j)]^2$$

The PSNR (in dB) is defined as:

$$PSNR = 20\log_{10}(MAX_1) - 10\log_{10}(MSE)$$

Here MAX_1 is the maximum possible pixel value of the image under consideration. In our experiment initially the original image pixels are represented using 8 bits per sample, hence MAX_1 is 255 and after bit width reduction the image pixels become 7 bits per sample, therefore MAX_1 is 128.

Table 2 shows the comparative study of the PSNR values for five different 256×256 gray scale images. PSNR0 is peak signal to noise ratio before approximation for the gray scale image and PSNR1 is peak signal to noise ratio after approximation for the gray scale image. From Table 2 it is observed that the PSNR1 for gray scale image after trade off level 3 is the best among all. For trade off level 4 the PSNR 1 is also satisfactory. Table 3 provides percentage (%) degradation in quality of the images between PSNR0 and PSNR1.

Original Image   MA 19.2571dB   AMA1 19.2821dB

AMA2 19.2378 dB   AMA3 19.3056 dB   AMA4 18.5837 dB

Fig. 16. Output quality of Image after applying the different level of approximation algorithms.

Table 2. PSNR (DB) calculation for 5 gray scale images for different trade off level

Sl. no.	Image (256 × 256)	MA		AMA1		AMA2		AMA3		AMA4	
		PSNR0	PSNR1	PSNR0	PSNR1	PSNR0	PSNR1	PSNR0	PSNR1	PSNR0	PSNR1
1	Leena	20.4209	19.2571	20.4444	19.2892	20.3984	19.2378	20.4089	19.3056	20.4444	18.5837
2	Brain	20.8530	20.0200	20.8670	20.0416	20.8561	20.0841	20.8574	20.0841	20.8615	18.3440
3	Barbara	20.0456	19.1846	20.0460	19.1900	20.0330	19.1710	20.0295	19.2112	20.0433	18.9800
4	Einstein	20.1900	18.9651	20.1786	18.9114	20.1895	18.8619	20.1914	18.9685	20.0295	19.2112
5	CKB	20.1666	20.0951	20.8514	20.1185	20.8574	20.0872	20.8666	20.1450	20.8622	18.2732

Table 3. Percentage (%) degradation in quality of images between the 5 gray scale images with before approximation and after approximation (Table 2)

Sl. no.	Image (256 × 256)	MA (% of Image quality degradation)	AMA1 (% of Image quality degradation)	AMA2 (% of Image quality degradation)	AMA3 (% of Image quality degradation)	AMA4 (% of Image quality degradation)
1	Leena	0.012	0.012	0.012	0.010	0.020
2	Brain	0.010	0.010	0.010	0.10	0.030
3	Barbara	0.010	0.010	0.010	0.010	0.011
4	Einstein	0.012	0.013	0.014	0.020	0.010
5	CKB	0.001	0.010	0.010	0.010	0.030

4.2   Layout Area Utilization

Area approximation after layout for the MA and its different level of approximations are observed in Fig. 17. It is observed from the graph that area approximation of the trade off level 3 for the MA cell occupies less area as compared to the trade off 4.

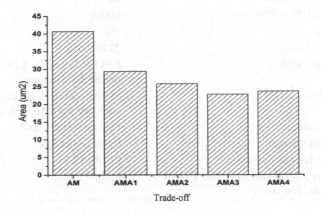

Fig. 17. Layout area of conventional and approximation MA cells

4.3   Parametric Analysis of the Design

Table 4 describes the different parametric analysis for the different trade off level. From the table we can wrap up that the trade off 3 and trade off 4 based adders are the best choice for DWT applications. But trade off 4 based adders is more promising for low power applications.

Table 4. Parametric analysis of the different trade off level

Trade off	Power dissipation (pW)	Average power reduction using voltage scaling technique		PSNR1(dB) (image: Barbara)	Area approximation (from layout) (μm^2)
		Transient power (average) (μW)	DC power (average) (mW)		
AMA4	134	0.0048	0.8	18.9800	23.5
AMA3	210	0.003	0.5	19.2112	23
AMA2	154	0.005	0.6	19.1710	25
AMA1	242	0.006	0.8	19.1900	28
MA	287	0.008	0.6	19.1846	42
FA	298	0.009	1.5	20.0456	-

4.4　Resource Utilization

Sl. no.	Resources	Hardware/Software
1.	Memory space allocated	105.6 MB
2.	No. of component	28
3.	No. of MOS or BIP cells	50089
4.	Latency	0%
5.	Operating frequency	2128 MHz
6.	Operating system	Red hat Enterprise Linux Server release 6.0 (Santiago)
7.	ASIC level design	Mentor Graphics Package Tool 6 with 180 nm CMOS Technology.
8.	For schematic design	Pyxis schematic tool
9.	For layout design	Pyxis layout tool
10.	For Pre Layout simulation	ELDO 12.2
11.	For Post Layout simulation and Layout Vs Schematic test (LVS)	Calibre tool

5　Conclusion

We execute an ASIC based design for dynamic bit width reduction of image through DWT process. Here we are utilizing the conventional approximate adder circuits for the bit width reduction of the image and make a comprehensive study based on power dissipation, area, DC and transient power analysis. Through the analysis we observe that trade off 4 introduce a satisfactory reduction of area and power dissipation with a minor degradation of image quality. As per our concern the work can be considered as a matchless proposal in the field of approximate computing for Digital Signal Processing.

Acknowledgment. The authors would like to thank SMDP-C2SD project, University of Calcutta funded by MeitY, Govt. of India for providing research facilities and also Xilinx CoreEL VLSI FPGA Center Of Excellence, Department of Electronics and Telecommunication, C.V. Raman College of Engineering, Bhubaneswar, India for their technical support.

We also thank Prof. (Dr.) Kaushik Roy, School of Electrical and Computer Engineering, Purdue University, USA for the encouragement and motivation provided to us.

References

1. Acharya, M., Pal, C., Maity, S., Chakrabarti, A.: Inexact implementation of wavelet transform and its performance evaluation through bit width reduction. In: Chakrabarti, A., Sharma, N., Balas, V.E. (eds.) Advances in Computing Applications, pp. 227–242. Springer, Singapore (2016). https://doi.org/10.1007/978-981-10-2630-0_14
2. Venkataramani, S., Roy, K., Raghunathan, A.: Approximate computing. Tutorial presentation at 29th International Conference on VLSI Design, Kolkata, India, 4–8 January 2016 (2016)
3. Gupta, V., Mohapatra, D., Raghunathan, A., Roy, K.: Low-power digital signal processing using approximate adders. IEEE Trans. Comput. Aided Des. Integr. Circuits Syst. **32**(1), 124–137 (2013)
4. Gupta, V., Mohapatra, D., Park, S.P., Raghunathan, A., Roy, K.: IMPACT: imprecise adders for low-power approximate computing. In: Proceedings of the 17th IEEE/ACM International Symposium on Low-Power Electronics and Design, 1 August 2011, pp. 409–414. IEEE Press (2011)
5. Jiang, H., Han, J., Lombardi, F.: A comparative review and evaluation of approximate adders. In: GLSVLSI 2015 Proceedings of the 25th Edition on Great Lakes Symposium on VLSI, pp. 343–348 (2015)
6. Jiang, H., Liu, C., Maheshwari, N., Lombardi, F., Han, J.: A Comparative study of Approximate Adders and Multipliers. A Tutorial
7. Gogoi, A., Kumar, V.: Design of low power, area efficient and high speed approximate adders for inexact computing. In: 2016 International Conference of Signal Processing and Communication (ICSC), Noida, India, 26–28 December 2016. IEEE Xlopre (2016)
8. Yang, Z., Jain, A., Liang, J., Han, J., Lombardi, F.: Approximate XOR/XNOR-based adders for inexact computing. In: 2013 13th IEEE Conference on Nanotechnology (IEEE-NANO), pp. 690–693. IEEE (2013)
9. Park, J., Choi, J.H., Roy, K.: Dynamic bit-width adaptation in DCT: image quality versus computation energy trade off. IEEE Trans. Very Large Scale Integr. (VLSI) Syst. **18**(5) (2010)
10. Gonzalez, R., Gordon, B.M., Horowitz, M.A.: Supply and threshold voltage scaling for low power CMOS. IEEE J. Solid-State Circuits **32**(8), 1210–1216 (1997)
11. Wu, K.-C., Marculescu, D.: Power-aware soft error hardening via selective voltage scaling. In: IEEE International Conference on Computer Design, ICCD 2008, Lake Tahoe, CA, USA, 12–15 October 2008 (2008)
12. Oboril, F., Shirvanian, A., Tahoori, M.: Fault tolerant approximate computing using emerging non-volatile spintronic memories. In: 2016 IEEE on 34th VLSI Test Symposium (VTS), Las Vegas, NV, USA, 25–27 April 2016 (2016)
13. Wunderlich, H.-J., Braun, C., Scholl, A.: Fault tolerance of approximate compute algorithms. In: 2016 IEEE on 34th VLSI Test Symposium (VTS), Las Vegas, NV, USA, 25–27 April 2016 (2016)
14. Adelson, E.H., Anderson, C.H., Bergen, J.R., Burt, P.J., Ogden, J.M.: Pyramid methods in image processing. RCA Eng. **29**(6), 33–41 (1984)

An Efficient Wireless Charging Technique
Using Inductive and Resonant Circuits

Purvi Agrawal$^{(\boxtimes)}$, Ruchi Dhamnani, Ananya Garg,
Shrivishal Tripathi, and Manoj Kumar Majumder

Department of Electronics and Communication Engineering,
DSPM International Institute of Information Technology (IIIT),
Naya Raipur, India
{purvi16101, ruchi16101, ananyag16101, shrivishal,
manojk}@iiitnr.edu.in

Abstract. This paper presents a novel wireless charging system by using the inductive and resonant circuits. The circuit primarily uses an electromagnetic field to trade energy between two objects through electromagnetic induction. Two inductors are designed by using copper coils with different number of turns using a *RLC* circuit resonant frequency. The measured resonant frequency serves as an input to the proposed metal oxide semiconductor field effect transistor (MOSFET) gate driver. Apart from this, an inductive charging is used to provide an input to bipolar junction transistor (BJT) and resistor based driver circuits. Using the proposed circuits, wireless induction is measured for different number of turns and distances between the inductive coils. Further, it is observed that the inductive circuit can provide the charging only for 12 cm, whereas a maximum of up to 1 m can be obtained using resonant frequency. Moreover, an approximate improvement of up to 54.6% can be achieved using more number of turns in the inductive based wireless charging system.

Keywords: Wireless charging ·
Metal oxide semiconductor field effect transistor (MOSFET) · Transistor ·
Copper coil · Light emitting diode (LED) · Intensity

1 Introduction

Wireless power transmission using inductive coupling, is a successful approach for exchanging power through devices [1] without utilizing ordinary wire framework [2]. It is viable in the areas, where wire framework is inaccessible or inconceivable [3]. The wireless charging, also called inductive power transfer (IPT) [4], in this method power source is transmitted electromagnetic energy to an electrical resistor across an air gap [5], without any interconnecting wires. Wireless charging is utilized when one to one wired connection is not acceptable [6] and the power transfer source that is battery resides in the product itself or it can be implemented in the areas, where products are not in reach [7]. This technique is applied in medical devices and food products where bacteria levels must be kept to a minimum and having electrical contacts between them is not allowed [8]. Currently, remote charging is quickly advancing from portable

© Springer Nature Singapore Pte Ltd. 2019
A. Sengupta et al. (Eds.): VDAT 2019, CCIS 1066, pp. 164–170, 2019.
https://doi.org/10.1007/978-981-32-9767-8_14

chargers to wireless power transfer in electric vehicles as it provides a substitute to lithium batteries that are far costly [9]. However, the wireless charging is economical as it helps curbing air pollution. The hidden standard behind wireless charging is the notable Faraday's law of induced voltage, ordinarily utilized in engines and transformers [10].

Earlier, Dai et al. [11] presented a brief description of different types of power transfer approach like static power charging, wireless power transmission, and the methods people have used till now for implementing it. The authors discussed only about the inductive and capacitive coupling and charging techniques without considering the number of turns in the inductive coils. Later Gao et al. [12] also investigated the wireless power transmission among inductive and capacitive coils. They created an inductive power transfer technique innovation for a long time with effectively popularized products at low power level. The authors neglected the resonant frequency based charging with number of turns in the coils. Recently, Ahamad et al. [13] provides a state-of-the-art review of all the wireless charging technologies without considering the impact of number of turns in the inductive coils. Therefore, the previous works [11–13] does not provide a comprehensive demonstration for wireless charging system using the inductive distance and number of turns in the coil.

This paper proposes the design of a transistor based circuit for efficient wireless charging systems. The system is analyzed by varying the number of turns, diameter as well as by using different transistors, for evaluating the performance of different inductive coils. Using the proposed technique, a relation has been established between conduction, number of turns, and diameter of the coil. The angular variation between the inductive coils has also been demonstrated in the intensity of light of the Light Emitting Diode (LED) for different circuits. Further, the overall area of the inductive coil is obtained in order to analyze the induction. The primary objective is charging a device by inductive coupling in an efficient manner so that it consumes minimum power and that also without any physical contact. The inspiration of picking "wireless charging pad" as the research is to understand the innovation that allows a power transferring source to transmit electromagnetic energy to an electrical load across an air gap, without interconnection or any physical contact.

This paper is organized in the following three sections including Sect. 1 as introduction to the current research scenario in the area of wireless charging. Section 2 provides a detail description of the proposed wireless charging techniques. The charging for different number of turns, diameter and height between the inductive coils are also explained in this section. Finally, Sect. 3 draws a brief summary of the paper.

2 Proposed Solution and Discussion

The proposed technique primarily has two parts, namely wireless power transmitter and receiver. The transmitter section of wireless charging circuit comprises of a Direct Current (DC) power source, oscillator, and a transmitter coil. A fixed DC voltage is provided by a DC power source, and this DC signal is served as the input to the oscillator circuit. The operation of the oscillator circuit is used to convert this input DC voltage to a high frequency alternating current (AC). This high frequency AC when passes through the transmitting coil, it generates a magnetic field and the coil behaves as an electromagnet. The change in the magnetic field induces Electromagnetic Field (EMF) as per the faraday's law. Due to this induced EMF, an alternating magnetic field is generated and a reverse phenomenon in the receiver coil occurs. The alternator current is induced that leads to glow the LED. The electromagnetic induction primarily occurs with the principle of Faraday's law that uses the primary idea from lines of force. This electric field can instigate an electrical flow in a nearby receiver section without really contacting it. This type of charging utilizes an electromagnetic field to exchange energy between the two lines. It is typically finished with a charging station. The energy is transferred through an inductive coil to an electronic gadget, which would then be able to utilize this transferred energy for the purpose to run the gadget or charge any battery. The general block diagram of the proposed wireless charging system using MOSFET gate driver circuit is shown in Fig. 1(a). The driver circuit (marked in Fig. 1(a)) primarily represents the transistor level diagram of MOSFET gate driver. Using the gate driver circuit the experimental set up is shown in Fig. 2. The components used for this experiment are described as follows [14]

I. *DC power Source:* It includes a step down transformer its objective is to lower the input voltage to a required level, and it comprises of a rectifier circuit which converts the AC voltage to DC signal. A power supply is an electrical device employed to provide the electric power to the transmitter section. The operation of a power supply is to vary over electric charge flow and frequency to power the load.

II. *Transmitter Coil:* Power is transferred to the transmitter section of the circuit it is designed by the copper coil wounded into a loop comprises of a fixed number of turns in according with the requirement. After the transmitter receives power, it energizes the coil and it is responsible for the magnetic coupling between the coil. Hence, by using this mechanism the power is transferred to the transmitter coil. It is connected via a 2N2222A transistor and a resistor of different values for the proposed circuits.

III. *Receiver coil:* The receiver coil is designed in a similar way as the transmitting coils. It is connected with an LED. Electromagnetic induction takes place via two coil and current transfer happens. This can be verified as the LED glows.

IV. *Resistor:* It is a passive electrical component that introduces resistance in the electric circuit. They are used to reduce the current flow, divide the voltage level and provides biasing to the active elements. High power resistors are used to dissipate several watts of electrical power in the form of heat. The resistor value changes with temperature and applied voltage. The quantitative value of resistances is obtained using the color-coding scheme.

V. *MOSFET:* The gate input of MOSFET is isolated from the principle current carrying channel, hence it is referred as an Insulated Gate Field Effect Transistor (IGFET). The most widely recognized kind of the protected gate FET that is utilized in a wide range of sorts of electronic circuits. The IGFET or MOSFET are voltage controlled device in contrast to BJT that is a current controlled device. It also comprises of a "Metal Oxide" gate which isolates the p or n channel of the semiconductor by an extremely thin layer commonly referred as glass.

VI. *Transistor*: A Bipolar Junction Transistor (BJT) primarily comprises of two different configurations namely PNP and NPN. The BJT generally has three terminals such as collector, emitter, and base wherein the current generally flows from collector to emitter. It works in either of the three region called as saturation, active, and cut off. This protected metal layer terminal can be considered as one of the two plates of a capacitor. The distance between these two gate decides the efficiency of the transistor.

Using the above-mentioned components, the electronic circuits for wireless charging is designed using a MOSFET gate driver and Inductive power transfer circuit as described in the following sub-sections.

2.1 Mosfet Gate Driver Circuit

In this subsection, the driver circuit of Fig. 1(b) and its experimental setup in Fig. 2 are demonstrated using PNP transistor BC557, NPN transistor BC547, different resistors (1 to 10 kΩ) and NMOS L7812CV. The working of this circuit can be analyzed, when a 2.4 V square wave signal is applied to R0 it turned on/off the transistor periodically and a constant 24 V is supplied by the power supply. Due to this signal, it activates the gate of the MOSFET the resultant is a square wave signal of 24 V. In this case MOSFET acts as an amplifier. In proposed circuit solution, it is observed that the conduction occurs only when one coil is vertically above the other. Mutual conduction did not occur when the coils are placed side by side. In a two coil wireless power transfer system consisting of the transmitting and receiving loops, the efficiency is proved to reach its maximum at the resonant frequency for both the loops. The two inductor coils primarily uses a resonant frequency 9.65 MHz in order to provide an input to the MOSFET gate driver circuit. A function generator is used to provide the input to the transmitter with a square wave signal of amplitude 2.4 V amplitude and frequency of 9.65 MHz. A LED is connected at the end of the receiver. The efficiency of a particular load can be determined by changing the driving frequency.

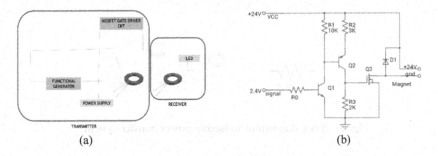

Fig. 1. (a) Block diagram of wireless charging system, (b) MOSFET gate driver circuit.

Fig. 2. Experimental setup for wireless charging system using MOSFET gate driver circuit.

2.2 Inductive Power Transfer Circuit

The block diagram of inductive power transfer system is shown in Fig. 3. Using the inductive power transmitter technique, Fig. 4 represents the experimental setup of power transfer circuit with different number of turns in copper coil. In order to design the circuit, two copper coils each of 64.5 gm of 22-gauge copper wire with 20 turns each and diameter of 7.76 cm is used. Along this NPN transistor of IC 2N2222A and a resistance of 30 K are used as shown in Fig. 4(a). Based on the designed prototype, it is analyzed that the LED is glowing for a maximum distance of up to 6 cm and an angular deviation of up to 48°. However, it is observed that the intensity of the LED is lesser for a 64.5 gm copper wire. Therefore, it can be inferred that a copper coil with more number of turns is required in order to obtain a relation of the turns and distance covered by the wireless charging.

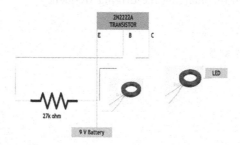

Fig. 3. Block diagram of inductive power transfer system.

In order to meet with the requirement, the experiment is also performed with two copper coils each of 125 gm of 22-gauge copper wire with 40 turns each and diameter 7.76 cm, NPN transistor of IC 2N2222A transistor and a resistance of 30 K as shown in Fig. 4(b). Based on the designed prototype, it is analyzed that the LED is glowing up to a distance of maximum 9 cm and an angular deviation of 52°. But since in this case, more number of turns are used, the LED is bright enough. Further, it is observed that on increasing the distance between the coils, the intensity of the glowing LED reduces substantially. The maximum intensity can be obtained when the two coil are in their closest proximity. Further, in order to improve the intensity, the experiment has also been performed with two copper coils each of 125 gm of 22 gauge of copper wire having 56 turns each and diameter of 4.5 cm as shown in Fig. 4(c). In this case, the LED is glowing for a maximum distance of up to 12 cm and an angular deviation of up to 69°. This is the best suited possible solution to provide the wireless charging with an improved distance and angular displacement between the coils.

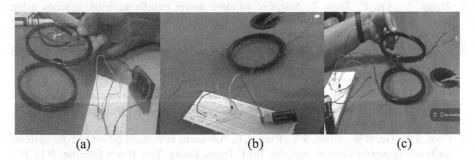

(a)   (b)   (c)

Fig. 4. Experimental set up wireless charging system using inductive power transfer circuit having copper coils of (a) 20 turns and distance 7.76 cm (b) 40 turns and distance 7.76 cm (c) 56 turns and distance 12 cm

Using the above experimental techniques, Table 1 summarizes the intensity of LED under the different conditions such as number of turns, height, and angular deviation between the inductive coils.

Table 1. Comparison for different number of turns in inductive coil.

S. no.	Number of turns	Diameter	Angular deviation	Height	Intensity of light
1	56	4.5 cm	69°	12 cm	Brightest
2	40	7.76 cm	52°	6 cm	Brighter
3	20	7.76 cm	48°	7.76 cm	Bright

3   Conclusion

In this work, an efficient method is proposed for wireless charging system using different technical aspects such as number of turns, angular variation, diameter, and height between the inductor coils. A number of experiments is performed using a MOSFET gate driver and inductive power transfer circuits. It is observed that the intensity of the load (LED) is varied for different number of turns in the transmitting and receiving coils. The maximum intensity is obtained for the inductive circuit that has the maximum number of turns in the coil. By performing the experiments, the inductive coil with 56 turns possesses an approximate of 54.6% and 15.9% improved wireless power transfer in comparison to the circuits having 20 and 40 turns, respectively. The proposed charge transfer technique is useful for a wide range of future applications such as mobile battery charging, LED glowing, Electric vehicles, computerized cameras, media players, gaming controllers, Bluetooth headsets, controlling instruments, therapeutic gadgets, and e-bicycles, etc.

References

1. Zhang, Y., Lu, T., Zhao, Z.: Selective wireless power transfer to multiple loads using receivers of different resonant frequencies. IEEE Trans. Power Electron. **30**(11), 6017–6029 (2015)
2. Miller, J.M., Onar, O.C., Chinthavali, M.: Primary-side power flow control of wireless power transfer for electric vehicle charging. IEEE Trans. Power Electron. **3**(1), 147–162 (2015)
3. Qiu, C., Chau, K.T., Liu, C., Chan, C.C.: Overview of wireless power transfer for electric vehicle charging. In: Proceeding of Electrical Vehicle Symposium Exhibition (EVS), vol. 7, pp. 1–9 (2013)
4. Choi, S.Y., Gu, B.W., Jeong, S.Y., Rim, C.T.: Advances in wireless power transfer systems for roadway-powered electric vehicles. IEEE Trans. Emerg. Top. Power Electron. **3**(1), 18–36 (2015)
5. Mi, C.C., Buja, G., Choi, S.Y., Rim, C.T.: Modern advances in wireless power transfer systems for roadway powered electric vehicles. IEEE Trans. Ind. Electron. **63**(10), 6533–6545 (2016)
6. Li, S., Liu, Z., Zhao, H., Zhu, L., Shuai, C., Chen, Z.: Wireless power transfer by electric field resonance and its application in dynamic charging. IEEE Trans. Ind. Electron. **63**(10), 6602–6612 (2016)
7. Choi, S., Huh, J., Lee, W.Y., Lee, S.W., Rim, C.T.: New cross-segmented power supply rails for roadway-powered electric vehicles. IEEE Trans. Power Electron. **28**(12), 5832–5841 (2013)
8. Bosshard, R., Kolar, J.W.: Multi-objective optimization of 50 kW/85 kHz IPT system for public transport. IEEE Trans. Power Electron. **4**(4), 1370–1382 (2016)
9. Budhia, M., Covic, G., Boys, J.: A new IPT magnetic coupler for electric vehicle charging systems. In: Proceeding of IEEE 36th Annual Conference on Electronic Conference (IECON), Cincinnati, OH, USA, pp. 2487–2492 (2010)
10. Liu, M., Zhao, C., Song, J., Ma, C.: Battery charging profile-based parameter design of 6.78 Mhz class E^2 wireless charging system. IEEE Trans. Emerg. Power Electron. **3**(1), 18–36 (2015)
11. Dai, J., Ludois, D.C.: A survey of wireless power transfer and a critical comparison of inductive and capacitive coupling for small gap applications. IEEE Trans. Power Electron. **30**(11), 6017–6029 (2015)
12. Gao, Y., Duan, C., Oliveira, A.: Three-dimensional coil positioning based on magnetic sensing for wireless EV charging. IEEE Trans. Emerg. Power Electron. **30**(11), 6017–6029 (2016)
13. Ahmad, A., Alam, M.: A comprehensive review of wireless charging technologies for electric vehicles. IEEE Trans. Transp. Electrif. **4**(1), 1–9 (2018)
14. Floyd, T.L.: Electronic Devices - Conventional and Current Version, 9th edn. Pearson, London (2015)

A Novel Gate-Level On-Chip Crosstalk Noise Reduction Circuit for Deep Sub-micron Technology

Swatilekha Majumdar[(✉)] [iD]

Indian Institute of Technology Delhi, New Delhi 110016, India
swatilekha.phd@gmail.com

Abstract. Deep sub-micron technology design presents great challenges to design engineers since the digital noise present on-chip becomes a crucial metric in handling signal integrity issues. On-chip noise contributes detrimentally to information being carried by a circuit net and also causes delay uncertainty. As the wires are placed close to each other, coupling capacitances (C_c) become significant leading to non-critical paths gaining critical path status. To address on-chip crosstalk noise problem, most design approaches involve layout optimization or post-layout corrections. This includes shielding wires from each other by placement of guard wires between two signal nets, a practice most common in PCB designs. However, with continued scaling, a lot of circuit nets would require noise corrections and layout optimization approach would cause area and timing issues. This work rectifies on-chip crosstalk noise at gate-level with special consideration to the worst case crosstalk effect when forbidden data streams '101' and '010' are transmitted by the adjacent wires. The paper presents a novel crosstalk reduction circuit that reduces crosstalk noise by 86%. By using the proposed circuit, the timing uncertainty was reduced to below 9%, with area and power penalties below 40%. All the simulations are carried out using silicon extracted spice models.

Keywords: Crosstalk · Deep sub-micron · Noise

1 Introduction

Crosstalk noise is one of the major concerns while designing a sub-nanometer technology chip. Presence of on-chip crosstalk noise not only compromises on the performance of VLSI digital circuits but also leads to incorrect bit-flips while data is being transmitted along the circuit nets. In deep sub-micron technology, coupling capacitance plays a dominant role in the total net capacitance offered by the routed lines [11]. A logical transition in the 'aggressor' line injects charges into the adjacent 'victim' line which leads to logic hazard on the victim lines [10]. These logic hazards are responsible for logic failures and erroneous bit-flips. Furthermore, if noise from the aggressor line is injected during the time a transition occurs at the victim line, it suffers from data uncertainty [1,7,9,14].

© Springer Nature Singapore Pte Ltd. 2019
A. Sengupta et al. (Eds.): VDAT 2019, CCIS 1066, pp. 171–179, 2019.
https://doi.org/10.1007/978-981-32-9767-8_15

This leads to non-critical path becoming a critical parameter when speed and performance of the chip are considered, further putting limitations on clock frequency among other critical issues.

Engineering optimization to mitigate crosstalk noise involves two different approaches – (1) post-layout verification wherein interconnect models and simplification methods have been utilized to calculate peak noise voltage and noise margin extraction to study the noise transients in logic circuits and, (2) pre-layout optimization, where design flow is introduced at the logic synthesis level on probabilistic crosstalk model [4,10]. Additional methodologies include increasing wire spacing, shield insertion, incremental routing and device sizing [2,5,6,8,13]. Since coupling information is unknown at the logic synthesis stage, probabilistic approaches [3] are often used to estimate crosstalk before routing is performed. Although post-layout verification has been an effective method to reduce on-chip noise, they have convergence problems which results in costly and lengthy number of iterations. To reduce the convergence issue, an alternative approach can be to have an intelligent compensation circuit that can be incorporated along with the drivers already present on-chip, which wakes up sporadically when critical or forbidden data streams are transferred. This technique will not only aid the existing crosstalk reduction mechanisms but will also contribute marginal power consumption as the circuit functions sporadically.

In this paper, we introduce a noise compensation circuit which will aid the existing on-chip crosstalk noise reduction technique and will take care of the worst case crosstalk noise, i.e. noise generated when forbidden codes '101' and '010' are transmitted. Our goal is to reduce the convergence issue that is associated with the post-layout verification methodology that is the most efficient way to reduce on-chip noise. The paper is organized as follows: Sect. 2 will provide a brief idea on the existing challenges due to crosstalk noise and introduce the circuit and its operation, Sect. 3 will discuss the performance of the circuit in reduction of noise. Section 4 will conclude the paper.

2   Crosstalk Noise and Gate-Level Solution

Figure 1 shows a typical scenario of an aggressor-victim model. Crosstalk occurs due to the presence of coupling capacitance between wires placed close to each other on-chip. The *aggressor* wire or the wire which injects charge into the affected wire or the *victim* wire is responsible for causing signal integrity issues that sprout from such interference. The degree to which this interference occurs determines the magnitude (V_p) of the crosstalk noise and also the delay uncertainty (Δt). In literature, several models have been presented that are used to examine the effects of crosstalk noise analytically. These models are based on Thevenin voltage source connected in series with a output resistance along with RC equivalent of the wire [10]. Considering Fig. 1, we analyze the peak noise magnitude (V_p) through an equation provided in [7,10,15] modified to 2 aggressor-1 victim scenario:

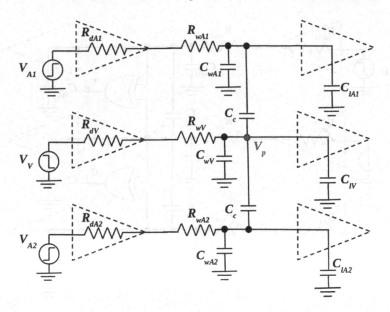

Fig. 1. Classic aggressor-victim wire model showing crosstalk noise at the victim line. V_p represents the maximum magnitude of the crosstalk noise.

$$\frac{V_p}{V_{dd}} = \frac{2(R_{dV} + R_{wV})C_c}{(R_{dA1} + R_{wA1})(C_{wA1} + C_{lA1} + C_c) + (R_{dV} + R_{wV})(C_{wV} + C_{lV} + 2C_c)} \quad (1)$$
$$+(R_{dA2} + R_{wA2})(C_{wA2} + C_{lA2} + C_c)$$

where, A1 and A2 are the two aggressor lines placed around victim line (V). R_{dA1}, R_{dA2} and R_{dV} are aggressor and victim driver resistances, R_{wA1}, R_{wA2}, R_{wV}, C_{wA1}, C_{wA2} and C_{wV} are aggressor and victim wire effective resistances and capacitances. C_c is the coupling capacitance between the aggressor and victim wires. C_{lA1}, C_{lA2} and C_{lV} are load capacitances of aggressor and victim fan-out gates. Additionally, delay uncertainty (Δt) is given by:

$$\Delta t_{max} = \tau_r ln\left(\frac{2V_p}{V_{dd}} + 1\right) \quad (2)$$

where,

$$\tau_r = (R_{dV} + R_{wV})(C_{wV} + C_{lV} + 2C_c)$$

If we keep the drivers constant, the wire resistance of the aggressors act as a shield to reduce the crosstalk noise. However, a similar shielding effect on victim wire will increase the effective wire resistance, increasing the noise magnitude. This in turn will also increase the delay uncertainty. An effective way therefore is to dynamically decrease the victim data path resistance only when the worst case data transmission occurs, i.e. opposite transition in aggressor and victim wires.

In this regard, we propose a dynamic noise suppression circuit that will be inserted before the victim wire load driver and will be active only when driver

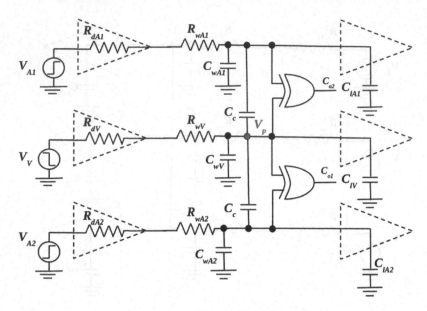

Fig. 2. Wire load model showing placement of two XOR cells between aggressor and victim wire to provide information to the reduction circuit when forbidden data is transmitted.

insertion/buffer insertion technique is unable to reduce the crosstalk noise below tolerable noise ranges. To start off, we perform a noise driven design synthesis flow, similar to that reported in [10]. Here, driver strength selection is performed and wire load model is generated in the first step while running a preliminary synthesis of each circuit. Placement and routing is then performed without considering any timing or crosstalk optimization. This step is followed by RC extraction of the design where static timing analysis is performed to identify the victim nodes where the effect of crosstalk is maximum [5]. At these victim nodes, the proposed circuit is inserted. Figure 2 shows the placement of the circuit in the design and Fig. 3 shows the proposed noise reduction circuit. The main purpose of this circuit is to reduce crosstalk by using large drive strength for sensitive signal carrying wires.

2.1   Operating Principle

If the aggressor and the victim driver strengths are same, the node closer to the victim wire load driver is affected maximum if the C_c at the node is high. The proposed noise reduction technique detects the peak crosstalk noise and discharges the charge that is injected by the aggressor wires. As the reduction circuit comes in picture when opposite transition or forbidden data '101' and '010' is transmitted, the circuit wakes up sporadically and contributes to overall less power.

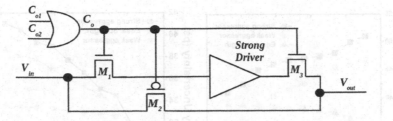

Fig. 3. Proposed noise reduction circuit that further aids the driver to reduce crosstalk noise.

Table 1. Data transmission affecting the crosstalk noise and delay uncertainty

Aggressor	Victim	$V_a - V_v$	C_{eff}	Delay Uncertainty
0	1	$2V_{dd}$	$C_a + 2C_c$	Yes (slowdown)
1	0	$2V_{dd}$	$C_a + 2C_c$	Yes (slowdown)
0	0	0	C_c	Yes (speedup)
1	1	0	C_c	Yes (speedup)

2.2 Working

Table 1 shows the equivalent capacitance (C_{eff}) contributing to crosstalk noise when different data bits are transmitted via the aggressor and victim lines. During worst case data transmission, there is logically opposite data on the aggressor and the victim wires. In such case, the XOR gate connected to the wires will give an output '1' at the output node C_{o1} and/or C_{o2}. These outputs are then transferred to an OR gate which will determine that an opposite data transmission is present on the wires. If the output of the OR gate is '1', transistors M1 and M2 are turned on in the noise reduction circuit. The excess charge injected by the aggressor is discharged to the ground due to the presence of a strong driver in victim line path. This reduces the crosstalk noise. In case the data transmission occurs in the same direction in both aggressor and victim wires, the output of XOR (C_{o1} and C_{o2}) and OR gates are '0'. Transistor M3 is activated which transfers the data to the victim load driver. A driver is not required in this path as the data transmitted will not be affected by the crosstalk noise (refer Table 1).

Considering Eq. (1), if the routing is made such that the aggressor wire is shorter than the victim wire (a common practice to reduce crosstalk [12]), $R_{wA} \approx 0$. If the victim wire resistance is also ignored ($R_{wV} = 0$), Eq. (1) becomes:

$$\frac{V_p}{V_{dd}} = \frac{2R_{dV}C_c}{R_{dA1}(C_{wA1} + C_{lA1} + C_c) + R_{dV}(C_{wV} + C_{lV} + 2C_c)} \atop + R_{dA2}(C_{wA2} + C_{lA2} + C_c)} \tag{3}$$

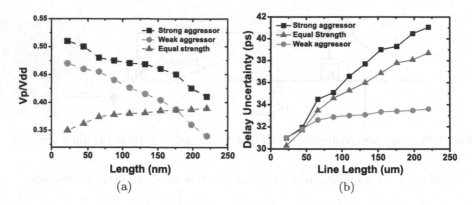

Fig. 4. (a) Normalized peak noise versus line length (b) Delay uncertainty versus line length with varying aggressor driver strength. The victim driver has $R_{dV} = 1200 \; \Omega$.

If we consider that the routing to reduce crosstalk is such that $C_{wA1} = C_{wA2} = C_{wA}$ and the load driver for both aggressor line are of similar strengths ($R_{dA1} = R_{dA2} = R_{dA}$ and $C_{lA1} = C_{lA2} = C_{lA}$), Eq. 3 modifies to

$$\frac{V_p}{V_{dd}} = \frac{2R_{dV}C_c}{2R_{dA}(C_{wA} + C_{lA} + C_c) + R_{dV}(C_{wV} + C_{lV} + 2C_c)} \tag{4}$$

From the above equation we can see that to reduce crosstalk noise, we can increase the victim driver strength with respect to aggressor driver to suppress the noise. But this modification may lead to aggressor becoming the victim. This issue can be solved by increasing victim driver strength only under certain cases when forbidden codes are transmitted.

For our case study, the aggressor and victim drivers are chosen such that the crosstalk noise is sufficient enough to affect the victim wire ($> 0.1V_{dd}$ between any two wires) and the aggressor wire does not become a victim wire on other data transmission. Figure 4(a) and (b) shows the significance of aggressor and victim driver ratio on crosstalk noise and delay uncertainty. The technology node considered for simulations is 22 nm. R_w is 260 Ω, C_w is 10 fF and coupling capacitance (C_c) is 30 fF. All these values are obtained from RC wire load model extraction at 22 nm technology node. Therefore will be able to discharge the extra charges quickly without adding much delay in the circuit.

3   Performance Analysis

Figure 5 shows the suppression of crosstalk noise by the proposed circuit when various driver strengths both aggressor and victim wires are considered. It can be seen that for worst case when aggressor driver is stronger than victim driver, the crosstalk noise is reduced by 71%. For equal drive strength of aggressor and victim, the crosstalk is reduced by 60% and when the aggressor is weaker than victim, the crosstalk is reduced by almost 85%. Data uncertainty is also reduced

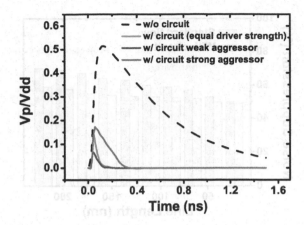

Fig. 5. Crosstalk noise suppression by the proposed circuit for different driver strengths of the aggressor. The crosstalk noise is considered for worst case data transmission ('1' at aggressor and '0' at victim net). The strength of the victim driver is kept constant.

Table 2. Performance evaluation when proposed noise reduction circuit is implemented

Parameter		Without circuit reduction	With circuit reduction
V_p/V_{dd}	Equal strength	53%	60 %
	Strong aggressor	20%	71%
	Weak aggressor	60%	85%
Δt	Equal strength	20%	11%
	Strong aggressor	2%	15%
	Weak aggressor	25%	9%
Power	-	2 µW	2.9 µW (when active)
Area	-	1×	1.39×

by 75% for worst case and by 91% for best case driver ratio. Although including the reduction circuit improves the performance in terms of noise reduction and delay uncertainty, it causes area and power penalty. Table 2 summarizes the performance.

For shorter wire length of the aggressor, the driver parameters (R_{dA} and C_{dA}) dominate the noise magnitude and delay uncertainty. But for longer wires, the R_{wA} and R_{wV} cannot be neglected. Figure 6 shows the noise reduction for varying line lengths. For standard flow it can be seen that as the line lengths increase, the percentage of crosstalk noise suppression saturates. This can also be derived from Eq. (1) where for longer wires, the wire related parameters can no longer be neglected and they play the dominant part in crosstalk noise. For very long wires and wires with weak aggressor drivers, $R_{dA} << R_{wA}$ and $C_{wA} \approx 0$. Therefore, Eq. (1) reduces to:

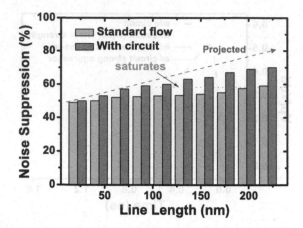

Fig. 6. Noise suppression of standard flow and with the proposed noise suppression circuit. The blue arrow line represents the projected direction of noise suppression. (Color figure online)

$$\frac{V_p}{V_{dd}} = \frac{2(R_{dV} + R_{wV})C_c}{2R_{wA}(C_{lA1} + C_c) + (R_{dV} + R_{wV})(C_{wV} + C_{lV} + 2C_c)} \tag{5}$$

Since, V_p/V_{dd} is still a function of R_{dV}, the proposed technique is still beneficial for longer line lengths as opposed to standard flow.

4   Conclusion

The paper presents a novel gate-level noise reduction circuit that can be implemented at the victim load driver end to reduce crosstalk noise. The circuit functions in sporadic manner and only comes into play when forbidden codes such as '101' and '010' are transmitted by the victim and aggressor lines. Using the circuit, the noise in the design is reduced by 86% while the delay uncertainty is below 9%. We have observed that while standard flow of placing buffers and drivers are efficient for shorter line lengths, the method fails when longer line lengths are considered. As our methodology does not involve strengthening the exiting buffers in the design but rather using an alternate path to discharge the extra charges injected by the aggressor line to the victim line, the proposed methodology is efficient even for longer line lengths. The only downside to this methodology is the penalty in terms of area and power.

References

1. Bang, S., Han, K., Kahng, A.B., Luo, M.: Delay uncertainty and signal criticality driven routing channel optimization for advanced dram products. In: 2016 21st Asia and South Pacific Design Automation Conference (ASP-DAC), pp. 697–704. IEEE (2016)

2. Becer, M.R., et al.: Postroute gate sizing for crosstalk noise reduction. IEEE Trans. Comput. Aided Des. Integr. Circuits Syst. **23**(12), 1670–1677 (2004)
3. Becer, M.R., Blaauw, D., Panda, R., Hajj, I.N.: Pre-route noise estimation in deep submicron integrated circuits. In: Proceedings International Symposium on Quality Electronic Design, pp. 413–418. IEEE (2002)
4. Chakraborty, M., Chakrabarti, A., Mitra, P., Saha, D., Guha, K.: Pre-layout module wise decap allocation for noise suppression and accurate delay estimation of SoC. In: 2016 20th International Symposium on VLSI Design and Test (VDAT), pp. 1–6. IEEE (2016)
5. Franzini, B., Forzan, C., Pandini, D., Scandolara, P., Dal Fabbro, A.: Crosstalk aware static timing analysis environment. SNUG Europe 2001 (2000)
6. Vaisband, I.P., Jakushokas, R., Popovich, M., Mezhiba, A.V., Köse, S., Friedman, E.G.: Shielding methodologies in the presence of power/ground noise. In: Vaisband, I.P., Jakushokas, R., Popovich, M., Mezhiba, A.V., Köse, S., Friedman, E.G. (eds.) On-Chip Power Delivery and Management, pp. 511–532. Springer, Cham (2016). https://doi.org/10.1007/978-3-319-29395-0_33
7. Kahng, A.B., Muddu, S., Vidhani, D.: Noise and delay uncertainty studies for coupled RC interconnects. In: Twelfth Annual IEEE International ASIC/SOC Conference (Cat. No. 99TH8454), pp. 3–8. IEEE (1999)
8. Kose, S., Salman, E., Friedman, E.G.: Shielding methodologies in the presence of power/ground noise. IEEE Trans. Very Large Scale Integr. (VLSI) Syst. **19**(8), 1458–1468 (2011)
9. Kumar, V.R., Alam, A., Kaushik, B.K., Patnaik, A.: An unconditionally stable FDTD model for crosstalk analysis of VLSI interconnects. IEEE Trans. Compon. Packag. Manuf. Technol. **5**(12), 1810–1817 (2015)
10. Milter, O., Kolodny, A.: Crosstalk noise reduction in synthesized digital logic circuits. IEEE Trans. Very Large Scale Integr. (VLSI) Syst. **11**(6), 1153–1158 (2003). https://doi.org/10.1109/TVLSI.2003.817551
11. Mukhopadhyay, A.K., Sarkar, A.: Comparative analysis of some crosstalk avoidance coding techniques in deep submicron VLSI interconnects. In: 2017 Devices for Integrated Circuit (DevIC), pp. 1–5. IEEE (2017)
12. Stöhr, T., Alt, M., Hetzel, A., Koehl, J.: Analysis, reduction and avoidance of crosstalk on VLSI chips. In: Proceedings of the 1998 International Symposium on Physical Design, pp. 211–218. ACM (1998)
13. Subrahmanya, P., Manimegalai, R., Kamakoti, V., Mutyam, M.: A bus encoding technique for power and cross-talk minimization. In: 17th International Conference on VLSI Design Proceedings, pp. 443–448. IEEE (2004)
14. Tang, K.T., Friedman, E.G.: Delay and noise estimation of cmos logic gates driving coupled resistive-capacitive interconnections. Integr. VLSI J. **29**(2), 131–165 (2000)
15. Vittal, A., Chen, L.H., Marek-Sadowska, M., Wang, K.P., Yang, S.: Crosstalk in VLSI interconnections. IEEE Trans. Comput. Aided Des. Integr. Circuits Syst. **18**(12), 1817–1824 (1999)

On-Chip Threshold Compensated Voltage Doubler for RF Energy Harvesting

Arun Mohan$^{(\boxtimes)}$, Saroj Mondal, and Surya Shankar Dan

Birla Institute of Technology and Science Pilani, Hyderabad Campus,
Hyderabad, India
p20170016@hyderabad.bits-pilani.ac.in

Abstract. This paper presents a new threshold voltage compensation scheme for voltage doubler in-order to convert radio frequency (RF) energy to direct current (DC) energy for RF energy harvesting applications. The proposed scheme utilizes a chain of diode connected MOS transistors instead of secondary battery or large off-chip resistors, for minimizing losses due to the MOSFET threshold voltage. The proposed doubler is suitable for RFID applications where targeted supply voltage is 0.5 V. The voltage doubler has been designed and simulated in UMC's 0.18 μm CMOS technology node. It achieves a peak power conversion efficiency (PCE) of 48% at an input power of −12 dBm for an output DC voltage of 0.5 V, and hence suitable for ultra-low power applications.

Keywords: Radio frequency · Direct current · Energy harvesting · RFID · Power conversion efficiency

1 Introduction

The proliferation of internet of things (IoT) into health care and health monitoring [14], wireless sensing [13], and radio frequency identification [3] has led to a demand for low form factor, self sustaining and energy efficient devices. Conventionally, such devices are dependent on battery power for their operation. However, the use of battery introduces a trade-off between operational life-time and form factor - a bigger battery ensures longer lifetime but results in large form factor and vice versa. Moreover, battery requires regular maintenance/replacement which adds additional overhead to the system and could have life threatening consequences in the case of bio-medical applications. Therefore, in order to have a self-sustainable, compact device, one may avoid battery by scavenging ambient energy. Based on the application and deployment area, one may choose the optimal energy source/sources (solar, thermal, vibrational, or RF) for powering an IoT node. Scavenging RF energy is a viable alternative in locations where solar, thermal, or vibrational energies are insufficient/absent. The process of extracting energy from radio frequency (RF) waves is widely known as wireless power transfer (WPT).

Supported by BITS Pilani, Hyderabad.

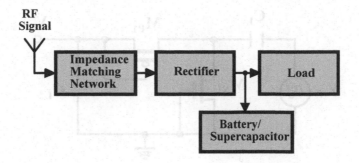

Fig. 1. Basic RF energy scavenging system for an IoT node.

The basic building blocks of a WPT system are shown in Fig. 1. RF signal/signals are received by the single/multi-band antenna. An impedance matching network provides optimal impedance to the antenna so as to extract maximum power from the RF signal received. The desired RF energy is then converted to DC by a rectifier. The output of the rectifier could be used to supply the load and/or the excess energy could be stored into a battery or a supercapacitor for future use. Such systems have been shown to be suitable for powering RFID tags [1,5] which can operate at ultra-low voltage and power levels.

Energy efficiency, low maintenance and form factor are the primary design goal of an RF energy harvesting system. The efficiency of such a system primarily depends on the power conversion efficiency (PCE) of the rectifier due to the non linear nature of RF to DC conversion. PCE of a rectifier could be improved by minimizing conduction losses of the rectifying element. For this, one could use a rectifying element which has a low turn-on voltage such as Schottky diode [6], zero threshold voltage MOSFETs [15] or tunnel field effect transistors [9]. However, these devices either entail additional processing steps adding to the cost or are incompatible with the current CMOS technology and hence are not preferred for on-chip applications. In CMOS rectifiers, conduction losses can be compensated by reducing the threshold voltage of the transistors used. This can be achieved by the use of proper compensation networks [8] or through body bias [10].

In this paper, we propose a novel rectifier circuit intended for ultra-low power RFID applications [2] that require a DC supply voltage of 0.5 V. The proposed rectifier topology is full on-chip, operating in the 915 MHz RFID band and is simulated using UMC 0.18 μm CMOS technology. The rest of the paper is organized as follows: Sect. 2 provides a background of various compensation techniques used for RFID applications. Section 3 discusses the proposed threshold voltage compensation technique. Results and a detailed comparison with the state-of-the-art is discussed in Sect. 4 followed by conclusion in Sect. 5.

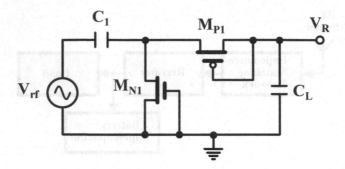

Fig. 2. Schematic of a voltage doubler using diode connected MOSFETs.

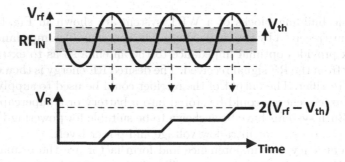

Fig. 3. Input-output waveforms associated with a voltage doubler.

2 Background Theory

Voltage doubler is generally preferred as the rectifier circuit for RF-DC conversion at ultra-low power conditions since it provides a DC output voltage which is twice the input voltage. Moreover, higher output voltages can be achieved by cascading multiple voltage doubler stages [7]. Generally, diode connected MOSFETs are used as the doubling element instead of conventional p-n junction diodes due to their lower turn-on voltage. A conventional single stage CMOS voltage doubler is shown in Fig. 2 [16]. It comprises of two diode connected MOS transistors, M_{N1} and M_{P1}, coupling and load capacitors, C_1 and C_L, respectively. V_{rf} represents peak voltage of the input RF signal received by the antenna and V_R represents the DC output voltage of the doubler. During the negative half-cycle of V_{rf}, C_1 is charged through the transistor M_{N1} while during the positive half-cycle of V_{rf}, C_1 discharges its energy to the load capacitor C_L or subsequent stages input capacitor through M_{P1} transistor. Therefore, DC output voltage V_R of the doubler can be written as

$$V_R = 2 \times (V_{rf} - V_{TN} - V_{TP}). \tag{1}$$

where V_{TP} and V_{TN} are the threshold voltages of PMOS and NMOS transistors, respectively. Ideally, V_{TN} and V_{TP}, should be equal to zero in order to get the $V_R = 2V_{rf}$; However, due to some finite threshold voltage of the MOS transistor, one would not be able to achieve the desired output voltage as stated above. In literature, this threshold voltage drop is termed as "rectifier dead zone". Figure 3 shows the input and output waveforms of the voltage doubler. The shaded portion of the input waveform represents the dead zone.

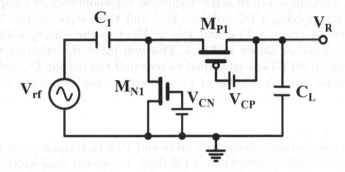

Fig. 4. Threshold voltage compensation scheme for a voltage doubler using a secondary battery.

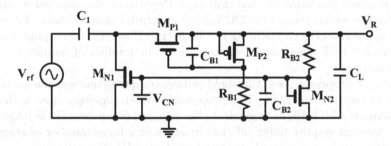

Fig. 5. Threshold voltage compensation scheme for a voltage doubler using MOSFETs and off-chip resistors.

The voltage doubler dead zone also limits the achievable PCE at ultra-low power levels. The PCE of a doubler is defined as

$$PCE = \frac{P_{OUT}}{P_{IN}} \times 100\%$$
$$= \frac{P_{OUT}}{P_{OUT} + P_{LOSS}} \times 100\%$$

(2)

where P_{OUT}, P_{IN} represents the output DC power and the input RF power of the voltage doubler, respectively. P_{LOSS} represents the losses in the doubler during power transfer. At ultra-low power, the doubler dead zone is the primary contributor in P_{LOSS}. Thus, PCE of a doubler could be improved by minimizing the doubler dead zone thereby reducing P_{LOSS}.

Techniques used to reduce threshold voltage of MOSFET devices and thereby minimize CMOS based voltage doubler dead zone are called as threshold voltage compensation techniques. They are classified into two categories: active [16] and passive techniques [11]. In active technique, threshold voltage compensation is achieved by applying a DC voltage (V_{CN} and V_{CP}) equal to the MOSFET threshold voltage ($V_{CN} = V_{TN}$ and $V_{CP} = V_{TP}$) to the corresponding MOS-FET gate terminal as shown in Fig. 4. This will make the effective threshold voltage of the MOSFETs nearly equal to zero and the output DC voltage will be approximately the ideal value of $2V_{rf}$. However, the compensation voltage is provided using a secondary battery, and hence, is unsuitable for self-powered applications. In order to avoid the usage of a secondary battery, a compensation scheme utilizing the output DC voltage proposed in [11], has two networks for providing compensation voltage to NMOS and PMOS transistors as shown in Fig. 5. Threshold voltage drops across the diode connected transistors M_{P2} and M_{N2} are used as the compensation voltage, which are connected to the gates of M_{P1} and M_{N1}, respectively. To minimize the current through the compensation networks, large (100s of kΩ) off-chip resistors (R_{B1} and R_{B2}) are used. However, high resistance values could potentially lead to a substantial increase in circuit power consumption and chip area. Papotto et al. proposed a compensation scheme which utilizes the DC voltage generated along a chain of cascaded voltage doublers as the compensation voltage [12]. However, this topology suffers from very low PCE since the losses increase as the number of doubler stages in cascade increases.

Hence, we propose a novel threshold voltage compensation scheme for voltage doubler to improve its PCE. The proposed doubler topology uses a chain of diode connected MOSFETs to generate the required compensation voltage. This scheme does not require bulky off chip resistors or a large number of stages for its operation making it suitable for low form factor RFID applications.

3   Proposed Self V_{TH} Compensation

In Fig. 2, the gate voltage of M_{P1} is V_R and gate voltage of M_{N1} is zero. However, NMOS and PMOS transistors require positive and negative gate-source voltages, respectively, to turn on. Hence, in-order to reduce the effective threshold voltage, the potential applied at the gate terminal of M_{P1} should be decreased and that of M_{N1} should be increased. If the DC voltage generated at the output of the designed voltage doubler is used to provide compensation voltage to the MOSFETs, such a scheme is popularly known as "self-threshold voltage compensation."

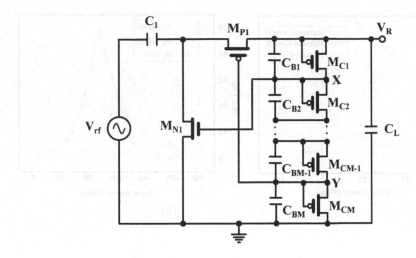

Fig. 6. Proposed self threshold compensated voltage doubler circuit.

Figure 6 shows the proposed voltage doubler scheme. It carries out self-threshold voltage compensation by sampling the output DC voltage using a chain of diode connected PMOS transistors. DC voltage drop along the chain are used as the compensation voltage for the MOSFETs M_{P1} and M_{N1}. Assuming that transistors M_{C1} to M_{CM} are identical, voltage drop at any node X due to N transistors starting from the ground terminal is given by:

$$V(X) = \left(\frac{N}{M}\right) \times V_R \qquad (3)$$

where M is the total number of diode connected MOSFETs in the compensation network. Based on the above observations, gate terminal of M_{N1} and M_{P1} are connected to node X and node Y, respectively for threshold compensation. This ensures that gate voltage of M_{P1} is reduced and that of M_{N1} is increased thereby reducing doubler dead zone.

While deciding on the value of M, impact of doubler dead zone and reverse leakage on PCE should be taken into account. For small values of M, compensation voltage is large resulting in increased reverse leakage current. On the other hand, large values of M leads to very low compensation voltage and hence ineffective in reducing doubler dead zone. For this work, 4 diode connected MOS transistors are used in series (M = 4) for optimizing the trade-off between doubler dead zone and reverse leakage.

The proposed threshold compensated voltage doubler circuit was designed and simulated using 0.18 μm CMOS technology node. Total channel widths of 10 μm and 21 μm were used for the rectifying NMOS and PMOS transistors, respectively to ensure nearly identical on-state resistance. A minimum channel width of 0.24 μm was chosen for the compensation MOSFETs to minimize their power consumption. For the purpose of comparison, level 1 and level 3 circuits

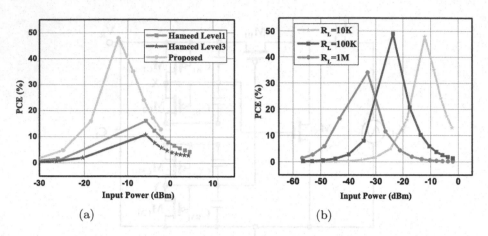

Fig. 7. PCE as a function of input power of (a) proposed design in comparison with state-of-the art for 10 kΩ load and (b) proposed design for different values of load resistances.

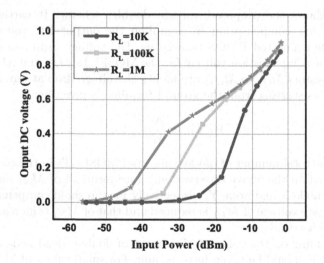

Fig. 8. Output DC voltage of the proposed circuit as a function of input power for different road resistances.

in [4] were simulated in 0.18 μm CMOS technology, using minimum of 2 and 3 stages, respectively in cascade.

4   Results and Discussions

Figure 7(a) shows PCE as a function of input RF power for the three rectifier configurations. A load resistance of 10 kΩ is chosen for comparison. The PCE of the proposed circuit increases as input power increases reaching a peak value and then decreases with further increase in input power. At lower input power levels, the output voltage generated is also low. This output voltage does not produce sufficient compensation voltage to overcome rectifier dead zone effectively. This limits the PCE at lower input power levels. At higher input power levels, output DC voltage is also high resulting in higher value of compensation voltage. This leads to increased reverse leakage currents, which limits the PCE. The proposed circuit achieves a peak PCE of 48.07% at an input power of −12 dBm (63 μW) with a 10 kΩ load. The peak PCE for level 1 and level 3 circuits are 16% @ −5.8 dBm and 10.77% @ −5.8 dBm input power, respectively. This shows that the proposed circuit can achieve a higher peak PCE at a lower RF input power level.

Table 1. Summary of the proposed circuit performance.

Load	Peak PCE @ Input power	Min Input power for $V_{DC} = 0.5V$	PCE @ min input power
10 kΩ	47.8% @ −12.15 dBm	−12.8 dBm	44.62%
100 kΩ	49% @ −23.66 dBm	−21.9 dBm	40.8%
1 MΩ	34.02% @ −33 dBm	−27 dBm	13.3%

Figure 7(b) shows the PCE characteristics of the proposed circuit for different values of load resistance. As the value of load resistance increases, peak PCE shifts to lower input power values. Load resistance of 100 kΩ achieves the highest peak PCE (48.6%), since it generates a compensation voltage which optimizes losses due to doubler dead zone and reverse leakage current effectively. At higher and lower values of load resistance, reverse leakage and doubler dead zone respectively limits the achievable PCE.

Output DC voltage of the proposed circuit as a function of RF input power for different values of load resistances is shown in Fig. 8. As the load resistance increases, the target output DC voltage of 0.5 V can be obtained at lower values of input RF power. Hence, the proposed circuit is suitable for ultra-low power levels of operation over a wide range of load resistances. A summary of the proposed work's performance is provided in Table 1. A comparison of the proposed work with the state-of-the-art is provided in Table 2.

Table 2. Performance comparison of Rectifier topologies.

Rectifier topologies	CMOS technology	Operating frequency	Load	# of Stages	Peak PCE @ Input power	Additional Requirements
This work	0.18 μm	915 MHz	10 kΩ	1	48.07% @ −12 dBm	-
Level 1 [4]	0.18 μm	915 MHz	10 kΩ	2	16% @ −5.8 dBm	Minimum 2 stages in cascade
Level 2 [4]	0.18 μm	915 MHz	10 kΩ	3	10.77% @ −5.84 dBm	Minimum 3 stages in cascade
Papotto [12]	90 nm	915 MHz	500 kΩ	17	16.1% @ −15.83 dBm	Triple well CMOS process
Nakamoto [11]	0.35 μm	953 MHz	-	1	36.6% @ −6 dBm	Large off chip resistors, Ferroelectric capacitors
Umeda [16]	0.3 μm	950 MHz	$I_O = 400$ nA	6	11% @ −6 dBm	Secondary battery

5   Conclusion

A self compensated voltage doubler with a chain of diode connected PMOS transistors as the compensation network was designed and simulated. The proposed circuit was designed using 0.18 μm CMOS technology and was compared with the state-of-the-art rectifier topologies. The proposed circuit was found to have higher value of peak PCE while delivering 0.5 V DC output voltage. The proposed scheme does not require the use of a secondary battery or large off-chip resistors or large number of cascaded stages. Thus the proposed circuit is suitable for ultra-low power 0.5 V applications requiring low form factor.

References

1. Amendola, S., Lodato, R., Manzari, S., Occhiuzzi, C., Marrocco, G.: RFID technology for IoT-based personal healthcare in smart spaces. IEEE Internet Things J. **1**(2), 144–152 (2014)
2. Dastanian, R., Abiri, E., Ataiyan, M.: A 0.5 V, 112 nW CMOS temperature sensor for RFID food monitoring application. In: 2016 24th Iranian Conference on Electrical Engineering (ICEE), pp. 1433–1438. IEEE (2016)
3. Finkenzeller, K.: RFID Handbook: Fundamentals and Applications in Contactless Smart Cards, Radio Frequency Identification and Near-Field Communication. Wiley, Hoboken (2010)
4. Hameed, Z., Moez, K.: Hybrid forward and backward threshold-compensated RF-DC power converter for RF energy harvesting. IEEE J. Emerg. Sel. Topics Circ. Syst. **4**(3), 335–343 (2014)

5. He, D., Zeadally, S.: An analysis of RFID authentication schemes for internet of things in healthcare environment using elliptic curve cryptography. IEEE Internet Things J. **2**(1), 72–83 (2015)
6. Karthaus, U., Fischer, M.: Fully integrated passive UHF RFID transponder IC with 16.7-μm minimum RF input power. IEEE J. Solid-State Circ. **38**(10), 1602–1608 (2003)
7. Le, T., Mayaram, K., Fiez, T.: Efficient far-field radio frequency energy harvesting for passively powered sensor networks. IEEE J. Solid-State Circ. **43**(5), 1287–1302 (2008)
8. Lin, H., Chang, K.H., Wong, S.C.: Novel high positive and negative pumping circuits for low supply voltage. In: Proceedings of the 1999 IEEE International Symposium on Circuits and Systems VLSI (Cat. No. 99CH36349), ISCAS 1999, vol. 1, pp. 238–241. IEEE (1999)
9. Liu, H., Li, X., Vaddi, R., Ma, K., Datta, S., Narayanan, V.: Tunnel FET RF rectifier design for energy harvesting applications. IEEE J. Emerg. Sel. Topics Circ. Syst. **4**(4), 400–411 (2014)
10. Moghaddam, A.K., Chuah, J.H., Ramiah, H., Ahmadian, J., Mak, P.I., Martins, R.P.: A 73.9%-efficiency CMOS rectifier using a lower DC feeding (LDCF) self-body-biasing technique for far-field RF energy-harvesting systems. IEEE Trans. Circ. Syst. I: Regular Papers **64**(4), 992–1002 (2017)
11. Nakamoto, H., et al.: A passive UHF RF identification CMOS tag IC using ferroelectric RAM in 0.35-μm technology. IEEE J. Solid-State Circ. **42**(1), 101–110 (2007)
12. Papotto, G., Carrara, F., Palmisano, G.: A 90-nm CMOS threshold-compensated RF energy harvester. IEEE J. Solid-State Circ. **46**(9), 1985–1997 (2011)
13. Sheng, Z., Mahapatra, C., Zhu, C., Leung, V.: Recent advances in industrial wireless sensor networks towards efficient management in IoT. IEEE Access **3**, 622–637 (2015)
14. Sundaravadivel, P., Kougianos, E., Mohanty, S.P., Ganapathiraju, M.K.: Everything you wanted to know about smart health care: evaluating the different technologies and components of the internet of things for better health. IEEE Consumer Electron. Mag. **7**(1), 18–28 (2018)
15. Theilmann, P.T., Presti, C.D., Kelly, D.J., Asbeck, P.M.: A μW complementary bridge rectifier with near zero turn-on voltage in SOS CMOS for wireless power supplies. IEEE Trans. Circ. Syst. I: Regular Papers **59**(9), 2111–2124 (2012)
16. Umeda, T., Yoshida, H., Sekine, S., Fujita, Y., Suzuki, T., Otaka, S.: A 950-MHz rectifier circuit for sensor network tags with 10-m distance. IEEE J. Solid-State Circ. **41**(1), 35–41 (2006)

Utilizing NBTI for Operation Detection
of Integrated Circuits

Ambika Prasad Shah(✉)🆔, Amirhossein Moshrefi🆔, and Michael Waltl🆔

Institute for Microelectronics, TU Wien, Vienna, Austria
ambika_shah@rediffmail.com, {moshrefi,waltl}@iue.tuwien.ac.at

Abstract. Counterfeiting of integrated circuits (ICs) has become a serious challenge in recent years, as the reuse of devices can affect the reliability and security of electronic systems. This is of particular importance for military, space, and financial applications. Nevertheless, it can be very difficult to detect recycled ICs, especially when they have been used for only a short period of time. To detect the reuse of ICs, we take advantage of the fact that the threshold voltage of single PMOS transistors change over time due to Negative Bias Temperature Instability (NBTI). As a consequence of a pure drift of the threshold voltage towards higher values, the standby leakage current decreases over time. We analyze the change of the standby leakage current of the c17 ISCAS'85 benchmark suite employing the PTM model implemented in HSPICE to estimate the operational time of the chip. Our results clearly demonstrate that the standby leakage current for worst case and minimum stress conditions increases by 20.5% and 10.08% after the stress time of 3 years, respectively. Thus the thorough investigation of the standby leakage current provides a measure for the operational time analysis of ICs.

Keywords: NBTI · Circuit simulation · Standby leakage current · Counterfeit · Recycled chip · Reliability · ISCAS'85 benchmark circuit

1 Introduction

The counterfeiting of Integrated Circuits (ICs) has been increased over the last decades and could not only affect the stable operation of integrated circuits but furthermore cause security leaks of electronic systems. Based on the recent report by the International Chamber of Commerce, the value traded for counterfeit and pirated goods could reach \$991 billion by 2022 [1]. One major concern for counterfeiting is its negative impact on innovation, but might also lead to a lowering of employment and economic growth [2]. On the other hand, according to January 2019 report from the World Economic Forum, e-waste is now the

The research leading to this work has received substantial funding from the Take-off program of the Austrian Research Promotion Agency FFG (projects no. 861022 and 867414).

© Springer Nature Singapore Pte Ltd. 2019
A. Sengupta et al. (Eds.): VDAT 2019, CCIS 1066, pp. 190–201, 2019.
https://doi.org/10.1007/978-981-32-9767-8_17

fastest growing waste in the world. Apparently, only 20% of global e-waste is formally recycled, but this could be significantly increased by reusing of electronic systems [3].

There are various types of counterfeit for electronic systems, for instance the ICs can be recycled, remarked, overproduced, cloned, tampered, etc. [4]. Among these, the recycled and remarked electronic components together cover more than 80% of counterfeit of the individual components [5]. However, counterfeiting of ICs is not straight-forward and might also suffers from the lack of proper test solution to prevent fraudulent of them. Thus a unique way for testing and detection of unwanted recycling of electronics systems has to be created to control the boom of counterfeiting ICs. So far, several detection techniques to identify recycled ICs have been proposed. Zhang et al. [6] proposed a path-delay fingerprinting approach for identifying recovered ICs by calculating the delay of fast aging gates. In [7], Guo et al. have used a SRAM cell which appeared most sensitive to aging mechanisms for the detection of possibly recycled ICs. In common, these two techniques are based on the statistical data analysis and require a pre-analysis of large number of pristine circuits. Zhang et al. [8] proposed a ring oscillator (RO) based light weight on-chip sensor to detect the reuse of ICs. This design contains a reference RO next to the normally used ROs, as the different structures ages with different rates, this can be used to detect counterfeit of electronics. However, although this approach is effective, it requires additional on-chip hardware and hence cannot be used for existing structures which are in use and already circulating in the market.

A new approach could take advantage of the aging of single transistors of the circuits over time. In detail, we use the change in parameters of the ICs due to Negative Bias Temperature Instability (NBTI) of individual transistors to detect possibly recycled ICs. Due to NBTI, the threshold voltage of PMOS transistor drifts over time, and if pure NBTI degradation is considered, the standby leakage current (I_{ddq}) of the transistor decreases at the same time [9, 10]. This decrease of I_{ddq} over time can be used as the parameter for detecting the operational time of the IC. So far we estimate the I_{ddq} of the entire chip by performing circuit simulations for a large number of transistors. To demonstrate the proposed methodology, we use c17 circuit from ISCAS'85 benchmark suite [11] and calculate the critical path, which is exposed to the worst case stress conditions, of the circuit, and compare the steady power consumption to the minimum stress case. Finally, we clearly reveal a significant reduction in the steady power consumption of the degraded circuit, which enables to detect the reuse of electronic chips.

2   ISCAS'85 c17 Benchmark Circuit

Figure 1 shows the circuit for c17 from the ISCAS'85 benchmark suite which consists of six NAND gates and is used for further analysis. For the c17 circuit one has to identify the critical path where the most PMOS transistors are stressed during normal operation. For this, the inputs of the single NAND gates are analyzed next. As we primarily focus on the NBTI for PMOS case, the transistors are stressed when a logical low state is applied at the respective inputs of the NAND blocks. Figure 2 shows the probabilities of getting logic high at each node of the circuit, P_1 through P_{11}, and are computed by applying all possible input pattern combinations to the inputs (I[1]–I[5]) of the circuit. Here P_i is the ratio of the number of 1's on the line i to the total number of input patterns. For this circuit, the total number of combinations are $2^5 = 32$. The signal probabilities for all the inputs are considered to be 0.5 as the probability of primary input being 0 or 1 is assumed to be equal.

The total degradation of the PMOS transistor due to NBTI depends on the input signal probability. The impact of NBTI on the entire c17 circuit depends on the input and output signal probability of each NAND gate, which is again the input probability of a subsequent NAND gate. The output signal probability for a logic '1' input of each NAND gate can be express as [12]

$$P(Y = 1) = 1 - P_A P_B. \tag{1}$$

where P_A and P_B are the input signal probabilities for being logic '1' at the inputs of the respective NAND gate. Considering Fig. 2, it can be observed that the gates G1 and G2 have the highest probability to be stressed, as one or both inputs see the logic '0' state more frequently than the inputs of other NAND gates. NAND gate G5 has the minimum probability of being stressed during operation. The NAND gates which are stressed mostly during operation are highlighted in red whereas NAND gate which are exhibit only minimum stress is highlighted in green.

For worst case stress patterns and the minimum stress patterns of the twelve PMOS transistors of six NAND gates of the c17 circuit are summarized in Table 1. There are two input patterns for each case, which are used for further analysis of the degradation of the c17 circuit.

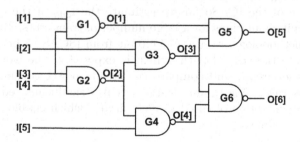

Fig. 1. c17 circuit from ISCAS'85 benchmark suite. G1-G6 are the two input NAND gates. I[1]–I[5] are the circuit inputs, O[1]–O[4] are the intermediate outputs of the single nodes, and O[5]–O[6] are the outputs of the entire circuit.

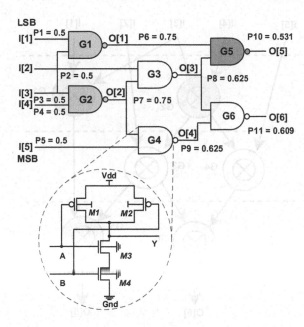

Fig. 2. Input and output signal probabilities for six NAND gates in c17 circuit. It has to be noted, that the PMOS devices are stressed when a logic '0' is applied at the respective inputs. (Color figure online)

Table 1. Stressed PMOS transistors (M_1 and M_2) in all NAND gates of c17 circuit for the four extreme input patterns

NAND gates	Maximum stress		Minimum stress	
	00010	10010	11110	11111
G1	M_1, M_2	M_1, M_2	M_1	–
G2	M_1, M_2	M_1, M_2	–	–
G3	–	–	M_2	M_2
G4	M_2	–	M_1	M_1
G5	M_2	M_2	–	M_1
G6	M_1	M_1, M_2	–	–

2.1 Static Timing Analysis of the c17 Circuit

Static timing analysis (STA) is one of the techniques to verify the timing of a digital design. STA is used at the gate level to derive the faults caused due to cross-talk delay effects [13]. The numbers of cross-talk faults between all possible combinations of inputs in a digital VLSI circuit can be very large and thus impractical to detect for large complex circuits. Therefore static timing analysis is typically used to get a reduced set of cross-talk delay faults [13]. The tree data structure is used to analyze the entire paths in the circuit more

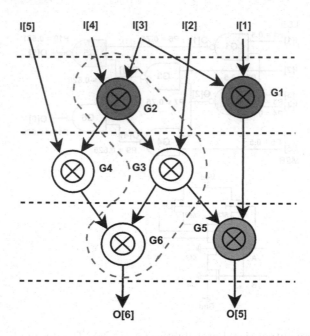

Fig. 3. Dataflow graph (DFG) for critical path of c17 benchmark circuit.

detailed. To calculate the total number of paths in the circuit the depth-first search algorithm is used. A set of critical paths from the total number of paths are detected which exhibit the largest delay of all the paths.

In VLSI design, data-flow graph (DFG) is typically used to represent the circuit netlist. The use of DFG is extended for logic synthesis, design verification, timing analysis, and post-manufacturing testing. DFGs can also be used for timing analysis of the c17 benchmark circuit [14], as shown in Fig. 3. By performing an STA, we note that the path I[4] → G2 → O[2] → G3 → O[3] → G6 → O[6] is the critical timing path for the underlying c17 circuit. The longest paths for the c17 circuit are indicated by the enclosed loop line, as shown in Fig. 3. We used this critical path for calculating the maximum delay of the circuit. Further, out of the two NAND gates, which exhibit the worst case stress conditions G1 and G2, the latter is part of the critical path and thus used for further analysis more closely.

2.2   Steady Leakage Current (I_{ddq}) Model for NAND Gate

Figure 4 shows the two input CMOS NAND gate with inputs A, B and output Y. In addition all the leakage current components present in the circuit for the four possible input bit combinations are also shown we have considered the subthreshold leakage current, the gate leakage and the junction leakage current for further analysis, as these are the major leakage current components [15]. The sum of all the components for each transistor for each particular input

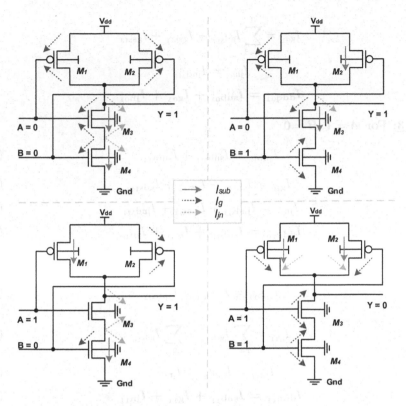

Fig. 4. Standby leakage current (I_{ddq}) model of a two input NAND gate for four different input combinations is shown. The currents I_{sub}, I_g and I_{jn} are the subthreshold leakage current, gate leakage current, and junction leakage current, respectively.

combination is considered as the overall standby leakage current, and can be calculated as follows:

<u>Case 1:</u> For $A = B = 0$

$$I_{sub_{00}} = I_{sub_{M3}} + I_{sub_{M4}} \tag{2}$$

$$I_{g_{00}} = \sum_{x=1}^{4} I_{gd_{Mx}} + \sum_{y=1}^{3} I_{gs_{My}} \tag{3}$$

$$I_{jn_{00}} = I_{jns_{M3}} + I_{jnd_{M3}} + I_{jnd_{M4}} \tag{4}$$

$$I_{ddq_{00}} = I_{sub_{00}} + I_{g_{00}} + I_{jn_{00}} \tag{5}$$

<u>Case 2:</u> For $A = 0, B = 1$

$$I_{sub_{01}} = I_{sub_{M2}} + I_{sub_{M3}} \tag{6}$$

$$I_{g_{01}} = \sum_{x=1}^{3} I_{gd_{Mx}} + I_{gs_{M1}} + I_{gs_{M3}} \tag{7}$$

$$I_{jn_{01}} = I_{jnd_{M1}} \tag{8}$$

$$I_{ddq_{01}} = I_{sub_{01}} + I_{g_{01}} + I_{jn_{01}} \tag{9}$$

<u>Case 3:</u> For $A = 1, B = 0$

$$I_{sub_{10}} = I_{sub_{M1}} + I_{sub_{M4}} \tag{10}$$

$$I_{g_{10}} = I_{gd_{M2}} + I_{gs_{M2}} + I_{gd_{M4}} \tag{11}$$

$$I_{jn_{10}} = I_{jnd_{M3}} + I_{jns_{M3}} + I_{jnd_{M4}} \tag{12}$$

$$I_{ddq_{10}} = I_{sub_{10}} + I_{g_{10}} + I_{jn_{10}} \tag{13}$$

<u>Case 4:</u> For $A = B = 1$

$$I_{sub_{11}} = I_{sub_{M1}} + I_{sub_{M2}} \tag{14}$$

$$I_{g_{11}} = \sum_{x=1}^{4} I_{gd_{Mx}} + \sum_{y=3}^{4} I_{gs_{My}} \tag{15}$$

$$I_{jn_{11}} = I_{jnd_{M1}} + I_{jnd_{M2}} \tag{16}$$

$$I_{ddq_{11}} = I_{sub_{11}} + I_{g_{11}} + I_{jn_{11}} \tag{17}$$

Table 2 summarizes the different leakage current components present for the different input combinations for the two input NAND gate. The cross ($\times$) represent the absence of any leakage component, a checkmark ($\checkmark$) represent the presence of subthreshold leakage component, bullet ($\bullet$) and circle ($\circ$) represent the gate and junction leakage components for source and drain side, respectively. Table 3 summarizes the resulting steady leakage current I_{ddq} for the four different input combinations of the two input NAND gate. I_{sub}^{N}, I_{jn}^{N}, I_{g}^{N} and I_{sub}^{P}, I_{jn}^{P}, I_{g}^{P} represents the subthreshold leakage current, the junction leakage current, and the gate leakage current components for the NMOS and PMOS transistors, respectively. Please note, that only the PMOS transitors leakage current are considered to change over time due to NBTI, whereas the NMOS leakage currents are considered stable in our analysis.

2.3   Effect of NBTI on the Steady Leakage Current (I_{ddq})

With the scaling of CMOS technology, variability and reliability issues of single transistors become more and more important for the performance and lifetime of integrated circuit. In this context, NBTI and positive BTI (PBTI) play an important role for NMOS and PMOS devices. However, extensive experimental investigations demonstrated that the effect of NBTI in PMOS is more sizable compared to the PBTI in NMOS case and is thus considered to be the dominant

Table 2. Presence of leakage current components for a NAND gate

Transistor	Leakage components	Input (A, B)			
		00	01	10	11
$M1$	I_{sub}	×	×	✓	✓
	I_g	● ○	● ○	×	○
	I_{jn}	×	×	×	○
$M2$	I_{sub}	×	✓	×	✓
	I_g	● ○	×	● ○	○
	I_{jn}	×	×	×	○
$M3$	I_{sub}	✓	✓	×	×
	I_g	● ○	○	×	● ○
	I_{jn}	● ○	○	● ○	×
$M4$	I_{sub}	✓	×	✓	×
	I_g	∪	● ∪	∪	● ∪
	I_{jn}	○	×	○	×

Table 3. Standby leakage current (I_{ddq}) model for 2 input NAND gate

A	B	I_{ddq}
0	0	$4I_g^P + 2I_{sub}^N + 3I_{jn}^N + 3I_g^N$
0	1	$I_{sub}^P + 2I_g^P + I_{sub}^N + I_{jn}^N + 3I_g^N$
1	0	$I_{sub}^P + 2I_g^P + I_{sub}^N + 3I_{jn}^N + I_g^N$
1	1	$2I_{sub}^P + 2I_{jn}^P + 2I_g^P + 4I_g^N$

limiting factor of a device/circuit lifetime [16]. NBTI refers to the stress case for PMOS transistors when a negative bias is applied across at the transistor's gate contact. This negative bias can trigger the creation of so called interface states and oxide defects, which lead to a drift of the threshold voltage, reduction of the sub-threshold slope and to a reduction of the on-current [16]. When the gate stress is released the shift of the threshold voltage accumulated during stress recovers partially, but also permanent degradation of the threshold voltage after each stress cycle is observed. The latter can lead to a significant permanent shift of the threshold voltage of PMOS over time, which can introduce some uncertainty in the device/circuit behavior and thus decrease the device/circuit lifetime. By considering a drift of the threshold voltage only, this behavior can cause a reduction of the standby leakage current of the transistor and hence a reduction of the overall I_{ddq} of the complete chip when the chip is used for a long time [10].

Following up the previous identification of the NAND gates which undergo the worst case stress conditions of the analyzed c17 circuit, we now want to take the change of the threshold voltage during device operation into account. As discussed, G2 and G5 are the NAND gates which are exhibited to the worst case and minimum stress conditions, respectively. Thus the maximum change in the steady power consumption follows from

$$\Delta I_{\mathrm{ddq}} = \left| I_{\mathrm{ddq}}|_{G_2} - I_{\mathrm{ddq}}|_{G_5} \right|. \tag{18}$$

When chip ages, I_{ddq} from G5 will decrease rapidly, whereas the I_{ddq} from G2 will not change as much. This will unavoidably result in an increase of ΔI_{ddq} which gets larger the longer the chip gets used.

In order to analyze the maximum change of the steady leakage current, the test pattern that selects the PMOS transistors leakage of fast aging gates, i.e. worst stress conditons, is identified (index F). Similarly, we also select a second test pattern that selects the PMOS transistors with the smallest leakage current increase, i.e. slow aging gates (denoted with index S).

The normalized ΔI_{ddq} for all the combinations are finaly used to detect the recycled IC and is calculated to

$$\Delta I = \frac{I_{\mathrm{S}} - I_{\mathrm{F}}}{I_{\mathrm{S}} + I_{\mathrm{F}}}. \tag{19}$$

3   Simulation Results and Discussion

To demonstrate the effectiveness of the proposed approach for detecting recycled ICs, the PTM 32 nm CMOS technology is used [17]. For the analysis of the device stress, the HSPICE MOSRA model has been used [18]. All the simulations are performed at an elevated temperature (T = 125 °C) for the stress time of three years.

Figure 5 shows the power dissipation of c17 benchmark circuit for input bit combinations leading to either the maximum or the minimum number of PMOS transistors stressed simultaneously. From results it is observed that the c17 has the maximum number of PMOS transistors is stressed for input combinations, '00010' and '10010'. From these bit-combinations the maximum power dissipation is for bit-combination '00010'. Similarly, if we consider the minimum number of PMOS transistor under stress, then the c17 has the minimum power dissipation, which is obtained for the input bit combination '11111'. From the maximum stress input pattern, it is also observed that the NAND gate G2 is always the one with the maximum stress as input I[3] and I[4] are always low for all the considered input bit combinations. Figure 5 furthermore reveals that the c17 circuit has the minimum power dissipation for the input bit-patterns '10010' and '11111' for the maximum and minimum number of stressed PMOS transistors, respectively. Thus these two combinations are considered as the fast aging pattern (T_{F}) case and the slow aging pattern (T_{S}) case.

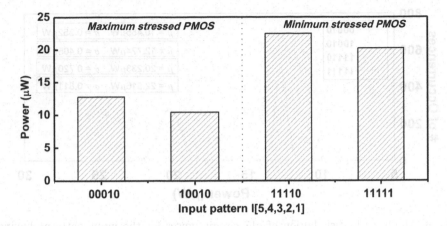

Fig. 5. c17 circuit power dissipation for the input patterns having maximum and minimum number of PMOS are under stress. As can be seen, the steady power consumption tends to decrease for the heavily stressed case.

Figure 6 shows the 5000 Monte Carlo simulations for analyzing the power consumption for different input patterns. As can be seen, the input patterns '00010' and '11110' have the highest deviation for the maximum and the minimum number of stressed PMOS, respectively, whereas the input pattern, '10010' and '11111' have the minimum deviation for the maximum and the minimum number of stressed PMOS, respectively. As we primarily focus on the analysis of the standby leakage current for estimating the lifetime of IC; we will consider the input patterns which exhibit less variation. The input pattern with respect to maximum degradation due to NBTI is '10010' and considered as a first test pattern (T_F). Similarly, for the reference input pattern '11111' is considered as the second test pattern (T_S), which shows only a small variation in the power consumption and furthermore triggers the c17 circuit path with minimum number of stressed PMOS devices.

Table 4 shows the normalized steady leakage current I_{ddq} based on the selected input patterns for the pristine, as well as stressed c17 circuit. One can observe that I_F reveals the higher effect of stress compared to I_S. The decrement in both, I_F and I_S, after three years of stress is 20.5% and 10.08%, respectively. Furthermore it can be observed that the ΔI increases with stress time. The $\Delta I\%$ for fress simulation is 77.88%, and it increases to 80.12% after the stress time of three years. Following from this trend, this cleverly method allows to detect whether the underlying electronic devices is in its virgin, or the device has already been used.

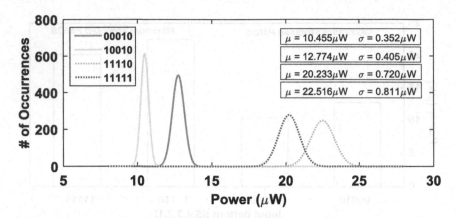

Fig. 6. Monte carlo distribution of c17 circuit power for the input patterns having maximum and minimum number of PMOS are under stress.

Table 4. Normalized I_{ddq} for new and used c17 circuit

Usage Time ↓	I_F (nA)	I_S (nA)	$\Delta I(\%)$
Fresh	1.824	14.67	77.88
1 Year	1.54	13.51	79.58
2 Years	1.49	13.31	79.90
3 Years	1.45	13.19	80.12

4   Conclusion

Counterfeiting of ICs might give rise for instable electronic applications but also might cause severe security leaks. To detect if any electronic circuit is still in its pristine state or has already been used a new approach based on analysis of the circuit's steady power consumption is discussed. Device aging is considered due to NBTI and is applied to the c17 benchmark circuit. For the analysis, the input patters leading to worst case stress conditions and minimum overall device stress are identified. Finally, the comparison of the standby leakage consumption for both cases clearly reveal that a significantly reduced standby power consumption is observed for the used devices compared to the pristine ones. This finally enables to distinguish between pristine and recycled integrated electronics circuits.

References

1. The economic impacts of counterfeiting and piracy. https://cdn.iccwbo.org/content/uploads/sites/3/2017/02/ICC-BASCAP-Frontier-report-2016.pdf. Accessed 09 Mar 2019
2. Frontier Economics: The economic impacts of counterfeiting and piracy. Frontier Economics, Melbourne (2017)

3. A New Circular Vision for Electronics. http://www3.weforum.org/docs/WEF_A_New_Circular_Vision_for_Electronics.pdf. Accessed 09 Mar 2019

4. Guin, U., DiMase, D., Tehranipoor, M.: Counterfeit integrated circuits: detection, avoidance, and the challenges ahead. J. Electron. Test. **30**(1), 9–23 (2014)

5. Kessler, L.W., Sharpe, T.: Faked parts detection. Printed Circ. Des. Fab **27**(6), 64 (2010)

6. Zhang, X., Xiao, K., Tehranipoor, M.: Path-delay fingerprinting for identification of recovered ICs. In: 2012 IEEE International Symposium on Defect and Fault Tolerance in VLSI and Nanotechnology Systems (DFT), pp. 13–18. IEEE (2012)

7. Guo, Z., Rahman, M.T., Tehranipoor, M.M., Forte, D.: A zero-cost approach to detect recycled SoC chips using embedded SRAM. In: 2016 IEEE International Symposium on Hardware Oriented Security and Trust (HOST), pp. 191–196. IEEE (2016)

8. Zhang, X., Tehranipoor, M.: Design of on-chip lightweight sensors for effective detection of recycled ICs. IEEE Trans. Very Large Scale Integr. (VLSI) Syst. **22**(5), 1016–1029 (2014)

9. Shah, A.P., Yadav, N., Beohar, A., Vishvakarma, S.K.: Process variation and NBTI resilient schmitt trigger for stable and reliable circuits. IEEE Trans. Device Mater. Reliab. **18**(4), 546–554 (2018)

10. Kang, K., Alam, M.A., Roy, K.: Characterization of NBTI induced temporal performance degradation in nano-scale SRAM array using I_{ddq}. In: 2007 IEEE International Test Conference, pp. 1–10. IEEE (2007)

11. ISCAS'85 Benchmark Circuits. http://www.pld.ttu.ee/~maksim/benchmarks/iscas85/. Accessed 9 Apr 2019

12. Ghavami, B., Raji, M., Saremi, K., Pedram, H.: An incremental algorithm for soft error rate estimation of combinational circuits. IEEE Trans. Device Mater. Reliab. **18**(3), 463–473 (2018)

13. Bhuvaneswari, M.C.: Application of Evolutionary Algorithms for Multi-objective Optimization in VLSI and Embedded Systems. Springer, Heidelberg (2014). https://doi.org/10.1007/978-81-322-1958-3

14. Neophytou, S.N., Michael, M.K.: Path representation in circuit netlists using linear-sized ZDDs with optimal variable ordering. J. Electron. Test. **34**(6), 667–683 (2018)

15. Islam, A., Hasan, M.: Leakage characterization of 10T SRAM cell. IEEE Trans. Electron Devices **59**(3), 631–638 (2012)

16. Schroder, D.K.: Negative bias temperature instability: what do we understand? Microelectron. Reliab. **47**(6), 841–852 (2007)

17. Zhao, W., Cao, Y.: Predictive technology model for nano-CMOS design exploration. ACM J. Emerg. Technol. Comput. Syst. (JETC) **3**(1), 1 (2007)

18. Synopsys: HSPICE user guide: Simulation and analysis (2010)

A Widely Linear, Power Efficient, Charge Controlled Delay Element for Multi-phase Clock Generation in 1.2 V, 65 nm CMOS

Raviteja Kammari(✉) and Vijaya Sankara Rao Pasupureddi

Center for Advanced Studies in Electronics Science and Technology,
University of Hyderabad, Hyderabad, Telangana, India
{raviteja.kammari,vijaysp}@uohyd.ac.in

Abstract. Voltage controlled delay element (VCDE) is a basic building block in clocking circuits, especially in delay-locked loops (DLL). The VCDE is intended to generate an accurate and precise delay from a reference clock and it is expected to have linear delay characteristics with respect to the control voltage over a wide range. In addition, the VCDE needs to be robust across the process and temperature corners with low power consumption. The conventional delay elements such as current-starved inverter (CSI), wide-range CSI, triply controlled delay cell and digital controlled delay element lack one or more of the above mentioned features. In this paper, a robust, low-power, widely linear (over rail-to-rail control voltage range), charge-controlled, differential delay element circuit topology is proposed. The proposed circuit topology consists of a differential transmission gates along with a variable capacitors and it is implemented in 1.2 V, 65 nm CMOS technology. The performance results shows that it has a delay range of 80 ps to 120 ps over a control voltage range from rail-to-rail. The designed circuit topology is robust over PVT corners and exhibits a bandwidth of 500 MHz (1 GHz to 1.5 GHz) with a power consumption of 0.6 μW and occupies an area of 0.0018 mm^2.

Keywords: Voltage controlled delay element ·
Multi-phase clock generation · Charge controlled · Delay locked loops

1 Introduction

The delay element is a circuit that produces an output waveform similar to the input waveform, only delayed by a certain amount of time [1]. The delay elements are broadly classified into two types: static delay element, where delay is constant and dynamic delay element, where delay is variable. The variable delay elements are used for fine, precise and accurate pulse delay control in high speed digital IC's. In order to achieve wide phase shift or to generate multiple phases, chain of delay elements are used as a delay line. The delay lines are essential building blocks in most of the high-speed digital IC applications, such as delay locked loops (DLLs), time-to-digital converters (TDCs), voltage controlled oscillators

© Springer Nature Singapore Pte Ltd. 2019
A. Sengupta et al. (Eds.): VDAT 2019, CCIS 1066, pp. 202–214, 2019.
https://doi.org/10.1007/978-981-32-9767-8_18

(VCOs), pulse-width control loops (PWCLs) [2]. In all the above mentioned applications, the variable delay elements determine the precise and accurate pulse time reference, hence their design need to be robust.

In high-speed digital IC applications, DLL is widely used for on-chip clock generation, to achieve synchronization and elimination of clock skew among different blocks [3]. The basic architecture of multi-phase clock generation (MPCG) using DLL is shown in Fig. 1 and in this architecture, the delay element is a critical building block. The delay element in MPCG-DLL should maintain fifty percent duty cycle over a wide range of input control voltage, otherwise, it leads to the generation of mis-aligned phases. In addition, if the delay element characteristics with respect to control input are non-linear, it leads to jitter in the DLL and long locking time of the loop. Moreover, the wide dynamic range for delay control results in wide locking range for the DLL. Also, it is well known that, delay line consumes major part of the total DLL power budget. Thus, there is a need for delay element, which is widely linear, duty cycle control circuitry (DCCC) free, wide dynamic range delay control along with low power consumption.

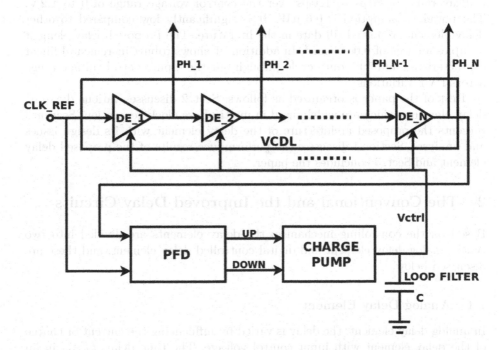

Fig. 1. Basic architecture of DLL for multi-phase clock generation

There are various dynamic delay elements which are widely used to partly achieve the above mentioned features. These delay elements are majorly categorized into analog [1,3–7], and digital [8] delay elements based on the control mechanism. However, all of these delay elements are lacking one or more of the above mentioned features. For example, conventional current starved inverter provides good delay range, but it exhibits non-linear delay-control voltage characteristics and also has mismatches in the duty cycle. The delay element proposed in [5] has good delay range with wide linearity but it consumes more power and it is not robust, especially, the signal integrity fails at slow-fast (SF) and fast-slow (FS) process corners. On the other hand, digital controlled delay elements provide full range of linearity, low-power. However, it is not possible to fine tune them precisely, which results in high jitter.

In a deep sub-micron CMOS process, it is well known that, time-domain resolution of a digital signal edge transition is superior to voltage resolution of analog signals [9]. By taking advantage of this new paradigm, this work proposes, a new DCCC free, robust, low-power, charge-controlled, rail-to-rail output swing, widely linear differential delay element for multi-phase clock generation. The proposed delay element circuit topology is built by using high speed switches and variable caps in 1.2 V, 65 nm CMOS technology, thanks to the availability of high precision capacitors and excellent MOS switches in sub-100 nm technologies. The proposed delay element is designed at 1.25 GHz center frequency and it has a delay range of 80 ps to 120 ps over the control voltage range of 0 to 1.2 V. The power consumption is 0.6 μW. It is significantly low compared to other delay elements reported till date in the literature. The proposed delay element occupies an area of 0.0018 mm². In addition, it shows robust incremental linear characteristics and 50% duty cycle through out the input control voltage range across PVT variations.

Rest of the paper is organized as follows: Sect. 2 discusses various dynamic delay elements which are widely used in multi-phase clock generation. Section 3 presents the proposed architecture of the delay element with its design issues and analyses. Section 4 discusses the performance results of the proposed delay element and Sect. 5 concludes the paper

2   The Conventional and the Improved Delay Circuits

Based on the controlling mechanism the delay elements are divided into two types: analog delay element and digital controlled delay element, and these are discussed below.

2.1   Analog Delay Element

In analog delay element, the delay is varied by influencing the current or charge of the delay element with input control voltage. The time delay, t_{delay}, in an analog delay element is defined by [10].

$$t_{delay} = \frac{CV_{sw}}{I_{cp}} \tag{1}$$

where C is the load capacitance and I_{cp} is the charging/discharging current, and V_{sw} is the swing voltage. The delay of the analog delay cell varies linearly with C and V_{sw}. It is to be noted that, V_{sw} is an input voltage at which the inverter output changes its state and for a standard inverter, it is commonly set to $V_{DD}/2$ and is not variable. Therefore, either the C or I_{cp} should be varied to adjust the delay. In current (I_{cp}) controlling technique, the required delay is achieved by limiting the current I_{cp} with input control voltage.

The current starved inverter (CSI) shown in Fig. 2 is the most widely used delay cell in DLLs, as it has advantages in terms of fine tuning, less area and high gain. However, it has the disadvantage of non-linear variation of delay with respect to control input, high power consumption and narrow range of delay control. The CSI also faces the duty cycle mismatches at PVT variations. To overcome these problems, various modified structures of CSI are proposed.

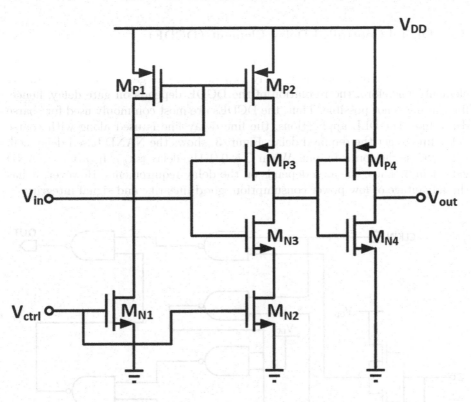

Fig. 2. Conventional current starved inverter

The duty cycle correction mechanism was employed in [3] and [4] to maintain the 50% duty cycle. In [3], the duty cycle correction was made by adding two more transistors in parallel with current limiting transistors and duty cycle control signal was generated by comparing the output of the delay line with reference clock. This makes the circuitry more complex, increased area and power. In [4], delay regulation for both rising and falling edges was reported. The rising and falling edges are corrected individually to make the duty cycle correction. It results in large area and high power consumption compared to CSI. In addition, the delay elements reported in [3] and [4] suffers from non-linear delay-control voltage characteristics.

The linearity and power consumption characteristics are improved in [5] by adding the auxiliary current sources in parallel with current limiting transistors. Therefore, a wide range of operation is achieved. However, the area is increased and for SF and FS process corners the duty cycle variations causes misaligned phases. Apart from CSI's, differential delay elements are reported in [6,7]. In these, voltage controlled resistors are placed to control the delay. it has a good range of delay but small range of linearity and this architecture needs $2V_{d,sat}$ headroom, therefore the output will not be from rail to rail.

2.2   Digital Controlled Delay Element (DCDE)

The delay provided by the DCDE depends on the signal propagation path from the input to output, that inherently depends on the gate delay of the delay element. Therefore, the resolution of the DCDE depends on gate delay, hence, fine tuning is not possible. Thus, the DCDEs are most commonly used for coarse delay line. For DLL applications, the fine delay line is used along with coarse delay line to get the required delay. Figure 3. shows the NAND based delay cell, where 'C' is the control input. When C is 0/1 the delay is $t_{gd}/4t_{gd}$ (t_{gd} - NAND gate delay). Thus, the area depends on the delay requirements. However, it has the advantage of low power consumption, good linearity and signal integrity.

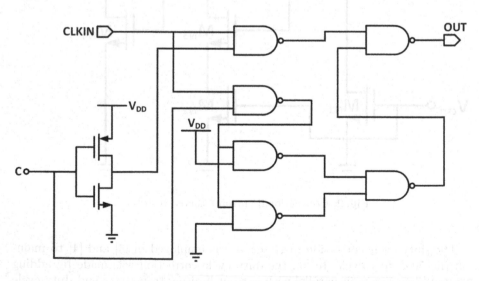

Fig. 3. Digital controlled delay element

3   Proposed Delay Element Circuit Topology

The modified CSIs and DCDE improve the weakness of the conventional CSI, However, they still lack one or more important features such as linearity, 50% duty cycle, wide dynamic range, and low power consumption across temperature and process corners. These features are crucial for delay element to employ in the design of MPCG-DLLs.

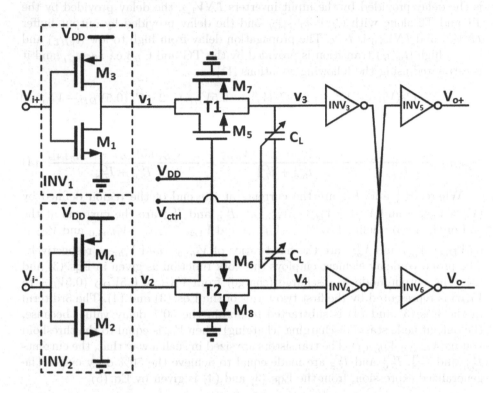

Fig. 4. Proposed delay element circuit topology

The proposed delay element architecture is shown in Fig. 4. Differential inputs V_{i+} and V_{i-} are applied to the two input inverters INV_1 and INV_2, which drive the transmission gates T1 and T2 respectively. The transmission gate NMOS($M_{5,6}$) and PMOS($M_{7,8}$) devices are controlled by supply voltage V_{DD} and 0 V respectively. Therefore, the transmission gates T1 and T2 are always turned ON and provide a constant ON-resistance which is equal to $r_{on5,6}||r_{on7,8}$. The key element of the proposed architecture is the variable capacitors C_L, thanks to the availability of high precision capacitors in sub-100 nm technologies. The variable load capacitance (C_L) is controlled by input controlled voltage (V_{ctrl}), which in turn controls the delay. The output voltage across the load capacitor is triangular in nature, since the output load capacitance is charged or discharged by the input. Hence, to make the signal rail-to-rail and also pass this output to the next stage, buffers $INV_{3,4}$ and $INV_{5,6}$ are placed. Thus, the output buffer along with input inverter causes fixed delay. Hence, the delay offered by the proposed delay element circuit topology is given by Eq. (2)

$$t_{delay} = t_{inv} + t_{TG+C_L} + t_{buf} \tag{2}$$

where the t_{delay} is the total delay of the proposed delay element. In which, t_{inv} is the delay provided by the input inverters $INV_{1,2}$, the delay provided by the T1 and T2 along with C_L is t_{TG+C_L} and the delay provided by output buffer $INV_{3,4}$ and $INV_{5,6}$ is t_{buf}. The propagation delay from high to low (t_{pHL}) and low to high (t_{pLH}) transition is provided by the TG and C_L i.e., t_{TG+C_L} and it is estimated using the following equations [11].

$$t_{pHL} = \frac{2 * C_L(V_{DD} - V_{out}^0)}{I_{7,8}^C} + \frac{2 * C_L(V_{out}^0 - 0.5V_{DD})}{I_{5,6}^C + I_{7,8}^C} - \frac{2 * C_L(0.5V_{DD} - V_{thn1,2})}{I_{5,6}^{C1} + I_{7,8}^{C1}} \tag{3}$$

$$t_{pLH} = \frac{2 * C_L V_{out}^{0'}}{I_{5,6}^{C1}} + \frac{2 * C_L(0.5V_{DD} - V_{out}^{0'})}{I_{5,6}^{C1} + I_{7,8}^{C1}} - \frac{2 * C_L(0.5V_{DD} - |V_{thp3,4}|)}{I_{5,6}^C + I_{7,8}^C} \tag{4}$$

Where, $I_{5,6}^{C1}$ and $I_{7,8}^C$ are the currents at the end of the region defined by ($V_i > V_{thn1,2}$ and $V_{1,2} \geq V_{DD} - V_{thn5,6}$). $I_{5,6}^C$ and $I_{7,8}^{C1}$ are the currents at the end of the region defined by ($V_i > V_{thn1,2}$ and $V_{1,2} \leq V_{DD} - V_{thn5,6}$ and $V_{3,4} \geq 0.5V_{DD}$). V_{out}^0 and $V_{out}^{0'}$ are the fixed ratios of $V_{thn5,6}$ and $V_{thp7,8}$ respectively. The proposed delay element employs the work function as given in Eqs. (3) and (4). The output node to discharge (charge) from V_{DD} to $0.5V_{DD}$ ($0.5V_{DD}$ to V_{DD}) is represented by the first two terms of the Eqs. (3) and (4). The 3rd term in the Eqs. (3) and (4) is subtracted to obtain the 50% delay value, because, the output node starts discharging (charging) when V_{in} is equal to the threshold voltage $V_{thn1,2}(V_{thp3,4})$. The transistors are sized in such a way that, the currents $I_{5,6}^{C1}$ and $I_{7,8}^C$, $I_{5,6}^{C1}$ and $I_{7,8}^C$ are made equal to achieve the 50% duty cycle. The generalized expression, from the Eqs. (3) and (4) is given by Eq. (5)

$$t_{TG+C_L} = \frac{0.5V_{DD}C_L}{I} \tag{5}$$

From the Eq. (5), the delay characteristics over the wide range of control input is achieved by linear variation of capacitance with control input. The power consumption in the proposed delay element circuit topology is significantly low, as there is no direct path between supply rails. In the proposed delay element most of the power is consumed in charging and discharging of the load capacitance (C_L) [1].

4   Performance Results

The proposed delay element is implemented in 1.2 V, 65 nm CMOS technology. The switches of the proposed architecture shown in Fig. 4 are supplied with constant supply rails. Differential inputs with a voltage swing from 0 to 1.2 V and frequency range from 1 GHz to 1.5 GHz are applied to inputs V_{i+} and V_{i-} of the delay element. The capacitance of the variable capacitors (C_L) is varied by applying the input control voltage (V_{ctrl}) from 0 to 1.2 V. The differential output is taken at the V_{o+} and V_{o-} of the proposed architecture.

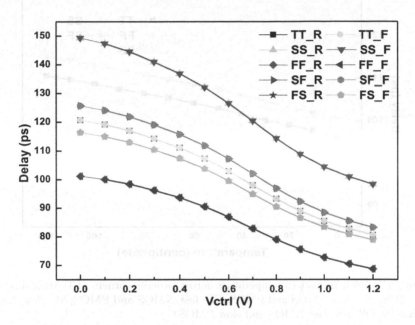

Fig. 5. Delay with respect to control voltage (V_{ctrl}) across all process corners (TT-typical NMOS and PMOS, SS- slow NMOS and PMOS, FF- fast NMOS and PMOS, SF- slow NMOS and fast PMOS, FS- fast NMOS and slow PMOS, R-t_{pLH}, F-t_{pHL})

The delay characteristics simulations are carried out for the control voltage (V_{ctrl}) sweep and also for robustness check. For checking the robustness against temperature variation, temperature is varied from 0 °C to 120 °C by fixing the V_{ctrl} to 650 mV, and V_{DD} to 1.2 V. Similarly, for checking the robustness against voltage variation, the V_{DD} is varied from 1.0 V to 1.3 V, by fixing the temperature and V_{ctrl} to 27 °C and 650 mV respectively.

Delay of the differential output with respect to control voltage across process corners is shown in Fig. 5. The trending of the delay characteristics for both t_{pHL} and t_{pLH} shows incremental linearity across the process corners. There is a delay range of 40 ps (80 ps to 120 ps) for control voltage range from 0 to 1.2 V and the delay characteristics of t_{pHL} and t_{pLH} are overlapped. This indicates that 50% duty cycle is maintained over the rail-to-rail input control voltage range. Similar delay characteristics with respect to V_{ctrl} are observed for the process corners. However, for SS corner these characteristics are shifted up and provides a delay of 51 ps (in the range from 98 ps to 149 ps), and for FF corner, the characteristics are shifted down and provides a delay of 33 ps (in the range from 68 ps to 101 ps) over the V_{ctrl} range from 0 to 1.2 V.

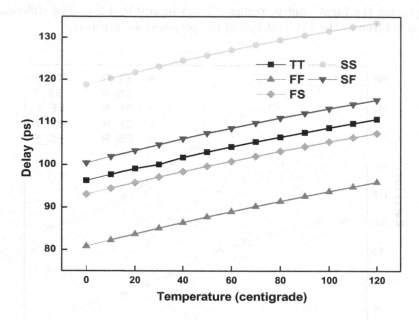

Fig. 6. Delay with respect to temperature across process corners (TT- typical NMOS and PMOS, SS- slow NMOS and PMOS, FF- fast NMOS and PMOS, SF- slow NMOS and fast PMOS, FS- fast NMOS and slow PMOS)

Delay characteristics with temperature variations from 0 °C to 120 °C across process corners is shown in Fig. 6. There is a 1 ps to 1.5 ps delay raise per 10 °C raise of temperature and total of 15 ps delay variation from 0^{circ}C to 120 °C. The delay characteristics for temperature variations across process corners shows the similar characteristics and the characteristics are shifted up to a maximum of 22 ps for SS process corner, and shifted down to a minimum of 16 ps for FF process corner from typical characteristics.

The delay characteristics with variation of supply voltage is shown in Fig. 7. There is linear variation of delay with supply across the process corners. There is 9 ps fall of delay from its typical value for 100 mV rise in V_{DD} and the 12ps rise of delay from its typical value for 100 mV fall in V_{DD}. The delay characteristics with respect to supply variations across process corners shows the similar characteristics, these are shifted up by maximum of 27 ps and minimum of 19 ps for V_{DD}, 1.1 V and 1.3 V respectively from typical characteristics for SS process corner and these are shifted down by maximum of 18 ps and minimum of 13 ps for V_{DD}, 1.1 V and 1.3 V respectively from typical characteristics for FF process corner.

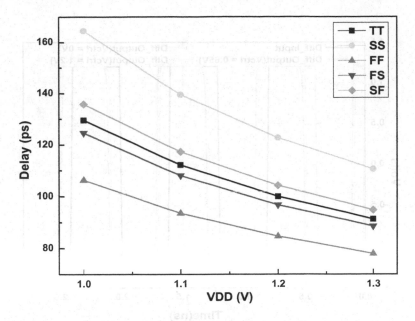

Fig. 7. Delay with respect to V_{DD} across process corners (TT- typical NMOS and PMOS, SS- slow NMOS and PMOS, FF- fast NMOS and PMOS, SF- slow NMOS and fast PMOS, FS- fast NMOM and slow PMOS)

Figures 5, 6, and 7 shows the variations of delay with respect to control voltage, temperature and supply voltage for SF and FS process corners are also similar to the typical (TT) corner. Figure 8 shows the differential output of the delay element at input control voltage of 650 mV and two extremes (0 V and 1.2 V). The differential transient response shows the output with the swing rail-to-rail. The CSI, wide range CSI [5] also simulated in 65 nm CMOS process along with the proposed architecture and the comparison of power consumption of these architecture with the proposed architectures is shown in Fig. 9. *The power metrics shows, the proposed delay element consumes 52 times lesser power consumption than conventional delay element (CSI) and 21 times lesser power consumption than wide-range CSI.* Figure 10 shows the layout of the proposed architecture. Core area of the delay element is 0.0018 mm², in that more than half of the area is occupied by the variable capacitors. The performance results of the proposed architecture are summarized in Table 1.

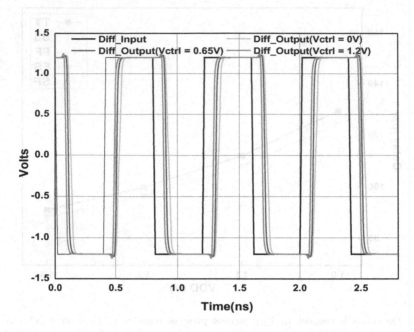

Fig. 8. Transient response of proposed architecture at $V_{ctrl} = 0\,\mathrm{V}$, $0.65\,\mathrm{V}$ and $1.2\,\mathrm{V}$

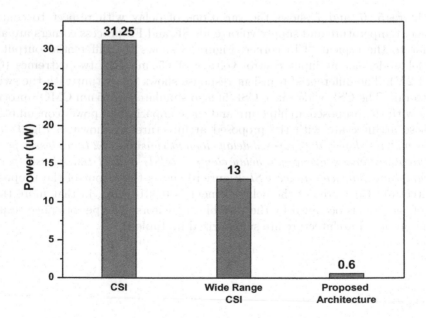

Fig. 9. Power consumption of CSI, wide-range CSI and proposed architecture

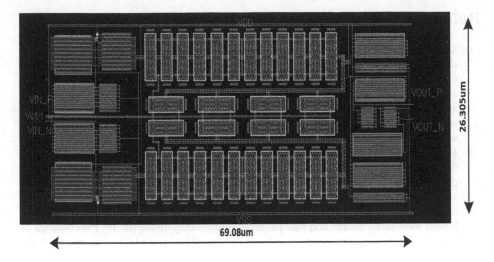

Fig. 10. Layout of the proposed delay element

Table 1. Performance summary of the proposed architecture

Technology	65 nm
V_{DD}	1.2 V
Power	0.6 μW
Area	0.0018 mm^2
Delay range	80 ps–120 ps
Control voltage range	0 V–1.2 V

5 Conclusion

A new robust, low-power, charge controlled, widely linear differential delay element for multi-phase clock generation in 1.2 V, 65 nm CMOS is proposed in this work. It introduces a novel technique to vary the delay by using transmission gates and variable capacitors with out the need for any duty cycle correction circuitry. These features enables the proposed design to employ in fine and coarse delay line to use in DLLs. To the best of authors knowledge, the proposed delay element circuit topology shows the lowest power consumption of 0.6 μW and wide linearity with robustness, while operating at a maximum frequency of 1.5 GHz with a bandwidth of 500 MHz. It occupies an area of 0.0018 mm^2 in 1.2 V, UMC 65 nm CMOS. Thus, the proposed delay element circuit topology is a good candidate for deploying in multi-phase clock generation delay locked loops (MPCG-DLL's)

References

1. Mahapatra, N.R., Tareen, A., Garimella, S.V.: Comparison and analysis of delay elements. In: The 2002 45th Midwest Symposium on Circuits and Systems, MWS-CAS 2002, Tulsa, OK, USA, p. II (2002). https://doi.org/10.1109/MWSCAS.2002.1186901
2. Jovanovic, G.S., Stojcev, M.K.: Linear current starved delay element. In: International Scientific Conference on Information Communication and Energy Systems and Technologies (2005)
3. Moon, Y., Choi, J., Lee, K., Jeong, D.-K., Kim, M.-K.: An all-analog multiphase delay-locked loop using a replica delay line for wide-range operation and low-jitter performance. IEEE J. Solid-State Circ. **35**(3), 377–384 (2000). https://doi.org/10.1109/4.826820
4. Jasielski, J., Kuta, S., Machowski, W., Kołodziejski, W.: An analog dual delay locked loop using coarse and fine programmable delay elements. In: Proceedings of the 20th International Conference Mixed Design of Integrated Circuits and Systems - MIXDES 2013, Gdynia, pp. 185–190 (2013)
5. Lu, C., Hsieh, H., Lu, L.: A 0.6 V low-power wide-range delay-locked loop in 0.18 μm CMOS. IEEE Microwave Wirel. Components Lett. **19**(10), 662–664 (2009). https://doi.org/10.1109/LMWC.2009.2029752
6. Foley, D.J., Flynn, M.P.: CMOS DLL-based 2-V 3.2-ps jitter 1-GHz clock synthesizer and temperature-compensated tunable oscillator. IEEE J. Solid-State Circ. **36**(3), 417–423 (2001). https://doi.org/10.1109/4.910480
7. Jacob Baker, R.: CMOS Circuit Design, Layout, and Simulation, 2nd edn, pp. 596–600. IEEE Press, Piscataway (2012)
8. Bayram, E., Aref, A.F., Saeed, M., Negra, R.: 1.5-3.3 GHz, 0.0077 mm^2, 7 mW all-digital delay-locked loop with dead-zone free phase detector in 0.13 μm CMOS. IEEE Trans. Circ. Syst. I: Regul. Pap. **65**(1), 39–50 (2018). https://doi.org/10.1109/TCSI.2017.2715899
9. Staszewski, R.B., et al.: All-digital TX frequency synthesizer and discrete-time receiver for Bluetooth radio in 130-nm CMOS. IEEE J. Solid-State Circ. **39**(12), 2278–2291 (2004). https://doi.org/10.1109/JSSC.2004.836345
10. Jovanović, G., Stojcev, M.: Voltage controlled delay line for digital signal. Facta universitatis - Ser.: Electron. Energetics **16**, 215–232 (2003). https://doi.org/10.2298/FUEE0302215J
11. Sharma, A., Alam, N., Bulusu, A.: Effective current model for inverter-transmission gate structure and its application in circuit design. IEEE Trans. Electron Devices **64**(10), 4002–4010 (2017). https://doi.org/10.1109/TED.2017.2742358

A CMOS Low Noise Amplifier
with Improved Gain

Sunanda Ambulker[1](✉) (iD), Jitendra Kumar Mishra[1] (iD),
and Sangeeta Nakhate[2]

[1] IIIT Allahabad, Prayagraj 211015, Uttar Pradesh, India
sunandaambulkar@gmail.com
[2] MANIT Bhopal, Bhopal 462003, Madhya Pradesh, India

Abstract. In this paper, an improved gain CMOS Low Noise Amplifier
(LNA) is presented. Here a single stage common source amplifier with common
gate as cascode circuit is used to design the LNA. It is having small signal gain
of 14.4 dB and covers the bandwidth from 4.47 GHz to 5.41 GHz. It has been
observed that at the center frequency of 5 GHz the input and output return loss
are −17.98 dB and −15.86 dB respectively. A 1 dB compression point is at
−14.85 dBm at 5 GHz input frequency. From 1.8 V supply voltage, 4.67 mA
current is drawn.

Keywords: Cascode amplifiers · Current source · Low Noise Amplifier (LNA) ·
CMOS · Noise figure

1 Introduction

In the RF front-end receiver the low noise, low cost and low power are basic performance requirements for the wireless communication applications. These requirements
depend on the various sub blocks of the RF front-end receiver. The Main building
blocks of the RF front-end receiver are Low Noise Amplifier (LNA), filter, mixer, ADC
etc. Being the first block of the receiver front end the design of the LNA plays the crucial
role in the overall performance of the wireless communication system. The design of
LNA is governed by certain performance parameters [1, 2] such as linearity, Noise
Figure (NF), stability, input return loss, output return loss, and gain. Power is also of
concern for wireless system. Several different LNAs have been reported in literature for
wireless communication application covering the millimeter wave (mmw) frequency
band. In [3] the Common Gate (CG) UWB LNA was designed. To improve the noise
figure and bandwidth a common-drain feedback and an inductive shunt peaking in the
load respectively is also proposed in [4]. In [5] to implement ultra wideband LNA based
on a new dual-channel shunt technique is presented. In this technique, two channels are
used in which one uses an inductive-series peaking technique and another channel uses a
resistive feedback technique. Using such techniques, it could achieve flat gain over the
intended frequency range and wideband input impedance matching respectively. An
Inductor-less low noise amplifier is used in [6], which can be used for wireless sensor
network where current reuse scheme and shunt feedback structure are utilized for low
power dissipation and good input matching respectively.

© Springer Nature Singapore Pte Ltd. 2019
A. Sengupta et al. (Eds.): VDAT 2019, CCIS 1066, pp. 215–223, 2019.
https://doi.org/10.1007/978-981-32-9767-8_19

In this paper, a low noise amplifier for mmw application is designed using 180 nm CMOS technology. In this design for input matching, a parallel capacitor is used and a parallel combination of two common gate NMOS transistor at output are used for reducing noise.

The rest of the paper is organized as follow: Sect. 2 gives the design of CMOS LNA and its analysis. Simulation results are presented in Sect. 3, which is followed, by conclusion and references.

2   Design of CMOS LNA and Its Analysis

Figure 1 shows the schematic of proposed LNA. A cascode configuration is used for the design of high gain LNA. Transistor NM1 is common source degeneration amplifier and NM2, NM3 are common gate amplifier, by using these cascode network reverse isolation is improved, C_{in} is the input dc blocking capacitor, C_{out} is output blocking capacitor, L_s is source degeneration inductor, which is used to give the input matching and high input impedance. For good and efficient input matching a capacitor, C_c in parallel with Ls is used. L_g is gate inductor used to tune out the effect of C_{in} and set the resonant frequency. L_d is drain inductor used to tuned the output and increase gain and also work as a band pass filter form with C_{Tune}. The overall performance of the low noise amplifier is determined by the gain, noise figure, input, and output reflection coefficients, stability factor. Hence the optimization of the circuit is done such a way to obtain moderate values of such parameters.

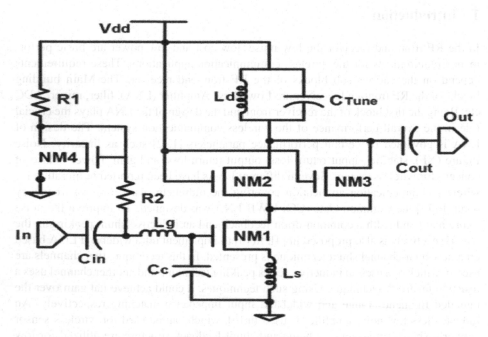

Fig. 1. Schematic of LNA

The optimized device sizes are given in Table 1. Minimum length of the all MOSFETs are chosen here. To increase the width of the transistor and reduce the resistive loss, multiple fingers are used. All the Inductors e.g. L_g, L_s and L_d are spiral in shape.

Table 1. Optimized device sizes.

Device	Size
NM1	27.5 * 4
NM/NM3	25 * 2
NM4	6 * 2
L_g	3.39 nH
L_s	585.83 pH
Cc	103 fF
R1	603 Ω
R2	603 Ω
L_d	3.39 nH
C_{in}	4.92 pF
C_{out}	180.88 fF

3   Simulation Results and Discussion

To validate the proposed CMOS LNA design, simulation is performed in cadence virtuoso environment with UMC 180 nm technology. With 1.8 V supply the proposed LNA consumes 8.42 mW of power. The different simulated gain plots of Available gain (GA), Power Gain (GP) and Transducer Gain (GT) are depicted in Fig. 2. As it can be seen in the plot that the gain GP is closer to GT, which indicates that the input matching is done properly. Figure 3 illustrates the variation of various S-parameters of LNA with respect to (wrt) input frequency. Figures 4 and 5 shows the VSWR curve and Noise Figure (NF) curve respectively wrt input frequency. Input referred 1 dB Compression point curve is illustrated in Fig. 6. The various important performance parameters of LNA are summarized in Table 2 at 5 GHz, frequency stability factor (kf) is greater than 1 i.e. 14.1, which indicates that the proposed LNA is stable. Table 2 represents the various performance parameters of proposed CMOS LNA design at 1.8 V supply voltage (Fig. 7).

Table 2. Performance summary of the proposed LNA.

S11 (dB)	−17.98
S12 (dB)	13.23
S21 (dB)	−39.788
S22 (dB)	−15.86
NF (dB)	2.045
IP3	−14.85 dBm
Power consumption (mW)	8.42
Stability factor (kf)	10.1
VSWR1 (dB)	2.20
VSWR2 (dB)	2.85
Gain (dB)	14.4
BW (GHz)	4.47 to 5.41

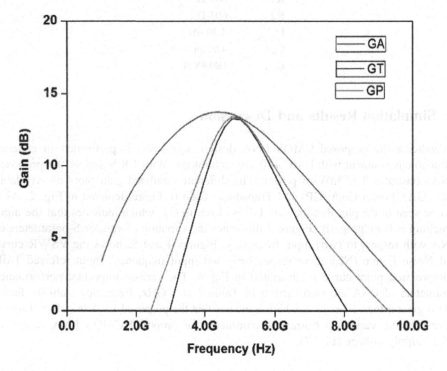

Fig. 2. GA, GP and GT vs frequency

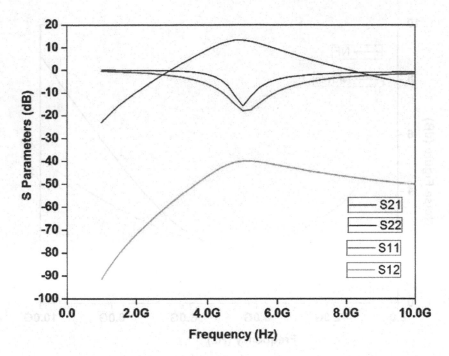

Fig. 3. S-Parameters

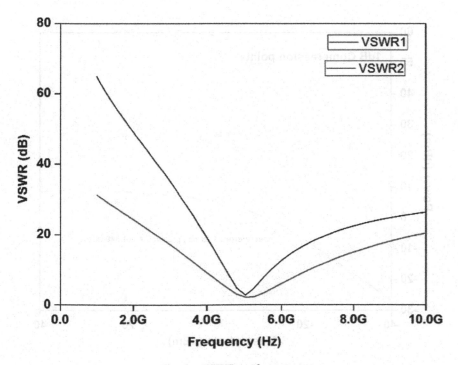

Fig. 4. VSWR vs frequency

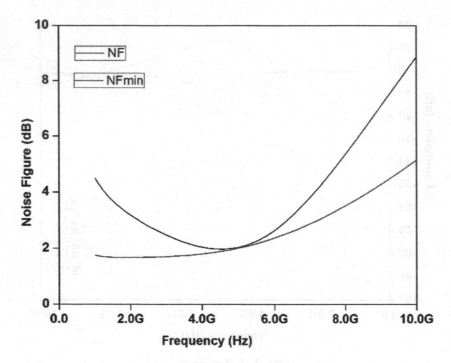

Fig. 5. NF vs input frequency

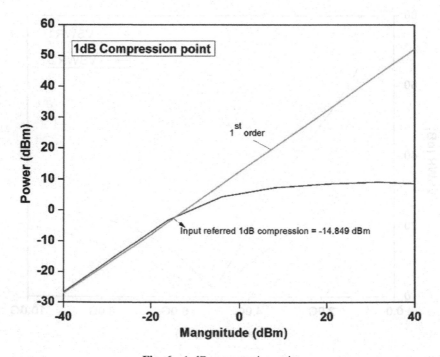

Fig. 6. 1 dB compression point

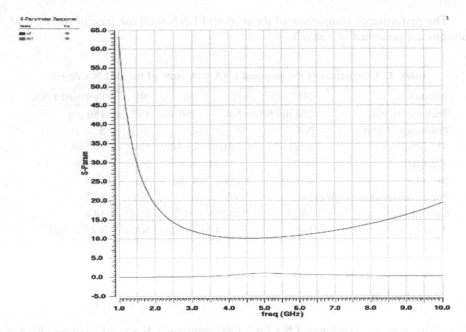

Fig. 7. Stability factor vs input frequency

Figure 8 shows the layout of proposed design, which consume the area about 0.9×1.5 mm^2.

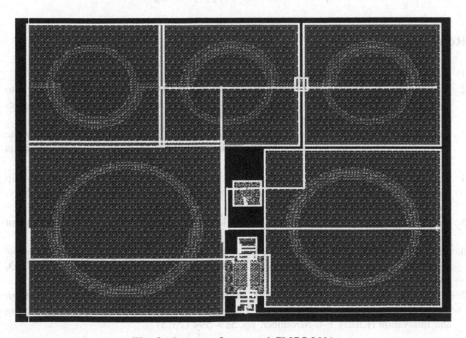

Fig. 8. Layout of proposed CMOS LNA

The performance comparison of the proposed LNA with the state of the art LNA designs are presented in Table 3.

Table 3. Comparison of the proposed LNA with state of the art LNA designs

Parameters	[4]	[7]	[8]	[9]	Proposed LNA
Technology (nm)	250 nm SiGe	NA	180 nm	180 nm	180 nm
Frequency (GHz)	NA	4	4	6	5
S11 (dB)	<−11	−61.11	<−10.3	NA	−17.98
S22 (dB)	<−35	−16.61	NA	NA	−15.86
NF (dB)	4.1/4.5	1.062	4 dB	5.5	2.04
Power consumption (mW)	24	NA	6	NA	8.42
Gain (dB)	14.25	10.288	10.5	13.1	14.4
Bandwidth (GHz)	5–6	3.5–4.5	3–5.6	NA	4.47 to 5.41
Supply voltage (V)	1.8	NA	1.8	1.8	1.8

4 Conclusion

This paper presents a high gain LNA for 5 GHz frequency. For good input matching, a parallel capacitor is used in the proposed design, which results in an improvement in the input matching of the circuit. For high gain a cascode configuration is utilized which provides a gain of 14.4 dB. At a targeted frequency of 5 GHz NF is 2.04 dB and it dissipates 8.42 mW of power from 1.8 V supply voltage.

References

1. Razavi, B.: RF Microelectronics. Prentice Hall, Upper Saddle River (1998)
2. Subramanian, V., Spiegel, S., Eickhoff, R., Boeck, G.: A CMOS low noise amplifier for 5 to 6 GHz wireless applications. In: SBMO/IEEE MTT-S International Microwave & Optoelectronics Conference (IMOC), pp. 778–781 (2007)
3. Fan, X., Sánchez-Sinencio, E., Silva-Martinez, J.: A 3 GHz–10 GHz common gate ultrawideband low noise amplifier. In: Proceedings of IEEE Midwest Symposium Circuits and Systems, August 2005
4. EL-Gharniti, O., Kerherve, E., Begueret, J.-B.: A 5 GHz low noise amplifier with on-chip transformer-balun. In: Proceedings of the 9th European Conference on Wireless Technology, pp. 353–356, September 2006
5. Lai, Q.-T., Mao, J.-F.: A 0.5–11 GHz CMOS low noise amplifier using dual-channel shunt technique. IEEE Microwave Wirel. Components Lett. **20**, 280–282 (2010)
6. khabbaz, A., Sobhi, J., Koozehkanani, Z.D.: A sub-mW 2.9-dB noise figure Inductor-less low noise amplifier for wireless sensor network applications. Int. J. Electron. Commun. (AEÜ) **93**, 132–139 (2018)
7. Charchian, M., Zakeri, B., Miar-niami, H.: Wideband noise figure low noise amplifier design for 3.5 GHz to 4.5 GHz. In: 2nd International Conference on Knowledge-Based Engineering and Innovation (KBEI), 5–6 November, pp. 589–594 (2015)

8. Zokaei, A., Afzali, M., Alvankarian, B.J., Dousti, M.: 3–5 GHz ultra wideband common-gate low noise amplifier. In: 2012 IEEE International Conference on Circuits and Systems (ICCAS), pp. 98–102 (2012)
9. Andersson, S., Svenson, C., Drugge, O.: Wideband LNA for a multi standard wireless receiver in 0.18 µm CMOS. In: Proceedings of the ESSC, pp. 655–658, September 2003

Radiation Hardened by Design Sense Amplifier

Avinash Verma[✉] and Gaurav Kaushal

ABV IIITM, Gwalior 474015, MP, India
imavinashverma99@gmail.com

Abstract. This paper presents a fully symmetrical radiation hardened sense amplifier is designed in and 32 nm FinFET Double gate PTM technology to tolerate single node upset and multiple-node upset.circuit. A 9 pC charge is used at critical node of the sense amplifier to analyse Single Event Transient. The Experimental results on sensing delay, input offset voltage, power comparision and critical charge demonstrated the effectiveness of the proposed scheme.

Keywords: SEU · FINFET · Double gate · Soft error · Critical charge

1 Introduction

MEMORIES are widely used in aerospace applications as the medium to store data in which single event upsets (SEUs) induced by radiation particles are becoming one of the most significant issues [1–5]. Performance of memory and its peripheral circuits like sense amplifier, row decoder and column decoder can be affected by these radiations. As When these radiations hits a node of a sense amplifier, the induced charge along its path can be collected and accumulated through drift processes. Once a transient current pulse generated by the accumulated charge is above the switching threshold of the circuit, the stored value in this node will be changed [6]. To prevent loss of data due to radiation, electronic design techniques are required. The technique of implementing a system which can tolerate radiation is called radiation hardening [7].

Sense Amplifier is the vital circuit in the periphery of CMOS memory as its job is to sense stored data from selected memory. As shown in Fig. 1 in one column of memory array multiple memory cells are connected. Thus the capacitance of bitline increases there by increasing the discharging time of bitline. To decrease the read access time of memory array sense amplifier is used for each coloumn of memory. The sense amplifier senses the difference of bitline voltages and produces the correct output in very less amount of time. Thus performance of sense amplifiers strongly affects memory read access time. Hence it is necessary to design robust sense amplifiers that can provide high radiation hardening capability.

The primary design concerns in radiation hardened sense amplifier are critical charge, sensing delay, input offset voltage and power consumption. [8–11]. The

© Springer Nature Singapore Pte Ltd. 2019
A. Sengupta et al. (Eds.): VDAT 2019, CCIS 1066, pp. 224–235, 2019.
https://doi.org/10.1007/978-981-32-9767-8_20

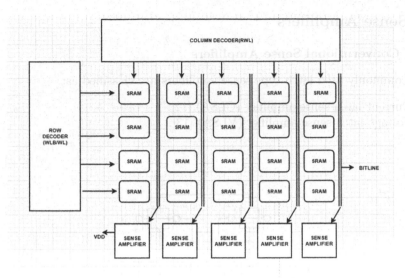

Fig. 1. Block diagram of memory array.

performance of radiation hardened sense amplifiers is determined primarily by the critical charge. As higher the critical charge higher SEU tolerance can be achieved. Another important parameter of sense amplifier is sensing delay. It is necessary to reduce the sensing delay to have a high performance sense amplifier. The robustness of the sense amplifier is determined by the input offset voltage i.e. the minimum voltage difference between the bit-lines that can be correctly sensed.

The double-gate concept considerably increases the efficiency of transistors as they are scaled down as compared to planar CMOS. Thus double-gate (DG) devices have emerged as a very promising candidate for circuit design. The gate to channel coupling is doubled and hence short channel effects are easily suppressed. The double-gate (DG) devices have good carrier mobility in reduced dimensions and hence better intrinsic switching time. Alse the leakage currents are reduced. The current driving capability of DGFET is twice that of planar CMOS and hence DGFETs can be operated at much lower input and threshold voltages. Thus power consumption is less in DGFETs.

To achieve high radiation tolerence with lower power consumption a radiation hardened sense amplifier is proposed by using the double gated FINFET technology.

The rest of the paper is described as follows. Section 2 includes the architecture of traditional Sense amplifiers and design of proposed radiation hardened sense amplifier. Section 3 consists of different analysis on proposed RHBD sense amplifier. Comparision with previous reported sense amplifiers is also presented. The conclusion is summarized in Sect. 4.

2   Sense Amplifiers

2.1   Converntional Sense Amplifiers

The commonly used latch type sense amplifiers are classified as:

(1) Current latch sense amplifier (CLSA) [12].
(2) Voltage latch sense amplifier (VLSA) [13].

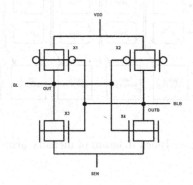

Fig. 2. Circuit diagram of DTVLSA.

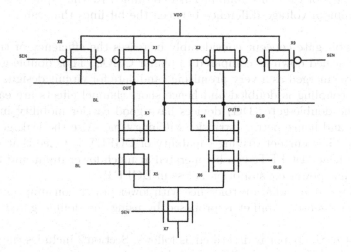

Fig. 3. Circuit diagram of DTCLSA.

VLSA and CLSA circuits designed in single gate technology are directly converted to Double gate-FinFET technology by changing each transistor with a tied gate (TG). These configuration are referred as DTVLSA (Directly Translated Voltage Latch Sense Amplifier) and DTCLSA (Directly Translated Current Latch Sense Amplifier) respectively. Figure 2 shows the direct translation of VLSA to DG-FinFET technology. DTCLSA has been reported [14,15] al., 2006 and the circuit diagram is reproduced in Fig. 3. The design of DTVLSA and DTCLSA has been based on the classic cross-coupled latch structure.

The current latch sense amplifier called independent gate sense amplifier (IGSA) has been reported [15]. Current difference in pull down paths is achieved by only one transistor in each pull down path in IGSA as compared to two transistors in each pull down path in DTCLSA. IGSA has primary advantage of an increased discharging current, reduced area as compared to DTCLSA and increased gain of the cross coupled inverters. This in turn reduces the sensing delay, increases the speed and reduces the switching power. Disadvantage of IGSA is that it is not tolerant to single event upset.

Another reported sense amplifier is the RHIGSA (Radiation hardened independent gate sense amplifier) design [16]. RHIGSA has separate input and output nodes. Hence RHIGSA has accelerated sensing speed, and it can be used for low voltage operation. RHIGSA design has 4 critical nodes which shows complete immunity against single event upset. Disadvantage of RHIGSA is that it is not tolerant to multi node upset.

2.2   Proposed Radiation Hardened by Design Sense Amplifier

The circuit is made of totally 11 double gated FinFet transistors, Six pMOS and five nMOS. OUT and OUTB are two primary nodes and A and B are the two secondary storage nodes. Nodes OUT and B maintain same logic values and nodes OUTB and A are at same logic values.

There are two access transistors M9 and M10 for read operation and inputs of sense amplifier are BL and BLB.

Node A and B of circuit is associated with only pMOS transistors which are used to avoid negative transient pulse. This idea is behind the fact that when ionizing particle striking on pMOS transistor produce only positive current pulses (Fig. 4).

2.3   Operation

The operation of sense amplifier has two phases namely pre-charge and sense signal amplification. In the pre-charging phase, SA signal is kept 'low' and the output nodes OUT and OUTB are charged to voltages same as bitlines. Bit-lines are used to transfer data between SRAM and sense amplifier. In the sensing phase, SEN signal goes 'high'. This activates the cross-coupled structure and drives the outputs to the appropriate values.

If voltage of BL is higher then BLB then node OUT is charged to VDD while voltage at OUTB goes to zero. This is called read 1 operation. Where as OUTB is charged to VDD if BLB voltage is higher then bl. This is called read 0 operation (Fig. 5).

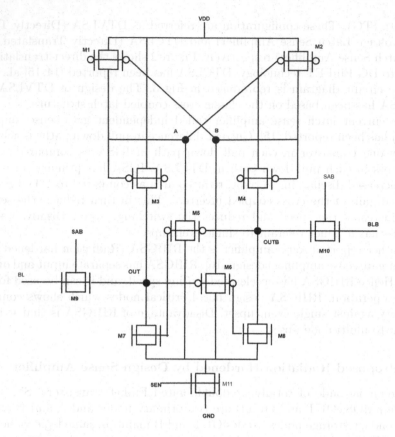

Fig. 4. Proposed radiation hardened by design sense amplifier

3   Analysis

This section includes the soft error, sensing delay, input offset voltage, power dissipation and critical charge analysis of proposed RHBD sense amplifier. The circuit is benchmarked with respect to conventional and reported sense amplifiers. All analysis are performed by using synopsys HSPICE tool by using 32 nm PTM double gated FinFet technology.

3.1   Soft Error Analysis of Proposed Sense Amplifier

A soft error is a particle strike that affects node of an sense amplifier and if its charge deposited value is greater than the critical charge than data will flip. The critical charge is defined as the minimum charge value needed to flip the state of sense amplifier. To model a particle strike by injecting a double exponential current pulse in a node.

In this section single node and multi node is discussed. Node A and B is associated with pMOS transistors thus only positive transient current 0 to 1 upset

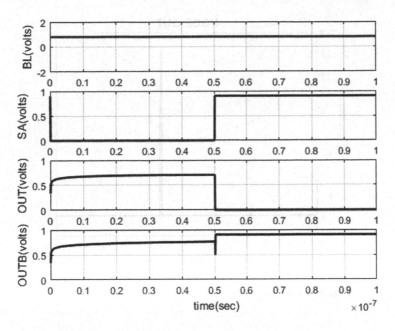

Fig. 5. Read 1 operation of proposed sense amplifier circuit

Table 1. Critical charge values of all nodes in proposed RHBD sense amplifier.

Node	Critical charge
A	900 fC
B	900 fc
OUT(0 to 1)	9 pC
OUT(1 to 0)	100 fC
OUTB(0 to 1)	9 pC
OUTB(1 to 0)	100 fC
OUT (1 to 0) and OUTB (0 to 1)	400 fC
OUT (0 to 1) and OUTB (1 to 0)	400 fC
OUT (0 to 1) and B (0 to 1)	298 fC
OUTB (1 to 0) and B (0 to 1)	298 fC
OUT (1 to 0) and A (0 to 1)	298 fC
OUTB (0 to 1) and A (0 to 1)	298 fC

will happen. For node OUT and OUTB both positive and negative transient upset is applied (Table 1).

1. **OUT (0 to 1)** When OUT is upset by a particle strike it will be pulled up to 1. But on the other side node OUTB remain same. As OUTB is 1 thus

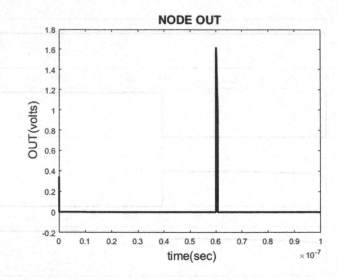

Fig. 6. Fault injection simulation of node OUT(0 to 1)

M7 remains ON there by discharging OUT and pulling back to initial state (Fig. 6).

2. **OUT (1 to 0)** When OUT is upset by a particle strike it will be pulled down to 0. But on the other side node A remain same. As A is 0 thus M3 remains ON there by charging OUT and pulling it back to previous state (Fig. 7).

3. **QUTB (0 to 1)** When OUTB is upset by a particle strike it will be pulled up to 1. But on the other side node OUT remain same. As OUT is 1 thus M8 remains ON there by discharging OUTBB and pulling it back to initial state (Fig. 8).

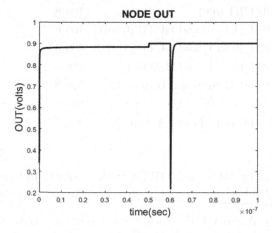

Fig. 7. Fault injection simulation of node OUT(1 to 0)

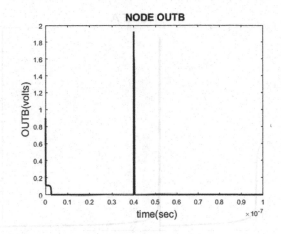

Fig. 8. Fault injection simulation of node OUTB(0 to 1)

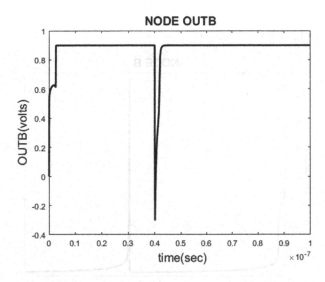

Fig. 9. Fault injection simulation of node OUTB(1 to 0)

4. **OUTB (1 to 0)** When OUTB is upset by a particle strike it will be pulled down to 0. But on the other side node B remain same. As B is 0 thus M4 remains ON thereby charging OUTB and pulling it back to initial state (Fig. 9).

5. **A (0 to 1)** When A is upset by a particle strike it will be pulled up to 1. But on the other side node OUTB remain same. As OUTB is 0 thus M5 remains ON there by discharging A and pulling it back to initial state (Fig. 10).

6. **B (0 to 1)** When B is upset by a particle strike it will be pulled up to 1. But on the other side node OUT remain same. As OUT is 0 thus M6 remains ON there by discharging B and pulling it back to normal state (Fig. 11).

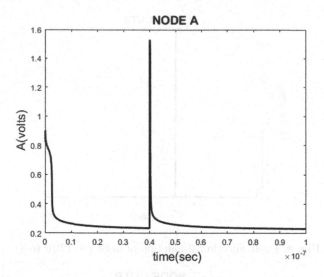

Fig. 10. Fault injection simulation of node A(0 to 1)

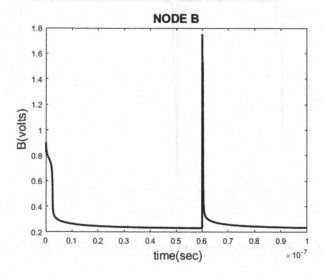

Fig. 11. Fault injection simulation of node B(0 to 1)

3.2   Sensing Delay

Sensing delay is one of the important parameter that decides performance of a sense amplifier. Sense delay is defined as time at which sense enable signal rises to Vdd/2 to the time at which output drops to Vdd/2 (Fig. 12).

The time taken for reading the data from memory cell is defined as read access time. The time taken for node to charge from 0 to 50% of power supply is called read 1 access time. Whereas time taken for node to discharge from 1

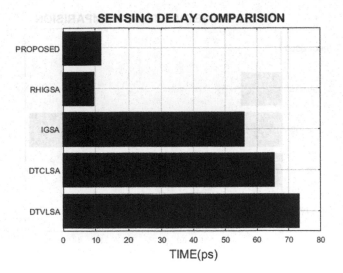

Fig. 12. Sensing delay of different sense amplifier.

to 10% of power supply is called read 0 access time. Sensing delay affects the access time of memory. Figure shows the result of sensing delay of different sense amplifier circuits. The sensing delay of proposed sense amplifier is found to be 11.23 ps.

3.3   Input Offset Voltage

The robustness of the sense amplifier is determined by the input offset voltage i.e. the minimum voltage difference between the bit-lines that can be correctly sensed. For input offset voltage calculation Bitline (BL) is provided with supply of VDD where as bitline bar (BLB) is charged from 0.88VDD to VDD. The input offset voltage of proposed sense amplifier is found to be 0.001 V (Fig. 13).

3.4   Power Comparision

The static power consumption of the circuit is measured by giving initial condition to bitlines and power supply is connected to circuit. Figure 14 shows the power consumption of different sense amplifier circuits.

3.5   Critical Charge Comparision

Node upset is checked by injecting a double exponential current pulse in both primary and secondary nodes of sense amplifier. The value of current pulse at which the circuit output node value starts to flip is taken for critical charge calculation. Critical charge value for various nodes of sense amplifier is shown (Table 2).

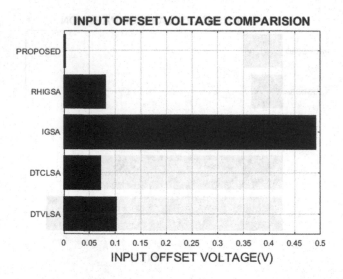

Fig. 13. Input offset voltage of different sense amplifier

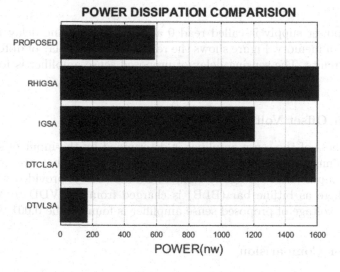

Fig. 14. Power comparision of different sense amplifier

Table 2. Critical charge comparision

Sense amplifier	Single node	Multi node
DTVLSA	0	0
DTCLSA	0	0
IGSA	10 fC	0
RHIGSA	Tolerant	0
PROPOSED	9 pC	400 fC

References

1. Ibe, E., Taniguchi, H., Yahagi, Y., Shimbo, K.-I., Toba, T.: Impact of scaling on neutron-induced soft error in SRAMs from a 250 nm to a 22 nm design rule. IEEE Trans. Electron Devices **57**(7), 1527–1538 (2010)
2. Dodd, P.E., Massengill, L.W.: Basic mechanisms and modeling of single-event upset in digital microelectronics. IEEE Trans. Nucl. Sci. **50**(3), 583–602 (2003)
3. Baumann, R.C.: Soft errors in advanced semiconductor devices part I: the three radiation sources. IEEE Trans. Device Mater. Rel. **1**(1), 17–22 (2001)
4. Hughes, H.L., Benedetto, J.M.: Radiation effects and hardening of MOS technology: devices and circuits. IEEE Trans. Nucl. Sci. **50**(3), 500–521 (2003)
5. Boatella, C., Hubert, G., Ecoffet, R., Duzellier, S.: ICARE on-board SAC-C: more than 8 years of SEU and MCU, analysis and prediction. IEEE Trans. Nucl. Sci. **57**(4), 2000–2009 (2003)
6. Yan, A., Huang, Z., Yi, M., Xu, X., Ouyang, Y., Liang, H.: Double-node-upset-resilient latch design for nanoscale CMOS technology. IEEE Trans. Very Large Scale Integr. (VLSI) Syst. **25**(6), 1978–1982 (2017)
7. Chen, Z., Lin, M., Ding, D., Zheng, Y., Sang, Z., Zou, S.: Analysis of single-event effects in a radiation-hardened low-jitter PLL under heavy ion and pulsed laser irradiation. IEEE Trans. Nucl. Sci. **64**(1), 106–112 (2017)
8. Chow, H.C., Chang, S.H.: High performance sense amplifier circuit for low power SRAM applications. In: Proceedings of IEEE International Conference ISCAS, pp. II-741–II-744 (2004)
9. Golden, M., Tran, J., McGee, B., Kuo, B.: Sense amp design in SOI. In: Proceedings of IEEE International SOI Conference, pp. 118–120 (2005)
10. Choudhary, A., Kundu, S.: A process variation tolerant self compensating sense amplifier design. In: Proceedings of IEEE Computer Society Annual Symposium on VLSI (ISVLSI 2009), pp. 263–267 (2009)
11. Choudhary, A., Kundu, S.: A process variation tolerant self compensating Fin-FET based sense amplifier design. In: Proceedings of ACM Great Lakes Symposium on VLSI (GLSVLSI 2009), pp. 161–164 (2009)
12. Kobayashi, T., et al.: A current-controlled latch sense amplifier and a static power-saving input buffer for low-power architecture. IEICE Trans. Electron. **76**(5), 863–867 (1993)
13. Sinha, M., et al.: High-performance and low-voltage sense-amplifier techniques for sub-90 nm SRAM. In: Proceedings of IEEE International [Systems-on-Chip] SOC Conference. IEEE (2003)
14. Yeung, J., Mahmoodi, H.: Robust sense amplifier design under random dopant fluctuations in nano-scale CMOS technologies. In: 2006 IEEE International SOC Conference. IEEE (2006)
15. Mukhopadhyay, S., Mahmoodi, H., Roy, K.: A novel high-performance and robust sense amplifier using independent gate control in sub-50-nm double-gate MOSFET. IEEE Trans. Very Large Scale Integr. (VLSI) Syst. **14**(2), 183–192 (2006)
16. Rathod, S.S., Saxena, A.K., Dasgupta, S.: A low-noise, process-variation-tolerant double-gate FinFET based sense amplifier. Microelectron. Reliab. **51**(4), 773–780 (2011)
17. Lupo, N., Bonizzoni, E., Maloberti, F.: A cross-coupled redundant sense amplifier for radiation hardened SRAMs. In: 2017 New Generation of CAS (NGCAS). IEEE (2017)

Delay Efficient All Optical Carry Lookahead Adder

Sayantani Roy[1(✉)], Arighna Deb[2], and Debesh K. Das[1]

[1] Department of Computer Science & Engineering, Jadavpur University,
Kolkata, India
sayantaniroy44@gmail.com, debeshd@hotmail.com
[2] School of Electronics Engineering, KIIT University, Bhubaneswar, India
arighna87@rediffmail.com

Abstract. Carry look ahead adders (CLA) are the fastest of all adders and achieve high speed through parallel carry computations. This method does not require the carry signal to propagate stage by stage. In this paper, an efficient all-optical realization of CLA is proposed using Mach–Zehnder interferometer (MZI) gates. Experimental results confirm the efficacy of the proposed design over similar existing designs.

Keywords: Carry Lookahead Adder (CLA) ·
Mach-Zehnder Interferometer (MZI) · Optical cost · Optical delay

1 Introduction

Optical circuits emerge as an alternative to current circuit technologies thanks to the advances in silicon photonics [1]. They allow for ultra-high speed network while having beneficial low power properties. In electronic digital systems, optical technology is already in use as ultra-fast interconnects [2, 3]. This requires conversion from the electrical to optical and optical to electrical domain at every interconnect interface. This is obviously a significant drawback which can easily be avoided if the underlying systems are realized by optical technologies only. This motivates research in the area of designing all-optical circuits.

Thus far, all-optical digital design involves the realizations of basic Boolean operations [4–6] and some important arithmetic units such as adder/subtractor [7–14], multiplexer [15, 16]. Since adders are the basic building blocks in the arithmetic logic units (ALUs), the designs of adder circuits, like in traditional technology, have also received significant attention in optical technology.

It is well-established that a Carry Look-ahead Adder (CLA) improves the speed of additions over a ripple carry adder (RCA) [17] by generating all the carry bits in parallel. This look-ahead carry generation method makes the CLA a high speed logic unit for addition. The advantage of CLA is that the additions is done in constant time, whereas it is O(n) in case of ripple carry adder. The disadvantage of CLA is that it needs more hardware to achieve the better timing performance.

Like traditional design the researchers also concentrated on the all-optical implementations of CLA. The all-optical implementations of CLA using Mach-Zehnder Interferometer (MZI) switches (or simply called as MZI gates) is reported in [13, 14].

© Springer Nature Singapore Pte Ltd. 2019
A. Sengupta et al. (Eds.): VDAT 2019, CCIS 1066, pp. 236–244, 2019.
https://doi.org/10.1007/978-981-32-9767-8_21

In this paper, we propose an all-optical realization of Carry Look-ahead Adder (CLA) using an optical gate library composed of MZI gate, splitter and combiner. Like traditional design CLA using MZI gates cannot offer constant time as MZI gates use only two inputs. We show that this time is at least $\lceil \log n \rceil + 2$ for an n-bit circuit. The proposed all-optical CLA circuit generates outputs with less delay as compared to the existing adder designs [11–13] proving the efficacy of our technique.

The rest of the paper is structured as follows. Section 2 reviews the basics on optical circuits and the commonly applied gate library. The proposed all-optical realization of CLA is introduced in Sect. 3. Different parameter calculation is summarized in Sect. 4 while the paper is concluded with a discussion on the future scope in Sect. 5.

2 Optical Circuits

To keep the paper self-contained, this section briefly reviews the common logic model and gate library used in the domain of optical logic synthesis. Mach-Zehnder Interferometer (MZI) can realize optical circuits. In the logic domain, this switch is abstracted to a so called MZI gate. Logically, an MZI gate is defined as follows [18, 19]:

Definition 1: An MZI gate as shown in Fig. 1(a) realizes a Boolean function composed of two optical inputs x and y as well as two optical outputs z and w. The absence of any input signal leads to the logic value 0 at the output z. The presence of input signal x and the absence of input signal y leads to the logic value 1 at the output w. In the presence of both input signals, the outputs z and w produce 1 and 0 respectively. Therefore, the functions, $z = x \& y$ and $w = z \& \sim y$ are realized.

Definition 2: A splitter as shown in Fig. 1(b) divides an optical signal into two signals – each with only half of the incoming signal power. In contrast, a combiner merges two optical signals into a single one and by this inherently realizes the OR-function. A splitter (combiner) may have more than two outputs (inputs). Then, in case of a splitter, the strength of the signal is divided by the number of outputs.

An MZI gate, splitter and combiner together form an optical gate library which can realize any Boolean function.

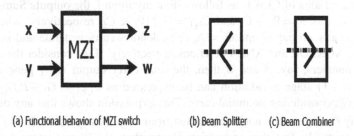

(a) Functional behavior of MZI switch   (b) Beam Splitter   (c) Beam Combiner

Fig. 1. Optical gate library

An EX-OR realization of $x \& y$ using MZI gates, a combiner and two splitters is shown in Fig. 2.

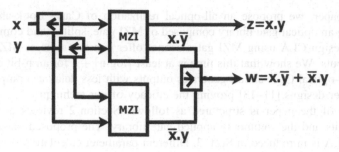

Fig. 2. Shows the EX-OR realization of x & y

The size of an optical circuit is determined in terms of number of MZI gates. Since splitters and combiners are significantly easier to realize than the MZI gates, the area combination of splitters and combiners are often considered negligible. Besides that, the delay of a longest path from primary input to the primary output is estimated in terms of the number of MZI gates those are present in the corresponding path [9]. Here, a delay of an MZI gate is considered as unity.

3   Proposed All-Optical Carry Lookahead Adder

In this section, we first review and illustrate the basic concepts of CLA. Afterwards, we present the proposed all-optical realization of the CLA.

3.1   Carry Look-Ahead Adder (CLA)

Carry propagation time is an important attribute which limits the speed of operation of the adders. To reduce the carry propagation time, the concept of Carry Look-ahead logic is employed which computes all the carry outputs in parallel. The concept of look-ahead in order to generate carry bits completely removes the carry propagation delay and thereby enhances the operational speed of the adder. Adders relying on this concept of carry generation are known as Carry Look-ahead Adders (CLAs) [17].

The general idea of CLA is as follows: For any input i, the outputs Sum and Carry can be defined as $S_i = P_i \oplus C_i$ and $C_{i+1} = G_i \mid (P_i \& C_i)$ respectively, where $P_i = A_i$ B_i denotes carry propagate and $G_i = A_i \& B_i$ denotes carry generate and symbols '$\oplus$, $\mid$, &' define XOR, OR and AND operations respectively. If we consider the addition of two n-bit numbers, say, A and B then, the final carry output C_{i+1} generated at the $i^{th} (0 \leq i \leq n - 1)$ stage of addition can be expressed as $C_{i+1} = G_i + P_i G_{i-1} + \cdots + P_i P_{i-1}..P_1 G_0$, considering no initial carry. This expression shows that any output carry C_{i+1} at any i^{th} stage needs not be computed from output carry C_i of $(i - 1)^{th}$ stage i.e. preceding stage. In fact this expression shows that, the output carry C_{i+1} of any i^{th} stage relies only on input carry G_0. For example, all the carry outputs $C_1, C_2, C_3, ..., C_{n-1}$ generated during the addition of two n-bit numbers, $A(a_{n-1}, a_{n-2}, ..., a_1, a_0)$ and $B(b_{n-1}, b_{n-2}, ..., b_1, b_0)$ can be expressed in terms of input carry as follows:

$$C_1 = G_0$$
$$C_2 = G_1 + P_1 C_1 = G_1 + P_1 G_0$$
$$C_3 = G_2 + P_2 C_2 = G_2 + P_2 G_1 + P_2 P_1 G_0$$
$$C_4 = G_3 + P_3 C_3 = G_3 + P_3 G_2 + P_3 P_2 G_1 + P_3 P_2 P_1 G_0$$
$$\vdots$$

$C_n = G_{n-1} + P_{n-1} G_{n-2} + P_{n-1} P_{n-2} G_{n-3} + \ldots + P_{n-1} P_{n-2} \ldots P_2 P_1 G_0$ where, $G_0 = A_0 B_0$, $G_1 = A_1 B_1$, $G_2 = A_2 B_2$, $G_3 = A_3 B_3$
and $P_0 = A_0 \oplus B_0$, $P_1 = A_1 \oplus B_1$, $P_2 = A_2 \oplus B_2$, $P_{n-1} = A_{n-1} \oplus B_{n-1}$

The result of the addition can be obtained now as $S_0 = A_0 \oplus B_0$, $S_1 = P_1 \oplus C_1$, $S_2 = P_2 \oplus C_2$, ..., $S_{n-2} = P_{n-2} \oplus C_{n-2}$, $S_{n-1} = P_{n-1} \oplus C_n$, $S_n = C_n$.

Now the adder circuit can be designed as shown in Fig. 3 that consist of three sub-circuits, the first one (P & G generator) produces P_i's and G_i's the second one called as Carry Generator of CLA produces carries of different levels. The third one sum generator generates the output sum result. Clearly first one or third one is providing single delay. The second one is basically a two level AND-OR circuit. Thus the total delay becomes 4. The problem in this CLA design is that to achieve the speed we need more hardware. Moreover in Carry Generator part are require AND and OR gates with higher inputs.

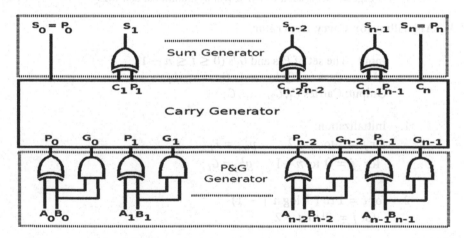

Fig. 3. Structure of Carry Lookahead Adder

3.2 Proposed All-Optical Realization of CLA

In this sub-section, we introduce the proposed design for all-optical CLA circuits. The expressions for CLA are mapped to the equivalent net lists of optical gates. The proposed all-optical designs for CLA utilize non-modular staircase like sub-circuits which finally leads to the improved all-optical realizations of CLAs.

The problem in the CLA design using MZI gates is that the MZI gates have only two inputs. In the traditional logic design, the carries are generated using two-level AND-OR realization where AND and OR gates are having more than two inputs. But as MZI gate realizing AND gate can have maximum two inputs, this AND realization itself requires more than one level.

To design AND gates with n inputs we require $\lceil \log n \rceil$ levels of MZI gates. For example if we like to design $P_3 P_2 P_1 G_0$ for traditional design it becomes as shown in the Fig. 4(a), but in case of MZI it is realized as in Fig. 4(b).

The implementation of the expression of carries as given in Sect. 3.1 may be done in several ways. As the goal of CLA is achieving the speed, our first target is to minimize the delay. Obviously this delay is $\lceil \log n \rceil$ as expressions for C_n requires an AND gate realization of n inputs which needs to be implemented by a tree of MZI gates of $\lceil \log n \rceil$ levels. Keeping this value $\lceil \log n \rceil$ as maximum allowable delay, we now try to optimize the number of MZI gates. To do it, we use the following algorithm to generate the carries at different levels as defined in Sect. 3.1 using only MZI gates, beam splitter and beam combiner.

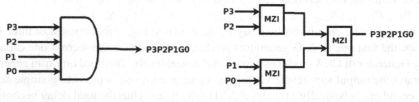

(a) Traditional design using logic gate   (b) Design using MZI switches

Fig. 4. Realization of $P_3 P_2 P_1 G_0$ by traditional and MZI

3.3 Algorithm for Carry Generator

Input : The set of P_i's and G_i's $(0 \leq i \leq n - 1)$,
where $P_i = a_i \oplus b_i$ and $G_i = a_i . b_i$
Output: Carries $C_1, C_2, \ldots \ldots, C_n$

1. Initialization:
    for $j = 1$ to $n - 2$ $p_{0,j}^1 = P_j$;
    for $j = 0$ to $n - 1$ $g_{0,j}^1 = G_j$;

2. for $i = 1$ to ($\lceil \log n \rceil - 1$)
    for $j = 2^i$ to $n - 2$

    $$p_{i,j}^2 = p_{i-1,j}^{2^{i-1}} \cdot p_{i-1,j-2^{i-1}}^{2^{i-1}} ;$$

3. for $i = 2$ to $(n - 1)$
    for $j = i - 1$ to $(n - 2)$

    $$g_{\lceil \log i \rceil, j}^{j} = p_{\lceil \log i \rceil - 1, j}^{2^{\lceil \log i \rceil - 1}} * g_{\lceil \log i \rceil - 1, 2^{\lceil \log i \rceil - 1} + (j-i)}^{2^{\lceil \log i \rceil - 1}} ;$$

4. $C_n = \sum g_{\lceil \log i \rceil, (n-1)}^{i}$
    where $i = 1$ to n and $\sum$ represents the OR operation.

5. End of the algorithm.

Each $p_{i,l}^{2^i}$ $(1 \leq i \leq \lceil \log n \rceil - 1)$, $(2^i \leq l \leq n - 2)$ obtained in step-2 of the algorithm is realized by an MZI gate to produce AND operation. Similarly, each $g^i_{\lceil \log i \rceil, j}$ obtained in step-3 of the above algorithm is realized by an MZI gate to produce AND operation. Each C_i obtained in step-4 of the algorithm is implemented by beam combiners.

We are using some beam splitters as shown in Fig. 1(b), when any signal line is used more than once.

The sum-result is obtained by EX-OR gates as shown in Fig. 3 and each EX-OR gate can be implemented as shown in Fig. 2.

A complete adder circuit for 8-inputs is shown in Fig. 5 using MZI gates, combiners and splitters.

4   Parameter Calculation

As the optical cost of beam splitter and beam combiner are relatively small, the optical cost of a given circuit is the number of MZI switches required to design that circuit.

Lemma 1: The number of MZI gates for the proposed design for an n-input adder is $\frac{n^2}{2} + n \lceil \log n \rceil + \frac{5n}{2} - 2^{\lceil \log n \rceil} - 1$.

Proof: The 1st stage ($P \& G$ generator) of Fig. 3 requires $2n$ MZI gates.

For the carry generator, the 2nd step of the **Algorithm Carry Generator** produces the number of gates

$$(n - 2) + (n - 2^2) + (n - 2^3) + \ldots + \left(n - 2^{\lceil \log n \rceil - 1}\right)$$
$$= n \lceil \log n \rceil - n - 2^{\lceil \log n \rceil} + 2$$

For the 3rd step of algorithm the number of AND gates produced is $= (n - 1) + (n - 2) + \ldots + 1) = \frac{n(n-1)}{2}$

The 3rd step of Fig. 3 requires $2(n - 1) - 1$ AND gates. One AND gate $P_1 G_0$ is actually produced in the first step of the algorithm.

Thus the total number of gates

$$= 2n + n \lceil \log n \rceil - n - 2^{\lceil \log n \rceil} + 2 + \frac{n(n-1)}{2}$$
$$= \frac{n^2}{2} + n \lceil \log n \rceil + \frac{5n}{2} - 2^{\lceil \log n \rceil} - 1$$

□

If $\log n$ = integer then,

Then the number of MZI gates $= \frac{n^2}{2} + n \log n + \frac{3n}{2} - 1$

Lemma 2: The delay of MZI adder is $\lceil \log n \rceil + 2$.

Proof: The optical delay is estimated as the number of stages of MZI switches multiplied by a unit Δ. The $P \& G$ generator and sum generator requires one unit delay each. The carry generator requires $\lceil \log n \rceil$ units Δ. Hence the result.   □

Figure 5 shows the complete realization of our proposed 8 bit Carry Look-ahead Adder.

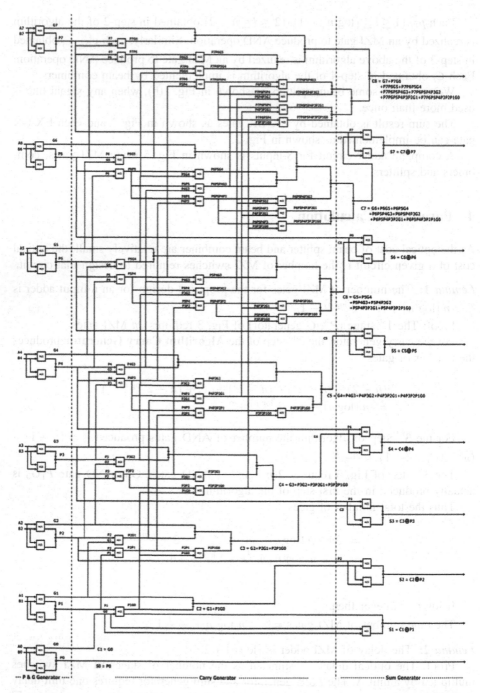

Fig. 5. All-Optical realization of 8 bit Carry Lookahead Adder using Mach Zehnder Interferometer

5   Comparative Results

The Table 1 shows the comparison of all-optical carry look-ahead adders with respect to delay and number of MZI gates.

We have compared the result with an earlier work [13]. The 2nd and 3rd columns in the Table 1 represent the result of [13] and our work respectively.

The Table 2 shows the comparison of three adder designs with respect to different values of $n = 8, 16, 32, 64$. The first column in Table 1 represents the value n. The 2nd, 3rd, 4th and 5th columns in the Table 2 represent the delay in [11–13] and proposed work respectively. The 6th, 7th, 8th and 9th columns represent the number of MZI gates required in [11–13] and proposed work respectively. As evident from the result our design is very efficient with respect to speed.

Table 1. Comparison of All-Optical Carry Look-ahead Adder with respect to number of MZI gates and delay.

	[13]	Proposed work
Delay	n	$\lceil \log n \rceil + 2$
No of MZI	$2n$	$\frac{n^2}{2} + n \lceil \log n \rceil + \frac{5n}{2} - 2^{\lceil \log n \rceil} - 1$

Table 2. Shows the comparison of different All-Optical Adder $n = 8, 16, 32, 64$

n	Delay				No of MZI			
	[11]	[12]	[13]	Proposed work	[11]	[12]	[13]	Proposed work
8	11	25	8	5	48	49	16	67
16	19	49	16	6	96	97	32	215
32	35	97	32	7	192	193	64	719
64	67	193	64	8	384	385	128	2527

6   Conclusion and Future Scope

In this paper, an efficient all-optical realization of Carry Look-ahead Adder (CLA) is proposed using Mach–Zehnder Interferometer (MZI) based switches along with analysis of the corresponding costs and delays. Design complexities presented ensure minimum delay in all optical carry look-ahead adder circuit realization. Our design technique has been compared with recently reported design techniques. The experimental results confirm the efficacy of the proposed design over similar existing designs with respect to speed. Though the number of MZI gates is more in our design, the low power properties of MZI gates do not demand much power. The work may be extended to find the techniques to reduce the number of MZI gates. The application of amplifiers may be done to improve the signal strength.

Acknowledgement. A part of this work is funded by DST project DST/ICPS/CPS-Individual/2018/403(G).

References

1. Pavesi, L., Lockwood, D.J.: Silicon Photonics. Topics in Applied Physics. Springer, Berlin (2004)
2. Ho, R., et al.: Silicon photonic interconnects for large-scale computer systems. IEEE Micro **33**(1), 68–78 (2013)
3. Sato, T., et al.: Photonic crystal lasers for chip-to-chip and on-chip optical interconnects. IEEE J. Sel. Top. Quantum Electron. **21**(6), 728–737 (2015)
4. Kim, J.Y., Kang, J.M., Kim, T.Y., Han, S.K.: All-optical multiple logic gates with XOR, NOR, OR, and NAND functions using parallel SOA-MZI: theory and experiment structures. J. Light. Technol. **24**(9), 3392–3399 (2006)
5. Martinez, J.M., Ramos, F., Mart, J.: 10 Gb/s reconfigurable optical logic gate using a single hybrid-integrated SOA-MZI. Fiber Integr. Opt. **27**(1), 15–23 (2007)
6. Taraphdar, C., Chattopadhyay, T., Roy, J.: Mach-Zehnder Interferometer based all-optical reversible logic gate. Opt. Laser Technol. **42**(2), 249–259 (2010)
7. Cherri, A.K., Al-Zayed, A.S.: Circuit designs of ultra-fast all-optical modified signed-digit adders using semiconductor optical amplifier and Mach-Zehnder Interferometer. Optik – Int. J. Light Electron. Opt. **121**(17), 1577–1585 (2010)
8. Sribhashyam, S., Ramachandran, M., Prince, S., Ravi, B.R.: Design of full adder and subtractor based on MZI—SOA. In: IEEE International Conference on Signal Processing and Communication Engineering Systems, pp. 19–21 (2015)
9. Al-Zayed, A., Cherri, A.: Improved all-optical modified signed-digit adders using semiconductor optical amplifier and Mach-Zehnder Interferometer. Opt. Laser Technol. **42** (5), 810–818 (2010)
10. Thapliyal, H., Ranganathan, N.: A new reversible design of BCD adder, pp. 1–4 (2011)
11. Datta, K., Chattopadhyay, T., Sengupta, I.: All optical design of binary adders using semiconductor optical amplifier assisted Mach-Zehnder Interferometer. Microelectron. J. **46** (9), 839–847 (2015)
12. Kotiyal, S., Thapliyal, H., Ranganathan, N.: Mach-Zehnder Interferometer based design of all optical reversible binary adder. In: Proceedings of the Conference on Design, Automation and Test in Europe. EDA Consortium (2012)
13. Dutta, P., Bandyopadhyay, C., Giri, C., Rahaman, H.: Mach-Zehnder Interferometer based all optical reversible carry-lookahead adder. In: IEEE Computer Society Annual Symposium on VLSI, pp. 412–417 (2014)
14. Miao, J., Li, S.: A novel implementation of 4-bit carry look-ahead adder. In: 2017 International Conference on Electron Devices and Solid-State Circuits (EDSSC). IEEE, pp. 1–2 (2017)
15. Maity, G., Chattopadhyay, T., Roy, J., Maity, S.: All-optical reversible multiplexer. In: Proceedings of Computers and Devices for Communication (CODEC), pp. 1–3 (2009)
16. Datta, K., Sengupta, I.: All optical reversible multiplexer design using Mach-Zehnder Interferometer. In: International Conference on VLSI Design, pp. 539–544 (2014)
17. Mano, M.M.: Digital Logic and Computer Design. Pearson Education India, Chennai (2017)
18. Scaffardi, M.P., Ghelfi, P., Lazzeri, E., Poti, L., Bogoni, A.: Photonic processing for digital comparison and full addition based on semiconductor optical amplifiers. IEEE J. Sel. Top. Quantum Electron. **14**(3), 826–833 (2008)
19. Wang, Q., et al.: Study of all-optical XOR using Mach-Zehnder Interferometer and differential scheme. IEEE J. Sel. Top. Quantum Electron. **40**(6), 703–710 (2004)

Computing Architecture and Security

Asynchronous Hardware Design
for Floating Point Multiply-Accumulate
Circuit

M. Mohamed Asan Basiri$^{(\boxtimes)}$

Department of Electronics and Communication Engineering, IIITDM, Kurnool
518007, India
asanbasiri@gmail.com

Abstract. This article explains an asynchronous hardware architecture
for floating point multiply-accumulate circuit (MAC) that is exploited
in many of the modern engineering applications such as voice/image
processing, noise cancellation, and so on. The proposed asynchronous
IEEE-754 single precision floating point MAC sends the previous result
to the present multiplication for accumulation purpose without synchronous registers, which causes much reduction in switching power
dissipations. Our proposed asynchronous design eliminates the *glitches*
and *metastability*. The Wallace structure based proposed asynchronous
IEEE 754 single precision floating point MAC achieves 91.8% of reduction in energy per operation (or power delay product) than base-32 based
design [5] using 45 nm CMOS technology.

Keywords: Asynchronous circuit · Digital filter · DSP ·
Multiply-accumulate circuit

1 Introduction

Digital signal processors (DSPs) [1] are crucial for performing the high performance arithmetic calculations used for engineering applications such as
image/video compression, multimedia, and etc. The most of the digital signal
processing operations such as filtering [2], convolution, correlation, and transformations [3] work with multiplication followed by repeated addition. So, MAC [4]
is the heart of digital signal processing hardware. The basic MAC operation is
shown in (1), where the inputs $U[i]$ and $V[i]$ will be multiplied. The multiplication result will be added with the previous MAC result $W[i-1]$ to produce
the present MAC result $W[i]$. So, m numbers of total MAC operations will be
performed in (1).

$$W_m = \sum_{i=1}^{m} U_i.V_i \tag{1}$$

© Springer Nature Singapore Pte Ltd. 2019
A. Sengupta et al. (Eds.): VDAT 2019, CCIS 1066, pp. 247–257, 2019.
https://doi.org/10.1007/978-981-32-9767-8_22

In the floating point MAC, three floating point operands are used. The two input operands will be multiplied and the result will be added to the third one (previous MAC result). Here, the main thing is to align the mantissas before the addition of third operand.

1.1   Related Work

In the past two decades, several hardware designs of MAC were proposed. In [5], base-32 conversion is taken for IEEE-754 floating point operands and that causes three special cases. In this work, the addition of previous MAC output is clubbed with current multiplication. A similar work is proposed in [6], where one of the serious problem called most significant bit prediction in the floating point MAC is addressed. In this paper, the floating point MAC design as shown in [6] is used to make an asynchronous hardware implementation. In [6], the mantissa alignment is done before the multiplication cum accumulation. In [7], the mantissa alignment is done after the multiplication of present operands. In [8], the mantissa alignment is done using the leading zero prediction of present operands. In the synchronous MAC as shown in Fig. 1(a), the adder will get previous immediate result $(z[i-1])$ and multiplication output $(x[i] \times y[i])$ from the clocked registers and multiplier respectively. The dynamic power is more due to the clocked registers. To reduce this dynamic power, we have proposed asynchronous MAC in Fig. 1(b), where the multiply-accumulate circuit will get previous immediate result $(z[i-1])$, $x[i]$, and $y[i]$ from the completion detection logic, primary input port, and primary input port respectively. In the multiply-accumulate circuit of Fig. 1(b), the addition of previous MAC result will be done along with present multiplication that causes a reduction of separate adder for accumulation.

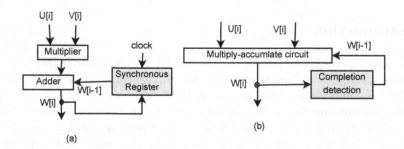

Fig. 1. (a) The clocked conventional and (b) asynchronous proposed multiply-accumulate circuit designs.

1.2   Contribution of This Paper

The aim of this research work is to enrich the performance of floating point MAC by using asynchronous hardware design. In other words, we have improved our

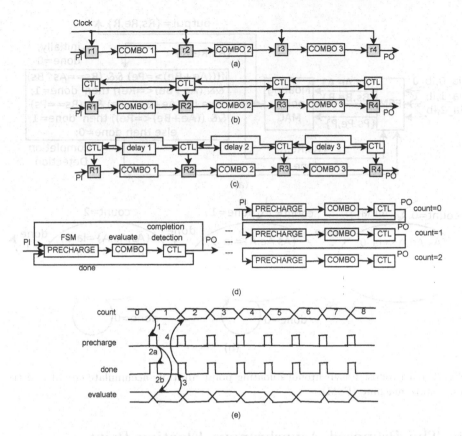

Fig. 2. (a) The synchronous circuit with pipeline, (b) the asynchronous pipelined circuit with the presence of *glitches*, (c) the existing asynchronous pipelined circuit without *glitches*, (d) the proposed asynchronous design without *glitches* [12,13], and (e) the protocol used in our proposed asynchronous design [12,13].

earlier synchronous floating point MAC design [6] using our own asynchronous logic [12] proposed earlier. Indeed, the asynchronous circuits are not many available. The proposed asynchronous IEEE-754 single precision floating point MAC sends the previous result to the present multiplication for accumulation purpose without synchronous registers, which causes much reduction in switching power dissipations. The synthesis results prove that the proposed MAC gives good performance than various previous designs with 45 nm CMOS technology.

This article is organized with four sections. The Sect. 2 explains the proposed asynchronous circuit design for MAC. The implementation details and synthesis results of various MACs are elaborated in Sect. 3. The conclusion in Sect. 4 gives the summary of this entire article.

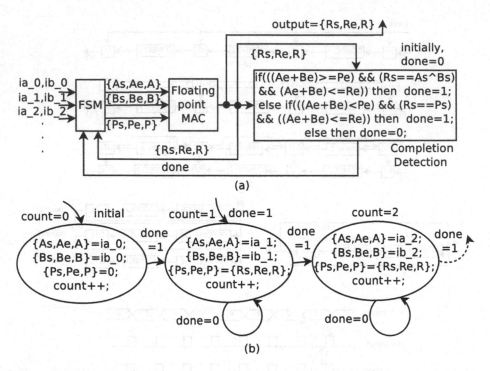

Fig. 3. (a) Proposed asynchronous floating point multiply-accumulate circuit and (b) finite state machine (FSM).

2   The Proposed Asynchronous Floating Point Multiply-Accumulate Circuit Design

In all the asynchronous circuit designs, there is no need for synchronous registers. As compared with synchronous designs, the asynchronous circuits [11] have several advantages such as lower dynamic power dissipation, elimination of the clock distribution & clock skew problems, and less emission of electromagnetic noise. One of the prominent advantage with asynchronous designs would be secured hardware design in side channel analysis. The power traces are the major sources in side channel analysis of any crypto design. The attacker can infer the secret key based on the power traces. The asynchronous designs can mitigate the power dissipation. So, the asynchronous circuits can be used eventually in many of the hardware security applications. Similarly, the disadvantages with asynchronous circuits are lack of EDA tools to do the synthesis, area overhead due to the completion detection, and lack of assurance of timing convergence.

Figure 2(a) shows the synchronous pipelined circuit design, where a common clock is connected with the registers (r1, r2, r3, and r4). Here the combination logics COMBO 1, COMBO 2, and COMBO 3 are used in between the registers (r1 & r2), (r2 & r3), and (r3 & r4) respectively. Whenever the clock is triggered, the data from one segment will be transferred into the another. Here the total

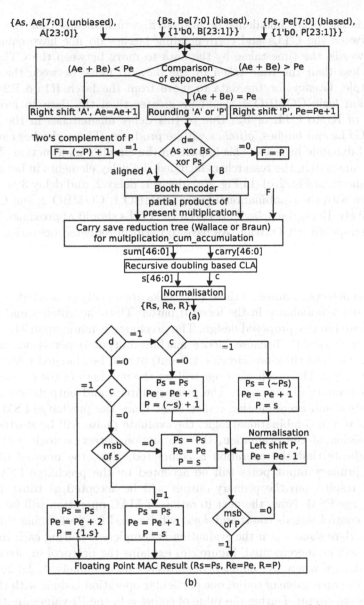

Fig. 4. (a) Proposed floating point multiply-accumulate circuit [6] without pipeline and (b) Normalization.

number of segments is three. The circuit with asynchronous pipeline is shown in Fig. 2(b), where the *glitches* are present due to the presence of delay mismatch. Here, the control logics (CTLs) instructs the latches to accept the data or not, whereas in Fig. 2(a), the clock signal instructs the registers to accept the data or not. The latches are represented as R1, R2, R3, and R4. The rigorous issue with

Fig. 2(b) is the delay imbalance or mismatch, which means that the forward paths between the CTLs and corresponding latches do not have equal delay. In other words, the time taken by the data to move between the CTLs would be much less than the time taken by the data to move between the latches. For example, latency for the data to move from the latch R1 to R2 via the combination logic COMBO 1 would be greater than the data to move from the CTL of R1 to CTL of R2. Due to this delay mismatches in the forward paths of CTLs and latches, *glitches* will be produces. These glitches causes the static and dynamic hazards. This impact on the circuit's malfunction. To avoid this delay mismatch, the researchers included the delay elements in between the CTLs as shown in Fig. 2(c). In Fig. 2(c), delay 1, delay 2, and delay 3 are used in accordance with the combinational logics COMBO 1, COMBO 2, and COMBO 3 respectively. Here, the delay in between the CTLs should approximately equal to the corresponding COMBO. We have to perform repeated operation such as multiplication and addition. So we use only one segment in Fig. 2(d) instead the multiple segments as shown in Fig. 2(c). Our single segment proposed design includes three serially connected sub blocks, they are precharge, evaluate, and completion detection. Since all these sub blocks are serially connected, we do not have any delay imbalance in the forward paths. Thus the glitches and hazards are eliminated in our proposed design. The precharge is made up of Moore finite state machine (FSM), because Moore machine output depends on the input as well. In the asynchronous circuits, the output will be changed whenever the input is changed. The precharge stage will get the inputs from the primary input ports and primary output port. The primary inputs and outputs are used for multiplication and accumulation respectively. Once the precharge FSM assigns the inputs to the combinational logic, the evaluate phase will be started. After the completion of the evaluation, the completion detection logic will raise a flag to indicate that the operation is completed. Now, the new set of inputs from the primary input ports will be accepted by the precharge FSM. Also, the MAC result from the primary output will be accepted as third input by the precharge FSM. Now, the next iteration of MAC operation will be started. Here, the control signals *count* and *done* will be used for performing this whole operation. Here *done* = 1 if the evaluation is completed. During each iteration, the *count* will be incremented. Figure 2(e) explains the protocol involved in the proposed design, where five numbers of states are used, namely, 1, 2a, 2b, 3, and 4. During the each value of *count*, one particular operation is done with the same combinational circuit. During the value of *count* = 0, the PI values are taken by the precharge stage and from *count* = 1 onwards, the PI and PO values are taken by the precharge stage. In Fig. 2(e), lets assume that the *count* = 1. Now, the precharge operation will be performed (state-1). After this precharge operation, the *done* = 0 (state-2a), in parallel, the combination logic operation will be performed in *evaluation* stage (state-2b). If the evaluation stage is completed, the *done* = 1 (state-3). After that the *count* value is incremented (state-4).

Figure 3(a) shows the proposed asynchronous floating point multiply-accumulate circuit, whose finite state machine (FSM) is shown in Fig. 3(b).

Initially, the *count* = 0 and *done* = 0. The FSM will start with the inputs ia_0 and ib_0 while $\{Ps, Pe, P\}$ = 0. After the MAC operation, the result $\{Rs, Re, R\}$ will be produced. Now, the resultant $\{Rs, Re, R\}$ will be used in the completion detection to produce *done*. Once *done* = 1, the next iteration will be started, where the *count* is incremented by one. Now, the inputs ia_1 and ib_1 will be assigned into $\{As, Ae, A\}$ and $\{Bs, Be, B\}$ respectively, while $\{Ps, Pe, P\} = \{Rs, Re, R\}$. This starts the second iteration. In the similar way, the whole operation will be done with the help of *count* and *done* without synchronous registers.

The entire floating MAC algorithm used in this paper follows our previous work [6]. Here the two input operands to be multiplied are $\{As, Ae, A\}$ and $\{Bs, Be, B\}$. Similarly, the operand of previous multiply-accumulation result is $\{Ps, Pe, P\}$. Since we use IEEE 754 single precision representation, three fields are used in each of the operands. They are sign bit, exponent, and mantissa. Here, the suffixes s and e are used to represent the sign bit and exponent respectively. Initially, we have right shifted the matissas B and P to the one position. During this right shift, we do not allow the increment in the exponents Be and Pe. This process is to avoid the *msb* prediction problem in the floating point multiply-accumulation. Usually, the multiplication of two n-bit numbers will produce the multiplication result with $2n$ or $2n - 1$-bit wide. Since the accumulation is clubbed with the present multiplication of our proposed design, we cannot obtain the multiplication result separately. So, we cannot exactly predict what would be the resultant width of the multiplication of the mantissas A and B. Since we use the floating point numbers, the *msb* of two numbers need to be aligned before they are added, but we cannot find the *msb* of the present multiplication result of the mantissas A and B. So to avoid this *msb* prediction, we have right shifted the matissas B and P upto one position. In the first stage of Fig. 4(a), comparison of exponents will be done. During the exponent comparison, the right shift of the mantissa A or P would be done with respect to the conditions associated with $(Ae + Be)$ and Pe. During the multiplication of the mantissas A and B, the mantissa of the previous MAC result (P) will be added in such a way that the *msb* of P is aligned with the *msb* of the final partial product of the multiplication result $A \times B$ to avoid this *msb* prediction. In the last step, the normalization procedure as shown in Fig. 4(b) is followed. To avoid the precision loss, we use three extra bits, namely guard bit, round bit, and sticky bit during the right shift of each mantissas. The IEEE 754 rounding technique is used here. The round up, round down, and round to even will be followed with respect to these three bits. Here, multiplication of A and B is done with Wallace structure or Braun structures. During the normalization process, we consider the *msb* of the multiplication result (s) and carry output (c) of the multiplication result. Based on these two values, we will be deciding what would be resultant sign bit and exponent. This entire step follows the standard signed fixed point arithmetic. After this entire process, we will obtain the resultant MAC operand $\{Ps, Pe, P\}$ that would be used as an input to the next round of MAC operation. Since we use clockless asynchronous logic, our completion detection unit will send this operand $\{Ps, Pe, P\}$ to the next round of MAC operation. This operation will be continued untill our required round of multiply-accumulation is completed.

During the multiplication of 24-bit mantissas $A \times B$, one of the partial products is to be considered as the previous MAC result. Therefore, the total number of partial products would be 25. So, the number of carry save stages in the Wallace and Braun structures would be $-1.71 + 1.71 log_2(25)$ and (25-2) respectively. Here, the first stage of Braun structure will accept three partial products. So, we have subtracted 2 from 25. In general, the number of carry save stages in the Wallace structure is much less than Braun structure. Here, we used the radix-4 modified Booth algorithm to reduce the partial products in both Wallace and Braun structures. We do not use the radix-2 Booth encoding, because radix-2 Booth encoding will act as a signed multiplication. Also, the raix-2 Booth encoding does not reduce the number of partial products.

Table 1. Performance analysis of various IEEE-754 single precision floating point MAC designs using Wallace tree and carry save array (Braun) multipliers with 45 nm CMOS technology.

Floating point MAC design	# synchronous pipeline stages	Critical path delay (ps)	Frequency (MHz)	Area-delay product $(\mu m^2.ps)$	Energy per operation (zJ)
Conventional (Wallace)	4	0637.4	1568.87	05846385.77	462933874.15
base-32 form [5] (Wallace)	3	0830.3	1204.38	10720642.63	804072550.02
[6] (Wallace)	2	1237.8	0807.88	08587113.72	613722517.78
[7] (Wallace)	3	1201.8	0832.09	08317181.28	606718312.83
[8] (Wallace)	2	1364.8	0732.71	09077233.22	724273110.52
Proposed asynchronous (Wallace)	**0**	**0167.7**	**NA**	**01115746.67**	**065772538.68**
Conventional (Braun)	5	0656.7	1522.76	07571422.65	197581808.39
base-32 form [5] (Braun)	4	0893.4	1119.31	13193615.05	959233484.58
[6] (Braun)	2	1433.8	0697.44	10696162.33	753866805.12
[7] (Braun)	3	1417.6	0705.41	10172312.13	721732199.92
[8] (Braun)	2	1568.9	0637.38	13894482.43	844611001.32
Proposed asynchronous (Braun)	**0**	**0194.6**	**NA**	**01305657.02**	**078414420.28**

In the conventional design (as shown in Fig. 1(a)), accumulation will be done separately after the multiplication. NA is not applicable.

3 Design Modeling, Implementation, and Results

The existing and proposed MACs are modeled in Verilog HDL. The Cadence (Genus/Innovus) ASIC design tool is used to simulate and synthesis these designs. The asynchronous design can be used in Cadence by eliminating the clock tree generation [14,15]. All MAC designs in Table 1 are implemented using

45 nm CMOS technology with $0.88\,v$ as the operating voltage. Here, the factors $Ip\_default\_probability$, $Ip\_default\_toggle\_rate$, $Ip\_toggle\_rate\_unit$, and $Ip\_default\_toggle\_percentage$ are taken as 0.5, 0.02, 1 ns, and 0.2 respectively.

Table 1 gives the synthesis result comparison between various floating point MAC architectures. Here, we have compared the critical path delay [16], area-delay product, and power delay product (PDP) [17]. The PDP is calculated by multiplying the total power with critical path delay, where the total power is the addition of switching and leakage powers. The several CMOS technologies are used to implement the existing MAC designs. Since we do not have all these CMOS libraries used in the existing papers, all the existing and proposed MAC designs are implemented as per the reference papers using one particular 45 nm library ($tcbn45gsbwpbc088ccs.lib$ with 0.88v). In all our implementations as shown in Table 1, the MACs are designed using Wallace tree [9] and carry save array (Braun) [10] multipliers. In Table 1, the Braun multiplier based MAC designs require more delay, area, and power dissipations because $n \times n$-bit Braun multiplier requires n-carry save stages, whereas the Wallace structure requires $O(log_2 n)$ carry save stages. The floating point MAC [6] requires more a critical path delay than base-32 based design [5], because [6] is designed only with two stages of pipeline, where the critical path includes the final addition followed by normalization, whereas [5] requires multiple pipeline stages (>2). Due to more pipeline stages (more registers), the area of [5] is greater than others. Since there is no clock, asynchronous circuits do not have to wait till the clock comes as in synchronous designs. The output changes immediately as the inputs change. Hence the time taken for asynchronous and synchronous designs will be different. The proposed Wallace tree based asynchronous IEEE-754 floating point single precision MAC achieves 91.8% of reduction in energy per operation as compared with base-32 based design [5] using 45 nm CMOS technology. Figure 5 shows the chip layout diagram for proposed asynchronous single precision floating point MAC using Wallace structure, where the aspect ratio and core utilization are 1 and 85% respectively. Therefore, the core area in the layout would be $\frac{6653.23}{0.85} =$ 7827.33 μm^2.

In our proposed asynchronous MAC, the -ve timing slack along with *glitches* are avoided. The glitches will be occurring due to the delay imbalance in the circuits. Also, the *metastability* and *unstability* are eliminated in the proposed design during the post layout simulation. Due to the continuous assignment of output as the input, the *unstability* is occurring in the asynchronous designs. In our proposed MAC design, the output is taken as input if the condition with the control signals *count* and *done* is satisfied. For example, there is no input assignment after $count = 15$ in Fig. 3(a). So, the final stable state will be reached at $count = 15$.

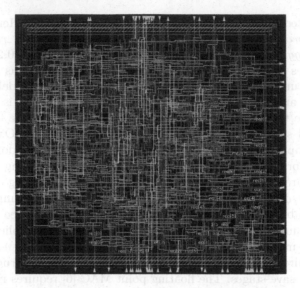

Fig. 5. Chip layout diagram of the proposed asynchronous single precision floating point MAC using Wallace structure: core area is 7827.33 μm^2, the die space around the core is 3 μm, and the total chip area is 8924.58 μm^2 with 45 nm CMOS technology.

4   Conclusion

This article explains an asynchronous hardware architecture for floating point multiply-accumulate circuit (MAC) that is exploited in many of the modern engineering applications such as voice/image processing, noise cancellation, and so on. The proposed asynchronous IEEE-754 single precision floating point MAC sends the previous result to the present multiplication for accumulation purpose without synchronous registers, which causes much reduction in switching power dissipations. Our proposed asynchronous design eliminates the *glitches* and *metastability*. The Wallace structure based proposed asynchronous IEEE 754 single precision floating point MAC achieves 91.8% of reduction in energy per operation (or power delay product) than base-32 based design [5] using 45 nm CMOS technology.

References

1. Smith, S.W.: The Scientist and Engineers Guide to Digital Signal Processing, pp. 551–566. California Technical Publishing, Poway (1997)
2. Mohamed Asan Basiri, M., Sk, N.M.: Configurable folded IIR filter design. IEEE Trans. Circ. Syst. II: Express Briefs **62**(12), 1144–1148 (2015)
3. Mohamed Asan Basiri, M., Sk, N.M.: An efficient VLSI architecture for lifting based 1D/2D-discrete wavelet transform. Microprocess. Microsyst. **47**, 404–418 (2016)

4. Mohamed Asan Basiri, M., Sk, N.M.: An efficient hardware based MAC design in digital filters with complex numbers. In: IEEE International Conference on Signal Processing and Integrated Networks (SPIN), pp. 475–480 (2014)
5. Vangal, S.R., Hoskote, Y.V., Borkar, N.Y., Alvandpour, A.: 6.2-GFlops floating-point multiply-accumulator with conditional normalization. IEEE J. Solid-State Circ. **41**(10), 2314–2323 (2006)
6. Mohamed Asan Basiri, M., Sk, N.M.: An efficient hardware based higher radix floating point MAC design. ACM Trans. Des. Autom. Electron. Syst. (TODAES) **20**(1), 15:1–15:25 (2014)
7. Li, G., Li, Z.: Design of a fully pipelined single-precision multiply-add-fused unit. In: IEEE 20th International Conference on VLSI Design Held Jointly with 6th International Conference on Embedded Systems (VLSID 2007), pp. 318–323 (2007)
8. Mei, X.-L.: Leading zero anticipation for latency improvement in floating-point fused multiply-add units. In: IEEE International Conference on ASIC, pp. 53–56 (2005)
9. Mohamed Asan Basiri, M., Nayak, S.C., Sk, N.M.: Multiplication acceleration through quarter precision wallace tree multiplier. In: IEEE International Conference on Signal Processing and Integrated Networks (SPIN), pp. 502–505 (2014)
10. Jones, C.M., Dlay, S.S., Naguib, R.G.: Berger check prediction for concurrent error detection in the Braun array multiplier. In: IEEE International Conference on Electronics, Circuits and Systems, pp. 81–84 (1996)
11. Nowick, S.M., Singh, M.: High-performance asynchronous pipelines: an overview. IEEE Des. Test Comput. **28**(5), 8–22 (2011)
12. Mohamed Asan Basiri, M., Shukla, S.K.: Asynchronous hardware implementations for crypto primitives. Microprocess. Microsyst. **64**, 221–236 (2019)
13. Mohamed Asan Basiri, M., Shukla, S.K.: Low power hardware implementations for network packet processing elements. Integr. VLSI J. **62**, 170–181 (2018)
14. Cortadella, J., Kondratyev, A., Lavagno, L., Lwin, K., Sotiriou, C.: From synchronous to asynchronous: an automatic approach. In: IEEE Design, Automation and Test in Europe Conference and Exhibition (2004)
15. Moreira, M., Calazans, N.: Comparing two asynchronous IC design flows. In: South Symposium on Microelectronics (2012)
16. Xia, Z., Ishihara, S., Hariyama, M., Kameyama, M.: Dual-rail/single-rail hybrid logic design for high-performance asynchronous circuit. In: IEEE International Symposium on Circuits and Systems (ISCAS), pp. 1–4 (2012)
17. Gonzalez, R., Gordon, B.M., Horowitz, M.A.: Supply and threshold voltage scaling for low power CMOS. IEEE J. Solid State Circ. **32**(8), 1210–1216 (1997)

A Unified Methodology for Hardware Obfuscation and IP Watermarking

Saurabh Gangurde and Binod Kumar$^{(\boxtimes)}$ ⓘ

Computer Architecture and Dependable Systems Lab (CADSL),
Department of Electrical Engineering, IIT Bombay, Mumbai, India
saurabhgangurde@iitb.ac.in, binodkumar@ee.iitb.ac.in

Abstract. Hardware security is a matter of increasing importance in the modern world. With increasing threats of piracy and theft, it is needed to devise methodologies to mitigate these concerns. Obfuscating the design netlist is a popular method to achieve this to a significant extent. However, full security guarantee is not provided with the encryption approach. Under this scenario, a watermarking method complements the security guarantee by providing claims of IP authorship. In this paper, we present a unified methodology for circuit encryption and watermarking to enhance hardware security. Experiments on several ISCAS'85 benchmark circuits show that the proposed methodology has average 8.2% area overhead and 11.3% power overhead.

Keywords: Hardware security · Obfuscation · Watermarking

1 Introduction

In the modern age, integrated circuits have been seriously hit by the growing concerns of information leakage and attack by unauthorized agents. This necessitates development of methods to ensure that these circuits can not be attacked and they are protected from illegal usage also [1–3]. Moreover, most of the design companies are fabless nowadays which results into involvement of many other companies which are even continents apart [4–6]. As a result of this, at times sharing of the designs is inevitable which can lead to IP (intellectual property) theft in various forms.

Circuit Obfuscation is one of the technique to mitigate hardware attacks as this technique encrypts the circuit/design. This leads to serious security concerns as the designs can be copied stealthily which leads to the original designers being bereft of their rights. Typically, the logic encryption is carried out by addition of extra XOR gates in the original circuit. The key acts as a switch for opening up the logic functionality of the circuit to its legal owner. We utilize a similar methodology for logic encryption and conjunct it with a methodology for watermarking the concerned design (or, IP). The objectives of the proposed logic encryption methodology are twofold. First, it enhances the security guarantee and second, it provides a scheme to ascertain the IP authorship. Since the IC

© Springer Nature Singapore Pte Ltd. 2019
A. Sengupta et al. (Eds.): VDAT 2019, CCIS 1066, pp. 258–271, 2019.
https://doi.org/10.1007/978-981-32-9767-8_23

design and fabrication process is typically spread out across many vendors and countries, it is necessary to have a mechanism to ascertain the design authorship through watermarking. Since area overhead is an unwilling manifestation of the obfuscation methodology, it is needed to minimize it as much as possible while ensuring that there is no decrease in the circuit delay. This is one of the reasons behind our motivation for attempting together logic obfuscation and IP watermarking. In this paper, we have applied the unified methodology on combinational circuits only. We strongly believe that the same methodology can be extended/adapted to sequential circuits also for unified obfuscation and watermarking. An unified methodology for logic encryption and watermarking solves these two issues in a manner such that overheads are contained within limits necessary to significantly enhance the security guarantee of the hardware designs.

The remainder of the paper is organized as follows. Section 2 summarizes some of the related work on hardware obfuscation and digital watermarking. Section 3 presents our unified methodology of obfuscation and watermarking. This section also provides an illustration of the proposed methodology. Section 4 presents our experimental results regarding area overhead and delay. Finally, Sect. 5 concludes the paper with some directions on future research.

2   Related Work

Logic obfuscation is a popular method for enhancing the design security through insertion of additional gates in the design [7]. By adding extra gates into the design, the functionality can be hidden significantly and it becomes easier to thwart attack attempts [1,8–11]. The goal here varies from avoiding IC overproduction (for illegal sales) to avoiding the reverse engineering of the designs. In previous years, many authors have suggested various techniques for obfuscation of circuits [12–15]. For example, similar to XOR cell, multiplexer cell is used as a target for obfuscation with correct key as the select input [3]. While there are approaches for functionality obfuscation, some proposals have also suggested layout obfuscation. Note that these logic obfuscation techniques incur area overhead with implications on power dissipation and delay parameters. Therefore, the minimization of overhead issues while enhancing the security guarantee in a maximal manner is an ongoing area of research. Performing the obfuscation at higher levels of design abstraction has also been proposed [16]. Logic obfuscation for sequential circuits has also been specifically addressed via physically unclonable functions (PUFs) in [17].

To ascertain authorship of an intellectual property (IP), watermarking can be very useful [18–22]. In the context of integrated circuit designs, we can say that even if someone breaks encryption of the obfuscated circuit we need some signature to prove our authorship. It is particularly very useful in cases of arbitration involving multiple parties. Watermarking a circuit is technically equivalent to embedding a secret message in the design netlist. The authors in [18] provide a detailed survey and comparison of various watermarking techniques for different kind of applications. The authors in [23] have proposed several methods of watermarking for sequential functions. Watermarking ensures continuance of trust between customers and IP producers. With watermarking, the customers can be sure that they have purchased a legitimate product while the IP creators/vendors are sure that customers can not resell the products illegally. Thus, the proposed unified methodology in the paper is aimed at preventing both hardware security attacks and IP theft.

3   Proposed Methodology

Obfuscation adds key bits in the primary inputs effectively making input vectors longer, thereby, enhancing the security guarantee. There is only one correct key vector for which the circuit works correctly and for all other key combinations outputs of the circuits are don't care situations (e.g., say we add n bit key to circuit which have m bit primary inputs so there are $(2^n - 1) * 2^m$ combinations for which outputs are don't care). For example, the input vector in Table 1 shows wrong key combinations and corresponding don't care outputs. These don't care situations are potential targets for watermarking as shown in green color in Table 1. Since, the corresponding outputs are don't cares (in the fourth and fifth rows of Table 1), we can perform the watermarking operation using them by specifying the don't cares corresponding to any one of these conditions. This may further depend on the choice of gates to be watermarked in the particular circuit.

Table 1. Truth table for obfuscated circuit

Primary Inp	Key Inp	output
10.....1	10110	1
10.....0	10110	0
10.....0	0XXXX	X
00.....1	11XXX	X
11.....1	10110	0
00.....0	10110	1

The proposed methodology maps the logic encryption problem to a stuck-at fault detectability task. The underlying motivation is the fact that a test vector capable to detect stuck-at faults at some nets in the circuit can identify primary outputs not affected by addition of extra gates. This assists in finding the obfuscation and watermarking positions in an unified manner. Proposed methodology is explained below stepwise with example of C17 circuit from ISCAS'85 combinational benchmark suite. The pseudo code for the proposed methodology is given as Algorithm 1.

Algorithm 1. Unified Methodology for logic encryption and watermarking

---

Result: Encrypted and Watermarked Circuit(EnWaC)

1 G=generate_graph(original_circuit);
2 V=one_random_test_vector;
3 obfuscation_targets=stuck_at_fault_simulator(G,V);
4 levelize_graph(G);
5 OWT=obfuscation_watermark_targets;
6 TPO=target_primary_output;
7 obfuscation_watermark_targets=[];
8 modified_graph=G;
9 **for** *target in obfuscation_targets* **do**
10   subgraph=subgraph(G,target);
11   components=connected_components(G);
12   **for** *component in components* **do**
13   target_primary_output=outputs(component);
14   OWT.add(target,target_primary_output);
15   add_key_and_xor_gate(target,modified_graph);
16   add_watermark(TPO,modified_graph);
17   **end**
18 **end**
19 **return** modified_graph;
20 EnWaC ← circuit as per modified_graph;

3.1 Step 1: Generate Circuit Graph

Given a netlist of circuit in hardware description language(VHDL/verilog or any other) construct a directed acyclic graph (G) of the circuit. Nodes of this graph are gates and primary inputs/outputs in the netlist and edges would correspond to the wires between gates. Figure 1 show the original circuit, C17 which we consider here for completely illustrating our unified watermarking and encryption methodology. We have to choose the targets for obfuscation and encryption. Further, we levelized the circuit graph (G) or the circuit with respect to fanout of the gates (which are nodes in the circuit graph). Primary inputs are nodes having level 0 and recursively we can levelize circuit using the following equation:

$$u.level = u.parent.level + 1$$

where u is node of graph (G). Here, parent refers to the preceding parent node of current node u. Figure 2 shows levelized C17 circuit.

3.2 Step 2: Generate Random Test Vector

Consider a random test vector (V) which detects stuck-at fault at some nets (N) in the circuit. Find those nets (N) for which stuck-at testability succeeds by V. For instance-Randomly generated test vector 11110 can test stuck at

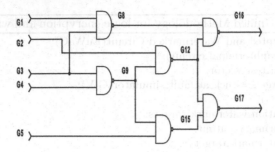

Fig. 1. C17 Circuit from ISCAS'85 benchmark.

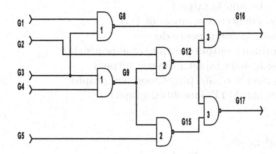

Fig. 2. Levelized C17 circuit

faults at $G9, G12, G15, G8$ as shown in red color in Fig. 3. Let's call these as *obfuscation_targets*. For each target in *obfuscation_targets* repeat step 4 which is basically finding the connected components in the logical fan-out of those nets.

3.3   Step 3: Connected Component Analysis of the Circuit

– Extract subgraph of the circuit iterating following criteria for each node in graph (G) built in step 1 for the selected target from step 3:

$$\text{If } node.level > target.level \text{ then } subgraph.add(node).$$

– Find connected components in the subgraph. Each component will have at least one primary output. Store these target and primary output pair for further analysis. These primary output(s) will have corresponding target from step 3. Note that after doing connected component analysis, we get primary output(s) such that these outputs are independent of the chosen target. This is because of the fact that the graph connectivity shows dependence on parent nodes only and thereby different components are independent of each other. For example, in C17 circuit target net $G15$ is chosen as target. After extracting subgraph with the above criteria, we can obtain the disconnected components which are shown in Fig. 4. This figure shows two disconnected components with respect to net $G15$ (which acts as a parent node in the subgraph).

Each component contains exactly one primary output of the circuit. We are going to use primary output $G16$ as it is independent of target $G15$ and we can easily watermark $G16$ with respect to $G15$ which is explained below in step 4.

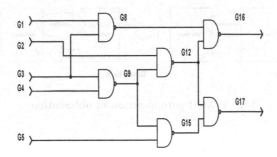

Fig. 3. Target net selection for C17 circuit (Color figure online)

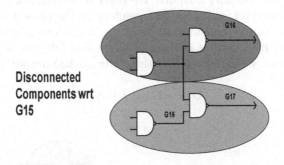

Fig. 4. Output of graph-based connection analysis

3.4   Step 4: Obfuscation and Watermarking Procedure

Final step consists of mixture of obfuscation as well watermarking using stored pairs of targets and corresponding primary outputs. For every target net, replace this net with XOR gate and add key bit in primary input. The methodology for XOR gate insertion is schematically illustrated in Fig. 5. Since the key can be either 0 or 1, we can have 2 different configurations for the obfuscated circuit. When the correct key is 0, the obfuscated circuit behaves in a way similar to a wire in all functional cases (which is shown on left hand side of Fig. 5). In a similar vein, when the correct key is 1, the obfuscated circuit behaves as if there is an inverter (NOT gate) at the site of obfuscation (which is shown on left hand

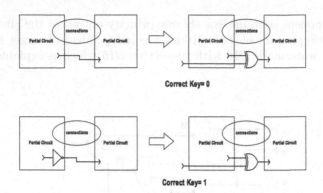

Fig. 5. XOR gate insertion in obfuscation

side of Fig. 5). Let's assume that the correct key bit to be 0. If target net is driven by NOT gate then replace the corresponding gate and net(s) with XOR gate and add key bit in primary input. Note that in this modified circuit, correct key bit will be 1 as explained in Fig. 5. Similarly for watermarking, we randomly choose one of the primary output from the target-output pairs. Note that a stored pair can consist of many primary outputs. We need to watermark the circuit using key bits added to target which are independent of the chosen primary output. In the running example, output $G16$ is chosen and corresponding (target net, key) pair is $(G15, K_0)$. Output is watermarked using OR gate and K_0 as shown in Fig. 6. Therefore, we can state that the watermarked output in this circuit is given by

$$G16 = G16_{old} + K_0$$

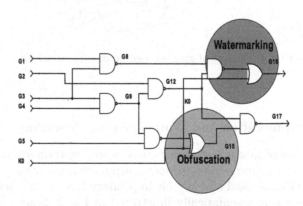

Fig. 6. Final obfuscated and watermarked C17 circuit

As the correct key bit is 0, for $K_0 = 1$ $G16$ is don't care for original C17 circuit. However, we are forcing $G16 = 1$ for all inputs where $K_0 = 1$ thus leaving watermark in the functionality of the circuit itself. We can do this only because $G16$ does not depend on K_0 which is extracted in step 4. Similarly, we can also watermark using AND gate as

$$G16 = G16_{old}.\bar{K}_0$$

Decision of watermarking will be entirely dependent on the designer (i.e., whether to choose OR gate or AND gate, which key bits should be chosen etc). This provides sufficient freedom to the designer to adjust the obfuscation level with the physical design parameters (area, delay etc.)

Through the above methodology, it is clear that circuit has obfuscated functionality (i.e., circuit will give correct output only if correct key is provided) as well as watermarked (i.e. for the special inputs chosen by designer and the corresponding outputs are actually don't cares for the original circuit but watermarked by designer or IP holder.) These special outputs would act as watermarked signature(s) for the particular circuit designer or the design company or the person who has acquired the IP in a legal manner.

4   Experiments and Results

4.1   Experimental Setup

We have used an in-house stuck-at-fault simulator to generate the target combinations for watermarking and encryption. For area and power overhead analysis, we used Synopsis Design Compiler(DC). NetworkX library in python is used for the connected component analysis of graph of the circuit. The characteristics of the benchmark circuits are reported in Table 2 which are obtained after synthesis with the GSCL 45 nm standard cell library by the DC tool. It is important to note that we have obfuscated only 2% of total cells (which is shown in third column of Table 2) of the complete circuit, whereas many of the previous techniques have proposed higher number of circuit cells to be encrypted such as 5% of cells have been obfuscated in [3]. Thus, the proposed methodology has lesser area overhead in comparison to [3] and other similar techniques targeting logic obfuscation.

4.2   Overhead Results for Benchmark Circuits

It is imperative that the security guarantee with the proposed method of obfuscation and watermarking depends on the length of the key which is utilized. Clearly, the length of the key becomes a critical factor for the associated area and power overheads. Therefore, we measure these overheads for all the benchmark circuits presented in Table 2 with respect to the number of key bits added to the original circuit. Normalized area and power overhead results are plotted in Figs. 7, 8, 9, 10, 11 and 12 (normalization is done with respect to the original circuit). The normalization has been carried out with respect the original circuit (i.e., non-obfuscated circuit). X-axis of each figure shows the number of

Table 2. ISCAS'85 benchmark circuits

Circuit	Number of nets	Number of cells
C17	12	7
C432	214	178
C499	270	229
C880	336	276
C1355	265	224
C5315	1021	843
C6288	2742	2710

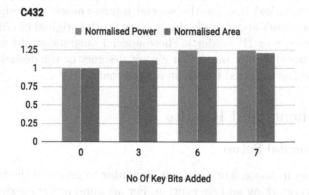

Fig. 7. Results for benchmark circuit C432

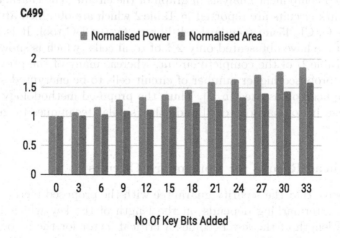

Fig. 8. Results for benchmark circuit C499

key bits added in circuit. This variable is changed to observe the manifestation in area and power overhead with respect to the number of key bits added. It is

C880

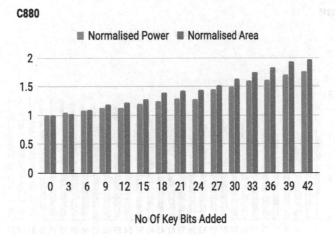

Fig. 9. Results for benchmark circuit C880

C1355

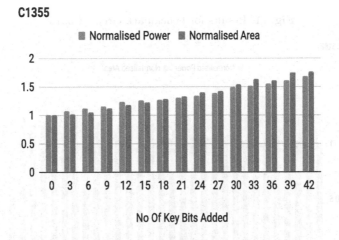

Fig. 10. Results for benchmark circuit C1355

observed that for larger circuit we can add more and more key bits without any significant increment in area or power overheads. We have obtained the power (static+dynamic) results using Design compiler tool. This tool reports static power in accordance with the standard cell library utilized during synthesis process and the dynamic power is computed by the probabilistic calculation of the resulting switching activity at the circuit nets.

For C432 circuit, there is a minuscule increase in the area and power even if seven key bits have been added. Due to the smaller size of the circuit, we did not try for larger number of key bits in this case. The power overhead is slightly larger than that of the area overhead. For C499 circuit, even if the number of keys are eighteen, the area overhead and the power overhead are within 50%.

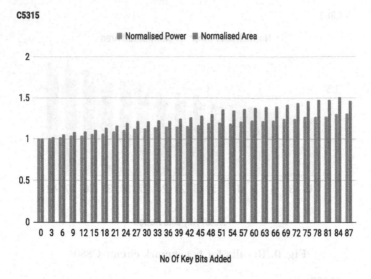

Fig. 11. Results for benchmark circuit C5315

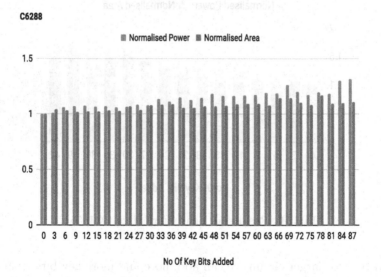

Fig. 12. Results for benchmark circuit C6288

When the number of key bits increases beyond eighteen, there is increase in the power overhead whereas area overhead is limited to 50% even if the key bits are increased to thirty. The increment in area and power overhead decreases when we are obfuscating larger sized circuits. For example- in C5315 circuit with in 50% limits of area and power overhead, as many as eighty-one key bits can be added. Note that unlike C432 and C499, the area overhead is larger than the power overhead. A similar trend is observed for the case of C6288 benchmark

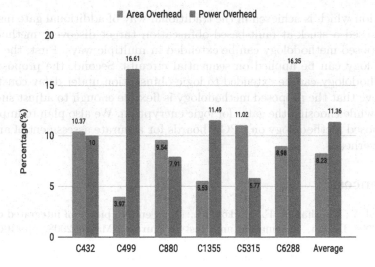

Fig. 13. Averaged overhead results

circuit. In this case, the final area remains close to the original area even if the number of keys are as high as seventy-five which definitely ensures higher security guarantee. These results showcase that the proposed methodology is scalable with the increase in circuit size. The proposed methodology attains a wider acceptability for large circuit sizes because of very less area overhead for them.

4.3 Averaged Overhead Results

Corresponding area and power overhead results are shown in Fig. 13 for all circuits considered for our experiments. On an average, 8.2% area overhead and 11.3 % power overhead is needed to implement the proposed methodology. For the circuit of large size, the area overhead is lesser (with in 10%) while power overhead is slightly larger. However, the increase in power can be traded off with the number of key bits to be added. Thus, with the proposed technique for watermarking and obfuscation in an unified manner, we can enhance the security guarantee at affordable overhead costs.

5 Conclusion

The growing attacks on integrated circuits across the globe have increased the impetus to look into hardware security measures. Moreover, because of decentralized design process and associated volume production of integrated circuits, the issue of IP theft has become also very serious. We presented an unified methodology for logic encryption and IP watermarking. By utilizing the don't care in input-output combinations, we can watermark the IP in addition to the logic obfuscation which is achieved in the traditional way of additional gate insertion. We proposed a stuck-at fault-based obfuscation target discovery methodology. The proposed methodology can be extended in multiple ways. First, the unified methodology can be applied on sequential circuits. Second, the proposed unified methodology can be extended to logic obfuscation under delay constraints. We believe that the proposed methodology is flexible enough to adjust such constraints while choosing the gates for logic encryption. We also plan to implement the proposed methodology on FPGA boards for accurate assessment of area and power overheads.

References

1. Roy, J.A., Koushanfar, F., Markov, I.L.: Epic: ending piracy of integrated circuits. In: 2008 Design, Automation and Test in Europe, March 2008, pp. 1069–1074 (2008)
2. Schulze, T.E., Kwiat, K., Kamhoua, C., Chang, S.-C., Shi, Y.: Record: temporarily randomized encoding of combinational logic for resistance to data leakage from hardware trojan. In: 2016 IEEE Asian Hardware-Oriented Security and Trust (AsianHOST), December 2016, pp. 1–6 (2016)
3. Zhang, J.: A practical logic obfuscation technique for hardware security. IEEE Trans. Very Large Scale Integr. (VLSI) Syst. **24**(3), 1193–1197 (2016)
4. Arafin, M.T., Stanley, A., Sharma, P.: Hardware-based anti-counterfeiting techniques for safeguarding supply chain integrity. In: 2017 IEEE International Symposium on Circuits and Systems (ISCAS), May 2017, pp. 1–4 (2017)
5. Rajendran, J.J.V.: An overview of hardware intellectual property protection. In: 2017 IEEE International Symposium on Circuits and Systems (ISCAS), May 2017, pp. 1–4 (2017)
6. Liu, B., Qu, G.: VLSI supply chain security risks and mitigation techniques: a survey. Integration **55**, 438–448 (2016). http://www.sciencedirect.com/science/article/pii/S0167926016300013
7. Rajendran, J., Pino, Y., Sinanoglu, O., Karri, R.: Security analysis of logic obfuscation. In: DAC Design Automation Conference, June 2012, pp. 83–89 (2012)
8. Alasad, Q., Yuan, J.: Logic obfuscation against IC reverse engineering attacks using PLGs. In: 2017 IEEE International Conference on Computer Design (ICCD), November 2017, pp. 341–344 (2017)
9. Chakraborty, R.S., Bhunia, S.: Hardware protection and authentication through netlist level obfuscation. In: 2008 IEEE/ACM International Conference on Computer-Aided Design, November 2008, pp. 674–677 (2008)
10. Tehranipoor, M., Koushanfar, F.: A survey of hardware trojan taxonomy and detection. IEEE Des. Test Comput. **27**(1), 10–25 (2010)
11. Rajendran, J., Sinanoglu, O., Karri, R.: VLSI testing based security metric for IC camouflaging. In: 2013 IEEE International Test Conference (ITC), September 2013, pp. 1–4 (2013)
12. Chakraborty, A., Xie, Y., Srivastava, A.: Template attack based deobfuscation of integrated circuits. In: 2017 IEEE International Conference on Computer Design (ICCD), November 2017, pp. 41–44 (2017)
13. Rajendran, J., Pino, Y., Sinanoglu, O., Karri, R.: Logic encryption: a fault analysis perspective. In: 2012 Design, Automation Test in Europe Conference Exhibition (DATE), March 2012, pp. 953–958 (2012)

14. Awan, S.M., Rashid, S., Gao, M., Qu, G.: Functional obfuscation of digital circuits using observability don't care conditions. In: 2016 IEEE International Conference on Information and Automation for Sustainability (ICIAfS), December 2016, pp. 1–6 (2016)
15. Meade, T., Zhao, Z., Zhang, S., Pan, D., Jin, Y.: Revisit sequential logic obfuscation: attacks and defenses. In: 2017 IEEE International Symposium on Circuits and Systems (ISCAS), May 2017, pp. 1–4 (2017)
16. Lao, Y., Parhi, K.K.: Obfuscating DSP circuits via high-level transformations. IEEE Trans. Very Large Scale Integr. (VLSI) Syst. **23**(5), 819–830 (2015)
17. Zhang, J., Lin, Y., Lyu, Y., Qu, G.: A PUF-FSM binding scheme for FPGA IP protection and pay-per-device licensing. IEEE Trans. Inf. Forensics Secur. **10**(6), 1137–1150 (2015)
18. Abdel-Hamid, A.T., Tahar, S.: IP watermarking techniques: survey and comparison. In: Proceedings of the 3rd IEEE International Workshop on System-on-Chip for Real-Time Applications, July 2003, pp. 60–65 (2003)
19. Kahng, A.B., Kirovski, D., Mantik, S., Potkonjak, M., Wong, J.L.: Copy detection for intellectual property protection of VLSI designs. In: 1999 IEEE/ACM International Conference on Computer Aided Design. Digest of Technical Papers (Cat. No. 99CH37051), November 1999, pp. 600–604 (1999)
20. Abdel-Hamid, A.T., Tahar, S., Aboulhamid, E.M.: A tool for automatic watermarking of IP designs. In: The 2nd Annual IEEE Northeast Workshop on Circuits and Systems, NEWCAS 2004, June 2004, pp. 381–384 (2004)
21. Publicly detectable watermarking for intellectual property authentication in VLSI design. IEEE Trans. Comput.-Aided Des. Integr. Circ. Syst. **21**(11), 1363–1368 (2002)
22. Fan, Y.: Testing-based watermarking techniques for intellectual-property identification in SOC design. IEEE Trans. Instrum. Measur. **57**(3), 467–479 (2008)
23. Torunoglu, I., Charbon, E.: Watermarking-based copyright protection of sequential functions. IEEE J. Solid-State Circ. **35**(3), 434–440 (2000)

Threshold Implementation of a Low-Cost CLEFIA-128 Cipher for Power Analysis Attack Resistance

S. Shanthi Rekha and P. Saravanan$^{(\boxtimes)}$ (iD)

Department of Electronics and Communication Engineering,
PSG College of Technology, Coimbatore 641 004, India
dpsaravanan@gmail.com

Abstract. Lightweight cryptography aims to satisfy the need for security and privacy in the resource constrained environment like smart cards, RFID and smart edge nodes in Internet of Things (IoT). CLEFIA is one of the ISO/IEC 29191-2 standard lightweight cryptographic algorithm suitable for these applications. Though CLEFIA is proven to be resistant to the cryptanalytic attacks, it is vulnerable to implementation attacks namely Side-Channel Attacks (SCAs). Power Analysis Attacks (PAAs) are the most popular type of SCA and the existing literature has shown successful PAA against CLEFIA. Hence there is a need for strong countermeasure against PAA. The contributions of this work are two-fold: (i) We have proposed a novel 16-bit serial architecture for CLEFIA-128 encryption with a Composite Field Architecture (CFA) based S1 box and Algebraic Normal Form (ANF) based S0 box (ii) A novel Threshold Implementation (TI) with 2-input shares is derived and implemented for the S0, S1 boxes. Thereby, two-shared top level CLEFIA architecture is constructed that shows sufficient first-order PAA resistance when validated using SAKURA-G FPGA board. The PAA categories considered are: (i) Evaluation style – Differential Power Analysis (DPA), Correlation Power Analysis (CPA), Mutual Information Analysis (MIA) with three different power models (ii) Conformance style –Test Vector Leakage Assessment (TVLA) Attack category. This work thereby becomes the first contribution to propose a first-order PAA resistance two-share TI-based CLEFIA implementation with a considerable area compromise, suitable for resource constrained applications.

Keywords: Power Analysis Attack · Threshold Implementation · Low-cost implementation · CLEFIA · Serial architecture

1 Introduction

The recent advancements in Internet of Things (IoT) leads to large number of resource constrained devices to connect to the Internet. To ensure security of these devices, the traditional algorithms are not suitable and hence there is a new class of cryptographic algorithms developed for these applications under the category of lightweight ciphers. Among the different lightweight ciphers developed, Sony Corporation's CLEFIA [1] is standardized by ISO/IEC 29192-2 in 2012 [2]. Further CLEFIA is a recommended

© Springer Nature Singapore Pte Ltd. 2019
A. Sengupta et al. (Eds.): VDAT 2019, CCIS 1066, pp. 272–285, 2019.
https://doi.org/10.1007/978-981-32-9767-8_24

cipher for lightweight cryptographic technology in e-government applications by the Japanese Cryptographic Research and Evaluation Committee (CRYPTREC) in 2013 [3]. Hence we have implemented CLEFIA in our work.

CLEFIA is a 128-bit block cipher with three different key lengths 128, 192 and 256-bits. Two types of keys namely round keys (RK) and whitening keys (WK) are used for encryption and decryption. The number of rounds of operation varies as 18, 22 and 26 rounds with the key length. The encryption/decryption architecture is based on Generalized Feistel Network (GFN) where a 4-branch Feistel structure is employed with two F-functions F0 and F1. Each of the two F-functions uses two Substitution boxes (S-box) S0 and S1 and two diffusion matrices M0 and M1. The key generation module is also based on the same 4-branch Feistel structure for 128-bit and 8-branch Feistel structure for 192/256-bit key. Decryption is the inverse of encryption where the round keys and whitening keys have to be given in reverse order. More detailed explanation of the round functions and key generation can be found in [1]. While most of the existing works have proposed iterative architectures for CLEFIA-128, the authors of [4] have reported three different 8-bit serialized ASIC implementations for the cipher on 130 nm technology.

The vulnerability of the CLEFIA cipher to Differential Attacks [5] and Fault Attacks [6] has been studied in detail. Side Channel Attacks (SCAs) are one class of attacks that exploits the implementation vulnerabilities of the cryptographic devices to extract the secret key. By monitoring the power consumption/electromagnetic radiations/time taken for execution, the key value can be monitored. These attacks are non-invasive and hence they cannot be detected. Among the different types of side channels, power analysis attacks (PAAs) are vast studied in literature. Authors of [7] have conducted a simulation based Differential Power Analysis (DPA) on the first round of CLEFIA to extract the first round key using a hamming weight model (HWM). The work in [8] demonstrates a Correlation Power Analysis (CPA) and electromagnetic attack on the CLEFIA implementation on 8-bit AVR processor based smart card. The attack is carried out on the last 3 rounds of encryption. Hence there is a strong need for efficient countermeasures to prevent PAA.

The PAA countermeasures can be implemented at different abstraction levels. We aim to implement it at RTL level in-order to implement and validate the same on a SCA standard SAKURA-G board. Two major countermeasures at RTL are Hiding and Masking. The work in [10] has shown first, second and third order masking technique for CLEFIA on FPGA and Intel platform, however there is no evaluation of PAA resistance by the authors. The Masking technique leaks information due to glitches. Threshold Implementation (TI), a variant of masking technique was proposed in [9] to overcome the leakage due to glitches and is proved to be the strongest countermeasure against PAA till date. As per the author's knowledge, there is no work in literature for a TI implementation of CLEFIA. The major contributions of this work are:

- A 16-bit novel serial architecture is proposed for CLEFIA-128 with a Composite Field Architecture (CFA) based S1 box and Algebraic Normal Form (ANF) based S0 box. The proposed architecture has achieved a very low area and a reasonable throughput.

- A novel 2-share based TI implementation is derived for CLEFIA S0 and S1 box for the first time in literature and integrated to derive a two-shared TI based CLEFIA architecture.
- The proposed first-order protected CLEFIA architecture is validated for PAA resistance against (i) Evaluation Style categories – DPA, CPA, Mutual Information Analysis (MIA) and (ii) Conformance Style categories – non-specific Test Vector Leakage Assessment (TVLA). The results show that the implementation is resistant against first-order PAAs.

The paper is organized as follows: Sect. 2 describes the novelty in CLEFIA architecture along with the result comparison. Section 3 explains in detail on the proposed TI implementation derivation and Sect. 4 presents the results of PAA evaluation. Section 5 presents the conclusion followed by references.

2   Proposed CLEFIA Architecture

We have proposed a serial CLEFIA architecture with a 16-bit data-path to perform encryption/decryption as shown in Fig. 1. The synthesis results are performed with Semi-Conductor Laboratory (SCL) [8] 180 nm technology using Cadence Encounter RTL Compiler. For comparison purposes, the area is reported in Gate Equivalence (GE) which is obtained by dividing the area reported in μm^2 by the area of the lowest driving strength 2-input NAND gate of that corresponding technology library.

The data-path is formed by using area efficient S0/S1 boxes as explained in Sect. 2.1, followed by M0/M1 matrix realizations using x2, x4 and x8 Galois Field (GF) multipliers. The register files R0–R7 are of 16-bit size and each line carries 16-bit data except the ones explicitly shown as 8-bits. The addition of R8 register file in our proposed serial architecture has reduced the critical path delay from 5.1 ns to 3.5 ns. Further the '16' 2x1 MUXes required for the product addition in M0/M1 matrix Multipliers are reduced to '2' MUXes by placing them before the 'R8' register. These optimization techniques along with the efficient realizations of the individual blocks to obtain a 16-bit CLEFIA data-path is one of our contribution.

2.1   ANF Based CLEFIA S0 Box

CLEFIA S0 box construction is based on 4 random S-boxes namely SS0, SS1, SS2 and SS3 which are further combined using $GF(2^4)$ multiplier. In this work, ANF based implementation is chosen for the S0 box realization. ANF representation of a Boolean function is useful to evaluate the algebraic degree and the linearity property of any function. ANF expressions are mainly useful to find shares of the Boolean function, when we adopt the countermeasure against SCA namely TI. The ANF implementation of S0 box requires only 115 GE, hence we have adopted the same for our serial architecture.

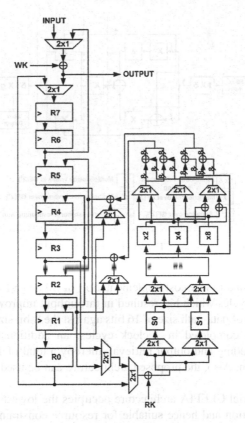

Fig. 1. Proposed 16-bit serial data-path of CLEFIA architecture

2.2 CFA Based CLEFIA S1 Box

CLEFIA S1 box construction is based on $GF(2^8)$ inversion using the polynomial $z^8 + z^4 + z^3 + z^2 + 1$ [2]. The CFA based realization of S-boxes are proved to achieve the lowest area in literature. The core of the CFA computation is the multiplicative inverse block preceded and followed by the affine transformation f and g respectively as shown in Fig. 2. Gate-level implementations of the $GF(2^4)$ arithmetic based blocks namely multiplier, squarer, constant multiplier, inverter, isomorphic and inverse iso-morphic mapping combined with affine f and g are adopted in this work. The CFA based S1 box architecture consumes an area of about 207 GE which is 50% less compared to the LUT approach. Hence we have chosen this for the top level serial architecture.

The proposed serial architecture after integration of the sub-blocks occupies 1345 GE and consumes a power of 1.3 mW. The performance comparison of the proposed serial CLEFIA architecture with the existing serial architecture [4] is shown in Table 1. It can be seen that, there is about 19% decrease in total area and a two-fold improvement in throughput calculated at 100 kHz. For comparison with [4], we have chosen the operating frequency of 100 kHz. The area decrease of the proposed

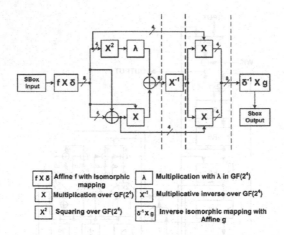

Fig. 2. Proposed CFA architecture of CLEFIA S1 box

architecture is attributed to low cost implementation of S0 and S1 boxes. The decrease in number of clock cycles which has resulted in throughput improvement is because of the optimal selection of data-path size of 16 bits against the 8-bit size in [4]. Each round computation can be completed in 7 clock cycles, an additional 8 clock cycles is required for input loading and output retrieval, thereby a total of 142 clock cycles for encryption/decryption. Also, the proposed architecture can be used for both encryption and decryption.

The proposed serial CLEFIA architecture occupies the lowest area and has a very low power consumption and hence suitable for resource constrained applications like edge nodes in IoT devices, RFID Tags, smart cards etc.

3   Proposed CLEFIA Threshold Implementation

The proposed serial architecture has comparatively less algorithmic noise that arises from parallel computation of data and hence has less resistance to PAA. This motivates us to derive a low-cost RTL countermeasure for the proposed serial CLEFIA archi-tecture which is explained in the subsequent section.

3.1   Threshold Implementation of CLEFIA

The objective of the countermeasures is to nullify the effect of data that the circuit processes on the power consumption. At the RTL level, the most efficient technique proposed so far till date is Threshold Implementation (TI), originally proposed by Nikova et al. in 2006 [9]. It involves splitting of the data into two or more shares and the computation data-path of each share runs in parallel. There are three basic requirements that any TI implementation should satisfy: Correctness, Non-completeness and Uniformity. The key features and advantages of TI techniques are (i) The intermediate results do not leak any information about the secret value since each share is independent of at least one input (ii) Even in the presence of glitches, sufficient first-order resistance is obtained. (iii) The technique is compatible with the standard RTL Design flow.

In general for a 'd'-th order security of any arbitrary function with algebraic degree 't', the TI scheme uses a minimum of (td + 1) shares. The work in [11] is to further reduce the number of shares from (td + 1) to (d + 1) provided that the input shares are independent. Hence the output share is independent of at least one share of input variable. In-order to satisfy the non-completeness property, the design has to be pipelined to sufficient number of stages. To ensure uniformity in all these cases, sufficient bits of randomness is introduced at each pipelined intermediate computation stage. The work in [12] has realized a 3-stage pipelined AES S-box with 2 shares with each stage requiring about 12, 24 and 28 bits of randomness. The authors claim to have achieved less area compared to the other AES TI implementations.

Based on this idea, ours is the first work to derive a TI implementation for a low-cost CLEFIA architecture. The TI implementation of the proposed CFA S1 box and ANF S0 boxes are derived and using the same, the two-share top level CI FFIA architecture is implemented. In this work, the shares of the inputs a, b are denoted as $\{a0, a1\}$ $\{b0, b1\}$; the shares of the output f[i], i = 0, 1, 2, 3 are denoted as $\{f3[i], f2[i], f1[i], f0[i]\}$ respectively.

TI Implementation of CLEFIA S1 box: The CFA Architecture of S1 box is shown in Sect. 2.2. The CFA architecture consists of linear blocks namely affine transformation f with isomorphic mapping, affine transformation g with inverse isomorphic mapping, square-scaler, addition blocks which are replicated directly for processing the two-shares. The non-linear blocks are the $GF(2^4)$ multiplier and inverter. Based on the work in [11], for the first-order security (d = 1), number of required input shares is d + 1=2, provided that the input shares are independent and hence the number of output shares is $(d + 1)^t = 2^t$, t is the algebraic degree of the function. It is observed that the algebraic degree of the $GF(2^4)$ multiplier is 2 and $GF(2^4)$ inverter is 3. Hence the TI multiplier implementation takes 2-input and produces 4-output shares as shown in (1), inverter implementation takes 2-input and produces 8-output shares. The 4-output shares of multiplier are further reduced to two by xoring with sufficient bits of randomness. Similarly the 8-output shares of inverter are reduced to two. Also, the number of pipeline stages is 3 similar to [12]. Due to space limitations, only the multiplier sharing expressions are given in (1). To satisfy the non-uniformity property, the 3-pipelining stages require 12, 28 and 24 bits of randomness each. The TI implementation of CFA S1 box occupies 1085 GE and consumes 6.2 mW power.

$$f[3] = (a[3] * b[3]) \oplus (a[3] * b[0]) \oplus (a[0] * b[3]) \oplus (a[2] * b[1]) \oplus (a[1] * b[2])$$
$$f[2] = (a[3] * b[3]) \oplus (a[3] * b[2]) \oplus (a[2] * b[3]) \oplus (a[2] * b[0]) \oplus (a[0] * b[2]) \oplus (a[1] * b[1])$$
$$f[1] = (a[3] * b[2]) \oplus (a[2] * b[3]) \oplus (a[3] * b[1]) \oplus (a[1] * b[3]) \oplus (a[2] * b[2]) \oplus (a[0] * b[1]) \oplus (a[1] * b[0])$$
$$f[0] = (a[3] * b[1]) \oplus (a[1] * b[3]) \oplus (a[2] * b[2]) \oplus (a[0] * b[0])$$

$$f0[3] = (a0[3] * b0[3]) \oplus (a0[3] * b0[0]) \oplus (a0[0] * b0[3]) \oplus (a0[2] * b0[1]) \oplus (a0[1] * b0[2])$$
$$f1[3] = (a0[3] * b1[3]) \oplus (a0[3] * b1[0]) \oplus (a0[0] * b1[3]) \oplus (a0[2] * b1[1]) \oplus (a0[1] * b1[2])$$
$$f2[3] = (a1[3] * b0[3]) \oplus (a1[3] * b0[0]) \oplus (a1[0] * b0[3]) \oplus (a1[2] * b0[1]) \oplus (a1[1] * b0[2])$$
$$f3[3] = (a1[3] * b1[3]) \oplus (a1[3] * b1[0]) \oplus (a1[0] * b1[3]) \oplus (a1[2] * b1[1]) \oplus (a1[1] * b1[2])$$

$$f0[2] = (a0[3] * b0[3]) \oplus (a0[3] * b0[2]) \oplus (a0[2] * b0[3]) \oplus (a0[2] * b0[0]) \oplus (a0[0] * b0[2]) \oplus (a0[1] * b0[1])$$
$$f1[2] = (a0[3] * b1[3]) \oplus (a0[3] * b1[2]) \oplus (a0[2] * b1[3]) \oplus (a0[2] * b1[0]) \oplus (a0[0] * b1[2]) \oplus (a0[1] * b1[1])$$
$$f2[2] = (a1[3] * b0[3]) \oplus (a1[3] * b0[2]) \oplus (a1[2] * b0[3]) \oplus (a1[2] * b0[0]) \oplus (a1[0] * b0[2]) \oplus (a1[1] * b0[1])$$
$$f3[2] = (a1[3] * b1[3]) \oplus (a1[3] * b1[2]) \oplus (a1[2] * b1[3]) \oplus (a1[2] * b1[0]) \oplus (a1[0] * b1[2]) \oplus (a1[1] * b1[1])$$

$$f0[1] = (a0[3] * b0[2]) \oplus (a0[2] * b0[3]) \oplus (a0[3] * b0[1]) \oplus (a0[1] * b0[3]) \oplus (a0[2] * b0[2]) \oplus (a0[0] * b0[1]) \oplus (a0[1] * b0[0])$$
$$f1[1] = (a0[3] * b1[2]) \oplus (a0[2] * b1[3]) \oplus (a0[3] * b1[1]) \oplus (a0[1] * b1[3]) \oplus (a0[2] * b1[2]) \oplus (a0[0] * b1[1]) \oplus (a0[1] * b1[0])$$
$$f2[1] = (a1[3] * b0[2]) \oplus (a1[2] * b0[3]) \oplus (a1[3] * b0[1]) \oplus (a1[1] * b0[3]) \oplus (a1[2] * b0[2]) \oplus (a1[0] * b0[1]) \oplus (a1[1] * b0[0])$$
$$f3[1] = (a1[3] * b1[2]) \oplus (a1[2] * b1[3]) \oplus (a1[3] * b1[1]) \oplus (a1[1] * b1[3]) \oplus (a1[2] * b1[2]) \oplus (a1[0] * b1[1]) \oplus (a1[1] * b1[0])$$

$$f0[0] = (a0[3] * b0[1]) \oplus (a0[1] * b0[3]) \oplus (a0[2] * b0[2]) \oplus (a0[0] * b0[0])$$
$$f1[0] = (a0[3] * b1[1]) \oplus (a0[1] * b1[3]) \oplus (a0[2] * b1[2]) \oplus (a0[0] * b1[0])$$
$$f2[0] = (a1[3] * b0[1]) \oplus (a1[1] * b0[3]) \oplus (a1[2] * b0[2]) \oplus (a1[0] * b0[0])$$
$$f3[0] = (a1[3] * b1[1]) \oplus (a1[1] * b1[3]) \oplus (a1[2] * b1[2]) \oplus (a1[0] * b1[0])$$

$$(1)$$

TI Implementation of CLEFIA S0 box: The ANF expressions of the CLEFIA S0 box has an algebraic degree of 3. Hence the SS0, SS1, SS2 and SS3 sub-blocks are shared with 2-input and 8-outputs (further reduced to 2) each and are combined using GF(2) multipliers to arrive at its TI implementation. Such an implementation has occupied about 581 GE with a power consumption value of 5.2 mW. Due to page limitations, ANF expressions of only SS0 and its corresponding two shared TI implementation expressions are shown in (2).

$$f0 = 1 \oplus a[0] \oplus (a[3] * a[2]) \oplus (a[3] * a[1]) \oplus (a[2] * a[1]) \oplus (a[1] * a[0]) \oplus (a[3] * a[2] * a[1]) \oplus (a[2] * a[1] * a[0])$$
$$f1 = 1 \oplus a[3] \oplus a[2] \oplus (a[3] * a[1]) \oplus (a[2] * a[0]) \oplus (a[1] * a[0]) \oplus (a[3] * a[2] * a[1]) \oplus (a[2] * a[1] * a[0])$$
$$f2 = 1 \oplus a[2] \oplus a[1] \oplus (a[3] * a[0]) \oplus (a[2] * a[0]) \oplus (a[1] * a[0]) \oplus (a[3] * a[2] * a[1])$$
$$f3 = a[3] \oplus (a[3] * a[1]) \oplus (a[2] * a[0]) \oplus (a[3] * a[2] * a[1]) \oplus (a[3] * a[2] * a[0])$$

$$f0[0] = 1 \oplus a0[0] \oplus (a0[3] * a0[2]) \oplus (a0[3] * a0[1]) \oplus (a0[2] * a0[1]) \oplus (a0[1] * a0[0]) \oplus (a0[3] * a0[2] * a0[1]) \oplus (a0[2] * a0[1] * a0[0])$$
$$f1[0] = a1[0] \oplus (a0[3] * a1[2]) \oplus (a0[3] * a1[1]) \oplus (a1[2] * a1[1]) \oplus (a1[1] * a1[0]) \oplus (a0[3] * a1[2] * a1[1]) \oplus (a1[2] * a1[1] * a1[0])$$
$$f2[0] = (a1[3] * a0[2]) \oplus (a1[3] * a1[1]) \oplus (a0[2] * a1[1]) \oplus (a1[1] * a0[0]) \oplus (a1[3] * a0[2] * a1[1]) \oplus (a0[2] * a1[1] * a0[0])$$
$$f3[0] = (a1[3] * a1[2]) \oplus (a1[3] * a0[1]) \oplus (a1[2] * a0[1]) \oplus (a0[1] * a1[0]) \oplus (a1[3] * a1[2] * a0[1]) \oplus (a1[2] * a0[1] * a1[0])$$
$$f4[0] = (a0[3] * a0[2] * a1[1]) \oplus (a0[2] * a1[1] * a1[0])$$
$$f5[0] = (a0[3] * a1[2] * a0[1]) \oplus (a1[2] * a0[1] * a0[0])$$
$$f6[0] = (a1[3] * a0[2] * a0[1]) \oplus (a0[2] * a0[1] * a1[0])$$
$$f7[0] = (a1[3] * a1[2] * a1[1]) \oplus (a1[2] * a1[1] * a0[0])$$

$$f0[1] = 1 \oplus a0[3] \oplus a0[2] \oplus (a0[3] * a0[1]) \oplus (a0[2] * a0[0]) \oplus (a0[1] * a0[0]) \oplus (a0[3] * a0[2] * a0[1]) \oplus (a0[2] * a0[1] * a0[0])$$
$$f1[1] = a1[3] \oplus a1[2] \oplus (a1[3] * a0[1]) \oplus (a1[2] * a1[0]) \oplus (a0[1] * a1[0]) \oplus (a1[3] * a1[2] * a0[1]) \oplus (a1[2] * a0[1] * a1[0])$$
$$f2[1] = (a0[3] * a1[1]) \oplus (a0[2] * a1[0]) \oplus (a1[1] * a1[0]) \oplus (a0[3] * a0[2] * a1[1]) \oplus (a0[2] * a1[1] * a1[0])$$
$$f3[1] = (a1[3] * a1[1]) \oplus (a1[2] * a0[0]) \oplus (a[1] * a0[0]) \oplus (a1[3] * a1[2] * a1[1]) \oplus (a1[2] * a1[1] * a0[0])$$
$$f4[1] = (a0[3] * a1[2] * a0[1]) \oplus (a1[2] * a0[1] * a0[0])$$
$$f5[1] = (a1[3] * a0[2] * a0[1]) \oplus (a0[2] * a0[1] * a1[0])$$
$$f6[1] = (a0[3] * a1[2] * a1[1]) \oplus (a1[2] * a1[1] * a1[0])$$
$$f7[1] = (a1[3] * a0[2] * a1[1]) \oplus (a0[2] * a1[1] * a0[0])$$

$$f0[2] = 1 \oplus a0[2] \oplus a0[1] \oplus (a0[3] * a0[0]) \oplus (a0[2] * a0[0]) \oplus (a0[1] * a0[0]) \oplus (a0[3] * a0[2] * a0[1])$$
$$f1[2] = a1[2] \oplus a1[1] \oplus (a0[3] * a1[0]) \oplus (a1[2] * a1[0]) \oplus (a1[1] * a1[0]) \oplus (a0[3] * a1[2] * a1[1])$$
$$f2[2] = (a1[3] * a0[0]) \oplus (a1[2] * a0[0]) \oplus (a1[1] * a0[0]) \oplus (a1[3] * a1[2] * a1[1])$$
$$f3[2] = (a1[3] * a1[0]) \oplus (a0[2] * a1[0]) \oplus (a0[1] * a1[0]) \oplus (a1[3] * a0[2] * a0[1])$$
$$f4[2] = (a0[3] * a0[2] * a1[1])$$
$$f5[2] = (a0[3] * a1[2] * a0[1])$$
$$f6[2] = (a1[3] * a0[2] * a1[1])$$
$$f7[2] = (a1[3] * a1[2] * a0[1])$$

$$f0[3] = a0[3] \oplus (a0[3] * a0[1]) \oplus (a0[2] * a0[0]) \oplus (a0[3] * a0[2] * a0[1]) \oplus (a0[3] * a0[2] * a0[0])$$
$$f1[3] = a1[3] \oplus (a1[3] * a0[1]) \oplus (a0[2] * a1[0]) \oplus (a1[3] * a0[2] * a0[1]) \oplus (a1[3] * a0[2] * a1[0])$$
$$f2[3] = (a0[3] * a1[1]) \oplus (a1[2] * a0[0]) \oplus (a0[3] * a1[2] * a1[1]) \oplus (a0[3] * a1[2] * a0[0])$$
$$f3[3] = (a1[3] * a1[1]) \oplus (a1[2] * a1[0]) \oplus (a1[3] * a1[2] * a1[1]) \oplus (a1[3] * a1[2] * a1[0])$$
$$f4[3] = (a0[3] * a0[2] * a1[1]) \oplus (a0[3] * a0[2] * a1[0])$$
$$f5[3] = (a0[3] * a1[2] * a0[1]) \oplus (a0[3] * a1[2] * a1[0])$$
$$f6[3] = (a1[3] * a0[2] * a1[1]) \oplus (a1[3] * a0[2] * a0[0])$$
$$f7[3] = (a1[3] * a1[2] * a0[1]) \oplus (a1[3] * a1[2] * a0[0])$$

$$(2)$$

The two-share S0 and S1 boxes are then integrated to form the top level two-share architecture by replicating the linear blocks namely key XORs, registers, x1, x4, x8 multipliers and multiplexers twice for processing the two input shares. The two shares of the plain text are derived by using a LFSR-based Pseudo-Random Number Generator (PRNG) block which generates a 16-bit random number. Thereby the top-level serial based two-shared CLEFIA Architecture occupies around 3955 GE which is about three times more than the unprotected implementation with a power consumption of 30 mW. The throughput decreases by 20% because of the extra clock cycles required due to the pipelined S0 and S1 boxes. Based on our survey, since there is no TI work on CLEFIA in the existing literature, we compare our results with that of AES cipher. A recent low-cost AES TI with similar number of shares have reported an area of 6053 GE on a byte serial architecture [12]. However the proposed lightweight CLEFIA cipher with an efficient TI implementation has 34% lesser area, making it still suitable for resource constrained applications. Since the power consumption is technology dependent, we do not attempt to compare the same with other works.

Table 1. Synthesis results comparison

Reference	Area (in GE)	No. of clock cycles	Throughput @ 100 kHz(kbps)	Efficiency
Existing serial [4]	1664	328	39	0.023
Our serial unprotected	**1345**	**142**	**90**	**0.067**
Our serial protected	**3955**	**178**	**71.91**	**0.018**

4   PAA Resistance Analysis

PAAs are Known Plain Text/Cipher Text attacks that recover the secret key byte-by-byte. The first part of this section explains the setup developed to perform the PAA while the second part describes the results obtained for protected and unprotected implementations.

4.1   PAA Setup

- Threat model: It is assumed that the attacker has physical access to the cryptographic device implementing the encryption algorithm and can control the data inputs. The attacker can also observe the outputs of the performed operation, without the knowledge of the secret key.
- Attack Data-path: The selection function in our work is the output of the 8-bit S-boxes S0/S1 of first round since S-boxes are responsible to induce the confusion property of the cipher. The data-path computes and stores one S-box computation per clock cycle.
- Predictions Phase: For 'm' plain-text values, the possible key values for an 8-bit attack path is $k_s(i) = 0$ to 255. The data-path is evaluated using MATLAB code and the S-box output values are obtained. The size of the S-box output matrix is m x 256. The DPA attack work on bit models (any bit of the S-box) and CPA/MIA can be performed using HWM or Hamming Distance Model (HDM) or Signed Bit Model (SBM).
- Measurement Phase: The implementation of the attack data-path is done on SCA Standard Evaluation Board (SASEBO) namely SAKURA-G which is embedded with two FPGAs: (i) The main FPGA namely Cryptographic FPGA – Spartan 6 xc6slx75 and (ii) The secondary FPGA namely Control FPGA – Spartan 6 xc6slx9. The amplified and de-noised supply current of the design implemented in Main FPGA is tapped through SMA coaxial cables. The current traces are captured using KeySight Mixed Signal Oscilloscope MSO6014A. The oscilloscope captures the trigger signal and the current trace from the FPGA board.
- Pre-processing and Attack Phase: The efficient pre-processing phase of our work consists of the following features: (i) The measured current samples contain very

little noise since all the capacitors on Vcore line are removed and voltage drop (power trace) caused by the 1-ohm shunt resistor inserted between the cryptographic FPGA and the Vcore line is captured. (ii) The measured current samples contain a sufficient current level for the attack since they are obtained from the in-built amplifier on the board with a bandwidth of 360 MHz and a gain of +20 dB. (iii) The required features of the measured current samples are extracted using Python. The pre-processed samples are then re-arranged into a trace matrix $m \times n$. The pre-processed traces are then analyzed using DPA-CPA/MIA/TVLA attack scripts in MATLAB.

4.2   Attack Results

With our developed attack setup, we have performed two styles of PAA: (i) Evaluation style attacks- which involves forming a theoretical model and evaluating the implementation against different attack strategies. The analysis types like DPA [13], CPA [14] and MIA [15] fall under this category. DPA uses difference of means (DoM) method to predict the key while CPA uses a statistical distinguisher namely Pearson's Correlation Coefficient (CC) to correlate between the measurements obtained and predictions made. The idea of using information theory metrics to quantify the dependence between the leakage and power consumption model was proposed by Benedikt et al., as MIA in [15]. The advantage of this method is that it relaxes the strict requirement of linear dependency between the measurements and predictions as in CPA and exploits comparatively more information than DPA. Hence the MIA based attacks are independent of the attacking platform and the variables need not be strictly linear. In our work, the Mutual Information (MI) between the random variable X (power consumption) and the leakage L (predictions) is calculated in bits using MATLAB code. For each secret key value, MI function processes the inputs column by column and returns an 'm x n' matrix, where 'm' corresponds to the number of traces and 'n' corresponds to the sampling points. The maximum value of MI is subsequently recorded, the index of which returns the key. Our work reports a metric named Minimum Time to Disclosure (MTD) that describes the cross-over point of the correct Correlation Coefficient (CC) with the CC curves of the other key guesses. We have used this metric to quantify the CPA and MIA attacks in our work. (ii) Conformance style attacks- which involves evaluating the leakages independently, to determine if there is a SCA vulnerability, rather than estimating the correct key. The very popular TVLA [16] falls under this category which performs t-tests using the statistical mean and variance parameters. Based on the literature, acceptable t-value across all the sampling points is $\leq \pm 4.5$. If t-value exceeds the threshold, the implementation is considered to be vulnerable to PAA. This methodology does not determine the exact secret key value or the number of traces required for successful key retrieval. In certain applications it is required to strongly determine the implementation vulnerability of a system and this methodology provides its usefulness in those scenarios.

Table 2 shows the metrics comparison of protected and unprotected implementations of a few keys. While the un-protected implementations have shown successful key recoveries with less than 768 traces for all the attack categories, the protected implementation does not reveal the secret key even with 100,000 traces for first-order attacks. Hence sufficient PAA protection is achieved using the proposed two-share CLEFIA architecture. Figures 3, 4 and 5 shows the attack results of CPA and TVLA.

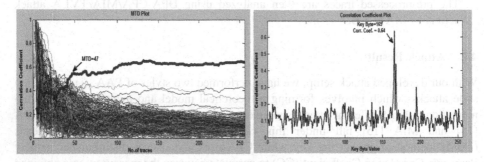

Fig. 3. (a) CPA-HWM CC plot (b) MTD plot for key byte = 165 on unprotected CLEFIA S0 box

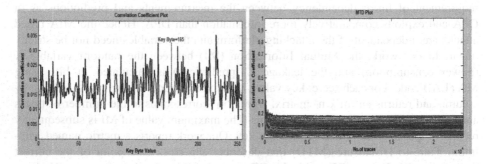

Fig. 4. (a) CPA-HWM CC plot (b) MTD plot for key byte = 165 on protected CLEFIA S0 box

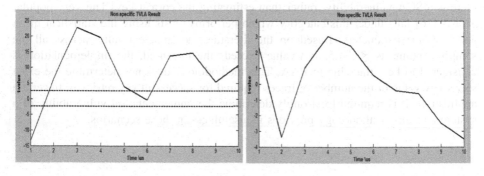

Fig. 5. Non-specific TVLA results for (a) un-protected (b) protected implementation

Table 2. PAA resistance analysis

Cipher	Attack category	Key-byte value (in Hex)	Metrics achieved	No. of traces used
Unprotected CLEFIA	DPA	90(S0 box)	Max. diff = 0.6	256
	CPA-HWM	90(S0 box)	CC = 0.6, MTD = 37	256
	CPA-HDM	165(S0 box)	CC = 0.35, MTD = 175	256
	CPA-SBM	90(S1 box)	CC = 0.26, MTD=182	256
	MIA-HWM	90(S0 box)	MI = 0.78, MTD = 240	768
	MIA-HDM	165(S0 box)	MI = 0.6, MTD = 540	768
	MIA-SBM	165(S0 box)	MI = 0.35, MTD = 225	768
	TVLA	90(S1 box)	t-value > -4.5	512
Protected CLEFIA	Evaluation style (First-Order)	90(S0/S1 box) 165(S0 box)	Unsuccessful	100,000
	Conformance style (First-order)	90(S0/S1 box) 165(S0 box)	t-value < 4.5	100,000

5 Conclusion

CLEFIA is an ISO/IEC standard lightweight cryptographic algorithm suitable for resource constrained applications. We have proposed a 16-bit novel serial CLEFIA architecture with a low-cost CFA based S1 box and ANF based S0 box. The proposed serial architecture has achieved a very low area of 1345 GE with a power consumption of 1.3 mW. Since PAA is shown to be a stronger threat to the cryptographic implementations, we have developed a novel two-share TI implementation for the proposed CLEFIA architecture to mitigate the same. The proposed TI implementation occupies an area of 3955 GE, which is 34% smaller than a similar AES TI implementation. We have briefed the PAA setup created using SAKURA-G board and performed the Evaluation and Conformance style attacks. While the unprotected implementation is easily attacked with less than 768 traces, the protected implementation shows resistance to PAA using 100,000 traces.

The first-order PAA resistant CLEFIA architecture is suitable for resource constrained applications. The higher order PAA resistance of the proposed TI implementation will be analyzed in future.

Acknowledgement. This work has been done from the grant received from Visvesvaraya PhD Scheme of Ministry of Electronics and Information Technology, Government of India, being implemented by Digital India Corporation. This work was also supported by Special Manpower Development Programme for Chips to System Design (SMDP-C2SD) project sponsored by the Department of Electronics and Information Technology (DeitY), Government of India. The authors would like to thank the contribution from the following people: Vidhya D, Aravindh M, Kirubhas Shankar R K, Lakshmanan G, Mahalakshmi S, Prashanth S and Rajesh Srivatsav S, Department of ECE, PSG College of Technology for their support in implementation of the proposed work.

References

1. Shirai, T., Shibutani, K., Akishita, T., Moriai, S., Iwata, T.: The 128-bit blockcipher CLEFIA (extended abstract). In: biryukov, a (ed.) FSE 2007. LNCS, vol. 4593, pp. 181–195. Springer, Heidelberg (2007). https://doi.org/10.1007/978-3-540-74619-5_12
2. ISO, ISO/IEC 29192-2:2012: Information Technology - Security Techniques - Lightweight Cryptography - Part 2: Block Ciphers (2012). http://www.iso.org/iso/home/store/catalogue_tc/catalogue_detail.htm?csnumber=56552
3. CRYPTREC: Cryptographic Technology Guideline. http://www.cryptrec.go.jp/report/cryptrec-rp-2000-2017.pdf
4. Akishita, T., Hiwatari, H.: Very compact hardware implementations of the blockcipher CLEFIA. In: Miri, A., Vaudenay, S. (eds.) SAC 2011. LNCS, vol. 7118, pp. 278–292. Springer, Heidelberg (2012). https://doi.org/10.1007/978-3-642-28496-0_17
5. Boura, C., Naya-Plasencia, M., Suder, V.: Scrutinizing and improving impossible differential attacks: applications to CLEFIA, camellia, LBlock and SIMON. In: Sarkar, P., Iwata, T. (eds.) ASIACRYPT 2014. LNCS, vol. 8873, pp. 179–199. Springer, Heidelberg (2014). https://doi.org/10.1007/978-3-662-45611-8_10
6. Chester, R., Mukhopadhyay, D.: Differential Cache Trace Attack against CLEFIA. IACR Cryptology ePrint Archive, 12, (2010)
7. Bai, X., Lu, H., Wang, Y., Xu, Y.: Differential power analysis attack on CLEFIA block cipher. In: IEEE International Conference on Computational Intelligence and Software Engineering, pp. 1–4 (2009)
8. Kim, Y., Ahn, J., Choi, H.: Power and electromagnetic analysis attack on a smart card implementation of CLEFIA. In: International Conference on Security and Management (SAM), p. 1 (2013)
9. Nikova, S., Rechberger, C., Rijmen, V.: Threshold implementations against side-channel attacks and glitches. In: Ning, P., Qing, S., Li, N. (eds.) ICICS 2006. LNCS, vol. 4307, pp. 529–545. Springer, Heidelberg (2006). https://doi.org/10.1007/11935308_38
10. Baihan, A., Duggirala, P.S., Baihan, M.: A high-order masking approach for CLEFIA implementation on FPGA and Intel. In: Proceedings of the International Conference on Security and Management (SAM), pp. 79–85 (2017)
11. Reparaz, O., Bilgin, B., Nikova, S., Gierlichs, B., Verbauwhede, I.: Consolidating masking schemes. In: Gennaro, R., Robshaw, M. (eds.) CRYPTO 2015. LNCS, vol. 9215, pp. 764–783. Springer, Heidelberg (2015). https://doi.org/10.1007/978-3-662-47989-6_37
12. Ueno, R., Homma, N., Aoki, T.: Toward more efficient DPA-resistant AES hardware architecture based on threshold implementation. In: Guilley, S. (ed.) COSADE 2017. LNCS, vol. 10348, pp. 50–64. Springer, Cham (2017). https://doi.org/10.1007/978-3-319-64647-3_4
13. Kocher, P., Jaffe, J., Jun, B., Rohatgi, P.: Introduction to differential power analysis. J. Cryptographic Eng. 1, 5–27 (2011)
14. Brier, E., Clavier, C., Olivier, F.: Correlation power analysis with a leakage model. In: Joye, M., Quisquater, J.-J. (eds.) CHES 2004. LNCS, vol. 3156, pp. 16–29. Springer, Heidelberg (2004). https://doi.org/10.1007/978-3-540-28632-5_2

15. Gierlichs, B., Batina, L., Tuyls, P., Preneel, B.: Mutual information analysis. In: Oswald, E., Rohatgi, P. (eds.) CHES 2008. LNCS, vol. 5154, pp. 426–442. Springer, Heidelberg (2008). https://doi.org/10.1007/978-3-540-85053-3_27
16. Roy, D.B., Bhasin, S., Patranabis, S., Mukhopadhyay, D., Guilley, S.: What Lies Ahead: Extending TVLA Testing Methodology Towards Success Rate. IACR Cryptology ePrint Archive, 1152 (2016)

Brain Inspired One Shot Learning Method for HD Computing

Devika R. Nair$^{(\boxtimes)}$ and A. Purushothaman

Department of Electronics and Communication Engineering,
Amrita School of Engineering, Amritapuri, Amrita Vishwa Vidyapeetham,
Vallikavu, India
devikanair18@gmail.com, ampurushothaman@gmail.com

Abstract. The brain's power of perception, learning, thought, language, concepts, adaptivity, ability to tolerate noise etc are amazing to the human kind for a long time and it is a big challenge for us to model a platform with these properties. In this work, we propose a new architecture for applications in high dimensional computing. The brain-inspired high dimensional computing architecture involves generation and storage of large strings of random bits using hypervectors. A True Random Number Generator (TRNG) using Fibonacci and Galois ring oscillator is for generating high dimensional vectors. Digital post processing of random data using Linear Feedback Shift Registers (LFSR) is also introduced. High dimensional binary vectors are then used for representing entities. High degree of parallelism, noise tolerance, learning by analogy are some of the characteristics that make it possible for use in brain inspired computing. Operations like superposition and binding are defined for High dimensional vectors. The algebra of high dimensional vectors make this architecture suitable for certain cognitive tasks such as learning by analogy, learning for classification, etc. The proposed high dimensional computing architecture can be used for language is implemented using 2-D architecture for High Dimensional (HD) computing and validated against the benchmark datasets. This architecture introduces a new method of learning known as one shot learning, considering the effectiveness in resource consumption and computation flexibility. The power consumption and related design issues are presented in this work. The experiments carried out for the language identification problem are motivating and opens up a new paradigm for machine learning and classification tasks such as cancer detection using benign and malignant cells, spam mail detection and so on.

Keywords: High Dimensional Computing (HDC) ·
True Random Number Generator (TRNG) ·
Linear Feedback Shift Register (LFSR) · One shot learning ·
Language hypervector · Search hypervector

© Springer Nature Singapore Pte Ltd. 2019
A. Sengupta et al. (Eds.): VDAT 2019, CCIS 1066, pp. 286–297, 2019.
https://doi.org/10.1007/978-981-32-9767-8_25

1 Introduction

For the last 50 years, the semiconductor industry has been focused on maximize the computational power at minimal cost using various technologies. Different levels of abstraction can be observed, starting from transistor-level switching circuits to scalable nanometre-circuit technologies. Deterministic Boolean algebra are replaced by more scalable stored 3D architectures [7], using Vertical Resistive Random Access Memories (VRRAM) [7]. These transformations in semiconductor and computational technologies have posed numerous challenges, all types of computation need to be supported with high precision at a low cost, energy efficiency and should satisfy concomitant requirements like reliability, noise immunity, operational stability with fewer deviations from the expected values.

With the recent evolution of machine learning approaches in deep learning [12], decision making, and recognition, Artificial Intelligence has entered a new era. These new approaches in machine learning using Internet of Things (IoT) demonstrate unrivalled performances in solving many issues in our day today life starting from automation of home appliances to detection of cancer. This new approach shows more advantages over conventional method of computation, which is mainly based on numbers.

Biological neural networks are always an unbelievable thing for engineers. From here comes the idea of artificial neural networks. It is now widespread in areas like language identification, hand gesture recognition, image recognition, autonomous cars. Power and energy savings are the main highlights of using machine learning approaches when compared to conventional methods. From these we can conclude that there is a need for some hierarchical changes in present computer architectures by combining the properties of digital computer and artificial intelligence. Utilization in terms of energy is very poor in current deep learning algorithms. So it is very useful to have new techniques with minimum utilization of energy by using one shot learning algorithms and computational methods [5] that emulate human brain.

Brain is the most amazing organ in human body that acts as the centre of our nervous system. It works by generating patterns of muscle activity controlled by neurons and it's secretions. Human brain consists of 40 billion neurons and 240 trillion synapses which constitutes the basics of computations. Brain have much faster computation as the computations are done using certain patterns of neural interactions instead of doing using proper calculations. From this comes the idea of high dimensional computing where calculations are done using vectors which are having high dimensions similar to brains large circuits. These high dimensional vectors are called hypervectors. These hypervectors can be used for classification, association, hierarchy formation.

RAM (Random Access Memory) of computers can be compared to human cerebellum with it's dense internal wiring network. The amazing factor is that even though our brain don't have any look up table like structures which is normally used as pointers to address arrays, computations are very fast and store huge data in memory. Human cerebellum can store millions of data elements without having equivalence of a lookup table that is commonly used to reduce run time computational time by using array indexing operations. Therefore, our computations should be analogous to that done by brains. To attain this astonishing networking property of brain, we are proposing hypervectors with properties like randomness and robustness. The basic question is why randomness is needed in our computation. This is because human brain determines many things through learning from surroundings are left to chances. Two brains are contradictory both in hardware and internal structures.

We are proposed to do computation with 10,000 bit. Normally bits greater than thousand bits are called high dimensional. Robustness property defines the ability to tolerate errors even if one third data is lost. To improve robustness property we are choosing 10,000 bit [6] and this type of computation is called high dimensional computing or hyperdimensional computing. The basic operations involved in high dimensional computing are addition or bundling, multiplication or binding and permutation. Using these simple mathematical operations we can make high dimensional architectures and can be used in different applications like language recognition systems, image processing and classification. In this we are modeling an architecture for language recognition using high dimensional computing. We are exploiting the one shot learning property of high dimensional vectors in the sense that all operations are doing at memory locations itself and results in fast computation.

As mentioned above random numbers are mandatory for High Dimensional Computing (HDC) [1]. A new technique for True Random Number Generation (TRNG) [2] is presented. The output of TRNG will be sequence of 0's and 1's with equal probability. Randomness can be increased by using a post processing unit. As random numbers are unavoidable part of high dimensional computing, it is implemented using a new method using Galois and Fibonacci ring oscillators [3]. The output of this combined ring oscillators [3] should be truly random. A post processing unit using Linear Feedback Shift Register (LFSR) is also explained. This random number generator has many applications in spam detection, cryptography, smart cards, computer games etc.

This paper structured as follows. Section 2 give an introduction to High Dimensional Computing. Generation of random data for language identification system is presented in Sect. 3. For increasing the randomness we use a post processing unit using LFSR covered in Sect. 4. Section 5 introduces 2D architecture for One Shot Learning Method. Experimental results are shown in Sect. 6. Section 7 concludes the work.

2   What Is HD Computing?

To emulate the human brain's enviable computational capabilities in deep learning applications, we need to move into high dimensional computing. A human brain's wiring system is composed of synapses interconnecting millions of neurons. Information processing and computations are accomplished based on some patterns generated by brain rather than calculation based on numbers. By using high dimensional vectors we can achieve our goal. Orthogonal property of high dimensional vectors can be seen when we multiply or bind two vectors and results in a third vector which will be dissimilar to the operands. A hypervector can be formed by various vector operations like multiplication, addition and permutation operations [1].

In this study, language recognition using HD vectors is demonstrated. The 21 European languages for this one shot learning method is obtained from a high data set called Wortschatz. Mainly training is done using this data set and testing is done using Europarl Parallel Corpus data base. Testing phase includes a total of 21,000 sentences from 21 languages that is each language have 1000 sentences. Europarl Parallel Corpus: http://www.statmt.org/europarl/ Wortschatz Corpora: http://wortschatz.uni-leipzig.de/en/download/. Languages can be identified from a sequence of three letters called trigrams [1]. If k + 2 is the length of a sentence, then there will be k trigrams. For example in the word "Welcome" there will be 5 trigrams like wel, elc, lco, com and ome. By comparing the trigram information of each of 21 European languages with the trigram information of the given test sentence, we can identify the languages. Therefore, the first step in HD computing will be generation of 10,000 random bits for each of the 26 Latin alphabets and space. This is explained in the next section. The total trigram count will be $27^3 = 19683$ and this count can be accumulated to a 19683 dimensional vector. This 19683 dimensional vector can act as a high dimensional vector as the dimension is greater than thousand. There is no correct limit for the dimension of vector. When dimensionality increases, accuracy also increases. To find the most similar character compare these high dimensional vectors. The 27 Latin letters acts as the seed vectors. By using each 3 letter from given test sentence, trigrams are formed each of 10,000 dimension [6]. The trigram HD vector obtained after permutation operations have equal probability of 0's and 1's. By adding the trigrams in the input text, a text profile called input text hypervector can be created. By comparing the test profile of input text with the already available language profile we can identify the language.

3   Generation of Random Data

The basic principle used in generation of random number sequences for high dimensional computing involves replacing conventional ring oscillator-based random number sequences by feedback-controlled asynchronous circuits [3]. These feedback controlled asynchronous circuits can provide more randomness as it involves many exclusive or (XOR) logical operations. Conventional type random number generators exploit noise generated as a result of variations in thermal noise or shot noise. However, a practical true random number generator can be made using digital integrated circuits. Ring oscillator based method mainly uses variations in frequency and phase, also called jitters [2] in free running oscillators. Oscillators are implemented as ring oscillators with odd number of inverters connected together to form a closed structure using XOR operation. Then output of ring oscillator can be sampled at a lower frequency using a separate system clock and D flip-flop. These types of TRNG have many disadvantages including low speed and mutual coupling between the ring oscillators. This results in reduced randomness of binary sequences.

Edge triggered flip-flops and metastable state of RS (SET/RESET) latches like D flip-flop can be used more precisely as random sequence of 0's and 1's. If the set up and hold times of data input and clock of such D flip-flops are intentionally violated, the output of flip-flop can be made unpredictable. These violations can be obtained, for example, if both input and clock are simultaneously varied at the same rate. The output should be random data [2] can be biased to a stable value. The metastability and jitter property of clock can be exploited together. The output random data can be sampled using D flip-flops. The metastability variations are very less compared to other variations like jitter. These metastability variations are sensitive to temperature and voltage.

The main principle used in this paper for random number generation lies in replacing classical method using ring oscillators by asynchronous circuits with feedback. Ring oscillator based circuits are less susceptible to coupling in terms of frequency and phase. Depending on asynchronous circuits used, randomness and pseudo-randomness [3], of the generator varies. Pseudorandom property is not actually random but it appears to be random and is generated by deterministic process. Along with the pseudo-randomness [3] properties, the delay generated in the internal logic gates of the oscillator circuit results in unpredictable variations. These variations are propagated through the internal feedback structures. If these delay levels are maintained within a tolerable level, then randomness can be achieved in the analog level also by using internal variations in metastability [3]. By using a sampling unit such as D flip-flop more randomness than obtained from oscillator circuits due to metastability can be achieved as the resulting oscillating signal is due to both digital and analog noises. The clock for sampling the output of ring oscillator that we are used here is using external clock having a frequency of 1000 MHz to meet the power consumption, set up and hold timings. This value may change according to the frequency of ring oscillators used. The coupling effects resulting from clock signal and input of D flip-flops used in the entire circuit resulting in pseudo-randomness, which reduces randomness properties. After sampling, we get the desired output binary sequence with comparatively high speed and large entropy for each bit.

3.1   Fibonacci and Galois Ring Oscillators

This work proposes a practical method for random number generation using Fibonacci and Galois ring oscillators in contrast to conventional type ring oscillators. These oscillators are more extended version of basic ring oscillator architecture as mentioned in [8]. The normal feedback structure is replaced by complex feedback consisting of different XOR gates. The configuration consisting of feed-backs using XOR are called Fibonacci and Galois configuration of LFSR's. Instead of delay elements, inverters are cascaded with feedback elements connected in between two inverters. The delay of individual inverters can be varied by specifying the required delay while writing Hardware Description Languages (HDL).

Fibonacci Ring Oscillator. Fibonacci Ring Oscillator shown in Fig. 1 shows cascading of r number of inverters connected one after another such that the last inverter is connected back to the first inverter via XOR gates. To specify the feedback connections, fi is used. When fi (i = 1, 2, 3, 4) is made 1, switch can be made ON and when fi = 0, switch will be OFF. In order to define the input to the first inverter, the last inverters output should be cascaded with the XOR whose fi are made 1. The feedback connections are from left to right. XOR operations are as usual the modulo-2-addition. The output of this ring oscillator [3] can be taken from output of any inverter.

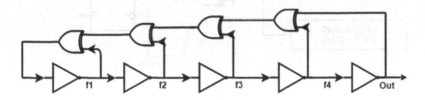

Fig. 1. Fibonacci ring oscillator

Galois Ring Oscillator. The Galois Ring Oscillator shown in Fig. 2 shows cascading of r number of inverters such that the last inverter act as the feedback to the system and serves as the input to the other inverters as well. To specify the feedback connections, fi (i = 1, 2, 3, 4) is used. When fi is made 1, switch can be made ON and when fi = 0, switch will be OFF. In order to define the input to the first inverter, the last inverters output should be cascaded with the XOR whose fi are made 1. The feedback connections [3] are from right to left. In this configuration, the output should be taken from the last inverter in cascade stages.

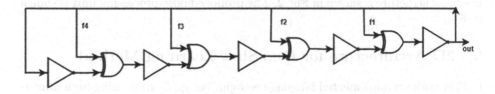

Fig. 2. Galois ring oscillator

Combined Ring Oscillator. The properties like robustness and randomness can be improved by modulo 2 addition using XOR by combining the output of Fibonacci and Galois ring oscillators. The output of these oscillators are fed to the inputs of a XOR gate and this XOR output is fed as the input to a D flip-flip-flop. The resulting configuration is shown in Fig. 3. It is sampled using external clock. Output will be random sequence of 0's and 1's.

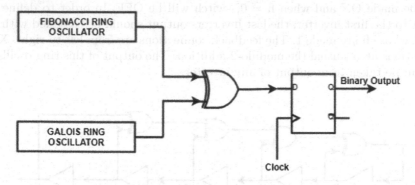

Fig. 3. Combined ring oscillator

4   Post Processing Unit Using LFSR

To enhance the randomness of output obtained after sampling in the combined ring oscillator structure a more energy efficient post-processing unit using Linear Feedback Shift Register [3] is implemented. D flip-flops are arranged serially and between each flip-flop XOR operation is carried out using feedback signal obtained from the last D flip-flop to the first register. Feedback signal is XOR with selected output of flip-flops. We will get maximum length sequence by using primitive polynomial. To improve the security of random numbers, suitable for many domains including cryptographic applications, this investigation uses 63 registers [2]. The LFSR's can be implemented in the Galois or Fibonacci architecture. However, this work mainly focuses on Galois type implementation. It's basic structure is shown in Fig. 2. The proposed post-processing unit is shown in Fig. 4.

5   2D Architecture for One Shot Learning Method

In this work we implemented language recognition application using high dimensional computing. The proposed architecture for language identification is shown in Figs. 5 and 6. This architecture is memory centric [4]. This high dimensional architecture mainly consists of two modules namely, encoder and search module. This hypervector obtained from encoding module is used in search module for comparison with already known hyper vectors of different languages. By calculating the hamming distance between given input language and already stored database of languages, the search module [1] identifies the language having closest match with input language.

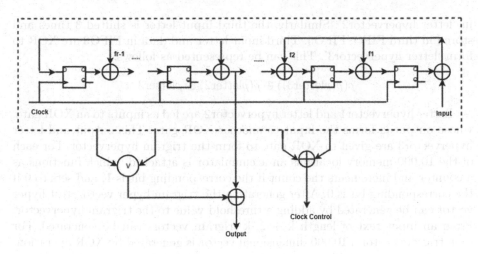

Fig. 4. Post processing unit using LFSR

Fig. 5. 2D architecture for language recognition: encoding module

5.1 Encoding Module

An Encoding module consists of storage unit for the input text in a memory called item memory [1] and finally forms a text hypervector by combining trigram hyper vectors. Encoding module produces hyper vector representation for each of the given input letter. Item memory found in the Encoding module stores the letter hypervector for each of the given 26 letters in the alphabet and space. A look up table is used for storing the hypervector having equal probability of zeros and ones and are orthogonal to each other.

From the true random number generated data obtained, first a 10000 bit vector is assigned for each of the 26 letters and space. In addition, this should be stored in 27 memory locations for further calculations. These 27 memory locations represents the item memory in the Encoding module. For generation of trigram hyper vectors, consecutive three letters from input text file are taken. First input letter should be shifted right once and stored in first First-In First-Out (FIFO) memory, FIFO1. First input letter and FIFO1 data are XOR to form the first letter hypervector. The second input letter should be shifted right twice and stored in second FIFO, i.e. FIFO2. The shifting operation is indicated by ρ. The second incoming letter and FIFO2 are given to XOR gate and stored in 'letter hypervector2'. Similarly, the third input letter is shifted 3 times and stored in third FIFO, FIFO3. Third input letter and data in FIFO3 are XOR to form 'letter hypervector3'. This can be represented as follows:

$$\rho(\rho(\rho\text{letter3})) \oplus \rho(\rho\text{letter2}) \oplus \rho\text{letter3}$$

Letter hypervector1 and letter hypervector2 are fed as inputs to an XOR gate, whose output is forms the input to another XOR gate. This output and letter hypervector3 are given to XOR gate to form the trigram hypervector. For each of the 10,000 memory locations an accumulator is attached, which functions as a counter and increments the count if the corresponding bit is 1, and sets to 0 if the corresponding bit is 0. After generating the trigram hyper vector, test hyper vector can be generated by adding a threshold value to the trigram hypervector. From an input text of length k + 2, k trigram vectors can be generated. For each trigram vector a 10,000 dimensional vector is generated by XOR operation. By applying a threshold value of k/2 to the accumulator, output the resultant binary vector can be generated. This is called input text hyper vector.

Training and testing can be implemented using the Encoding module as shown in Fig. 5. If the language of the input text is known, we call them as language hyper vector [1]. These hyper vectors are already stored in similarity search module. During the testing phase, the language is unknown and hyper-vector is called query hypervector [1]. To identify the closest matching language, the query hyper vector is passed to the search module.

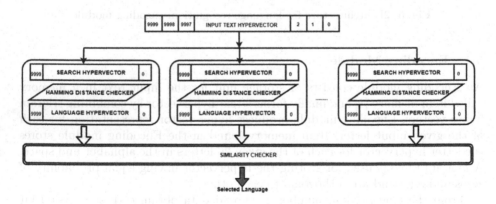

Fig. 6. 2D architecture for language recognition: search module

5.2 Similarity Search Module

The language hypervector formed by the Encoding module is stored in the memory block of Similarity Search Module [1] in the training phase. It is also generated in the same way as input text hypervector formed in the Encoding module and it's shown in Fig. 6. We have 21 European languages and we have obtained 21 hypervector for each of these languages and are stored in corresponding row in the search module. When search hyper vector is sent to the search module to identify the language, it is compared with all the available language hypervectors. An associative memory is used for comparison purposes. The language of closest similarity is checked using Hamming distance approach.

The search module uses 10,000 XOR gates for mismatch identification. We can count the number of positions in the query hypervector and language hyper vector that disagrees by using Hamming distance. During each clock cycle, the similarity measurement module compares each input text hypervector and already stored hypervectors of languages. A total of 21 similarity measurement blocks are needed as here we are using 21 European languages to complete the recognition process. The measurement process is carried out in the same time period as the query hypervector is broadcasted. Finally, a comparison module selects the least Hamming distance and identifies the language of the unknown input text (language to be found).

6   Experimental Results

This section mainly focuses the experimental results of the proposed 2D architecture for language recognition system. For implementing the high dimensional architecture for language recognition standard ASIC (Application Specific Integrated Circuits) flow [9] is used. For simulation and synthesis purpose Cadence®Encounter®RTL Compiler is used. The true random numbers for high dimensional computing were generated by replacing the conventional free running oscillator based TRNG. This new method for random numbers is robust and are efficient in terms of speed also.

The Cadence Encounter tool is used to synthesize language recognition architecture using high dimensional computing. Human power of identifying the objects from a very few examples(one shot learning) are clearly modelled using high dimensional computing. For training and testing purpose we used 21 European languages. By reading an input text, the proposed architecture using HDC can correctly identify the language it belongs to. This is achieved by using a hamming distance checker. This identification technique using HDC takes only considerable amount of time. It takes a total time around 8,50,000 ns to identify the given input text's language after clock is applied. In this work we are using input text containing 30 letters only. From this few length of input text itself language identification is possible. This shows the robustness property of high dimensional vectors. This architecture is found to be more efficient when comparing with other machine learning methods [1]. Considering memory requirement and accuracy we are using trigram for generating hypervectors. It's a memory centric architecture. The proposed architecture includes computing and storing of these HD vectors within the same memory locations itself. Hence the name memory centric. The proposed architecture takes a total area of 3166 cell size [10]. A standard cell consist of transistors and interconnects connecting them together to implement a particular logic function.

We can see that different instances as mentioned in Table 1, in proposed architecture drew 19227.124 nw leakage power and 88799.457 nw dynamic power. Thus HD architecture consumes 108026.581 nw power in total. Leakage power mainly depends on supply voltage, threshold voltage [11] for switching the circuit.

Table 1. Power consumption report

Instance	Cells	Leakage power (nw)	Dynamic power (nw)	Total power consumption
Main module	247	17843.414	83362.833	101206.2
Post processing unit using LFSR	15	303.742	958.463	1262.205
Fibonacci ring oscillator	4	55.51	216.48	271.99
Galois ring oscillator	4	55.67	215.89	271.56

7 Conclusion

This paper has presented an efficient method for language recognition using different properties of high dimensional computing like multiplication, addition and permutation. For identification purpose we used 21 European languages. Random numbers which forms the basis of high dimensional is implemented using a new method for true random number generation is implemented using a combined design of Fibonacci and Galois ring oscillators. To add more randomness uses a post-processing unit using LFSR. The proposed method can clearly identify the given input European language by calculating the hamming distance with the language hypervector stored in the memory. This architecture have is efficient in terms of power, area and timing when compared with conventional machine learning methods. Future applications of HD computing includes cancer cell detection, pneumonia detection using chest x-ray and so on.

References

1. Rahimi, A., Datta, S., Kleyko, D., Frady, E.P., Olshausen, B., Kanerva, P., Rabaey, J.M.: High-dimensional computing as a nanoscalable paradigm. IEEE Trans. Circ. Syst.-I Reg. Pap. **64**, 2508–2521 (2017)
2. Liu, Y., Cheung, R.C., Wong, H.: A bias-bounded digital true random number generator architecture. IEEE Trans. Circ. Syst.-I: Reg. Pap. **64**(1), 133–144 (2017)
3. Golic, J.D.: New methods for digital generation and post processing of random data. IEEE Trans. Comput. **55**(10) (2006)

4. Tanner, A., Tan, J., Holmes, S.: Automatically Generated VLSI Memory. University of Utah CS/EE 6710 Digital VLSI Design, Fall 2003, December 2003
5. Rahimi, A., Benatti, S., Kanerva, P., Benini, L., Rabaey, J.M.: Hyperdimensional biosignal processing: a case study for EMG-based hand gesture recognition. In: IEEE Conference on Electromagnetic Field Computation (CEFC), November 2016
6. Kanerva, P.: Computing with 10,000-bit words. In: Fifty-second Annual Allerton Conference Allerton House, UIUC, Illinois, USA, October 2014
7. Li, H., Wu, T.F., Rahimi, A., Li, K.-S.: Hyperdimensional computing with 3D VRRAM in-memory kernels: device-architecture co-design for energy-efficient, error-resilient language recognition. In: IEDM 2016, p. 412 (2016)
8. Liu, D., Liu, Z., Li, L., Zou, X.: A low-cost low-power ring oscillator-based truly random number generator for encryption on smart cards. IEEE Trans. Circ. Syst.-II: Express Briefs **63**(6), 608–612 (2016)
9. Auer, D., Buer, M.: A design flow for embedding the ARM processor in an ASIC. In: Proceedings of Eighth International Application Specific Integrated Circuits Conference (1995)
10. Ichihashi, M., Woo, Y., Parihar, S.: SRAM cell performance analysis beyond 10-nm FinFET technology. In: International Symposium on VLSI Technology, Systems and Application (VLSI-TSA) (2016)
11. de Carvalho Ferreira, L.H., Cleber Pimenta, T.: A CMOS voltage reference based on threshold voltage for ultra low-voltage and ultra low-power. In: International Conference on Microelectronics (2005)
12. Warrier, S.R., Murugan, S: Implementing a neural processor for accelerating deep learning. In: 9th International Conference on Computing, Communication and Networking Technologies (ICCCNT) (2018)

Dual-Edge Triggered Lightweight Implementation of AES for IoT Security

Sajid Khan[1], Neha Gupta[1], Abhinav Vishvakarma[1], Shailesh Singh Chouhan[2], Jai Gopal Pandey[3], and Santosh Kumar Vishvakarma[1(✉)]

[1] Nanoscale Devices, VLSI Circuit and System Design Lab,
Discipline of Electrical Engineering, Indian Institute of Technology Indore,
Indore 453552, M.P., India
{phd1601102015,phd1701202008,abhinavvishvakarma,skvishvakarma}@iiti.ac.in
[2] EIS Lab, Department of Computer Science, Electrical and Space Engineering,
Lulea University of Technology, 97187 Luleå, Sweden
shailesh.chouhan@ltu.se
[3] Integrated Systems Group, CSIR- Central Electronics Engineering Research
Institute (CEERI), Pilani 333031, Rajasthan, India
jai@ceeri.res.in

Abstract. Internet of Things (IoT) is now a growing part of our life. More than 10 billion devices are already connected, and more are expected to be deployed in the next coming years. To provide a practical solution for security, privacy and trust is the main concern for deploying IoT in such a large scale. For security and privacy in IoT, cryptography is the required solutions. AES algorithm is a well known, highly secure and symmetric key algorithm, but the area and power budget of AES makes it unsuitable for IoT Security. In this paper, we have presented a lightweight implementation of AES, with dual-edge triggered S-box. The proposed architecture has been implemented on FPGA as well as in ASIC on 180 nm technology. The proposed architecture uses a 32-bit data path to encrypt 128-bit plain-text with 128-bit cipher-key. ASIC implementation of the proposed architecture results in low-power (122.7 μW at 1 V) consumption with a reduction in the hardware overhead by 30% and a throughput of 23 Mbps at 10 MHz clock frequency.

Keywords: Lightweight · Dual-edge triggered · AES · Architecture · IoT · Security

1 Introduction

Internet of things (IoT) is expected to use in a variety of emerging applications, such as smart cities, wearable electronics, remote health care, agriculture, and many more [1]. The IoT technology utilizes real-time analysis with machine learning method to process data and make decisions. Security failure of these devices can affect billions of lives as well as a huge financial loss with privacy invasion [2], [3]. Thus, data security is one of the main concern in the effective

© Springer Nature Singapore Pte Ltd. 2019
A. Sengupta et al. (Eds.): VDAT 2019, CCIS 1066, pp. 298–307, 2019.
https://doi.org/10.1007/978-981-32-9767-8_26

and meaningful deployment of IoT devices on a large scale level [4], [5]. To secure sensitive data, cryptography provides an efficient solution. However, the hardware cost and power budget of conventional cryptography implementations limit the use of conventional cryptography algorithm in IoTs [6].

Advanced Encryption Standard (AES) has been standardized by NIST in year 2001 [7]. Traditionally, the AES cipher is the most widely used algorithm implemented on various devices to secure wired as well as wireless communicated data. However, most of the IoT devices are battery powered and smaller in size; hence, the utmost priority for the IoT constrained devices is to consume minimum power with a minimum area overhead. In this concern, a lightweight variant of the AES like cipher is very much needed.

In this paper, we propose a low-power architecture for AES-like cipher and its hardware implementation. Here, we have selected 32-bit datapath based architecture to achieve low-power and high throughput. By using clock gating, minimizing the number of datapath registers, and reducing the unnecessary transitions, a sufficient amount of power has been saved. Here, dual-edge triggered D-flip flops have been used in S box datapath; hence, the proposed architecture requires only two S-boxes instead of four. It results in less area overhead as compared to the other 32-bit datapath architectures. Rest of the paper is organized as follows: in Sect. 2, the standard AES algorithm is discussed. Section 3 describes the proposed architecture and selected optimization strategies. The post-layout simulation results are discussed in Sect. 4 and finally the paper is concluded in Sect. 5.

2   The Standard AES Algorithm

AES is a symmetric block cipher algorithm because it uses the same key for both the encryption and decryption operations. The cipher can process 128-bit data with 128, 192, and 256-bit key with 10, 12, and 14 number of rounds respectively. Accordingly, the cipher is referred as AES-128, AES-192, and AES-256 respectively. The each round is consist of four transformations: *SubBytes*, *ShiftRows*, *MixColoumns* and *AddRoundKey*. Each round of the cipher goes through all the above transformation with a new transformed key except in the last round. The last round does not go through the *MixColumn* transformation as shown in Fig. 1. 128-bit data is arranged in a 4 × 4 matrix by dividing the 128-bit in 16, 8-bit blocks. The matrix is called a state matrix.

The *AddRoundKey* transformation is just XOR of the state matrix with a 128-bit key. The *SubByte* transformation is a byte-by-byte substitution of state matrix using a mapping function which is nonlinear by nature. The nonlinear mapping function can be implemented as a look-up-tables (LUTs) or by using arithmetic in a finite field using irreducible polynomial $(x^8 + x^4 + x^3 + x + 1)$ in $GF(2^8)$ and an affine transformation. *ShiftRows* transformation is the circular shift of rows using offset 0, 1, 2 and 3 for first, second, third, and fourth row respectively. For encryption, rows are shifted to the left and for decryption shifted to the right. In *MixColumn* transformation each column of state matrix is treated as a four-term polynomial and then multiplied by $p(x) = 3x^2 + x^3 + x + 2$ using multiplication modulo $x^4 + 1$ in $GF(2^8)$. This can be considered as a matrix multiplication, as given in (1).

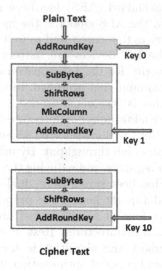

Fig. 1. The standard AES algorithm.

$$\begin{bmatrix} 2 & 3 & 1 & 1 \\ 1 & 2 & 3 & 1 \\ 1 & 1 & 2 & 3 \\ 3 & 1 & 1 & 2 \end{bmatrix} \begin{bmatrix} b_{00} & b_{04} & b_{08} & b_{12} \\ b_{01} & b_{05} & b_{09} & b_{13} \\ b_{02} & b_{06} & b_{10} & b_{14} \\ b_{03} & b_{07} & b_{11} & b_{15} \end{bmatrix}$$

(1)

Here the *SubByte* transformation is the only nonlinear transformation while all other transformations are linear. Each round requires a different round key which can be generated by the *KeyExpansion* process with three operations namely, *RotWords*, *SubWords* and XOR. The *RotWords* is shifting of bytes and the *SubWord* is word substitution using the S-box. Keys can be generated on-the-fly or they can be generated once, then stored and later given to the encryption or decryption module. In the proposed architecture, the round keys are generated on-the-fly.

3   Proposed Architecture

For IoT applications, the primary concern is power and area. Here, high throughput is not much required, hence pipelined and unrolled architectures are unsuitable for most of the IoT applications. For this reason, we implemented the AES cipher with 32-bit datapath based architecture. The architecture is based on dual-edg (DE) flip flop that is shown in Fig. 2 similar to [8]. Since memory consumes a lot of power, so instead of storing all the round keys to a large memory, keys are generated on-the-fly (OTF) which prevents the hardware redundancy as well as area overhead. Also, the architecture is iterative in nature that runs for ten rounds.

In the hardware implementation, among all of the transformations, *SubByte* and *SubWords* are the only transformations which are implemented as a sequential circuit, rest all are implemented in the form of combinational circuits. In AES, S-box implementation has a huge impact on the area as well as on power consumption. It has been found that approx 40% to 50% of the total area is occupied by the S-box only [8]. A 32-bit datapath architecture requires at-least four S-boxes to substitute 32-bit data coming from *ShiftRows* block, in the proposed architecture, to reduce hardware overhead we have used only two S-boxes in *Key Expansion* as well as in *Encryption* which are dual-edge triggered.

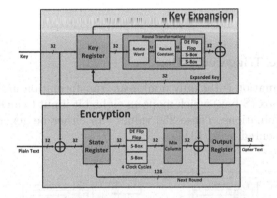

Fig. 2. An architecture for the lightweight implementation of the AES algorithm.

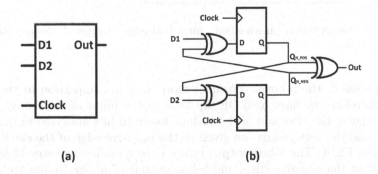

Fig. 3. Dual-edge triggered D-flip flop (a) Symbol (b) Circuit.

3.1   Dual-Edge Triggered D-Flip Flop

In the proposed architecture the Pseudo Dual-edge (DE) flip flop given in [9] is slightly modified for its subsequent and use. The modified DE flipflop is shown in Fig. 3 which is synthesizable for ASIC as well as for FPGA devices. The DE flip flop is consist of three XOR gates and two D-flip flops, one is positive edge triggered, and another one is negative edge triggered. The output of the positive edge triggered D-flip flop can we written as:

$$Q[n+1]_{POS} = Q[n]_{NEG} \oplus D1[n] \tag{2}$$

Similarly, The output of the negative edge triggered D-flip flop can we written as:

$$Q[n+1]_{NEG} = Q[n]_{POS} \oplus D2[n] \tag{3}$$

(2) and (3) can be XORed to get the final output ot the modified DE flip flop, as shown in 4.

$$Out = D1[n] \oplus D2[n] \oplus Q[n]_{NEG} \oplus Q[n]_{POS} \tag{4}$$

3.2   Dual-Edge Triggered S-Box

SubByte transformation is the only nonlinear transformation in AES. It consists of Substitutions box (S-box) which maps an eight-bit input to an eight-bit output and has 256 combinations. These 256 values can either be generated on-the-fly or can be implemented using LUTs.

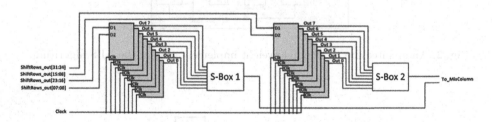

Fig. 4. A computation mechanism for dual-edge triggered S-box and its implementation.

As discussed, the S-boxes consumes more area in comparison to the other blocks; therefore, we have used DE flip flops at the input of the S-box. At the positive edge of the clock out of the 32-bits, lower 16-bits are given to the input of S-box and the rest 16-bits are given at the negative edge of the clock which is shown in Fig. 4. The S-box output values corresponding to lower 16-bits are registered at the negative edge, and S-box output of upper 16-bits are passed to *MixColumn* as it is. We have generated the S-box values in two ways: with LUTs and on-the-fly. The LUT based approach saves power while the later one saves the hardware area.

3.3 The Key Expansion Process

Using the AES Key expansion process, all round keys are generated. The Key Expansion process includes four operations: *RotWords*, *RoundConstant*, *Sub-Word* and XORing. In *SubWord* 32-bit is substituted using S-box. In the key expansion, S-box is used to substitute the 32-bits data coming from *RoateWord*, here also, instead of four S-boxes, we have used only two DE flip flop based S-boxes to reduce the cell area. Also, the S-boxes are used only for one clock cycle. To prevent unrequited transitions, the S-box block has been disabled for the rest of the clock cycles; hence, power is further reduced (Fig. 5).

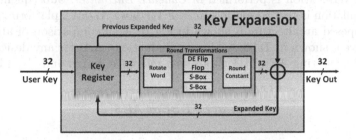

Fig. 5. Architecture of key expansion algorithm.

4 Implementation Results and Discussion

4.1 An FPGA Implementation

The proposed architecture has been implemented on Basys3 FPGA platform by using Xilinx Vivado tool. Since there is a limited number of I/O pins available on Basys3 board, we used UART to transmit and receive, plain text, user key, and ciphertext, respectively. Table 1 shows the FPGA resources utilization and timing report.

Table 1. Basys3 utilization and timing report

Design	Resource utilization		Design timing @ 100 MHz	
	No. of LUTs	No. of flip flops	Worst negative slack	Worst hold slack
AES (LUT S-box)	1028	537	6.082 ns	0.127 ns
AES (OTF S-box)	753	537	5.461 ns	0.127 ns
DE-AES (LUT S-box)	598	621	2.531 ns	0.132 ns
DE-AES (OTF S-box)	522	621	1.256 ns	0.138 ns

From Table 1, it can be seen that the for AES and DE-AES, on-the-fly S-box has lower area overhead and smaller setup slack in comparison to the LUT based

S-box. Small setup slack is due to the propagation delay of combinational circuit used to generate S-box values on-the-fly, which is not the case with LUT based S-box. The DE-AES has even smaller value of setup slack because it operates on both of the clock edges.

4.2 An ASIC Implementation of the Architecture

For a fair comparison, we have implemented all the four architectures of Table 1 in ASIC. These architectures have been modeled in Verilog HDL and synthesized using 180 nm PDK of SCL using *Cadence RTL Compiler*. Layout generation and functional verification is performed in *Cadence Encounter*. Subsequently, post-layout simulation is carried out in *Cadence Virtuoso ADEXL* platform. A layout of the proposed architecture is shown in Fig. 6. Area comparison of above four architecture is shown in Table 2. The area reduction (ΔA) for any design can be calculated by setting AES LUT S-box as a reference design and given by:

$$\Delta A = \frac{(Area\ of\ LUT\ SBox\ AES) - (Area\ of\ design)}{Area\ of\ LUT\ SBox\ AES} \times 100\% \qquad (5)$$

Fig. 6. Layout of the DE-AES architecture using SCL 180 nm Technology.

Table 2 shows that among all the four architectures, the LUT-based architecture occupies largest area. For LUT S-box and on-the-fly S-box, the proposed DE-AES occupies 83.13% and 70% smaller area, respectively when it is compared with the LUT-based conventional S-box. The FPGA implementation also confirms the ASIC area results. Also, when the S-boxes are implemented in LUTs, the proposed architecture consumes 25 μW power that is more than the conventional AES as a penalty to save 16.87% area. However, when on-the-fly S-boxes are used, the proposed architecture saves 6.66% area and consumes 87.1 μW less power. By this we can say that, when on-the-fly S-box is used, the proposed DE-AES architecture is the best candidate to save power as well as the area.

Table 2. ASIC area and power comparison

Design	Layout area	Tech.	Area reduction	Power @1.8 V
AES (LUT S-box)	0.160 mm^2	180 nm	-	578.5 μW
AES (OTF S-box)	0.120 mm^2	180 nm	25%	819.6 μW
DE-AES (LUT S-box)	0.133 mm^2	180 nm	16.87%	603.5 μW
DE-AES (OTF S-box)	0.112 mm^2	180 nm	30%	732.5 μW

We have also analyzed the power at various process corners at different supply voltages. Although the PDK works at 1.8 V power supply voltage, we are able to scale it down at lower values without affecting its performance. Power for all the five corners at various supply voltage is shown in Fig. 7, all the process corner works well at 1 V.

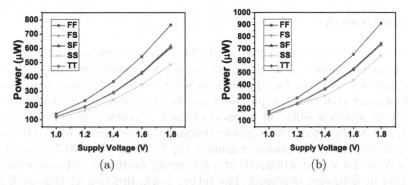

Fig. 7. Power consumption analysis for different supply voltages for (a) DE-AES LUT S-box (b) DE-AES on-the-fly S-box

Since the proposed design is implemented at 180 nm technology, at 1.8 V it consumes 732.6 μW and 603 μW of power for on-the-fly S-box and LUT S-box respectively. The power consumption is much higher than the other implementations listed in Table 3. This is due to the fact that the other architectures have been implemented at lower technology nodes. To make a fair comparison we have used scaling theory [10] to theoretically approximate power consumption of our design at the same technology node. Power approximation using scaling theory shows that if the designs are implemented on the same technology node our design will consume lesser power in comparison to than all the others architectures as listed in Table 3.

Table 3. Performance comparison of the proposed architecture with other architectures

Parameters	Design					
	DE-AES (LUT)	DE-AES (OTF)	[11]	[12]	[13]	[14]
Block size (bit)	128	128	128	128	128	128
Key size (bit)	128	128	128	128	128	128
Technology (nm)	180	180	90	40	65	22
Latency (Clock cycle)	55	55	44	337	160	336
Frequency (MHz)	10	10	10	122	32	76
Power (μW)	603@1.8 V 122.4@1 V	732.6@1.8 V 157.3@1 V	-	100 @0.45 V	67.7 @0.6V	170 @0.34V
Throughput (Mpbs)	23	23	-	46.2	25.6	20
Technology Scaling Factor	-	-	2	4.5	2.76	8.18
Approx. power for our design at the same technology node* (μW)	-	-	-	29.77 (LUT) 36.17 (OTF)	79.15 (LUT) 96.17 (OTF)	9.01 (LUT) 10.94 (OTF)

*using scaling theory

5   Conclusion

In this paper, we have presented a DE-AES architecture and its FPGA and ASIC implementations. The design consumes low hardware area and power which makes it suitable for applications where area and power requirements are of primary concern. The proposed architecture provides moderate level of throughput, which is sufficient for most of the IoT nodes. The post-layout simulation results show that the complete design consumes about $732.5\,\mu$W power. With voltage scaling the design consumes $122.7\,\mu$W at 1 V, $190.7\,\mu$W at 1.2 V, $289.3\,\mu$W at 1.4 V and $419.2\,\mu$W at 1.6 V using on-the-fly S-boxes with 30% reduction in hardware overhead. The future work direction of this work is to further reduce the power by investigating different low-power design techniques.

Acknowledgment. The authors would like to thank UGC, Govt. of India under the JRF Scheme for providing financial support (Ref. No. 3548/NET-DEC. 2015). We also extend our sincere gratitude to SMDP-C2SD programme, sponsored by MeitY, Govt. of India providing the required tools to carry out this work and Semiconductor Laboratory (SCL), India for providing PDK.

References

1. Zanella, A., Bui, N., Castellani, A., Vangelista, L., Zorzi, M.: Internet of things for smart cities. IEEE Internet Things J. **1**(1), 22–32 (2014)
2. Sadeghi, A.R., Wachsmann, C., Waidner, M.: Security and privacy challenges in industrial internet of things. In: Proceedings of the 52nd Annual Design Automation Conference, p. 54. ACM (2015)

3. Halak, B., Murphy, J., Yakovlev, A.: Power balanced circuits for leakage-power-attacks resilient design. In: Science and Information Conference (SAI), pp. 1178–1183. IEEE (2015)
4. Xu, T., Wendt, J.B., Potkonjak, M.: Security of IoT systems: design challenges and opportunities. In: Proceedings of the 2014 IEEE/ACM International Conference on Computer-Aided Design, pp. 417–423. IEEE Press (2014)
5. Sicari, S., Rizzardi, A., Grieco, L.A., Coen-Porisini, A.: Security, privacy and trust in Internet of Things: the road ahead. Comput. Netw. **76**, 146–164 (2015)
6. Vahedi, E., Ward, R.K., Blake, I.F.: Security analysis and complexity comparison of some recent lightweight RFID protocols. In: Herrero, Á., Corchado, E. (eds.) CISIS 2011. LNCS, vol. 6694, pp. 92–99. Springer, Heidelberg (2011). https://doi.org/10.1007/978-3-642-21323-6_12
7. Daemen, J., Rijmen, V.: Aes proposal: Rijndael (1999)
8. Bui, D.H., Puschini, D., Bacles-Min, S., Beigné, E., Tran, X.T.: AES datapath optimization strategies for low-power low-energy multisecurity-level internet-of-things applications. IEEE Trans. Very Large Scale Integr. (VLSI) Syst. **25**(12), 3281–3290 (2017)
9. Hildebrandt, R.: The Pseudo Dual-Edge D-Flipflop. http://www.ralf-hildebrandt.de/publication/publication.html. Accessed 02 June 2019
10. Dennard, R.H., Gaensslen, F.H., Yu, H.N., Rideout, V.L., Bassous, E., LeBlanc, A.R.: Design of ion-implanted MOSFET's wi th very small physical dimensions. IEEE J. Solid-State Circ.**SC-9**(5), 256–268 (1974)
11. Banik, S., Bogdanov, A., Regazzoni, F.: Exploring energy efficiency of lightweight block ciphers. In: Dunkelman, O., Keliher, L. (eds.) SAC 2015. LNCS, vol. 9566, pp. 178–194. Springer, Cham (2016). https://doi.org/10.1007/978-3-319-31301-6_10
12. Zhang, Y., Yang, K., Saligane, M., Blaauw, D., Sylvester, D.: A compact 446 Gbps/W AES accelerator for mobile SoC and IoT in 40 nm. In: 2016 IEEE Symposium on VLSI Circuits (VLSI-Circuits), pp. 1–2. IEEE (2016)
13. Zhao, W., Ha, Y., Alioto, M.: AES architectures for minimum-energy operation and silicon demonstration in 65 nm with lowest energy per encryption. In: 2015 IEEE International Symposium on Circuits and Systems (ISCAS), pp. 2349–2352. IEEE (2015)
14. Mathew, S., et al.: 53 Gbps native GF (2 4) 2 composite-field AES-encrypt/decrypt accelerator for content-protection in 45 nm high-performance microprocessors. In: 2010 IEEE Symposium on VLSI Circuits (VLSIC), pp. 169–170. IEEE (2010)

2L-2D Routing for Buffered Mesh Network-on-Chip

Rose George Kunthara[1](✉)[iD], K. Neethu[1][iD], Rekha K. James[1],
Simi Zerine Sleeba[2][iD], Tripti S. Warrier[3], and John Jose[4][iD]

[1] Division of Electronics, School of Engineering, CUSAT, Cochin, India
rosekunthara87@gmail.com, neethukuriyedam@gmail.com, rekhajames@cusat.ac.in
[2] Viswajyothi College of Engineering and Technology, Muvattupuzha, India
simi.abie@gmail.com
[3] Department of Electronics, CUSAT, Cochin, India
tripti@cusat.ac.in
[4] Indian Institute of Technology Guwahati, Guwahati, India
johnjose@iitg.ac.in

Abstract. The rise in complexity and number of processing cores in
SoC has paved way to the development of efficient and structured on-
chip communication framework known as Network on Chip (NoC). NoC
is embraced as an interconnect solution for the design of large tiled chip
multiprocessors (TCMP). It is characterized by performance metrics such
as average latency, throughput and power dissipation which depend on
underlying network architecture. In this paper, we propose 2L-2D (Two
Layer Two dimensional) architecture to enhance performance of conventional buffered 2D mesh NoC where two identical layers of 8×8 meshes
are stacked one on top of the other. 2L-2D uses conventional 5-port
virtual channel router (VCR) architecture and vertical interconnections
are made by utilizing unused ports at edge routers only. Experimental
results indicate that our proposed approach improves throughput and
network saturation point whereas average flit latency and power dissipation is considerably reduced when compared with standard 5-port 2D
mesh and torus designs.

Keywords: Network-on-Chip · Virtual channel router ·
Average latency · Throughput

1 Introduction

Rapid progress and innovations in IC technology have led to massive rise in
transistor integration which resulted in the evolution of complex System-on-
Chip (SoC) comprising of IP (Intellectual Property) cores that are connected
either by classical shared bus or point to point intercommunication architectures.
Network-on-Chip (NoC), a packet-switched network, has emerged to overcome
integration restrictions of SoC and interconnect associated issues like global

© Springer Nature Singapore Pte Ltd. 2019
A. Sengupta et al. (Eds.): VDAT 2019, CCIS 1066, pp. 308–320, 2019.
https://doi.org/10.1007/978-981-32-9767-8_27

wire delay problem which arise due to technology scaling. NoC communication is widely employed owing to its better scalability over conventional forms of on-chip interconnect, improved performance, built-in fault tolerance, better load handling ability, modular topology to connect the processing elements, concurrent communication between several pairs of processing cores and improved parallelism [1,2].

Scalable homogeneous NoC architecture comprises of several processing cores integrated on a single chip which are interconnected by a two dimensional mesh topology. High-speed routers, network interfaces (NI) and communication links are the basic components of regular tile-based NoC. The processing cores are attached to routers and the routers are connected by bi-directional links to exchange data between various processing elements (PE) in the form of packets. A packet is subdivided into flits (flow control units), which is the basic unit of data transfer in NoC. NoC network traffic is due to cache misses and coherence transactions. Each router has 5 bi-directional ports, North, South, East, West that are connected to neighbouring routers and a local port attached to corresponding PE [1,3]. The conventional VCR based NoC design employ input buffers to improve throughput, network bandwidth utilization rate, load handling ability and thereby raise network performance. 2D mesh NoC architecture is widely used in TCMP due to its regular structure and scalability.

In this paper, we propose a novel design approach based on traditional VCR based NoC, where two layers of 2D mesh network are stacked on top of each other, without altering standard 5-port router microarchitecture. Comparison of our proposed design with a planar 2D mesh network and 2D torus network engaging equal number of routers show improved network saturation point and throughput with minimal average latency, power consumption and footprint while running at similar frequency as conventional 2D design.

The rest of this paper is organized as follows: In Sect. 2 gives an overview about the related work and Sect. 3 describes motivation behind our design. Section 4 present features of proposed design. Section 5 gives a description about experimental methodology followed. The results are discussed in Sect. 6 and Sect. 7 concludes the paper.

2   Related Work

As 2D integrated circuits (IC) have limited floor planning choices, performance improvements occurring from NoC designs is restricted. The developments made in 3D IC technology has paved the way for routers used in 2D NoC topology to migrate towards 3D based topology. 2D NoC architectures use links made of global copper wires whereas 3D NoC comprises of both copper links and vertical TSV interconnects. 3D ICs can improve system performance manifold as they consists of several layers of active devices. Due to decrease in interconnect length, 3D ICs has improved performance, reduced power due to shorter interconnects, better packaging density and greater noise immunity [4,5].

Stacked Mesh or Hybrid 3D NoC-Bus mesh structure is proposed in [6] which is a combination of packet-switched network and bus structure. 7-port symmetric 3D NoC router is replaced with 6-port hybrid NoC-Bus 3D switch to exploit small interlayer distance in a 3D IC for improving performance. Their approach uses addition arbiter for each pillar or vertical bus for improved integration between NoC and bus structures. The authors in [7] compare 2D mesh NoC structures and corresponding 3D structures by evaluating power consumption, speed and zero-load latency to indicate 3D NoC advantages over 2D NoC. They also developed an analytical model for zero-load latency of each network under consideration which takes into account the topology effects on 3D NoC performance. An exhaustive study of inter-strata communication architectures in 3D NoC is described in [8]. Several design options such as a hop-by-hop symmetric 3D design, a simple bus-based vertical connection and a 3D crossbar structure are explored in their work. They also propose an improved partially-connected 3D crossbar structure called DimDe, to deliver better performance and energy-delay product characteristics.

MIRA (Multi-layered on-chip Interconnect Router Architecture) proposed by [9] is a stacked 3D NoC structure which is optimized to minimize power consumption and the area requirements thereby enhancing performance and thermal behaviour. Feero et al. [10] analyse performance of different 3D NoC architectures to exhibit their improved functionality in contrast to conventional 2D structures. They have introduced a novel architecture termed as ciliate 3D mesh which is basically a 3D mesh with several IP blocks per each switch. Each router is comprised of 7 ports, but their architecture has reduced overall bandwidth owing to multiple IP blocks per router and minimal connectivity when compared to a complete 3D mesh network. The authors in [11] report several application mapping and TSV placement strategies for 3D NoC systems. They also propose exact and heuristic techniques to address thermal-aware system design and test methods for both 2D and 3D NoC based architectures.

The effects of minimizing number of Through-Silicon-Via (TSV) to half and quarter on functionality of 3D NoC are assessed in [12]. Unbalanced distribution of 3D switches and random delays for different applications are main drawbacks of their architectures. Authors in [13] employ partition islands of switches to form areas for allocating same TSV pad for communication between interlayers, which are managed by serialization logic. But the average packet delay tends to exponentially rise with increase in number of switches per TSV bundle owing to serialization across TSV bundle. Contrary to 3D NoC employing vertical arbitration, a novel arbitration-free design is proposed for shared vertical links in [14]. Their proposed design has better performance in energy, throughput and latency when compared with symmetric 3D NoC with same area footprint.

3   Motivation

In a 2D NoC architecture, as the number of processing cores grows, there is significant increase in average packet latency whereas the communication quality

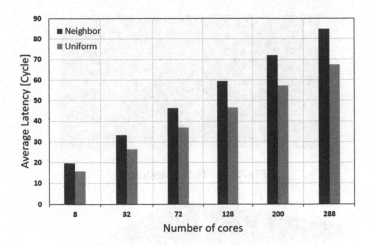

Fig. 1. Latency versus number of processing cores for different synthetic traffic patterns

decline due to rise in average number of hops between routers. Figure 1 clearly depicts the rise in flit latency with increasing number of cores for different synthetic traffic patterns in a planar 2D mesh NoC network. In contrast to 2D NoC network, 3D NoC designs will have minimal packet latency and smaller area footprint. But, 3D integration in NoC incur extra challenges as packets have to traverse along third dimension for which 3D router architectures have to be used. This increases arbitration, number of interconnections and ports in routers. The authors in [15], clearly indicate that crossbars used in 3D routers have increased power dissipation and area in contrast to 2D NoC routers.

The performance and area benefits of 2D NoC and 3D NoC architectures are put to use in our approach for enhancing functionality of 2D virtual channel routers. 5-port router architecture of conventional VCR based NoC is used in our design to build 2 identical layers of 8 × 8 meshes. The inter-layer communication is by vertical interconnections using TSVs made at edge routers through their unused ports thereby, improving routing efficiency.

4   Proposed Design

As mesh topology has a regular structure and routers are interconnected by short wires, we have taken mesh network for our proposed work. Figure 2 shows 8 × 16 2D mesh NoC and Fig. 3 details our new structure: 2L-2D. The proposed structure is formed by stacking 2 layers of 8 × 8 2D mesh NoC network. Both the layers are connected only through edge routers using vertical interconnect such as TSV. In a conventional 2D mesh NoC, all the 5-ports of routers, excluding the edge routers, are fully utilized in forming on-chip interconnect structure. But the edge routers have unused ports, which we have utilized in our design, to make connection between two layers through vertical interconnection links. Thus instead of having a 7-port router structure as in a 3D mesh NoC network,

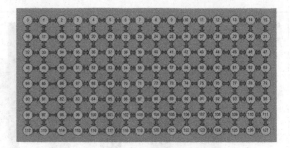

Fig. 2. 8 × 16 2D Mesh NoC

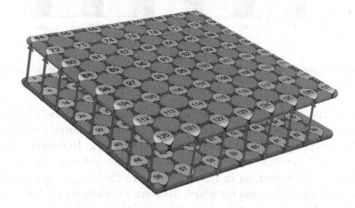

Fig. 3. 2L-2D 8 × 8 Mesh NoC

routers in our proposed design can have the same 5-port router architecture as in a 2D mesh NoC.

The 5-port router used in this design is same as that of traditional virtual channel router as shown in Fig. 4. Conventional VC routers employ buffers at their input ports so that flits can stay in them till they attain a productive port. Complex buffer management circuitry is required in addition to buffers, consuming significant portion of on-chip power and occupying large footprint on the chip [16,17]. The routing unit calculates required output port for the packet. Virtual Channel (VC) allocator unit does the task of reserving a VC in downstream router for each packet. Switch Allocation (SA) module performs arbitration to pick the winning packet when several packets require same downstream router. 5 × 5 crossbar is employed as switching fabric.

Flit is routed to nearby router based on XY routing algorithm in 8 × 16 2D mesh and torus NoC whereas a modified XY routing algorithm is employed in our design for efficient routing. Simple static XY routing is used for intra-layer routing. When the source and destination routers are in different layers, flits advance to nearest edge router in X-dimension which gives minimal Manhattan

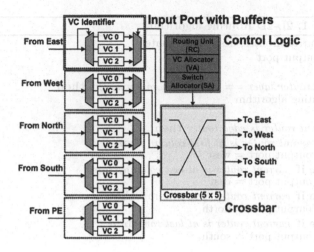

Fig. 4. Virtual channel router of [1]

distance across source and destination routers, as shown in algorithm aside. The above design approach can be implemented for bufferless mesh NoC as well.

5   Experimental Methodology

We employ Booksim 2.0 [18], an open source cycle accurate NoC simulator which models conventional VC based NoC router [1]. For our evaluations, we have used folded torus topology as in [1], to remove lengthy end-around link at the cost of doubling the span of other links. We then make necessary alterations to model our proposed design.

5.1   Synthetic Workload

The performance of 2L-2D is compared against VCR for mesh and torus topologies with size 8 × 16 (128 nodes) using standard synthetic workloads like uniform, tornado, bit-reverse, bit-complement, shuffle, neighbor and hotspot. After sufficient warm up time, average latency of flits and throughput readings are taken for all the traffic patterns by varying injection rates between zero and network saturation. Due to space limitations, results plotted for few traffic patterns only are shown.

5.2   Real Workloads

We also evaluate the performance of our new design against baseline VCR of size 8 × 16 for both mesh and torus topologies using real application mixes such as multi-programmed SPEC CPU2006 [19] benchmark application suite and multi-threaded PARSEC benchmarks [20]. Multi2Sim [21] simulator is used to model

---

Algorithm 1. 2L-2D Routing algorithm

Input   : current_router, destination_router
Output: output port

if *(current_router_layer == destination_router_layer)* then
| XY routing algorithm
else
| if *current router is edge router* then
| if *current router is at first column* then
| | output port = west
| else if *current router is at last column* then
| | output port = east
| else if *current router is at first row* then
| | output port = north
| else if *current router is at last row* then
| | output port = south
| end
| else
| output port taken as east or west depending on shortest Manhattan
| distance between source and destination router
| end
end

---

a 128-core multiprocessor system where every processing core comprises an out-of-order x86 processing module with 64 KB, 4-way set-associative private L1 cache and 512 KB, 16-way set-associative shared distributed L2 cache. One of the benchmark applications from SPEC CPU2006 suite is run on each processing core. Depending on misses per kilo instructions (MPKI) values, we divide applications into Low, Medium and High MPKI. 7 multiprogrammed workload mixes are produced by combining the different applications from application suite. We also run multithreaded workloads on an equivalent setup with minor alterations to create sufficient traffic for our analysis. Network events produced by running these workloads are then fed as traffic to NoC simulator.

6   Results and Analysis

The performance of 2L-2D is compared against VCR based NoC for both mesh and torus topologies of size 8×16 (128 nodes). For VC router (VCR), we assume 16 VCs per input port for our analysis purpose. We employ deadlock free, deterministic, minimal path XY routing algorithm in VCR to analyse the performance improvement of our proposed design.

6.1   Effect on Average Latency

Flit latency is computed as the time instant at which flit is first created in network to the time instant when flit reaches destination core, including queuing

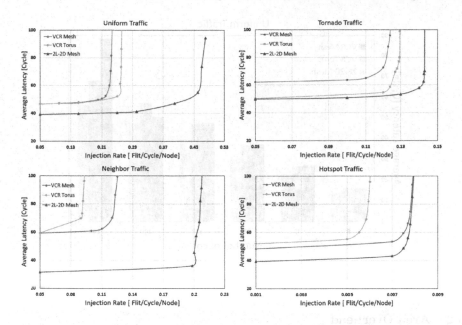

Fig. 5. Average latency comparison for different synthetic traffic patterns.

time at source node. Wider and lower latency curve indicates that router performance is better. Average flit latency comparisons between 8×16 2D mesh VCR, 8×16 2D torus VCR and our proposed design under some of the typical synthetic traffic patterns are shown in Fig. 5. 2L-2D reduces average latency by 17%, 20% and 18% for uniform, tornado and hotspot traffic respectively, compared to VCR mesh. The average latency reduction of 2L-2D compared to VCR torus is 16%, 7% and 24% for the same traffic patterns. When injection rate nears saturation, there is exponential increase in average latency due to flooding of network with flits. Higher the saturation injection rate in a router better is its load handling capacity. It is quite evident from Fig. 5 that our proposed design has much improved saturation injection rate compared to VCR mesh and torus networks.

Figure 6 depicts comparison of average latency values as the number of processing cores is increased. On scaling number of cores, our 2L-2D design has better reduction in average latency over other two designs. The reduction in average latency of flits compared to VCR mesh and torus networks for multiprogrammed and multithreaded workloads are shown in Fig. 7. There is significant decrease in average flit latency values for all the mixes using our design approach. As in multi-dimensional architectures, this reduced latency is due to reduced hop count and more number of NoC links in our design where edge routers are interconnected through TSVs.

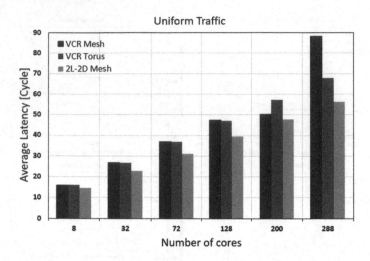

Fig. 6. Average latency versus number of processing cores

6.2 Area Overhead

In a NoC network, router overhead and wiring overhead contributes to total area overhead. Overall router area is based on total number of routers used in the network and area overhead per router, which is dependent on number of ports. 2D NoC architecture generally uses 5-port router architecture for mesh network whereas in 3D NoC designs, generally 7-port routers are utilized. Our proposed design has used same 5-port router architecture of 2D design thus, saving on router area overhead. There is negligible hardware router area overhead for our proposed work due to the modified routing logic which is overshadowed by remarkable reduction in average latency and throughput improvement.

For a 2D mesh NoC, wiring overhead includes overhead due to horizontal wirings only (8×16 2D mesh employs 232 horizontal links). For 3D NoC, in addition to area due to horizontal and vertical wirings, there is inter-layer via footprint. 2L-2D uses twice the number of horizontal links present in 8×8 mesh network (224 horizontal links) and some additional vertical wirings (28 vertical links) for connecting edge routers, thereby raising total wiring overhead. TSV has been utilized to connect inter-layer routers, which consumes some amount of silicon area and metal area. But our 2 layer design has reduced footprint as two 8×8 networks are stacked on top of each other.

6.3 Effect on Throughput

Network throughput is calculated as number of flits ejected from network per router per cycle. For a multi-layer NoC network, throughput improvement depends on average hop count and number of physical links. Throughput delivered by an ideal NoC network will be same as the flit injection rate. As 2L-2D has more physical links and less average number of hops, our proposed design

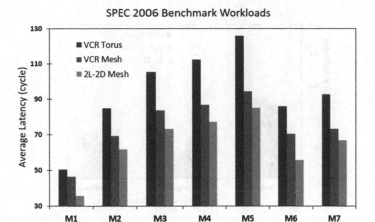

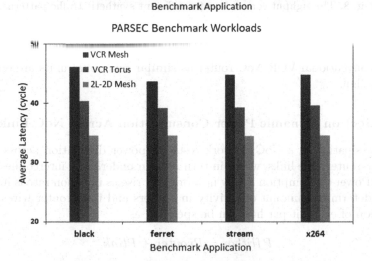

Fig. 7. Average latency for real applications

has better throughput indicating better quantity of sustainable traffic. Comparison with synthetic traffic patterns such as uniform, neighbor and bit-complement indicate throughput improvement of 2L-2D over other designs as shown in Fig. 8.

6.4 Effect on Router Pipeline Delay

Verilog HDL models of a router used in VCR based NoC and our proposed work is implemented and synthesized using Xilinx Vivado Design Suite-HLx to calculate pipeline latency of the router. Router delay is calculated as the time that a flit takes to traverse across router input port to router output port. The same functional units that are used in VCR are also employed in our design since both of them make use of 5-port router structure, only difference being in the

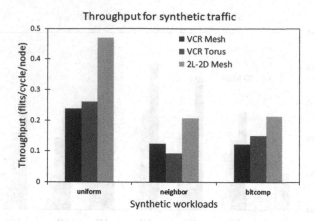

Fig. 8. Throughput comparison for different synthetic traffic patterns.

routing logic used. Thus, our router pipeline frequency also remains the same as that of conventional VCR NoC router as similar functional units are employed in our design.

6.5   Effect on Dynamic Power Consumption Across NoC Links

Power dissipation in a NoC network rests on power dissipation across routers and inter-router wire links, which in turn rely on underlying, interconnect architecture. Power consumption in any network will rise as injection rate is increased since it determines amount of activity in routers and inter-router wires. Power dissipation of each flit per hop can be specified as

$$Pflithop = Prouter + Plink \tag{1}$$

where Prouter denotes power dissipation across each router and Plink is across inter-router links. Since identical routers are used for both 8×16 VCR and our design, power dissipation across router is going to be the same. Power dissipation of a flit which takes n number of hops can be given as

$$Pflit = \sum_{i=1}^{n} Pflithop, i \tag{2}$$

The average power dissipation per flit when N flits are transmitted is specified as

$$Pflitavg = \frac{1}{N} \sum_{j=1}^{N} Pflit \tag{3}$$

Thus average power dissipation of each flit depends on number of hops between the source and destination nodes.

The area and power is calculated and compared using Orion [22]. We presume 65 nm technology at 1 GHz operational frequency with one cycle inter-router link delay. Router area is same for all the designs as we have employed the same 5-port router microarchitecture in our design also. Dynamic power dissipation reduces by 23% for uniform traffic, 26% for tornado and 25% for hotspot traffic when compared with VCR mesh network. There is power dissipation reduction of 7%, 8% and 16% for uniform, tornado and hotspot traffic respectively when compared with torus network. Thus, our proposed design has significant reduction in dynamic power consumption across NoC links due to reduced average number of hops.

7 Conclusion

NoC has emerged as a promising solution to overcome scalability and bottleneck challenges faced by conventional SoC architectures. In this paper, we proposed 2L-2D, where two similar layers of 8 × 8 mesh NoC are placed on top of each other and minimal TSV based vertical interconnections are made through the unused ports of edge routers only. The performance and area advantages of 2D and 3D architectures are exploited in our approach using minimal number of TSVs and employing conventional 5-port VCR based NoC router. This design can be further extended to 3D NoC structure where multiple layers are stacked on top of each other and communication between layers are only through edge routers so that the same 5-port router architecture can be employed. The thermal issues associated with our proposed design can be evaluated as a future work.

References

1. Dally, W., et al.: Principles and Practices of Interconnection Networks. Morgan Kaufmann, Burlington (2004)
2. Dally, W.: Route packets, not wires: on-Chip interconnection networks. In: Design Automation Conference (DAC-2001), pp. 684–689. ACM Press, New York, June 2001. https://doi.org/10.1109/DAC.2001.156225
3. Dally, W.: Virtual-channel flow control. IEEE Trans. Parallel Distrib. Syst. 3(2), 194–205 (1992). https://doi.org/10.1109/71.127260
4. Topol, A.W., et al.: Three-dimensional integrated circuits. IBM J. Res. Dev. 50(4/5) (2006). https://doi.org/10.1147/rd.504.0491
5. Davis, W.R., et al.: Demystifying 3D ICS: the pros and cons of going vertical. IEEE Des. Test Comput. 22(6), 498–510 (2005). https://doi.org/10.1109/MDT.2005.136
6. Li, F., et al.: Design and management of 3D chip multiprocessors using network-in-memory. In: Proceedings of International Symposium Computer Architecture, pp. 130–141 (2006). https://doi.org/10.1109/ISCA.2006.18
7. Pavlidis, V.F., et al.: 3-D topologies for networks-on-chip. IEEE Trans. Very Large Scale Integr. (VLSI 2007), 1081–1090 (2007). https://doi.org/10.1109/TVLSI.2007.893649

8. Kim, J., et al.: A novel dimensionally-decomposed router for on-chip communication in 3D architectures. In: Proceedings of International Symposium on Computer Architecture, pp. 138–149 (2007). https://doi.org/10.1145/1273440.1250680
9. Park, D., et al.: MIRA: a multi-layered on-chip interconnect router architecture. In: Proceedings of International Symposium on Computer Architecture, pp. 251–261 (2008). https://doi.org/10.1109/ISCA.2008.13
10. Feero, B.S., et al.: Networks-on-chip in a three-dimensional environment: a performance evaluation. IEEE Trans. Comput. 32–45 (2009). https://doi.org/10.1109/TC.2008.142
11. Manna, K., et al.: Thermal-aware design and test techniques for two- and three-dimensional networks-on-chip. In: 2016 ISVLSI, pp. 583–586 (2016). https://doi.org/10.1109/ISVLSI.2016.76
12. Xu, T., et al.: A study of through silicon via impact to 3D network-on-chip design. In: Proceedings of Conference on Electronics Information Engineering, pp. 333–337 (2010). https://doi.org/10.1109/ICEIE.2010.5559865
13. Wang, Y., et al.: Economizing TSV resources in 3D network-on-chip design. IEEE Trans. Very Large Scale Integr. Syst. 23(3), 493–506 (2015). https://doi.org/10.1109/TVLSI.2014.2311835
14. More, A., et al.: Vertical arbitration-free 3-D NoCs. IEEE Trans. Comput.-Aided Des. Integr. Circ. Syst. 37(9), 1853–1866 (2018). https://doi.org/10.1109/TCAD.2017.2768415
15. Agyeman, M.O., et al.: Performance and energy aware inhomogeneous 3D networks-on-chip architecture generation. IEEE Trans. Parallel Distrib. Syst. 27(6), 1756–1769 (2016). https://doi.org/10.1109/TPDS.2015.2457444
16. Hoskote, Y., et al.: A 5-GHz mesh interconnect for a teraflops processor. IEEE Micro 27(5), 51–61 (2007). https://doi.org/10.1109/MM.2007.4378783
17. Taylor, M.B., et al.: Evaluation of the raw microprocessor: an exposed wire-delay architecture for ILP and streams. In: ISCA 2004. https://doi.org/10.1109/ISCA.2004.1310759
18. Jiang, N., et al.: A detailed and flexible cycle-accurate network-on-chip simulator. In: IEEE International Symposium on Performance Analysis of Systems and Software (2013). https://doi.org/10.1109/ISPASS.2013.6557149
19. SPEC2006 CPU benchmark suite. http://www.spec.org
20. Bienia, C., et al.: The PARSEC benchmark suite: characterization and architectural implications. In: PACT, pp. 72–81 (2008)
21. Ubal, R., et al.: Multi2sim: a simulation framework to evaluate multicore-multithreaded processors. In: SBAC-PAD, pp. 62–68 (2007). https://doi.org/10.1109/SBAC-PAD.2007.17
22. Kahng, A.B., et al.: ORION 2.0: a fast and accurate NoC power and area model for early-stage design space exploration. In: Design, Automation Test in Europe (DATE), pp. 423–428 (2009). https://doi.org/10.1109/DATE.2009.5090700

Efficient Low-Precision CORDIC Algorithm for Hardware Implementation of Artificial Neural Network

Gopal Raut, Vishal Bhartiy, Gunjan Rajput, Sajid Khan, Ankur Beohar, and Santosh Kumar Vishvakarma[✉]

Nanoscale Devices, VLSI Circuit and System Design Lab,
Discipline of Electrical Engineering, Indian Institute of Technology Indore,
Indore 453552, MP, India
{phd1701102005,skvishvakarma}@iiti.ac.in

Abstract. An efficient FPGA or ASIC based hardware implementation of deep neural networks face the challenge of limited chip area, and therefore an area efficient architecture is required to fully harness the capacity of parallel processing of FPGA and ASIC in contrast to general purpose processors. In literature, the challenges are to investigate a generalized mathematical model and architecture for neuron block in an ANN implementation. We have proposed a generalized architecture for neuron implementation based on the shift-and-add algorithm, collectively known as Coordinate Rotation Digital Computer (CORDIC) algorithm, having a wide range of application. The look-up-table (LUT) based approach with a shift-and-add algorithm is an alternative technique for polynomial approximation and implementation. Paper explains how the CORDIC algorithm works and investigates the power and area efficient versatile computational unit for ANN application. The derived model proves that for the hyperbolic tangent function required a double pseudo-rotation and additional subtraction compares to the sigmoid function. In this reference versatile approach based optimized sigmoid activation function is implemented. The function is synthesized and validate on Xilinx zynq XC7Z010clg400 SoC and result reveals the minimum resources utilization.

Keywords: Artificial neural networks · ASIC/FPGA hardware · Shift-and-add algorithm · CORDIC algorithm · Activation function

1 Introduction

Many researchers developed attractive hardware architecture for real-time inference of deep neural network. An artificial neural network (ANN) is very popular for many problems that are very difficult for the other computational model like image processing, pattern recognition, prediction, and classification [1]. The use of hardware architectures gives a more parallel structure of ANNs for the desire

© Springer Nature Singapore Pte Ltd. 2019
A. Sengupta et al. (Eds.): VDAT 2019, CCIS 1066, pp. 321–333, 2019.
https://doi.org/10.1007/978-981-32-9767-8_28

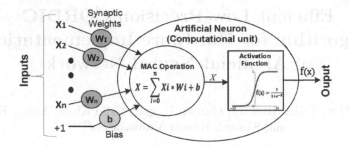

Fig. 1. Artificial single neuron model architecture

to optimize performance or reduce the cost of the implementation, particularly for applications demanding high parallel computation. Consequently, a significant amount of research effort has been spent on the hardware implementation of neural networks to achieve high energy and area efficient. However, many unique disadvantages are with the hardware platforms such as limitations with high data precision which has relation to hardware cost of the necessary computation, and the reconfigurability in the hardware implementation compared to software [2]. The neural network has been implemented using both software and hardware. However, researchers focused on hardware implementation as it is faster than the software part (Fig. 1).

The implementing of digital circuits using conventional digital design procedure tends to take more chip area on Field Programmable Gate Arrays (FPGAs) than the semi-custom or full custom Application Specific Integrated Circuits (ASICs) design approach [3]. Moreover, it is efficient, flexibility to reuse and reconfigure to optimize performance for any specific type of application [4]. The main focus of this article is on accelerating ANN on small-sized FPGAs [5], each neuron contains a computational unit having multiply-accumulate (MAC) followed by activation function (AF) shown in Fig. 1. Whereas, each MAC unit is relatively expensive in terms of power and area of hardware floor area (i.e., large numbers of gates) in FPGA and ASIC. The architecture of the computational unit and type of AF is the choice for design. However, the mostly "sigmoid" or "squashing" functions are used which compresses an infinite input signal range to finite output signal range, e.g., $[-1, +1]$. Research on ANN architecture is well enough; the MAC unit is still untouched. Many methods are implemented for elementary function evaluation like look-up-table based interpolation [6], CORDIC and Polynomial approximations.

In many application such as a built-in multiplier or dedicated hardware for sigmoid function, the CORDIC algorithm is having a good compromise of accuracy versus speed. The neural network has been implemented on both digital and analog platforms, but because digital circuits are easy to design, cheaper, and have noise immunity, they are preferred over analog implementation. For many controllers and FPGAs, logic implementation using the CORDIC algorithm is

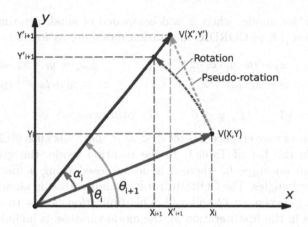

Fig. 2. The rotation and pseudo-rotation of a vector of length about an angle with the origin. The pseudo-rotation is the key idea about the CORDIC circuit for computation and realization of mathematical functions

over four times more efficient [7]. The size of the LUTs will decide the accuracy of the evaluated function. A CORDIC uses only adders to compute the result, with the benefit that it can, therefore, be implemented using relatively basic hardware. The CORDIC algorithm is used especially for trigonometric calculation which also can calculate other useful operation such as arithmetic operation, logarithmic and hyperbolic function calculation, and exponentiation listed by [8]. The CORDIC algorithm is based on the rotation and pseudo-rotation of a vector of length about an angle with the origin. The pseudo-rotation shown in Fig. 2 is the key idea about the CORDIC circuit for computation and realization of mathematical functions.

The rest of this brief is organized as follows. Section 2 describes the CORDIC algorithm. Section 3 will provide computation unit implementation using a CORDIC algorithm explanation. Section 4 will cover generalized approaches activation function of its implementation using CORDIC. In Sect. 5, we will give the analysis and discussion of proposed design architecture. Finally, Sect. 6 concludes this brief.

2   Cordic Algorithm Explanation

The CORDIC algorithm is an iterative convergence algorithm that offers effective low-cost implementation of a all types of complex trigonometric function. A CORDIC has three inputs, x_0, y_0, and z_0. Depending on the inputs to the CORDIC, various results can be produced at the outputs x_n, y_n, and z_n. CORDIC can be used to realized the fast (digital) DSP modules with minimum resources utilization [9–11]. CORDIC algorithm is designed in two modes, namely rotation mode and vectoring mode. The vector is rotated through an angle z in rotation mode, where z is decomposed of small rotating angle. The general equation [12] of CORDIC in rotation mode are as follows.

$$x_{i+1} = x_i - m \cdot y_i \cdot d_i \cdot 2^{-i} \qquad\qquad y_{i+1} = y_i + x_i \cdot d_i \cdot 2^{-i}$$
$$z_{i+1} = z_i - d_i \cdot tan^{-1} 2^{-i} \qquad\qquad z_n = z_0 + tan^{-1}(y_0/x_0)$$

where $d_i = +1$ if $y_i \leq 0$ -1 otherwise

The domain of convergence is $-99.7° < z_0 < 99.7°$ because $99.7°$ is the sum of all angles in the list of Table 1. In the rotation mode, the given vector is rotated through an angle h, where h is decomposed using a finite number of small elementary angles. The CORDIC rotation and vectoring algorithms having rotation angle between $-\pi/2$ and $\pi/2$. This limitation is due to the use of 2^0 for the tangent in the first iteration. m the mode variable, is included in general equation to realize trigonometric, inverse trigonometric, linear and hyperbolic functions. Here trigonometric and inverse trigonometric functions are realized using $m = -1$. Whereas, linear and hyperbolic functions are realized using $m = 0$ and 1 respectively.

Table 1. Step 'i' of the process, at each step to force the angle to converge to the desired final rotation.

i	$\alpha_i = tan^{-1}(2^{-i})$	
	Degrees	Radians
0	45.00	0.7854
1	26.57	0.4636
2	14.04	0.2450
3	7.13	0.1244
4	3.58	0.0624
5	1.79	0.0312
6	0.90	0.0160
7	0.45	0.0080
8	0.22	0.0040
9	0.11	0.0020

3   Exploration of Computational Unit for ANN Using CORDIC Algorithm

It says one neuron is critical if small jitter on this neuron'computation introduces large final output quality degradation otherwise it is resilient. Each neuron having a computational unit which includes the MAC and activation function.

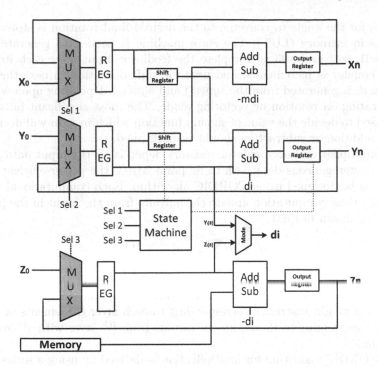

Fig. 3. CORDIC algorithm based proposed architecture for versatile computation

The multiplications and accumulations are performed in each MAC. Moreover, multiplier and adder can be implemented with different techniques that are accurate or approximate depending on the design objective. The design parameters will be area, power, response time, reliability, accuracy, etc. The energy and area improvements in operation can be achieved using the approximation technique. The fixed point computational unit (MAC) is designed, as floating point MAC has high complexity and power consumption. The limitation with the fixed-point based system cannot express the wide range of the variable. Moreover, weight/bias constants precision selection is one of the important choices in resource-limited hardware implementation.

The MAC operation can be realized using CORDIC based proposed architecture (Fig. 3) in Linear mode. In linear mode, the mode variable $m = 0$ modifies the general linear mode equation as follows:

$$x_n = x_0$$
$$y_n = y_0 + x_0 * z_0$$
$$z_n = 0$$

where z_0 and y_0 represent the corresponding weight and bias value and x_0 represents the input. In Fig. 3 shows the input and output parameters and the constants for the angle to converge to the desired final rotation is stored look-up-values in memory (LUT). The state machine is needed to generate select signals sel1, sel2 and sel3 to complete the feedback input after each iteration and the counter is incremented and used for shift operation in next the iteration. The d_i is generated from the $sgn(y_i)$ and $sgn(z_i)$ depending upon whether it is operating on rotation or vectoring mode. The most significant bit (MSB) will be used to decide the value of signum function which in turn will decide the whether addition or subtraction should be performed.

The multiplier and accumulator resistors depends on the input data width. Applying heterogeneous data path to fix-point MAC, the power efficient architecture can be designed using CORDIC algorithm. Each computational unit is performing their computation update the outputs from the input in the preceding layer as shown in Eq. 1.

$$a_j^l = \sigma(\sum \omega_{jk}^l a_k^{l-1} + b_j^l) \tag{1}$$

where σ is the squashing function (sigmoid) of computational unit k, corresponds to overall neurons in $(l\text{-}1)^{th}$ layer. To formulate this equation in matrix form, we assume a weight matrix ω^l corresponding to each layer l. Elements of weight matrix ω^l are weights to the inputs of neurons from l^{th} layer with j^{th} row and k^{th} column.

The CORDIC algorithm for multiplication is derived by using a series representation for weight in the l_{th} layer as shown in Eq. 6 as follows:

$$x_j = x_k * w_{jk} \tag{2}$$

$$= \omega_{jk} * \sum_{i=1}^{j} a_i * 2^{-i} \tag{3}$$

$$= \sum_{i=1}^{j} \omega_{jk} * a_i * 2^{-i} = \sum_{i=1}^{j} a_i * \omega_{jk} * 2^{-i} \tag{4}$$

The equation state that x_j is composed of a shifted version of weight ω. The unknown coefficient a_i may be found by driving x to zero one bit at a time. If the ith bit of input x_k is non-zero, y_i is first right shifted by i bits and added to the current value of x_j. When x has been driven to zero all bits have been examined and x_j contains the signed product of input vector and weight. The implementation is based on the standard shift and add multiplication. The calculation is considered for the weight ranges from -1 to $+1$.

4   Activation Function Design Technique

The hardware implement of activation function, various approaches have been proposed. Moreover, these methods are fall in to two categories piecewise linear approximation and Look-up table based approaches [13]. In this work, we consider the four mostly used approaches to make review concise.

4.1 LUTs Based Implementation by Storing Function Values

The most common method used is look-up tables based hardware implementation of activation function. The continuous function is approximated into discrete values of the function and store in the LUT. However, LUT implementations required more storage and increasing latency. The technique

4.2 LUTs Based Implementation by Storing Parameters

The activation function is a continuous function. Instead of storing the function values directly, this method keeps the function slope and the function intercept in the LUT. The outlook for implementation is storing function in piecewise with a different slope, value can be calculated using Eq. 5.

$$y = kx + c \tag{5}$$

where k is the slope and c is the function intercept. The output calculation depends on the above parameters and this approach leads to higher accuracy. However, used data by the multiplier and adder to calculate the equation needs more storage.

4.3 Approximation in Calculation

The approximation is done in many ways, the exponential function implementation is expensive but if it is converted into base-2 exploration, which is efficient to implement on hardware. In [14] used the following a formula to approximate the exponential function.

$$e^x \approx exp(x) \approx 2^{1.44x} \tag{6}$$

The sigmoid function can be calculated using this approximated function as:

$$Sigmoid(x) \approx \frac{1}{1 + 2^{-1.44x}} \approx \frac{1}{1 + e^{-1.5x}}$$

similarly for tanh function can be calculated using this approximation. Approximation technique can realized sigmoid and tanh function in single block with different operation but it requires more clock cycle. Where base-2 calculation and addition/subtraction required different clock cycle which decreases the overall performance. For the tanh function required one more clock cycle for an additional block. It takes minimum hardware utilization but has more latency which affects learning period.

4.4 Implementation Using CORDIC Algorithm

The sigmoid function presents a problem for direct hardware implementation since both the division and exponential operation. The tanh function passes through zero and can be treated as y = x around to zero unlike to sigmoid function. However, the implementation of sigmoid function in piece-wise linear (PWL) approximation, the non-linear model is divided into several approximate linear segments. Research done in [15,16] shows that non-linear activation function increases learning performance and provide higher accuracy. However, hardware implementation of non-linear activation function will lead to high silicon area consumption and reduced the speed of operation.

The sigmoid or hyperbolic tangent activation function is realized by making mode variable $m = -1$, and operating in vectoring mode where d_i will be decided by signum of y_i. The equation for realizing hyperbolic tangent is given by equation of Z_n from the following equation.

$$x_n = A_n\sqrt{x_0^2 - y_0^2}$$
$$y_n = 0$$
$$z_n = z_0 + tanh^{-1}(y_0/x_0)$$
$$A_n = \prod_n \sqrt{1 - 2^{-2i}}$$

The sigmoid function is realized through tan hyperbolic as follows:

$$sinh(x) = \frac{e^x - e^{-x}}{2} \quad \& \quad cosh(x) = \frac{e^x + e^{-x}}{2} \tag{7}$$

$$sinh(x) + cosh(x) = e^x \quad \& \quad sinh(x) - cosh(x) = e^{-x} \tag{8}$$

$$f(x) = tanh(x) = \frac{e^x - e^{-x}}{e^x + e^{-x}} \tag{9}$$

$$g(x) = Sigmoid(x) = \frac{1}{1 + e^{-x}} = \frac{e^x}{1 + e^x} \tag{10}$$

By solving the Eqs. 9 and 10, the relation between the tan hyperbolic and sigmoid is

$$tanh(x) = 1 - 2\ Sigmoid(-2x) \tag{11}$$

$$Sigmoid(x) = \frac{1 + tanh\,(x/2)}{2} \tag{12}$$

We should have generalized design for sigmoid function approximation which should be applicable for a variety of activation function. The tanh function passes through zero and can be treated as y = x around to zero unlike to sigmoid function [17]. In principle, sigmoid and tanh have likely expressive ability, but in practice, sigmoid is just a activation function with constant. When the output of neuron is restricted [0, 1], the neuron activation is more likely closed to 0.5. The activation range need more saturation with sigmoid than with tanh using the conventional technique [18]. However, the implementation of sigmoid function requires half pseudo-rotation steps compare to the tan hyperbolic function shown

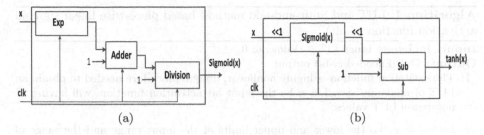

(a)   (b)

Fig. 4. CORDIC algorithm based (a) sigmoid activation function (b) hyperbolic tangent activation function

in Eq. 12. It can be concluded that for the best learning, in terms of resources utilized and speed. We can conclude that the sigmoid activation function is the best choice for implementation using the CORDIC algorithm.

5   Implementation of Efficient LUT and Shift-and-Add Algorithm Based Activation Function

The direct hardware implementation of sigmoid function is challenging since both the division and exponential operations are present in function. The practical option for implementation in hardware is linearly approximate the function [19]. In piece-wise linear (PWL) approximation, the non-linear model is divided into several approximate linear segments. Research done in [15,16] shows that non-linear activation function increases learning performance and provide higher accuracy. However, the hardware implementation of the non-linear activation function will lead to high silicon area consumption and reduced the speed of operation. It is demanded for generalized design exploration for approximate activation function which can explore different variety activation function.

The LUT based piece-wise-linear approximation of activation function is the best way to implement for less hardware utilization. When the number of neurons is lower than the total BRAM blocks available in the FPGA circuit, the best way to approximate the sigmoid function is the lookup table based method. Based on the size, speed and accuracy, we have implemented the linear approximation in resulting activation function shown in Algorithm 1. The LUT-based approach works much faster than piece-wise linear approximation but LUT consumes memory. The activation function design using mix model using the CORDIC algorithm and LUT based approach of sigmoid activation function will be the best choice. We choose the angles so that the required angle will be constructed from the sum of all them, with appropriate signs. The multiplication can be performed by the shift-and-add of binary number whereas $\tan\alpha_i$ is realized using a power of 2 for the above application.

It can be concluded that the best approximation method, in terms of resources utilized and errors introduced, PWL approximation is the option especially when the number of the neurons that use sigmoid function is larger than the

Algorithm 1. LUT and Shift-and-add method based piece-wise linear sigmoid activation function (8-bit)

Input: In: Integer range $(2^n - 1)$ downto 0;
Output: Out: Encoded N-bit output

1: The excitation function is highly nonlinear, unique procedure needed to obtain an LUT of minimum size. Let n be the input bit activation function, will having 2^n number of LUT values.

2: Let x_1 & x_2 be the lower and upper limits of the input range and the range of output (y) is between 2^{-N} and $1 - 2^{-N}$, It is found that $x_1 = +ln(2^n - 1)$ and $x_2 = -ln(2^n - 1)$.

3: To produce change in quantize output (Δy) equals to 2^{-n} for the log-sigmoid activation function for the change in input (Δx) i.e gap between the two input points for N-bit LUTs.

$$(\Delta x) = \frac{2 \times Input\ Margin(IM)}{2^n} \tag{13}$$

4: *Generation of Look-Up-Table with shift-and-add Property (Slope at the origin=0.5).*

begin
for index In $-2^{(Nbit-1)}$ *to* $2^{(Nbit-1)}$-1 **do**

$$y <= \frac{2.0}{1.0 + exp^{\left(\frac{-4.0 \times Slop}{Input\ Range}\right) \times x}} - 1 \tag{14}$$

$w <= y * \left(2.0^{(Nbit-1)}\right)$ ... shifts bits to the left
$t <= Round(w)$
$z <= Integer(t)$
$x := x + input\ scale(\Delta x)$ ... add scale value
end for

---

number of the BRAM blocks available in the FPGA circuit. When the number of neurons is lower than the total BRAM blocks available in the FPGA circuit, the best way to approximate the sigmoid function is the lookup table based method. Based on size, speed and accuracy, we have implemented the linear approximation in resulting activation function shown in Algorithm 2. We include the linear interpolation along with the LUTs. LUT-based approach works much faster than piece-wise linear approximation, though LUT consumes memory. So, if there is not much concern about memory, LUT based approach is preferred. An analysis of the trade-off between the hardware cost, look-up-table based approximate activation function is also implemented and its hardware resource utilization as shown in Table 2 (Fig. 5).

6   Results and Discussion

The dominant computation part in the ANN is multiplier, adder and activation function. However all these function can be realized on the same hardware in

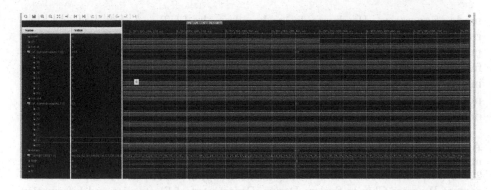

Fig. 5. Simulation validation of sigmoid activation function based on Algorithm 1.

CORDIC algorithm based architecture. By selecting the mode of operation any function can be realized using the proposed architecture shown in Fig. 3. The CORDIC algorithm based proposed architecture for versatile computation is the key point for hardware reutilization. An analysis of the trade-off between the hardware cost, look-up-table based approximate activation function is implemented. The sigmoid function implementation take the half rotation for logic evaluation compares to tanh function using CORDIC algorithm which concluded that the time and value taken by the algorithm is less case of sigmoid activation function. In this regards the algorithm for 8-bit integer piece-wise linear sigmoid activation function have been implemented using LUT and shift-and-add property for multiplication which takes least hardware resource utilization for Zynq XC7Z010clg400 SoC, Zybo board as shown in Table 2.

Table 2. LUT based sigmoid function implementation

Features/resources	Utilization	Available
LUT	1	17600
FF	1	35200
BRAM	0.5	60

7 Conclusion

This paper provided a methodology for the design of power and area efficient versatile computational unit implementation for ANN application. Hardware implemented activation function performance and analysis shows the correct functionality based on the CORDIC algorithm. The different logic function is implemented on the same hardware using a CORDIC algorithm based on the mode of operation. Hardware design based on the LUT and shift-and-add algorithm approach based hybrid architecture for sigmoid activation function is proposed. The deep neural network architecture contains numerous mathematical functions such as multiplication, addition, trigonometric function, etc. And it implemented on the same hardware using the CORDIC algorithm. The proposed technique for logic implementation saved resources utilization by realizing different functions on the same hardware.

Acknowledgment. The authors would like to thank the University Grant Commission (UGC) New Delhi, Government of India under JRF scheme with award no. 22745/(NET-DEC. 2015) for providing financial support and Special Manpower Development Program Chip to System Design, Department of Electronics and Information Technology (DeitY) under the Ministry of Electronics and Information Technology, Government of India for providing necessary Research Facilities.

References

1. Mukta, P., Kumar, U.A.: Neural networks and statistical techniques: a review of applications. Expert Syst. Appl. **36**(1), 2–17 (2009)
2. Herbordt, M.C., et al.: Achieving high performance with FPGA-based computing. Computer **40**(3), 50–57 (2007)
3. Wong, H., Betz, V., Rose, J.: Comparing FPGA vs. custom CMOS and the impact on processor microarchitecture. In: Proceedings of the 19th ACM/SIGDA International Symposium on Field Programmable Gate Arrays. ACM (2011)
4. Nurvitadhi, E., et al.: Accelerating binarized neural networks: comparison of FPGA, CPU, GPU, and ASIC. In: 2016 International Conference on Field-Programmable Technology (FPT). IEEE (2016)
5. Liu, J., Liang, D.: A survey of FPGA-based hardware implementation of ANNs. In: International Conference on Neural Networks and Brain, ICNN&B 2005, vol. 2. IEEE (2005)
6. Sadeghian, M., Stine, J., Walters, E.: Optimized linear, quadratic and cubic interpolators for elementary function hardware implementations. Electronics **5**(2), 17 (2016)
7. Cockrum, C.K.: Implementation of the CORDIC algorithm in a digital downconverter (2008)
8. Andraka, R.: A survey of CORDIC algorithms for FPGA based computers. In: Proceedings of the 1998 ACM/SIGDA Sixth International Symposium on Field Programmable Gate Arrays, pp. 191–200. ACM (1998)
9. Despain, A.M.: Fourier transform computers using CORDIC iterations. IEEE Trans. Comput. **100**(10), 993–1001 (1974)
10. Duh, W.-J., Wu, J.-L.: Implementing the discrete cosine transform by using CORDIC techniques. In: International Symposium on VLSI Technology, Systems and Applications, pp. 281–285. IEEE (1989)
11. Hu, Y.H., Naganathan, S.: A novel implementation of a chirp Z-transform using a CORDIC processor. IEEE Trans. Acoust. Speech Sig. Process. **38**(2), 352–354 (1990)
12. Walther, J.S.: A unified algorithm for elementary functions. In: Proceedings of the Spring Joint Computer Conference, 18–20 May 1971, pp. 379–385. ACM (1971)

13. Zhang, M., Vassiliadis, S., Delgado-Frias, J.G.: Sigmoid generators for neural computing using piecewise approximations. IEEE Trans. Comput. **45**(9), 1045–1049 (1996)
14. Gomar, S., Mirhassani, M., Ahmadi, M.: Precise digital implementations of hyperbolic tanh and sigmoid function. In: 2016 50th Asilomar Conference on Signals, Systems and Computers, pp. 1586–1589. IEEE (2016)
15. Basterretxea, K.: Recursive sigmoidal neurons for adaptive accuracy neural network implementations. In: NASA/ESA Conference on Adaptive Hardware and Systems (AHS). IEEE (2012)
16. Basterretxea, K., et al.: An experimental study on nonlinear function computation for neural/fuzzy hardware design. IEEE Trans. Neural Netw. **18**(1), 266–283 (2007)
17. Yang, T., Wei, Y., Tu, Z., et al.: Design space exploration of neural network activation function circuits. IEEE Trans. Comput.-Aided Des. Integr. Circ. Syst., 1 (2018). https://doi.org/10.1109/TCAD.2018.2871198
18. LeCun, Y.A., Bottou, L., Orr, G.B., Müller, K.-R.: Efficient backprop. In: Montavon, G., Orr, G.B., Müller, K.-R. (eds.) Neural Networks: Tricks of the Trade. LNCS, vol. 7700, pp. 9–48. Springer, Heidelberg (2012). https://doi.org/10.1007/978-3-642-35289-8_3
19. Ferreira, P., et al.: A high bit resolution FPGA implementation of a FNN with a new algorithm for the activation function. Neurocomputing **71**(1–3), 71–77 (2007)

An Ultra Low Power AES Architecture for IoT

Sajid Khan[1], Neha Gupta[1], Gopal Raut[1], Gunjan Rajput[1],
Jai Gopal Pandey[2], and Santosh Kumar Vishvakarma[1(✉)]

[1] Nanoscale Devices, VLSI Circuit and System Design Lab,
Discipline of Electrical Engineering, Indian Institute of Technology,
Indore 453552, Madhya Pradesh, India
{phd1601102015,phd1701202008,phd1701102005,phd1601102014,
skvishvakarma}@iiti.ac.in
[2] Integrated System Group, CSIR-CEERI, Pilani 333031, Rajasthan, India
jai@ceeri.res.in

Abstract. Internet of Things (IoT) is now becoming a part of our
life. Many devices are already connected, and more are expected to be
deployed in the next coming years. The main concern for IoT is to provide
a practical solution for security, privacy, and trust. The science of cryptography plays an important role for providing security in IoTs. AES
algorithm is a well known symmetric key, block cipher that is highly
secure. In this paper, we present an ultra-low power architecture for
the AES cipher that is need for most IoT applications. The proposed
architecture has been implemented on SCL 180 nm technology. We have
used 4-bit serializer and deserializer (SerDes) to send and receive 128-bit
data. The proposed AES architecture uses 32-bit data path in SubByte
transformation, and it requires 44 clock cycles for encryption of 128-bit
plaintext with a 128-bit cipher key. To deserialize 128-bit plaintext and
cipher key, the architecture requires 32 clock cycles. Similarly, to serialize 128-bit ciphertext, 32 clock cycles are overlapped by 44 clock cycles
required by AES module. By this, once, after the first 32 clock cycles,
the use of SerDes does not affect on the throughput of the system. At
10 MHz the ASIC implementation of the proposed architecture on SCL
180 nm PDK consumes 52.2 μW and 194.7 μW power at 1 V and 1.8 V
respectively and provides a throughput of 28 Mbps.

Keywords: Lightweight · AES · Architecture · IoT · Security

1 Introduction

Internet of things (IoT) refers to the ever-growing network and is expected to
use in a variety of emerging applications, such as smart cities, wearable electronics, remote health care, agriculture, and many more [1]. This adds a level
of intelligence to the devices, enabling them to communicate even without the
involvement of a human being. It utilizes real-time analysis with machine learning method to process data and make decisions. Security failure of these devices

© Springer Nature Singapore Pte Ltd. 2019
A. Sengupta et al. (Eds.): VDAT 2019, CCIS 1066, pp. 334–344, 2019.
https://doi.org/10.1007/978-981-32-9767-8_29

can affect billions of lives as well as a huge financial loss with privacy invasion [2,3]. Thus, avoiding security failure is considered as a serious issue in the effective and meaningful deployment of IoT devices on a large scale [4,5]. To secure sensitive data, cryptography provides an efficient solution. However, the hardware cost and power budget of conventional cryptography implementations limit the use of conventional cryptography algorithm in most of the IoT applications [6]. In year 2001, the advanced encryption standard (AES) whas been formally approved as a US federal standard [7]. The current issue on the security of the IoTs can be solved by using the available AES cipher algorithm. It is considered as a strong and secure cipher. But majority of the IoT devices are battery powered. So, minimizing power consumption is the utmost priority for the IoT constrained devices to keep the battery life longer. In this concern, an ultra-low power architecture of AES-like cipher is very much needed.

This paper aims to propose a low-power architecture for AES cipher and its hardware implementation. Here, a 32-bit datapath architecture for SubByte transformation is chosen to achieve low-power and high throughput requirements. We used 4-bit serializer and deserializer (SerDes) to deserialize 128 bit plaintext, cipher key and serialize 128-bit ciphertext. The 32 clock cycles needed to deserialize plaintext and cipher key, are overlapped by the 44 clock cycles that are required to perform encryption operation. By this, 370 I/O pads have been saved without affecting the throughput of the system. For power optimization, we used clock gating, minimized the number of datapath registers and reduced the unnecessary transitions. To reduce transitions, we have applied an *enable* signal to various blocks so that they can be disabled when they are not needed. The design uses 32-bit architecture in SubByte transformation; hence it is at least four times faster than the 8-bit datapath architectures at the same clock frequency. With these optimization, high throughput of 28 Mbps at 10 MHz has been achieved along with at extreme low-power of 52.2 μW at 1 V.

This paper is organized as follows: in Sect. 2, an overview of the standard AES algorithm is provided. Section 3 describes the proposed architecture and related optimization strategies. An ASIC post-layout simulation results are discussed in Sect. 4 and finally, conclusion is drawn in Sect. 5.

2   An Overview of the AES Algorithm

AES is a symmetric block cipher algorithm that can process 128-bit data with 128, 192 and 256 bit key with 10, 12 and 14 number of rounds respectively, which is referred as AES-128, AES-192, and AES-256. Each round is consist of four transformations: *SubBytes*, *ShiftRows*, *MixColoumns* and *AddRoundKey*. To convert a plaintext with 128-bit key into a ciphertext the AES core runs for ten rounds, where each round goes through all the above transformation with a new transformed key except the last round. The last round does not require the *MixColumn* transformation as shown in Fig. 1.

The 128-bit data is arranged in a 4 × 4 matrix by dividing the 128-bit in 16, 8-bit blocks. The matrix is called as state matrix. *AddRoundKey* transformation

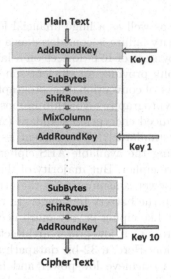

Fig. 1. The standard AES algorithm.

is just the XOR of state matrix with 128-bit key. *SubByte* transformation is the byte-by-byte substitution of state matrix using a mapping function that is nonlinear in nature. The function can be implemented as a lookup table (LUT) or using arithmetic in finite field using irreducible polynomial $(x^8+x^4+x^3+x+1)$ in $GF(2^8)$ and an affine transformation. *ShiftRows* transformation is the circular shift of rows. For encryption rows are shifted to left and for the decryption they are shifted to right. In *MixColumn* transformation each column of state matrix is treated as a four term polynomial and then multiplied by $p(x) = 3x^2+x^3+x+2$ using multiplication modulo x^4+1 in $GF(2^8)$. This can be considered as a matrix multiplication as shown in (1).

$$\begin{bmatrix} 2 & 3 & 1 & 1 \\ 1 & 2 & 3 & 1 \\ 1 & 1 & 2 & 3 \\ 3 & 1 & 1 & 2 \end{bmatrix} \begin{bmatrix} b_{00} & b_{04} & b_{08} & b_{12} \\ b_{01} & b_{05} & b_{09} & b_{13} \\ b_{02} & b_{06} & b_{10} & b_{14} \\ b_{03} & b_{07} & b_{11} & b_{15} \end{bmatrix} \tag{1}$$

Each round requires a different round key which can be generated by *Key-Expansion* algorithm. The operation consists of three other operations that are *RotWords*, *SubWords* and XOR. *RotWords* is shifting of bytes and *SubWord* is word substitution using S-Box. Here, the round keys can be generated on-the-fly or can be generated once, then stored and later utilized for encryption or decryption modules. As we know memory consumes a large amount of power, therefore, instead of storing all the round keys in a large memory, keys are generated on-the-fly.

3   Proposed Architecture

We have proposed a low-power architecture of AES for IoT constrained devices where power consumption is a serious issue. For IoTs, high throughput is not much required; therfore pipelined and loop-unrolled architectures are not much suitable for general-purpose IoT applications. The architecture shares hardware in different rounds, this reduces hardware as well as power overhead. The architecture runs in iterative fashion for ten rounds using the same hardware for all the rounds. In the implementation, we have used two 4-bit deserializer to deserialize 128-bit plaintext and cipher key and one serializer to re-serialize the 128-bit ciphertext in 32 clock cycles that is shown in Fig. 2.

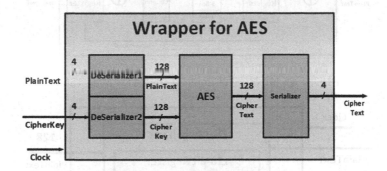

Fig. 2. SerDes wrapper for proposed AES architecture.

Here, all the blocks are combinational except the *SubByte*, which is sequential in nature. The *SubByte* block uses 32-bit data path with four S-Boxes and takes four clock cycles to substitute 128-bit data. After four clock cycles all the 128 bits are passed to *ShiftRows* blocks. Since data is available after three clock cycles, all the other blocks are disabled for three clock cycles to prevent unnecessary transitions to achieve power reduction. It this context, the *ShiftRows* block is implemented by using wires only. Figure 3 shows the proposed architecture of our AES implementation.

To keep the memory usage minimum, all the *RoundConstants*, in key expansion are generated on-the-fly instead of storing them into memory. Some of the optimization details are provided below.

3.1   Serializer

The proposed architecture uses two 4-bit serializers to receive 128-bit plaintext and cipher key. Here we have used two 128-bit temporary registers to store plaintext and cipher key. Once all the 128-bit data is received from plaintext and cipher key serializer, AES module starts working. Figure 4 shows the architecture of deserializer used for cipher key and plaintext.

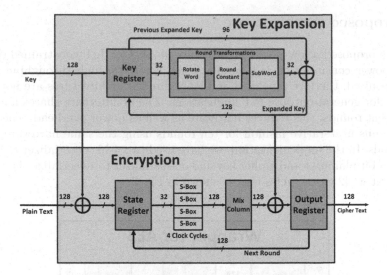

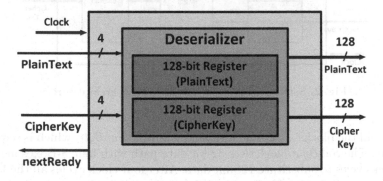

Fig. 3. Architecture of implemented AES algorithm.

Fig. 4. Architecture of deserializer.

To overlap the clock cycles of deserializer, after 32 clock cycles, *nextReady* signal is asserted and *wrapper module* is ready to capture new plaintext and cipher key. Similarly once the ciphertext is ready, *cipherReady* signal is asserted and 128-bit ciphertext is delivered in 32 clock cycles while next data is being processed. Hence use of serializer/deserializer does not affects on system throughput and the architecture is able to perform encryption at very low power consumption.

3.2 *SubByte* transformation

The *SubByte* transformation is only nonlinear transformation in AES. It consists of substitutions box (S-Box) which maps an eight bit input to eight bit output and has 256 combinations. These 256 values can either be generated on-the-fly or can be implemented using LUT.

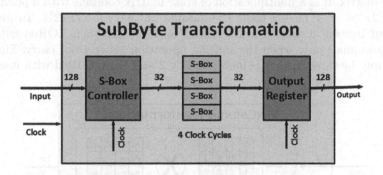

Fig. 5. Architecture of *SubByte* transformation.

We have implemented S-Box using LUT approach, which takes eight-bit input and provides corresponding eight-bit value. Here four S-Boxes have been utilized for SubByte transformation, and they requires four clock cycles to substitute the 128-bit input data (Fig. 5).

3.3   *ShiftRows* transformation

In *ShiftRows* transformation, each row of state matrix is shifted to left with the offset of 0, 1, 2 and 3 for first, second, third and froth row respectively. In the design we have implemented *ShiftRows* with wires only (Fig. 6).

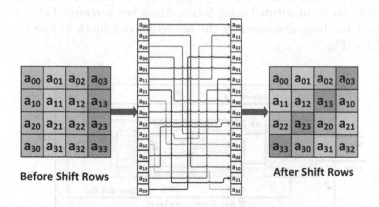

Fig. 6. Architecture of *ShiftRows* transformation.

3.4 *MixColumn* transformation

The *MixColumn* transformation is a linear transformation applied to the columns of state matrix. It is a multiplication of state matrix columns with a polynomial $a(x) = 3x^3 + x^2 + 1x + 2$ using the modulo $(x^4 + 1)$ in $GF(2^8)$. To multiply the input by two, it has been left-shifted by 1-bit and then XORed with '1B' (in hexadecimal) only when the shifting operation generates a carry. Similarly to multiply by three, first it is multiplied by 2 and then XORed with itself.

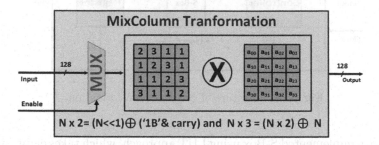

Fig. 7. Architecture of *MixColumn* transformation.

Since *MixColumn* transformation is only required at the fourth clock cycle of every round, we disabled it for the rest three clock cycles to save power (Fig. 7).

3.5 Key Expansion

Using key expansion all the round keys are generated. The key expansion process includes four operations: *RotWords*, *RoundConstant*, *SubWord* and XORing. In *SubWord* 32-bit is substituted using S-Box. Since key is required after four clock cycles, so it has been generated by the key expansion block in four consecutive clock cycles (Fig. 8).

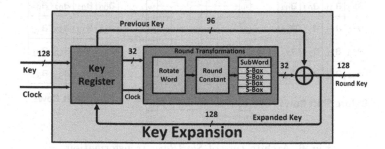

Fig. 8. Architecture of key expansion algorithm.

Table 1. Utilization report on Basys3 platform

S. no.	Resource	Available	Utilization	Utilization %
1	Slice LUTs	20800	1278	6.14
2	Slice Register	41600	1137	2.73
3	F7 Muxes	16300	80	0.49
4	F8 Muxes	8150	32	0.39
5	IOs	106	16	15.09

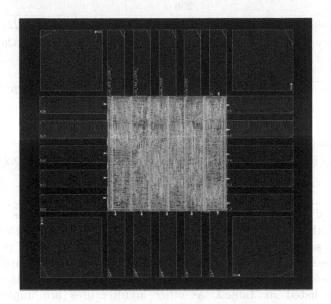

Fig. 9. Layout of the proposed architecture.

4 Implementation Results and Discussion

4.1 FPGA Implementation

We have implemented the proposed architecture on Basys3 FPGA using Xilinx Vivado tool. Table 1 shows the FPGA resources utilization report.

4.2 An ASIC Implementation of the Architecture

The proposed architecture is modeled into Verilog HDL and synthesized for SCL 180 nm PDK using *Cadence RTL Compiler*. *Cadence Encounter* is used for layout generation and functional verification. The ASIC post-layout simulation is carried out in *Cadence Virtuoso ADEXL* platform. The layout of the proposed architecture is shown in Fig. 9.

Table 2. Performance comparison of the proposed architecture with Other architectures

Parameters	Design					
	This work	[8]	[9]	[10]	[11]	[12]
Block size (bit)	128	128	128	128	128	128
Key size (bit)	128	128 192 256	128	128	128	128
Technology (nm)	180	28	90	40	65	22
Latency (Clock cycle)	44	44 52 60	44	337	160	336
Frequency (MHz)	10	10	10	122	32	76
Power (µW)	52.2 @ 1 V	20 @0.6 V	-	100 @0.45 V	67.7 @0.6 V	170 @0.34 V
Throughput (Mbps)	28	28	28	46.2	25.6	20
Energy (pJ)	5.2	2	-	0.81	1.9	2.23

Analysis of various process corners at different supply voltages is presented in Fig. 10. Although the PDK works at 1.8 V power supply voltage, we have been able to scale it down at lower values without affecting the performance. All the process corner works well at 1 V. Since the design is implemented at 180 nm technology it consumes 194.7 µW at 1.8 V which is higher than the other architectures listed in Table 2, as other architectures are implemented on lower technology node. If we approximate power using scaling theory [13] our architecture will consume the lowest power among all the architectures listed in Table 2.

The analysis of various process corners at different supply voltages, and different operating temperatures are shown in Fig. 10. From these figures, it can be observed that the power consumption for proposed architecture increases with supply voltage and operating temperature. At room temperature power deviation between fast-fast and slow-slow process corner is 4.17 µW at 1 V and 26.3 µW at 1.8 V respectively. As the operating temperature increase the power deviation also increases, at 100 °C the power deviation between fast-fast and slow-slow process corner is 24.48 µW at 1 V and 74.6 µW at 1.8 V respectively.

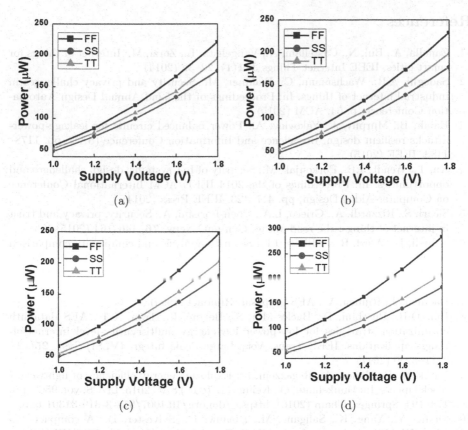

Fig. 10. Power consumption analysis for different supply voltages at (a) 25 °C (b) 50 °C, (c) 75 °C, (d) 100 °C

5   Conclusion

In this paper, we have presented a low-power architecture of AES that is suitable for IoT applications. The proposed architecture is implemented on SCL 180 nm technology and it provides moderate throughput, which is sufficient for most of the IoT nodes. The ASIC post-layout simulation results show that the complete design consumes about 194.7 µW but after applying voltage scaling the design consumes 52.2 µW at 1 V, 77.35 µW at 1.2 V, 108.7 µW at 1.4 V and 142.5 µW at 1.6 V.

Acknowledgment. The authors would like to thank the UGC, Government of India under the JRF Scheme for providing financial support (Ref. No. 3548/NET-DEC. 2015). We also extend our sincere gratitude to SMDP-C2SD programme, Government of India and Semiconductor Laboratory (SCL) India for providing PDK.

References

1. Zanella, A., Bui, N., Castellani, A., Vangelista, L., Zorzi, M.: Internet of things for smart cities. IEEE Internet Things J. **1**(1), 22–32 (2014)
2. Sadeghi, A.R., Wachsmann, C., Waidner, M.: Security and privacy challenges in industrial internet of things. In: Proceedings of the 52nd Annual Design Automation Conference, p. 54. ACM (2015)
3. Halak, B., Murphy, J., Yakovlev, A.: Power balanced circuits for leakage-power-attacks resilient design. In: Science and Information Conference (SAI), pp. 1178–1183. IEEE (2015)
4. Xu, T., Wendt, J.B., Potkonjak, M.: Security of IoT systems: design challenges and opportunities. In: Proceedings of the 2014 IEEE/ACM International Conference on Computer-Aided Design, pp. 417–423. IEEE Press (2014)
5. Sicari, S., Rizzardi, A., Grieco, L.A., Coen-Porisini, A.: Security, privacy and trust in internet of things: the road ahead. Comput. Netw. **76**, 146–164 (2015)
6. Vahedi, E., Ward, R.K., Blake, I.F.: Security analysis and complexity comparison of some recent lightweight RFID protocols. In: Herrero, Á., Corchado, E. (eds.) CISIS 2011. LNCS, vol. 6694, pp. 92–99. Springer, Heidelberg (2011). https://doi.org/10.1007/978-3-642-21323-6_12
7. Daemen, J., Rijmen, V.: AES proposal: Rijndael (1999)
8. Bui, D.H., Puschini, D., Bacles-Min, S., Beigné, E., Tran, X.T.: AES datapath optimization strategies for low-power low-energy multisecurity-level internet-of-things applications. IEEE Trans. Very Large Scale Integr. (VLSI) Syst. **25**(12), 3281–3290 (2017)
9. Banik, S., Bogdanov, A., Regazzoni, F.: Exploring energy efficiency of lightweight block ciphers. In: Dunkelman, O., Keliher, L. (eds.) SAC 2015. LNCS, vol. 9566, pp. 178–194. Springer, Cham (2016). https://doi.org/10.1007/978-3-319-31301-6_10
10. Zhang, Y., Yang, K., Saligane, M., Blaauw, D., Sylvester, D.: A compact 446 Gbps/W AES accelerator for mobile SoC and IoT in 40nm. In: 2016 IEEE Symposium on VLSI Circuits (VLSI-Circuits), pp. 1–2. IEEE (2016)
11. Zhao, W., Ha, Y., Alioto, M.: AES architectures for minimum-energy operation and silicon demonstration in 65nm with lowest energy per encryption. In: 2015 IEEE International Symposium on Circuits and Systems (ISCAS), pp. 2349–2352. IEEE (2015)
12. Mathew, S., et al.: 53Gbps native GF (2 4) 2 composite-field AES-encrypt/decrypt accelerator for content-protection in 45nm high-performance microprocessors. In: 2010 IEEE Symposium on VLSI Circuits (VLSIC), pp. 169–170. IEEE (2010)
13. Dennard, R.H., Gaensslen, F.H., Yu, H.N., Rideout, V.L., Bassous, E., LeBlanc, A.R.: Design of ion-implanted MOSFET's with very small physical dimensions. IEEE J. Solid-State Circuits SC **9**(5), 256–268 (1974)

Efficient Closely-Coupled Integration of AES Coprocessor with LEON3 Processor

Rajul Bansal(✉) and Abhijit Karmakar

CSIR - Central Electronics Engineering Research Institute (CEERI),
Pilani 333031, India
rajulbansal@gmail.com

Abstract. This paper proposes an efficient closely-coupled method for integrating the widely used Advanced Encryption Standard (AES) hardware as a coprocessor IP core in the LEON3 processor-based System-on-Chip (SoC) design. As AES is increasingly being used in Internet of Things (IoT) and Edge computing devices to secure transmission of sensitive data, this method can be used to reduce the energy consumption in embedded applications. The closely-coupled method presented in this paper combines the benefits of both the traditional tightly-coupled and the industry prevalent bus-coupled approaches. The proposed method provides higher performance along with portability, to address the demand of higher processing power and reduced time-to-market. A maximum of 10% reduction in number of clock cycles was achieved in our experiments which translates to significant energy saving compared to industry prevalent bus-coupled hardware coupling method.

Keywords: AES · Closely-coupled · LEON3 · SPARCv8 · SoC · Coprocessor

1 Introduction

In today's online world, the Advanced Encryption Standard (AES) is widely used to secure different types of sensitive data in multitude of embedded applications ranging from Internet of Things (IoT) and Wireless Sensor Networks (WSN) to space applications and onboard data storage. Growing need of higher performance with lower power has necessitated the use of application specific hardware for AES algorithm. These AES IP-cores are then integrated into the modern-day System-on-Chip (SoC) designs as coprocessors.

AES hardware accelerator module implementation of AES coprocessor is presented in [1]. In this paper, easy interfacing of the coprocessor is achieved using Avalon system bus interface. In [2] AES is used for wireless sensor networks and is interfaced with MicroBlaze using Advanced eXtensible Interface (AXI) [3] bus. An application-specific instruction set coprocessor design presented in [4] utilizes instruction and data ram within the coprocessor module to reduce the instruction transfer between embedded processor and the coprocessor. The authors claim good flexibility, high energy efficiency and low latency. However, we believe that the performance of the systems to which these AES coprocessors are integrated, can be further enhanced though our proposed coprocessor coupling interface alone.

© Springer Nature Singapore Pte Ltd. 2019
A. Sengupta et al. (Eds.): VDAT 2019, CCIS 1066, pp. 345–356, 2019.
https://doi.org/10.1007/978-981-32-9767-8_30

Coupling methods of coprocessors in an SoC environment have been categorized into three domains, namely, *tightly-coupled*, *bus-coupled* and *closely-coupled*, within the purview of this paper. In *tightly-coupled* method the processor and the coprocessor pipelines are intermingled and common resources are utilized [4, 5]. The disadvantage of this method is major redesign and verification of the hardware along with compiler re-design, which can be man-hour intensive and impacts time-to-market. On the contrary, the *bus-coupled* method prevalent in the industry, provides a common interface so that rapid IP-cores integration can be achieved and time-to-market is reduced [6, 7]. This method has a disadvantage of lower performance when compared to tightly-coupled implementations.

We have proposed a method where performance benefits of tightly-coupled coprocessor is combined with ease-of-integration property of bus-coupled coprocessor designs in a LEON3-based [8] SoC. The proposed *closely-coupled* method utilizes separate register file for coprocessor, and does not implement processor register to coprocessor register transfer instructions, thereby minimizing communication between the two. The coupling method has also the benefit that it does not require any modification in the compiler design. Other common shared resources in instruction fetch stage and execute stage are still used for synchronizing the coprocessor instructions and data load/store operations. In this paper, we have also presented the performance benefits of closely coupled AES IP-core through total cycle count and Cycles per Instructions (CPI) based comparison results.

After introduction in Sect. 1, the details of the closely-coupled integration method has been explained in Sect. 2. In Sect. 3, we have explained the high-level modelling approach used for the purpose of system-level performance evaluation. Hardware of our design has been explained in Sect. 4. The results of running applications on hardware with closely-coupled as well as bus-coupled AES coprocessor are given in Sect. 5. We have concluded in the last section.

2 Coprocessor Integration

The AES coprocessor was integrated using both the Advanced High-performance Bus (AHB) and the coprocessor interface in the LEON3 processor-based SoC design. The AES core configuration and the integration method along with register file arrangement and management of data transfers, are briefly described in this section.

2.1 AES Core

The AES core used for our implementation is the OpenCores [9] implementation. It includes cipher feedback (CFB) mode, output feedback (OFB) mode, and counter (CTR) mode. The benefit is that the same hardware can be used for both encryption and decryption. Among the 128-, 192- and 256-bit key options, we used the 128-bit key for our experiment which is four times the bus width and the LEON3 processors data handling capacity per cycle. The AES core pipeline itself requires a latency of 21 cycles to produce the first output and thereafter 128-bit cipher-text at each cycle [9].

2.2   Integration of AES Core as a Coprocessor

Interface wrappers are required for coupling the above AES core to the LEON3-based SoC. The two integration methods implemented by us are depicted in Fig. 1. In order to implement the bus-coupled method, wrappers are designed to encapsulate the AES core such that the input and output registers are linearly mapped on the AHB bus starting at 0xA0000000 address location. Also, a control register mapped at subsequent address location is used to control the executions in the coprocessor pipeline and manage the flow of data to and from the AES core. This management is required because of the difference in data bandwidth of the AHB bus (32-bit) and the AES core (128-bit). The AES pipeline being much faster is stalled when input data is not available. Clock gating is used during the stalled phase to reduce power consumption.

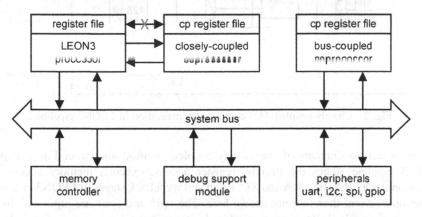

Fig. 1. Coprocessor integration in a LEON3 processor based SoC.

Another wrapper was designed to integrate the same AES core with similar configuration that implements our proposed closely-coupled method. The logic inside the wrapper taps instructions and necessary signals from various stages of the LEON3 processor pipeline as shown in Fig. 2. These tapped instructions are then decoded in the AES coprocessor module. The implemented bus-coupled method discussed in the previous paragraph works by writing data values to the address where coprocessor control register is mapped. These data values act as instructions to the bus-coupled coprocessor. Whereas, in the closely-coupled integration method, the coprocessor-operate instructions directly control the operations of AES core coupled to LEON3 processor. The coprocessor Load/Store instructions are used to load and store data directly from memory to the coprocessor register file. Direct transfers between processor register file and coprocessor register file is not allowed in our implementation as shown in Fig. 1, so as to selectively decouple the processor and the coprocessor register files. In other words, instructions corresponding to such transactions are not implemented.

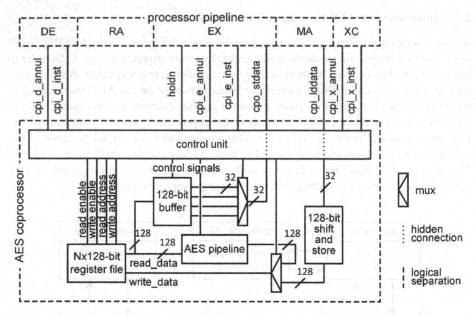

Fig. 2. Closely-coupled AES coprocessor integration in LEON3 pipeline.

The interface diagram of the closely-coupled method shown in Fig. 2 depicts LEON3 pipeline stages the decode, register access, execute, memory access and exception as DE, RA, EX, MA and XC. Fetch and writeback stages of LEON3 processor are untouched and therefore not shown here. The cpi* and cpo* are input and output coprocessor signals. Instructions from decode stage of the processor are forwarded to coprocessor control unit. The coprocessor control unit decodes the coprocessor instructions and in-turn provides addresses and control signals to various blocks within the coprocessor. For coprocessor Load/Store instructions, data needs to be loaded or stored from common data cache which is accessed only in MA stage of the processor.

The coprocessor control unit shown in Fig. 2 keeps a tap on the current instruction being executed in the LEON3 processor pipeline through cpi_x_inst for load operation and cpi_e_inst for store operations. The read and write cycle of coprocessor register file and the data muxes are controlled in synchronization to these signals. After the coprocessor-operate instruction is forwarded by the processor in the decode stage, further execution of coprocessor-operate instructions do not require synchronization with the processor. Rest of the working of the coprocessor is independent of the processor. As a result, when an instruction is annulled or processor pipeline is halted due to unavailability of resources, the coprocessor pipeline can continue to run in the operate state. This enhances the number of instructions executed per second. However, it must be noted that the coprocessor pipeline halts during Load/Store operations in order to maintain the synchronization with processor pipeline.

In addition to having a separate register file for coprocessor, we have restrained the use of coprocessor condition codes in the proposed integration method. As a result, the additional coprocessor instructions that we have added to the processor do not alter the condition codes. In other words, software flow-control instructions are dependent only on results generated by the processor instructions and not on results generated by the coprocessor instructions. The benefit gained is that we do not need any modification in the compiler design. The additional coprocessor instructions are incorporated in the software tool-chain through use of leaf subroutines. This guarantees hassle-free closely coupled integration of the coprocessor in LEON3 processor pipeline.

Another interesting aspect of this method is that it is independent of the length of the coprocessor pipeline. Therefore, it can be used to integrate different types of coprocessors such as DWT [10], CORDIC, PRESENT [11], ECC [12], hashing, etc., in order to quickly tweak a given processor for efficient execution in such different application scenarios. The effect on hardware utilization due to increase or decrease in the pipeline depth of coprocessor remains similar to the bus-coupled case.

2.3   AES Coprocessor Configuration

We have tested two strategies in order to manage the execution in AES core while maintaining continuous data flow. First: the core is made to run at a quarter of system clock frequency when continuous stream of data is to be encrypted and the output is immediately required by the application. Second: the register file is filled completely with input data and then execution is started by running AES core at system clock frequency. In order to maintain the bandwidth of AES core i.e. 128-bit per cycle, there is a requirement of four-port register file of 32-bit each. The alternative is to have a 128-bit register file with 32-bit load and store managed through shift and store module.

In order to maximally utilize the AES pipeline, a minimum of 21 samples of 128-bit each have to be stored in the register file. This requires a minimum register file size with $N = 21$ (here N is the number of words) and 128-bit data width. The AES core is executed for 42 cycles so as to flush the pipeline and store results back to register file. After this, the data is stored back to memory through common data cache. Following this, the next set of data is loaded in the coprocessor register file. This process can run in loop in order to encrypt desired length of data.

In the scenario where only a single sample of data is to be encrypted, the AES core pipeline stages are not utilized efficiently and as a result the hardware utilization was found to be very poor. Also, the hardware utilization worsens depending on the increase in the length of the coprocessor pipeline. In such cases, software-based AES encryption may be used. Integration of this AES core with future version of the LEON3 processor which can fetch 64-bit data in a single cycle may provide better performance and as a result, the AES core can be run with higher hardware utilization.

3   High-Level System Modelling

RTL-level simulations are extremely slow; and running complete applications on the RTL model of complete SoC requires excessive time. A less-detailed design or a model with fast execution rates is required in order to run meaningful application code. In order to cater to this requirement, we have developed an Instruction Set Simulator (ISS) based model of the entire SoC for the purpose. An ISS is a functional model of an

Instruction Set Architecture (ISA) that implements most of the instructions defined in that particular ISA standard. The model defines only the coarse-grained functionality of the processor while ignoring the fine-grained data handling of the actual hardware. This model runs at much higher speed that enables fast application software execution and debugging.

We have modelled the working of AES core and the different coprocessor integration methods using TSIM2 [13] (ISS for LEON3 processor). The AHB interface was emulated and our custom memory map along with integration of custom IP-cores is as shown in Fig. 3. We have defined different memories as arrays and their addresses as variables to emulate desired system memory configuration. IP-cores that connect to the system bus in the hardware are also connected using this interface. Our high-level model exports functions that forwards the registers and data structures inside the IP core model to TSIM2. There are three interfaces, namely, the processor interface, coprocessor interface and the AHB bus interface as shown in Fig. 3.

The processor interface is modelled to access processor internal functionalities to control interrupts and coprocessor instructions. The AHB bus interface is modelled to read, write and initialize emulated memories connected directly to AHB bus. In addition to this, simulation interface is used to read status and control the simulation time, events, interrupts, system reset, simulation stop, etc. of the TSIM2 ISS. This interface is also used to connect and synchronize our high-level model of bus-coupled coprocessor.

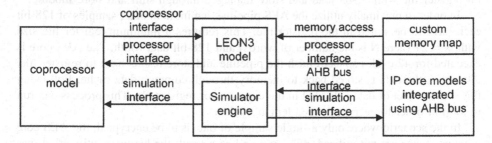

Fig. 3. TSIM2 ISS based modelling of coprocessor coupled designs.

A dedicated coprocessor interface integrates the modelled coprocessor subsystem which emulates the coarse-grained working of AES core. The processor interface links the working of coprocessor core to the processor core. The coprocessor interface exports coprocessor registers, execution, status, initialization and reset functionalities of the coprocessor model to the processor model. The position independent compiled binaries, shared objects, namely, io.dll/io.so, ahb.dll/ahb.so, fp.dll/fp.so and cp.dll/cp.so with appropriate endianness were generated for the purpose to make it run on a host PC with x86 architecture. Application code was run on this modelled system and the results are discussed in subsequent sections.

4 Hardware Implementation

The hardware design has been done on GRXC6S Board from Pender Electronics, that contains Spartan6 XC6SLX75 FPGA device. The hardware requirement for complete system including all the IP-cores is 5666 slice registers, 20891 slice LUTs and 42 RAM blocks. The design is synthesized to run at 50 MHz on Xilinx ISE 13.1. The pipelined AES takes 5344 slice registers, 9104 slice LUTs and 43 RAM blocks. The test system is as shown in Fig. 4.

Fig. 4. Test system for speech encryption.

4.1 Test Application

Our implementation was tested in a system used to encrypt the uncompressed speech samples. The 21-stage AES pipeline outputs 128-bit cypher-text per cycle. Considering 30 ms pseudo-stationary speech length sampled at 8 kHz with a resolution of 8-bits per sample, 1920 bits are required to be encrypted. In order to efficiently utilize the 21-stage AES core, we have implemented 21-word (N = 21) register file with 128-bit word width as discussed in Sect. 2.1. Therefore, the total number of bits that can be processed in a single loop is 2688, which is more than required.

For 16-bit data width, 3840 bits are to be encrypted for a 30 ms frame at 8 kHz sampling rate. In order to process this frame of 3840 bits in a single loop, a register file with N = 30 is required. For register file with words greater than 32, the standard coprocessor Load/Store operations require change in the standard SPARCv8 ISA format along with corresponding changes in the decoding style. The related process has been well explained in the paper [14].

4.2   Test Setup

The block diagram of entire system is as shown in Fig. 5. Voice is captured through electret microphone. The amplitude of signal is regulated using MAX9814 with Automatic Gain Control (AGC) and microphone amplifier. The analog signal is passed through a series capacitor to block DC bias of the microphone. The analog signal is then read through ADC in PCF8591. The PCF8591 is a data acquisition device controlled through I2C bus. The I2C IP-core within the SoC is enabled in full speed mode (400 kbit/s). The timer unit is initialized to generate 8 kHz timer interrupts. Single sample is read from the ADC and is stored in memory as part of interrupt subroutine.

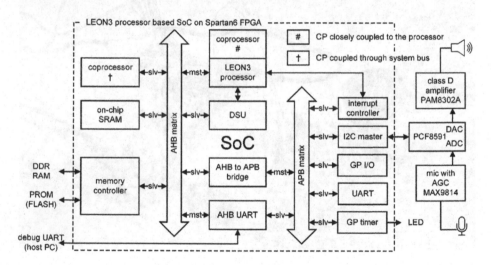

Fig. 5.   Block diagram of complete system.

The stored data (sample audio) is then read from memory and encrypted frame-by-frame as discussed in previous subsection. A single loop consists of loading data from memory to coprocessor register file, running the coprocessor for desired clock cycles and then storing the data back to memory. This loop is repeatedly called for encrypting longer sequence of input data. The single loop code is entirely written in assembly with certain parts (custom coprocessor instructions) hardcoded in hex. This is necessary since assembler does not support custom coprocessor opcodes by default. The assembly code is integrated to the main C code as in-line assembly. Thus, we do not require any modification in the compiler design in order to incorporate the custom coprocessor instructions. The cypher-text is then decrypted using similar process and the resultant values are stored back to memory. After this, we reinitialize the timer unit and the I2C IP-cores in order to send data to DAC on PCF8591 at 8 kHz sampling rate. The analog waveform from the DAC is then fed to speaker through class D amplifier (PAM8302A). The output is the original recorded audio.

5 Results

To evaluate the actual performance benefits, timer-based operations in the application code were removed and ISRs were replaced by simple functions. This was done so as to run the code at maximum possible speed. Application code for both bus-coupled and closely-coupled coprocessor hardware was executed for varying time periods. Number of cycles, number of instructions, CPI, cache hit percentage and AHB bandwidth utilization obtained from running the application code on the developed high-level model is presented in the Table 1 shown below.

Table 1. Performance comparison of proposed closely-coupled with bus-coupled coprocessor integration

Length of speech encoded	Coupling	Cycles	Instructions	CPI	Cache hit %	Bus BW utilization %
1 s	Bus	211551	116112	1.82	97.3	90.6
	Closely	196718	109808	1.79	96.4	93.5
2 s	Bus	370735	207152	1.79	97.6	91.7
	Closely	341262	194320	1.76	96.6	95.3
4 s	Bus	688137	388772	1.77	97.8	92.3
	Closely	629994	363156	1.73	96.7	96.3
8 s	Bus	1322941	752012	1.76	97.9	92.7
	Closely	1207494	700828	1.72	96.7	96.9
16 s	Bus	2592591	1478490	1.75	98.0	92.9
	Closely	2362464	1376170	1.72	96.8	97.2
32 s	Bus	5131807	2931450	1.75	98.0	93.0
	Closely	4672320	2726858	1.71	96.8	97.4
64 s	Bus	10210239	5837370	1.75	98.0	93.1
	Closely	9292032	5428234	1.71	96.8	97.5
128 s	Bus	20367103	11649210	1.75	98.0	93.1
	Closely	18531456	10830986	1.71	96.8	97.5
256 s	Bus	40680831	23272890	1.75	98.0	93.1
	Closely	37010304	21636490	1.71	96.8	97.5
512 s	Bus	81308287	46520249	1.75	98.0	93.1
	Closely	73968000	43247497	1.71	96.8	97.5

When comparing results from bus-coupled with closely-coupled we found significant increase in performance. We also found that the percentage of performance improvement increases with the increase in the length of speech. The increase in percentage is the reduction in the number of clock cycles for a similar task. This percentage reduction in number of clock cycles increases with time and stabilizes around approximately 10% and is as shown in Fig. 6.

The maximum cache hit rate reached 98% for bus-coupled and 96.8% for closely-coupled applications. The AHB bus bandwidth reached 93.1% for bus-coupled and 97.5% for closely-coupled cases. From Table 1 it can also be observed that when longer data set is used, the CPI of the system decreases. Since larger number of coprocessor instructions are required for encrypting a larger data, it can be said that the reduction in CPI is due to coprocessor instructions. Thus, custom coprocessor instructions not only reduce the number of cycles but also enhance the overall efficiency of the LEON3 processor.

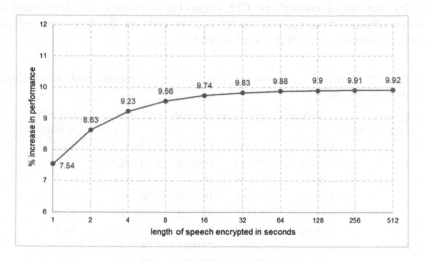

Fig. 6. Percentage increase in performance.

6 Conclusion

The performance of embedded systems that integrate AES core over the standard bus-coupled interface, has been significantly enhanced. Through use of proposed closely-coupled method described in this paper and the adjoining results, we have demonstrated how useful features of both tightly-coupled and bus-coupled coprocessors can be combined. The performance benefit of tightly-coupled coprocessors have been preserved in the proposed closely-coupled method while also retaining the portability aspect of bus-coupled coprocessors. The proposed method involves using separate register file for coprocessors and exclusion of coprocessor condition codes in order to selectively decouple the processor and coprocessor pipelines. Also, the integration process is independent of the length of the coprocessor to be integrated, thus making it highly portable. The minimal changes required in the processor pipeline can be included as standard part of processor design. We must promote the support for such closely-coupled interfaces in all future processor designs that target embedded to deeply embedded applications.

Acknowledgement. We would like to thank Director CSIR-CEERI for providing the requisite lab facilities to carry out the presented work. We would also like to acknowledge the MeitY sponsored SMDP-C2SD program for providing the required CAD tools and FPGA boards.

References

1. Feng, B., Haiwen, H., Qi, D.Y.: Parallel and multiplex architecture of AES-CCM coprocessor implementation for IEEE 802.15.4. In: 2013 Fourth International Conference on Emerging Intelligent Data and Web Technologies, Xian, China (2013)
2. Abdelmoghni, T., Mohamed, O.Z., Billel, B., Mohamed, M., Sidahmed, L.: Implementation of AES coprocessor for wireless sensor networks. In: 2018 International Conference on Applied Smart Systems (ICASS), Medea, Algeria (2018)
3. AMBA AXI Protocol Specification ARM Limited. http://infocenter.arm.com/help/index.jsp? topic=/com.arm.doc.ihi0022b/index.html. Accessed 01 Dec 2018
4. Wang, W., Han, J., Xie, Z., Huang, S., Zeng, X.: Cryptographic coprocessor design for IoT sensor nodes. In: 2016 International SoC Design Conference (ISOCC), Jeju, South Korea (2016)
5. Irwansyah, A., Nambiar, V.P., Khalil-Hani, M.: An AES tightly coupled hardware accelerator in an FPGA-based embedded processor core. In: International Conference on Computer Engineering and Technology, Singapore (2009)
6. Ramdani, A.Z., Rois, M., Adiono, T.: A real time AMBA based audio coprocessor for System-on-Chip. In: International Conference on Electrical Engineering and Computer Science (ICEECS), Kuta, Indonesia (2014)
7. Zhang, W., Yuan, Y., Liu, Y., Zhang, Y., Jiang, X.: A security coprocessor embedded system-on-chip architecture for smart metering, control and communication in power grid. In: IEEE International Conference on Solid-State and Integrated Circuit Technology (ICSICT), Guilin, China (2015)
8. LEON3 Processor, Gaisler Research. https://www.gaisler.com/index.php/products/processors/leon3. Accessed 01 Dec 2018
9. Homer, H.: AES: Overview, OpenCores. https://opencores.org/projects/tiny_aes. Accessed 01 Dec 2018
10. Bansal, R., Jatav, M.K., Karmakar, A.: A lifting instruction for performing DWT in LEON3 processor based System-on-Chip. In: Kaushik, B.K., Dasgupta, S., Singh, V. (eds.) VDAT 2017. CCIS, vol. 711, pp. 731–736. Springer, Singapore (2017). https://doi.org/10.1007/978-981-10-7470-7_68
11. Bogdanov, A., et al.: PRESENT: an ultra-lightweight block cipher. In: Paillier, P., Verbauwhede, I. (eds.) CHES 2007. LNCS, vol. 4727, pp. 450–466. Springer, Heidelberg (2007). https://doi.org/10.1007/978-3-540-74735-2_31

12. Guo, X., Fan, J., Schaumont, P., Verbauwhede, I.: Programmable and parallel ECC coprocessor architecture: tradeoffs between area, speed and security. In: Clavier, C., Gaj, K. (eds.) CHES 2009. LNCS, vol. 5747, pp. 289–303. Springer, Heidelberg (2009). https://doi.org/10.1007/978-3-642-04138-9_21

13. TSIM2 ERC32/LEON Simulator, Gaisler Research. https://www.gaisler.com/index.php/products/simulators/tsim. Accessed 01 Dec 2018

14. Bansal, R., Karmakar, A.: Efficient integration of coprocessor in LEON3 processor pipeline for System-on-Chip design. Microprocess. Microsyst. 51, 56–75 (2017)

Investigating the Role of Parasitic Resistance in a Class of Nanoscale Interconnects

Shah Zahid Yousuf[1(✉)], Anil Kumar Bhardwaj[1], and Rohit Sharma[2]

[1] School of Electronics and Communication,
Shri Mata Vaishno Devi University, Katra 182320, India
shahzahid2016@gmail.com
[2] Department of Electrical Engineering, Indian Institute of Technology Ropar,
Rupnagar 140001, India

Abstract. In nanoscale interconnects parasitic components are becoming drastically important with geometrical scaling. This work presents a comprehensive study of copper (Cu), SWCNT bundle, MWCNT, SC-MLGNR and TC-MLGNR nano interconnect in deep submicron (DSM) regime. We have extracted parasitic resistance of the above mentioned interconnects using physics based equivalent circuit models and investigated the effective resistivity of these interconnects at different technology nodes in DSM regime. It must be noted that when the dimensions of interconnect follow nanoscale, resistivity becomes the function of grain size. The nanoscale dimensions result in edge scattering and grain boundary scattering which inculcates tremendous effect on effective MFP. We examined the effect of grain size in scaled interconnects and analyzed the effect of edge and grain boundary scattering on resistivity of nanoscale interconnect. In our work we have look over five different interconnect geometries for the parasitic resistive component at 7 nm node and 14 nm node. We take Cu as a reference interconnect in our analysis. Our analysis show that the parasitic resistance of SWCNT Bundle, MWCNT, TC-MLGNR, SC-MLGNR interconnect is reduced by 77%, 84%, 59%, 80% compared to Cu interconnect at 7 nm node respectively. Our results also indicate a decrease of parasitic resistance by 70%, 80%, 35%, 60% compared to Cu interconnect at 14 nm node respectively. These calculations are valid below width of 14 nm. In this paper we have presented some Graphene counter parts which make it more promising candidate than CNT bundle interconnect apart from having greater p. u.l. resistance. We have analyzed the effects of Fermi energy and width on number of conduction channels for different technology nodes. This paper also shows comparable resistance of MWCNT and SWCNT due to reduced MFP of former interconnect.

Keywords: Chip-to-chip interconnects · Deep sub-micron (DSM) regime · Multilayer Graphene Nano-ribbon (MLGNR) · Parasitic resistive parameter · Side-contact MLGNR (SC-MLGNR) · Top-contact MLGNR (TC-MLGNR) · Mean free path (MFP) · Edge scattering · Grain size

© Springer Nature Singapore Pte Ltd. 2019
A. Sengupta et al. (Eds.): VDAT 2019, CCIS 1066, pp. 357–370, 2019.
https://doi.org/10.1007/978-981-32-9767-8_31

1 Introduction

Evolution of technology leads to shrinking of feature size with the scaling of devices. Unlike device scaling, the scaling of interconnects severely increases time parasitic components. The performance of a device is dominantly limited in present very large scale integration (VLSI) chip design [1]. From the last decade numerous innovative conductive materials have been introduced which seem to have future interconnect applications. As an example, as the effective silicon area of the nanoscale copper interconnect is drastically limited, two-dimensional (2D) and one-dimensional (1D) materials promise as potential diffusion barrier layer for Copper and low-k interconnect materials [2]. The main advantage of these interconnects is their thin atomic properties [1–4]. Moreover, CNTs and MLGNR possess many brilliant physical properties, making them as an idiom candidate for the upcoming nanoscale interconnect technology [4, 5]. CNTs can be classified in to two classes, one is single-walled CNT (SWCNT) and another is multi-walled CNT (MWCNT). This classification is based on the number of graphene sheets [9]. SWCNT are fabricated by a single graphene sheet. This single sheet is rolled into cylinder with diametric ranging from 0.4 nm to 4 nm. While as MWCNTs are fabricated by cylindrical coaxial assembly of SWCNTs [9–11]. Till date lot of study has been done in modelling and analysis of CNT interconnect. Also lot of efforts have been carried out in fabrication and evaluating reliability of the CNT interconnects [20]. It has manifested that the CNT interconnects held admirable properties over Cu interconnects [20]. But due to complicated fabrication process and imperfect contact resistance of CNTs, other materials like GNRs and Co have been investigated for potential of interconnects under 20 nm width. Apart from Cu and CNT, MLGNR have gained potential interest for the use of fast and energy efficient interconnect applications due to its simplicity in fabrication compared to CNTs and low parasitic resistance than nanoscale Cu interconnects [20]. As GNR have potentially high effective mean free path (MFP) and low resistivity compared to Cu, these have attracted great attention of researchers towards their interconnect application for future generations [16].

In Cu interconnects as the cross-sectional dimensions are approaching in the order of MFP, electron resistivity is increasing rapidly [13]. This is because of mingled aftermath of scattering of carriers along grain boundary, presence of high diffusion barrier layer and surface scattering [3]. This leads to increase in parasitic resistance on global level as well as local level. Due to increasing resistivity there arises a reliability involvement due to joules heating resulting in compelling rise in metal temperature [14]. Due to these limitations of Cu, novel materials like GNRs and CNTs came into picture. It was reported that GNR show slightly deviated electrical properties than ideal graphene [4–16]. Also patterning of graphene leads to rough edges in GNR interconnects [4]. Apart from that high mobility and large MFP make GNRs extremely good candidate for nano scale interconnects. Vast research interest has been seen in metallic CNTs for the application of nanoscale interconnects from last decade [11]. This is due to marvelous properties of thermal carriers, excellent transport of current and highly valid stable nature of CNTs [9–21]. The reported current density of isolated CNT was noted to be 10^{10} A/cm^2 and more. No damage was seen at elevated temperatures in

CNT interconnects [9]. At room temperature significant effects were seen due to scattering from grains and twin boundaries. Size dependent increase in resistance has been reported [2]. This is the result of external and internal surfaces scattering of electrons in nanoscale interconnects.

Readers must note that, we have primarily focused on width of interconnect as this is the only parameter that the circuit designer can decide. So far there has been limited focus on the effect of grain size and edge scattering on the nanoscale interconnects, which establishes the natality in our work.

The remaining study is organized in following manner: In Sect. 2, we describe physics based circuit model of interconnect structures investigated in this study. Section 3, present the results and discussion highlighting parasitic resistive. The effect on the performance metric of nanoscale interconnects is illustrated in this section. Important conclusions have been epitomized in Sect. 4.

2 Model Description of Interconnects

Figure 1 shows a typical interconnect geometry where W is interconnect width, H represents interconnect thickness and S = W is the spacing between adjacent interconnects. The inter-layer dielectric thickness (ILD) is denoted by T_{OX} and the relative permittivity of the medium surrounding the conductor is denoted by ε_r. These parameters are as per the ITRS projections [ITRS 2013] listed in Table 1 [12].

Table 1. Global interconnect parameters as per ITRS [12]

Technology node	14 nm	7 nm
Interconnect width (W)	21.5 nm^{-1} µm	10.5 nm^{-1} µm
Aspect ratio (H/W) WIRE	2.35	2.41
Aspect ratio (T_{OX}/W) ILD	1.55	1.55
Effective dielectric constant ε_r	2.09	1.66

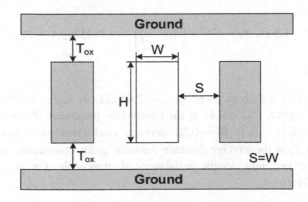

Fig. 1. Geometrical view of on-chip interconnect system.

2.1 Nanoscale Copper Interconnect

Copper (*Cu*) is the industry standard material for local, intermediate as well as global interconnect technology. However, copper intrinsically suffers from dramatic rise in resistivity at nanoscale with sizing down the dimensions of interconnect. This is due to comparable increase in scattering of electron from surface and grain boundary with scaling. Small grain size gives rise in scattering of electrons at boundary and hence leads to more scattering of electron than bulk scattering. Moreover, barrier layer occupying higher chunk of interconnect which cannot be scaled down with the interconnect dimensions increase silicon area and decrease performance. The geometrical view of Cu interconnect is shown in Fig. 2 with barrier thickness denoted as T_b, interconnect effective width as $W_{Cu}(= W - 2T_b)$ and height $H_{Cu}(= H - 2T_b)$, respectively.

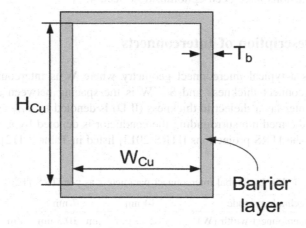

Fig. 2. Schematic of Copper nano-interconnect system.

The effective Cu resistivity is given by the combined Mayadas-Shatzkes (MS) model as [13]

$$\rho_{Cu} = \rho_0 \left\{ \left[1 - 1.5\alpha + 3\alpha^2 - 3\alpha^3 ln\left(1 + \frac{1}{\alpha}\right) \right]^{-1} + 0.45\lambda_{Cu}(1 - P_{Cu})\frac{W_{Cu} + H_{Cu}}{W_{Cu}H_{Cu}} \right\}$$

(1)

Where ρ_0 is bulk resistivity given by $\rho_0 = 2.04\,\mu\Omega.cm$, $\lambda_{Cu} = 37.3\,nm$ is mean free path (MFP) of copper, $P_{Cu} = 0.41$ is the specularity parameter of the copper surface and $\alpha = \lambda_{Cu}R_f/d_g(1 - R_f)$, $R_f = 0.22$ denotes coefficient of reflection of grain boundaries and d_g is the average distance between grain boundaries, which is set as W_{Cu} [14]. The per unit length resistance of nanoscale Cu is calculated by $(R_{Cu} = \rho_{Cu}L/W_{Cu}H_{Cu})$.

2.2   Multi-layer Graphene Nanoribbon Interconnect

According to the studies single layer graphene nano- ribbon (SL-GNR) show relatively high electrical resistance when compared to Cu. The reduced equivalent resistance in multilayer GNR (MLGNR) seems to be more applicable for nanoscale interconnect applications [15]. The inverse relation of the number of layers and scaling of the MLGNR interconnects has been reported [16]. The multiple layers of are patterned into a ribbons of width of few tens-of-nanometres. This provides a promising solution to the scaling issues of nanoscale interconnects due to ballistic transport of charge carriers [17]. According to the circuit analysis perspective, consecutive types of contact technology are known, (i) "top contact (TC) technology" and (ii) "side contact (SC) technology". In the former one from the top surface of MLGNR metal contacts are taken as shown in Fig. 3(a), while as in latter one metal contacts are taken from two sides of the GNR stack, shown in Fig. 3(b). In TC technology, there is very easy contact formation due to horizontal fabrication with the drawback of high effective resistance due to coextensive sequence of layers of GNR. In contrast, SC technology has very low value of effective resistance due to coextensive region of layers of GNR with in dual contacts as shown in Fig. 3(b) with the sacrifice of difficult fabrication technology [16].

The inter-layer spacing between coextensive layers equals $\delta = 0.34$ nm, a Vander Waal's gap and total number of layer N is chosen in between 10 to 40 [16]. The experimental resistivity along c-axis of Highly Oriented Pyrolytic Graphene (HOPG) has been reported as $0.3\,\Omega$.m [16]. Various papers have reported it to be $0.2\,\Omega$.m [16]. The R_X resistance for small width of dx in the figure is given as [16]

$$R_X = \lim_{\Delta x \to 0} \frac{R_Q dx}{N_{Ch} \lambda_{eff}} = \frac{h}{2e^2} \frac{1}{N_{ch}} \left[\frac{1}{\lambda_{eff}} \right] \tag{2}$$

Where $R_Q = \frac{h}{2e^2} = 12.9$ kΩ, is the quantum resistance of graphene layer, h is planks constant, e is the electronic charge, N_{ch} is number of conduction channels and λ_{eff} is effective MFP of MLGNR.

The number of conducting channels (N_{ch}) in each layer is a function of width w and Fermi energy (E_F) as stated in [18], which is given as:

$$N_{ch} = \begin{cases} a_0 + a_1 w + a_2 w^2 + a_3 E_F + a_4 w E_F + a_5 E_F^2 & \text{for } E_F > 0 \\ b_0 + b_1 w + b_2 w^2 & \text{for } E_F = 0 \end{cases}$$

Where a_0 to a_5 and b_0 to b_2 are known as fitting parameters [19] E_F is Fermi-energy which has values from 0.2 to 0.8 according to reports [16].

The effective MFP λ_{eff} of MLGNR is dependent on defect induced MFP λ_d and edge scattering MFP λ_{edge} in the interest of diffusive scattering near GNR edges [16].

$$\lambda_{eff} = \left[\frac{1}{\lambda_{edge}} + \frac{1}{\lambda_d} \right]^{-1} \tag{4}$$

The defects-induced MFP $\lambda_d = 300$ nm, depends on type of substrate. In case of hexagonal boron nitride substrate, defect-induced MFP $\lambda_d = 300$ nm and this value is

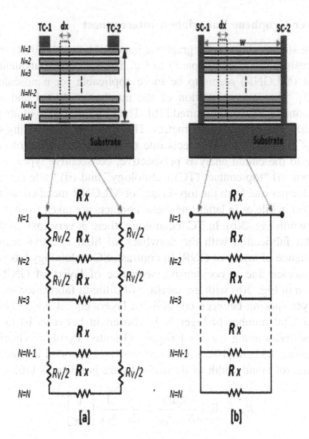

Fig. 3. Schematic view of multilayer graphene nano-ribbon (MLGNR) interconnect with physic based equivalent resistive network for (a) Top contact (TC) technology (TC-MLGNR) (b) Side contact (SC) technology (SC-MLGNR).

suggested for MLGNR interconnects [17]. For GNRs MFP by cause of edge scattering λ_{edge} is expressed as

$$\lambda_{edge} = \frac{w}{p} \sqrt{\left(\frac{E_F / \Delta E}{i + \beta} \right) - 1} \tag{5}$$

Where w represents GNR width, p represents the backscattering probability of the electron near GNR edges. The Fermi energy is E_F and ΔE represent the sub-band energy of metallic GNR. Also the inter-layer vertical resistance can be calculated by $R_V = \rho_c \delta / w dx$, where ρ_c, δ, w and dx are same parameters as mentioned above. For TC-MLGNR with N number of graphene layers equivalent resistance p.u.l. is given as

$$R_{TC-MLGNR} = R_{TGNR} + \frac{R_Q + R_{C1} + R_{C2}}{N} \tag{6}$$

Where $R_{TGNR} = (1/R_V + 1/R_X)^{-1}$ and R_{C1} and R_{C2} are contact resistances. For SC-MLGNR with N number of graphene layers, equivalent resistance p.u.l. is given as

$$R_{SC-MLGNR} = R_{SGNR} + \frac{R_Q + R_{C1} + R_{C2}}{NN_{ch}} \tag{7}$$

Here $R_{SGNR} = R_X/N$ and N_{ch} is the number of conduction channels.

2.3   CNT Interconnect

Figure 4(a) illustrates the cross-section of SWCNT bundle interconnect. The gap between the CNTs give rise to interlayer resistance. The CNTs are densely packed in the given structure. In the given figure, D is the diameter if SWCNT, the Vander Waals gap between CNT's is denoted by $\delta = 0.34$ nm, Vander Waal's gap. The metallic SWCNTs in the bundle are illustrated in terms of variable N given as [20]

$$N = F_F \left(N_w N_h - int \left[\frac{N_h}{2} \right] \right) \tag{8}$$

Where

$$N_w = int \left[\frac{w - D}{D + \delta} \right] + 1 \tag{9}$$

And

$$N_h = int \left[\frac{2H - D}{\sqrt{3}(D + \delta)} \right] + 1 \tag{10}$$

F_F is the fraction value of metallic SWCNTs in the nanoscale bundle of CNT. This value is taken as unity [20] and int[.] denote integral part to be taken. In case of SWCNT bundle, contact resistance is estimated by

$$R_C = \frac{1}{2N} \left(R_\delta + \frac{R_Q}{N_{ch}} \right) \tag{11}$$

Where $R_Q = h/2e^2 = 12.9$ kΩ is quantum resistance, h is planks constant, R_δ is imperfect contact resistance which depends on fabrication process and $N_{ch} = 2$ represents number of conduction channels for detached SWCNT.

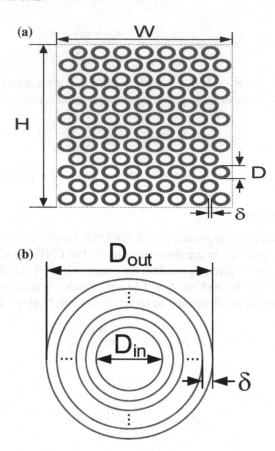

Fig. 4. (a) Schematic for cross-sectional view of SWCNT nanoscale interconnect bundle. (b) Schematic for cross-sectional view of MWCNT nanoscale interconnect.

The p.u.l. resistance of nanoscale SWCNT interconnect is modeled as

$$R_{p.u.l.} = \frac{R_Q}{\lambda_{SWCNT}} \tag{12}$$

Where $\lambda_{SWCNT} = 1000D$ is effectual MFP of SWCNT with diameter D.

Figure 4(b) illustrates the cross-sectional representation of MWCNT interconnect. MWCNT is explained as coaxial assembly of multiple cylindrical SWCNT with increasing diameter of twice Vander Waals gap. In the figure inner diameter and outer diameters are denoted by D_{in} and D_{out}, respectively. Number of MWCNT shells [20] is $N = 1 + int\lceil(D_{out} - D_{in})/2\delta\rceil$ and n_{th} shell diameter of MWCNT is given by $D_n = D_{in} + 2(n - 1)\delta$.

Equivalent single conductor transmission line model has been reported for modeling of contact resistance [21] given by

$$R_c = \frac{1}{4} \left[\sum_{n=1}^{N} \left(R_{icr} + \frac{R_Q}{N_{ch}} \right)^{-1} \right]^{-1} \tag{13}$$

N_{ch} depends on shell diameter and represents number of conduction channels for n_{th} shell expressed as [21]

$$N_{ch} = \left\langle \left\{ \begin{array}{ll} 2/3 & D_n < 6\,\mathrm{nm} \\ aD_n + b & D_n > 6\,\mathrm{nm} \end{array} \right\} \right\rangle \tag{14}$$

Here $a = 0.0612\,\mathrm{nm}^{-1}$ and $b = 0.425$. The resistance p.u.l. of MWCNT nanoscale interconnect is reckoned as

$$R_{p.u.l.} = \frac{R_Q}{2} \left[\sum_{n=1}^{N} \lambda_n N_{ch} \right]^{-1} \tag{15}$$

Key pursuance parameters for intermediate and global interconnects include parasitic resistance, parasitic capacitance and parasitic inductance. After extraction of effective parasitic R p.u.l., we investigate effect of width and conduction channels for various structures mentioned. Readers must note that we are taking effective grain size in to consideration which results in change in resistance p.u.l. at nano-metric scale.

3   Results and Investigation

For the nanoscale interconnect shown in Fig. 1, the consequence of parasitic resistance on pursuance metrics of different structures is presented in this section.

3.1   Effect on Resistivity

From the last decade, elevated resistivity has become one of the serious problem in the current on-chip interconnects like W and Cu. The tremendous elevation in resistivity due to consequence of scattering of carriers from grain boundary and side-walls. Novel materials like MLGNR and CNTs show lower resistance values compared to carbon. The resistance is an inverse function of width of interconnect. CNTs and MLGNRs have large MFP and carrier mobility compared to carbon interconnects but due to edge scattering there is cutback in effectual MFP of MLGNRs compared to CNTs. Also there is lowering of mobility in MLGNRs with increase in width. A high quality strips of graphene and SWCNT seems to conduct with large current density and on the verge of similar magnitude. Researchers have preferred GNRs over CNTs due to straight forward fabrication, well defined chirality whereas irregular chirality and legitimate control of band gap in CNTs. In the theoretical comparison of performance calculated values of global resistance or per unit length resistance ($\Omega/\mu m$) of different nanoscale interconnect structures are described as a function of width in which we have considered length to be larger than MFP. The thickness (H) of structure is taken as per the ITRS 2013 listed in Table 1. For our analysis we have varied width to only 100 nm but according to ITRS projections width of global interconnects varies from several tens of nanometers to few micrometers. We have analyzed different structures at two technology nodes of 7 nm node and 14 nm. As illustrated in Fig. 5(a) and (b) MLGNR interconnects exhibit superior performance over copper counterparts.

Apart from that, our analysis show that SC-MLGNRs have lower resistance than TC-MLGNRs. This is due to introduction of R_V resistive component which results in non-parallel resistive combination. From Fig. 5(a) and (b), it is clearly visible that for w<20 nm MLGNRs offer a lower resistance than Cu interconnects and SC-MLGNRs have very low resistance compared to TC-MLGNRs in addition to Cu interconnects. Records also show that resistance p.u.l. shows dramatically increase from 14 nm node to 7 nm node.

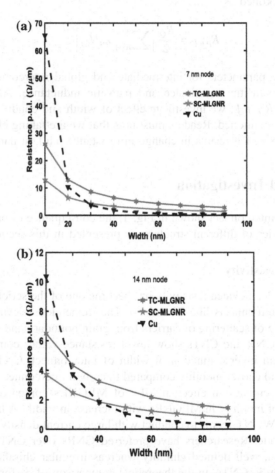

Fig. 5. (a) Resistance *(p.u.l.)* as a function of width. T = 300 K for TC-MLGNR, SC-MLGNR and Cu Nanoscale interconnect at 7 nm technology node. (b) Resistance *(p.u.l.)* as a function of width. T = 300 K for TC-MLGNR, SC-MLGNR and Cu Nano interconnect at 14 nm technology node.

Number of conduction channels (N_{ch}) depend on two parameters interconnect width (w) and Fermi energy (E_F) (3). Variation of N_{ch} for different values of w and Fermi energy (E_F) was considered between 0.2 eV to 0.8 eV is shown in Fig. 6(a) and (b) for 7 nm node and 14 nm node technology respectively. From the investigation we have seen that increasing the Fermi energy increase the number of conduction channels. This results in more conduction of charge carriers in GNR interconnects with increased value of Fermi energy. Also higher values of width show more availability of conduction channels. So in case of GNR interconnects more number of channels can be made available for conduction by increasing the Fermi energy.

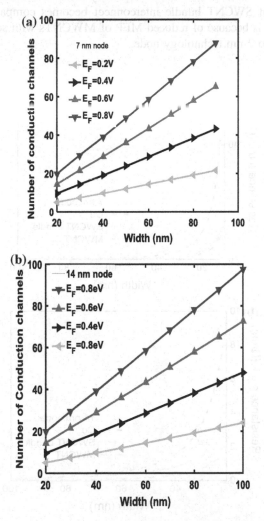

Fig. 6. (a) Number of conduction channels as a function of width and Fermi-energy. T = 300 K for MLGNR Nanoscale interconnect at 7 nm node. (b) Number of conduction channels as a function of width and Fermi-energy. T = 300 K for MLGNR Nanoscale interconnect at 14 nm node.

In case of CNT interconnects, width is varied from few tens of nanometers to hundred nanometer. In our research we have taken two types of CNT interconnects into account that is, SWCNT bundle and MWCNT interconnects. From Fig. 7(a) and (b) we illustrate variation of resistance per unit length as a function of width. We have plotted the resistance p.u.l. as a function of width for 7 nm node and 14 nm node technology. From plots given above it is evident that CNT interconnect exhibits superior properties than copper counterparts but this advantage becomes less significant with increase in width. From the plot we have also investigated a flit of the curve in case of SWCNT bundle nanoscale interconnect which determine width as an inconsistent function of interconnect. Figure 6(a) and (b) also shows that by means of this advent of technology node, resistance of SWCNT bundle interconnect becomes comparable to MWCNT interconnect. This is because of reduced MFP of MWCNTs with scaling from 14 nm technology node to 7 nm technology node.

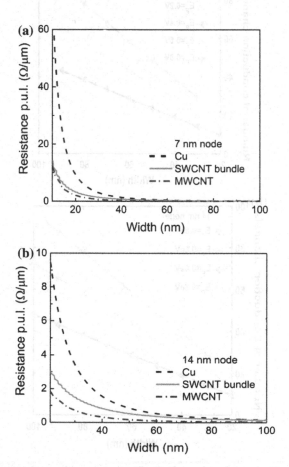

Fig. 7. (a) Resistance (*p.u.l*). as a function of width. T = 300 K for Cu, SWCNT bundle and MWCNT Nanoscale interconnect at 7 nm node. (b) Resistance *p.u.l.* as a function of width. T = 300 K for Cu, SWCNT bundle and MWCNT Nanoscale interconnect at 14 nm node.

4 Conclusion

In this work, we have investigated Cu, MLGNR and CNT nanoscale interconnect models for 7 nm node and 14 nm nodes. We have highlighted the penalty induced due to interconnect width on interconnect performance parameters. Moreover, we correlate different MLGNR and CNT structures with Cu. It is seen that resistance is an inconsistent function of width in case of SWCNT bundle interconnects. We have also analyzed the effect of width on number of conduction channels in case of MLGNR interconnects. Our work shows that CNTs provide excellent improvement for nanoscale interconnects but due complexity in fabrication and diameter alignment MLGNRs are preferred. Techniques for making negligible surface scattering are important parameters that are required to be addressed in future.

Acknowledgement. The authors gratefully acknowledge the help received from Vipul Kumar Nishad during our technical discussions.

REFERENCES

1. Nishad, A.K., Sharma, R.: Analytical time-domain models for performance optimization of multilayer GNR interconnects. IEEE J. Sel. Top. Quantum Electron. **20**(1), 17–24 (2013)
2. Zhao, W.S.: Electrical modeling of on-chip cu-graphene heteriogenious interconnects. IEEE Electron Device Lett. **36**(1), 74–76 (2015)
3. Lo, C.L., et al.: Studies of two dimensional h-BN and Mo S2 for potential diffusion barrier application in copper interconnect technology. NPJ 2D Matter. Appl. **1**, 42 (2017)
4. Nishad, A.K., Sharma, R.: Lithium-intercalated graphene interconnects: prospects for on-chip applications. IEEE J. Electron Devices Soc. **4**(6), 485–489 (2016)
5. Naeemi, A., Meindl, J.D.: Compact physics based models for graphene nanoribbon interconnects. IEEE Trans. Electron Devices **56**(9), 1822–1833 (2009)
6. Zhao, W.S.: Verticle graphene nanoribbon interconnect at the end of the roadmap. IEEE Trans. Electron Devices **65**(6), 2632–2637 (2018)
7. Farahani, E.K.: Design of n-tier multilevel interconnect architectures by using carbon nanotube interconnects. IEEE Trans. VLSI Syst. **23**(10), 2128–2134 (2015)
8. Rakheja, S., et al.: Evaluation of the potential performance of graphene nanoribbons as on-chip interconnects. In: IEEE Proceedings, vol. 101, no. 7, pp. 1740–1764, July 2013
9. Banerjee, K., et al.: Are carbon nanotubes the future of VLSI interconnects. In: DAC, vol. 47, no. 2, pp. 809–814 (2006)
10. Avouris, P., et al.: Carbon based electronics. Nat. Nanotechnol. **PP**, 605–615 (2005)
11. Li, H., et al.: Carbon nanomaterial for next generation interconnects and passives. IEEE Trans. Electron Devices **56**, 1799–1821 (2009)
12. International Technology Roadmap For Semiconductors (2013). http://www.itrs2.net
13. Steinhogl, W., et al.: Comprehensive study of the resistivity of copper wires with lateral dimensions of 100 nm and smaller. J. Appl. Phys. **97**(2), 023706-1–023706-7 (2005)
14. Im, S., et al.: Scaling analysis of multi-level interconnect temperatures for high performance ICs. IEEE Trans. Electron Devices **52**(12), 2710–2719 (2005)
15. Xu, C.: Modeling analysis and design of graphene nanoribbon interconnects. IEEE Trans. Electron Devices **56**, 1567–1572 (2009)

16. Kumar, V.: Performance and energy-per-bit modeling of multilayer graphene nanoribbon conductors. IEEE Trans. Electron Device **59**, 904–915 (2012)
17. Jiang, J., et al.: Intercalation doped multilayer graphene nanoribbons for next generation interconnects. Nano Lett. **17**, 1482–1488 (2017)
18. Kumar, R., et al.: Performance analysis of top-contact MLGNR based interconnect. In: IEEE Symposium on Nanoelectronic and Information System, pp. 11–16 (2016)
19. Nasiri, S.H., et al.: Compact formulae for number of conduction channels in various types of graphene nanoribbons at various temperatures. Mod. Phys. Lett. B **26**(1), 1150004 1-5 (2012)
20. Srivastava, N.: On the applicability of single-walled carbon nanotubes as VLSI interconnects. IEEE Trans. Nanotechnol. **8**(4), 542–559 (2009)
21. Sarto, M.S., Tamburrano, A.: Single-conductor transmission-line model of multiwall carbon nanotubes. IEEE Trans. Nanotechnol. **9**(1), 82–92 (2010)

A True Single-Phase Error Masking Flip-Flop with Reduced Clock Power for Near-Threshold Designs

Priyamvada Sharma$^{(\boxtimes)}$ and Bishnu Prasad Das

Indian Institute of Technology Roorkee, Roorkee, Uttarakhand, India
psharma@ec.iitr.ac.in, bpdasfec@iitr.ac.in

Abstract. The near-threshold computing is popular for energy-efficient designs. In this paper, an error masking flip-flop is proposed which uses true single-phase of the clock. The proposed flip-flop (FF) consists of a true single-phase FF, an error detector and an error correction module. The error detector flags an error signal using the internal nodes of the true single-phase FF and error correction module corrects the output state of the FF. The simulation results in 28 nm CMOS process shows that the proposed error masking FF consumes 81% lesser clock power compared to traditional transmission gate based FF whereas it consumes 83% lesser clock power compared to existing error masking FF. The proposed design is evaluated for its improved performance across different process corners and voltages. Hence, it is suitable for near-threshold designs.

Keywords: Near-threshold voltage · Resilient design · Error masking flip-flop · Low power · True single-phase clock

1 Introduction

The conventional integrated circuit requires large timing margins for proper functionality of the chip under severe process, voltage, temperature and aging (PVTA) variation. Especially these variations become severe in near-threshold region of operations as the amount of variation increases at reduced supply voltage. It leads to reduced performance and higher energy consumptions in the near-threshold designs. So, special attention is needed for near-threshold designs which can have improved performance and better energy-efficiency.

To handle this challenge, many resilient circuit techniques, which adaptively regulates the supply voltage and frequency of the design, are available in literature. The resilient circuit techniques such as in-situ timing error monitors available in literature are in [1–6]. However, these monitors dissipate more clock power as it requires both clock and inverted clock for its implementation. Several true single-phase flip-flops (FF) have been proposed in [7–9] to reduce clock power. In this paper, we are concentrating in designing an error masking FF

© Springer Nature Singapore Pte Ltd. 2019
A. Sengupta et al. (Eds.): VDAT 2019, CCIS 1066, pp. 371–382, 2019.
https://doi.org/10.1007/978-981-32-9767-8_32

which can correct output of the FF in the same clock cycle after the occurrence of timing error. A modified true single-phase FF along with error masking capability has been proposed to reduce the clock power of the FF.

This paper aims at providing a single-phase clocked error masking FF to address the issue of increased clock power in near threshold designs. The major contributions of this paper are as follows:

1. As true single-phase clock is used in the proposed FF, the clock power of the design is reduced significantly.
2. It is area-efficient compared to existing error masking FF.
3. It works from near-threshold to super-threshold supply voltages which is suitable for dynamic voltage and frequency scaling applications.

The proposed error masking FF uses true single-phase clock that helps in reducing the energy consumption of the design. The proposed error masking FF along with state-of-the-art EMFF are designed in 28 nm CMOS technology.

2   Proposed Error-Masking Flip-Flop

The proposed single-phase error masking flip-flop (SPEMFF) consists of a true single-phase FF, an error detector, and an error correction module. The block diagram of the SPEMFF is shown in Fig. 1. The data (D) and clock (CLK) signals are the inputs whereas error (ERROR) and the FF output (Q) are the output signals of SPEMFF. The FF behaves similar to conventional rising edge-triggered FF in the case of no timing violations. i.e. Data transition happens at the input of the FF during low phase of the clock. When data transition occurs in the high phase of the clock, the error detector module in the proposed SPEMFF flags an error to indicate late data arrival. The output of the FF is then updated by the error correction module of the SPEMFF.

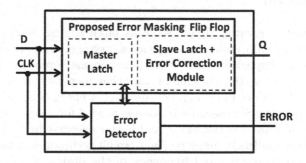

Fig. 1. Block diagram of the proposed error masking FF (SPEMFF)

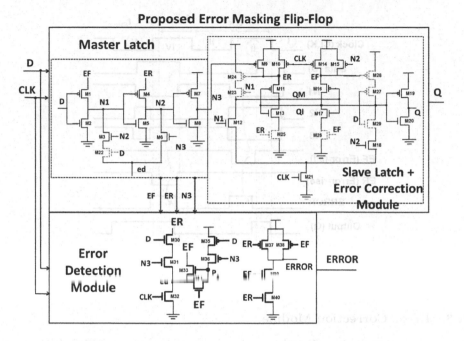

Fig. 2. Transistor level schematic of the proposed SPEMFF

2.1 Flip-Flop Design

The FF consists of master-slave version of single-phase FF. As single-phase of the clock is used for operation of the FF, the clock power dissipation is reduced significantly compared to the conventional transmission gate based FF (TGFF). The number of clocked transistor in the proposed FF is 4, whereas the TGFF requires 12 clocked transistors. Hence the clock power of the proposed FF is reduced significantly. The single-phase FF is appropriately modified to add error masking feature. Eight extra transistors are added in the FF level to the conventional single-phase FF [7] to make it error resilient. The schematic with transistor level implementation of the SPEMFF is shown in Fig. 2.

2.2 Error Detector Module

The error detector module (EDM) in SPEMFF uses the internal nodes of the FF to generate two error signals i.e. error-rise (ER) and error-fall (EF) signal for the detection of data rise and fall transition, respectively. These two signals are active low signals. To obtain the final error signal, ER and EF signals are given as the inputs to a NAND gate whose output is an active high signal. If the data transition occurs during high phase of the clock, the EDM flags an error signal, *ERROR*. If the data transition happens in low phase of the clock, the ERROR signal is not flagged. A total of 11 transistors (M30-M40) are used to implement the EDM and are marked in bold.

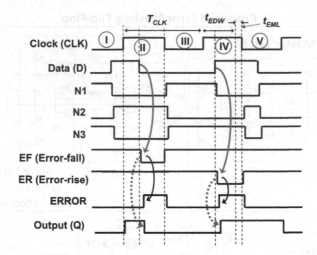

Fig. 3. Conceptual timing diagram of the proposed SPEMFF

2.3   Error Correction Module

Error correction module (ECM) is used to correct the output of SPEMFF whenever there is a timing violation. The circuit of ECM is integrated in the slave latch and uses 8 additional transistors (M22-M29) to correct the erroneous output state of the FF. The transistors in red colour represented with dotted lines are the part of ECM (M22-M29). They are active only when there is timing violation. When there is no timing violation, this module is inactive and SPEMFF behaves as a positive edge-triggered master-slave FF.

3   Operation of the Proposed SPEMFF

The complete transistor level schematic of SPEMFF is shown in Fig. 2. The SPEMFF works as positive edge-triggered master-slave FF when there is no timing violation. It flags an error and corrects the output of the slave latch when there is a data transition in high phase of the clock. The conceptual timing diagram showing different states of the intermediate nodes of SPEMFF is shown in Fig. 3. The data rise transition during the high phase of the clock discharges the node ER and flags the ERROR signal high, whereas a data fall transition discharges the node EF to ascertain the ERROR signal. The basic operation of the proposed SPEMFF is given in Table 1. The operating states of various modules such as master and slave latch, EDM and ECM are briefed with the error signal values. The detailed operation of EMFF for different data and clock conditions is discussed in the following subsection.

Table 1. Operation of the proposed SPEMFF.

Modules	Data transition	Data transitions in low phase of the clock		Data transitions in high phase of the clock	
		CLK = 0	CLK = 1	CLK = 0	CLK = 1
Master latch	Rise/Fall	Transparent	Hold	Transparent	Hold
Slave latch	Rise/Fall	Hold	Transparent	Hold	Correction
EDM	Fall	EF = ER = 1, ERROR = 0	EF = ER = 1, ERROR = 0	EF = ER = 1, ERROR = 0	EF = 0, ER = 1, Error = 1
	Rise				EF = 1, ER = 0, Error = 1
ECM	Fall	Inactive	Inactive	Inactive	QI charged & QM discharged
	Rise		Inactive		QM charged & QI discharged

3.1 Normal Operation (No Error Case)

The SPEMFF works as a positive edge-triggered master-slave FF when there is no error i.e. the data transitions occur in low phase of the clock (Timing windows I and V in Fig. 3). When the clock is low, the PMOS transistors connected to Clk are ON (M10 and M14) which charges both EF and ER nodes to VDD. The master latch becomes transparent during the low phase of the CLK and data is sampled. Node N3 stores the data sampled during the low phase of the clock and passes the data to slave latch during the high phase of the clock. There is no discharge path for the nodes N1 and N2 as the clock is low. As signals EF and ER are at logic "1", the output of the NAND gate is "0" and ERROR signal is not flagged. During the low phase of the clock, nodes EF and ER do not have any discharge path. The state of the transistors in ECM is inactive for low phase of the clock.

When the clock goes high, slave latch becomes transparent to the master latch output. As PMOS transistors M10 and M14 are OFF, one of the nodes QM or QI gets discharged based on the master latch output at the positive edge of the clock. Either QM discharges through M12 and M21 or QI discharges through M29, M18 and M21. Cross-coupled inverters (M11-M13 and M16-M17) update the output of the slave latch according to the master latch output. The transistors used for error correction (M22-M29) are inactive in this case and do not alter the slave operation. Transistors M25 and M26 are ON, whereas M24 and M28 are OFF. Transistor M29 remains in the same state as that of M18 in the case of no error. On the other hand, in the error detector module, the nodes EF and ER do not discharge through either of the paths M30, M31 and M32 or M33(active through M35-M36) and M32, as D and N3 are not at same logic value when the data transition happens in low phase of the clock. As the output of the slave latch follows the master latch output and master latch is in hold mode during the high phase of the clock, SPEMFF behaves as a conventional master-slave FF.

3.2   Error Masking Operation (Error Case)

The SPEMFF detects timing violation when the data transition happens in high phase of the clock and flags the ERROR signal. The output state of the FF is corrected using the transistors (M22-M29) and the signals EF, ER control the error correction. In the case of the timing violation, the slave latch samples the input data D instead of the master latch output N3. The error detection module detects both high-to-low and low-to-high transitions of the data by generating error-fall (EF) and error-rise (ER) signals, respectively.

Data Rise Transition Detection. Initially when the clock is low, EF and ER nodes are charged to VDD by M10 and M14. When clock signal goes high and assuming the data is low initially (Timing window IV in Fig. 3), the nodes N1 and N3 are charged to VDD by M1 and M7, respectively. Node N2 is discharged through M5 and also through M6 and M32. When CLK becomes high, the slave latch follows the output of master latch as D and N3 are at different logic levels. When the rise transition happens during high phase of the clock, node N1 discharges via M2, whereas node N2 remains discharged due to logic high value at node N3. The node ER starts discharging to GND voltage through the transistors M4, M6 and M32 as well as through transistors M30 and M31 of error detector. In this way, a timing violation due to rise transition is detected.

After detecting the timing violation, the output of the FF is corrected using the error correction module. The node QM charges to VDD through the transistors M23 and M24 as nodes N1 and ER are at logic low voltage. Moreover, the node QM does not have discharge path as transistor M25 is OFF. The node QI is discharged through transistors M17 and M26. The output of SPEMFF becomes high as transistor M19 charges the output to VDD. In this way, the output of the FF is corrected after detecting a timing violation due to a data rise transition. Nodes N1, N2 and N3 are updated during the low phase of the clock.

Data Fall Transition Detection. Initially when the clock is low, EF and ER nodes are charged to VDD by M10 and M14. When clock becomes high and assuming the data is high initially (Timing window II in Fig. 3), the node N1 is discharged through M2 and also through M3, M22 and M32 (N2 and D are high). Node N3 is discharged through M8. As nodes D and N3 are at opposite logic, the ERROR is not high. Thus the slave latch follows a normal operation and gives the output based on master latch output. When the data changes from high to low logic in the high phase of the clock, node EF gets discharged through M33 and M32. The transistor M33 is switched ON as node P1 is charged to VDD through M35 and M36. The transistor M34 becomes OFF as EF gets discharged. The nodes N3 and N1 remain discharged via transistor M8 and the path M3,

M22, M32 respectively, whereas N2 is charged through M4. The ERROR is flagged high as the signal EF becomes low.

In this way, the data transition from high to low is detected in the high phase of the clock. An active low EF signal initiates the error correction process. In this case, M28 is switched ON and charges QI node to VDD via M28 and M27 (D is low), whereas M26 closes the discharge path of QI as EF is low. Another discharge path for QI i.e. M29 and M18 is also closed as D is low. Therefore, the EMFF output (Q) is low as transistor M20 discharges the output to ground.

3.3 Glitch Sensitivity Analysis

The proposed SPEMFF can detect the data path glitches that occur in high phase of the clock. The ERROR signal is flagged whenever a rise or a fall glitch is encountered. The output is corrected with the help of correction module of SPEMFF. The minimum required glitch width ($P_{W,min}$) which can propagate to the output of the FF is approximately equal to data to Q delay of FF, whereas the minimum glitch width required to flag an ERROR signal is approximately equal to data to error detection delay. If the width of glitch is less than $P_{W,min}$, the presence of glitch may not be detected at the output of the FF. The conceptual timing diagram showing the glitch sensitivity of SPEMFF is presented in Fig. 4. In timing window II, as the glitch width is less than $P_{W,min}$, the ERROR signal is flagged, but there is no glitch at the output of the FF. In timing window IV, a fall glitch is shown which is wide enough to flag the ERROR signal and for the glitch to appear at the output of the FF. The value of $P_{W,min}$ for the proposed SPEMFF is found to be 2.9 ns and 2.4 ns for a fall and a rise glitch, respectively at a supply of 0.4 V with a glitch height of 0.4 V, in TT process corner at 25 °C.

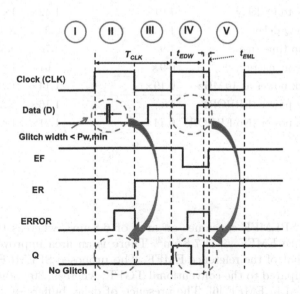

Fig. 4. Conceptual timing diagram for glitch analysis

3.4 Effective Timing Error Monitoring Window

The effective timing error monitoring window or error detection window (t_{EDW}) is a function of duty cycle of the clock and the time required to correct the output state of the FF after detecting a timing violation. The time required for the error correction (t_{EML}) includes the time delay required to discharge ER or EF and the time required to provide a valid logic value at the output of the FF, as represented in Fig. 4.

4 Simulation Results

The efficiency of SPEMFF is analyzed based on various performance parameters such as delay, power, area, etc. at FF level. The proposed SPEMFF is designed in industrial 28 nm CMOS technology along with a conventional TGFF and the error masking FF designed in [6] for comparison. The simulations have been performed on parasitic extracted netlists of the designs using Synopsys HSPICE. The quantitative results of various performance parameters studied at a supply voltage of 0.4 V are given in Table 2.

Table 2. Comparison of various performance parameters of EMFFs at 0.4 V.

Parameter	Proposed SPEMFF	Ref [6]	TGFF
Area (Layout)	1.92×	2.2×	1×
Clocked transistors (#)	4	14	12
Extra transistors (#)	16	30	NA
CLK to Q delay	1.01×	1.42×	1×
D to Q delay	1×	0.9×	NA
Setup time (ns)	1.95	4.76	0.88
Average energy	0.9×	1.61×	1×
Clock power at 10 MHz	0.19×	1.14×	1×
Peak power (ERROR)	1×	1.16×	NA
Peak power (No ERROR)	0.44×	1.21×	1×

4.1 Area

The proposed SPEMFF consumes an area of 6.8 um², whereas the area occupied by reference EMFF [6] is 7.8 um². There is an area improvement of 13% compared to that of the reference EMFF. The proposed SPEMFF has 16 extra transistors compared to the conventional TGFF, whereas, 30 additional transistors are required in EMFF [6]. The presence of delay buffers in [6] causes high area overhead in its implementation.

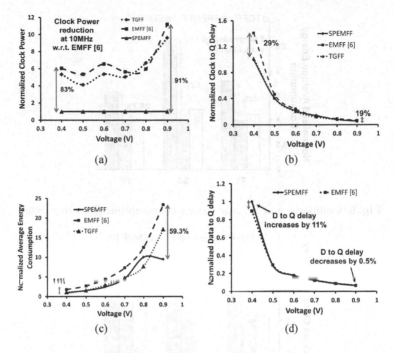

Fig. 5. Comparative study of performance characteristics for proposed SPEMFF with TGFF and EMFF [6] at TT process corner (a) Clock power evaluated at 10 MHz (b) CLK to Q delay (c) Average energy consumption (Error = 0) (d) Data to Q delay

4.2 Average Energy

The comparison of average energy consumption of SPEMFF is done with the reference EMFF and conventional TGFF for different process corners at 0.4 V as shown in Fig. 6. SPEMFF is highly energy efficient compared to TGFF and EMFF [6]. It is observed that SPEMFF consumes 44%, 62% and 36.7% lesser average energy compared to EMFF [6] at TT, SS, FF process corner respectively. On the other hand, SPEMFF consumes 10.7% and 18% lesser energy at TT and SS corners when compared to conventional TGFF. However, the energy consumption at FF corner is found to be 2% higher in the case of SPEMFF. The higher energy savings obtained in SPEMFF is due to low number of clocked transistors that significantly reduces the power penalty related to the toggling of clock signal in the design. Average energy consumption of three designs is also studied across voltage to study the effect of voltage scaling at TT process corner as shown in Fig. 5(c). It is observed that the energy consumption reduces with lowering of the supply voltage. The energy consumption of SPEMFF is found to be lesser in comparison to that of other two designs. SPEMFF consumes 44% and 59.3% lesser energy at 0.4 V and 0.9 V, respectively compared to the reference EMFF [6].

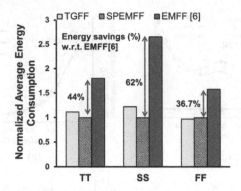

Fig. 6. Comparison of average energy consumption (No error case)

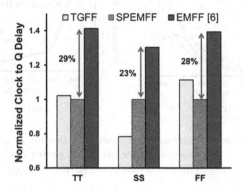

Fig. 7. Comparison of Clock to Q delay (No error case)

4.3   Clock Power

The clock power of SPEMFF is found at a clock frequency of 10 MHz for a supply voltage of 0.4 V. SPEMFF consumes 81% and 83% lesser clock power in comparison to that of TGFF and the reference EMFF. The use of true single-phase clock with only 4 transistors connected to clock leads to very low clock power in SPEMFF, making it suitable for energy efficient designs at lower supply voltages. The clock power for all the designs is studied across voltage in Fig. 5(a). The proposed FF shows higher power efficiency at 0.4 V as well as at the nominal voltage 0.9 V. The power savings of 91% is obtained by the proposed SPEMFF compared to reference EMFF [6] at 0.9 V. The peak power in SPEMFF is studied for different cases. In the case of no timing violation, the proposed SPEMFF consumes 63% and 56% lower peak power compared to EMFF [6] and TGFF, respectively. When there is timing violation, SPEMFF is found to have 13.8% lower peak power compared to the reference EMFF [6].

4.4 Delay

The CLK to Q delay of SPEMFF is compared with that of reference EMFF [6] and conventional TGFF, for different process corner at 0.4 V as shown in Fig. 7. The CLK to Q delay of SPEMFF is found to be 29% lesser compared to the EMFF [6] at TT process corner, whereas, a delay reduction of 23% and 28% is observed in SS and FF corners, respectively. The CLK to Q delay and D to Q delay have been studied for proposed design across voltage as shown in Fig. 5(b) and Fig. 5(d). The proposed SPEMFF shows a CLK to Q delay reduction of 29% and 19% at 0.4 V and 0.9 V, respectively compared to EMFF [6]. In the case of timing violation, the data (D) to Q delay of SPEMFF has a delay penalty of 11% at 0.4 V in comparison to EMFF [6]. However, the D to Q delay values are comparable for the voltage range of 0.5 V-0.9 V. The proposed SPEMFF shows better CLK to Q delay and higher energy savings with lower clock power consumption which ensures better performance and higher energy efficiency compared to the reference EMFF [6] and TGFF in near-threshold region.

5 Conclusions

This paper proposes a true single-phase clocked, energy-efficient error masking flip-flop with reduced clock power for near-threshold computing. The proposed SPEMFF is designed in 28 nm technology node and simulated under all the process conditions. The proposed flip-flop consumes 81% lesser clock power compared to the traditional transmission gate based flip-flop whereas it consumes 83% lesser clock power compared to existing error masking flip-flop. The proposed SPEMFF is found to be highly energy efficient and suitable for the designs operating in near-threshold region.

Acknowledgement. Authors would like to thank Science and Engineering Research Board (SERB), Department of Science and Technology, Government of India for funding support from project number ECR/2015/000422 for part of this work.

References

1. Zhang, Y., et al.: iRazor: 3-transistor current-based error detection and correction in an ARM cortex-R4 processor. In: Proceedings of IEEE International Solid-State Circuits Conference (ISSCC), pp. 160–162. IEEE, San Francisco (2016). https://doi.org/10.1109/ISSCC.2016.7417956
2. Kwon, I., Kim, S., Fick, D., Kim, M., Chen, Y., Sylvester, D.: Razor-lite: a light-weight register for error detection by observing virtual supply rails. IEEE J. Solid-State Circuits **49**(9), 2054–2066 (2014). https://doi.org/10.1109/JSSC.2014.2328658
3. Das, B.P., Onodera, H.: Frequency independent warning detection sequential for dynamic voltage and frequency scaling in ASICs. IEEE Trans. Very Large Scale Integr. (VLSI) Syst. **22**(12), 2535–2548 (2014). https://doi.org/10.1109/TVLSI.2013.2296033

4. Shang, X., Shan, W., Shi, L., Wan, X., Yang, J.: A 0.44V-1.1V 9-transistor transition-detector and half-path error detection technique for low power applications. In: Proceedings of IEEE Asian Solid-State Circuits Conference (A-SSCC), pp. 205–208. IEEE, Seoul (2017). https://doi.org/10.1109/ASSCC.2017.8240252
5. Huang, C., Liu, T., Chiueh, T.: An energy-efficient resilient flip-flop circuit with built-in timing-error detection and correction. In: Proceedings of International Symposium VLSI Design, Automation Test (VLSI-DAT), pp. 1–4. IEEE, Hsinchu (2015). https://doi.org/10.1109/VLSI-DAT.2015.7114574
6. Sannena, G., Das, B.P.: Metastability immune and area efficient error masking flip-flop for timing error resilient designs. Integration 61, 101–113 (2018). https://doi.org/10.1016/j.vlsi.2017.11.006
7. Kawai, N., et al.: A fully static topologically-compressed 21-transistor flip-flop with 75% power saving. IEEE J. Solid-State Circuits 49(11), 2526–2533 (2014). https://doi.org/10.1109/JSSC.2014.2332532
8. Cai, Y., Savanth, A., Prabhat, P., Myers, J., Weddell, A.S., Kazmierski, T.J.: Ultra-low power 18-transistor fully static contention-free single-phase clocked flip-flop in 65-nm CMOS. IEEE J. Solid-State Circuits 54(2), 550–559 (2019). https://doi.org/10.1109/JSSC.2018.2875089
9. Lin, J., Sheu, M., Hwang, Y., Wong, C., Tsai, M.: Low-power 19-transistor true single-phase clocking flip-flop design based on logic structure reduction schemes. IEEE Trans. Very Large Scale Integr. (VLSI) Syst. 25(11), 3033–3044 (2017). https://doi.org/10.1109/TVLSI.2017.2729884

Hardware Design and Optimization

ASIC Based LVDT Signal Conditioner for High-Accuracy Measurements

K. P. Raghunath[2]($\boxtimes$), K. V. Manu Sagar[1], T. Gokulan[1], Kundan Kumar[1], and Chetan Singh Thakur[1]

[1] Department of Electronic Systems Engineering, Indian Institute of Science, Bengaluru 560012, Karnataka, India
{manuk,gokulant,kundankumar,csthakur}@iisc.ac.in
[2] Department of Electrical Communication Engineering, Indian Institute of Science, Bengaluru 560012, Karnataka, India
raghunathp@iisc.ac.in

Abstract. A novel Application-Specific Integrated Circuit (ASIC) based signal conditioning system for closed loop control of Linear Variable Differential Transformer (LVDT) for sensor interface application is presented in this paper. The LVDTs are used for measuring linear displacement in industrial, military, aerospace, sub-sea, downhole drilling, nuclear power and process control applications. The signal conditioning is achieved through an ASIC-based digital signal processing unit. The existing commercially available Integrated Circuits (ICs) for LVDT signal conditioning are mostly analog and additional external circuitry is required for processing. The proposed system is a digital implementation of the LVDT signal conditioner with a better dynamic response and linearity through closed loop control. A unique feature of this ASIC is the use of synchronous demodulation technique using ADC sampling, reducing the complexity involved in conventional AM demodulation circuits. One of the major advantages of digital implementation is that the system can be reconfigured through external supervisory control. In this implementation, this is enabled by a universal asynchronous receiver-transmitter (UART) interface. This makes the system suitable for a wide range of applications. The functionality of the system was verified through a Verilog implementation on ARTIX-7 Field Programmable Gate Array (FPGA). The ASIC design is implemented in SCL-180 nm technology with an area 1 mm X 1 mm and the power utilization is 285 μW.

Keywords: LVDT · Signal conditioner · ASIC

1 Introduction

The linear variable differential transformer (LVDT) is a displacement transducer that accurately measures position and is extensively used in various industries

INSPIRE faculty fellowship (DST/INSPIRE/04/2016/000216) from the Department of Science Technology.

© Springer Nature Singapore Pte Ltd. 2019
A. Sengupta et al. (Eds.): VDAT 2019, CCIS 1066, pp. 385–397, 2019.
https://doi.org/10.1007/978-981-32-9767-8_33

for displacement measurement. The working principle of LVDT is detailed in [1]. Many applications require reading uncertainty as low as a few micrometers and also may require the transducer to be located in harsh and crammed environments, for instance, the case of the Large Hadron Collider (LHC) collimators position survey system [2]. In such cases, locating the reading electronics far from the transducer might tamper the accuracy. Further, locating the modules too near may not be possible due to space constraints. Such applications demand the signal conditioning module to be integrated with the transducer. As a result, a highly miniaturized and application specific module is necessary. Hence an ASIC based implementation is chosen. ASIC has several advantages over microcontroller/Digital Signal Processing (DSP) based solutions. ASIC is more suitable for hard real time applications as it is a hardware implementation and hence more deterministic whereas microcontroller/DSP requires software development. Also with the continuous increase in demand across industries, ASIC based solutions are economically more viable. The schematic of an LVDT integrated with an ASIC based signal conditioner is shown in Fig. 1. Other implementations of LVDT signal conditioner are discussed below.

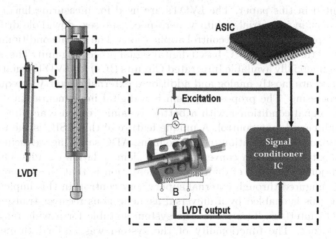

Fig. 1. LVDT integrated with signal conditioner ASIC

A Digital Signal Processing (DSP) based LVDT signal conditioner is presented in [1,9]. The FPGA based implementations of the LVDT are presented in [3,11–14]. The paper [3] presents a phase compensated signal conditioner, while [11] presents a non-linearity compensator of an LVDT sensor based on Artificial Neural Network (ANN). The LVDT for various applications can be found in the literature. A high precision radiation LVDT conditioning presented in [10,13,14] talks about the measurement of position, velocity and acceleration of a rotating shaft and [8] presents an accurate linear measurement using LVDT.

The LVDT output is a double sideband suppressed carrier amplitude modulated (DSBSC-AM) signal. The core displacement information is modulated by the precision sine wave excitation signal, which is given to the transformer primary winding. The sine wave is generated using direct digital synthesis (DDS) [6]. The modulated signal is obtained at the differential output of the secondary winding.

The objective of LVDT signal conditioning system is to measure the output voltage from the modulated wave at the transformer secondary that represents the movement of the core. The measured output will undergo required signal processing and is transmitted serially. There are two existing, well-documented approaches for LVDT signal conditioning. One is the ratio-based method [3] and the other is the synchronous demodulation method [4]. The ratio-based method computes position as the ratio of the transformer secondary output and primary input excitation.

However, ratio-based methods are noisy and in case there is a sensor-induced phase lag in the secondary differential waveform, the secondary to primary ratio does not give an exact measure of position, and a phase correction is required to produce the correct output. The second approach applies the standard phase-sensitive demodulation technique to the LVDT secondary output, a DSBSC-AM waveform.

The scheme is insensitive to sensor induced phase errors. However, this scheme necessitates the use of high performance floating point DSPs, and hence, may not be commercially viable for single channel LVDT signal conditioning. Two commercially available monolithic LVDT signal conditioners are AD598 and AD698 from Analog Devices. The AD598 and AD698 utilize the ratio-based method and their implementation details are documented in their respective datasheets [4,5]. Both implementations generate a primary excitation that varies from 20 Hz to 20 kHz, and a dc voltage proportional to the LVDT core position. The AD598 is insensitive to sensor-induced phase errors. The AD698 requires external RC network to eliminate sensor-induced phase lag. The proposed system implements an LVDT signal conditioner based on phase synchronous demodulation. It is The sine wave for exciting the transformer primary winding, as well as the three-phase square wave for driving the motor connected to the core, are generated using Direct Digital Synthesis (DDS). The differential output at the secondary winding of the transformer is demodulated using digital synchronous demodulation technique. There is also closed loop control to make the system linear and more dynamic. UART interface is an additional feature for external communication. The system will send output and health monitoring data to an external monitoring module where the data analysis is carried out. Based on the analysis, appropriate control inputs can be sent to the system.

2   System Description

The system block diagram is shown in Fig. 2. The DDS output, which is a sine wave at user-defined frequency ranging from 10 kHz to 20 kHz, is used to excite the LVDT primary winding. This waveform is functioning as the carrier wave for modulating the signal corresponding to the core movement. Based on the core movement, the transformer secondary produces a modulated output. This output is given as input to the Analog to Digital Converter (ADC). The ADC is sampled at positive and negative peaks of carrier signal. The output is reconstructed using sample values at the positive peak and inverted sample values at the negative peak. Since the carrier signal is generated by the ASIC, the peak points are readily available. This synchronous method avoids complex operation required for phase-sensitive demodulation architecture [7]. The demodulated output is applied to the filter and controller unit, which will remove unwanted harmonics signal present in the demodulated signal. The filtered output is fed to a controller for generating the necessary signal required for the closed loop control. This is to increase the dynamic range of the LVDT and also to increase the dynamic range of the system. The filtered output is decimated using a moving average filter and it is sent to an external monitoring system by a UART Transmitter. Health monitoring signals are also sent along with the filtered output. The UART Receiver module receives the control variables and filter coefficients from the external unit to get desired outputs.

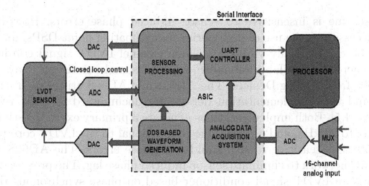

Fig. 2. Block diagram of the LVDT signal conditioning system

3   Components of the System

The major components of the system are listed and explained in this section.

3.1   Direct Digital Synthesis (DDS)

Direct digital synthesis is a well-known technique for generation of standard waveforms. It basically is a look up table (LUT) based method where the sample values of the desired waveform are stored in an LUT and the user can generate the output waveform at the desired frequency required by the user. The block diagram describing DDS is shown in Fig. 3. The frequencies that can be obtained are derived from the master clock (16 MHz) and the selection of the specific frequency is done by feeding a 4-bit input to this module. This method generates frequencies in the range 10 kHz to 20 kHz. The 4-bit input corresponds to the address of the LUT that stores the factor by which the master clock is to be divided to obtain the sampling rate corresponding to the desired frequency. The waveform of our interest is the sine wave input to the primary winding of the LVDT. In the second LUT 64 samples corresponding to this sine waveform is stored.

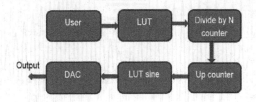

Fig. 3. DDS module

3.2 Sensor Processing

The function of the sensor processing block, shown in Fig. 4, is to demodulate the sensor output, filter the output data for removing the unwanted harmonics and provide feedback signal for closed loop application. The data is decimated at a user-defined rate and is sent to the UART controller. The operation of ADC, DAC and multiplexer are controlled by timing control signals. The major functions of sensor processing module are explained below:

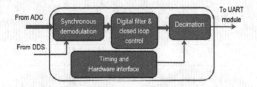

Fig. 4. Functional block diagram of the sensor signal processing

Phase-Sensitive Demodulation

Phase-sensitive demodulation, also known as synchronous demodulation, is a technique for envelope detection of the modulated differential output signal received from the LVDT. The analog output from the LVDT is sampled periodically at the positive and negative peaks of the digitized modulated signal obtained from the ADC and the original carrier waveform from the DDS module are the inputs to this block. The carrier and the modulated waveform are multiplied for demodulation. The process involves sampling the negative peaks of the received signal and inverting it. Subsequently, the inverted negative samples are interleaved between the positive peak values to reconstruct the envelope. As discussed earlier, the envelope corresponds to the linear motion of the core of the LVDT. The pictorial representation of the above demodulation process and the obtained simulation response of the same in MATLAB and ModelSim are shown in Figs. 5, 6 and 7 respectively.

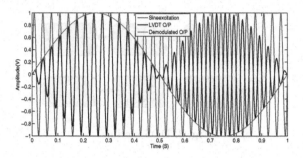

Fig. 5. Phase-sensitive demodulation technique

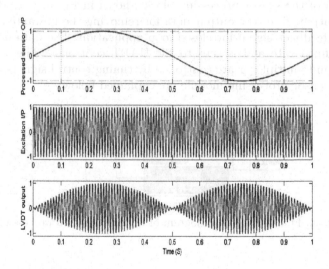

Fig. 6. Simulated response of the demodulation scheme in MATLAB

Digital Filter and Closed Loop Control

An Infinite Impulse Response (IIR) filter is implemented in the system to filter the LVDT displacement signal. The transfer function of the IIR filter is shown in Fig. 8. In this module the command output generation for closed loop control

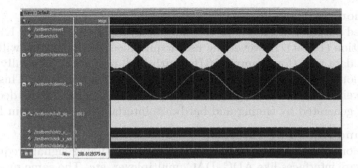

Fig. 7. Simulated response of the demodulation scheme in ModelSim

of the LVDT core displacement is also implemented. The filter coefficients and control loop tuning parameters are fed into the system after calibration. The command signal is given to a torque generator to generate a force which prevents the core from moving outside its dynamic range. For obtaining the frequency response, the input signal frequency is varied with respect to time and filter output is plotted. The obtained simulation waveform is shown in Fig. 9.

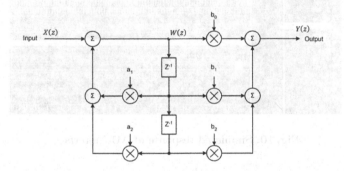

Fig. 8. IIR filter

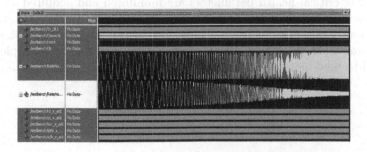

Fig. 9. Frequency response of IIR Filter

Decimation

The filtered output is available to this module at high data rate (10 KHz) with low resolution (10-bit). However the user requirement of the output will be normally low data rate (for example 50 Hz) with high resolution (typically 24-bit). The function of this module is to achieve these user requirements. This is done by using weighted block averaging. The precise timing signal for the decimation interval is generated by timing and hardware interface block shown in Fig. 4.

Timing and Hardware Interface

The function of timing block is to generate precise timing signals required for the hardware interfaces like ADC, DAC, multiplexer, etc. The same module will generate periodic pulses for the decimation interval. The ADC requires start of conversion, read and chip select pulses for the operation. Similarly, for closed loop operation, DAC write signal and data inputs are also to be provided. Also, control signals are to be generated for multiplexing the health monitoring channels for data acquisition. The simulated response of ADC interface is shown in Fig. 10. The interface is having clock, data and strobe signals. The data is sampled at the rising edge of the clock whenever the strobe signal is high.

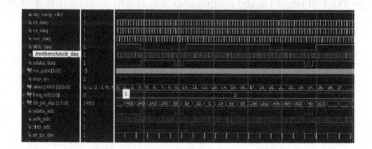

Fig. 10. Simulated response of ADC interface

3.3 System Health Monitoring

A number of critical health parameters are monitored and acquired along with the displacement information. These include power supply level status, temperature, reference voltage levels (data acquisition), carrier amplitude level, etc. The health parameters are analog signals, and a 16-channel analog multiplexer and ADC can be used along with the proposed ASIC for data acquisition.

3.4   Communication Interface

The ASIC is implemented with a UART communication interface. The entire set of data, which includes the demodulated received signal, filter and control loop constants, health parameters, etc are packaged into packets and transmitted via the UART transmitter. The baud rate for the data transmission and reception is made selectable externally by the operator. As mentioned earlier, an operator can monitor the system parameters and provide supervisory correction inputs. The supervisory inputs could be received through the UART receiver module and will be used for the subsequent sensor output processing operation. The response of the UART transmission at a baud rate of 19.2Kbps at a periodicity of 20ms is shown in Fig. 11.

Fig. 11. Simulated response of UART module

4   Implementation

The standard ASIC design flow was followed for the design and implementation. The design flow is represented in Fig. 12. The register transfer level (RTL) implementation was done using verilog in Xilinx VIVADO environment. The various modules in the system were implemented and simulated using Modelsim. The logic was synthesized for ARTIX-7 FPGA and outputs were verified in the hardware. The RTL synthesis was carried out in Cadence environment using RTL compiler. The synthesis was performed for 100 MHz and timing margins were verified. The physical design was carried out in Cadence Encounter. The floor plan area was set based on the utilization of logic. Power and timing parameters were extracted from Cadence Encounter. The graphic data system (GDS) was streamed into Virtuoso after sign off checks. The design rule checks (DRC), layout versus schematic (LVS) and antennae violations were cleared using Calibre SCL-rule deck. The final graphic data system (GDS) was streamed out from Virtuoso for tapeout.

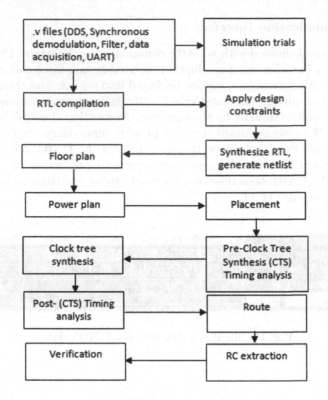

Fig. 12. ASIC design flow

5   Results

The results obtained during physical design on cadence at the different stages like synthesis, timing analysis, power planning and verification are presented. The power plan report is given in Table 1. The timing analysis results were verified at all stages of physical design till sign off. The sign-off timing results for hold and setup analysis are separately shown in Tables 2 and 3. The worst case negative slack (WNS) and total negative slack (TNS) are reported as positive in all the cases. The resource utilization of chip with CMOS SCL-180 nm technology and that on Artix-7 FPGA are shown in Tables 4 and 5 respectively. The layout view of the GDS generated after verification is shown in Fig. 13.

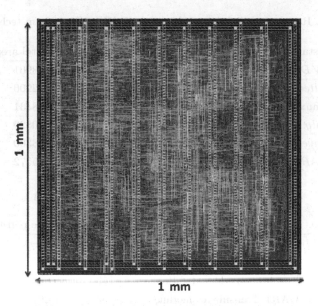

Fig. 13. Layout view of chip

Table 1. Power summary

Sl. no.	Title	Power (nW)
1	Cells	2976
2	Leakage	198.08
3	Internal	124340.01
4	Net	17220.26
5	Switching	141560.27

Table 2. Sign-off timing analysis report (hold)

Setup mode	All	Reg2Reg	Default
WNS (ns)	3.634	4.439	3.634
TNS (ns)	≈ 0	≈ 0	≈ 0
Voilating paths	≈ 0	≈ 0	≈ 0
All paths	245	245	11

Table 3. Sign-off timing analysis report (setup)

Setup mode	All	Reg2Reg	Default
WNS (ns)	0.020	0.070	0.020
TNS (ns)	≈ 0	≈ 0	≈ 0
Voilating paths	≈ 0	≈ 0	≈ 0
All paths	504	245	271

Table 4. Resource utilization of chip with CMOS SCL-180 nm technology

Instance	Cells	Cell area	Net area	Total area
LVDT_sigconditnr	9017	255267	143633	398901
filter_0	7177	194501	118399	312900
dmux16_1	221	17292	1139	18431
anlg_daq_0	216	7994	2835	10829
waveform_gen_1	233	4858	3442	8300
UART_Transmitter_0	156	3559	2012	5572

Table 5. Resource utilization on Artix-7 FPGA

Sl. no.	Name of the module	Slice LUT	Slice registers
1	Analog data acquisition module	65	61
2	IInd order bi-quad IIR filter	51	192
3	Synchronous demodulation	113	93
4	UART Transmitter module	55	29
5	Waveform generation module	26	17
6	LVDT signal conditioner	1092	785

6   Conclusion

A novel ASIC-based digital signal conditioner for linear variable differential transducer is designed and developed. The design has been implemented in FPGA ARTIX-7 and the functionality verification was done after interfacing with LVDT sensor. Subsequently, ASIC design was done following the standard ASIC design methodology, in the Cadence environment. The developed signal conditioner provides a low power and miniaturized solution and offers a direct serial interface to the processor. The direct interface minimizes any possible interference to the sensitive output of the sensor. This makes it suitable for high precision applications. The programmability of the filter coefficients, baud rate of the data transmission and frequency selection of sine wave through external UART interface makes it a superior choice for a wide range of applications. The closed loop control provision implemented in the system helps in achieving better dynamic response and linearity. A 16-channel analog data acquisition system also has been implemented in the system which can be used for monitoring various health parameters associated with the sensor and its environment. The chip consumes 285 μW power and area of 1 mm² in SCL -180 nm technology.

References

1. Ford, R.M., Weissbach, R.S., Loker, D.R.: A novel DSP-based LVDT signal conditioner. IEEE Trans. Instrum. Meas. **50**(3), 768–773 (2001)
2. Masi, A., Danzeca, S., Losito, R., Peronnard, P., Secondo, R., Spiezia, G.: A high precision radiation-tolerant LVDT conditioning module. Nucl. Instrum. Methods Phys. Res. A
3. Banerjee, K., Dam, B., Majumdar, K.: A novel FPGA-based LVDT signal conditioner
4. Analog Devices: LVDT Signal Conditioner. AD598 Application Note (1989)
5. Analog Devices: Universal LVDT Signal Conditioner. AD698 Application Note (1995)
6. Murphy, E., Slattery, C.: Direct digital synthesis (DDS) controls waveforms in test, measurement and communications. Analog Dialogue **39**, 12–15 (2005)
7. Dam, B., Banerjee, K., Majumdar, K., Banerjee, R., Patranabis, D.: A zero phase-lag homodyne demodulation technique for synchronous measurement applications and its FPGA implementation. J. Circuits Syst. Comput. **14**(4), 771–791 (2005)
8. Novacek, G.: Accurate linear measurement using LVDTs. Circuit Cellar Ink **100**, 20–27 (1999)
9. Flammini, A., Marioli, D., Sisinni, E., Taroni, A.: A multichannel DSP-based instrument for displacement measurement using differential variable reluctance transducer. IEEE Trans. Instrum. Meas. **54**(1), 178–183 (2005)
10. Masi, A., Danzeca, S., Losito, R., Peronnard, P., Secondo, R., Spiezia, G.: A high precision radiation-tolerant LVDT conditioning module. Nucl. Instrum. Methods Phys. Res. Sect. A: Accel. Spectrom. Detect. Assoc. Equip. **745**, 73–81 (2014). https://doi.org/10.1016/j.nima.2014.01.054. ISSN 0168–9002
11. Misra, P., Mohini, S.K., Mishra, S.K.: ANN-based non-linearity compensator of LVDT sensor for structural health monitoring. In: Proceedings of the 7th ACM Conference on Embedded Networked Sensor Systems - SenSys 2009 (2009)
12. Petchmaneelumka, W., Songsuwankit, K., Rerkratn, A., Riewruja, V.: Simple LVDT signal conditioner. In: 2017 3rd International Conference on Control, Automation and Robotics (ICCAR), Nagoya, pp. 758–761 (2017). https://doi.org/10.1109/ICCAR.2017.7942799
13. Banerjee, K., Dam, B., Majumdar, K.: An FPGA-based integrated signal conditioner for measurement of position, velocity and acceleration of a rotating shaft using an incremental encoder. In: 2016 IEEE First International Conference on Control, Measurement and Instrumentation (CMI), Kolkata, pp. 440–444 (2016). https://doi.org/10.1109/CMI.2016.7413786
14. Debnath, D.S., Pal, M., Banerjee, K., Dam, B., Majumdar, K.: An FPGA-based incremental encoder signal conditioner with reduced error in rotational rate estimation over a wide range of rotational speeds. In: 2016 2nd International Conference on Control, Instrumentation, Energy & Communication (CIEC), Kolkata, pp. 120–124 (2016). https://doi.org/10.1109/CIEC.2016.7513785

Quality Driven Energy Aware Approximated Core Transform Architecture for HEVC Standard

Neelam Arya[✉][iD], Anil Kumar Rajput[iD], Manisha Pattanaik, and G. K. Sharma

ABV-Indian Institute of Information Technology and Management, Gwalior 474015, India
{neelam,anil,manishapattanaik,gksharma}@iiitm.ac.in

Abstract. In order to support real-time HD video requirements for mobile and real time applications, energy-efficient design is the need of the hour for such low-cost devices. HEVC is the latest video compression standard that achieves high compression ratio and high bit-rate over existing architecture(H.264) but at the cost of higher computational complexity. HEVC incorporates integer DCT as an essential transform scheme for compressing the successive video frames. Approximate Integer DCT implementations with quality as a major constraint are proposed which consider the properties of transform matrices as prescribed by HEVC. A systematic approximation strategy has been introduced to achieve a reasonable quality-energy trade-off. The proposed 1-D architectures have reduced arithmetic complexity and less hardware resources when implemented on Artix-7 FPGA. A 56% reduction in resource utilization and 62% reduction in ASIC power when implemented on CMOS 180 nm technology is obtained compared with the reference DCT implementations and an improvement in coding performance is achieved as compared with the current work on approximated DCT architectures.

Keywords: DCT · HEVC · Energy aware architecture · Approximate computing · DCT approximation · FPGA

1 Introduction

Signal Processing for low power applications is an extremely important necessity in most of the applications particularly involving multimedia. High efficiency video coding (HEVC) is the latest video compression standard. HEVC has been designed for achieving increased video resolution and increased use of parallel processing architectures over the existing H.264 video standard. In HEVC, both DCT and IDCT are flexible for adopting approximation. In this paper, DCT is approximated due to its larger hardware cost. In real-time encoder architectures such as in HEVC, DCT is basically used in both mode decision and reconstruction loop, while IDCT is adopted in the reconstruction loop only [14]. One of the

© Springer Nature Singapore Pte Ltd. 2019
A. Sengupta et al. (Eds.): VDAT 2019, CCIS 1066, pp. 398–412, 2019.
https://doi.org/10.1007/978-981-32-9767-8_34

most repeatedly executed and therefore power hungry operations is the Discrete Cosine Transform (DCT) Block. DCT is a dominant transformation operation used to convert signal values from spatial to frequency domain incorporating properties like good energy compaction, basis vectors orthogonality etc. which is necessary for attaining high compression efficiency. Integer DCT used in HEVC [4] is capable of reducing the complexity in transformational kernel by eliminating the need for floating point multiplications. Also, the integer DCT possesses variety of properties which are useful for compression efficiency and for efficient implementation.

DCTs are combination of several data points represented in form of cosine functions oscillating at different frequencies. The HEVC Standard allows to use DCT of lengths of N = 4, 8, 16 and 32. The High Efficiency Video Coding Standard (HEVC) uses core transform matrices which reduces the number of arithmetic operations [4]. Despite this fact, the dynamic range of integer DCT is large leading to higher hardware cost. Moreover, integer DCT increases data-path length [5] which increases circuit delay. The selection of proper coefficients is non-trivial as the distance between original and approximated coefficients should be acceptable. Approximation computing techniques can produce far-reaching improvements for DCT of higher sizes, as the computational complexity of DCT increases quadratically with transform length [2]. The literature for HEVC-Compliant approximation is limited. Thus, this work addresses energy-efficient HEVC-Compliant 1-D Approximate DCT architectures.

Approximate Computing can be leveraged to improve circuit performance by accepting inaccuracies in the calculations. DCT can benefit greatly form Approximate Computing, since it is inherently inexact, compute intensive and energy-constrained. There is a considerable scope for power consumption reduction in HEVC video codec through means of algorithmic and architectural level optimizations. As multimedia applications are error-resilient due to limited capability of human perception, a few small errors while compressing/decompressing images and videos can be allowed while maintaining acceptable quality. Error resiliency also implies that it is possible to apply approximate computing techniques in intermediary computations of such algorithms without causing any major changes in the output quality. Quality bound approximations which are also energy aware is undertaken in this work. Approximate computing approach is applied and analyzed for design of 4-point, 8-point and 16-point 1-D DCT architectures with quality conservation as a major objective while achieving favorable energy-quality trade-off. Further, the approximation strategy proposed can be extended to 32-point DCT architecture as well.

The remaining paper is arranged as follows. Section 2 briefly surveys relevant DCT architectures. Section 3 proposes new approximate energy-efficient DCT architectures. Proposed approximate DCT Architectures for N = 4, 8 and 16 are discussed in Sect. 3.2. Experimental setup and results are reported and discussed in Sect. 4. Section 5 summarizes the work and presents scope for future work for the same.

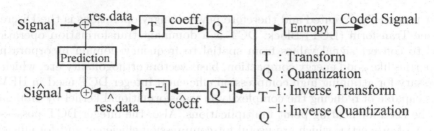

Fig. 1. Dataflow for HEVC video encoder

2   Background and Related Work

Figure 1 shows the dataflow for HEVC Encoder, the flow involves prediction, transform (T), quantization(Q), inverse quantization (Q^{-1}), inverse transform (T^{-1}) and entropy coding unit. The input to the transform unit is the residual data which is the difference between actual and predicted data. Profiling of HEVC is performed using $IntelvTune^{TM}Amplifier$, and the results clearly indicate that TComTrquant C++ class is the most time consuming, using almost 25% of the total time spent in various classes. Transforms amount to a total time which is around 9% in additional to this, the results clearly indicates that finding suitable implementation strategies for forward core transforms is indispensable.

2.1   DCT for HEVC

For a given input vector X $= [x_0, x_1, ...x_{N-1}]^T$, its corresponding DCT output Y $= [y_0, y_1, ..., y_{N-1}]^T$ is given by :

$$Y = C_N X, \tag{1}$$

where $C_{ij}\epsilon C_N$ represents different DCT coefficients in N-point DCT matrix C_N of size N × N, here N is the length of DCT.

$$C_{ij} = \frac{A}{\sqrt{N}} \cos[\frac{\pi}{N}(j + 0.5)i], \tag{2}$$

where i, j $= 0,1,........,$N-1 , A is equal to 1 and $\sqrt{2}$ for $i = 0$ and $i > 0$ respectively. The integer DCT matrix for HEVC V_N is obtained by multiplying the matrix C_{ij} by a scaling factor n $= 2^{6+M/2}$ where M $= log_2N$. The matrix elements are further tuned to satisfy the relevant DCT properties as mentioned in [4].

$$V_N = round\{2^n * C_N\}, \tag{3}$$

Any N-point integer DCT matrix can be further decomposed by exploring the even-odd decomposition property [5]. The DCT matrix is decomposed as:

$$
\begin{bmatrix} y0 \\ y2 \\ \cdot \\ \cdot \\ yN-4 \\ yN-2 \end{bmatrix} = \mathbf{C}_{N/2} \begin{bmatrix} a0 \\ a1 \\ \cdot \\ \cdot \\ aN/2-2 \\ aN/2-1 \end{bmatrix}, \tag{4}
$$

$$
\begin{bmatrix} y1 \\ y3 \\ \cdot \\ \cdot \\ yN-3 \\ yN-1 \end{bmatrix} = \mathbf{M}_{N/2} \begin{bmatrix} b0 \\ b1 \\ \cdot \\ \cdot \\ bN/2-2 \\ bN/2-1 \end{bmatrix}, \tag{5}
$$

where,

$$a(i) = x(i) + x(N-i-1), \tag{6}$$

$$b(i) = x(i) - x(N-i-1), \tag{7}$$

$M_{N/2}$ is a matrix of size $N/2 \times N/2$ for odd coefficient calculation and $C_{N/2}$ is a matrix of $N/2 \times N/2$ for even part calculation. $M_{N/2}$ can be further decomposed into $C_{N/4}$ and $M_{N/4}$ and so on to produce all lower DCT's in HEVC. HEVC standard employs DCT computation for 4-point, 8-point, 16-point and 32- point for its forward (video coder) as well as inverse (video decoder) form. The DCT basis vectors (rows of V_N) follows the symmetry property that greatly expedites the transform complexity to be reduced. The technique that utilizes this symmetry property is referred to as the even-odd decomposition (also known as partial butterfly during HEVC development) [4]. A 1-D forward transform using the even-odd decomposition technique follows these major steps which are also shown in Fig. 2:

1. An input adder unit (butterfly unit) responsible for add/subtract input signals $(X_0, X_1....X_n)$ to generate an N-point intermediate vector.
2. The even part is computed using the $N/2 \times N/2$ subset matrix formed by the even rows of the $N \times N$ transform matrix, the multiplication is realized using shifters.
3. The odd part is computed using the $N/2 \times N/2$ subset matrix formed by the odd rows of the $N \times N$ transform matrix. A Multiplier-less multiple constant multiplier unit (MCM) is designed for odd-part computation.
4. An output adder unit is responsible for addition/subtraction of the results of the even and the odd part.

The odd part realization through MCM unit takes the majority of hardware resources, as it uses adders and shifters. The design for approximate core transform and MCM unit is the major objective of this work.

2.2   Related Work

The work in [11] discusses approximate adaptive architectures and reconfigurable architectures for various DCT sizes. But, the work discussed in [11] does not hold the properties for making the transform HEVC-compliant. The work in [7] illustrates various simplified and approximated transistor-level implementations of a 1 bit full adder which are used in DCT implementation for JPEG encoder. An efficient integer DCT architecture implementation for different lengths has been presented in [12] along with the reconfigurable architectures. In [8] and [13] it has been proposed to extend the concept of approximate circuit evolution from the gate level to the functional level. In [10,11,15] full parallel, flexible and area-constrained architectures are proposed. The approximate technique discussed in [9] uses modified 4-point kernel for DCT computations. Higher length architectures are derived using these approximated 4-point transforms. The approximate scheme saves hardware cost and reduces power utilization at the cost of reduced coding performance of the video coder.

An approximate approach has been proposed in this paper to achieve favorable quality-energy trade-off while maintaining the integrity of core transforms in context of HEVC. The major contributions of this paper are as follows:

1. Approximate DCT Kernel for 4×4, 8×8 and 16×16 matrices are proposed based on systematic methodology to achieve approximate core transforms. The proposed approach can be extended to 32-point DCT for making the design HEVC complaint. Due to brevity, hardware implementations of 4, 8 and 16-point DCT are discussed.
2. The proposed approximate core transform is significantly closer to integer DCT of HEVC and demonstrates a better coding performance signifying improved quality.
3. Energy-aware hardware architectures are designed based on the proposed approximate technique to compute DCT of length N using an (N/2)-point DCT unit for N = 8 and 16.
4. A thorough comparison of complexity, energy-efficiency, area and power of different DCT implementations for HEVC is presented. Further, the experimental validation of proposed implementation on HM-13 reference software has been carried out and is briefly described.

3   Proposed DCT Approximation for HEVC

There is wide scope to redesign the transform kernel for DCT used in HEVC such that computational complexity and energy is reduced while maintaining reasonable quality trade-off. Preserving DCT properties and correctness upto some extent are primary challenges. To address these issues, energy-aware DCT architectures with a new set of approximated fixed point coefficients are proposed. The magnitude of each coefficient is fixed using a systematic approximate methodology such that coding performance is improved and energy saving is maximized while reducing hardware complexity.

All the new integers in approximated transform kernel are modified in multiples of '8' as it is closest to the smallest integer '9' in DCT-16 matrix (which is considered for implementation in this paper). Since, '8' is a dyadic number, all the elements can be factorized using a common denominator. This facilitates absorption of scaling factor in subsequent stages of encoding pipeline.

The approximation strategy used has following benefits:

- The number of adder/subtractors have been reduced in proposed approximated DCT architectures compared to reference algorithm [4] and reference architecture in [12].
- The coefficients are approximated to maintain the minimum distance with original set of coefficients.
- The elements of first basis vector remains '64' (also it is a multiple of '8') thus maintaining the property of orthonormality.
- Each core transform matrix coefficient comprises of '8' bits including sign bit as per HEVC specification.
- Similar concept can be extended to DCT-32 matrix by approximating coefficients in multiples of '8' keeping the basis vector same. Thus, making the approach HEVC compliant.

3.1   Proposed 4-Point DCT Architecture

A modified 4-point DCT architecture using approximated kernel is proposed, the architecture consists of adders/subtractors and MCM block. A 4-point 1-D forward transform architecture with output matrix Y and DCT kernel C_4 is defined as follows:

$$Y = C_4 X, \qquad (8)$$

where

$$\begin{bmatrix} Y_0 \\ Y_1 \\ Y_2 \\ Y_3 \end{bmatrix} = \begin{bmatrix} 64 & 64 & 64 & 64 \\ 83 & 36 & -36 & -83 \\ 64 & -64 & -64 & 83 \\ 36 & -83 & 83 & -36 \end{bmatrix} \begin{bmatrix} X_0 \\ X_1 \\ X_2 \\ X_3 \end{bmatrix},$$

The approximated transform matrix $C_4{}'$ is obtained by modifying the original transform matrix C_4, where the coefficient '83' is modified as '80' and '36' as '32' to get the approximated kernel matrix as:

$$Y = C_4{}' X, \qquad (9)$$

where

$$\begin{bmatrix} Y_0 \\ Y_1 \\ Y_2 \\ Y_3 \end{bmatrix} = \begin{bmatrix} 64 & 64 & 64 & 64 \\ 80 & 32 & -32 & -80 \\ 64 & -64 & -64 & 80 \\ 32 & -80 & 80 & -32 \end{bmatrix} \begin{bmatrix} X_0 \\ X_1 \\ X_2 \\ X_3 \end{bmatrix},$$

Even-Odd decomposition technique [4] is employed to reduce the computational complexity of DCT. The 4-point 1-D forward transform can then be rewritten as:

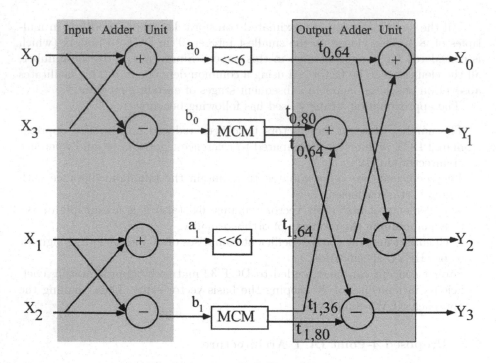

Fig. 2. 4-point 1-D DCT architecture

$$\begin{bmatrix} Y_0 \\ Y_2 \end{bmatrix} = C_2{}^o \begin{bmatrix} a_0 \\ a_1 \end{bmatrix} = \begin{bmatrix} 64 & 64 \\ 64 & -64 \end{bmatrix} \begin{bmatrix} a_0 \\ a_1 \end{bmatrix},$$

$$\begin{bmatrix} Y_1 \\ Y_3 \end{bmatrix} = C_2{}^e \begin{bmatrix} b_0 \\ b_1 \end{bmatrix} = \begin{bmatrix} 80 & 32 \\ 32 & -80 \end{bmatrix} \begin{bmatrix} b_0 \\ b_1 \end{bmatrix},$$

where the coefficients a_0, a_1, b_0, b_1 are given by following equations:

$$a_0 = X_0 + X_3 \quad (10),$$
$$a_1 = X_1 + X_2 \quad (11),$$
$$b_0 = X_0 - X_3 \quad (12),$$
$$b_1 = X_1 - X_2 \quad (13),$$

The MCM block (Fig. 3) is frequently used in DCT hardware realization where the multiplications with fixed coefficients can be replaced by network of shift and adders, thereby reducing hardware complexity. The Approximate MCM hardware for 4-point DCT in this work uses one adder and three shifters in comparison with three adders and four shifters of the reference implementation [12].

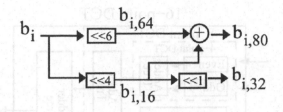

Fig. 3. Proposed approximate MCM (64, 80, 32) block

3.2 Architectures for DCT of Higher Lengths N = 8,16

The modified 4-point DCT architecture can be extended to 8-point architecture as shown in Fig. 4. As visible in the architecture implementation of 8-point DCT, it requires two 4-point DCT modules. The even-odd decomposition uses proposed approximated 4-point DCT module for even decomposition and the odd module uses modified approximated MCM unit realizing the odd coefficients in the DCT-8 matrix. The odd coefficients are derived to be multiples of '8'. The intermediate signals are computed as follows:

$$a_0 = X_0 + X_7 \quad (14),$$
$$a_1 = X_1 + X_6 \quad (15),$$
$$a_2 = X_2 + X_5 \quad (16),$$
$$a_3 = X_3 + X_4 \quad (17),$$

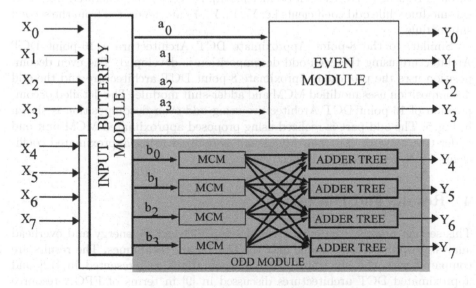

Fig. 4. 8-point DCT architecture

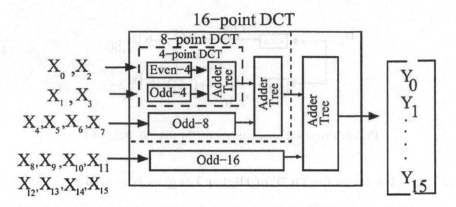

Fig. 5. Sixteen-point 1-D DCT architecture using even-odd decomposition technique

Similarly b_0, b_1, b_2 and b_3 were calculated.

$$b_0 = X_0 - X_7 \quad (18),$$
$$b_1 = X_1 - X_6 \quad (19),$$
$$b_2 = X_2 - X_5 \quad (20),$$
$$b_3 = X_3 - X_4 \quad (21),$$

The coefficients $(a_0 - a_3)$ act as an input to even module i.e. proposed 4-point DCT and $(b_0 - b_3)$ act as an input to MCM and Adder tree unit. After processing through respective DCTs even coefficients Y_0, Y_2, Y_4, Y_6 are generated from first sub-module while odd coefficients i.e. Y_1, Y_3, Y_5, Y_7 are generated from the second sub-module.

Similar, to the 8-point Approximate DCT Architecture a 16-point DCT Architecture using the even-odd decomposition is developed. The even decomposition uses the proposed approximate 8-point DCT architecture and the odd decomposition uses modified MCM and adder-shift module. The detailed decomposition of 16-point DCT Architecture using odd-even decomposition is shown in Fig. 5. The odd part is realized using proposed approximated MCM unit and adder tree network. The new MCM unit is realized using approximated coefficients for N = 4, 8 and 16 respectively.

4   Results and Discussion

This section presents the experimental setup followed by energy and overhead analysis of proposed technique over the benchmark techniques. The results are compared with the efficient DCT implementations as presented in [12] and approximated DCT architectures discussed in [9] in terms of FPGA resource utilization and ASIC performance for CMOS 180 nm technology node. The application level analysis is performed using the proposed approximated implementations with reference algorithm [4] and with the architectures implemented in [9] in HEVC HM-13 reference software. The proposed approximated core transform matrices uses multiplier less implementation as in [12], while the original algorithm in [4] is implemented using multipliers, adders and shifters. The proposed approximated transform uses 28% less adders and shifters compared to the 16-point 1-D DCT architectures in [12]. Table 1 shows the arithmetic complexity comparison with the reference algorithm in [4] and reference architecture in [12]. The approximate architecture in [9] is based on DCT of length 4 derived from the 4-point DCT of HEVC, the application level analysis therefore considers similar modifications in the HM software. To justify the results only 4-point approximations discussed in this paper are compared with those in [9]. The architectures proposed in this paper shows a balanced quality-energy trade-off as compared to [9] where the approximation technique degrades coding performance in lieu of reducing hardware complexity.

4.1   Experimental Setup and Tool Flow

The experimental setup in detail is presented in Fig. 6. The Verilog HDL description of accurate and different approximate DCT variants are developed and synthesized using: (1) ASIC design flow with cadence RTL Compiler, using TSMC 180 nm technology (2) FPGA design flow with Vivado 2018.1 for Artix-7 (XC7A35T) FPGA device. The designs are verified through gate-level simulations with various test inputs and detailed area, power/energy, delay estimation is performed to obtain SAIF (Switching Activity Interchange Format) files, which is then used for power estimation using Vivado Power Analyzer. For application evaluation, the equivalent behavior models of approximate DCT modules (in C++) are integrated into HEVC HM Test Model [6]. The quality evaluation, in terms of bit rate, and video quality (PSNR), is performed three test video sequences of different classes for sixteen point DCT architectures.

4.2   FPGA Implementation

The proposed 1-D 4-point, 8-point and 16-point DCT architectures have been implemented in Verilog. These Verilog HDL modules are simulated and verified in Xilinx Vivado 2018.1. For comparison purposes, the architecture of [12] and approximated architecture of [9] are also realized. The designs are synthesized and implementated on Artix-7 FPGA family. It is evident from Table-1 that the proposed technique achieves improvement of 56% in terms of number of LUTs required for FPGA implementation compared with [12] and a slightly greater LUT utilization when compared with [9]. As the work in [9] uses approximate coefficients which are in power of '2' and hence can be implemented through shift operations only which obviously will be lower than the implementation proposed in this paper (Tables 2 and 3).

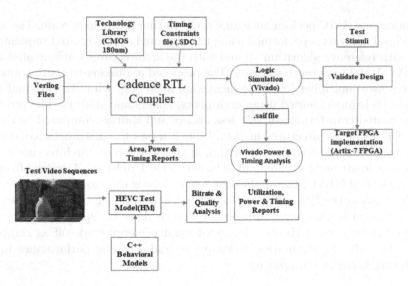

Fig. 6. Experimental flow showing the hardware (FPGA) and software (ASIC and HEVC HM Model) tools

The FPGA results obtained for 8-point 1-D forward transform shows an improvement of 48.29% for LUT utilization reduction. The architecture for 16-point 1-D transform shows an improvement of 55% over the reference architecture [12]. The power reported basically is the dynamic power considering 25% switching activity whereas the static power is not considered. Key metrics like Area-Delay product (ADP) and Energy which is power-delay product is also computed for detailed FPGA implementation analysis. The proposed 16-point architecture shows an improvement of 61% in power dissipation over reference architecture [12] and an performance improvement of about 44% over [12]. The approximated architectures in [9] typically shows less hardware resources due to use of approximated DCT coefficients in powers of '2' which uses only shifters for MCM realization, thereby reducing hardware resources but at the cost of decreased coding performance which is highlighted in application analysis.

Table 1. Arithmetic complexity of proposed & reference 1-D DCT algorithms

N	[4]			[12]		Proposed	
	MULT	ADD	SHIFT	ADD	SHIFT	ADD	SHIFT
4	4	8	2	14	10	11	8
8	20	28	2	50	30	41	24
16	84	100	2	186	86	141	56

Table 2. FPGA synthesis results for approximated & reference architectures for 1-D DCT of various sizes (N = 4, 8 & 16)

Architecture	Size of DCT	Area (LUT)	Power (mw)	Delay (ns)	ADP (No. of LUT's-ns)	Energy (pJ)
Proposed	4	91	130	5.97	543	776.75
	8	424	200	5.98	2535	1197.60
	16	**1457**	**341**	**6.10**	**8887**	**2081**
[12]	4	167	153	7.39	1234	1130.67
	8	820	268	7.570	6207	2028
	16	3308	400	14.284	47251	5713
[9]	4	62	92	4.01	248	365.47
	8	188	95	5.61	1054	533.23
	16	504	156	7.98	4021.92	1244.08

Table 3. Implementation results of proposed & approximated DCT architectures in 180-nm CMOS

Architecture	Size of DCT	Area (um^2)	Power (nw)	Delay (ns)	ADP (um^2-ns)	Energy (pJ)
Proposed	4	8273	1625116.445	5.378	44492	8.739
	8	31787	7425173.53	5.9	187543	43.85
	16	**131596**	**33357198.69**	**8.193**	**1078166**	**273.29**
[12]	4	19509	2946412	7.864	153418	23.17
	8	70483	16566452	8.334	587405	138.064
	16	256406	74571707	9.688	2484061	722.45
[9]	4	5256	583926.532	3.382	17775	1.974
	8	17008	2744881.68	4.9	83339	13.449
	16	47142	10279770.41	5.0	235710	51.39

Table 4. Average PSNR difference & bit-rate variation of proposed & reference approximated transforms

Class of video sequence	Architecture	BD-PSNR	BD-RATE	BD-PSNR*	BD-RATE*
B (1920 × 1080)	**Proposed**	**−0.01**	**0.25**	**−0.39**	**0.71**
	[9]	−0.15	0.26	—	—
E (1280 × 720)	**Proposed**	**−0.09**	**0.01**	**−0.90**	**0.34**
	[9]	−1.12	0.27	—	—

*(Evaluation using approximated 16-point DCT transform)

4.3   CMOS 180 nm ASIC Results

The Verilog netlist of each implemented DCT architecture is synthesized using Cadence Encounter(R) RC 14.27 RTL Compiler. All the designs are implemented on CMOS 180 nm technology and the results are compared with the existing architectures in [12]). Table 4 shows the comparison of worst path delay, total area, net power and power delay product(PDP) between various sizes of 1-D architectures. The PDP is calculated by multiplying worst path delay with net power. The proposed 4-point 1-D forward DCT achieves 35% improvement in worst path delay as compared with architectures in [12]. The proposed design for 4-point 1-D forward DCT also achieves improvement in area of about 58% as compared with [12] and about 45% reduction in power as compared with [12]. The proposed design of 8-point 1-D forward transform achieves 29% improvement in worst path delay as compared with architectures in [12]. The proposed design for 8-point 1-D forward DCT also achieves improvement in area reduction of 55% as compared with designs presented in [12] and a power reduction of about 55% as compared with [12]. The proposed design of 16-point 1-D forward transform achieves 15% improvement in worst path delay as compared with design in [12]. The proposed design for 16-point 1-D forward DCT also achieves area improvement of 48.67% as compared with architecture in [12] and power reduction of 55.2% as compared with [12].

4.4   Application Analysis

The application level performance of the proposed approximation method is compared with [9]. All the experiments are performed on HEVC HM-13 reference software with common test conditions as mentioned in [3]. Three input sequences of class B (1920×1080p) and class E (1280×720p) are used. The videos have a bit-depth of 8 with varying quantization parameters 22, 27, 32 and 37. The standard BD-rate approach [1] is used to measure PSNR variation and bit-rate loss. The results are calculated and presented in Table 4. The negative PSNR indicates PSNR degradation and positive values of bit-rate variation indicates coding loss compared to reference algorithm. The application results for only approximate four point transform from [9] is compared and the results for proposed approximated sixteen point transform work is compared with the reference algorithm in [4]. The results shows an improvement in PSNR and bit-rate over [9] since it uses approximated DCT coefficients with larger distance between original and the approximated core matrices while the proposed work maintains a reasonable distance between original and approximated matrices and while maintaining DCT integrity in HEVC. Thus, the proposed implementation shows an improved coding performance over [9].

5   Conclusion and Future Work

This paper proposes approximated 1-D DCT architectures for N = 4, 8 and 16 with approximated set of DCT coefficients. The proposed work uses systematic approximation strategy for obtaining DCT kernels which are according to

HEVC standard and holds approximately all the core transform properties. The architectures also have less arithmetic complexity compared to reference algorithm and architecture. The hardware implementations of the proposed architectures on FPGA and ASIC along-with experimental validation clearly shows a trade-off between quality and energy with better quality metrics than the existing approximate integer DCT architecture. The proposed 1-D architecture when implemented on Artix-7 FPGA, shows an ADP improvement of 75% over the existing reference architecture. CMOS 180-nm ASIC implementation shows an energy saving of 38% over the reference architecture. It is evident that the proposed approximation scheme saves hardware resources and improves energy efficiency while maintaining superior coding performance. The proposed research work can be extended for realization of 2-D 32-point reconfigurable DCT architectures in the future while exploiting approximation schemes for even better quality-energy trade-offs.

References

1. Bjontegaard, G.: Calculation of average PSNR differences between RD-curves. VCEG-M33 (2001)
2. Bossen, F., Bross, B., Suhring, K., Flynn, D.: HEVC complexity and implementation analysis. IEEE Trans. Circuits Syst. Video Technol. **22**(12), 1685–1696 (2012)
3. Bossen, F., et al.: Common test conditions and software reference configurations. JCTVC-L1100 **12** (2013)
4. Budagavi, M., Fuldseth, A., Bjontegaard, G., Sze, V., Sadafale, M.: Core transform design in the high efficiency video coding (HEVC) standard. IEEE J. Sel. Top. Signal Process. **7**(6), 1029–1041 (2013)
5. Chatterjee, S., Sarawadekar, K.: An optimized architecture of HEVC core transform using real-valued DCT coefficients. IEEE Trans. Circuits Syst. II: Express Briefs **65**, 2052–2056 (2018)
6. Fraunhofer, H.: HEVC test model (HM) v. 13 (2017)
7. Gupta, V., Mohapatra, D., Raghunathan, A., Roy, K.: Low-power digital signal processing using approximate adders. IEEE Trans. Comput.-Aided Des. Integr. Circuits Syst. **32**(1), 124–137 (2013)
8. Jridi, M., Alfalou, A., Meher, P.K.: A generalized algorithm and reconfigurable architecture for efficient and scalable orthogonal approximation of DCT. IEEE Trans. Circuits Syst. I: Regul. Pap. **62**(2), 449–457 (2015). https://doi.org/10.1109/TCSI.2014.2360763
9. Jridi, M., Meher, P.K.: Scalable approximate DCT architectures for efficient HEVC-compliant video coding. IEEE Trans. Circuits Syst. Video Technol. **27**(8), 1815–1825 (2017). https://doi.org/10.1109/TCSVT.2016.2556578
10. Kalali, E., Mert, A.C., Hamzaoglu, I.: A computation and energy reduction technique forHEVC discrete cosine transform. IEEE Trans. Consum. Electron. **62**(2), 166–174 (2016). https://doi.org/10.1109/TCE.2016.7514716
11. Masera, M., Martina, M., Masera, G.: Adaptive approximated DCT architectures for HEVC. IEEE Trans. Circuits Syst. Video Technol. **PP**(99), 1 (2016). https://doi.org/10.1109/TCSVT.2016.2595320
12. Meher, P.K., Park, S.Y., Mohanty, B.K., Lim, K.S., Yeo, C.: Efficient integer DCT architectures for HEVC. IEEE Trans. Circuits Syst. Video Technol. **24**(1), 168–178 (2014). https://doi.org/10.1109/TCSVT.2013.2276862

13. Sanchez-Clemente, A.J., Entrena, L., Hrbacek, R., Sekanina, L.: Error mitigation using approximate logic circuits: a comparison of probabilistic and evolutionary approaches. IEEE Trans. Reliab. **65**(4), 1871–1883 (2016). https://doi.org/10.1109/TR.2016.2604918
14. Sun, H., Cheng, Z., Gharehbaghi, A.M., Kimura, S., Fujita, M.: Approximate dct design for video encoding based on novel truncation scheme. IEEE Trans. Circuits Syst. I: Regul. Pap. **66**(4), 1517–1530 (2019)
15. Vasicek, Z., Sekanina, L.: Evolutionary approach to approximate digital circuits design. IEEE Trans. Evol. Comput. **19**(3), 432–444 (2015). https://doi.org/10.1109/TEVC.2014.2336175

Identification of Effective Guidance Hints for Better Design Debugging by Formal Methods

V. S. Vineesh⑩, Binod Kumar(✉)⑩, and Jay Adhaduk⑩

Computer Architecture and Dependable Systems Lab (CADSL),
Department of Electrical Engineering, IIT Bombay, Mumbai, India
{vineeshvs,binodkumar,jayadhaduk}@ee.iitb.ac.in
https://www.ee.iitb.ac.in/student/~cadsl/

Abstract. Achieving complete design verification by formal methods remains a daunting goal to date. With advancements in model checkers and other formal techniques, large designs can be verified in a partial or semi-formal manner. However, it is well known that exhaustive exploration of design state space is still prohibitive. In this paper, we revisit the concept of guided state space exploration which holds the promise of complete formal verification. Since it is not trivial to devise guidance strategies in an automatic manner, identification of the guidance hints becomes very crucial for a directed traversal of the state space. This directed traversal can ultimately reduce the time spent in formal verification and also assist in better design debugging. We propose a methodology for identification of such guideposts and utilize them for debugging purpose. Our goal is to achieve faster counter-example generation by the usage of guideposts. Experiments on a complex design show that guidance hints identified with the proposed methodology provide significant gains during model checking for different error traces.

Keywords: Formal verification · Model checking · Temporal logic

1 Introduction

Functional verification is one of the most challenging tasks in the modern design development cycle. While considerable progress has been made in the area of model checking to handle the state space explosion problem, developing automatic methodologies for achieving complete design verification still needs great attention [12,15]. By utilizing simulation, formal techniques like model checking can be guided and made more usable for successfully verifying larger designs. However, discovering such guidance strategies in an effective manner is not a trivial exercise [6,7]. Therefore, two important problems emerge out of this methodology for design verification by formal methods. First, generation of some guidance for assisting the model checking process. Second, developing techniques for

© Springer Nature Singapore Pte Ltd. 2019
A. Sengupta et al. (Eds.): VDAT 2019, CCIS 1066, pp. 413–427, 2019.
https://doi.org/10.1007/978-981-32-9767-8_35

further pruning out the state space with the help of obtained traversal (reachability) guidance. The second step is required because the guidance generation step is never a complete one and leads to a large number of possibilities remaining in the state space which serve as a hindrance in achieving higher speed-ups during model checking. This paper proposes a Signal Dependency Graph (SDG)-based methodology for solving the second challenge. With the help of Signal Dependency Graph built from the RTL (Register Transfer Level) design, the guidance (i.e., the list of internal signals and their values which act as guidance hints) help us to perform a partially directed analysis of the design state space. This directed state space search leads to significant gains in CPU time during model checking for properties. As a result, we succeed in generating counter-examples in lesser time.

The remainder of the paper is organized as follows. The preliminary concepts on waypoints are covered in Sect. 2 and the proposed methodology is elaborately explained in Sect. 3 with a detailed discussion on a case study. Experimental results and observations are presented in Sect. 4. The related work is briefly mentioned in Sect. 5. Finally, the paper is concluded in Sect. 6 with a discussion regarding the limitations of the proposed waypoint identification methodology and its possible extensions.

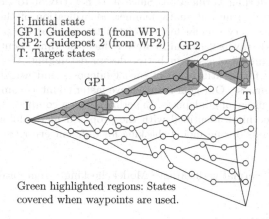

Fig. 1. Guidance-based state space traversal (For illustration purposes only). (Color figure online)

2   Illustrating Guidance-Based State Space Traversal

We refer to the guidance hints as "waypoints" hereafter. For the sake of brevity, we put forward the following definition:

Let S be the set of reachable states in design. A waypoint WP_k is a set of fully or partially specified signals $(s_1, s_2, ..., s_n)$ that correspond to a set of states $S^K = \{S_1, S_2, ..., S_n\} \in S$.

S^K is also referred to as guidepost (GP) in this paper. Let us consider the diagram given in Fig. 1 which illustrates guidance-based state space traversal. The set of states in the blue boxes (except for the leftmost and rightmost ones which are the initial and target states) are examples of guideposts (S^K) for reaching the target states T which satisfy the property ϕ. Along with identifying the waypoints, it is also important to select one state from the set of states represented by the guideposts (S^K) for the traversal to the subsequent guideposts. This concept is explained next with an example.

2.1   Concept of Waypoints

We have designed a system of two counters for explaining the identification of the starting state for the traversal to the next waypoint. The first counter counts in steps of 15 and the second one in steps of 5. The maximum counts allowed for counters 1 and 2 are 150 and 90 respectively. We have another feature in the design according to which the output of the counter 2 will not go beyond 80 if counter 1 is already full. The target state (ϕ) is any state which satisfies the following property.

$$EF(count2(c2) == 90)$$

The fully specified hints (i.e., signal with their values) selected for debugging are as follows:

- Initial state (I): count2 = 0
- Waypoint 1 (WP1): count2 = 45
- Waypoint 2 (WP2): count2 = 60

As per our assumption, all the states with $count2 = 45$ will be included in GP1. Let's say there are two states $S1$ and $S2$ in GP1 (there can be many more states in reality). Note that we did not use any particular criteria in selecting the starting state while traversing to GP2 and selected $S1$ arbitrarily. As shown in the Fig. 2, f1 (status full signal of counter 1) will become 1 just after GP1 and hence $c2$ will be stuck at the value 80 (because of the particular nature of the design due to which $c2$ will not count above 80 if $f1=1$). Hence, we would never reach any of the target states T (state where $c2=90$) if such a state space traversal strategy is applied.

This problem could be addressed by selecting the right set of signals which can help us identify the starting state from waypoint for further traversals, using Signal Dependency Graphs (SDG) (discussed in Sect. 3.1). It is clear from the SDG generated for the signal $count2$ (Fig. 4) that the signal $count2$ depends on $full\_1$ which in turn depends on $en1$. In short, we should have considered the value of the signal $en1$ also while picking the states from $S1$ and $S2$. This example is just for illustration purposes. However in practice, we should consider all the dependent signals and it's values for better SDG pruning.

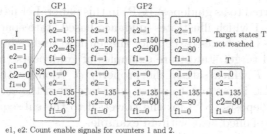

e1, e2: Count enable signals for counters 1 and 2.
c1, c2: Outputs of the counters 1 and 2.
f1: Status full ouput of counter 1.

Fig. 2. FSM showing Waypoints for the design *counters*

2.2 Utility of Waypoints

An Example Design with Four Parallel Counters. To further elucidate the advantages in using waypoints, we have designed a system with multi 13-bit counters which has the same clock. The four counters numbered as 1, 2, 3 and 4 count in steps of 1, 2, 3 and 4 respectively. The target property (ϕ) is,

$$EF(output_{any\ counter} >= 8188)$$

We performed model checking for the above design for the property specified above. In the first iteration, we did not apply any waypoint. We have performed model checking using the open source model checker, Yosys [13]. As mentioned in the Table 1, the BMC (Bounded Model Checker) tool took 224 s to check the property. We experimented with different number of waypoints. Initially, we have selected one waypoint ($output_{any\ counter} = 8188/2$), which reduced the time to check the property by almost half (115 s). More experiments were carried out with two, three and four number of waypoints. Waypoints for these cases were the nearest integer multiples of 8188/3, 8188/4 and 8188/5 respectively. The reduction in time can be explained from the fact that at each stage of model-checking, the state space is getting reduced successively.

Table 1. BMC time for different number of waypoints (Counters)

Waypoints	0	1	2	3	4	BMC time (s)
0	224					224
1	58	57				115
2	26	27	27			80
3	16	16	15	15		62
4	10	10	11	10	10	51

3   Proposed Methodology

The proposed methodology of waypoint identification involves a SDG-based filtering of the internal signals of the design. The primary motive behind this filtering is to obtain a list of signals (used to form waypoints) which would guide the model checking process for counter-example generation in lesser time. Given an error trace, we formulate the property which is to be formally checked. From this property, we obtain the Signal Dependency Graph for the target variables which are further analyzed to select the waypoints. Figure 3 shows a high level overview of the proposed methodology which is illustrated in Sect. 3.3.

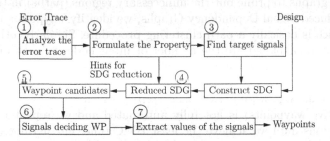

Fig. 3. Proposed methodology of waypoint identification

3.1   Signal Dependency Graph (SDG)

SDG is defined as a directed graph (G) with signals (in the RTL description) as Vertices (V) and the dependence between nodes as directed edges (E). If there is a directed edge $v_i \rightarrow v_j$, it means that the signal v_j depends on the signal v_i, where $v_i, v_j \epsilon V$ and $(v_i, v_j) \epsilon E$.

To generate the SDG, we first generate the CDFG (Control Data Flow Graph) of all the modules in the design. After that the intra-module dependency is derived by parsing the CDFGs and the inter-module dependencies are extracted by parsing the RTL description. We derive the final SDG by combining both.

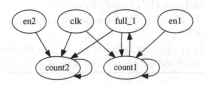

Fig. 4. Signal Dependency Graph for the signal "count2" (count value of the counter 2) of the design discussed in Sect. 2.1

3.2   Proposed Methodology for Identifying Waypoints

The concept of waypoint is represented in Fig. 1 in accordance with the terminology adopted in [6]. As it is clear from this diagram, the goal is to identify waypoints (the blue boxes, except for the leftmost and rightmost one which are the initial and target states) which assist in reaching from the reset state (or, otherwise a predefined state) to the target state which satisfies the property.

The proposed methodology takes as input an error trace (ETr) and the RTL design to find the waypoints. These waypoints assist us in finding a counterexample within lesser CPU time as compared to conventional model checking. After construction of SDG for target variables involved in the property, we need to reduce these graphs to prune out the unnecessary regions (paths) in the graphs. From the reduced Signal Dependency Graphs, we identify waypoints based on a heuristic which is basically a path clustering procedure. Similarly, other heuristics which can be explored are the number of input nodes to each one of waypoint candidates ($WPcand$) and the number of toggles in signal values of each one of $WPcand$ in any simulation trace($SiTr$). The proposed methodology is presented here as Algorithm 1. Note that step-6 (which is concerned with selection of effective waypoints) is not fully automated and we repeat the process for few iterations until we achieve the least BMC time. Furthermore, it can be argued that multiple error traces are possible which if not accounted for, may affect this algorithm. However, we observed that multiple error traces lead to the same property formulation in most of the cases as the final error state remains same. It is worth to note the practical usage of the proposed methodology lies in obtaining counter-examples in lesser CPU time.

Algorithm 1. *FindWaypoints*

Input: *ErrorTrace(ETr),Design(D)*
Output: *Waypoints(WP)*
1 analyze the error behavior(ETr) observed in the design(D) simulation;
2 formulate properties(P) related to step1 which are to be given to model checking;
3 select signal(s) from P and construct their Signal Dependency Graph (SDG) using D;
4 reduction of SDG in step3 to generate the reduced SDG (SDG') with the help of abstraction techniques(modular similarity, bit-width minimization and slicing);
5 identify waypoint candidates ($WPcand$) from SDG';
6 from $WPcand$, select WP using distance based clustering of signals in the longest K paths of SDG'. ;
7 for waypoints of the form $sig_i = m$, $sig_i \neq n$ or sig_i in the numerical/bit-width range of q to r, D is analyzed to obtain the values of m,n,q,r etc.

3.3   Case Study: Design, Bugs and Properties

The MESI Coherency Intersection Controller (MESI-ISC). We have used the MESI Coherency Intersection Controller [1] shown in Fig. 5 for our experiments with waypoints. The coherence system ensures consistency between different copies of data with same memory address. The MESI-ISC supports MESI coherence protocol [9] which is widely employed for performing coherency maintenance tasks in systems with multiple masters having local caches. Any cache line in this protocol can have four different states: *M*odified, *E*xclusive, *S*hared and *I*nvalid. In this implementation of the coherency system, there are two buses: main bus and coherency bus. The transactions in the main bus are initiated and driven by the masters. They communicate with the main memory, and the coherency controller (i.e., cache controller). The transactions in the main bus are the following: *write access, read access, write broadcast* and *read broadcast*. The coherency bus which is the core of the MESI protocol is driven by the coherency controller. The transactions done in this bus are the following: *write snoop, read snoop, enable write* and *enable read*. The round-robin priority logic in the design ensures that the requests from all the four CPUs are served without starving any of the CPUs. Later in the paper, we will discuss a bug which we have introduced into this priority logic which results in the miss of all requests from the CPU2. The MESI-ISC system [1] works as follows. The operation starts with the master initiating a memory access. Prior to that master sends a broadcast request to the main memory. The coherence controller communicates with the other masters and collects their response(s). Then the controller enables the initiator to perform the memory access. Note that the verification of cache coherence protocols is a challenging task [11]. This means that verifying the implementation of such coherence protocols is equally difficult which necessitates verification by formal methods for completeness. Moreover, the subtle complexity of cache coherence protocols makes MESI-ISC an ideal design for our case study during model checking experiments.

Properties Selected for Model Checking. We have identified two difficult properties for our experiments. To generate counter-examples, we intentionally injected one subtle design bug (separately during each property checking experiment) so that design functionality deviates from the desired specifications. For bringing out the differences between model checking with and without waypoints, we perform model checking, first by just providing the design and property to the model checker tool and then repeating the same with waypoints.

Bug 1: We have introduced a bug in the *status_full_o*[1] signal of FIFO_2. Because of this bug, the *status_full_o* never becomes high and FIFO_2 will keep accepting new entries even if it is full. The new entries will replace the last stored entry. For this reason, there is a chance that the requests coming from CPU 2 (which is stored in FIFO_2) will get replaced with subsequent requests.

Manifestation of Bug: This bug can be noticed by the occasional misses of the requests from CPU2.

   Property 1. We have designed a property (as shown in Listing. 1.1) which will expose this bug. In this property we have a request from CPU0 followed by

---

[1] The signal which goes high when the FIFO is full.

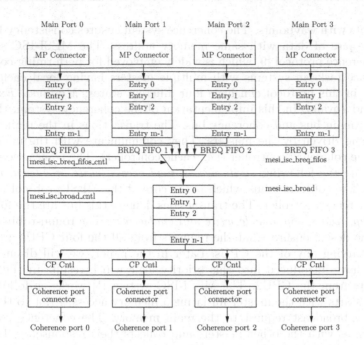

Main Port 0   Main Port 1   Main Port 2   Main Port 3

Fig. 5. The MESI Coherency Intersection Controller [1]

another request from CPU2. After sometime CPU0 sends another request. This request from CPU2 does not reach the BROAD FIFO and hence will be missed at the MESI OUTPUT also. As shown in Tables 2 and 3, this property takes few hours for model checking (Fig. 6).

Listing 1.1. property1

```
assert property (
not(
// ------------------BREQ FIFOs------------------
// FIFO_0 contains WR req. from CPU0 to addr 0
(mesi_isc_breq_fifos.fifo_0.data_o==41'h83
// FIFO_2 contains WR req. from CPU2 to addr 2
and mesi_isc_breq_fifos.fifo_2.data_o==41'h4c1)
// FIFO_0 contains WR req. from CPU0 to addr 2
[*1:$]##1 mesi_isc_breq_fifos.fifo_0.data_o==41'h483

// ------------------BROAD FIFO------------------
// WR req. from CPU0 to addr 0
##[1:$](mesi_isc_broad.broad_fifo.data_o==41'h83)
// WR req. from CPU0 to addr 2
[*1:$]##1 (mesi_isc_broad.broad_fifo.data_o==41'h483)

// ------------------MESI OUTPUT------------------
// WR req. from CPU0 to addr 0
##[1:$] (cbus_cmd0_o==3'b011 and cbus_addr_o==32'h0)
// WR req. from CPU0 to addr 2
[*1:$]##[1:$] (cbus_cmd0_o==3'b011 and cbus_addr_o==32'h2))
);
```

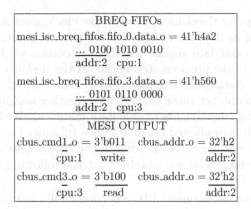

Fig. 6. Encoding of the signals used in Property 2

Identification of Waypoints Using the Proposed Algorithm. We have followed the steps mentioned in the Algorithm 1 to find the appropriate signals which decide waypoints.

1. The *Error Trace* obtained by simulating the design reveals that there could be some problems with the requests from CPU 2. Note that this *Error Trace* is provided by simulators like Modelsim and not the BMC tool.
2. Out of many possibilities where the bug could be, we have shortlisted the area between BROAD FIFO and the primary inputs as the buggy region. A property was designed (Listing. 1.1) to check the possible miss of requests from CPU 2 targeting this area. As per the proposal, other possible buggy regions could be explored if the assumption turned out to be wrong (i.e., if no counter-example was generated for the property by the end of this iteration). It's important to note that if we fail to cover all possible buggy areas for designing the property at this step, we might miss out a region where the actual bug is and end up with not catching the bug.
3. We have selected the signal *cbus_cmd0_o* and *cbus_addr_o* as the target variables since they are the ones which are closest to the primary output and hence the SDG corresponding to that will include all the potential signals for waypoints. Selection of these signals from the property is done by analyzing the RTL and identifying the signals which are structurally near to the primary output. An SDG for illustration is given in Fig. 7. The actual SDGs used for this work are not shown here since they are too large.
4. We used slicing techniques for reducing the size of the SDG generated in the previous step. This step required extra set of hints which are to be used as the slicing criteria. The hint which we used from the *ErrorTrace* is the following: the regions in the design which doesn't deal with the data from CPU 2 could be discarded from the SDG. The slicing of the SDG is done resulting producing a modified SDG (SDG') which does not have the signals related to BREQ FIFO 1 and BREQ FIFO 3.

5. All signals (except for the elementary ones like clock, reset etc.) in the reduced SDG are selected as the potential signals for the waypoints.
6. To identify the candidate signals for the waypoints, we have grouped the signals obtained in the previous step based on the *distance* in SDG from the root signal. The *distance* is determined by the number of nodes in the path from one node to another (note that we have neither assigned any weights to the edge nor using edge weights to calculate *distance*). We have used each of those signals with their allowed range of values (discussed as the next point) in the property and compared the speedup in the Model Checker. Higher speed-up in model checking time was obtained for the following set of signals(i.e., waypoints):
   - BREQ (Broadcast Request) FIFO becomes full (*status_full*).
   - Data output of the BROAD (Broadcast) FIFO (*broad_fifo.data_o*).

As mentioned previously, the selection of the signal which decides waypoint is very important. For example, the model checking when done using *status_full* signal, the obtained speedup in CPU time was significant. However, when it was done with *ptr_wr* (the write pointer for the BREQ FIFO 2) (which is also there in *WPcand*) the Model checker went for a time out (T.O).

7. The data values assigned to each signal is chosen using the design knowledge and the property. The final waypoints are as follows: *status_full* = 1, *broad_fifo.data_o* =41'h83[2]. Here the Guidepost 1 (GP1) is a set of states where the signals *status_full* is equal to 1 and Guidepost 2 (GP2) is a set of states where the signal *broad_fifo.data_o* is equal to 41'h83.Please note that

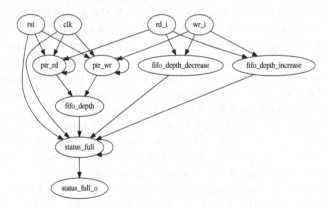

Fig. 7. Signal Dependency Graph for the signal 'status_full_o' in the design 'mesi_isc_basic_fifo' of MESI-ISC design [1]

---

[2] For this particular case, WP2 happens to be there in the property as well. We had to use *broad_fifo.data_o* in property 1 to ensure that the final output signals are generated by the requests 41'h83 and 41'h483, and not one of the many other possible requests which might give the same output values for *cbus_cmd0_o* and *cbus_addr_o* at MESI OUTPUT.

obtaining these data values itself is a hard problem and we have not addressed it in this paper. We are currently working on techniques to solve this problem.

For comparative evaluation, Property1 is checked via the following 2 ways. The same is repeated for property 2 (corresponding to Bug 2) as well.

1. Without any waypoint.
2. With waypoints (Property is broken down into 3 parts).
   (a) Reach the case where *status_full* of BREQ FIFO 2 is *1*.
   (b) Initialize the signal *status_full* of BREQ FIFO 2 to *1* in the design and check if the data is correctly transferred from all BREQ FIFOs to BROAD FIFO by specifying the value of *broad_fifo.data_o*.
   (c) Check for the transfer of data from BROAD FIFO to the MESI OUTPUT.

Bug 2: We introduced another bug in the priority logic of the BROAD FIFO controller of MESI-ISC design. It decides the priority at which the requests from the BREQ FIFOs are passed to the BROAD FIFO. Accordingly, the requests from BREQ FIFO 2 will always be neglected. In terms of implementation, it is done by introducing a simple *AND* gate with one of it's inputs tied to *4'b1011* and the other one connected to the output of the existing priority logic.

Manifestation of Bug: Due to this bug, the requests from CPU 2 never reach the MESI OUTPUT resulting in unexpected results (For example, if CPU 2 writes some data to a particular address and another CPU reads it, the data which is read will be the one which existed previous to the write by CPU 2. The effects can be in many other ways).

Listing 1.2. property2

```
assert property(
not(
// ------------------BREQ FIFOs------------------
// fifo_1 contains WR req. from CPU1 to addr 2
(mesi_isc_breq_fifos.fifo_1.data_o==41'h4a2
// fifo_2 contains WR req. from CPU2 to addr 2
and mesi_isc_breq_fifos.fifo_2.data_o==41'h4c1
// fifo_3 contains RD req. from CPU3 to addr 2
and mesi_isc_breq_fifos.fifo_3.data_o==41'h560)

// ------------------BROAD FIFO------------------
// WR req. from CPU1 to addr 2
[*1:$]##[1:$](mesi_isc_broad.broad_fifo.data_o==41'h4a2
// RD req. from CPU3 to addr 2
##1 mesi_isc_broad.broad_fifo.data_o==41'h560)

// ------------------MESI OUTPUT------------------
// WR req. from CPU1 to addr 2
[*1:$]##[1:$](cbus_cmd1_o==3'b011 and cbus_addr_o==32'h2)
// RD req. from CPU3 to addr 2
[*1:$]##[1:$] (cbus_cmd3_o==3'b100 and cbus_addr_o==32'h2))
);
```

Property 2: FIFO_1 will write at address 2 and then BREQ FIFO 2 will also write at the same address. Then BREQ FIFO 3 will read the value from the address 2. As there is a bug in the priority logic BREQ FIFO 3 will read the value which is written by BREQ FIFO 1 instead of BREQ FIFO 2. As in the case with property 1, there is a significant improvement in time when we use waypoints.

The waypoint used for checking property 2 is following:

- Data from BREQ FIFO reaches BROAD (Broadcast) FIFO. (WP1: *broad_fifo.data_o* with the values *41'h4a2* and *41'h560*).

4   Experimental Results

We utilized JasperGold (from Cadence) as the model checker tool for our experiments with the MESI-ISC design. All the model checking experiments were carried out on Intel-i7 machine running at 3.4 GHz with 16 GB RAM and booting on CentOS. The Tables 2 and 3 discusses the improvements in BMC time and memory usage for the property 1. Similarly Tables 4 and 5 discuss the results for the property 2. For property 1, we get a speed up of 11.44x in time. The reduction of memory usage is 2.34x. Moreover, it is important to note that the property 2 goes for BMC timeout (after running for more than 10 h) without waypoints (Table 4). Using waypoints it was completed in 215.9 s. Another set of results for property 2 is available in Table 5.

Table 2. Improvements in Bound, Time and Memory usage for property 1 (with BREQ FIFO size 2 and BROAD FIFO size 4)

Method		Bound	Time (s)	Memory (MB)	Bound (reduction)	Time (reduction)	Memory (reduction)
Without Waypoint		53	7947.6	365.28	0	1x	1x
With Way point	FIFO_Full	5	0.02	4.25	11	11.44x	2.34x
	BREQ FIFO to BROAD	38	515.6	49.45			
	BROAD FIFO to Final o/p	42	178.9	102.37			
	Total	42	694.52	156.07			

Comparison for Bound, Time and Memory usage is omitted in Table 4 since the Model checker goes for timeout (T.O.) for the case without waypoints, leaving us no data to compare against. This case strongly shows the benefits of

Table 3. Improvements in Bound, Time and Memory usage for property 1 (with BREQ FIFO size 2 and BROAD FIFO size 8)

Method		Bound	Time (s)	Memory (MB)	Bound (reduction)	Time (reduction)	Memory (reduction)
Without Waypoint		50	1370.4	151	0	1x	1x
With Way point	FIFO_Full	5	0.03	3.93	4	3.01x	0.81x
	BREQ FIFO to BROAD	40	249.3	124.58			
	BROAD FIFO to Final o/p	46	204.5	56.71			
	Total	46	453.83	185.22			

using waypoints as compared to the original model checking experiment (i.e., model checking without using waypoints). Note that the experimental results presented here consider only the model-checking time and not the time taken by the algorithm for the generation of waypoints. Also, the manual effort required in the proposed semi-automatic method of effective waypoint identification is not accounted for in these results.

Table 4. Improvements in Bound, Time and Memory usage for property 2 (with BREQ FIFO size 2 and BROAD FIFO size 4)

Method		Bound	Time (s)	Memory (MB)
Without Waypoint		T.O	T.O	-
With Way point	BREQ FIFO to BROAD	32	215.8	102.30
	BROAD FIFO to Final o/p	18	0.1	16.08
	Total	18	215.9	118.38

5   Related Work

The usage of semi-formal methods can ease out the challenges of state space exploration of the designs in many ways. One of them is generating high quality inputs used for functional verification. Plethora of work has been reported in this direction which utilize abstraction techniques in addition to guiding the random simulation-based state space search [3,4,12,14]. Similarly, supplying guidance assists in faster state space traversal also. Yang et al. [15] proposed the idea of

Table 5. Improvements in Bound, Time and Memory usage for property 2 (with BREQ FIFO size 2 and BROAD FIFO size 8)

Method		Bound	Time (s)	Memory (MB)	Bound (reduction)	Time (reduction)	Memory (reduction)
Without Waypoint		24	2	28.48	0	1x	1x
With Way point	BREQ FIFO to BROAD	13	0.4	14.77	6	3.33x	0.86x
	BROAD FIFO to Final o/p	18	0.2	18.12			
	Total	18	0.6	32.89			

a guidance based search strategy for invariant proving and bug finding. Typically, this scheme is highly successful in discovering subtle design bugs which are missed out by random or constrained-random simulation [5,7,10]. Various strategies for generation of guidance for a successful verification methodology based on semi-formal techniques are summarized in [2,7,16]. Abstraction is one of the most common ways to glean some hints which can assist in directed state space traversal. Techniques of abstraction are also useful for the minimization of the length of error traces. However, abstraction techniques are generally very useful for circuits dominated by data paths such as arithmetic circuits only. In this regard, guidance-based verification becomes essential for semi-formal/formal verification of circuits dominated by control paths. Note that abstraction can still be used in conjunction with guidance-based methodologies [5,7,8].

6   Conclusion

This paper proposed a methodology for identifying guidance hints, known as waypoints for better design debugging by model checking. With the help of waypoints, the state space traversal becomes faster leading to significant speed-up while property checking. With the proposed semi-automatic methodology for the identification of waypoints, we achieved significant speedup during counterexample generation. For large designs, a larger number of waypoints can significantly reduce the achievable gain in model checking time (i.e., CPU time). We are working on a simulation-based strategy which assists the Signal Dependency Graph-based analysis. The methodology involves generation of constrained-random simulation traces from the initial state to the first waypoint, from the first to second waypoint and so on. After careful analysis of these simulation traces, the subset of states corresponding to the intermediate waypoints can be identified automatically. Thus, we are actively pursuing full automation of the proposed effective guidance generation methodology. We are also looking at utilization of waypoints in fine-grained error localization at RTL abstraction of the design.

References

1. http://www.opencores.org/projects/mesi_isc
2. Choi, H., Yun, B.W., Lee, Y.T.: Simulation strategy after model checking: experience in industrial soc design. In: Proceedings IEEE International High-Level Design Validation and Test Workshop (Cat. No. PR00786), pp. 77–79, November 2000. https://doi.org/10.1109/HLDVT.2000.889563
3. De Paula, F.M., Hu, A.J.: An effective guidance strategy for abstraction-guided simulation. In: 2007 44th ACM/IEEE Design Automation Conference, pp. 63–68, June 2007
4. Fraer, R., Kamhi, G., Ziv, B., Vardi, M.Y., Fix, L.: Prioritized traversal: efficient reachability analysis for verification and falsification. In: Emerson, E.A., Sistla, A.P. (eds.) CAV 2000. LNCS, vol. 1855, pp. 389–402. Springer, Heidelberg (2000). https://doi.org/10.1007/10722167_30
5. Ganai, M.K., Aziz, A., Kuehlmann, A.: Enhancing simulation with BDDs and ATPG. In: Proceedings 1999 Design Automation Conference (Cat. No. 99CH36361), pp. 385–390, June 1999. https://doi.org/10.1109/DAC.1999.781346
6. Ho, C.R., et al.: Post-silicon debug using formal verification waypoints. In: DVCon (2009)
7. Nalla, P.K., Gajavelly, R.K., Baumgartner, J., Mony, H., Kanzelman, R., Ivrii, A.: The art of semi-formal bug hunting. In: 2016 IEEE/ACM International Conference on Computer-Aided Design (ICCAD), pp. 1–8, November 2016. https://doi.org/10.1145/2966986.2967079
8. Nanshi, K., Somenzi, F.: Guiding simulation with increasingly refined abstract traces. In: Proceedings of the 43rd Annual Design Automation Conference, DAC 2006, pp. 737–742. ACM, New York (2006). https://doi.org/10.1145/1146909.1147097
9. Papamarcos, M.S., Patel, J.H.: A low-overhead coherence solution for multiprocessors with private cache memories. In: Proceedings of the 11th Annual Symposium on Computer Architecture, Ann Arbor, USA, June 1984, pp. 348–354 (1984)
10. Ho, P., et al.: Smart simulation using collaborative formal and simulation engines. In: IEEE/ACM International Conference on Computer Aided Design. ICCAD - 2000, IEEE/ACM Digest of Technical Papers (Cat. No. 00CH37140), pp. 120–126, November 2000. https://doi.org/10.1109/ICCAD.2000.896461
11. Pong, F., Dubois, M.: The verification of cache coherence protocols. In: Proceedings of the Fifth Annual ACM Symposium on Parallel Algorithms and Architectures, SPAA 1993, pp. 11–20 (1993)
12. Shyam, S., Bertacco, V.: Distance-guided hybrid verification with GUIDO. In: Proceedings of the Design Automation Test in Europe Conference, vol. 1, pp. 1–6 (2006). https://doi.org/10.1109/DATE.2006.244050
13. Wolf, C.: Yosys open synthesis suite. http://www.clifford.at/yosys/
14. Yalagandula, P., Singhal, V., Aziz, A.: Automatic lighthouse generation for directed state space search. In: Proceedings Design, Automation and Test in Europe Conference and Exhibition 2000 (Cat. No. PR00537), pp. 237–242, March 2000. https://doi.org/10.1109/DATE.2000.840045
15. Yang, C.H., Dill, D.L.: Validation with guided search of the state space. In: Proceedings 1998 Design and Automation Conference, 35th DAC. (Cat. No. 98CH36175), pp. 599–604, June 1998. https://doi.org/10.1145/277044.277201
16. Yuan, J., Shen, J., Abraham, J., Aziz, A.: On combining formal and informal verification. In: Grumberg, O. (ed.) CAV 1997. LNCS, vol. 1254, pp. 376–387. Springer, Heidelberg (1997). https://doi.org/10.1007/3-540-63166-6_37

Comparative Analysis of Logic Gates Based on Spin Transfer Torque (STT) and Differential Spin Hall Effect (DSHE) Switching Mechanisms

Piyush Tankwal$^{(\boxtimes)}$ ⓘD, Vikas Nehra$^{(\boxtimes)}$ ⓘD,
and Brajesh Kumar Kaushik$^{(\boxtimes)}$ ⓘD

Department of Electronics and Communication Engineering, IIT Roorkee,
Roorkee 247667, India
{ptankwal, vnehra}@ec.iitr.ac.in, bkk23fec@iitr.ac.in

Abstract. Conventional complementary metal oxide semiconductor (CMOS) based memory and logic gates, has a major issue of large static power dissipation below 45-nm technology nodes. The most attractive property of CMOS technology was scalability. However, with continuous scaling short channel effects (SCEs) (like quantum mechanical tunneling, mobility degradation, hot carrier effects, drain induced barrier lowering) deteriorate the functionality of logic circuits. Hence, the researchers are looking for a possible substitute of conventional CMOS technology, as it is approaching towards its physical limit. The most promising substitute of the CMOS among the novel technologies is spintronics due to low power dissipation, non-volatility, high density, high endurance, and its easy integration with CMOS. There are two methods of switching: Spin Transfer Torque (STT) and Spin Hall Effect (SHE). This paper aims to analyze and compare the characteristics of hybrid CMOS/MTJ logic gates based on STT and Differential Spin Hall Effect (DSHE) magnetic random access memories (MRAMs). The logic gates based on STT-MRAM have certain limitations related to reliability and high write energy. The SPICE simulations using 45-nm standard CMOS design kit have been carried out to show that the power dissipation reduction is 95.6% in DSHE as compared to STT based logic gates. Moreover, write circuit for DSHE-MRAM consumes only 5.28 fJ energy per bit.

Keywords: Differential Spin Hall (DSH) MRAM ·
Magnetic Tunnel Junction (MTJ) · Spin Transfer Torque (STT)

1 Introduction

According to Moore's law, in the former few decades, CMOS technology has scaled rapidly [1]. However, CMOS technology approaches to its physical limit due to various issues such as short channel effects (SCEs), leakage power dissipation, and device reliability [2–4]. To mitigate these issues various emerging non-volatile technologies such as resistive random access memory (RRAM), phase-change RAM (PCRAM),

© Springer Nature Singapore Pte Ltd. 2019
A. Sengupta et al. (Eds.): VDAT 2019, CCIS 1066, pp. 428–441, 2019.
https://doi.org/10.1007/978-981-32-9767-8_36

spin transfer torque (STT)-MRAM were explored. Among these non-volatile memories alternatives, STT-MRAM is the most suitable candidate due to its non-volatility, high endurance, small on-chip area, and compatibility with CMOS fabrication [5].

The Magnetic Tunnel Junction (MTJ) is a most fundamental spin-based device that utilizes the quantum mechanical spin property of the charge carrier for storing the information. It contains three layers. Two of them are ferromagnetic (FM) layers namely free layer (FL) and pinned layer (PL) and one is insulating tunnel barrier implanted between ferromagnetic layers as shown Fig. 1.

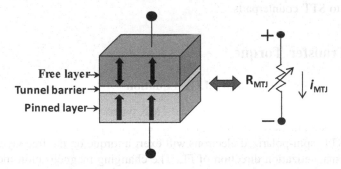

Fig. 1. Magnetic Tunnel Junction (MTJ).

The magnetization of PL is fixed due to high coercivity designed by using anti-ferromagnetic layers like FeMn or IrMn adjacent to ferromagnetic layer [6]. While, the magnetization of FL can be alter. The relative orientation of the magnetization of PL and FL is used to store logic '0' and logic '1' in the device. For parallel magnetization, resistance is low because tunneling probability is high as both FM layers have an equal density of states (DOS) for the up spin and down spin of electrons. On the other hand, anti-parallel magnetization resistance is high because tunneling probability is low for the up spin and down spin electrons in FM layers.

STT-MRAM cell have a MTJ and an access NMOS transistor as shown in Fig. 2 (a). STT and TMR are the two phenomenon that are used for writing and reading the bit

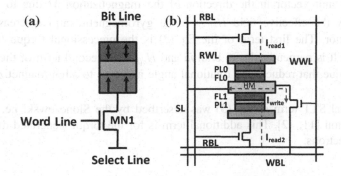

Fig. 2. (a) STT-MRAM cell, (b) DSHE-MRAM cell.

cell. However, STT-MRAM consumes high write energy and takes the large on-chip area due to transistor size of driver [7]. It limits the wide use of STT-MRAM for logic applications. In order to overcome the issue of high write energy DSHE based MRAM was proposed [8]. It provides an efficient switching mechanism by decoupling the read and write path. Owing to spin Hall effect (SHE), it is induced the spin current in the heavy metal (HM). It provides the more than 100% spin injection efficiency and low resistance track because of that it provides fast and efficient switching.

In the following paper, we have discussed the STT-MRAM, DSH-MRAM based memory cell, and logic gates. DSHE based logic gates are more energy efficient in comparison to STT counterparts.

2 Spin Transfer Torque

2.1 Spin Transfer Torque and LLGS Equation

STT phenomena is opposite to the GMR and TMR where conduction of electrons relies on the relative alignment of magnetization direction in ferromagnetic layers of MTJ. In the case of STT, spin-polarized electrons will exert a torque on the free layer (FL) that changes the magnetization direction of FL. The changing magnetization moment also affects the relative resistance of MTJ and is defined by a tunnel magnetoresistance (TMR) effect [9, 10], and can be expressed below:

$$TMR = \frac{R_{AP} - R_P}{R_P} \tag{1}$$

R_P and R_{AP} are the resistance of MTJ in case of parallel and the anti-parallel magnetization orientation respectively.

Landau-Lifshitz-Gilbert (LLG) equation as shown in Eq. 2.

$$\frac{\partial \vec{m}}{\partial t} = \underbrace{-|\gamma|(\vec{m} \times \vec{H}_{eff})}_{Precession} + \underbrace{\alpha \vec{m} \times \frac{\partial \vec{m}}{\partial t}}_{Damping} \tag{2}$$

$\vec{m}$ is the unit vector in the direction of the magnetization $\vec{M}$ due to the torque generated by the effective field $\vec{H}_{eff}$. γ is the gyromagnetic ratio whereas, α is the damping factor. The first term of the Eq. (2) is the precessional torque that rotates around $\vec{H}_{eff}$. It is perpendicular to both $\vec{m}$ and $\vec{H}_{eff}$. The second term of the Eq. (2) is damping torque that reduces the rotational angle and tries to align magnetization with $\vec{H}_{eff}$.

Additional STT term in Eq. (3) was described by the Slonczewski i.e. known as LLGS equation [11, 12]. This additional term is for the torque generated due to spin-polarized electrons.

$$\frac{\partial \vec{m}}{\partial t} = \underbrace{-|\gamma|(\vec{m} \times \vec{H}_{eff})}_{Pr\,ecession} + \underbrace{\alpha \vec{m} \times \frac{\partial \vec{m}}{\partial t}}_{Dampimg} + \overrightarrow{STT} \tag{3}$$

$$\overrightarrow{STT} = |\gamma|\beta(\underbrace{\hat{m} \times \varepsilon \hat{m} \times \hat{m}_p}_{1} + \underbrace{\varepsilon' \hat{m} \times \hat{m}_p}_{2}) \tag{4}$$

The first term in STT Eq. (4) is in-plane spin torque that is similar to the damping torque. This torque is due to the interaction of injected spin-polarized electrons and bounded electrons in the ferromagnetic layer. The second term denotes the exchange interaction between ferromagnetic layers termed as 'field-like' spin torque. It is perpendicular to both the layers. In most of the cases, the value of field like torque is neglected.

2.2 Comparison Between Write Circuit for STT and DSHE MRAM

The STT-MRAM based circuits utilize four NMOS transistors for write logic into the MTJs [11]. While the DSHE circuits use only two NMOS transistors as shown in Fig. 3.

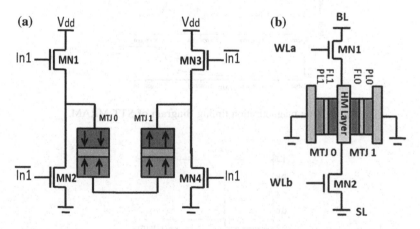

Fig. 3. (a) Write circuit of STT MRAM, (b) Write circuit of DSHE-MRAM.

In STT, when $In1$ is high the current is flowing in the direction of MTJ0 to MTJ1 as result of that logic '0' write in MTJ0 and logic '1' write in MTJ1. Conversely when $\overline{In1}$ is high current start flowing in the opposite direction and as a result logic '1' write in MTJ0 and logic '0' write in MTJ1. In DSH-MRAM, WL_b is always high for both reading and writing operations, while WL_a is set high for the period of a writing operation. A write voltage (V_{BL} or V_{SL}) of 0.4 V with 300 ps pulse width is used to change the free layer magnetization of MTJ0 and MTJ1. The logic state of MTJs is governs by the voltage on SL and BL terminal.

The STT-MRAM write circuit contributes significantly in the overall power calculation. DSH-MRAM based design overcomes this drawback by the using low value of write voltage (0.4 V) and narrow pulse width (300 ps) for switching. Energy

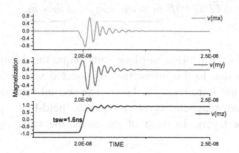

Fig. 4. Magnetization timing diagram of DSHE-MRAM.

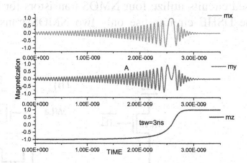

Fig. 5. The magnetization timing diagram of STT-MRAM.

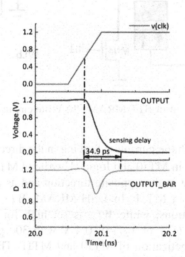

Fig. 6. Sensing delay of DSHE based (Pre-charge amplifier) PCSA.

consumed per bit by the write circuit of STT-MRAM is 115.7 fJ [13] whereas, DSHE-MRAM write circuit consumed 5.28 fJ, that is comparatively lower than the energy consumption of STT-MRAM write circuit. The consumption of power in the area efficient write circuit of DSHE shown in Fig. 3(b) is almost negligible. Low write voltage (0.4 V) and ultra-fast switching as shown in Fig. 4 foster the efficient working of the logic circuits based on DSHE-MRAM at lower supply voltages. Whereas, high write voltage (1.5 V) in conventional STT-MRAM bound its working at a low supply voltage as shown in Figs. 5 and 6.

2.3   STT-MRAM Based Logic Gates

The hybrid CMOS/MTJ circuits have four parts. The pre-charge sense amplifier (PCSA) for evaluating the complementary outputs. The combination of NMOS transistors used to get the desired output. Write circuit is used to write a particular bit among the pair of MTJs. Pair of MTJs to store the non-volatile complementary bits. Read and write current works in alternate clock cycles. Circuit configuration of hybrid MTJ/CMOS for Buffer/NOT the gate is shown in Fig. 7. It works in two phases: precharge and evaluation phase. B and $\overline{B}$ are the nonvolatile inputs realized using complementary MTJs. For the duration of the precharge phase (clk = 0), both the outputs will remain at the high logic level. Outputs are evaluated during the evaluation phase (clk = 1) based on the inputs. In MTJ device high resistance state (R_{AP}) of MTJs is considered as logic low '0' (antiparallel state of magnetization) and low resistance state (R_P) as logic high '1' (parallel state of magnetization).

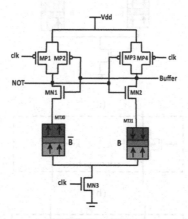

Fig. 7. STT-MRAM based Buffer/NOT gate.

The simulation result of Buffer/NOT circuit realized using hybrid MTJ/CMOS is shown in Fig. 8. For the input state 0, the resistance value of the right branch is lesser value than the left branch. Hence, output *NOT* remains at a high logic level while the output *Buffer* is discharged through MN2 and MTJ1. In the case of input state 1, the resistance value of the right branch is higher value than the left branch so the output *Buffer* remains at a high logic level while *NOT* is discharged through MN1 and MTJ0.

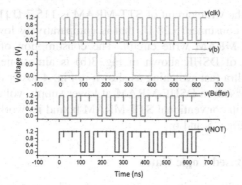

Fig. 8. Simulation results of STT-MRAM based Buffer/NOT gate.

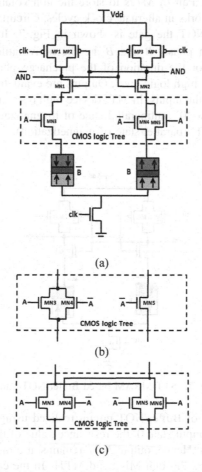

Fig. 9. STT-MRAM based logic circuits (a) AND gate, (b) OR gate, (c) EXOR gate.

AND/NAND circuit realized using hybrid MTJ/CMOS is shown in Fig. 9(a). When volatile input *A* is at logic low '0', NMOS transistors MN3 and MN5 will be in OFF mode. Hence, the left branch will be an open circuit resulting in no discharge path through the right branch. Therefore, the output *AND* will be connected to the ground through MN2 and MN4 transistors. For input combinations '10' and '11', outputs will depend on the resistance state of nonvolatile inputs through MTJ. For input combination 10 current will pass through both the branches as MN3 and MN5 both are ON. The resistance value of the right branch is lesser than that of the left branch. Hence, the output *AND* node will be discharged to ground and output $\overline{AND}$ will remain at a high logic level. Similarly, during 11 input state resistance value of the right branch will be higher than that of the left one. Hence, the output *AND* will remain at a high logic level while $\overline{AND}$ will be connected to ground through MN1 and MN3 transistors (Fig. 10).

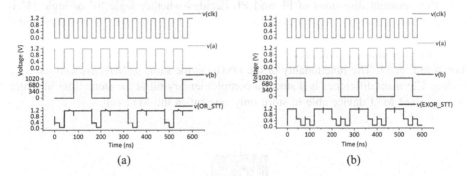

Fig. 10. Simulation results of STT-MRAM based (a) OR gate, (b) EXOR gate.

OR/NOR circuit realized using hybrid MTJ/CMOS is shown in Fig. 9(b). For the input state, 00 resistance value of the left branch is higher than the right branch. Hence, output $\overline{OR}$ remains at a high logic level while the output *OR* is discharged through MN2 and MN5 NMOS transistor. In the case of 01, the resistance of the right branch is higher than the left branch so the output *OR* remains at a high logic level while $\overline{OR}$ is discharged through MN1 and MN4 NMOS transistor. During 10 and 11 input state NMOS transistor, MN5 will be in OFF mode and the hence right branch will open circuit So Output *OR* will remain at the high logic level.

EXOR/EXNOR circuit realized using hybrid MTJ/CMOS is shown in Fig. 9(c). NMOS transistor MN4 and MN6 constitute the left branch while the right branch consists of MN5 and MN3 transistors. For the duration of the evaluation phase (clk = 1), the output *EXOR* will be discharged as the resistance value of the right branch is smaller than the left branch for 00 and 11 state.

Similarly, for input combinations, 01 and 10 output $\overline{EXOR}$ will be discharged because the resistance value of the left branch is smaller than a right branch.

3 Differential Spin Hall Effect (DSHE)

In two terminal MTJ, when STT is used as a switching mechanism has some draw-backs. It requires high write energy and there is also the possibility of oxide breakdown due to high current. To diminish these effects, SHE is used as a switching mechanism. The basic structure of SHE based MTJ has Hall metal (HM) plate with MTJ.

It uses STT+SHE both as a switching mechanism. The write energy for SHE+STT MRAM is lower in comparison to the STT-MRAM. When writing current start flowing into the HM because of that the spin current generates in the opposite direction of the charge current and electrons spin start splitting, up spin start moving in an upward direction and down spin start moving in a downward direction.

The reason of this splitting of the spins is the spin Hall effect (SHE). As the electron exerts the force the magnetization moment of the FL layer is changed. These mag-netization moment directions of FL and PL decides whether logic '0' or logic '1' is stored. If magnetization moment direction is parallel it means logic '0' is stored and if magnetization moment direction is anti-parallel it means logic '1' is stored.

The four terminal device DSHE consists of HM layered in between two PMTJs as shown in Fig. 11. The functionality of the DSHE is the same as SHE assisted the MTJ device. The main difference is it stores a complementary bit at the same time in which SHE assisted MTJ device able to store only one bit in the MTJ cell.

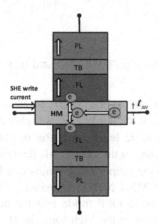

Fig. 11. DSHE Structure.

3.1 DSHE Based Basic Logic Gates

Circuit configuration of hybrid MTJ/CMOS for Buffer/NOT the gate is shown in Fig. 12.

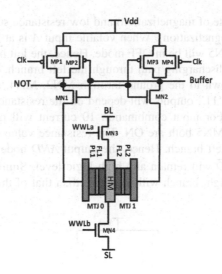

Fig. 12. DSHE-MRAM based Buffer/NOT gate.

For the input state 0, the resistance value of the right branch is lesser than the left branch. Hence, output *NOT* remains at a high logic level while the output *Buffer* is discharged through MN2 and MTJ1. In the case of state 1, the resistance value of the right branch is higher than the left branch so the output *Buffer* remains at a high logic level while *NOT* is discharged through MN1 and MTJ0 (Fig. 13).

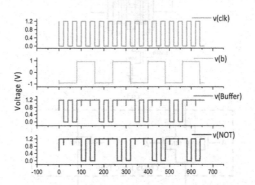

Fig. 13. Simulation results of (a) DSHE-MRAM based Buffer/NOT gate.

Circuit configuration of hybrid MTJ/CMOS for AND/NAND the gate is shown in Fig. 14(a). It works in two phases Precharge phase and Evaluation phase.*B* and $\bar{B}$ are the nonvolatile inputs realized using complementary MTJs using the DSHE mechanism. For the duration of the precharge phase (clk = 0), both the outputs will remain at the high logic level. Outputs are evaluated during the evaluation phase (clk = 1) based on the inputs. In MTJ device high resistance state (R_{AP}) of MTJs is considered as logic low '0' (antiparallel state of magnetization) and low resistance state (R_P) as logic high '1' (parallel state of magnetization). When volatile input A is at logic low '0', NMOS transistors MN3 and MN5 will be in OFF mode. Hence, the left branch will be an open circuit resulting in no discharging path through the left branch. Therefore, the output AND will be pulled down to the ground through MN2, MN4, and MTJ1. For input combinations '10' and '11', outputs will depend on the resistance state of nonvolatile inputs through MTJs. For input combination 10 current will pass through both the branches as MN3 and MN5 both are ON. The resistance value of the right branch is lesser than that of the left branch. Hence, the output AND node will be connected to ground and output $\overline{AND}$ will remain at a high logic level. Similarly, during 11 input state resistance of the right branch will be higher than that of the left one. Hence, the

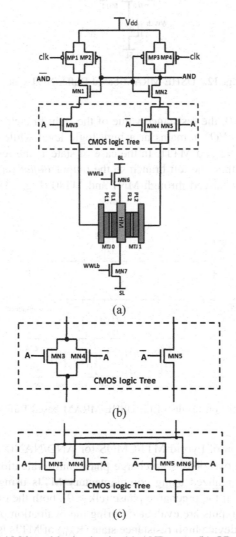

Fig. 14. DSHE-MRAM based logic circuits (a) AND gate, (b) OR gate, (c) EXOR gate.

output *AND* will remain at a high logic level while $\overline{AND}$ will be connected to ground through MN1, MN3, and MTJ0.

Similarly, OR/NOR, EXOR/EXNOR circuit realized by hybrid MTJ/CMOS using DSHE mechanism is represent in Fig. 14(b), (c).

4 Simulation Results and Model Parameters

The simulations are performed with HSPICE using 45-nm standard CMOS design kit at 1.2 V supply voltage and Verilog –A models of STT-MRAM [13] and DSHE-MRAM [14]. Device parameters for STT and DSHE-MRAM are represent in Tables 1 and 2 (Fig. 15).

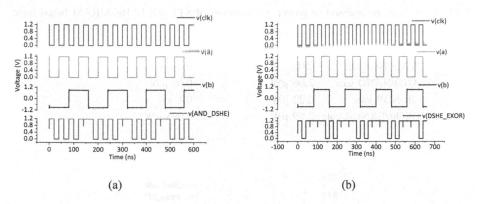

(a)   (b)

Fig. 15. Simulation results of DSHE-MRAM based (a) AND gate, (b) EXOR gate.

Table 1. STT-MRAM device parameters

Parameters	Value
MTJ surface area (nm^2)	40×40
Oxide barrier thickness (nm)	0.85
Free layer thickness (nm)	1.3
MTJ resistance (KΩ)	3.9(P), 7.9(AP)
Write voltage (V)	1.5
CMOS technology	45 nm

The simulations are performed by varying the power supply (Vdd) from 0.6 V to 1.4 V of the pre-charge sense amplifier (PCSA) based on STT and DSHE-MRAM. The simulations result shows delay is inversely proportional to Vdd and delay is more in case of STT in comparison of DSHE as shown in Fig. 16 (Table 3).

Table 2. DSHE-MRAM device parameters

Parameters	Value
Heavy metal volume (nm³)	50x40x3
Heavy metal resistance (Ω)	833
MTJ surface area (nm²)	40x40
Oxide barrier thickness (nm)	0.85
Free layer thickness (nm)	1.3
MTJ resistance (KΩ)	6.14(P), 14.1(AP)
Write voltage (V)	0.4
CMOS technology	45 nm

Table 3. Relative comparison of power consumption of STT and DSHE-MRAM based logic gates at 1.2 V

Basic logic gates	Based on STT-MRAM	Based on DSHE-MRAM
Buffer/Not gate	2.02 μW	0.092 μW
AND/NAND gate	2.06 μW	0.09 μW
OR/NOR gate	2.22 μW	0.1 μW
EXOR/EXNOR gate	2.69 μW	0.093 μW

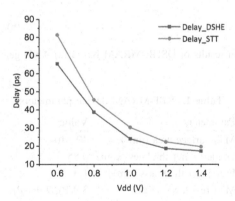

Fig. 16. Variation in the delay of DSHE and STT-MRAM based PCSA with power supply

5 Conclusions

The STT-MRAM and DSHE-MRAM are the most prominent candidates to replace MOSFET technology in the future. In this paper, we compare STT-MRAM and DSHE-MRAM based basic logic gates. The simulation results have shown that DSHE-MRAM has dissipated less power in comparsion to STT-MRAM based basic logic gates. Moreover, less write voltage is required in DSHE based logic circuits. The DSHE based circuits are very fast as they take comparatively less writing time. Hence, the DSHE-MRAM based circuits are more reliable and power efficient than STT-MRAM logic circuits.

References

1. Auth, C., et al.: A 22 nm high performance and low-power CMOS technology featuring fully-depleted tri-gate transistors, self-aligned contacts and high density MIM capacitors. In: IEEE Symposium on VLSI Technology, pp. 131–132 (2012)
2. Kim, N.S., et al.: Leakage current: Moore's law meets static power. IEEE Comput. **36**(12), 68–75 (2003)
3. Roy, K., Mukhopadhyay, S., Mahmoodi-Meimand, H.: Leakage current mechanisms and leakage reduction techniques in deep-submicrometer CMOS circuits. Proc. IEEE **91**(2), 305–327 (2003)
4. Young, K.K.: Short-channel effect in fully depleted SOI MOSFET's. IEEE Trans. Electron Devices **36**(2), 399–402 (1989)
5. Endoh, T., Koike, H., Ikeda, S., Hanyu, T., Ohno, H.: An overview of nonvolatile emerging memories-spintronics for working memories. IEEE J. Emerg. Sel. Top. Circuits Syst. **6**(2), 109–119 (2016)
6. Tang, D.D., Lee, Y.J.: Magnetic Memory Fundamentals and Technology, 1st edn. Cambridge University Press, Cambridge (2010). chap. 3–6
7. Oboril, F., Bishnoi, R., Ebrahimi, M., Tahoori, M.B.: Evaluation of hybrid memory technologies using SOT-MRAM for on-chip cache hierarchy. IEEE Trans. Comput.-Aided Des. Integr. Circuits Syst. **34**(3), 367–380 (2015)
8. Liu, L., Pai, C.F., Li, Y., Tseng, H.W., Ralph, D.C., Buhrman, R.A.: Spin-torque switching with the giant spin Hall effect of tantalum. Science **336**(6081), 555–558 (2012)
9. Ikeda, S., Hayakawa, J., Lee, Y.M., Matsukura, F., Ohno, Y.: Magnetic tunnel junction for spintronic memories and beyond. IEEE Trans. Electron Devices **54**(5), 991–1002 (2007)
10. Dorrance, R.: Modelling and design of STT-MRAM. M.S. thesis, Department of Electrical Engineering, University of California, Los Angeles (2011)
11. Gilbert, T.L.: A Lagrangian formulation of the gyromagnetic equation of the magnetization field. Phys. Rev. **100**, 1243 (1955)
12. Beaujour, J.-M.L., Bedau, D.B., Liu, H., Rogosky, M.R., Kent, A.D.: Spin-transfer in nanopillars with a perpendicularly magnetized spin polarizer. In: SPIE Proceedings, vol. 7398, p. 73980D
13. Deng, E., Zhang, Y., Klein, J.O., Ravelosona, D., Chappert, C., Zhao, W.: Low power magnetic full-adder based on spin transfer torque MRAM. IEEE Trans. Magn. **49**(9), 4982–4987 (2013)
14. Prajapati, S., Zilic, Z., Kaushik, B.K.: Area and energy efficient magnetic full adder based on differential spin hall MRAM. In: 16th IEEE International New Circuits and Systems Conference, NEWCAS 2018, Montreal, QC, Canada, pp. 317–321 (2018)

Multi-application Based Fault-Tolerant Network-on-Chip Design for Mesh Topology Using Reconfigurable Architecture

P. Veda Bhanu[1]([envelope])[ID], Pranav V. Kulkarni[1], Sai Pranavi Avadhanam[1],
J. Soumya[1], and Linga Reddy Cenkeramaddi[2]

[1] BITS-Pilani, Hyderabad Campus, Hyderabad 500078, Telangana, India
vedabhanuiit2010@gmail.com, kulkarni.pranav2@gmail.com,
pranavi11196@gmail.com, soumyatkgp@gmail.com
[2] University of Agder, Jon Lilletuns vei 3, 4879 Grimstad, Norway
linga.cenkeramaddi@uia.no

Abstract. In this paper, we propose a two-step fault-tolerant approach to address the faults occurred in cores. In the first stage, a Particle Swarm Optimization (PSO) based approach has been proposed for the fault-tolerant mapping of multiple applications on to the mesh based reconfigurable architecture by introducing spare cores and a heuristic has been proposed for the reconfiguration in the second stage. The proposed approach has been experimented by taking several benchmark applications into consideration. Communication cost comparisons have been carried out by taking the failed cores as user input and the experimental results show that our approach could get improvements in terms of communication cost after reconfiguration compared to before reconfiguration by providing fault-tolerance to the design.

Keywords: Mesh · Reconfiguration · Particle swarm optimization · Multi-application · Network-on-chip · Fault-tolerance

1 Introduction

Recent developments in the technology have led to shrink in the size of a chip. With increased application requirements, more number of IP cores are stacked on to a single chip, and the communication between them is highly challenging [6]. In a System-on-Chip (SoC) the communication between different IP cores is based on bus architecture [10] and they do not scale well with huge communication bandwidth requirements between the IP cores. To satisfy the current application requirements and to address the communication challenges, Network-on-Chip (NoC) has been proposed [4]. NoC mainly consists of three

This work is partially supported by the research project No. ECR/2016/001389 Dt. 06/03/2017, sponsored by the SERB, Government of India.

components Network Interface (NI), Routers or Switches and Interconnection links. The communication in NoC is achieved through packets using routers via links [2]. In the deep sub-micron level NoCs are prone to faults [15]. Faults can be categorized as Permanent, Intermittent and Transient. Permanent faults can be of logic faults, delay faults caused by the transistors or wires which are permanently open or short. The temporary interferences like voltage noise, EMI and cross talk can lead to Transient faults. Due to marginal or unstable hardware intermittent faults can occur at any component level in NoC which can affect the system performance and reliability [3]. Hence, there is a need to develop efficient fault-tolerant techniques which can address the faults. NoCs are designed to run single application at a time. In the multi-application environment, generic NoC fails to meet the requirements of other applications. Hence, reconfiguration is essential at the architecture level where NoC can cater the requirements of different applications.

In this paper, we propose a fault-tolerant methodology for mesh based reconfigurable NoC architecture while considering permanent faults in cores. Faults in the interconnection links and routers are considered as extension to our work. We have assumed that each core can have one router connected to it and failed cores are taken as input from the user. Spare cores are introduced at suitable positions in the architecture to take care of the communications associated with the failed cores. Our proposed approach works in two stages. In the first stage, a Combined Core Graph (CCG) is formed by considering multiple applications, and its mapping (including spare core) on to reconfigurable mesh network is performed using Particle Swarm Optimization (PSO). In the second stage, reconfiguration of cores (including spare core) is done using iterative heuristic such that the communication cost [12] is minimized. The reconfiguration is achieved using multiplexers by changing the connections between the cores and routers available in mesh network. According to the input application requirements, the core positions in the mesh network are changed using the multiplexers in an architecture. The reconfiguration stage is independent of first stage and thus it can be combined with any mapping algorithm reported in the literature. The rest of the paper is organized as follows. Section 2 describes literature survey. Section 3 gives brief overview of the reconfiguration architecture. Section 4 details about PSO approach and iterative heuristic. Section 5 discusses the experimental results. Section 6 concludes the paper.

2 Literature Survey

The efficient design of NoC architectures depends on mapping of the applications and routing techniques deployed. In case of multi-application mapping, it is important to make the chip reconfigurable to improve the efficiency. Since the efficient mapping of one application may not result in improvement for other applications. There have been many works reported in the literature which have explored the concept of reconfigurability. In [13], they have proposed Reconfigurable NoC architecture (ReNoC) that enables the topology to be reconfigured using topology switches. In [8], they have proposed a NoC architecture which tailors its topology according to the traffic of the input application. This reconfiguration has been done by changing the inter-router connections. Another work [11] proposes a run-time reconfigurable NoC which can dynamically create/delete links with a limited area overhead. This reconfiguration has been achieved through partial dynamic reconfiguration capabilities of the FPGAs. In [9], uDIREC technique has been proposed for fault diagnosis and reconfiguration. In this technique, reconfiguration has been implemented by 2 ways i.e., software and hardware based design. Both these implementations have been compared with respect to the complexity involved and the time taken for execution. The work reported in [14] has virtually divided the NoC network into different partitions wherein each partition serves a specific application and traffic flow. The reconfiguration is achieved by dynamic allocation of resources to different partitions according to the applications needs. The work reported in [1] presents a reconfigurable NoC based on mesh topology. The reconfigurability has been achieved with the help of multiplexers through which the connections between the cores and the routers can be changed. Most of works reported in the literature have not focused on the permanent faults that may occur in the application cores, whereas in our work permanent faults in cores have been addressed by introducing spare cores using PSO and reconfiguration is achieved using heuristic. This adds robustness to our system and makes the system reliable.

3   Design Methodology

In this section we present basic reconfigurable NoC architecture used and design flow followed in our approach.

3.1   Reconfigurable NoC Architecture

The reconfiguration methodology used in our approach is based on the architecture proposed in [1]. It is a mesh based architecture where different cores are connected to routers via multiplexers. The interconnections between the routers, routing algorithm utilized remains the same as that of [1]. The work reported in [13] have used switches for reconfiguration while the architecture reported in [1] have used multiplexers for the reconfiguration. Figure 1 shows fault-tolerant reconfigurable architecture for 4×4 mesh topology used in our approach.

From Fig. 1, it is evident that to accommodate a single spare core, there should exist at least one available router in the mesh network. Similarly, for n spare cores there should exist at least n available routers in the mesh network for mapping. Since the failed core is taken as input from the user, for n failed cores there will be n spare cores placed in efficient positions using the proposed approach. According to the number of spare cores to be placed, the size of the reconfigurable architecture varies. With reference to the standard mesh topology, each router contains maximum of four global ports to connect to four neighbor routers and one local port to connect to one core via multiplexer. The multiplexers allow the changes in the connections between the cores and routers.

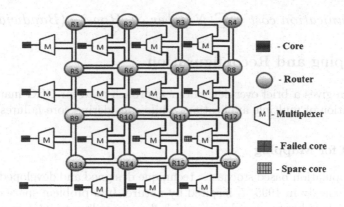

Fig. 1. 4×4 mesh based fault-tolerant reconfigurable NoC architecture

These connections are changed using the proposed heuristic for minimizing the communication cost according to the input applications.

3.2   Design Flow

The design flow followed in our approach is shown in Fig. 2. Our approach takes the inputs as multiple application core graphs, failed cores and performs the mapping and reconfiguration in two stages. First stage performs CCG mapping with spare core using PSO and in the second stage, reconfiguration is performed using the proposed heuristic, explained in Sect. 4.2. The communication cost is defined as the multiplication of number of hops and communication bandwidth between the source and destination cores after mapping onto routers in the given mesh topology.

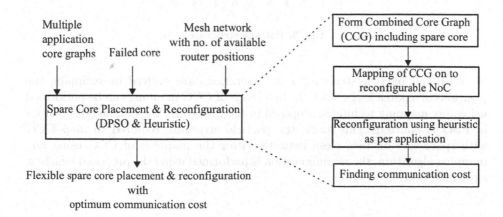

Fig. 2. Design flow followed in our approach

$$Communication\ cost = \sum(Number\ of\ Hops) * (Bandwidth) \quad (1)$$

4   Mapping and Reconfiguration

This section gives a brief overview of our approach used for CCG mapping and reconfiguration of multiple applications while considering core failures.

4.1   PSO for Mapping

PSO is a population based stochastic technique designed and developed by Eberhart and Kennedy in 1995 [7] inspired by nature. In a problem space each individual particle is known as solution which flies according to its own experience and as well as its neighboring particles. Each particle has a fitness value which determines its quality. Using Discrete PSO (DPSO) formulation proposed in [1], we have extended it to mapping of CCG onto the reconfigurable NoC architecture by including the spare cores. We have modified the particle structure defined in [1] to include spare cores, the rest of the process followed in our approach is same as that of [1].

Particle is an array of number of cores available in the CCG with an additional entry for the spare core. The contents of the array represent core number and the index of the array represents the router number in architecture. For a CCG of nine number of cores, the length of the particle will be ten, if we assume that there is a single spare core for the failed core. Depending on the number of failed cores, the length of the particle is extended to accommodate more number of spare cores. An example particle structure is shown in Fig. 3 for a CCG of nine cores and a single spare core.

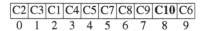

C2	C3	C1	C4	C5	C7	C8	C9	**C10**	C6
0	1	2	3	4	5	6	7	8	9

Fig. 3. Particle structure

With this particle structure, new generations are evolved by swapping the positions of a particle [1]. Since the first stage of CCG mapping can be performed using any mapping technique proposed in the literature, the detailed discussions of PSO is omitted. This forms the particle structure required to map CCG with spare core on to a mesh network. After the mapping of CCG using any mapping algorithm, the reconfiguration is performed using the proposed heuristic explained next.

Algorithm 1. Reconfiguration Heuristic

    Input: Combined core graph mapping including spare core
    Output: Reconfigured mapping with spare core

1 **Begin**
2 **for** *Each application core graph (includes spare core)* $G_i = (C_i, E_i)$ *of* A_i **do**
3   **Begin**
4   Mark all cores of C_i as unlocked for *Each edge (e)* $= (C_s^a, C_d^b)$ ϵ E **do**
5   **Begin**
6   Communication cost of edge *(e)* = Bandwidth(*e*) * Hop distance
        between the routers *a* and *b* to cores C_s^a and C_d^b are mapped

7   Sort all edges in E_i as a decreasing order of communication cost **for** *each*
     edge $e = (C_s^a, C_d^b)$ ϵ E *taken in the decreasing order* **do**
8   **Begin**
9   **if** C_s^a *and* C_d^b *are both locked* **then**
10   continue with next edge
11   **if** C_s^a *and* C_d^b *mapped to same router* **then**
12   Mark both cores are locked
13   **else**
14   **Begin if** C_s^a *is unlocked* **then**
15   **Begin**
16   Find the position of candidate with minimum cost of C_s^a
17   MPos = Position of candidate with minimum cost of *e*
18   Mapping of C_s^a to MPos
19   Lock core C_s^a
20   **if** C_d^b *is unlocked* **then**
21   **Begin**
22   Find the position of candidate with minimum cost of C_d^b
23   MPos = Position of candidate with minimum cost of *e*
24   Mapping of C_d^b to MPos
25   Lock core C_d^b

4.2   Reconfiguration Heuristic

In this section we present the proposed heuristic which performs the reconfiguration. CCG mapping from the first stage is taken as input to the heuristic. It picks up each application in CCG and does reconfiguration. For an application A_i the core graph is represented as $G_i = (C_i, E_i)$ where C_i represents the core number and E_i represents the respective edge. From the mapping information of the first stage, it computes the communication cost of an application by using the Eq. 1 and notes the position of the cores. Before invoking the heuristic, all the cores of an application are unlocked, meaning they are free to move from one router to other router with the flexibility provided by the multiplexers.

The edges E_i of the application are sorted in the decreasing order of the communication cost. The edge with highest communication cost (first edge in the order) is taken and the corresponding core positions are checked whether they are locked or not. If two cores corresponding to a single edge are locked then it continues for the next edge. If both cores pertaining to single edge are mapped to same router then mark the two cores as locked and continue for the next edge. If the source and destination core of the edge are unlocked, then source core is moved to the best position by changing the connection between routers using multiplexers. Similarly, if the destination core is unlocked then move to the best possible position using multiplexers and then mark the cores as locked. Moving to a better position with in the neighbouring router positions may result in decrease in the communication cost. Similarly, cores associated with remaining edges in the application are taken to lock their position. Once reconfiguration of one application is completed, remaining applications are taken, and the reconfiguration is performed using the same procedure. The proposed heuristic is presented in Algorithm 1.

5   Experimental Results

In this section we present the results obtained by applying our approach on various application benchmarks reported in the literature [12] and synthetic benchmarks generated using TGFF tool [5]. Since there are no approaches reported in the literature to compare with our approach, therefore we compared our approach in terms of communication cost obtained before reconfiguration and after reconfiguration. We have used high level language to generate a code for PSO and heuristics. The techniques have been implemented on a PC with Intel Xeon processor operating at 3.5 GHz having 32 GB internal memory. The results are organized as follows. Section 5.1 shows the comparison of communication cost in case of failed core common to all input applications. Section 5.2 shows the comparison of communication cost in case of failed core is common to few of the applications. Section 5.3 describes the case failed cores are in one application.

5.1   Failed Cores Are Common to Multiple Applications

In this section we present our results by considering the failed core is common to given input applications. Tables 1 and 2 shows the communication cost for the single failed core and multiple failed cores which are common to multiple applications respectively. As we can observe from Table 1, for multiple applications there is an improvement in terms of communication cost after reconfiguration. For multiple applications like MPEG+MWD the total number of cores in fault-free case are 21. In case of single core failure, a spare core is added to combined core graph. Therefore the number of cores has been increased to 22. The global communication cost for MPEG+MWD is 17391. Since MEM1 core is failed, a spare core having the functionality of MEM1 has been added to the design. MEM1 is common to both MPEG and MWD applications, therefore an improvement of 11.93% and 11.11% in communication cost has been achieved after reconfiguration respectively. This shows that our approach provides flexibility in placing the spare core in the CCG and reconfigured according to application requirement. Similarly, this can be applied to other applications reported in Table 1. On an average we have achieved an 11.31% improvement after reconfiguration.

Table 1. Communication cost with failed core common to different applications

Application	Cores	Faulty core	B.R[a]	A.R[b]	% Improvement
MPEG(MPEG+MWD)	22	Mem1	13935	12272	11.93
MWD(MPEG+MWD)	22	Mem1	3456	3072	11.11
MP3Enc(MP3+263Enc+263Dec)	30	Bitres1	58.41	47.59	18.52
263Enc(MP3+263Enc+263Dec)	30	Bitres1	488.88	450.86	7.77
263Dec(MP3+263Enc+263Dec)	30	Bitres1	107.96	96.19	10.89
G_1(G_1+G_2+G_3)	37	T0	90194.48	83852.81	7.03
G_2(G_1+G_2+G_3)	37	T0	38970.49	34646.07	11.09
G_3(G_1+G_2+G_3)	37	T0	30762.33	25283.45	17.81
G_1(G_1+G_4)	40	T0	77017.61	00954.49	11.50
G_4(G_1+G_4)	40	T0	189432.77	178961.01	5.52
				Average Improvement	11.31%

[a]Before Reconfiguration, [b]After Reconfiguration

As we can observe from Table 2, for two core failures the number of cores in the CCG have been increased by 2 (two spare cores are added to the design during CCG mapping stage). The average improvement in communication cost for two core failures is higher compared to single core failure. For MPEG+MWD application with MEM1, MEM2 as common cores failed, the improvement in terms of communication cost after reconfiguration is 12.78% and 6.13%. Similarly, we can see improvement in each application after reconfiguration. This is due to the efficient placement of spare cores using our approach. This shows that scalability of our approach while providing the improvement in communication cost after reconfiguration. Next we look into the case where failed core is common to few of the input applications.

5.2   Failed Cores Are Common to Few of the Input Applications

In this section experiment has been carried out by considering the failed core is common to few of the input applications. We have considered same set of benchmark applications reported in Tables 1 and 2. Due to page limit constraint we are not able to provide complete results for all applications. For one set of the input applications generated using TGFF tool [5] (G1+G2+G3), communication cost has been calculated. Figure 4 shows the failed cores are common to two of the three applications G1, G2, and G3.

In Fig. 4, first set of three applications show that two failed cores are common to G1 and G2 where as G3 is fault-free. In the next set of three applications, G2 and G3 are having two failed cores in common while G1 is fault-free. Similarly for the next set of three applications, G1 and G3 are having two failed cores

Table 2. Communication cost with multiple failed cores which are common to different applications

Application	Cores	Faulty core	B.R[a]	A.R[b]	% Improvement
MPEG(MPEG+MWD)	23	Mem1, Mem2	14985	13069	12.78
MWD(MPEG+MWD)	23	Mem1, Mem2	5216	4896	6.13
MP3Enc(MP3+263Enc+263Dec)	31	Bitres1, Bitres2	62.43	51.11	18.13
263Enc(MP3+263Enc+263Dec)	31	Bitres1, Bitres2	527.33	447.65	15.11
263Dec(MP3+263Enc+263Dec)	31	Bitres1, Bitres2	141.97	115.88	18.37
G_1(G_1+G_2+G_3)	38	T0, T2	91970.80	80145.89	12.85
G_2(G_1+G_2+G_3)	38	T0, T2	34439.28	28810.42	16.34
G_3(G_1+G_2+G_3)	38	T0, T2	29923.31	27806.83	7.07
G_1(G_1+G_4)	41	T0, T1	90708.20	78942.64	12.97
G_4(G_1+G_4)	41	T0, T1	218422.87	207951.10	4.79
				Average Improvement	**12.45%**

[a]Before Reconfiguration, [b]After Reconfiguration

in common while G2 is fault-free. We can observe from Fig. 4, our approach is providing the improvement in communication cost after reconfiguration in all the cases with faulty and fault-free applications. This shows the applicability of our approach to different core failures in multi-application environment. Next we look into failed cores present in one of the input applications.

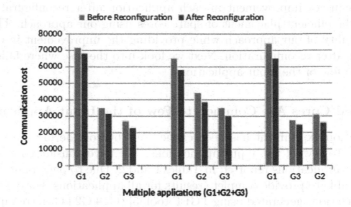

Fig. 4. Failed cores common to two applications

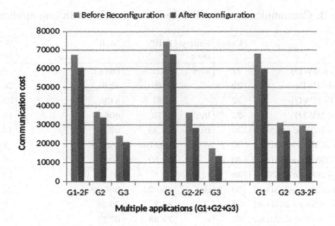

Fig. 5. Failed core is in one application

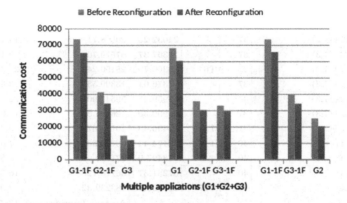

Fig. 6. Multiple core failures in two of the three input applications

5.3   Failed Cores Present in One Application

In this section we have experimented with the failed cores present in one application. We have considered the same set of applications used in Tables 1 and 2. We have assumed one failed core which is unique and not common to the given applications. Table 3 shows the comparison of the communication cost before and after reconfiguration. As we can observe from the Table 3, the average improvement we could achieve is 13.56% after reconfiguration. This is due to reconfiguration of an application by placing the spare cores in best suitable position.

Figure 5 shows the results of the communication cost for multiple core failures in one application. In this case the core failures are not common and unique to each application. For the set of three applications G1+G2+G3, in first case we have assumed two cores are failed in G1 while G2 and G3 are fault-free. In the second case we have assumed two cores have been failed in G2 while G1

Table 3. Communication cost if failed core is present in one application

Application	Cores	Faulty core	B.R[a]	A.R[b]	% Improvement
MPEG(MPEG+MWD)	22	idct	6821.5	6611.5	3.07
MWD(MPEG+MWD)	22	-	4160	3296	20.76
MPEG(MPEG+MWD)	22	-	6581.5	4138	37.12
MWD(MPEG+MWD)	22	hvs	4576	4064	11.18
Mp3Enc(MP3+263Enc+263Dec)	30	fft	79.38	67.55	14.9
263Enc(MP3+263Enc+263Dec)	30	-	480.76	438.58	8.77
263Dec(MP3+263Enc+263Dec)	30	-	99.59	80.26	19.41
Mp3Enc(MP3+263Enc+263Dec)	30	-	70	60.25	14.28
263Enc(MP3+263Enc+263Dec)	30	dct	856.24	666.29	22.19
263Dec(MP3+263Enc+263Dec)	30	-	84.2	76.38	9.28
Mp3Enc(MP3+263Enc+263Dec)	30	-	79.38	67.55	16.39
263Enc(MP3+263Enc+263Dec)	30	-	480.76	438.58	8.76
263Dec(MP3+263Enc+263Dec)	30	mem2	99.59	80.26	14.21
G_1(G_1+G_2+G_3)	37	T7	67312.33	60306.59	10.4
G_2(G_1+G_2+G_3)	37	-	36796.44	33761.78	8.24
G_3(G_1+G_2+G_3)	37	-	24032.23	20568.71	14.41
G_1(G_1+G_2+G_3)	37	-	74367.37	67570.70	9.1
G_2(G_1+G_2+G_3)	37	T6	36300.79	28190.24	22.34
G_3(G_1+G_2+G_3)	37	-	17376.01	13300.53	23.45
G_1(G_1+G_2+G_3)	37	-	67959.43	59547.90	12.37
G_2(G_1+G_2+G_3)	37	-	30909.30	126696.39	11.92
G_3(G_1+G_2+G_3)	37	T22	29496.48	26735.67	9.3
G_1(G_1+G_4)	40	T16	72174.44	66740.60	7.5
G_4(G_1+G_4)	40	-	178497.01	171599.92	3.86
G_1(G_1+G_4)	40	-	67281.37	56126.12	16.58
G_4(G_1+G_4)	40	T17	188706.78	183239.32	2.9
				Average Improvement	**13.56%**

[a]Before Reconfiguration, [a]After Reconfiguration

and G3 are fault-free. In the third case we have assumed two cores have been failed in the G3 application while G2 and G1 are fault-free. In all three cases our approach provides the flexibility in placing the spare core by performing PSO+Reconfiguration in the mesh network, so that the communication cost after reconfiguration is minimized. Next we look into core failures occurred in two of the three applications.

Figure 6 shows the communication cost if the failed cores are in two applications out of three. The results reported in Fig. 6 are for G1, G2, and G3 applications, generated by TGFF [5]. For the first case the core failures are in G1 - 1 fault, G2 - 1 fault while G3 is fault-free. In the second case G2 - 1 fault, G3 - 1 fault while G1 is fault-free. In the third case G1 -1 fault, G3 - 1 fault while G2 is fault-free. All these cases constitute two core failures in combined application. As we can observe from Fig. 6, there is an improvement in communication cost for all the three different cases of core failures. This is due to placement of cores using our approach such that after reconfiguration there is an improvement in communication cost.

6 Conclusion

In this paper we have proposed a reconfiguration technique along with a spare core for multi-application mapping. The reconfiguration provides flexibility while the introduction of a spare core provides a degree of fault tolerance in the architecture. The initial mapping has been done with the help of PSO while the reconfiguration has been done with the iterative heuristic technique. The results show significant improvement in terms of communication cost after reconfiguration. Future works includes, proposing exact techniques like Integer Linear Programming for reconfiguration.

References

1. Multi-application network-on-chip design using global mapping and local reconfiguration. ACM Trans. Reconfigurable Technol. Syst. **7**(2), 7:1–7:24 (2014)
2. Benini, L., Micheli, G.D.: Networks on chips: a new SoC paradigm. Computer **35**(1), 70–78 (2002)
3. Constantinescu, C.: Trends and challenges in VLSI circuit reliability. IEEE Micro **23**(4), 14–19 (2003)
4. Dally, W.J., Towles, B.: Route packets, not wires: on-chip inteconnection networks. In: Proceedings of the 38th Annual Design Automation Conference, DAC 2001. pp. 684–689. ACM, New York (2001)
5. Dick, R.P., Rhodes, D.L., Wolf, W.: TGFF: task graphs for free. In: Proceedings of the Sixth International Workshop on Hardware/Software Codesign, (CODES/CASHE 1998), pp. 97–101, March 1998
6. Islam, A.: Technology scaling and its side effects. In: 2015 19th International Symposium on VLSI Design and Test, p. 1, June 2015
7. Kennedy, J., Eberhart, R.: Particle swarm optimization. In: IEEE International Conference on Neural Networks, Proceedings, vol. 4, pp. 1942–1948, November 1995
8. Modarressi, M., Tavakkol, A., Sarbazi-Azad, H.: Application-aware topology reconfiguration for on-chip networks. IEEE Trans. Very Large Scale Integr. (VLSI) Syst. **19**(11), 2010–2022 (2011)
9. Parikh, R., Bertacco, V.: Resource conscious diagnosis and reconfiguration for noc permanent faults. IEEE Trans. Comput. **65**(7), 2241–2256 (2016)
10. Pasricha, S., Dutt, N., Ben-Romdhane, M.: Using TLM for exploring bus-based SoC communication architectures. In: 2005 IEEE International Conference on Application-Specific Systems, Architecture Processors (ASAP 2005), pp. 79–85, July 2005
11. Rana, V., Atienza, D., Santambrogio, M.D., Sciuto, D., De Micheli, G.: A reconfigurable network-on-chip architecture for optimal multi-processor SoC communication. In: Piguet, C., Reis, R., Soudris, D. (eds.) VLSI-SoC 2008. IAICT, vol. 313, pp. 232–250. Springer, Heidelberg (2010). https://doi.org/10.1007/978-3-642-12267-5_13

12. Sahu, P.K., Chattopadhyay, S.: A survey on application mapping strategies for network-on-chip design. J. Syst. Archit. **59**(1), 60–76 (2013)
13. Stensgaard, M.B., Sparsø J.: Renoc: a network-on-chip architecture with reconfigurable topology. In: Second ACM/IEEE International Symposium on Networks-on-Chip (nocs 2008), pp. 55–64, April 2008
14. Trivino, F., Alfaro, F.J., Sánchez, J.L., Flich, J.: Noc reconfiguration for CMP virtualization. In: 2011 IEEE 10th International Symposium on Network Computing and Applications, pp. 219–222, August 2011
15. Wang, J., Ebrahimi, M., Huang, L., Jantsch, A., Li, G.: Design of fault-tolerant and reliable networks-on-chip. In: 2015 IEEE Computer Society Annual Symposium on VLSI, pp. 545–550, July 2015

A Realistic Configurable Level Triggered Flip-Flop in Quantum-Dot Cellular Automata

Mrinal Goswami[1,2][✉], Mayukh Roy Choudhury[1], and Bibhash Sen[1]

[1] Department of Computer Science and Engineering,
National Institute of Technology, Durgapur, India
bibhash.sen@cse.nitdgp.ac.in
[2] School of Computer Science, Department of Systemics,
University of Petroleum and Energy Stuides, Dehradun, India
mgoswami@ddn.upes.ac.in

Abstract. Quantum-dot cellular automata (QCA) is a likely candidate for future low power nano-scale electronic devices. Recently, configurable QCA designs are studied due to its low device cost, low power consumption and efficient utilization of device area. In this direction, a design of level triggered configurable flip-flop (LTCFF) is proposed which can be configured to D, T and JK flip-flop. A realistic version of the proposed LTCFF is also implemented using a universal, scalable and efficient (USE) clocking scheme. The performance of the proposed LTCFF is evaluated in terms of area occupied, no. of cells and delay which shows significant improvement over existing designs. The design flexibility of LTCFF is further tested realizing n-bit Counter/Shift Register. Moreover, the single stuck-at faults of the proposed LTCFF are tested with the help of its control inputs. All the proposed designs are verified using QCADesigner simulator.

Keywords: Configurable logic ·
Quantum-dot cellular automata (QCA) · Flip flop · Counter ·
Register · Nanotechnology

1 Introduction

CMOS based VLSI designs play a significant role in digital design. The operation of computer chips has shown outstanding growth in the last few decades. However, the exponential increase of computing power over the last decades has relied on shrinking the transistor. The recent survey of International Technology Roadmap for Semiconductors (ITRS-2015) shows that the transistor could face the challenge of feature size limitation by 2021. Due to this limitation of CMOS technology, various nanoscale technologies such as NML, SET, QCA, CNT, etc. are investigated to increase the computing power of data processing. Among

© Springer Nature Singapore Pte Ltd. 2019
A. Sengupta et al. (Eds.): VDAT 2019, CCIS 1066, pp. 455–467, 2019.
https://doi.org/10.1007/978-981-32-9767-8_38

them, Quantum-dot Cellular Automata (QCA) is the most promising field coupled nanotechnology with extremely small feature size and ultra-low power consumption [6]. Research suggests that QCA can also supplement CMOS with some specific application where CMOS fails due to the power-hungry behavior of it [1].

With the advancement of IOT, *field programmable gate arrays* (FPGAs) are gaining more importance due to its flexibility. Flexibility and performance are the two significant issues of any digital logic circuit. The intermediate trade-off between flexibility and performance is the utmost necessity for a current digital logic circuit which can be attained by reconfigurable circuits like FPGA. The core of FPGAs is configurable logic blocks (CLBs). Several investigation have been done on QCA CLB related to FPGA [4,5]. The primary components of QCA based CLBs are LUT (look up table) and D flip-flop. Therefore, to increase the flexibility of CLB in FPGA, more flexible components need to be built. Recently, Pandiammal et al. proposed the design of 8-bit reconfigurable ALU in QCA [12]. The ALU is capable of performing four arithmetic and logical operations such as binary addition, logical AND, OR and EXOR.

On the other hand, QCA based flip-flops were studied extensively [7,15, 16]. However, all the previous designs realized different flip-flops with disparate designs, and thus they differ in terms of area and latency. The interconnection of the different flip-flops (SR, D, T, and JK) is another significant issue. Most of the previous designs are not robust and highly error-prone due to defective wire-crossing employed in their designs.

All these above factors motivate us to design a configurable as well as robust QCA flip-flop which can address the disparate behavior of existing designs as well as defective wire-crossing in QCA. The main contribution of this research is as follows:

- A configurable level triggered QCA flip-flop (**LTCFF**) is designed which can be configured to JK, D and T flip-flop.
- A regular symmetric version of the proposed LTCFF is also realized utilizing USE clocking scheme which advocates the flexibility of LTCFF.
- Considering LTCFF as a basic element, n-bit Counter/Shift Register is realized.
- Single stuck-at faults of the proposed ConFF is also analyzed.

The rest of the paper is organized as follows: Sect. 2 introduces fundamentals of quantum-dot cellular automata (QCA). Existing works based on reconfigurable logic are discussed in Sect. 3. The proposed design of level triggered configurable flip-flop (LTCFF) is introduced in Sect. 4. The higher order QCA configurable circuits are proposed in Sect. 5. Section 6 investigates the single stuck-at faults of the LTCFF. Finally, Sect. 7, concludes the paper.

2   Basics of QCA

A QCA cell comprises of four quantum dots (Fig. 1(a)) which can carry two free electrons. These free electrons can move between the four quantum dots. As

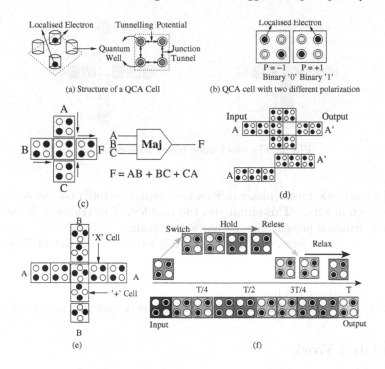

Fig. 1. The basic structures in QCA

shown in Fig. 1(b), the two polarization states of a QCA cell can be represented as P = −1 (logic 0) and P = +1 (logic 1). The basic structures of QCA technology are majority voter (Fig. 1(c)) and inverter (Fig. 1(d)). The QCA majority voter (MV) can be expressed as,

$$MV(A, B, C) = AB + BC + CA$$

A majority voter can serve as a 2-input AND gate if one of the inputs is fixed at P = −1. Alternatively, if anyone input of the majority voter is fixed at P = +1, then the modified majority voter can serve as a 2-input OR gate. There are two different types of inverter available in QCA technology as shown in Fig. 1(d). The possible two orientations ("+") and ("×") (90⁰ and 45⁰ respectively) of QCA cell are shown in Fig. 1(e). There are two fundamental wire-crossing techniques (co-planar and multi-layer) available in QCA. As shown in Fig. 1(e), the co-planar wire-crossing can be implemented with the mix combination of two different orientations (90⁰ and 45⁰) of QCA cells. However, production of 90⁰ cell needs a high level of precision in placing which increases the overall cost and the implementation complexity [3]. The multi-layer wire-crossing can be implemented with the help of two or more different layers. Multi-layer wire-crossing has several fabrication limitations due to which it is not considered here. Because of the several issues of coplanar as well as multi-layer wire-crossing, clock-zone based wire-crossing technique is considered here. It can be implemented using

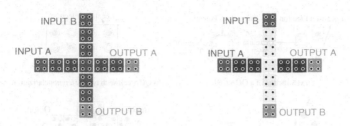

Fig. 2. The clock zone based wire-crossing

non-adjacent clock zones (phase difference is equal to 180^0) on the same plane [14] as shown in Fig. 2. This eliminates the problem of interference between the QCA cells which is present in coplanar wire-crossing.

The QCA clock controls the flow of information within the circuit. The circuit information is carried from one end to another with the help of a clock. The clock zones of QCA are distinct and 90^0 phase shifted. At the time of computation, the previous clock zone must hold its output, which can be achieved by splitting the clock into four phases: switch, hold, release and relax which is shown in Fig. 1(f).

3   Related Work

Limited attempts have been made to realize reconfigurable designs in QCA [8–11,13]. An And-OR-Inverter (AOI) logic is proposed in [8] whereby fixing one or more input various logic functions can be implemented such as OR-AND, NAND-OR, NOR-NAND, etc. which is shown in Fig. 3(a). In [9], a complex 7-input QCA configurable gate (out of 7 inputs, 3 inputs are used as control inputs)

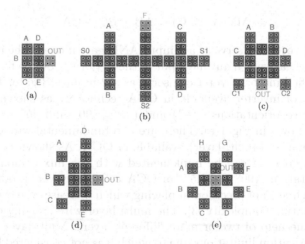

Fig. 3. Previous reconfigurable gates (a) AOI (b) 7-input complex gate (c) RFTG gate (d) PRC gate (e) Reconfigurable majority gate

is proposed by cascading three 3-input majority voter as shown in Fig. 3(b). The sum of product, product of sum, four-input AND, four-input OR logic, etc. can be constructed by fixing control inputs to "0" or "1". In [13], under the presence of different QCA defects, a symmetric configurable fault tolerant reconfigurable gate (RFTG) has been proposed as shown in Fig. 3(c). A novel configurable QCA design is proposed in [11]. The design (Fig. 3(d)) is capable of realizing various logic functions such as 2-input OR, 3-input AND, 2-input OR, 3-input OR etc. A reconfigurable majority gate (Fig. 3(e)) is presented in [10].

4   Level Triggered Configurable Flip-Flop

The QCA representation of the proposed level triggered configurable flip-flop (LTCFF) is shown in Fig. 4. The proposed LTCFF has 4 inputs (A, B, C1 and C2) and two outputs (Q and $\overline{Q}$) where C1, C2 are control inputs. The correct behaviour of the proposed LTCFF is verified using QCADesigner 2.0.3 and is shown in Fig. 5. The primary output of the proposed LTCFF is as follows:

$$Q_{t+1} = \{A.\overline{Q_t} + (\overline{B.C1 + A.C2.\overline{C1} + \overline{A}.\overline{C1}.\overline{C2}})Q_t\}CLK + \overline{CLK}.Q_t \tag{1}$$

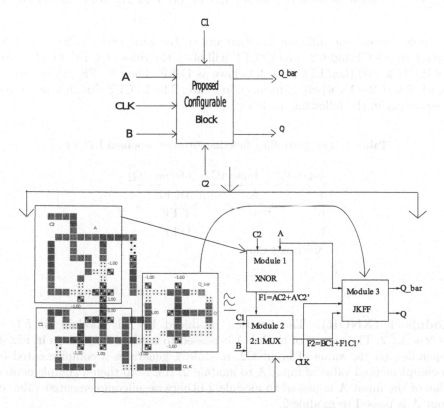

Fig. 4. The QCA layout of level triggered configurable flip-flop (LTCFF)

$$Q_{t+1} = \{A.\overline{Q_t} + \{\overline{A}.\overline{B}(C1 + C2) + A.\overline{B}(C1 + \overline{C2}) +$$
$$\overline{B}.C1 + \overline{C1}(\overline{A}.C2 + A.\overline{C2})\}Q_t\}CLK + \overline{CLK}.Q_t$$

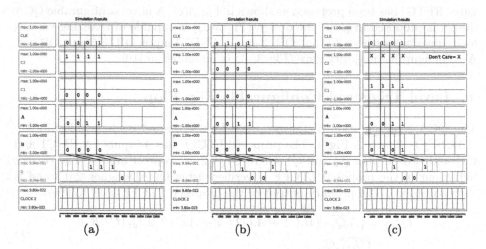

Fig. 5. The simulation result of proposed LTCFF (a) T FF (b) D FF and (c) JK FF

Table 1 shows the different functionality of the proposed LTCFF based on control inputs C1 and C2. The LTCFF will obey the rules of T FF if C1C2 = 01 and if C1C2 = 00 then LTCFF will behave as D FF. The LTCFF will behave as JK FF if C1C2 = 1X where X means don't care. The LTCFF design is described more deeply in the following modules:

Table 1. The controlling functionalities of proposed LTCFF

Input (C1)	Input (C2)	Output (Q)
1	X	JK FF
0	1	T FF
0	0	D FF
X = Don't Care		

Module 1 (XNOR). The function produced by this module is: $F1 = A.C2 + \overline{A}.\overline{C2}$. The output of module 1 is passed to module 2 as shown in Fig. 4. Depending on the value of input C2, module 1 generates a complemented or un-complemented value of input A to module 2. If C2 = 0 then a complemented value of the input A is passed to module 2 otherwise uncomplemented value of input A is passed to module 2.

Module 2 (2:1 MUX). The output function of this module is: $F2 = B.C1 + F1.\overline{C1}$. If $C1 = 1$, input B will be selected and module 3 will behave according to JK flip-flop. On the other hand, if $C1 = 0$, module 3 will behave either D flip-flop or T flip-flop depending on the output F1. If $F1 = \overline{A}$ then the module 3 will behave as a D flip-flop otherwise it will behave as a T flip-flop.

Module 3 (JK FF). This module follows the instructions of module 1 and 2. Module 3 behaves as T flip-flop if module 1 produces $F1 = A$ and at the same time module, 2 produces $F2 = F1$. Alternatively, if module 1 produces $F1 = \overline{A}$ and at the same time module 2 produces $F2 = F1$ then module 3 behaves as a D flip-flop. Finally, if module 2 produce $F2 = B$ (module 1: $F1 = $ don't care), then module 3 behaves like a JK flip-flop.

Table 2. Parformance of proposed LTCFF design

Design	Area μm^2	Cells	Layer	Configurable
The existing level edge triggered D FF				
In [7]	0.20	104	Single	No
In [16]	0.08	66	Single	No
The existing level edge triggered T FF				
In [7]	0.20	108	Single	No
In [16]	0.10	90	Single	No
The existing level edge triggered JK FF				
In [15]	0.75	415	Single	No
In [7]	0.12	80	Single	No
In [16]	0.10	68	Single	No
Proposed LTCFF	0.20	159	Single	Yes

The advantage of configurable memory units lies in its application domain. These can be used to design circuits with structural similarity eliminating the need to design separate hardware performing a specific function. For example, counters and shift registers can be implemented in a single design with the option to configure the flip-flop according to the need. The biggest advantage of the proposed LTCFF is that a single module can serve as a D, T and JK FF. Table 2 shows the performance of LTCFF with the existing D, T and JK FF. The proposed LTCFF consists of 2.75 delay covering an area of 0.20 μm^2 with 159 QCA cells. Although the proposed LTCFF exceeds in all the respect compared to existing designs, these small overheads can be accepted due to the configurable superiority of LTCFF over the existing designs. All the previous designs [7,15,16] are not configurable in nature and can produce only one function whereas LTCFF can produce three functions.

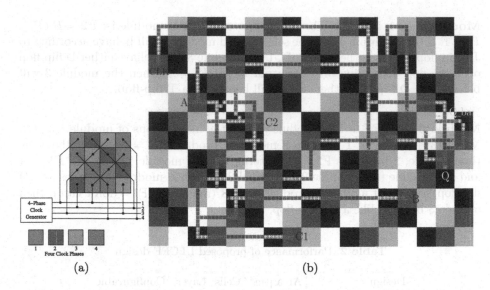

Fig. 6. (a) The USE clocking scheme [2] (b) The LTCFF layout under USE clocking scheme (LTCFF-USE)

On the otherhand, all the previous designs (Table 2) utilized random, irregular clocking without considering the proper layout of the underlying clocking circuit required for it. Using irregular/random clock zone, it is possible to simulate a circuit which is more compact. However, to maintain proper routing channel and a regular structure, it is the utmost necessity to follow a realistic clocking scheme. The development of the QCA circuit based on the realistic clocking scheme will bring the more laurel in the circuit synthesis process. In this direction, a universal, scalable, efficient (USE) realistic clock distribution scheme for QCA is proposed in [2]. The LTCFF layout under the USE clocking scheme (LTCFF-USE) is shown in Fig. 6. The proposed LTCFF-USE consists of 541 QCA cells covering an area of 1.81 μm². The LTCFF-USE allows us to present an all in one flip-flop, which can also be perceived as a standard universal design.

5   Design of Configurable n-bit Counter/Shift Register

Counter and registers are widely used sequential circuits in the digital system. In this section, the level of sensitive LTCFF is used as a fundamental building block to design the configurable n-bit counter/register. In order to synchronize the clock of the proposed configurable counter/register one additional delay control circuit (Fig. 7) is needed. The additional delay circuitry is used to delay the clock (fixing C3 = 0) by one complete cycle so that the clock can be synchronized. This delay circuit operates based on the operation table shown in Table 3. If C3 is set to zero then the delay clock (CLK_{t-1}) is propagated to the output; otherwise the current clock (CLK_1) is passed to the output.

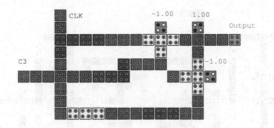

Fig. 7. The delay circuit

Table 3. The operation table of delay circuit

C3	Delay (CLK_{t-1})	Current (CLK_t)	Output
0	0	0	0
0	0	1	0
0	1	0	1
0	1	1	1
1	0	0	0
1	0	1	1
1	1	0	0
1	1	1	1

The Working Function of n-bit Counter/Shift Registrar. The proposed configurable 2-bit Register/Counter is shown in Fig. 8. It can be configured to a register or a counter as necessary. The proposed configurable 2-bit Register/Counter have five control inputs and two primary inputs. The basic unit of the proposed counter/register is LTCFF. In the proposed counter/register, C1 and C2 (C1 = C1 and C2 = C2) inputs are used to adjust the circuit to the required flip-flop whereas C3 input defines the behavior of the circuit as a register or a counter, i.e., if C3 = 0 then the circuit behaves as a register otherwise it behaves as a counter. The simulation result of the configurable 2-bit counter/register is shown in Fig. 10. The simulation result of the unidirectional shift register is shown in Fig. 10(a). The two LTCFF (configured as a D FF) is cascaded to design the proposed 2-bit shift register. The output Q_0 served as an input to the next LTCFF. The input data (0101) is shifted in the right direction by one-bit position with every clock cycle. Figure 10(b)(c) shows the two different waveforms for the proposed configurable 2-bit counter. The proposed 2-bit counter can be constructed using either T FF or JK FF as shown in Fig. 10(b)(c).

The 3-bit design of the proposed configurable counter/register is shown in Fig. 9. To synchronize the input and output of the 3-bit configurable counter/register circuit, two delay circuits are utilized. The top delay circuit is used to synchronize the output of the first module with rest modules, whereas the

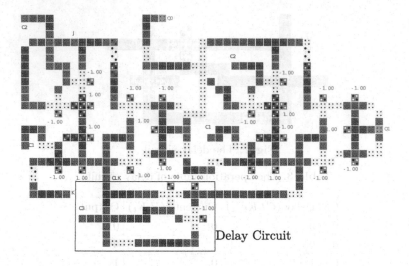

Delay Circuit

Fig. 8. The Proposed QCA configurable 2-bit Counter/Register

bottom two delay circuits are used to synchronize clock signal (CLK) of the proposed circuit. In the case of the 3-bit configurable counter/register if $C3 = C4 = 0$ then the circuit behaves as a register whereas if $C3 = C4 = 1$ than the proposed 3-bit configurable counter/register will behave as a counter. Similarly, cascading n-modules, it is possible to construct an n-bit configurable counter/register using the same logic.

The performance of the proposed configurable counter/register is shown in Table 4. Table 4 indicates that the proposed design outperforms the existing designs in terms of the area. Moreover, the advantage of using the proposed design is that the same design also can act as a shift register.

Table 4. Performance of counter/register

Design	Area μm^2	Cells	Layer
2-bit Counter in [17]	0.62	328	Single
Proposed Counter/Register	0.52	377	Single
3-bit Counter in [17]	1.20	616	Single
Proposed Counter/Register	0.97	702	Single

6 Testing of LTCFF

Generally, cell deposition defects are more likely to occur in QCA. In QCA technology, there is no concept of stuck-at faults, but due to some unknown faults, the QCA devices behave as like as stuck-at fault. However, the phenomenon

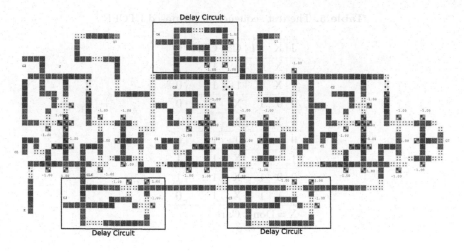

Fig. 9. The Proposed QCA configurable 3-bit Counter/Register

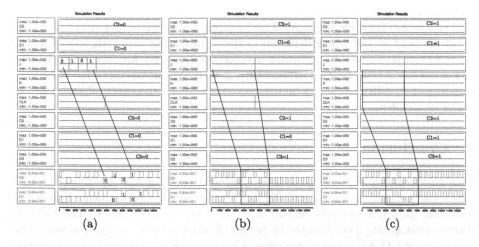

Fig. 10. The simulation result of 2-bit Counter/Register (a) Register using D FF (b) Counter using T FF and (c) Counter using JK FF

like stuck-at-faults may occur in the QCA logic circuit due to cell displacement between two different data paths. The most significant feature of the proposed LTCFF is that it can be tested with the help of its control inputs itself. The presence of faults can be detected in the proposed LTCFF only monitoring its control input and its corresponding output(Q).

The initial state of the flip flop is not known. Assuming there is no fault in the LTCFF, we apply input $JK = 1X$ ($C1 = C2 = 0$) to set the flip flop (Table 5). This means the proposed LTCFF will behave as D FF and pass the value at input J to the output Q. In the next second iteration, the control inputs are changed to $C1 = 0$ and $C2 = 1$. This will change the LTCFF will to T FF which is reflected

Table 5. The test sequence of proposed LTCFF

J	K	C1	C2	CLK	Q
1	X	0	0	1	1
1	X	0	1	1	0
0	0	1	X	1	0
1	X	0	0	1	1
0	X	0	0	1	0
1	1	1	X	1	1
0	0	1	X	1	1
1	1	1	X	1	0

X = Don't Care

in the output (Q = 0) and at the same time this ensures that the Q is not in stuck-at-1. The input vector JK = 00 test the stuck-at-1 fault for the input J. The stuck-at-0 fault for the input J and output Q can be analyzed applying the input JK = 1X in the fourth iteration in the Table 5. The input JK = 00 (C1 = 1, C2 = X) can be applied to test stuck-at-1 for the input K. Alternatively, JK = 11 (C1 = 1, C2 = X) can be used to detect stuck-at-0 fault at the input K. Therefore, the output < 10010110 > can be used as a test bench to detect all the stuck-at faults in LTCFF.

7   Conclusion

This work attempts to design a level-triggered configurable flip-flop (LTCFF) which can be used as a D, T and JK flip-flop as per the requirement. Further, a universal as well as scalable version of LTCFF is also investigated. The LTCFF shows outstanding performance in terms of area as well as clock zones. The flexibility of LTCFF is tested realizing n-bit counter/register within one circuit. Also, LTCFF is completely testable under single stuck-at faults.

Acknowledgment. This entire research has been carried out under the Visvesvaraya PhD scheme which is managed by the Media Lab Asia, India and is under the supervision of the Electronics and IT Department, Ministry of Communications and IT, Government of India.

References

1. Bernstein, G., et al.: Magnetic QCA systems. Microelectron. J. **36**(7), 619–624 (2005). https://doi.org/10.1016/j.mejo.2004.12.002. European Micro and Nano Systems

2. Campos, C.A.T., Marciano, A.L., Neto, O.P.V., Torres, F.S.: Use: a universal, scalable, and efficient clocking scheme for QCA. IEEE Trans. Comput.-Aided Des. Integr. Circuits Syst. **35**(3), 513–517 (2016). https://doi.org/10.1109/TCAD.2015. 2471996
3. Chaudhary, A., Chen, D.Z., Hu, X.S., Niemier, M.T., Ravichandran, R., Whitton, K.: Fabricatable interconnect and molecular QCA circuits. Trans Comp-Aided Des. Integr Circuits Syst. **26**(11), 1978–1991 (2007). https://doi.org/10.1109/TCAD. 2007.906467
4. Ghosh, B., Chandra, J.S., Salimath, A.K.: Design of a multi-layered QCA configurable logic block for FPGAs. J. Circuits Syst. Comput. **23**(06), 1450089 (2014)
5. Kianpour, M., Sabbaghi-Nadooshan, R.: A conventional design for CLB implementation of a FPGA in quantum-dot cellular automata (QCA). In: 2012 IEEE/ACM International Symposium on Nanoscale Architectures (NANOARCH). pp. 36–42, July 2012. https://doi.org/10.1145/2765491.2765499
6. Lent, C.S., Tougaw, P.D., Porod, W., Bernstein, G.H.: Quantum cellular automata. Nanotechnology **4**(1), 49 (1993)
7. Lim, L.A., Ghazali, A., Yan, S.C.T., Fat, C.C.: Sequential circuit design using quantum-dot cellular automata (QCA). In: 2012 IEEE International Conference on Circuits and Systems (ICCAS), pp. 162–167, October 2012
8. Momenzadeh, M., Huang, J., Tahoori, M.B., Lombardi, F.: Characterization, test, and logic synthesis of and-or-inverter (AOI) gate design for QCA implementation. IEEE Trans. Comput.-Aided Des. Integr. Circuits Syst. **24**(12), 1881–1893 (2005)
9. Motameni, H., Montazeri, B.: Reconfigurable logic based on quantum-dot cellular automata. J. Appl. Sci. Res. **7**, 1817–1823 (2011)
10. Navi, K., Mohammadi, H., Angizi, S.: A novel quantum-dot cellular automata reconfigurable majority gate with 5 and 7 inputs support. J. Comput. Theor. Nanosci. **12**(3), 399–406 (2015)
11. Navi, K., Roohi, A., Sayedsalehi, S.: Designing reconfigurable quantum-dot cellular automata logic circuits. J. Comput. Theor. Nanosci. **10**(5), 1137–1146 (2013)
12. Pandiammal, K., Meganathan, D.: Design of 8 bit reconfigurable ALU using quantum dot cellular automata. In: 2018 IEEE 13th Nanotechnology Materials and Devices Conference (NMDC), pp. 1–4, October 2018. https://doi.org/10.1109/ NMDC.2018.8605892
13. Roohi, A., Sayedsalehi, S., Khademolhosseini, H., Navi, K.: Design and evaluation of a reconfigurable fault tolerant quantum-dot cellular automata gate. J. Comput. Theor. Nanosci. **10**(2), 380–388 (2013)
14. Shin, S.H., Jeon, J.C., Yoo, K.Y.: Wire-crossing technique on quantum-dot cellular automata. In: 2nd International Conference on Next Generation Computer and Information Technology, vol. 27, pp. 52–57 (2013)
15. Venkataramani, P., Srivastava, S., Bhanja, S.: Sequential circuit design in quantum-dot cellular automata. In: 2008 8th IEEE Conference on Nanotechnology, pp. 534–537, August 2008. https://doi.org/10.1109/NANO.2008.159
16. Vetteth, A., Walus, K., Dimitrov, V., Jullien, G.: Quantum-dot cellular automata of flip-flops. In: ATIPS Laboratory 2500 University Drive, NW, Calgary, Alberta, Canada T2N 1N4 (2003)
17. Yang, X., Cai, L., Zhao, X., Zhang, N.: Design and simulation of sequential circuits in quantum-dot cellular automata: falling edge-triggered flip-flop and counter study. Microelectron. J. **41**(1), 56–63 (2010). https://doi.org/10.1016/j.mejo.2009. 12.008

User Guided Register Manipulation in Digital Circuits

Priyanka Panigrahi$^{(\boxtimes)}$ (iD), Rajesh Kumar Jha$^{(\boxtimes)}$ (iD), and Chandan Karfa$^{(\boxtimes)}$ (iD)

IIT, Guwahati, Assam, India
{priya176101006,rajes174101007,ckarfa}@iitg.ac.in

Abstract. Retiming is a widely used optimization technique in any electronic design automation (EDA) tools. Retiming primarily moves registers in digital circuit to improve the timing of the circuit. Retiming does not always produce the desired result due to various factors. As a result, the designer sometimes needs to insert register(s) into specific location(s) or delete or move register(s) from specific location(s) in order to break critical paths. This task has to be done along with register balancing i.e. the designer also needs to add or delete or move registers in all parallel paths as well to keep the functionality of the design unchanged. Manual register balancing in all parallel paths is complex and error prone due to the complexity of the design. So, this task has to be automated. The proposed method in this paper automatically inserts or deletes or moves register(s) to or from user specified location(s) and also does the register balancing in all parallel paths automatically. A Python based implementation has also been presented for the proposed method.

Keywords: Register balancing · Retiming · Critical path · Clock frequency

1 Introduction

1.1 What Is Retiming?

Retiming [4] is the process of moving registers in the circuit such that the overall functionality is preserved in the design. Its goal is to minimize latency, area, power, etc. Leiserson and Saxe in 1981 [3] provided the first formulation as well as the theoretical solution to retiming. Their later paper [4] has a better and wide overview of the subject. Narendra Shenoy in 1997 [5] covered the entire topic of retiming with elegance and ease. Retiming can be either forward or backward. In forward retiming, if each input is driven by a register, then it moves to all the outputs and vice versa for backward retiming. Here, we choose to perform backward retiming i.e. we aim to move a group of registers from output to all the inputs. Retiming can have an impact on number of registers. It may increase the number of registers in the circuit but the behaviour of the design remains intact. Retiming is primarily used for maximizing the target clock frequency by

© Springer Nature Singapore Pte Ltd. 2019
A. Sengupta et al. (Eds.): VDAT 2019, CCIS 1066, pp. 468–481, 2019.
https://doi.org/10.1007/978-981-32-9767-8_39

moving registers in the circuit to break the critical path(s). We have shown an example of backward retiming in Fig. 1. The locations of the nodes and registers before retiming are shown in Fig. 1a. After backward retiming, one register will move to the middle of the circuit which reduces the maximum circuit latency to half. The resultant circuit after retiming is shown in Fig. 1b.

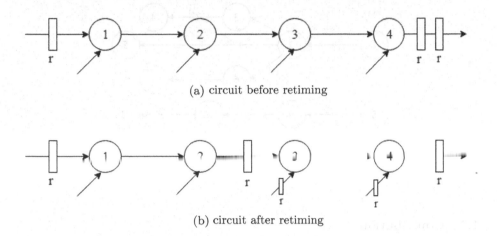

(a) circuit before retiming

(b) circuit after retiming

Fig. 1. An example of backward retiming

1.2   The Problem at Hand

During synthesis, the EDA tools calculate the critical path(s) based on some estimated delay of each combinational component of the circuit. However, performance of retiming depends on the delays of the corresponding combinational nodes of the design. The estimated delays in an EDA tool may not be accurate always. Specifically, with various versions of FPGA boards of various companies (say Intel-Altera, Xilinx, etc.), it is difficult for an independent EDA tool provider (such as Synopsys, Cadence, etc.) to obtain accurate delay of all FPGA components in all FPGA boards of all companies. The delay estimation of the EDA tool does not always reflect the actual physical delay of the combinational components. In addition, there is routing delay which is not considered during retiming. As a result, retiming may not always break the critical path(s). In such scenario, the designer may want to fine tune his circuit by adding or deleting registers in specific locations to break the critical path(s). This leads to register balancing in all parallel paths to keep the functionality intact in the circuit. We have shown an example of register balancing in Fig. 2. Let the user wants to insert a register in the edge $e_{3,4}$. Then, user also needs to insert one register each in the edges $e_{2,5}$, $e_{2,6}$ and $e_{8,9}$ in order to balance the parallel paths. The parallel paths can be found out by a cut which is shown using a dotted line. So, register balancing is complex and error prone due to the complexity of circuit design as there can be thousands of parallel paths in a real design. Moreover, a small mistake or imbalanced circuits can totally alter the functionality of the design. The objective of this work is to automate the register balancing task to help the designer from making last moment mistakes.

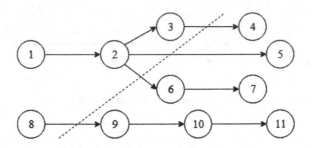

Fig. 2. An example of register balancing

1.3   Contribution

We term register manipulation as insertion or deletion or movement of registers in a digital circuit. Manipulation of registers in a digital circuit serves a crucial role. Register manipulation leads to register balancing in all parallel paths. Manual register balancing is almost impossible in complex circuits. So, this process has to be automated. The main contributions of the paper are as follows.

1. We presented a method to insert registers at user specified locations automatically with the help of register insertion constraints. This ensures automatic register balancing also.
2. We presented a method to delete registers from user specified locations automatically with the help of register deletion constraints. This ensures automatic register balancing also.
3. We also conclude that we can move registers in a circuit with user specified locations. Here, we need both the proposed constraints i.e. insertion constraint and deletion constraint as we move the register from one specific location to another in the circuit.
4. We have shown that our proposed constraints can be solved along with retiming constraints using any existing retiming engine.
5. We implemented the proposed methods in Python and tested using Xilinx Vivado synthesis tool [14] on several ISCAS89 benchmark circuits [13].

The proposed methods work on any design size preserving the core functionality of the circuit. To the best of our knowledge, this is the first solution to the register balancing problem which solves along with retiming.

1.4   Section Organisation

The rest of the paper has been organized as follows. Section 2 gives a basic idea of retiming. Section 3 presents the proposed method of automatic register manipulation. Some experimental results are presented in Sect. 4. Section 5 discusses the related work. Finally, the conclusion of the paper with the future work is given in Sect. 6.

2   Basics of Retiming

Retiming [2,4,5] is a transformation of the design which alters the sequential elements (registers) present in the circuit preserving the overall functionality of the circuit. In this section we give a brief idea of retiming to minimize the target clock period.

Any given sequential circuit can be represented using a directed graph $G(V, E)$, where each vertex $v \in V$ corresponds to the given design unit. Abstraction level decides the design unit which can be gates for gate level design and can be functional units, multiplexers, etc for register transfer level (RTL) design.

Each edge $e_{u,v} \in E$ represents the flow of signal from the output of node u to the input of node v. Each edge assigns with a weight which represents the number of registers in that edge. Weight of an edge must be non-negative i.e. $w(e_{u,v}) \geq 0, \forall e_{u,v} \in E$. Each vertex has a constant computational delay $d(v)$. It should not be negative i.e. $d(v) \geq 0, \forall v \in V$. Retiming aims to map the design G to a retimed design G_r. A retiming is labelling of the vertices to a set of integers. The weight of the retimed design is as follows:

$$w_r(e_{u,v}) = r(v) + w(e_{u,v}) - r(u)$$

where $w(e_{u,v})$ and $w_r(e_{u,v})$ are weight of the edge $e_{u,v}$ in the original design and retimed design respectively.

The retiming label $r(v)$, for any vertex v originally depicts the number of registers moved from its output towards its input which is called backward retiming. So, the task of retiming is to allocate retiming labels to all the combinational blocks of the design.

A path p can be defined as a sequence of alternating edges and vertices such that fan in of a vertex is fan out of its predecessor. The weight of a path $w(p)$ can be defined as the summation of the weights of the edges in the path. similarly, computational delay of a path $d(p)$ is the summation of the computational delays of all the vertices in the path. So, the clock period c of a path p can be found out by:

$$c = \max_{p|w(p)=0} d(p)$$

The goal of minimum latency global retiming is to minimize the clock period c.

Two important matrices $W(u, v)$ and $D(u, v)$ are required for formulation of retiming. $W(u, v)$ specifies the minimum number of registers on any path from node u to node v. $D(u, v)$ denotes the maximum computational delay incurred among all the paths from node u to node v with weight $W(u, v)$.

The matrix W can be calculated using algorithms for all pair shortest path like Floyd Warshall [16] since edge weights are zero or positive.The shortest path among each vertex pairs will give the solution. But, computation of D can not be solved as computation of W since each entry in D matrix depends on the corresponding value of W. There exists a unified method to compute both the matrices W and D simultaneously [15].

Now the constraints of retiming for a specific target clock period c can be formulated using a set of two inequalities.

- *(feasibility constraint): The edge-weight must be non-negative after retiming. Formally, $w_r(e_{u,v}) \geq 0, \forall e_{u,v} \in E$. So, $r(u) - r(v) \leq w(e_{u,v}), \forall e_{u,v} \in E$.*
- *(critical path constraint): The computational delay of zero-weight paths after retiming must be less than or equal to c. If $D(u, v) > c$, then $r(v) + w(e_{u,v}) - r(u) \geq 1$ must hold for the critical path to have computation time less than or equal to c. Formally, $r(u) - r(v) \leq w(e_{u,v}) - 1$ for all paths from u to v with $D(u, v) > c$.*

The aim here is to get the values of retiming labels r for all vertices satisfying the above two sets of constraints. These values can be constructed using a graph called constraint graph which can be generated using the above set of inequalities and solving the same using a single source shortest path algorithm, like Bellman-Ford algorithm [16]. Ekpanyapong et al. in 2006 [6] showed how Bellman ford can be used in case of retiming for finding the shortest path. Moreover, Busato et al. provided an efficient way to run Bellman-Ford in GPU enabled systems in 2016 [7].

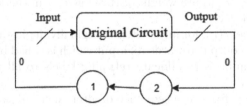

Fig. 3. Generating retiming circuit

3   Automatic Register Manipulation

In this paper, we term register manipulation as insertion, deletion or movement of register(s) in a digital circuit. In order to improve the designer mistakes in manual manipulation, this process has to be automated. In this section, we propose different constraints for insertion and deletion of registers in a circuit. We

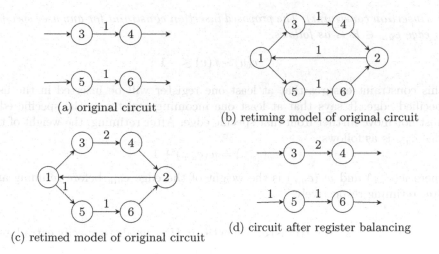

(a) original circuit

(b) retiming model of original circuit

(c) retimed model of original circuit

(d) circuit after register balancing

Fig. 4. An example of register balancing after register insertion

have shown that register manipulation is possible by specifying our proposed constraints along with the existing feasibility constraints and critical path constraints of a given circuit. Our method of register manipulation works along with register retiming. By virtue of retiming, all the parallel paths are also balanced. Thus, it does automatic register balancing. We discuss next the three register manipulations i.e. insertion, deletion and movement in following subsections.

3.1   Register Insertion

Retiming works on estimated delays of the nodes in the circuit. Sometimes the estimated delays are not actual delays. As a result, retiming may not break all critical paths in the circuit. In order to break those critical paths, the designer wants to insert register(s) at specific location(s). Register balancing automate this process of inserting registers at specified location and also balances registers in all parallel paths automatically. Following tcl command can be followed by users to specify the register balancing constraints.

$$define\_attribute < e_{u,v} > insert\_reg\_balance\_parallel\_paths$$

where $e_{u,v}$ denotes an edge from node u to v in which the user wants to insert an additional register. If user wants to insert registers at more than one location in a circuit, then user must specify one tcl command for each location.

Problem Formulation: User has to specify the edge in which he wants to insert a register. We create a suitable retiming model of the original circuit. Then any existing retiming algorithm can be applied to retime the circuit. After retiming, new registers will be inserted and parallel paths will be balanced.

– *(insertion constraint): The proposed insertion constraint for any user specified edge $e_{u,v} \in E$ is as follows.*

$$r(u) - r(v) \leq -1$$

This constraint ensures that at least one register will be inserted in the user specified edge. It says that at least one incoming register to the specific edge must not move further from that specific edge. After retiming, the weight of the edge $e_{u,v}$ is as follows:

$$w_r(e_{u,v}) = w(e_{u,v}) + 1$$

where $w(e_{u,v})$ and $w_r(e_{u,v})$ is the weight of the edge $e_{u,v}$ before retiming and after retiming respectively.

Retiming Model for Register Insertion: User needs to specify extra latencies if he wants to insert registers in the circuit. As parallel paths will be balanced after retiming, so there is no need of inserting unnecessary extra latencies in the circuit. This can be achieved by identifying the maximum number of constraints specified among all paths from input ports to output ports [1]. This maximum number of constraints is the minimum number of latencies to be inserted.

A retiming model must be created from the original circuit to insert extra latencies in the circuit. The retiming circuit can be generated by adding two dummy nodes 1 and 2 as shown in Fig. 3. The retiming circuit must be a closed loop to apply any existing register retiming algorithms [2]. To make the circuit closed all the input nodes of the circuit are connected from node 1 and all the output nodes of the circuit are connected to node 2. Also there is an edge from node 2 to node 1 and extra latencies are placed in this edge. All other new edges assigned with a weight of zero.

Let us consider the circuit given in Fig. 4a with two parallel edges $e_{3,4}$ with weight one and $e_{5,6}$ with weight one. Assume user wants to insert a register in the edge $e_{3,4}$. The retiming model of the original circuit is given in Fig. 4b. It may be noted that two dummy nodes 1 and 2 are inserted to make the circuit a closed loop as retiming algorithms can move registers in closed loop only [2]. As discussed earlier, all the input nodes of the circuit i.e. 3 and 4 are connected from node 1 and all the output nodes of the circuit i.e. 5 and 6 are connected to node 2. Also there is an edge from node 2 to node 1. All other new edges assigned with a weight of zero. Here, the minimum extra latencies required is one. The extra latency inserted in the edge $e_{2,1}$. This extra latency inserted is moved into the original circuit. After retiming we get back the original circuit by removing the dummy nodes 1, 2 and its associated edges. The retimed model is given in Fig. 4c. The circuit after register balancing is given in Fig. 4d.

A Case Study: Let us consider again the circuit given in Fig. 4a. Suppose, user wants to insert a register in the edge $e_{3,4}$. Here, we need to show how the register inserted into the specific edge and how the parallel paths are balanced due to our proposed register insertion constraint.

The retiming model of the original circuit is given in Fig. 4b. First, we must consider all the feasibility constraints i.e. $r(u) - r(v) \leq w(e_{u,v})$ for all edge $e_{u,v} \in E$. The feasibility constraints for the given circuit is as follows.

$$r(1) - r(3) \leq 0, \quad r(3) - r(4) \leq 1, \quad r(4) - r(2) \leq 0$$

$$r(1) - r(5) \leq 0, \quad r(5) - r(6) \leq 1, \quad r(6) - r(2) \leq 0$$

$$r(2) - r(1) \leq 1$$

The register insertion constraint i.e. $r(u) - r(v) \leq -1$ for the given edge $e_{3,4}$ is as follows.

$$r(3) - r(4) \leq -1$$

If we combine the insertion constraint of the edge $e_{3,4}$ i.e. $r(3) - r(4) \leq -1$ with its feasibility constraint i.e. $r(3) - r(4) \leq 1$, the final inequality is as follows: $r(3) - r(4) \leq -1$.

Here, we ignore the critical path constraints for simplicity of presentation. Our motive here is to show that register insertion is possible with our insertion constraint. However, we can consider the critical path constraints as well.

The constraint graph for the above inequalities are shown in Fig. 5. The constraint graph can be obtained by following procedures:

1. Draw a node i for each $r_i, i = 1, ..., N$.
2. Draw an extra node $N + 1$.
3. For each inequality of the form $r_i - r_j \leq k$, draw an edge from node j to node i with a weight of k.
4. For each node $i, i = 1, ..., N$, draw an edge from node $N + 1$ to node i with weight 0.

The retiming solution is the solution to the single source shortest path problem with node 7 as source in the constraint graph. The retiming solution for the given circuit is $r(1) = -1$, $r(2) = 0$, $r(3) = -1$, $r(4) = 0$, $r(5) = 0$ and $r(6) = 0$. The weights of the retimed circuit are as follows: $e_{2,1} = 0$, $e_{1,3} = 0$, $e_{3,4} = 2$, $e_{1,5} = 1$, $e_{5,6} = 1$, $e_{4,2} = 0$ and $e_{6,2} = 0$. The retimed model is given in Fig. 4c. The circuit after register balancing is given in Fig. 4d.

3.2 Register Deletion

Sometimes the critical path latency specified is much more than the actual critical path. In those cases user can delete some unwanted registers from the circuit. For example, let the target clock period of a given circuit is 20 ns. Let the largest delay in the circuit is 7 ns. If we delete a register from that path, the largest delay becomes 14ns. So, user can achieve the target clock cycle even after deleting the register from the circuit. Then its always a better choice to delete such register

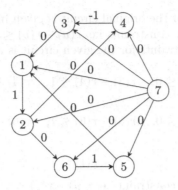

Fig. 5. Constraint graph

in order to save hardware. Following tcl command can be followed by users to specify the register balancing constraints.

$$define\_attribute < e_{u,v} > delete\_reg\_balance\_parallel\_paths$$

where $e_{u,v}$ denotes an edge from node u to v from which the user wants to delete a register. If user wants to delete registers from more than one location in a circuit, then user must specify one tcl command for each location.

Problem Formulation: User has to specify the edge from which he wants to delete a register.

– *(deletion constraint): The proposed deletion constraint for any user specified edge $e_{u,v} \in E$ is as follows.*

$$r(v) - r(u) \leq -1$$

This constraint ensures that one register will be deleted from the user specified edge. It says that the outgoing registers from that edge must be at least one more than the incoming registers to that edge. After retiming, the weight of the edge $e_{u,v}$ is as follows:

$$w_r(e_{u,v}) = w(e_{u,v}) - 1$$

where $w(e_{u,v})$ and $w_r(e_{u,v})$ is the weight of the edge $e_{u,v}$ before retiming and after retiming respectively.

Retiming Model for Register Deletion: The retiming model for deletion is same as register insertion i.e. a retiming circuit must be generated from the original circuit and two dummy nodes 1 and 2 are added to make the circuit closed. The only difference here is, there is no need of extra latency insertion. So, the weight of the edge $e_{2,1}$ is always 0. The dummy nodes and its associated edges are removed after retiming to get back the original circuit.

Register deletion can also be solved by deletion constraints which will be specified along with feasibility constraints and critical path constraints. After retiming, the additional register is deleted and also parallel paths are balanced.

3.3 Register Movement

Register movement implies deleting a register from one specific edge and inserting it to another specific edge. This can be specified by the following tcl command.

$$define\_attribute < from >< to > move\_reg\_balance\_parallel\_paths$$

As we need to do both insert and delete, the tool effectively use a insertion constraint and a deletion constraint for each move command. We can perform multiple movements in a single circuit. In order to achieve multiple movement we must add a move constraint for each edge.

3.4 Breaking Critical Path Using BFS

The main aim of this paper is to enable users to manipulate registers in a given circuit. A user can insert, delete or move registers form or to a given location. Usually registers are added in order to break the critical path(s). But finding the critical path is itself a hard task to do. However, the tool can assist the user to identify the critical path(s). Here we assume that the node delays are known. Then the user can specify the constraints as below.

$$define\_attribute < target\_clock\_period > finds\_all\_critical\_paths$$

The tool will list down all the paths having delay more than the specified delay. The user can decide which path to choose for inserting additional registers.

In order to help the developers, a method based on BFS [12] has been developed which finds all the critical paths with delays more than the specified target clock period. We find the critical path using a Breadth First Algorithm which searches the entire circuit. BFS can be used in two ways. It can find all paths having delay more than the specified delay or it can output all those paths and user can manually inserts registers in those path(s).

4 Experimental Results

We have implemented our proposed method in Python and the generated results have been tested on Xilinx Vivado 2018.2 [14]. In our experiment, standard ISCAS89 [13] benchmark circuits have been used. The ISCAS89 circuits have gate level design abstraction. In our implementation, ISCAS89 circuit is converted to an internal netlist structure. The retiming and register balancing works on this internal netlist. After that the netlist is converted to ISCAS89 format again. Finally to convert the ISCAS89 to Verilog for further synthesis, we have written a ISCAS89 to Verilog converter. All the experiments are performed on Intel x64 machine with 8GB primary memory and 3 GHz refresh rate. We have considered few ISCAS89 benchmarks [13] as shown in first column of Tables 1, 2 and 3. A benchmark, for example, s27 represents 27 number of nodes are present in that design.

4.1   Experiment 1

Table 1 shows the results for our register insertion constraints. Here, we show the critical path minimization where user knows the critical path(s) and inserts registers at specific locations to break the critical path. The observations are tabulated in Table 1. Before retiming the number of nodes in a critical path are shown in second column. Note that, we considered 5ns as the target clock period for first two set of benchmarks and 10ns for the rest of benchmarks taken for our experiment. The delay of each node has been kept as 1ns and each experiment has been performed 3 times and average values have been considered. It may be noted in column three that the critical paths are minimized due to user added insertion constraints. The results were generated and then converted automatically to Verilog and then synthesized using Xilinx Vivado. In Table 1, it may be notice that, the timing is not showing drastic improvement. For small circuits its not possible to show major improvements. However, for complex circuits we can get major timing improvements.

Table 1. Retiming for register insertion

Benchmark	Critical path (Before)	Critical path (After)	Time (Before)	Time (After)
s27	8	5	5.97	5.97
s298	8	5	6.01	6.01
s344	18	10	6.33	6.33
s820	12	10	6.41	6.301
s953	13	10	6.49	6.47
s1494	16	10	6.673	6.607
s1423	26	10	6.713	6.589

4.2   Experiment 2

We considered a trio, for example, 1I-2D-0M represents one register insertion operation, two register deletion operations and zero register movement operation. We have considered a number of trios for different benchmarks of ISCAS89 as shown in Table 2. Based on this trio, the result for LOC (lines of code) in Verilog,

LUT (look up table) and FF (flipflops or registers) are also shown in Table 2. We can see that, LUT is the same for a specific benchmark irrespective of the trio operations. This is because retiming does not change the functionality of the circuit i.e. the number of gates are unchanged after register manipulation. But, number of FF's (registers) change due to register balancing in all the parallel paths. We can notice that, there is a increase in FF (6 to 15 and 6 to 21) for the last benchmark considered i.e. s1494 due to the automatic register balancing. This is because the registers are inserted in all parallel paths by the retiming engine to balance the parallel paths.

4.3   Experiment 3

We considered our previously discussed BFS method in Sect. 3.4 to identify and break the critical path(s) in the circuit. This method finds all the critical paths. The results are shown in Table 3. We can find the critical paths and add delays to them using the proposed insertion register method or the same BFS algorithm can be used to insert delays in all the critical paths. BFS method gives a guidance to the user to identify the critical paths and where to insert the registers. It may be noticed that the number of critical paths reduced when we increase the target clock. For example, when the target clock for the benchmarks change from 5ns to 15ns, the number of critical paths reduced from 311 to 0 for benchmark s953 and from 165 to 1 for benchmark s1494. Here, we considered delay of all nodes to be 1ns but we can assign variable delay to different nodes in the procedure.

For deletion, smaller circuits are not producing an impact worth to report here. But it can be used to remove redundant registers from a circuit.

Table 2. Experiments on ISCAS89 standard circuits

Benchmark	Operation	LOC in Verilog	LUT	FF
s298	0I 0D 0M	321	119	14
	2I 1D 0M	332	119	19
	1I 2D 1M	331	119	20
s444	0I 0D 0M	484	181	21
	2I 1D 0M	502	181	25
	1I 2D 1M	509	181	26
s953	0I 0D 0M	979	395	29
	2I 1D 0M	989	395	36
	1I 2D 1M	990	395	35
s1494	0I 0D 0M	1356	647	6
	2I 1D 0M	1373	647	15
	4I 2D 1M	1401	647	21

Table 3. Finding critical paths

Benchmark	Target clock = 5	Target clock = 10	Target clock = 15
s27	8	0	0
s298	9	0	0
s400	23	0	0
s526	21	0	0
s820	91	5	0
s953	311	31	0
s1494	165	70	1

5 Related Work

This work is an improvement over [1]. In [1], author has presented a method for inserting register(s) after specific node(s). Their method does automatic register balancing by inserting a dummy node after each user specified node. They assigned computational delays as same as target clock period to the specific combinational node and the dummy node inserted after that and zero for all other nodes. It fails to work along with retiming as it locks all the existing registers in the circuit. The proposed method here can work along with retiming without use of dummy nodes after each user specified edge. Here also, there is no need of forcefully assigning specific delays to the combinational nodes. They only considered insertion of registers in a circuit. This paper presents different approaches for insertion, deletion and movement of registers and does automatic register balancing along with retiming.

6 Conclusion and Future Work

Manual insertion or deletion or movement of registers is a challenging task as it leads to register balancing in all parallel paths. So, this process has to be automated. In this paper, we proposed two constraints for automatic register insertion, deletion and movement in a circuit with user specified edges. This problem is solved along with existing retiming algorithms. Retiming model for insertion and deletion of registers is also discussed in the paper. We implemented both insertion and deletion of registers in Python and tested our approach using Xilinx Vivado. In future an algorithm can be proposed to automatically identify the specific location to insert or delete register to or from the circuit. Machine learning [10,11] can also play a crucial part in this problem. Vanilla Recurrent Neural Network [8,9] can be developed which can learn from various circuits regarding the most optimal place to put registers and perform the same during synthesis.

References

1. Karfa, C.: Automatic register balancing in model-based high-level synthesis. In: 6th Asia Symposium on Quality Electronic Design, Kula Lumpur, pp. 43–49 (2015). https://doi.org/10.1109/ACQED.2015.7274005
2. Malik, S., Sentovich, E.M., Brayton, R.K., Sangiovanni-Vincentelli, A.: Retiming and resynthesis: optimizing sequential networks with combinational techniques. IEEE Trans. Comput.-Aided Des. Integr. Circuits Syst. **10**(1), 74–84 (1991). https://doi.org/10.1109/43.62793
3. Leiserson, C.E., Saxe, J.B.: Optimizing synchronous systems. In: 22nd Annual Symposium on Foundations of Computer Science, Nashville, TN, USA, pp. 23–36 (1981). https://doi.org/10.1109/SFCS.1981.34
4. Leiserson, C.E., Saxe, J.B.: Retiming synchronous circuitry. Algorithmica **6**(1), 5–35 (1991)
5. Shenoy, N.: Retiming: theory and practice. Integr. VLSI J. **22**, 1–21 (1997)
6. Ekpanyapong, M., Waterwait, T., Lim, S.K.: Statistical Bellman-Ford algorithm with an application to retiming. In: Asia and South Pacific Conference on Design Automation, Yokohama, p. 6 (2006). https://doi.org/10.1109/ASPDAC.2006.1594810
7. Busato, F., Bombieri, N.: An efficient implementation of the Bellman-Ford algorithm for Kepler GPU architectures. IEEE Trans. Parallel Distrib. Syst. **27**(8), 2222–2233 (2016). https://doi.org/10.1109/TPDS.2015.2485994
8. Dongare, A.D., Kharde, R.R., Kachare, A.D.: Introduction to artificial neural network. Int. J. Eng. Innov. Technol. **2**(1) (2012)
9. Sinha, B.K., Sinhal, A., Verma, B.: A software measurement using artificial neural network and support vector machine. Int. J. Softw. Eng. Appl. **4**(4) (2013)
10. Blei, D.M., Ng, A.Y., Jordan, M.I.: Latent Dirichlet allocation. J. Mach. Learn. Res. **3**, 993–1022 (2003)
11. LeCun, Y.A., Bottou, L., Orr, G.B., Müller, K.-R.: Efficient backprop. In: Montavon, G., Orr, G.B., Müller, K.-R. (eds.) Neural Networks: Tricks of the Trade. LNCS, vol. 7700, pp. 9–48. Springer, Heidelberg (2012). https://doi.org/10.1007/978-3-642-35289-8_3
12. Pai, S.: An operational performance model of breadth-first search (2017)
13. ISCAS89 Sequential Benchmark Circuits. http://www.pld.ttu.ee/maksim/benchmarks/iscas89/verilog. Accessed 01 Mar 2019
14. Vivado Design Suite - HLx Editions. https://www.xilinx.com/products/design-tools/vivado.html. Accessed 01 Mar 2019
15. Parhi, K.K.: VLSI Digital Signal Processing Systems: Design and Implementation. Wiley, Hoboken (1999)
16. Cormen, T.H., Leiserson, C.E., Rivest, R.L., Stein, C.: Introduction to Algorithms. The MIT Press, Cambridge (2001)

RISC-V Half Precision Floating Point Instruction Set Extensions and Co-processor

Aneesh Raveendran[1(✉)], Sandra Jean[2], J. Mervin[1], D. Vivian[1], and David Selvakumar[1]

[1] Centre for Development of Advanced Computing, Bangalore, India
{raneesh,mervinj,viviand,david}@cdac.in
[2] College of Engineering, Anna University, Chennai, India
sandrajeanedward@gmail.com

Abstract. Recent times low/variable precision floating point operations have found its significance in the areas of AI, ML and IoT which need a balanced criterion like low-power/energy, area, high-performance, variable dynamic range/precision depending on the applications. The options are IEEE 754-2008 half (HP)/single (SP)/double (DP) precision floating point (FP) or the new data-type, POSIT [20]. Moreover, instructions set enabled computations provide flexibility for the applications. This paper presents a design of IEEE 754-2008 [11] half precision floating point (HP-FP)instruction set extensions (ISE) for RISC-V ISA [1] and details the architectures of various functional units of the co-processor. The out-of-order execute, in-order commit/retire co-processor supports half-precision addition, subtraction, division, square root, multiplication, fused multiply and accumulate, sign injection and compare. The co-processor accepts three half precision data operands, rounding mode and the associated op-code fields for computation. Each floating point computation is tagged with an instruction token to enable out-of-order execution, in-order completion and commit. The proposed modular floating point co-processor enables integration with integer pipeline. The RISC-V instruction set enabled half-precision co-processor has been verified using Berkeley soft-float test suites, synthesized for ASIC and FPGA and implemented on FPGA. A performance of 236 MHz on Xilinx Virtex-6 xcvlx550t FPGA and 555 MHz on 65 nm had been achieved.

Keywords: Floating point Co-processor · RISC-V instruction set extension · Instruction set extension for half precision ·
Half precision floating point co-processor · Processor micro-architecture ·
Out-Of-Order processor · IEEE 754-2008 compliant FPU

1 Introduction

Floating point numbers provide a wider dynamic range which offers better precision than the same length fixed point numbers. Floating point operations are used for applications such as embedded signal processing, graphic processing [2], digital image processing [3], and arithmetic protocols for secured data analysis [4] and also for astronomical and scientific calculations. Over the years, the requirements on precision

© Springer Nature Singapore Pte Ltd. 2019
A. Sengupta et al. (Eds.): VDAT 2019, CCIS 1066, pp. 482–495, 2019.
https://doi.org/10.1007/978-981-32-9767-8_40

range, rounding schemes, exceptions handling etc. of floating point and its arithmetic varied with every application. Some critical applications cannot tolerate rounding and truncation errors because of great number of calculations. For example, basic linear algebra subprograms (BLAS) based on Bailey's arithmetic uses Quadruple precision (QP) numbers to improve accuracy of calculations in supercomputers [5].

Besides these higher precision requirements, many applications do not require bulky (double or quadruple) floating point numbers consisting of larger precision/ range. IoT, AI/ML and embedded applications require energy efficient processors in their SoC platform; hence, for 16 or 32-bit processors, lower floating point computations are ideal. Namely, processors such as MSP430 [6] and ARM CORTEX-M3 are preferred for IoT and embedded systems with single precision (SP) computations. To facilitate the need of further lower precision floating point computation in such processors, FP16or FP8 can be adopted. Lower precision floats results in reduction in storage space, less computational time and decrease in implementation cost and area. IEEE 754 proposes a half precision FP to represent 16-bit FP numbers [11]. RISC-V specification [1] details instructions for SP FP, DP FP computations and highlights for HP FP operations.

Three basic components in IEEE 754 representation are sign (S), exponent (E) and mantissa (M) as shown in Table 1.

Table 1. Floating point number representation.

Precision	Sign(S)	Exponent(E)	Mantissa(M)	Bias(B)
Half	1[15]	5[14:10]	10[9:0]	15
Single	1[31]	8[30:23]	23[22:0]	127
Double	1[63]	11[62:52]	52[51:0]	1023

FP Number = $(-1)S* 2(E\text{-}Bias) * (H.M)$ where H is hidden bit which is always 1.

IEEE 754-2008 standard specifies all floating point operations. It accommodates all special inputs like sNaN, qNaN, +Infinity, –Infinity, positive zero and negative zero. It specifies five exceptions namely, overflow, underflow, invalid, inexact and division by zero. It facilitates five different rounding modes.

2   Literature Survey

Article [7] projects the effort of adding two half-precision floating point Numbers, employs round-to-zero, and treats de-normalized numbers as underflow. The verification has been carried out using hand generated test vectors (few hundreds) to test few corner cases involving NaN and Infinity and Perl script based auto test vector generator (2 million) to test wide variety of test cases. Article [8] argues that HP-FP arithmetic offers larger dynamic range than fixed point and fewer hardware resources than SP-FP/DP-FP and enough precision for certain applications. It reports a low latency HP-FP reciprocal square root (RSR) unit on FPGA and compares the performance with Intel and Xilinx RSR IP core. Literature [9] depicts HP-FP multiply-accumulate unit and adopts an innovative technique on pre-compute adjustment of the operands to utilize only DSP blocks of FPGA for performing mantissa multiplication and accumulation. The thesis [10] elaborates on the FPGA implementation of variable precision FP divide and square root for image and signal processing algorithms. It demonstrates a fully pipelined design with good tradeoff between area, latency and throughput and to enable integration with complex and pipelined designs. A half-precision floating point arithmetic unit [12] on 350 nm CMOS technology has been proposed, which supports operations such as addition, subtraction, multiplication and division using FMA techniques and adopts custom design approach. The multiplier is based on Wallace Tree configuration and Divider adopts an iterative algorithm based on Newton-Raphson technique.

An implementation [13] proposes a half precision floating point multiplier on 130 nm CMOS processes; it has a delay of 5 ns, suitable for low power, low-computational and low accuracy tolerant IoT applications. An ASIC implementation of floating point functional unit [14] proposes a combined half and single precision floating point multiplier for deep learning applications. The core runs on HP mode to conserve energy and SP mode to have better accuracy. An integrated approximate division and square root operation [15] with support of half, single and double precision floating point by varying precision (trans-precision) were presented with approximate computing method for RISC-V ISA. To achieve energy efficiency trans-precision is introduced with variable precision mantissa, the key contribution of the paper. The unit is integrated with multi-core RISC-V processor cluster as shared unit. The division adopts non-restoring binary divisor (NRBD) and square root follows non-restoring square root calculation (NRSC) algorithms with radix-2. In our earlier paper, RISC-V compliant FPU co-processor without precision control is presented in [16] which support all RISC-V floating point SP and DP instructions and achieved a throughput of 180 MFLOPS. Mr. Wolf [17], a PULP SoC targeted for IoT applications obtained a throughput of 1 GFLOP/s - with an energy-efficiency up to 15 MMAC/s/mW and 9 MFMAC/s/mW. It has 8 cores of low power RISC-V RVC32IMFX which has ISE for DSP operations and has 2 shared FPUs (common operations and FMAC). A RISC-V implementation (ROCKET Core – 64bit dual core) [18] details a single/double precision floating point co-processor with FMA at 45 nm SOI process and achieved a throughput of 16.7GFLOPS per watt. The FPU supports de-normal numbers and other exceptional values on hardware.

Our work focuses on architecting an out-of-order execute, in-order commit/retire FP co-processor supporting half-precision FP addition, subtraction, division, square root, multiplication, fused multiply and accumulate, sign injection and compare as an ISE for RISC-V. RISC-V ISA [1] states that half-precision scalar values are only supported as part of Vector Extension. Besides, it states that adding vector extension to any machine with floating-point support adds support for the IEEE HP-FP data type including a set of scalar half-precision instructions [21]. The ISA specification does not describe the HP-FP instructions separately as scalar extensions like SP (F)/DP (D), but follows the same template of other precisions. Our HP-FP co-processor is based on scalar half-precision instructions. However, the co-processor can be integrated as a functional unit for vectorized data/computations with a suitable converter to bundle the operands from vector register file.

Section 3 highlights RISC-V HP-FP ISE in-line with SP/DP FP instructions. Section 4 details the out-of-order coprocessor. Section 5 narrates the micro-architectures of various functional units. Section 6 explains the rationale on the adopted verification methodology. Section 7 presents the results on FPGA and 65 nm CMOS. Section 8 concludes and briefs further works.

3   RISC-V Half Precision Instruction Set Extension

3.1   Half Precision Floating Point Instruction

As mentioned earlier, HP-FP instructions are not defined as a separate scalar extension to reduce the number of standard instruction set variants. It's supported as part of Vector extensions [1, 21]. Figure 1 shows the instruction formats for scalar floating point operations. Bit position 25 to 26 (funct2 field) specifies the type of the floating operations and possible scalar/vector options which is referred by decodes are shown in Table 2. RS1, RS2 and RS3 are the source registers and RD is the destination register. funct3 field can be used to indicate rounding mode.funct 2 fields could be used to indicate HP operations.

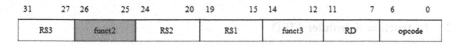

Fig. 1. RISC-V floating point instruction format.

3.2   Register File Organization (HP - Scalar Extensions)

RISC-V proposes 32 GPRs (x0 – x31) of size 32bit/64bit (XLEN) that store integer values that are visible to the user for 32-bit/64-bit user level address spaces. For FP ISE, 32 FP registers (f0 – f31), of FLEN bit length are added. FLEN can be of 32, 64 & 128-bit, for single, double and quad-precisions respectively. The effective register length is Maximum of (XLEN, FLEN).

3.3   Register File Organization (HP - Scalar Extensions)

For HP Fused Multiply-Accumulate (FMA), except funct2 (10) the remaining fields are same as SP/DP FP FMA. Table 3 depicts the proposed HP-FP ISE (scalar) for other operations.

4   RISC-V Half Precision Out of Order FP Co-processor

Top level architecture of pipelined out-of-order half precision floating point co-processor is depicted in Fig. 2. FPU co-processor contains instruction decoder, instruction scheduler FIFO, floating point functional units for each operation and an

Table 2. Instruction encoding format for SP/DP/HP-FP.

Funct2 Field	Mnemonic	Meaning
00	F	32-bit Single Precision
01	D	64-bit Double Precision
10	H	16-bit Half Precision
11	Q	128-bit Quad Precision

output decoder. FPU co-processor accepts the floating point instruction in-order, performs the computation out-of-order, and commits the results in-order.

4.1   Instruction Decoder

FPU instruction decoder decodes the input instruction and generates the enable signal for the corresponding functional unit. FPU input request contains, three half precision floating point data inputs along with 7-bit opcode, 7-bit F7 field, 5-bit F5 field, 3-bit F3 field and 3-bit rounding mode from RISC-V instruction. Rounding mode is instruction-wise or based on global flag.

4.2   Instruction Scheduler FIFO

The instruction scheduler FIFO stores the decoded instruction token/identifier in-order. The input valid signal given at the input acts as the write enable. Based on the identifier on top of the scheduler FIFO, FPU co-processor reads the results from corresponding individual floating point unit and commits the results in-order.

4.3   Functional Units

Proposed HP-FP pipelined arithmetic unit consists of seven concurrent units namely, Adder/Subtractor, Multiplier, Fused Multiplier and accumulator, Divider, Square root, Sign Injection and Operand Comparator to achieve high throughput for independent/concurrent HP-FP computations. FIFO is placed at the end of each functional unit to store the outputs from each unit. FIFOs are placed at the end of each unit to maintain the balance between individual floating point functional units. Addition/subtraction, multiplication units have a latency of 6 and 5 clock cycles respectively. Division and square root operation takes 19clock cycles. Sign injection and comparator takes 1 clock cycle and Fused Multiply-Accumulate module takes 8 clock cycles.

Table 3. Proposed HP floating point instruction set extension (scalar).

Opcode [6:0]	Funct7 [31:25]	Funct5 [24:20]	Funct3 [14:12]	Instruction
1010011 (computational)	0000010	RS2	RM	FADD.H
	0000110	RS2	RM	FSUB.H
	0001010	RS2	RM	FMUL.H
	0001110	RS2	RM	FDIV.H
	0101110	00000	RM	FSQRT.H
1010011 (sign injection)	0010010	RS2	000	FSGNJ.H
			001	FSGNJN.H
			010	FSGNJX.H
1010011 (minimum and maximum)	0010110	RS2	000	FMINS.H
			001	FMAX.H
1010011 (Comparison)	1010010	RS2	010	FEQ.H
			001	FLT.H
			000	FLE.H
1010011 (classification)	1110010	00000	001	FCLASS.H
1010011 (float to float conversion)	0100000	00010	RM	FCVT.S.H
	0100001	00011	RM	FCVT.D.H
	0100010	00100	RM	FCVT.H.S
		00101	RM	FCVT.H.D
1010011 (HP float to 32/64-bit integer)	1100010	00100	RM	FCVT.W.H
		00101	RM	FCVT.WU.H
		00110	RM	FCVT.L.H
		00111	RM	FCVT.LU.H
1010011 (32/64-bit integer to HP float)	1101010	00100	RM	FCVT.H.W
		00101	RM	FCVT.H.WU
		00110	RM	FCVT.H.L
1010011 (move)	1110010	00000	000	FMV.X.H
	1111010			FMV.H.X

4.4   Output Decoder

The output decoder reads the instruction token from the scheduler FIFO and checks whether the corresponding functional units FIFO is empty or not. If the FIFO is empty, the decoder waits till FIFO gets an element or if FIFO is not empty; it reads the entry from the FIFO and gives as 16-bit HP-FP result along with 5-bit exception.

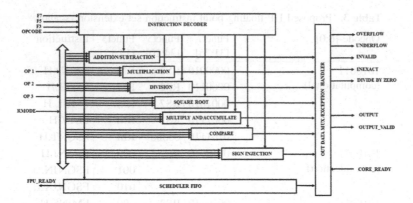

Fig. 2. HP-FP RISC-V Out-Of-Order coprocessor

5 Micro-architecture of HP-FP Functional Units

5.1 Adder and Subtractor Unit

Inputs: Two HP-FP operands, rounding mode, add/sub. Outputs: HP-FP result, 5 bits exception. Figure 3 depicts the micro-architecture of Adder/Subtractor functional unit.

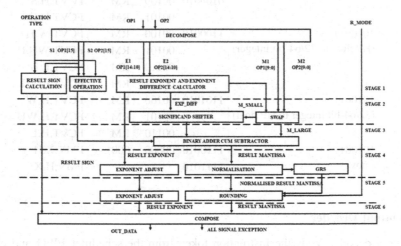

Fig. 3. Micro-architecture of Adder/Subtractor unit

In stage-1, the input operands are decomposed and classified into six formats: Zero, Infinity, qNaN, sNaN, Subnormal and normal numbers. The signs along with the input operation type are used for calculating the result sign. The effective operation to be carried out is determined by the XOR of the input signs and the operation type. Also the exponents are compared and the exponent differences are computed, larger exponent is set as the result exponent; hidden bit is appended to the mantissa based on whether it is a normal number or a subnormal number.

In stage-2, the mantissas (M1 and M2) are swapped such that the mantissa with the larger exponent is M1 and the mantissa with the smaller exponent is M2. M2 is shifted left by the exponent difference times for exponent matching. In stage-3 the mantissas are added or subtracted based on the effective operation to be performed as computed in stage-1. Stage-4 computes the leading one position (LOD) of mantissa and the exponent is adjusted based on the leading one position. Also mantissa is normalized such that the hidden bit is set to one. Guard bit and round bit are the last two bits shifted out. Sticky bit is the OR of all the remaining bits shifted out.

In stage-5 the rounding is performed on normalized mantissa which makes use of the guard, round and sticky bit; if required, the exponent is adjusted again after rounding. In final stage 6, the outputs of special operands are generated based on the number formats arrived in stage 1. If both the numbers are normal or subnormal, the result mantissa and exponent obtained are from stage-5, and along with the result sign the output is reconstructed in IEEE format and given as the output. Otherwise predefined special numbers along with exceptions will be given as output.

5.2   Multiplier Unit

Inputs: Two HP-FP operands, rounding mode. Outputs: HP-FP result, 5 bit exception. Figure 4 depicts the micro-architecture of half precision floating point multiplier unit.

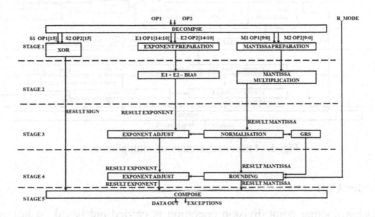

Fig. 4. Micro-architecture of multiplier unit

In stage-1, the two operands are decomposed and number format of each operand are noted. Result sign is calculated by XORing the signs of the input operands. In stage-2, the result exponent is calculated by adding two exponents, and subtracting half precision bias value. Result exponent is checked for overflow or underflow. Also multiplication of two mantissas is performed.

In stage-3, the position of leading one (LOD) is computed such that the leading significant bit is set to one. Based on the leading one position value, the mantissa and the exponent are adjusted. Guard, round and Sticky bit is calculated as in addition. In stage-4, rounding is performed based on the user specified rounding mode. Exponent is adjusted after rounding if required and will perform overflow or underflow checks. In final stage, the generation of special case outputs and reconstruction of the processed result to fit the 16-bit IEEE format were performed. Exception signals namely overflow, underflow, inexact, and invalid is raised whenever required.

5.3 Fused-Multiply Add Unit

Inputs: Three HP-FP operands, rounding mode, operation type – add/sub/negate add/negate sub. Outputs: HP-FP result, 5 bit exception. Rounding operation is performed only after addition to increase the precision and accuracy. Figure 5 depicts the micro-architecture of floating point multiply-accumulate unit. MAC unit combines the functionality of Multiplication and Addition/subtraction as section A and B.

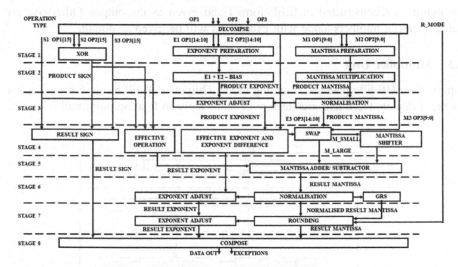

Fig. 5. Micro-architecture of multiplier unit

5.4 Divider Unit

Half-precision floating point division operation is carried out based on non-restoring binary division algorithm (NRBD). Inputs: Two HP-FP operands, rounding mode, Outputs: HP-FP result, 5 bits exception. Figure 6 depicts the micro-architecture of division unit.

In stage-1, inputs operands are decomposed and classified into six formats. If subnormal numbers are detected, the exponent is normalized to IEEE standard Emin value. Leading Zero Detectors (LZD) is used to count the leading zeros in mantissa. Quotient sign is the XOR of input operands sign. In stage-2, result exponent is calculated by subtracting the two exponents and adding a bias value. The exponent overflow or underflow is checked and the mantissa is normalized by shifting left based on leading zeros.

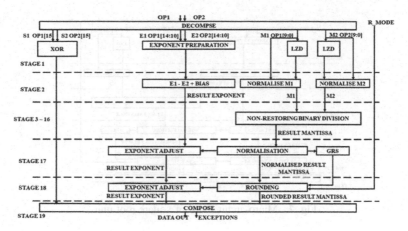

Fig. 6. Micro-architecture of division unit

In stage-1, inputs operands are decomposed and classified into six formats. If subnormal numbers are detected, the exponent is normalized to IEEE standard Emin value. Leading Zero Detectors (LZD) is used to count the leading zeros in mantissa. Quotient sign is the XOR of input operands sign. In stage-2, result exponent is calculated by subtracting the two exponents and adding a bias value. The exponent overflow or underflow is checked and the mantissa is normalized by shifting left based on leading zeros.

From stage-3 to stage-16, a non-restoring binary division algorithm is used, which produces a 14-bit of quotient from 14 iterations. In each iteration the dividend is shifted left once, the divisor is added or subtracted based on the previous quotient bit and the compliment of MSB of the resulting value is the quotient bit generated.

In stage-17, normalization is done by detecting the leading one in the mantissa. If the resulting quotient is less than one, the mantissa is shifted left and the exponent is decremented. The three bits after the required quotient are the guard, round and sticky bits. In stage 18, rounding is performed based on the specified rounding mode. Guard bit, Round bit and sticky bit decides whether 0 or 1 must be added to the normalized mantissa. After rounding, if required this stage performs the normalization operation. In stage-19, resultant values of sign, mantissa and exponent are reconstructed into the IEEE format and given as data out along with 5-bit exceptions. Results of special cases are also generated in this stage and sent as data out along with particular exception.

5.5   Square Root Unit

Inputs: One HP-FP operand, rounding mode, Outputs: HP-FP result, 5 bits exception. Square root is also computed in similar fashion to that of division. Figure 7 shows the micro architecture of half precision floating point square root operation.

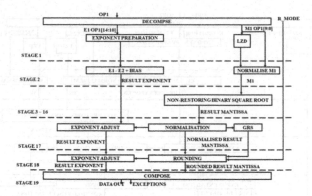

Fig. 7. Micro-architecture of square root unit

In stage-1, the input operand is decomposed and determined under which number format it falls. Negative numbers, operands with sign bit 1 is also detected. Result exponent is calculated by adding a bias to it and dividing the resulted exponent value by two if the input exponent is odd. If the input exponent is even, bias – 1 is added to it and the resulted exponent value is divided by two. The mantissa is shifted left by once in case of even exponents for normalization. A leading zero detector (LZD) is used to detect the leading zeros in the mantissa.

In stage-2: mantissa is shifted left based on the value of the leading zero detector. Stage-3 to stage-18 uses non-restoring square root algorithm (NRSC) and the operation is similar to division operation mentioned in section D. In stage-19, resultant values is reconstructed by padding sign, exponent and mantissa IEEE format and gives as data out along with 5-bit exceptions.

5.6   Comparator Unit

Comparator performs five different two operands (OP1 and OP2) HP-FP instructions – FLT.H (Less than), FLE.H (less than equal), FEQ.H (equal to), MIN.H (minimum of two numbers) and MAX (maximum of two numbers). The exponents and mantissa are compared separately. If OP1 is less than/less than equal/equal to OP2, a 16 bit data with LSB set as '1' is given as output. For minimum/maximum, the operand which is minimum/maximum of the two operands is given out as output.

5.7   Sign-Injection Unit

Sign injection module receives two input operands (OP1 and OP2), operation type signal. FSGNJ.H instruction computes the result sign as operand 2 sign. FSGNJN.H computes the result sign as compliment of operand 2 sign. FSGNJX.H operation computes the result sign as XOR of the sign of operand1 and sign of operand2. Mantissa and exponent of result will be same as that of operand 1. Latency for the operation is one clock cycle.

6 Verification of HP FPU

Verification of HP-FP adder/subtractor in article [7] has been carried out using hand generated test vectors (few hundreds) to test few corner cases involving NaN and Infinity and Perl script based auto test vector generator (2 million) to test wide variety of test cases. The reference model adopted for validating the output is not mentioned in [7]. Article [9] has not mentioned about verification. In article [13] the uniformly distributed pseudo-random test vectors has been generated using Matlab and Matlab output based on double precision processor has been adopted as reference.

In article [14] the combined SP and HP multiplier has been tested with Hauser's SoftFloat [19] suite for nearly 50 K test vectors. The performance has been compared with Synopsys Designware 32 bit multiplier. In [15] the approximate divider and square root unit for RISC-V ISA has been analyzed for performance and verification suite adopted has not been mentioned. In [17] and [18] FPU is part of a SoC and articles details more on SoC. Our functional units for RISC-V ISE HP-FP computations were developed on Verilog and were tested with Berkeley testFloat Release 3e [19]. The testfloat program is an all-in-one tool for testing floating-point arithmetic and generates 47,000 test operand values and reference results for each operation. Other popular floating point arithmetic unit test suites referred as [22] and [25] does not support HP-FP. Further, the RISC-V processor test suite [24] doesn't have routines to test HP-FP units. Similarly, RISC-V simulator [23] doesn't have HP-FP component.

7 FPGA and ASIC Synthesis Results

The proposed HP-FP co-processor was implemented on Xilinx Virtex-6 xc6vlx550-2ff1759 FPGA and achieved a throughput of 236 MFLOPS. Table 4 depicts the results (Table 5).

Table 4. FPGA synthesis results

Functional units	Area utilization			Max. frequency
	Slice register	Slice LUTs	DSP48E1	
Integrated HP-FP Co-processor	2200	5984	4	236 MHz

Table 5. ASIC synthesis results

Functional Unit	This work 65 nm	Work [13] '18 130 nm	Work [14], '17 32 nm	Work [15], '17 65nmLP
	(Total Power, Area, CP delay/Freq.)			
HP-FP ADD/SUB	2162 μW, 14905 μm^2, 1200 ps	–	–	–
HP-FP-MUL	1788 μW, 14277 μm^2, 1800 ps	820 μW, 29058 μm^2, 200 MHz	818 μW, 3309 μm^2, 450 ps	–
HP-FP-DIV	9459 μW, 37273 μm^2, 1600 ps	–	–	9500 μm^2, 357 MHz (5 Stages)
HP-FP-SQRT	9876 μW, 40432 μm^2, 1600 ps	–	–	9500 μm^2, 357 MHz (5 Stages)

8 Conclusion and Future Works

In this paper, a half precision instruction set extension (scalar) for RISC-V ISA has been proposed and micro-architected as a pipelined, out-of-order, HP-FP co-processor. The individual functional units of the HP-FP unit were verified using "testfloat" test suite [19]. Proposed co-processor design was implemented targeting Xilinx Virtex-6 FPGA device and 65 nm ASIC library. The design was able to achieve a throughput of 236 and 555 MFLOPS, respectively. Future works includes more rigorous verification of HP functional units, integration of HP-FP co-processor with a RISC-V processor, and running benchmark suites to determine HP-FP performance.

References

1. Waterman, A., Lee, Y., Patterson, D.A., Asanovic, K.: The RISC-V instruction set manual, vol. I: base user-level ISA. V2.2, '17
2. Hinds, C.N.: An enhanced floating point coprocessor for embedded signal processing and graphics applications. In: IEEE ACSS (1999)
3. Palekar, S., et al.: 32-bit RISC processor with floating point unit for DSP applications. In: IEEE IRTEICT (2016)
4. Lui, Y., Chiang, Y., et al.: Floating point arithmetic protocols for constructing secure data analysis application. In: 17th IEEE KES (2013)
5. Yamada, S., Ina, T., et al.: Quadruple-precision BLAS using Bailey's arithmetic with FMA instruction: its performance and applications. In: IEEE IPDP Symposium Workshops (2017)
6. Roy, A., Grossmann, P.J., et al.: A 1.3µW, 5pJ/cycle sub-threshold MSP430 processor in 90 nm xLP FDSOI for energy-efficient IoT applications. In: 17th IEEE ISQED, Santa Clara, CA (2016)
7. McAuley, T.: Half-Precision Floating Point Addition Unit. http://pages.hmc.edu/harris/class/e158/proj2/fpadder.pdf
8. Aguilera-Galicia, C.R., et al.: IEEE-754 half-precision floating-point low-latency reciprocal square root IP-core. In: 2018 IEEE 10th Latin-American Conference on Communications (2018)
9. Amaricai, A., et al.: FPGA implementations of low precision floating point multiply-accumulate. Int. J. Microelectron. Comput. Sci. 4(4) (2013)
10. Wang, X.: Variable precision floating-point divide and square root for efficient FPGA implementation of image and signal processing algorithms, Ph.D. thesis, Northeastern University Boston, Massachusetts, December 2007. http://www.ece.neu.edu/groups/rcl/theses/xjwang_phd2007.pdf
11. IEEE standards Board and ANSI, IEEE Standards for Binary Floating-point Arithmetic, 2008, IEEE Std., 754-2008
12. Kannan, B.: "The design of an IC Half Precision Floating Point Arithmetic Logic Unit", PhD Thesis 2009
13. Aguilera-Galicia, C.R., Lonuoria-Gandara, O., Pizano-Escalante, L.: Half-precision floating-point multiplier IP core based on 130 nm CMOS ASIC technology. In: IEEE LATINCOM (2018)
14. Nguyen, T.D., et al.: A combined IEEE half and single precision floating point multipliers for deep learning. In: IEEE Asilomar (2017)

15. Li, L., Gautschi, M., Benini, L.: Approximate DIV and SQRT instructions for the RISC-V ISA: an efficiency vs. accuracy analysis. In: 27th PTMOS (2017)
16. Raveendran, A., Patil, V.B., et al.: Out Of order floating point coprocessor for RISC V ISA. In: IEEE VLSISATA (2015)
17. Pullini, A., et al.: Mr. Wolf: a 1 GFLOP/s energy-proportional parallel ultra low power SoC for IoT edge processing. In: IEEE ESSCIRC (2018)
18. Lee, Y., et al.: A 45 nm 1.3 GHz 16.7 double-precision GFLOPS/W RISC-V processor with vector accelerators. In: IEEE ESSCIRC (2014)
19. BerkeleyTestFloat. http://www.jhauser.us/arithmetic/TestFloat.html
20. Next Generation Arithmetic UNUM & POSIT. https://posithub.org/
21. RISC-V "V" Vector Extension. https://github.com/riscv/riscv-v-spec/blob/master/v-spec.adoc
22. FPGen. https://www.research.ibm.com/haifa/projects/verification/fpgen/ieeets.html
23. SPIKE Simulator for RISC-V ISA. https://github.com/riscv/riscv-isa-sim
24. RISC-V Tests. https://github.com/riscv/riscv-tests/tree/master/isa
25. IEEE Floating Point Test Software. http://www.math.utah.edu/~beebe/software/ieee/

Functional Simulation Verification of RISC-V Instruction Set Based High Level Language Modeled FPU

Aneesh Raveendran$^{(\boxtimes)}$, Vinay Kumar, D. Vivian,
and David Selvakumar

Centre for Development of Advanced Computing, Bangalore, India
{raneesh, vinaym, viviand, david}@cdac.in

Abstract. Verification of a Floating point Unit is a challenging and unique task. Major challenges are the selection of reference model for verification and coverage domains and space of test vectors. The proposed paper considers a RISC-V compliant floating point unit modelled using a high level language, Bluespec System Verilog as Design Under Test (DUT) for verification. A reference model of floating point unit is developed in 'C' compliance with RISC-V ISA. To fulfil the requirements of test vector coverage domain and space, we have adopted four different kinds of test vectors schemes for verification. At first, a pseudo random verification approach is used to reduce the initial errors in design. In step-2, a RISC-V test suite was used to verify the proposed design for compliance with RISC-V ISA. In step-3, FPgen/IBM floating point test vectors were used to test for corner case test vectors, for better coverage space. Further, we adopted a unique approach to validate the RISC-V FPU in FPGA by providing the above three kinds of test vectors as inputs through 'C' application code on host machine. The outputs are compared with the above 'C' based reference model/FPgen output vectors/RISC-V test suite output vectors. In step-4, FPU on FPGA is validated using Whetstone code on host-machine FPU and redirected Whetstone floating point computations to FPU DUT on Xilinx Virtex-6 vc6lx550T FPGA device. Finally, the RISC-V FPU is integrated with dual issue out-of-order execute, in-order commit RISC-V processor and demonstrated a whetstone benchmarking application on FPGA. Major benefits of the proposed floating point verification can be extended to an application based RISC-V compliant floating point unit validation on FPGA without the use of RISC-V processor pipeline.

Keywords: RISC-V ISA · IEEE 754-2008 ·
Floating point processor verification · Formal verification of FPU ·
RISC-V processor · High level language verification ·
Verification of bluespec models

1 Introduction

Verification of Floating Point Unit (FPU) has been identified as a challenging task. In particular the difficulty arises in covering the test space of floating point numbers and several corner cases where floating point numbers tends to infinity or Not a Number

© Springer Nature Singapore Pte Ltd. 2019
A. Sengupta et al. (Eds.): VDAT 2019, CCIS 1066, pp. 496–509, 2019.
https://doi.org/10.1007/978-981-32-9767-8_41

(NaN) or denormals. Further, when the FPU is modelled as instruction set enabled unit additional verification challenges include generating appropriate instruction sequences model. Floating point unit can be verified using two methodologies i.e. either using formal verification methods [37–40] or using test vector based functional simulation method [15]. Formal verification methods for FPU tries to prove the functional correctness of the design, which generates the test vectors to reach approximately 100% coverage on design, but fails to cover the corner and extreme corner cases. Such corners cases require a significant amount of handwork which makes the task of FPU verification as a combined approach adopting both formal verification and test vector simulation based verification considering corner cases as well.

Simulation based methods involves generation of input test vectors to stimulate the design and verification of the results. Typically, FPU operands are generated by a constrained random generator while a scoreboard collects information from reference model and FPU device under test (DUT). The FPU DUT results are checked against a validated reference model. Combination of formal and simulation based approach for verification helps to identify and track the bugs in floating point unit.

The proposed strategies for FPU verification focuses on verification of an IEEE 754-2008 [41] compliant, instruction set enabled (RISC-V ISA based FP computations add, sub, mul, div, sqrt, convert, compare, min/max, signinject – single precision (SP) and double precision (DP)) and modelled with a high level hardware description language, BlueSpec [20], our FPU which is detailed in [35]. The FPU fully adheres to IEEE 754 standard for SP-FP, DP-FP representations and computations, special operands (sNaN, qNaN, +infinity, −infinity, +Zero, −Zero), rounding modes support and exception handling schemes. All the computations related to "denormal" numbers are also handled in hardware. RISC-V ISA is based on fixed length instructions and supports compressed 16 bit instructions. The ISA supports 32 and 64 bits data and adopts separate FP register file (32 bits/64 bits).

Section 2 details the literatures on the topic and Sect. 3 briefs the design of RISC-V ISA compliant FPU and detailed in [35]. Section 4 details the reference model for the RISC-V FPU verification. Section 5 briefs the various methods and schemes used for RISC-V FPU verification. Section 6 details FPGA prototyping and FPU instructions validation on FPGA using Whetstone benchmark code by substituting our FPU instead of host machine FPU. Section 7 compares our approaches with other related published works. Section 8 concludes and future works.

2 Literature Survey

Article [1] details the design basis and implementation of a general purpose functional verification monitors written in System Verilog with Cover Points and Coverage Collector to verify FPU described using HDL. Further, methodologies for the input and output test vectors domain coverage, identification of corner cases are defined. The output of FPU, the Device Under Verification (DUV) is compared with an already verified reference model FPU. The reference model FPU adopted to test the designs is based on Soft Float library [2] for binary representation and the IBM's DecNumber library [3] for decimal arithmetic. As case studies only addition and subtraction had been evaluated. Article [4] depicts the design and verification of a FPU modelled in VHDL to be used as reusable IP block called Milk co-processor. The implementation is compliant with IEEE Std. 754-1985. The code has been verified initially using generic test vector based simulation to identify larger bugs and further code-based analysis to verify for the corner cases. Recent times High Level Languages based hardware design has been adopted to speed up the product development time. In the similar angle article [5] articulates a High Level Synthesis (HLS) framework based on commercial tool, designs and verifies a FPU complaint with IEEE Std. 754-1985 using the HLS framework from behavioural model to gate level netlist. FPU code had been developed using System C as a behavioural model and synthesized till gate level netlist using the proposed HLS framework of the article which is based on commercial tool. RTL generated from HLS had been simulated with Commercially-off-the-shelf (COTS) tool. The RTL has been tested with a ported EEMBC FPMark [6] (dedicated to FPU) to target design. COTS LEC tool has been adopted to prove the design between netlist and RTL. The paper suggests adopting a formal verification tool to prove the logic equivalence between high level behavioral model of FPU written in System C and HLS generated RTL and make the framework more robust.

Article [7] describes a coverage model for the verification of FPU (IEEE Std. 754-2008) and verifies model with FP addition (binary 16). It presents a heuristic approach for coverage models based on equivalence classes (partitioning) and boundary value analysis. The test bench is written in System Verilog which generates the test vectors based on the proposed coverage models, provides them as input to the DUV, and compares the output with the output of the reference model for the FPU. The paper doesn't suggest the kind of reference model used for final checking the validity of the DUV output. Further, in order to establish the confidence on the coverage models envisaged in the paper, it has been compared with FPGen v1.1 [8] and lists the discrepancy between the two coverage models viz. the one proposed in the paper and the FPGen coverage models. It has been mentioned that FPGen targets coverage models based on rounding modes and intermediate operands defined by standard as well which the article [7] did not consider. Literature [9] describes the a mixed strategy for the coverage models by combining the Constrained Random Tests (CRT) which is materialized by the input test vector generator and Coverage Driven Verification (CDV) which is taken care by the verification monitor. CDV gives feedback to CRT generator about the coverage achieved and based on that the CRT tunes the test vector generation strategies. Broadly the paper targets the simulation based verification of FPU which includes the input generation, simulation of DUV with generated test inputs, and analysis of the DUV outputs which is done by a monitor. The monitor compares the output with a reference model. The paper does not mention about the adopted reference model. CRT and CDV have been developed with System Verilog. The two DUV are decimal and binary FPU compliant with IEEE Std. 754-2008 supporting ADD and SUB operations. The paper argues by citing various other references that, simulation based verification of FPU remains the primary means despite few successes of formal methods based verification of FPUs. The reasons cited is that the corner cases of input vectors require significant time in the execution of formal methods.

All the references [1, 4, 5, 7, 9] focus on FPU verification based on simulation and the FPU DUV that has been considered is neither instruction set enabled or pipelined.

Further, those papers focus proving the verification methodologies limited to few FPU operations and only data paths of FPU and not control path-data path together.

The paper [10] details a formal approach, based on equivalence checking. The article considers instructions sequence enabled, pipelined design of FPU which is closer to industrial processors. Such models enable verification of not only complex data paths of FPU, but also the control paths of the FPU. Further, it overcomes the limitation of verifying single instruction issued on empty pipeline. It considers stressing the pipeline/control paths and thereby FP instructions sequence by adding non-FP instructions ahead and after. It's an automated bit level formal verification of end-to-end. Two instances of the FPU is used, one serves as a reference and the other actual DUV. Execution of instruction sequences is equivalence checked between both. Proof of correctness of each individual instruction is considered from which the paper infers that the entire FPU is verified formally. Article [11] argues that not all FP operations are implemented as a logic circuit. For example, divide and square root operations are implemented as "micro-coded" sequences based on the adopted iterative approximate algorithms viz. Newton-Raphson method. The paper describes a method to do verification in such scenarios and modifies FPGen [8] suitably. Article [12] discusses implementation and verification of decimal FPU in System Z9, the first IBM processor supporting decimal FP arithmetic.

The paper [13] provides a fully automated formal verification methodology for fused-multiply-add (FMA) FP operation. Verification is carried out by comparing with a simple reference model derived from processor architectural specification. The processor adopts BDD and SAT based symbolic simulation and uses a combination of case splitting, multiplier isolation and automatic model reduction. Article [14] presents FPGen a test generation framework for verifying FP data paths and covers any FP architectural coverage model. The tool is based on strong constraint solving capabilities. FPGen had been widely used for simulation based verification of many hardware based FPUs. The paper [15] mentions that FP division has exceptional corner cases verification challenges despite remarkable advances in formal methods based techniques. Further, it details the relevant verification tasks and the algorithms as part of FPGen for FP division. The paper [16] details ACL2 theorem proving based verification of low power x86 FP multipliers which has been implemented based on iterative algorithms and gives intermediary results in redundant representation. Article [17] formulates Symbolic Trajectory Evaluation (STE) based formal verification of new generation FPUs data paths at Intel. The article opines that formal techniques based verification arithmetic units had matured over the period of time.

Articles [10, 13, 16, 17] articulate verification of FPUs (designed using low level RTL) based on various formal methods based techniques.

Article [18] proposes a formal verification framework to verify systems designed using SysML [19] and encoded in BlueSpec [20] a high level specification language. The paper proposes an efficient encoding framework (but not verified formally) for SysML to BSV [20] and SysML is verified with a probabilistic symbolic model checker, PRISM. Since, the SysML model is verified with a model checker that concludes the formal verification of the design in BSV as well. Formal verification of the generated BSV code is not proposed. The paper [21] briefs on the verification of hardware designs represented with high level specification language such as BSV. Traditional model checker based verification adopted for low level RTL code is generally amenable to verification of high level (HL) modelling language based designs. HL language abstracts many of the low level artefacts of RTL. The paper suggests using formal verification tools such as SMV and Spin to verify the correctness properties of such high-level behavioral models. Further, the article proposes an approach to convert a transactions-based description of a design into an appropriate mode suitable for model checking using Spin. SystemC is being increasingly adopted for description of abstract algorithmic blocks. SystemC blocks are abstract and loosely timed. Lack of tools hampers verification at SystemC models itself and forces post synthesis based verification

The article [22] presents a native SystemC formal based approach. SV assertions have been used to demonstrate the types of properties of SystemC blocks and how they execute in a formal environment. Automated formal checks and proof evaluations have been demonstrated on codes which uses SystemC fixed point arithmetic classes. The paper [23] presents a different FP hardware verification approach based on reusable IEEE 754 std. compliant SystemVerilog arithmetic library (assertion based verification IP-ABVIP) with an application demo of an industrial design. The tool does not cover iterative algorithm involved in division and square root. The tool consists of a set of packages defining data types encoding IEEE 754 FP operands, exceptions flags, rounding modes, and functions capturing expected results of FP operations. The assertion based library implements IEEE 754-2008 and verified with other FPUs. The ABVIP (treated as reference) and FPU to be tested is given as inputs to a formal tool. The paper [24] introduces a formal sequential equivalence checking tool and present how it is used. Sequential Equivalence Checking is the process of proving formal equivalence between two non-state matching implementations of a given design specification.

Articles [18, 19, 21–24] articulate formal verification of FPUs modelled using High Level Languages. Articles [25–28] details model checker based verification of SystemC based designs. Articles [21, 29–34] details model checker based approaches on formal verification of BSV [20] based designs. Article [29] defines a formal semantics based on natural semantics to BSV language and uses that as an input to a model checker to verify any unwanted properties. Article [30] proposes a scheme for mapping the constructs of BSV to Uppaal, a modelling language for validating and verifying real-time system. Article [31, 34] propose a methodology to verify BSV models using another model checking tool, Spin. BSV model is converted to PROMELA which is an input specification language for Spin. Article [32] presents a prototype to shallow embed BSV for PVS theorem prover compatible with PVS model checker. Article [33] presents a prototype to shallow embed BSV for SAL model checker.

3   RISC-V ISA- FPU–in Brief

Top level architecture of RISC-V ISA compliant floating point unit is depicted in Fig. 1 and detailed in [35]. It is modelled using Bluespec System Verilog [20]. FPU accepts the input operand in order, executes out-of-order and commits in-order. Input request contains operands, op-code and function fields. Each FPU request is stored in an input FIFO of depth 2. Input operand width is fixed to 192-bit which holds 3 data operands

(32/64 bits), op-code, f7, f5, and f3 fields which a decoder decodes. Instruction token for each specific functional unit is stored in the scheduled instruction FIFO (depth of six which is max. number of pipeline stages in functional units) which specifies the current computations in the functional units. Each computation has dedicated functional unit. On each clock cycle an instruction will be issued till instruction scheduler queue is not full. Since depth of this queue should be equal to maximum clock latency of all operations to operate without any bubble in pipeline. As instructions are issued on every clock cycle, they can execute in parallel and out of order. They may finish even out of order but they cannot commit out of order.

Output decoder commits the oldest instruction from pipeline. To ensure in-order commit, output decoder in the pipeline reads the scheduled instruction from top of the scheduled instruction FIFO and polls the completion signal from the matching functional unit. Once the floating point operation is completed, the result (32-bit or 64-bit), exceptions (5-bit) from the functional unit is read and stored in output FIFO which has a depth of 2. On completion of instruction execution, first token from the top of the instruction scheduler FIFO is removed. FPU outputs the numeric results and exceptions, if any. Table 1 shows the device utilization of RISC-V compliant FPU DUT targeted at 160 MHz on Virtex-6 XC6VLX550T FPGA device.

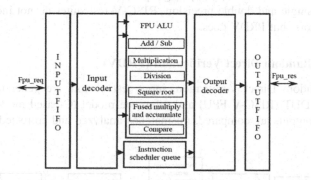

Fig. 1. Architecture of out-of-order FPU

Table 1. Device utilization of FPU DUT on Xilinx Virtex-6 XC6VLX550T FPGA.

Parameter	Utilization count	Total count
Slice register	52997	687360
Slice LUTs	74379	343680
Block RAMs	3	632
DSP48E1S	23	864

4   RISC-V FPU Reference 'C' Model

For verification of instruction set enabled FPU, a reference model (instructions based functional model) which performs floating point arithmetic has been developed with 'C' as part of this work and the result of reference model is treated as a golden reference and compared against DUT response. From known published research works, the reference model for FPU verification could possibly be, (1) translated Verilog model from high level FPU code, (2) netlist generated after ASIC/FPGA synthesis. This reference model accepts three operands along with instruction fields (opcode, f7, f3, f5 and rm) and generates the output with host machine CPU hardware.

5   RISC-V Fpu Verification Basis

RISC-V FPU DUT could possibly be driven with inputs of 3 different kinds to achieve more coverage on test vectors for verification and compatibility with IEEE 754. The 3 kinds of inputs are: Pseudo Random Direct Verification (PRDV) which minimizes the generic functional errors, RISC-V test suites to ensure compliance with RISC-V ISA, and IBM floating point test suites to ensure corner cases testing. Each of these test suites validates the functionality through High Level Language BlueSpec simulator, "bsim". The basis for different kinds of inputs is as follows:

PRDV inherently considers generating instruction sequences which stresses the FPU functional unit pipelines which is not taken care by FPgen and RISC-V test suites. FPgen generates test vectors only for single precision. RISC-V test suites and PRDV supports both single and double precision. RISC-V test suites do not include "denormals" test vectors, but PRDV does.

5.1   Pseudo Random Direct Verification (PRDV)

In Pseudo Random Direct Verification, input test vectors are generated randomly, applied to the DUT (RISC-V FPU) and reference model (C-based model of RISC-V FPU) and the outputs are compared, mismatches analyzed and corrected.

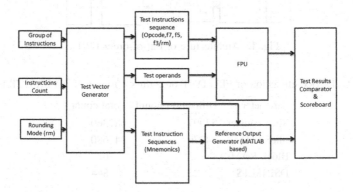

Fig. 2. Pseudo Random Direct Verification Flow

Figure 2 depicts the flow of pseudo random direct verification. It has 4 components: Test Vector Generator (TVG), FPU (DUT), Reference Output Generator (ROG) and test result comparator with a scoreboard.

Test Vector Generator (TVG)

TVG accepts a set of test instructions to be verified, number of random instructions to be generated and rounding mode. TVG outputs test instructions (opcodes, function fields) sequence, operands (both binary and decimal) and test sequences (instruction mnemonics). TVG is developed in 'C'. Figure 3 depicts the TVG flow for PRDV. The operands are generated by initially generating a 192 bits random number and partitioning into 3 operands (32 bits/64 bits) and utilized for two/three operands instructions. The operands are composed as binary (for DUT) and decimal for reference generator.

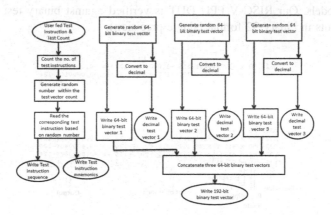

Fig. 3. Test Vector Generation Framework

Reference Output Generator (ROG)

Reference output generator is developed in 'C' which models RISC-V floating point instructions. It accepts the test instruction sequences and the test operands from TVG and computes the instructions on host CPU hardware and outputs the results and exceptions, if any.

Test Result Comparator and Scoreboard

This component accepts the outputs from FPU DUT, ROG output and test instruction sequence etc. The unit compares both outputs and reports errors. Further, indicates the instruction in the sequence that caused the mismatch.

5.2 RISC-V Floating Point Test Suites

RISC-V tool chain provides standard test suites. It specifies the test cases for various single and double precision RISC-V FP operations (RV32uf, RV32ud, RV64uf, RV64ud), provides test vectors and results. Test vectors are applied to the FPU DUT and results compared with RISC-V test suite standards.

5.3 FPgen Floating Point Test Suites

FPgen is a floating point tool from IBM, provides a test-suite to verify basic formats specified in the IEEE 754. The approach used in this test-suite is to first define a high level test-plan, and then to generate a suite of test-cases that covers the test plan. The test plan is a coverage model which is a set of tasks targeting a certain floating- point operations with most of the corner cases. The models are of two types: (a) Operation-general models which is applicable to all floating-point operations. (b) Operations-specific models which is applicable for one or more specific floating-point operations. Every test case in a model specifies values for the rounding mode, the enable bits, and the operands. The test cases are given for all the rounding modes specified by IEEE 754.

The test suite comprises a set of files that corresponds to either binary or decimal coverage models. Our RISC-V FPU DUT is verified against binary test suite which supports inputs in binary-32 format (single precision).

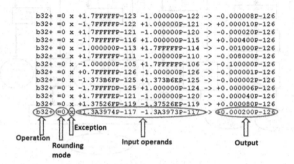

Fig. 4. IBM test case representation for FP operations

Each test case appears on a separate line that contains: operation, rounding mode, exceptions, input operands and output which is separated by "->" sign as depicted in Fig. 4.

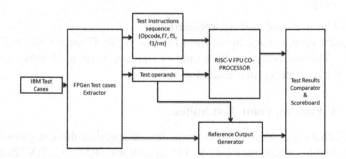

Fig. 5. IBM test cases based verification flow for RISC-V FPU DUT

These FPgen test cases are golden model for the design which is verified against the output generated by the RISC-V FPU. The approach is depicted in Fig. 5.

6 RISC-V FPU Validation on FPGA

6.1 FPU Validation on FPGA

FPU has been configured on FPGA with a host machine interface through PCIe. PRDV, FPgen and RISC-V test suites based test vectors has been given FPGA based FPU DUT and the respective outputs are compared with the respective references viz. 'C' model output, FPgen and RISC-V suite.

6.2 Whetstone Benchmarking Code Validation on FPGA

Any host machine based application which has floating point operations infers either CPU hardware or software FP libraries. We have redirected the FP operations to our FPU DUT on FPGA through PCIe and obtained the results back.

One instance of Whetstone code was compiled to use hardware FPU on host machine. Another instance of the Whetstone code was compiled to use equivalent software floating point library or functions instead of hardware floating point unit. In software floating point library or function calls, PICO FPGA APIs were used to redirect the floating point operations. Steps to be performed to redirect FP computations to FPU DUT in FPGA are listed below:

Step 1: Download libgcc library, modify the floating point functions (_Z3adddd for addition, _Z3subdd for subtraction, _Z3muldd for multiplication etc.).

Step 2: Compile the open-source software floating point library (libgcc) with -msoft-float flag using gcc compiler and create libsoft-fp library

Step 3: Compile application code using -msoft-float gcc flag to disable hardware floating point instructions and infers software floating point function calls

Step 4: Also while compilation use -m32 and -m64 flag to generate 32 bit or 64 bit assembly instructions

Step 5: Compile Whetstone benchmarking code using libsoft-fp library

Step 6: Compile the whetstone benchmarking code as a generic c code using gcc commands

gcc −g −m32 −msoft-float whets.c −lsoft-fp −L

After step 5, compiler generates calling functions in assembly like addition (function: _Z3adddd), subtraction (function: _Z3subdd), multiplication (function: _Z3muldd) and division (function: _Z3divdd). Modify these calling functions without changing the function name to invoke FPGA and pass the arguments to the FPGA. Convert the result obtained from FPGA from IEEE to decimal value and forward as return argument. Replace the INTEL hardware floating point instructions such as addsd, divsd, subsd, mulsd with calling functions _Z3adddd, _Z3divdd, _Z3subdd, _Z3muldd respectively. These soft-float functions uses PICO interfaces and APIs to invoke the PICO FPGA board and run the operation on the board. Final result of this function will be written back to the destination register.

addsd 16(%rbp), %xmm0 with movsd 16(%rbp), %xmm1 and call _Z3adddd addsd adds the value in 16(%rbp) with 64 bit register %xmm0 and stores back into same register %xmm0. Function _Z3adddd takes double precision input from %xmm0 and %xmm1 and stores back in %xmm0. Figures 6 and Fig. 7 show the experimental results of Whetstone code run on host machine and the results for the RISC-V FPU DUT on FPGA and both matches.

```
aneesh@uchr1-ws8:~/FPU/Board_Test/01_Whetstone_C_code$ ./a.out 10

      0         0         0   1.0000e+00  -1.0000e+00  -1.0000e+00  -1.0000e+00
    120       140       120  -6.8342e-02  -4.6264e-01  -7.2972e-01  -1.1240e+00
    140       120       120  -6.8342e-02  -4.6264e-01  -7.2972e-01  -1.1240e+00
   3450         1         1   1.0000e+00  -1.0000e+00  -1.0000e+00  -1.0000e+00
   2100         1         2   6.0000e+00   6.0000e+00  -7.2972e-01  -1.1240e+00
    320         1         2   4.9041e-01   4.9041e-01   4.9039e-01   4.9039e-01
   8990         1         2   1.0000e+00   1.0000e+00   1.0000e+00   1.0000e+00
   6160         1         2   3.0000e+00   2.0000e+00   3.0000e+00  -1.1240e+00
      0         2         3   1.0000e+00  -1.0000e+00  -1.0000e+00  -1.0000e+00
    930         2         3   8.3467e-01   8.3467e-01   8.3467e-01   8.3467e-01
```

Fig. 6. Whetstone testing on host machine CPU (without FPU on FPGA)

```
aneesh@uchr1-ws8:~/FPU/Board_Test/02_Whetstone_FPU_Test$ sh run.sh

Opening stream1
      0         0         0   1.0000e+00  -1.0000e+00  -1.0000e+00  -1.0000e+00
    120       140       120  -6.8342e-02  -4.6264e-01  -7.2972e-01  -1.1240e+00
    140       120       120  -6.8342e-02  -4.6264e-01  -7.2972e-01  -1.1240e+00
   3450         1         1   1.0000e+00  -1.0000e+00  -1.0000e+00  -1.0000e+00
   2100         1         2   6.0000e+00   6.0000e+00  -7.2972e-01  -1.1240e+00
    320         1         2   4.9041e-01   4.9041e-01   4.9039e-01   4.9039e-01
   8990         1         2   1.0000e+00   1.0000e+00   1.0000e+00   1.0000e+00
   6160         1         2   3.0000e+00   2.0000e+00   3.0000e+00  -1.1240e+00
      0         2         3   1.0000e+00  -1.0000e+00  -1.0000e+00  -1.0000e+00
    930         2         3   8.3467e-01   8.3467e-01   8.3467e-01   8.3467e-01
```

Fig. 7. Whetstone testing on FPU DUT on FPGA

7   Comparison with Other Work

The Table 2 shown below compares our approach with other published relevant works on the aspects of FPU reference model, test vectors generation schemes, verification approaches and hardware validation. References [1, 3, 8, 10, 13, 15] are from IBM, [17] from Intel and [16] from AMD.

Table 2. Comparison: proposed approach versus published work.

Parameters	[3, 8, 10, 12, 13, 15] IBM	[17] INTEL	[16] AMD	[This Work] RISC-V FPU
Reference model	Reference FPU is developed using HDL	Reference FPU is developed using C++ language	ACL2 based formal FPU model	Reference FPU is developed using C language
Test vectors generation schemes	Random Test vectors, FPGen test suites, AVPgen	Random test vectors, Proprietary tools generated vectors	Formal methods for verification	PRDV FPGen RISC-V Test suites

(*continued*)

Table 2. (*continued*)

Parameters	[3, 8, 10, 12, 13, 15] IBM	[17] INTEL	[16] AMD	[This Work] RISC-V FPU
Verification approaches	Both formal and simulation based verification	Formal verification only	Formal verification only	Simulation based verification
Hardware validation	Uses sixth sense tool for validation	Not mentioned	Not mentioned	FPGAs for hardware validation

8 Conclusion and Future Work

This paper presents a verification flow for an instruction set enabled FPU modeled using BlueSpec System Verilog, a high level hardware description language. Pseudo Random Direct Verification (PRDV) uses a 'C' FPU reference model compliant with RISC-V ISA. PRDV corrects the initial design errors, RISC-V test suites and FPgen test suites were used to test corner cases and improve the test vector coverage. PRDV inherently considers generating instruction sequences which stresses the FPU functional unit pipelines which is not taken care by FPgen and RISC-V test suites. FPgen generates test vectors only for single precision. RISC-V test suites and PRDV supports both single and double precision. RISC-V test suites do not include "denormals" test vectors, but PRDV does. With the above test vectors/model validated the design on FPGA.

Finally, Whetstone application is been modified to utilize FPU DUT on FPGA and compare the result with Whetstone code which uses host CPU. FPU DUT has been integrated with our dual issue, out-of-order execute, in-order commit RISC-V processor and demonstrated a whetstone benchmarking application. Proposed floating point verification approach can be extended to an application based RISC-V com-pliant floating point unit validation on FPGA without the use of RISC-V processor pipeline

Currently the test instruction sequence comprise only FP instructions and future work could include integer instructions, load/store instructions etc. to emulate real scenario micro-architecture. Further, adopting Formal Methods Tools like NuSMV to model the RISC-V ISA based FPU and verify the correctness of the FPU properties using model checker.

References

1. Goni, O., Todorovich, E., et al.: Generic construction of monitors for floating point unit designs. In: 2012 VIII Southern Conference on Programmable Logic (2012)
2. Hauser, J.: "Softfloat" technical Report - International Computer Science Institute (2010). http://www.jhauser.us/arithmetic/SoftFloat.html
3. Cowlishaw, M.: The decNumber C library, 3rd ed. IBM Corp. (2008). https://www.ibm.com/support/knowledgecenter/en/SSB23S_1.1.0.15/gtpa2/pkdecsp.html, http://mirrors.josefsipek.net/speleotrove.com/decimal/decnumber.pdf

4. Brunelli, C., Nurmi, J., et al.: Design and verification of a VHDL model of a floating-point unit for a RISC microprocessor. In: IEEE International Symposium on System-on-Chip (2016)
5. Chen, C.I., Yu, C.Y., Lu, Y.J., Wu, C.F.: Apply high-level synthesis design and verification methodology on floating-point unit implementation. In: International Symposium on VLSI Design, Automation and Test (VLSI-DAT) (2014)
6. EEMBC FPMark. https://www.eembc.org/fpmark/
7. Pachiana, G., Rodriguez, J.A.: Coverage modeling for verification of floating point Arithmetic units. In: Argentine School of Micro-Nanoelectronics, Technology and Applications (2014)
8. IBM Floating Point Test Generator. https://www.research.ibm.com/haifa/projects/verification/fpgen/
9. Goñi, O., Todorovich, E., et al.: Components for coverage-driven verification of floating-point units. In: IEEE IX Southern Conference on Programmable Logic (SPL) (2014)
10. Krautz, U., Paruthi, V., et al.: Automatic verification of floating point units. In: Proceedings of 51st Annual Design Automation, DAC 2014 (2014)
11. Guralnik, E., Birnbaum, A.J., Koyfman, A., et al.: Implementation specific verification of divide and square root instructions. In: 19th IEEE International Symposium on Computer Arithmetic (2009)
12. Duale, A.Y., Decker, M.H., et al.: Decimal floating-point in z9: an implementation and testing perspective. http://research.ibm.com/haifa/projects/verification/fpgen/papers/duale.pdf
13. Jacobi, C., et al.: Automatic formal verification of fused-multiply-add FPUs. https://www.research.ibm.com/haifa/projects/verification/SixthSense/papers/flavor_date_05.pdf
14. Aharoni, M., et al.: FPgen – a test generation framework for datapath floating-point verification. In: Eighth IEEE International High-Level Design Validation and Test Workshop (2003)
15. Guralnik, E., et al.: Simulation-Based Verification of Floating-Point Division (2011). https://www.research.ibm.com/haifa/projects/verification/fpgen/papers/Simulation_Based_Verification_of_Floating_Point_Division.pdf
16. Seidel, P.-M.: Formal verification of an iterative low-power x86floating-pointmultiplier with redundant feedback. https://arxiv.org/pdf/1110.4675.pdf
17. Kiran Kumar, M.A., et al.: Symbolic trajectory evaluation: the primary validation vehicle for next generation intel® processor graphics FPU. http://www.cs.utexas.edu/~hunt/fmcad/FMCAD12/025.pdf
18. Ouchani, S., et al.: A formal verification framework for bluespec system verilog in specification & design languages (FDL) (2013)
19. OMG: OMG Systems Modelling Language (OMG SysML) Specification, Object Management Group. http://www.omgsysml.org/
20. Bluespec inc. http://www.bluespec.com
21. Singh, G., et al.: Model-checking based verification for hardware designs specified using bluespec system verilog. In: IEEE 8th International Workshop on Test and Verification (2007)
22. Beyer, S.: The application of formal technology on fixed-point arithmetic systemC designs. In: Design and Verification Conference and Exhibition. One spin soluution (2015)
23. Ram, R.: Formal verification of floating point hardware with assertion based VIP. In: Design and Verification Conference and Exhibition. One spin solutions (2018)
24. Travis, W., Pouarz, V., et al.: Efficient and exhaustive floating point verification using sequential equivalence checking. In: DVCon (2017)
25. Cimatti, A., et al.: Software model checking SystemC. IEEE Trans. Comput.-Aided Des. Integr. Circuits Syst. 32, 774–787 (2013)

26. Cimatti, A., Griggio, A., Micheli, A., Narasamdya, I., Roveri, M.: Kratos – a software model checker for SystemC. In: Gopalakrishnan, G., Qadeer, S. (eds.) CAV 2011. LNCS, vol. 6806, pp. 310–316. Springer, Heidelberg (2011). https://doi.org/10.1007/978-3-642-22110-1_24

27. Herber, P., et al.: Formal verification of SystemC designs using the BLAST software model checker. In: International Workshop on Model-Based Architecting and Construction of Embedded Systems (ACES-MB) (2013)

28. Ngo, V.C., et al.: Statistical model checking for SystemC models. In: IEEE 17th International Symposium on High Assurance Systems Engineering (HASE) (2016)

29. Oscar, O.: On the Formal Semantics of Bluespec System Verilog, Thesis (2013)

30. Hauksson, H.: Towards model checking BSV in Uppaal, MscThesis (2013)

31. Singh, G., et al.: Model checking bluespec specified hardware designs. In: Eighth International Workshop on Microprocessor Test and Verification (2017)

32. Richards, D., et al.: A prototype embedding of bluespec system verilog in the PVS theorem prover. In: Second NASA Formal Methods Symposium, NFM 2010 (2010)

33. Richards, D., et al.: A prototype embedding of bluespec systemverilog in the SAL model checker. http://www.cs.ox.ac.uk/dcc2010/slides/richards.pdf

34. Singh, G., Shukla, Sandeep K.: Verifying compiler based refinement of bluespec^{TM} specifications using the SPIN model checker. In: Havelund, K., Majumdar, R., Palsberg, J. (eds.) SPIN 2008. LNCS, vol. 5156, pp. 250–269. Springer, Heidelberg (2008). https://doi.org/10.1007/978-3-540-85114-1_18

35. Raveendran, A., Patil, V.B., et al.: Out of order floating point co-processor for RISC V ISA. In: IEEE VLSISATA (2015)

36. Waterman, A., Lee, Y., Patterson, D.A., Asanovi, K.: The RISC-V instruction set manual. Base User-Level ISA. V2.2, vol. I (2017)

37. Clarke, E., German, S.: Verifying the SRT division algorithm using theorem proving techniques. Formal Methods Syst. Des. **14**, 7–44 (1999)

38. Fournier, L., Arbetman, Y., et al.: Functional verification methodology for microprocessors using the genesys test program generator. Application to the x86 microprocessors family. In: DATE99 (1999)

39. Harrison, J.: Formal verification of IA-64 division algorithms. In: Aagaard, M., Harrison, J. (eds.) TPHOLs 2000. LNCS, vol. 1869, pp. 233–251. Springer, Heidelberg (2000). https://doi.org/10.1007/3-540-44659-1_15

40. Jerinic, V., Langer, J., Heinkel, U., Muller, D.: New methods and coverage metrics for functional verification. In: IEEE Design, Automation and Test in Europe (2006)

41. IEEE standards Board and ANSI. IEEE Standards for Binary Floating-point Arithmetic, IEEE Std., 754-2008 (2008)

42. Whetstone. https://www.netlib.org/benchmark/whetstone.c

Real Time Implementation of Convolutional Neural Network to Detect Plant Diseases Using Internet of Things

Govind Bajpai, Aniket Gupta, and Nitanshu Chauhan[✉]

Department of Electronics Engineering,
National Institute of Technology Uttarakhand, Srinagar, India
nitanshu.chauhan@nituk.ac.in

Abstract. In this paper, we have described the real time implementation of machine learning on identification of plant disease. This is done by using the concept of transfer learning with Convolutional Neural Networks (CNNs) on self-designed drone. In order to achieve high crop yield, the time management and robust diagnosis of the plant disease is a crucial factor along with the inspection of their nutrient deficiencies. We have designed and trained a novel real time system using machine learning with deep convolutional networks to identify the plant diseases for the diagnosis. This is based on a concept of leaf image classification. The trained system is processed on an open source development board and it is mounted on self-design automated drone and uses Internet of Things (IoT) to transfer the captured images to a local database which is connected to a global Server.

Keywords: Deep learning · Transfer learning ·
Convolutional Neural Network (CNN) · Internet of Things (IoT) ·
Plant disease · Drone

1 Introduction

Machine learning [1, 2] with Artificial Intelligence (AI) [3] is a fine example of an automated world. The implementation of an automated computational system on a drone for the detection and diagnosis of the plant diseases, would offer a valuable assistance to farmers and using IoT [2, 4] provides a medium to connect it globally and making it mobile. This introductory section is bifurcated in two parts:

1.1 Introduction to Machine Learning

In recent years, learning based AI [3] applications have achieved tremendous growth providing a research in development of novel methodologies and models. Machine learning trains the system to develop the ability of automatic learning and improve the results from its own experience without the help of any other programmed hardware. Researchers had demonstrated the use of machine learning in the artificial intelligence. In the field of computer vision and image classifications, researchers have made steady progress from simple CNN model [5, 6] like ImageNet [5] to more complex CNN

© Springer Nature Singapore Pte Ltd. 2019
A. Sengupta et al. (Eds.): VDAT 2019, CCIS 1066, pp. 510–522, 2019.
https://doi.org/10.1007/978-981-32-9767-8_42

models [7, 8] like Quiche [9], AlexNet [10, 11], Inception (GoogLeNet) [12, 13], ResNet [14], and BN-Inception-V3 [15, 16] are proposed to show the continuous improvements to achieve a new state-of-art but the real time results are still hard to reproduce [17, 18]. In the entire process of machine learning data play an important role using data-set machine learning model is trained. In this manuscript, "Plant Village Dataset" [19] is used which includes a huge collection of thirty different types of images of plant diseases such as diseases in Apple, Blueberry, Corn, Tomato etc. are used for the training of CNN Models. The ANNs (Artificial Neural Networks) are the models that mathematically imitate the general principles of brain functioning with neurons and provide a platform that interconnect them. They are generally trained by the process of supervised learning while CNN Models are used to train the system for dealing with images. These models are having networks that can differentiate among different diseases [20–22]. During the process of the transfer learning various files like bottlenecks, retrained graph etc. are created which are further used at the time of classification of unseen images. After the training process, new final layer gets added and this layer is trained on the leaf's images in the dataset. During training process, it finds the bottleneck from the cache and finally feeds them into final layer to get predictions. Those predictions can be compared with actual labels, and the results of comparison are used to update the final layer's weight through back-propagation process.

1.2   Internet of Things (IoT) and Unarmed Aerial Vehicles (UAV)

Internet of Things means global connectivity to all over the globe and represents the ability to collect and share the data across the internet where it can be used for various applications. In past two decades, IoT has been providing continuous impact in solving daily live problems and in various applications [23, 24] such as connecting home appliances with network, health-care, utilities, transport, etc. This manuscript includes the use of its application such as transfer of data from one place to another and data base management using IoT [25]. In the past few years drone technology is widely used in various fields such as in the field of agriculture and more precisely termed as Precision Agriculture to optimize harvests [26–28]. This paper presents how drone technology in combination with IoT and machine learning [28] is used for faster detection of agricultural diseases, as there are some diseases which are having devastating and costly consequences if not detected at right time. Fast reaction is a key to allow the farmer to control the disease and limit the damage. The potential benefits for the farmer are substantial, connected to an alert system a drone could save a farmer significant time by autonomously detecting the diseases.

2   The Complete Process Flow

In Fig. 1 we have explained the basic process flow of the entire system on board design and its functionality.

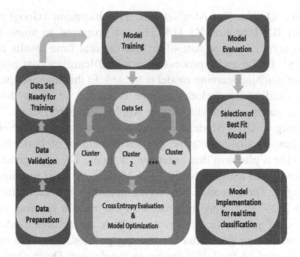

Fig. 1. A complete process flow diagram.

2.1 Data Preparation

Data frame is the fulcrum of all the machine learning algorithms. Some pre-processing on the data needed to be done to make a valid data set. The entire database is initially divided into three sub-datasets: the training set, validation set and the testing set. This can be done by randomly splitting [29] the entire data set in the ratios of 60%, 20% and 20% of the data in training data validation set and the testing set, respectively. The 60, 20 and 20 splitting ratios of training, validation and testing dataset is the most commonly used in neural network applications. The similar splitting ratios (e.g. 50, 25, and 25) should not have a significant impact on the performance of the developed models [12]. The development board is programmed to create two datasets which produce uniformly distributed pseudorandom numbers for the random image selection. One of the sample images of infected leaves of tomato which comes in the class of Septoria Lycopersici is shown in Fig. 2.

Fig. 2. Septoria Lycopersici infected tomato leaves.

2.2   Training, Testing and Validation Data Set

Training data (or training set) refers to that fragment of data which is used to train the model. Test data (or test set) refers to that segment of the data which is used only at the end of the model to evaluate the model's accuracy. Validation data (or validation set) refers to that portion of the data used to assess how well the model is developed.

2.3   Training, Testing and Validation Data Set

The ultimate aim of any CNN model is to minimize the value of loss function so that it can provide better classification accuracy. The technique used in CNN for its optimization is the back propagation. In the back propagation technique the gradient of weights and bias of each layer are evaluated which are used to update the model parameters so as to minimize the loss function. After optimization model evaluation is done in which accuracy is calculated by supplying some sample data.

2.4   Training, Testing and Validation Data Set

This subsection deals with the testing of robustness of the model in which the data is divided in several parts known as clusters. These clusters are supplied to the models which in turn calculate the final accuracy of the models.

2.5   Training, Testing and Validation Data Set

All the above steps have been applied on the various models such as AlexNet [10, 11], GoogLeNet [12, 13], ResNet [14] etc. Accuracy of the models is evaluated and based on the acquired results the most accurate model is selected for image classification. The selection of the best model is performed on the fulcrum of the two parameters:

(a)   Training Accuracy

It is the accuracy which is achieved while the model is being trained on the training data and can be expressed mathematically as a fraction of instances classified correctly:

$$Accuracy = \frac{TheAmountofCorrectClassifications}{TheTotalNumberofClassifications} \tag{1}$$

In Figs. 3, 4, and 5, the training accuracy of the models versus its training time for all the three models is shown. It is clear from the respective figures that the accuracy increases with the training time. The accuracy of the model is directly dependent on the training data as a higher amount of data provides a higher data accuracy [5]. Moreover, the conclusion drawn from the figures is that the most accurate model in terms of testing accuracy is ResNet CNN model.

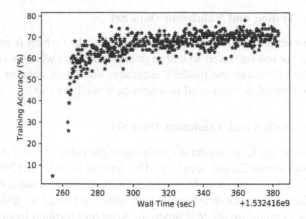

Fig. 3. Training Accuracy vs Wall Time for AlexNet model.

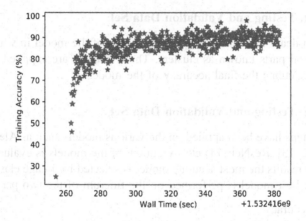

Fig. 4. Training Accuracy vs Wall Time for GoogLeNet model.

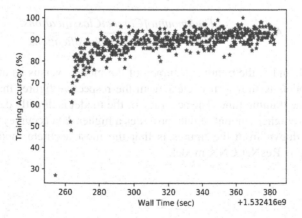

Fig. 5. Training Accuracy vs Wall Time for ResNet model.

(b) Cross Entropy

The cross entropy is the value of cost function evaluated while training the model [5] between the two probability distributions p and q over the same underlying set of events. These events are measured the average number of bits needed to identify an event drawn from the set in which a coding scheme is used which is optimized for an "artificial" probability distribution q rather than the "true" distribution p. The cross entropy for the distributions p and q over a given set is defined as follows:

$$H(p,q) = E_p[-logq] = H(p) + D_{kl}(p \| q) \tag{2}$$

where H(p) is the entropy of p, and $D_{kl}(p \| q)$ is the Kullback–Leibler divergence of q from p (also known as the relative entropy of the p with respect to q).

For discrete p and q this means

$$H(p,q) = -\sum_x p(x) \log q(x) \tag{3}$$

The situation for continuous distributions is analogous. We have to assume that p and q are absolutely continuous with respect to some reference measure r (usually r is a Lebesgue measure on a Borel σ-algebra). Let P and Q be probability density functions of p and q with respect to r.

$$-\int P(x) log Q(x) dr(x) = E_p[log Q] \tag{4}$$

Therefore, the notation H (p, q) is also used for a different concept of the joint entropy of p and q. The validation of error in predicting the feature is also verified with the cross-entropy extraction as shown in Fig. 7. This figure shows the value of cross entropy around 0.28 and it leads to 28% feature loss during the training of the model, which is quite appreciable. Therefore, a lower value of cross entropy makes a better model. The cross entropy decreases drastically with the training time and weights which are adjusted such that to minimize the loss as shown in Figs. 6, 7, and 8. The point where gradient descent of Loss Function becomes zero provides the optimized weights of the model. Therefore, it can be concluded that the best fit model according to Cross Entropy parameter is ResNet CNN Model.

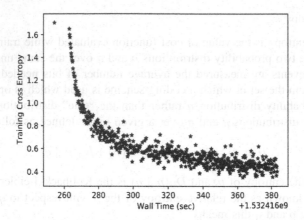

Fig. 6. Cross Entropy vs Wall Time for AlexNet model.

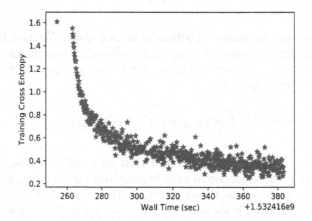

Fig. 7. Cross Entropy vs Wall Time for GoogLeNet model.

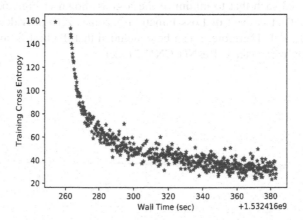

Fig. 8. Cross Entropy vs Wall Time for ResNet model.

In Table 1, we have shown the model and their evaluated accuracy. The conclusion drawn from the Table 1 is that the best Fit Model is ResNet CNN model on which the further process is done.

Table 1. CNN training parameters.

S. no.	CNN model	Training accuracy	Cross entropy
1	AlexNet	0.81	0.1 – 0.01
2	GoogLeNet	0.89	0.01 – 0.001
3	ResNet	0.95	0.001 – 0.0001

2.6 Real Time Implementation of Trained Model on an Automated Drone

Figure 9 illustrates the complete real time implementation process which is divided into four major sections as given below:

(a) Field Surveillance by Drone

Nowadays the automation of a drone is no longer a big task due to the availability of high-performance flight controller in the market. This paper presents the realization of an automated drone facilitated with the GPS module using which it can move over the desired fields while maintaining its proper altitude so as to take clear photographs. In Table 2, some of the required specifications of the drone are mentioned.

Fig. 9. Self-designed automated drone.

Table 2. Drone Specifications

S. no.	Parameter	Value
1	Max ascent speed	13.4 mph
2	Max descent speed	8.9 mph
3	Satellite systems	GPS
4	Battery specs	2200 mAh, 12 V
5	Remote frequency	2.400–2.483

(b) Image Capturing and Sending Them to the Local Network and Processing Unit (LNPU) Using IoT

For capturing a high quality image, the OpenMV Cam is used which is a high-quality camera runs on the Micro Python Operating System which allows to program the camera using python according to applications [30]. The whole package of the camera includes an OpenMV Cam M7, LCD and Proto Shield, Wi-Fi shield, Servo Shield, Pan and Tilt shield, Motor Shield and various lenses as shown in Fig. 10. Python program is developed for capturing the images and transmitting it to the Local Network and Processing Unit as in Fig. 11 by using Wi-Fi shield through IoT.

Fig. 10. Various components of an OpenMV Cam.

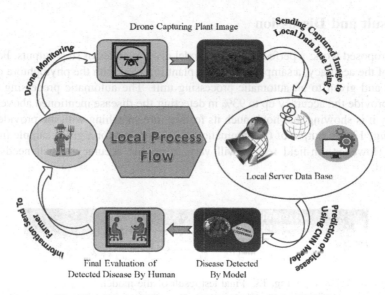

Fig. 11. A Local Network and Processing Unit (LNPU).

(c) Prediction of the Disease by an Automatic Data Processing Unit

This subsection deals with the final prediction of the plant disease by an automatic data processing unit which is trained with the selected model.

(d) Connecting the Local and Global Server for Increasing the Data-Set and Accuracy

Finally, the multiple LNPUs are connected to the Global Network via IoT which would increase the data collection rate (Fig. 12).

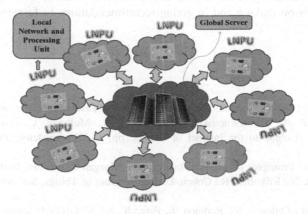

Fig. 12. Linking of the LNPUs to the Global Server.

3   Result and Discussion

In our proposed work, a perfectly trained model gives a series of step outputs. For final testing of the accuracy, a sample image of a plant infected with the phytophtora disease is taken and given to an automatic processing unit. The automatic processing unit is able to provide the accuracy up to 93% in detecting the disease mentioned above. More precisely it is showing that how much its features are matching with the provided data set. In Fig. 13, the output of the automatic processing unit for a given sample image is shown. However, on-field results will vary from this accuracy which needs to be addressed.

```
phytophthora infestans (score = 0.93803)
tomato mosaic virus tomv (score = 0.05852)
alternaria solani (score = 0.00195)
septoria lycopersici (score = 0.00106)
tetranychus urticae (score = 0.00043)
```

Fig. 13.   Final test result of the model.

4   Conclusion

With the advancement of the powerful computing techniques, we are able to automate the tasks that are very challenging and costly to the mankind. Convolutional Neural Networks act as the Artificial Neuron in the Artificial Intelligent systems. We have designed the very efficient models to automate the tedious tasks like disease detection using Neural Network and IoT. Through IoT the process of creating a local data server is done which can serve the purpose of disease detection. Moreover, the IoT serves the purposed to update the farmers with required solutions which are the low-cost alternatives to the human experts. It helps to detect the early onset of the crop diseases with aids faster decision making and in giving recommendations to farmers to curb yield loss.

References

1. Quinlan, J.R.: C4. 5: Programs for Machine Learning. Elsevier, Amsterdam (2014)
2. Höller, J., Boyle, D., Karnouskos, S., Avesand, S., Mulligan, C., Tsiatsis, V.: From Machine-to-Machine to the Internet of Things, pp. 1–331. Academic Press, Cambridge (2014)
3. Nilsson, N.J.: Principles of Artificial Intelligence. Morgan Kaufmann, Burlington (2014)
4. Gershenfeld, N., Krikorian, R., Cohen, D.: The Internet of Things. Sci. Am. **291**(4), 76–81 (2004)
5. Rastegari, M., Ordonez, V., Redmon, J., Farhadi, A.: XNOR-Net: imagenet classification using binary convolutional neural networks. In: Leibe, B., Matas, J., Sebe, N., Welling, M. (eds.) ECCV 2016. LNCS, vol. 9908, pp. 525–542. Springer, Cham (2016). https://doi.org/10.1007/978-3-319-46493-0_32
6. Anderson, A.: An Introduction to Neural Networks. PHI Publication, Amsterdam (1998)

7. Cireşan, D.C., Meier, U., Masci, J., Gambardella, L.M., Schmidhuber, J.: High-performance neural networks for visual object classification. Arxiv preprint arXiv:1102.0183 (2011)
8. Szegedy, C., et al.: Going deeper with convolutions. In: Proceedings of the IEEE Conference on Computer Vision and Pattern Recognition, pp. 1–9 (2015)
9. Gomez, R., Gomez, L., Gibert, J., Karatzas, D.: Self-Supervised Learning from Web Data for Multimodal Retrieval. arXiv preprint arXiv:1901.02004
10. Iandola, F.N., Han, S., Moskewicz, M.W., Ashraf, K., Dally, W.J., Keutzer, K.: SqueezeNet: AlexNet-level accuracy with 50x fewer parameters and <0.5 mb model size. arXiv preprint arXiv:1602.07360 (2016)
11. Yuan, Z.W., Zhang, J.: Feature extraction and image retrieval based on AlexNet. In: Eighth International Conference on Digital Image Processing, ICDIP 2016, vol. 10033, p. 100330E. International Society for Optics and Photonics (2016)
12. Singla, A., Yuan, L., Ebrahimi, T.: Food/non-food image classification and food categorization using pre-trained googlenet model. In: Proceedings of the 2nd International Workshop on Multimedia Assisted Dietary Management, pp. 3–11. ACM (2016)
13. Tang, P., Wang, H., Kwong, S.: G-MS2F: GoogLeNet based multi-stage feature fusion of deep CNN for scene recognition. Neurocomputing 225, 188–197 (2017)
14. Wu, Z., Shen, C., Van Den Hengel, A.: Wider or deeper: revisiting the resnet model for visual recognition. Pattern Recognit. 90, 19–133 (2019)
15. Xia, X., Xu, C., Nan, B.: Inception-v3 for flower classification. In: 2017 2nd International Conference on Image, Vision and Computing (ICIVC), pp. 783–787. IEEE (2017)
16. Barratt, S., Sharma, R.: A note on the inception score. arXiv preprint arXiv:1801.01973 (2018)
17. Singh, V., Misra, A.K.: Detection of plant leaf diseases using image segmentation and soft computing techniques. Inf. Process. Agric. 4(1), 41–49 (2017)
18. Mohanty, S.P., Hughes, D.P., Salathé, M.: Using deep learning for image-based plant disease detection. Front. Plant Sci. 7, 1419 (2016)
19. Available online: plantvillage.psu.edu
20. Sladojevic, S., Arsenovic, M., Anderla, A., Culibrk, D., Stefanovic, D.: Deep neural networks based recognition of plant diseases by leaf image classification. In: Computational Intelligence and Neuroscience (2016)
21. Barbedo, J.G.: Factors influencing the use of deep learning for plant disease recognition. Biosyst. Eng. 172, 84–91 (2018)
22. Ferentinos, K.P.: Deep learning models for plant disease detection and diagnosis. Comput. Electron. Agric. 145, 311–318 (2018)
23. Miorandi, D., Sicari, S., De Pellegrini, F., Chlamtac, I.: Internet of Things: vision, applications and research challenges. Ad Hoc Netw. 10(7), 1497–1516 (2012)
24. Zanella, A., Bui, N., Castellani, A., Vangelista, L., Zorzi, M.: Internet of things for smart cities. IEEE Internet Things J. 1(1), 22–32 (2014)
25. Mohammed, J., Lung, C.H., Ocneanu, A., Thakral, A., Jones, C., Adler, A.: Internet of Things: remote patient monitoring using web services and cloud computing. In: 2014 IEEE International Conference on Internet of things (iThings) and Green Computing and Communications (GreenCom), IEEE and Cyber, Physical and Social Computing (CPSCom), pp. 256–263. IEEE (2014)
26. Vattapparamban, E., Güvenç, İ., Yurekli, A.İ., Akkaya, K., Uluağaç, S.: Drones for smart cities: issues in cybersecurity, privacy, and public safety. In: 2016 International Wireless Communications and Mobile computing Conference (IWCMC), pp. 216–221. IEEE (2016)

27. Dang, C.T., Pham, H.T., Pham, T.B., Truong, N.V.: Vision based ground object tracking using AR. Drone quadrotor. In: 2013 International Conference on Control, Automation and Information Sciences (ICCAIS), pp. 146–151. IEEE (2013)
28. www.pwc.be/en/documents/20180518-drone-study.pdf
29. Reitermanova, Z.: Data splitting. In: WDS, vol. 10, pp. 31–36 (2010)
30. www.openmv.io/

A Novel 20nm FinFET Based 10T SRAM Cell Design for Improved Performance

Anushka Singh[1]($\boxtimes$), Yash Sharma[1], Arvind Sharma[2],
and Archana Pandey[1]

[1] Department of Electronics and Communication Engineering,
Jaypee Institute of Information Technology, Noida 201309, India
anushka1996@gmail.com, 15102230yash@gmail.com,
archana.pandey@jiit.ac.in
[2] University of Minnesota, Minneapolis, MN 55455, USA
arvuce22@gmail.com

Abstract. Static Random Access Memory cell has been under immense design updation recently with an aim to enhance its performance, to withstand the device level process variations and simultaneously support low power applications. SRAMs are used as memory reserve in digital processing systems due to their high speed performance. But, standard 6T SRAM bit-cells suffer from sizing issue which further results in a trade-off between the write ability and read stability of the cell. In this paper, we propose a 20 nm FinFET based 10 transistor (10T) SRAM bit-cell design based on single ended sensing. The read stability has increased significantly in the proposed SRAM design in comparison to standard 6T SRAM bit-cell since it has a separate bit line discharging path for decoupling the data storage-nodes completely from the read path. Data cognizant word lines and PMOSs as power gating transistors are used to enhance the write ability. Hence, it gives better read and write static noise margin (RSNM and WSNM) as compared to standard 6T SRAM cell. In comparison to previous 10T SRAM bit-cells, the proposed bit-cell design shows enhanced read-write operations. The simulations have been performed using Predictive Technology Model (PTM) files for 20 nm FinFET on HSPICE. The supply voltage has been kept at 0.9 V for the proposed bit-cell. The area of proposed bit-cell has been found to increase by 1.55 times in comparison to standard 6T SRAM cell and has been found to be similar to that of previous 10T SRAM bit-cell.

Keywords: FinFET · SRAM · Power gating · Static noise margin

1 Introduction

Continuous scaling of transistors has enabled reduction of costs along with increased speed and higher density of metal oxide semiconductor field effect transistors (MOSFET) on a chip. As put forth by Moore's Law, due to scaling, the count of transistors per chip approximately doubles every eighteen months. Hence, FinFETs have been proposed as a promising alternative of standard MOSFET based circuits and further study is being done to enhance the FinFET based circuit performances in today's technological era.

© Springer Nature Singapore Pte Ltd. 2019
A. Sengupta et al. (Eds.): VDAT 2019, CCIS 1066, pp. 523–531, 2019.
https://doi.org/10.1007/978-981-32-9767-8_43

The role of Static Random Access Memories (SRAMs) in modern digital gadgets and systems is increasing day by day. Hence, the chip area used for SRAMs in these devices will increase substantially. Due to rapid scaling in nanometre regime, SRAM is becoming vulnerable to noise sources. SRAM reliability at lower voltages has become a major concern in modern technology. The reduced supply and threshold voltage makes the task of designing a stable SRAM cell difficult [1].

In 6 transistor (6T) SRAM Cell, it becomes onerous to assure reliability during read-write operations, which may lead to read/write failures. In order to overcome these challenges, various SRAM bit-cell design topologies have been proposed such as 7 transistors (7T) [2], 8 transistors (8T) [3], 9 transistors (9T) [4], 10 transistors (10T) [5] which are based either on differential sensing or single-ended sensing bit-cells. 10T PMOS-PMOS-NMOS (PPN) based differential sensing bit-cells, which provide an isolation between the storage nodes and bit-lines to enhance the read stability was proposed [6]. But these bit-cells have poor write margin because they have similar configuration as that of standard 6T SRAM cell. For further increasing read stability, a 10T SRAM cell design which uses 6T SRAM cell design with 4 additional transistors which decouple the storage-nodes from bit line at the time of read operation was proposed [7]. To achieve improved write ability, SRAM bit-cell with Data-Cognizant Power Gating Write Assist was proposed recently [8].

Static Noise Margin (SNM) is a criteria used for measuring the cell stability. Maintaining adequate RSNM has always been a substantial challenge for obtaining stability in an SRAM cell. Moreover, WSNM impacts the stability of SRAM during the write operation on the cell [9]. Hence, in the proposed cell design we aim to obtain desirable WSNM and RSNM.

Hence, in our paper, we propound a single ended sensing based 10T SRAM bit-cell based on 20 nm FinFET technology which has enhanced read and write performance.

Further on, the paper has been divided into the following sections: Sect. 2 discusses about the proposed bit-cell design, its read, write and hold operations. In Sect. 3 the simulation and results of all the operations have been described and thus compared to standard 6transistor (6T) SRAM bit-cell. Finally, Sect. 4 concludes the paper.

2   Proposed 10T SRAM Bit Cell

In our work, we propose a 10T SRAM bit-cell design based on single ended sensing (Fig. 1). The proposed bit-cell has been designed using different word-lines for performing the read-write operations. It consists of PPN inverter circuits in the core of the cell structure. It has a separate bit-line discharging path for decoupling data storage node completely from the read path. Data cognizant word-lines and PMOSs as Power-gating transistors are used to improve the write ability.

2.1   Read Operation

In Fig. 2, the read 0 operation of the proposed bit-cell design has been illustrated. At the time of read operation, read word-line (RW) is enabled for turning on the read access transistor (RAC) and VVSS is forced to 0 i.e. grounded. The write word-line left (WWL) as well as the write word-line right (WWR) are set to 0. The bit-line discharges via the read pass gate transistor (RPG) based on the value of voltage at node QB.

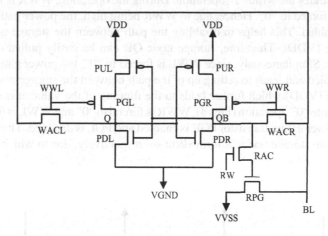

Fig. 1. Proposed 10T SRAM bit-cell design.

2.2 Hold Operation

At the time of hold operation, initially stored data is retained by the inverter and the storage-nodes are secluded from the bit-line by switching-off the access and pass gate transistors. Moreover, for reducing the leakage current VVSS is kept HIGH.

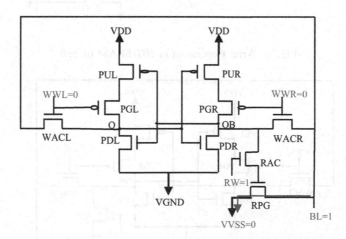

Fig. 2. 10T SRAM bit-cell during the read 0 operation.

2.3   Write Operation

At the time of write operation, in the proposed bit-cell design, bit-line (BL) is always set to "0". The RW is also simultaneously set to "0" to disable the read discharging path. Figure 3 illustrates the write "1" operation. During the operation, WWR is forced to "1" and WWL is forced to "0". Hence, due to WWR being high, the power gating transistor (PGR) is disabled. This helps in disabling the path between the storage node QB and power source (VDD). Therefore, storage node QB can be easily pulled down to "0" through VBL. Simultaneously, since WWL is forced to "0", the power gating transistor (PGL) is enabled and leads to setting up of the path between the storage node Q and the power source (VDD) which further leads to the flipping of the value at node Q to "1".

During write "0" operation (Fig. 4), WWR is forced to "0" and WWL is forced to "1". Hence, the power gating transistor PGR is enabled and PGL is disabled. Thus, the path of power source to storage nodes is formed/cut-off respectively, due to which the value of the storage node QB flips to "1" and value of storage node Q drains to "0" through BL.

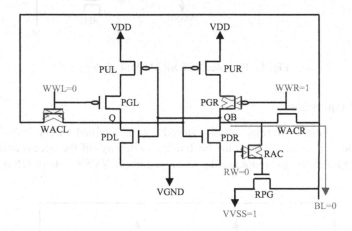

Fig. 3. Write 1 operation in 10T SRAM bit-cell.

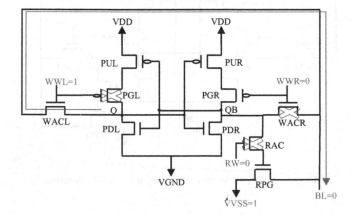

Fig. 4. Write 0 operation in 10T SRAM bit-cell.

3 Simulation Setup and Results

In the study, the simulations have been performed on HSPICE using PTM-MG model files for 20-nm FinFETs [10]. The transistor sizing criteria for 10T SRAM cell is illustrated in Table 1. In our work, for analyzing the stability of read-write operation in the proposed 10T SRAM bit-cell, the read and write static noise margin (RSNM and WSNM) have been calculated and studied using the butterfly curve approach at VDD = 0.9 V. The circuit for butterfly curve measurement for read operation is illustrated in Fig. 5.

3.1 Read Operation

In our 10T SRAM cell design, the storage-nodes (QB and Q) are separated from the read path. Hence, during read operation there is no effect of the bit-line (BL) on the storage-nodes due to which the cell stability increases. The RSNM of proposed SRAM cell design, the standard 6 transistor (6T) SRAM design and previous 10T SRAM designs [7, 8] is calculated using the butterfly plot as illustrated in Fig. 6. The RSNM for the proposed SRAM cell design has been found to be greater than the 6T SRAM bit-cell and almost equal to previously proposed 10T SRAM bit-cell designs [7, 8].

Table 1. Transistor sizing for the proposed 10T SRAM.

SRAM CELL	NFin = 1	NFin = 2	NFin = 3
Proposed 10T	PUL, PGL, PUR, PGR	WACL, WACR, RPG	PDL, PDR, RAC

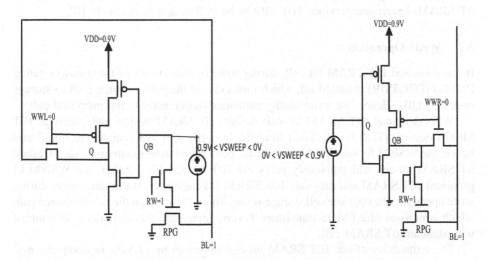

Fig. 5. Bit-cell circuit for butterfly curve measurement for read operation.

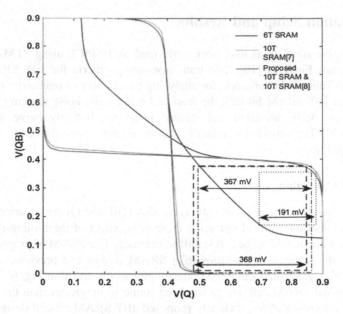

Fig. 6. RSNM Comparison

Moreover, the bit-line discharge takes place via a single transistor, which leads to a considerable reduction of the read delay in comparison to standard 6T SRAM cell and previously proposed 10T SRAM bit-cell designs. The read delay of proposed 10T SRAM bit-cell significantly improves by 30.78% and 39.37% in contrast with standard 6T SRAM design and previous 10T SRAM bit-cell design respectively [8].

3.2   Write Operation

In the proposed 10T SRAM bit-cell, during write operation, one of the 2 power gating PMOSs (PGL/PGR) is turned off, which thus cuts off the power source path to storage nodes (Q/QB). Hence, the write ability enhances significantly in the proposed cell.

WSNM of our 10T SRAM bit-cell design, 6T SRAM design and previous 10T SRAM designs [7, 8] is calculated from the butterfly plot as illustrated in Fig. 7 and hence, the WSNM for our SRAM bit-cell has been found to be greater than the standard 6T SRAM bit-cell and previously proposed 10T SRAM [7]. Further, the WSNM of proposed 10T SRAM and previous 10T SRAM [8] are equal. At the same time, during write operation, the opposite cell storage-nodes flip to "1" through the power source path which comprises of 2 PMOS transistors thereby increasing the write delay in contrast with standard 6T SRAM cell.

The write delay of our 10T SRAM bit-cell improves by 21.57% in comparison to the write-delay of previous 10T SRAM bit-cell [8].

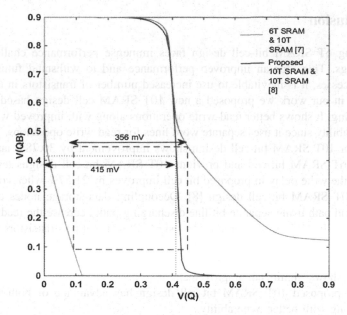

Fig. 7. WSNM Comparison

3.3 Dependence of Read Delay on NFin of RPG Transistor in the Proposed Bit-Cell

During simulation of read operation, it was observed that the read delay for NFin = 2 of read pass gate (RPG) transistor was 1.44 times the read delay for NFin = 1. Therefore, on increasing the size (NFin) of the RPG transistor, the read delay increases in the proposed 10T SRAM cell design.

3.4 Area Consideration

The area occupied by our cell design has been compared to the area of standard 6T SRAM bit-cell and thus found to be higher by 1.55 times due to increased number of transistors in the proposed bit-cell design. Also the area of proposed bit-cell is 16.18% less than the previous 10T SRAM bit-cell design [7]. Whereas when compared to previous 10T SRAM bit-cell design [8], the areas are found to be equal (Table 2).

Table 2. Comparison of SRAM cell designs at VDD = 0.9 V

SRAM CELL	RSNM (mV)	WSNM (mV)	Area	Read delay	Write delay
6T	191	356	X1	8.1 ps	8.3 ps
10T [7]	367	356	X1.84	4.08 ps	9.16 ps
10T [8]	368	415	X1.55	7.15 ps	23.1 ps
Proposed 10T	368	415	X1.55	5.13 ps	19 ps

4 Conclusion

The existing 6T SRAM bit-cell design faces immense performance challenges and shortcomings. Thus, for an improved performance and to withstand future technological processes, it is inevitable to use increased number of transistors in the SRAM cell. Thus, in our work we proposed a new 10T SRAM cell design based on single ended sensing. It shows better read-write operations along with improved write ability and read stability since it uses separate word lines for read-write operations. Thus, read delay of our 10T SRAM bit-cell design shows improvement by 30.78% and 39.37% relative to 6T SRAM bit-cell and previous 10T SRAM bit-cell designs respectively. Moreover, the write delay in proposed bit cell improves by 21.57% when compared to previous 10T SRAM bit-cell design [8]. Decoupling data-storage nodes completely from the read path using separate bit line discharging path decrease the read delay and increases the RSNM in the proposed design. Power gating transistors assists in improving the write ability as shown in the results for WSNM. Thus, the RSNM and WSNM of proposed 10T SRAM cell design is coherent to the latest 10T SRAM bit-cell design but shows significant improvement in read-write delay compared to it [8]. Hence, the proposed 10T SRAM bit-cell design has advantage of both-better read stability along with better write ability.

References

1. Rahaman, M., Mahapatra, R.: Design of a 32 nm independent gate FinFET based SRAM cell with improved noise margin for low power application. In: Proceedings of International Conference on Electronics and Communication Systems (ICECS), pp. 1–5. IEEE, Coimbatore (2014)
2. Ansari, M., Afzali Kusha, H., Ebrahimi, B., Navabi, Z., Kusha, A.A., Pedram, M.: A near-threshold 7T SRAM cell with high write and read margins and low write time for sub-20 nm FinFET technologies. Integr. VLSI J. **50**, 91–106 (2015)
3. Chang, L., Montoye, R.K., Nakamura, Y., Batson, K.A., Eickemeyer, R.J., Dennard, R.H., et al.: An 8T- SRAM for variability tolerance and low-voltage operation in high-performance caches. IEEE J. Solid-State Circuits **44**(4), 956–963 (2008)
4. Liu, Z., Kursun, V.: Characterization of a novel nine-transistor SRAM cell. IEEE Trans. Very Large Scale Integr. (VLSI) Syst. **16**(4), 488–492 (2008)
5. Chang, I.J., Kim, J., Park, S.P., Roy, K.: A 32 kb 10T sub-threshold SRAM array with bit-interleaving and differential read scheme in 90 nm CMOS. IEEE J. Solid-State Circuits **44**, 650–658 (2009)
6. Lo, C.-H., Huang, S.-Y.: P–P–N based 10T SRAM cell for low-leakage and resilient subthreshold operation. IEEE J. Solid-State Circuits **46**(3), 695–704 (2011)
7. Limachia, M., Viramgama, P., Thakker, R., Kothari, N.: Characterization of a novel 10T low-voltage SRAM cell with high read and write margin for 20 nm FinFET technology. In: Proceedings of 30th International Conference on VLSI Design and 16th International Conference on Embedded Systems (VLSID), pp. 309–314. IEEE, Hyderabad (2017)

8. Oh, T.W., Jung, S.: SRAM cell with data-aware power-gating write-asist for near-threshold operation. In: Proceedings of IEEE International Symposium on Circuits and Systems (ISCAS), pp. 1–4. IEEE, Florence (2018)
9. Jiajing, W., Nalam, S., Calhoun, B.H.: Analyzing static and dynamic write margin for nanometer SRAMs. In: Proceedings of IEEE International Symposium on Low Power Electronics and Design (ISLPED), pp. 129–134. IEEE, Bangalore (2014)
10. Predictive Technology Model (PTM). http://ptm.asu.edu/modelcard

Design of a Power Efficient Pulse Latch Circuit as a Solution for Master Slave Flip-Flop

Muneeb Sulthan[1]([✉]), Shubhajit Roy Chowdury[1], Rajnish Garg[2], and Alok Tripathi[2]

[1] Indian Institute of Technology, Mandi, India
muneebbai86@gmail.com
[2] STMicroelectronics Pvt Ltd, Greater Noida, India

Abstract. The recent trend in minimizing power dissipation of digital integrated circuits through low power clock storage has motivated the design of a conditional scan pulsed latch circuit. In this paper, a power efficient two bit conditional scan pulsed latch circuit as a solution For Master Slave Flip-Flop with a conditional pulse generator circuit has been proposed for the generation of clock signal which will drive the scan latch circuit as the input clock signal. This conditional pulse generation circuit will generate a pulse signal based on the mismatch between input data and the output data at the active clock edge. With this scan pulsed latch circuit 65% power savings has been achieved when compared with traditional SCAN Master Slave Flip-Flop and 54% when compared with our own one bit conditional scan pulsed latch circuit designed using 28 nm FDSOI CMOS LVT technology.

Keywords: Flip-flop · Pulse generator · Scan latch ·
Time borrowing · Power consumption

1 Introduction

In the recent years, Researches and Designers have changed this outline and given more importance for circuit designs with low power consumption and reduced area. The continuous trend in miniaturising of integrated circuits has led to leakage and other issues becoming more and more prominent over time. Hence minimization of power dissipation of digital integrated circuits has become the need of the hour. Digital circuit involves consideration of basic parameters like, power dissipation, area of implementation, leakage of power, speed and the efficiency of the circuit. These parameters are co-related, often trade off with each other, So depending on application some parameter are given more importance than other.

Supported by STMicroelectronics Pvt Ltd.

A. Sengupta et al. (Eds.): VDAT 2019, CCIS 1066, pp. 532–540, 2019.
https://doi.org/10.1007/978-981-32-9767-8_44

A crucial design requirement in the field of a deep sub-micron CMOS technology is the power dissipation and the area reduction, not only in transferable products but also in high performance VLSI systems. The power consumption of clock networks contributes 20% to 45% of overall system power dissipation in most of the highly synchronous system. Out of this, the clock storage part consumes 90% power dissipation in the clock network. We can reduce this power from 4% to 9% of the total power if the design is a low power clock storage part. However there is a potential to reduce the power dissipation in the clock network, If the design involves a low power clock storage component [1].

The recent advances in VLSI design and the increased number of battery based applications have set the goal of designing higher performance circuits coupled with lower power consumption [3]. The fundamental building block of any sequential digital circuit are Flip-Flops and Latches. The speed of these flip-flops thus determines the timing of a circuit design. Flip-flops also have a major contribution in the total power consumption of the design [4]. Conventional flip-flops are mainly implemented using Master-Slave Latch. In a Master Slave Latch, the data is latched to the master end at the rising edge of the clock, similarly the data will be available at the slave at the falling edge of clock pulse. In case of latches which is level sensitive, they consume less power when compared with Flip-flops. But, because of their data transparent nature it is difficult to perform timing verification on such type of latches.

A pulsed latch circuit is a latch circuit which is an intermediate alternative approach between latches and Flip-Flops using the benefits of both in timing as well as in power. In a pulsed latch circuit, a glitch signal which is generated from a pulse generator is used as a clock for the level sensitive latch. Since the pulse generator used in pulse latch is also power consuming the design of such circuit is also critical for a robust design.

In this paper, the design of a two bit conditional scan pulsed latch circuit is proposed together with a conditional pulse generator for the generation of clock signal that would drive the scan latch circuit as the clock signal. The whole circuit is divided into two parts. The first part is the generation of pulse signal through a pulse generator circuit and the next part is the scan latch to store the data. The two components are thereafter combined to make these two circuits act like a whole pulsed latch circuit. A two bit pulsed latch circuit has been designed which is giving a gain in power of 65% when compared with traditional scan master slave flip-flop and a 54% when compared with our own one bit conditional scan pulsed latch circuit.

2   Design of 2-Bit Conditional Pulse Latch

2.1   Design of Unconditional Clock Pulse Generator

A one-bit unconditional clock pulse generator is designed to have low power and low clock loading is shown in Fig. 1. It consist of 3 stacked NMOS transistors. The clock pulse(CP) is fed into inverter and its delayed version is available at the output(CPI) which is connected as the input to the stacked NMOS transistors.

These stacked NMOS transistors decide the width of the pulse that is generating from the pulse generator which will feed as the input clock to the latch circuit.

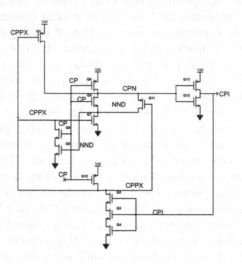

Fig. 1. Unconditional clock pulse generator.

The length of all transistors (NMOS and PMOS) are kept same(30 nm) to reduce the total power consumption. The width of the transistor are sized according to the requirement of latch circuit to store the data correctly. But the power of this unconditional clock pulse generator is getting increased because of the width used to store the data in the latch when it compared with the Traditional flip-flop. So our ultimate aim is to reduce the overall power. Hence, we decide to go for the design of conditional pulse generator.

2.2   Design of 1-Bit Conditional Scan Pulse Latch

Figure 2 show the design of the 1-bit conditional clock pulse generator. The name conditional is coming because, here the pulse will generate only when the condition of Data and output is satisfied. The circuit is similar to unconditional pulse generator circuit, the difference is that in place of the stack, this circuit will depend on the conditional transistors. The RN pin is the reset pin. The CPI output from this pulse generator will act as the clock signal for the scan latch in Fig. 3. The output and input of the scan latch circuit will form the conditional pulse generator circuit.

The function of the conditional pulse generator is as follows. At the rising edge of the every clock signal, the conditional pulse generator will generate a pulse signal when there is a mismatch between the input data signal and the output signal. This pulse will be used as input to the scan latch circuit to generate the output signal which will be same as the input. Similarly, when the input data and the output data is matched the pulse generator will not give any output

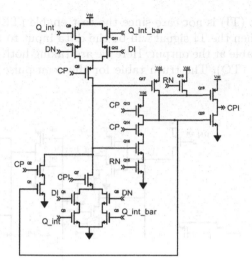

Fig. 2. 1-bit conditional clock pulse generator.

signal so that there is no triggering for the latch circuit. Hence, the output will remain as the previous output signal.

Table 1. Truth table for scan pulse latch

Truth table					
TE	TI	CLK	D	Q	TQ
0	X	0	0	Q	Q
0	X	0	1	Q	Q
0	X	1	0	0	0
0	X	1	1	1	1
1	0	0	X	Q	Q
1	1	0	X	Q	Q
1	0	1	X	0	0
1	1	1	X	1	1

The reset pin RN is which shown in the Figs. 2 and 4 is used to pull down the pulse signal to low. The multiplexer shown in the Figs. 3 and 5 will help to multiplex the input data signal D and D1 and to test the electronics device with 10 different known test input can be given trough TI with the help of the enable signal TE.

Figure 3 shows the 1-bit scan latch circuit in which it have the data input signal along with a test input signal. The data input(D) is fed into the bi-stable inverter when the pulse from the pulse generator goes high. At that time what ever the test input (TI) is not care since the test enable (TE) is off. When the test mode is ON then the TI signal will be the data input to the bi-stable latch which will be available at the output. Here we are taking both output(Q) as well as the test output (TQ). The truth table for the scan pulse latch is shown in Table 1.

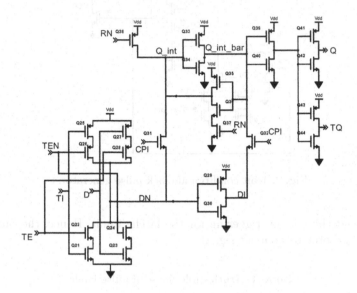

Fig. 3. Scan latch circuit.

2.3   Design of 2-Bit Conditional Scan Pulse Latch

Figure 4 shows the design of conditional two bit pulse generator. Here the condition will depend upon the 2 output signal and the 2 input data signal coming from the scan pulse latch. The circuit is similar to 1 bit conditional pulse generator except the conditional circuit which is given as the parallel to the earlier one. In a 2-bit scan pulse latch, it consist of two scan pulse latch circuit to store the two bit data separately. The data signal DN, DI, Q-int and Q-int-bar is coming from the first scan pulse, Similarly the DN-1, DI-1, Q-int-1 and Q-int-bar-1 are the signals coming from the second scan pulse latch circuit. This pulse signal CPI from the pulse generator will feed to the clock input to the different scan pulse latch. The most advantage of this type of pulse generator is that, by using this single pulse generator it can drive upto 10 scan pulse latches and hence the area is saved [2].

From the one-bit conditional pulsed latch itself we are getting a power saving of 25% when it is compared with industrial standard 28 nm FDSOI CMOS LVT technology scan master slave flip-flop and when it transferred to two-bit conditional scan pulsed latch we got a gain in power of 65% when compared

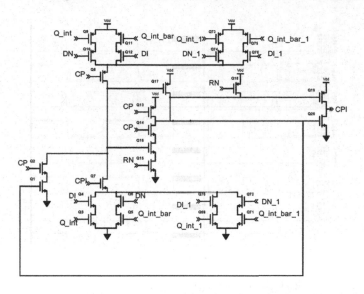

Fig. 4. 2-bit conditional pulse generator.

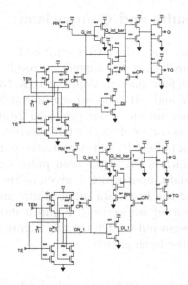

Fig. 5. 2-bit scan latch circuit.

with same and a gain of 54% in power when compared with our own one-bit conditional pulsed latch. Length of all the transistors are kept 30 nm (minimum length of a transistor in 28 nm FDSOI CMOS technology). Width of the transistors are sized so as to store the output data signal correctly. Transistor sizing is crucial for our the low power 2bit conditional pulse latch design to ensure correct functionality and robustness.

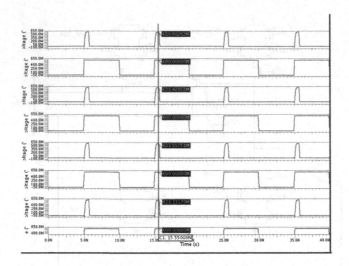

Fig. 6. 2-bit conditional clock pulse generator.

3   Simulation Results and Comparison

The advantage of our 2-bit scan pulse latch circuit is that it can work even for low voltage application. Figure 6 show the simulation result of the 2-bit conditional clock pulse generator with four different slopes (100 ps, 130 ps, 175 ps and 200 ps) with a voltage of 600 mV and 1 fF load capacitance at SS corner.

Figure 8 show the final output of our proposed 2-bit scan pulse latch with 750 mV Vdd at the process corner of SS at a temperature of −40°C. In the figure the first signal is the clock pulse(CP) which fed to the pulse generator to produce the pulse signal(CPI) which is fed to the scan pulse signal as the input clock. Third signal is the first data input which is given as the data signal and fourth one is the output(Q) for the first data input. Fifth and sixth signals are the second data input and output respectively. Figure 9 shows the complete layout of the 1-bit conditional scan pulse latch circuit. Figure 10 shows the layout for 2-bit conditional scan pulse latch circuit.

Table 2. Post layout comparison of 2-bit scan pulse latch with convectional flip-flops.

	Gate strength	Leakage power (mW)	Active power (mW)	Setup time (ps)	Hold time (ps)	C to Q delay (ps)	D to Q delay (ps)	Area (μm^2)
1-bit Scan Flip Flop	X8	1.01E-03	3.40E-03	0.428	0.355	0.171	0.599	4.57
1-bit conditional scan pulse latch	X8	1.12E-03	2.53E-03	0.613	0.559	0.215	0.828	5.06
2-bit conditional scan pulse latch	X8	1.04E-03	1.16E-03	0.554	0.516	0.269	0.823	4.40

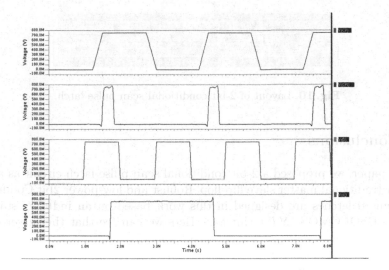

Fig. 7. 1-bit conditional scan pulse latch.

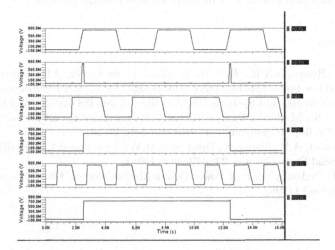

Fig. 8. 2-bit conditional scan pulse latch.

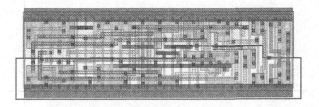

Fig. 9. Layout of 1-bit conditional scan pulse latch.

Fig. 10. Layout of 2-bit conditional scan pulse latch.

4   Conclusions

In this paper, we proposed a 2-bit conditional scan pulse latch circuit as a solution for traditional master slave flip-flop. Robust and low-power 2bit Conditional Scan pulsed latches are designed in this work based on an industry standard 28-nm FDSOI CMOS LVT technology. Here we can see that the power of our proposed 2-bit scan pulse latch is reduced about 65% and 54% from the our own 1-bit traditional scan master slave flip-flop and with 1-bit conditional scan pulse latch respectively. Table 2 shows the post layout comparison results of 2-bit scan pulse latch with scan master slave flip flop and our own conditional pulse latch circuit and also this circuit can be used for low voltage devices.

References

1. Singh, K., Rosas, O.A.R., Jiao, H., Huisken, J., de Gyvez, J.P.: Multi-bit pulsed-latch based low power synchronous circuit design. In: 2018 IEEE International Symposium on Circuits and Systems (ISCAS) 978-1-5386-4881-0/18/. IEEE (2018)
2. Tripathi, A.K., Mathuria, P.: Conditional pulse generator circuit for low power pulse triggered flip flop, Patent number: 9401715, July 26 2016
3. Chandrakasan, A.P., Sheng, S., Brodersen, R.W.: Low power CMOS digital design. IEEE J. Solid State Circuits **27**, 473–484 (1995)
4. Rabaey, J., Pedram, M.: Low Power Design Methodologies. Kluwer Academic Publishers, Norwell (1996)

Design and Analysis for Power Reduction with High SNM of 10T SRAM Cell

Kamini Singh, R. S. Gamad[(⊠)], and P. P. Bansod

Shri G. S. Institute of Technology and Science, Indore, Madhya Pradesh, India
kaminisingh1006@gmail.com, rsgamad@gmail.com,
pbansod@sgsits.ac.in

Abstract. This paper presents a study and analysis of 10T SRAM (static random-access memory) cell and also comparison has been done with conventional 6T SRAM and it also gives good Read stability and Write Margin with 34.21% and 33.33% respectively and less power. Proposed design is used as a part of memory with single purpose devices which requires low power consumption and reliability because memories are integrated part of digital circuits. Analysis and design of this circuit is done by using cadence tool at 180 nm technology. Simulation-based results are represented in this paper.

Keywords: Read stability · Write ability · Power consumption · Butterfly diagram

1 Introduction

In today's world microelectronics are found in a wide area of devices. Due to rapid growth in electronic devices wide, an evaluation in new technology has been triggered, with a particular focus on memory. Now a day's memories are widely used in biomedical, wireless and implementable devices. Modern VLSI system has individual part of memory Organization. Semiconductor memories are act as an integrated portion of VLSI framework. There are two types of RAM (random access memory) SRAM (static random-access memory), DRAM (dynamic random-access memory), here dynamic word means it require periodically refresh the charge of ideal storage capacitors because of that reason DRAMs are not frequently used memory even it contains less area than the SRAM [1], For improving stability and power consumption many SRAM Cell designs have been proposed, but Conventional 6T cell is still provided a good balance between size and performance because conventional 6T cell has a very compact and simple structure but it's operation of voltage is minimum and limited by conflicting requirements for read and write stability because of that reason it is not use for ultra-low voltage operation [2]. There are many proposed designs for memory cells design to improve speed and power in which one method is 10T (other memory configuration (7T, 8T, 9T) have there-own advantages and limitations) which focuses on increasing SNM low power.

A typical SRAM cell is made up of six MOSFETs. One bit is stored by four transistors (PM0, PM1, NM0, and NM1) forms two cross-coupled inverters. There are two stable states which is denoted by 0 and 1. Conventional 6T cell is simple but it has

© Springer Nature Singapore Pte Ltd. 2019
A. Sengupta et al. (Eds.): VDAT 2019, CCIS 1066, pp. 541–549, 2019.
https://doi.org/10.1007/978-981-32-9767-8_45

poor stability at minimum voltage due to which we always try to improve its read and write stability and introduces various methods in which some methods are dual rail power supply, negative bit line, single bit line with dynamic feedback control etc. But power supply of the 6T SRAM cannot reduced less than 0.6 V for successful operation.

2 Conventional 6T Transistors

Conventional 6T cell contains two back to back CMOS inverters. The output of one inverter is connected to another inverter as an input. Working operation for 6t SRAM cell: During write operation BL (bit line) will be charged to '1' or lowered to be '0' depending upon storing the data, and BLB (bit line bar) is charged complemented to the BL (Fig. 1).

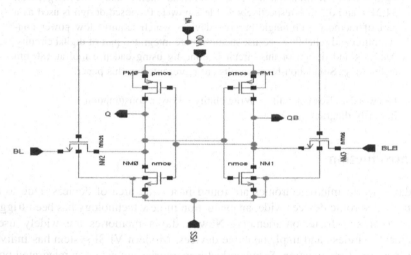

Fig. 1. Conventional 6T SRAM cell

To write '1' BL will be charged to VDD and BLB will be lowered to '0' and WWL charged to VDD and value will be stored at terminal Q and complemented value will be stored at terminal Q. For read operation BL and BLB will be charged to VDD and WL charged to '1' it provides a path from BL to ground through NM2 and NM3 which shows a cell is contained '1' at Q terminal and complimented value at QB. This Conventional 6T SRAM cell gives very less read noise margin (RNM) for better noise margin it requires width of pull-down transistor (NM0 and NM1) should be increase but due to increase area of the SRAM which in turn increases the leakage currents. As per requirement of less power consumption during active condition of circuit requires low supply voltage, due to voltage scaling reliability of circuit is reduced SRAM reliability is more suspect at lower voltages VDD min is the minimum supply voltage for an SRAM for read stability and write ability. Therefore, the analysis of read/write stability is essential for low power SRAMs [3, 4].

3 Proposed Cell Design of 10T SRAM

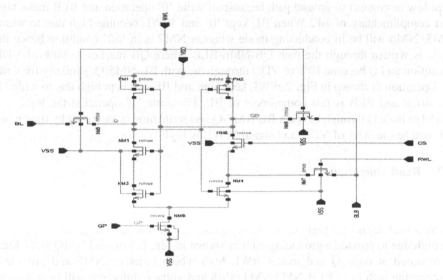

Fig. 2. Proposed 10T SRAM Cell

Figure 2 represents a schematic of 10T SRAM Cell which is proposed in this paper Contains 10 transistors in which PM1, PM2, NM3, NM4 create a cross coupled inverters and acts as storing cell where PM1, PM2 are pull-up transistors and NM3, N4 are poll down transistors. The BL contains data which we want to write for '1' it will be charged to VDD and for '0' it will be lowered to '0' and at the same time BLB will be complementary of that. Where NM1 is cascaded with NM3 and NM8 transistors in ground path which provides a cascading effect and used to reducing power consumption. Transistor NM2 is used for control signal during read operation and it provides an isolation between VDD to ground path which provides an interrupt free read operation and gives a good RNM (read noise margin). Transistor NM7 provide an access path for read operation whereas NM8 acts as sleep transistor during hold operation and stacking effect as well, which provides a low leakage current during hold operation due to which power consumption will be less for proposed cell design [5, 6].

4 Operations of Propose 10T SRAM Cell

This gives the operation of proposed SRAM Cell, Table 1. Illustrates the working operation of proposed 10T cell for read and write condition.

4.1 Write Operation

According to Fig. 2. Write operation of proposed SRAM Cell, when we write a '0' WWL is kept high to get access transistor to provide connection between bit line and cell, RWL makes '0' because it is write operation, CS kept high which provides a path from access transistor to ground and GP is kept which provides a grounding path. BL is kept low or connect to ground path because of write '0' operation and BLB make high just complimentary of BL. When BL kept '0' and WWL become high due to which NM5, NM6 will be in conducting mode whereas NM7 is in 'off' condition hence the logic is written through the path QB-NM6-BLB where QB reaches to 90% of VDD condition and Q become 10% of VDD through the path BL-NM5-Q. similarly for write '1' operation as shown in Fig. 2 WWL kept high and BL will kept high due to write '1' operation and BLB is just compliment of BL. For write '1' operation the logic 1 is stored at node Q through the path BL-NM5-Q and write time is measured by time when 'Q' reaches to 90% of VDD and signal WWL is high.

4.2 Read Operation

Before read operation first of all both BLB and BL are precharged to VDD. For read operation keeping WWL (write word line) will be '0' because of read operation, RWL (read word line) is kept high, CS (control signal) will be low and GP (ground path) will be high due to provide a grounding path as shown in Fig. 2. For read '1' (Q = 1), logic 1 is stored at node Q and makes RWL high which turns on NM7 and provide a discharging path from BLB-NM7-NM4-NM8 and voltage difference will be generated between BL and BLB and it is sensed by sense amplifier and decision taken by sense amplifier. The read time is measured by discharging of BLB through the discharging path from 90% to 10% of VDD.

Table 1. Table for various operations performed by proposed 10T SRAM Cell

	Data stored			
	Write 1	Write 0	Read	Hold
WWL	1	1	0	0
BL	1	0	1	0
BLB	0	1	"Discharge"	0
RWL	0	0	1	0
CS	1	1	0	1
GP	1	1	1	0

5 Simulation Results

To evaluate the proposed 10T SRAM cell is design Cadence Tool. Waveforms are generated by Cadence SPECTRE simulator. In this paper, comparison of 6T and 10T has been done in terms of static power, average power, total power consumption, write margin (WM) and RSNM of proposed 10T and conventional 6T SRAM cell in 180 nm (gpdk) technology as discussed above gives result of comparison between conventional 6T and proposed 10T SRAM cell. Transient analysis read and write operation of 6T and proposed 10T SARM are shown below where Figs. 3 and 4 gives write and read operation respectively and Figs. 5 and 6 gives Write and Read operation of proposed 10 SRAM.

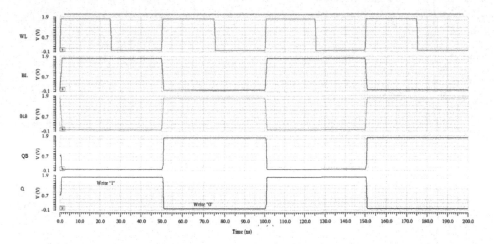

Fig. 3. Write operation of 6T SRAM Cell

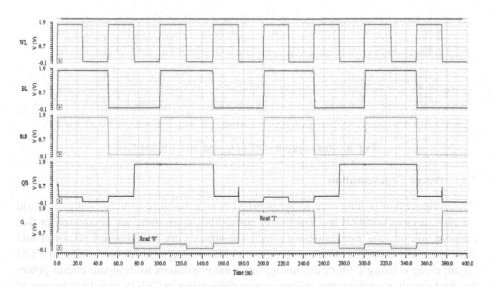

Fig. 4. Read operation of 6T SRAM Cell

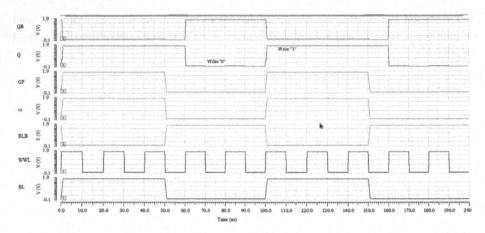

Fig. 5. Write operation of proposed 10T SRAM Cell

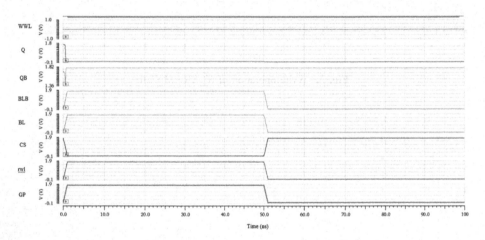

Fig. 6. Read operation of proposed 10T SRAM Cell

5.1 Power Consumption

Power dissipation is important factor in VLSI design because in today's digital world portable devices are used and low power consumption are more advantageous for that purpose. We always need a device which consumes very less amount of power and there are many methods of circuit design to reduce leakage power in circuits. In VLSI circuit designs using CMOS technology have many sources to dissipate circuit power by short circuit, switching and leakage power dissipation in CMOS mainly two types of power dissipations are Dynamic and Static power dissipation, where static power consumption occurs when circuit is in static condition no input/output changes. Static power is also called as DC power and calculated by the Dynamic power consumption is also called as active power or charging and discharging capacitors [7, 8]. Total power is calculated by sum of Dynamic and Static power. Figure 7 gives a graph for total power versus VDD for both proposed 10T and conventional 6T.

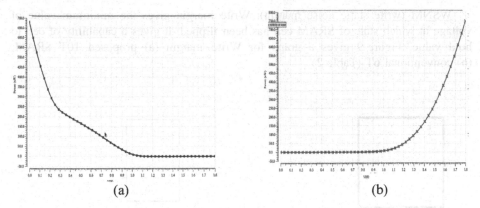

(a)   (b)

Fig. 7. Power versus VDD graph for SRAM Cells (a) proposed 10T SRAM (b) conventional 6T SRAM

5.2 Static Noise Margin (SNM)

SNM is used to check for cell stability of SRAM during read, write and hold operation. It gives information about the stability of cell by tolerance level of noise voltage at each storage node for DC analysis which can be tolerated by the circuit without flipping of stored data. There are two methods of measuring SNM of SRAM Cell. First method is graphical method which is VTC behaviour of cross coupled inverters is commonly called as Butterfly curve. The Static Noise Margin or SNM of an inverter device can be graphically represented by this butterfly curve, and second method is N-curve method. SNM can be calculated by measuring the side length of the square smaller of two side length becomes the actual SNM [9].

RSNM (read static noise margin): RSNM is used to characterisation of data retention capability it is gives the noise voltage at each storage node for DC analysis that can be tolerated without changing the stored bit. Figure 8 shows butterfly diagram for read stability.

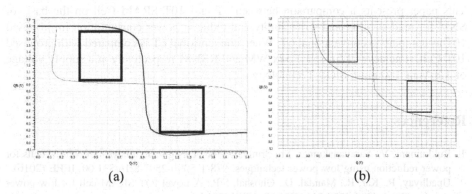

(a)   (b)

Fig. 8. Butterfly diagram of read operation (a) proposed 10T SRAM, (b) conventional 6T SRAM

WSNM (write static noise margin): Write margin gives the minimum value of voltage at which state of SRAM cell has been flipped. It gives a capability of cell to hold value. Figure 9 gives a graph for Write margin (a) proposed 10T SRAM, (b) conventional 6T (Table 2).

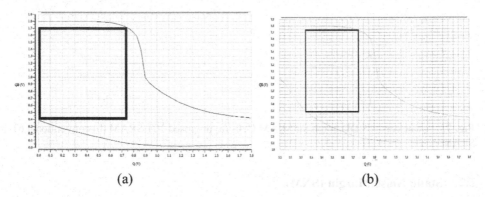

(a)   (b)

Fig. 9. Butterfly diagram of write operation (a) proposed 10T SRAM, (b) conventional 6T SRAM

Table 2. Result for different SRAM Cells

SRAM cells	Parameters				
	Technology	Power supply	SNM		Power
			Write	Read	
6T	180 nm	1.8	500 mV	250 mV	751 uW
10T	180 nm	1.8	750 mV	380 mV	1.299e−11

6 Conclusion

This paper presents a comparison between 6T and 10T SRAM Cell on the basis of SNM for read stability and write ability and reduced power consumption in proposed 10T as compare to conventional 6T. When conventional 6T is compared with proposed 10T Cell, it achieves 1.5x and 1.52x WM and RSNM respectively at a supply voltage of 1.8 V in 180 nm CMOS Technology.

References

1. Rukkumani, V., Saravanakumar, M., Srinivasan, K.: Design and analysis of SRAM cells for power reduction using low power techniques. 978-1-5090-2597-8/16/$31.00. IEEE (2016)
2. Upadhyay, P., Kar, R., Mandal, D., Ghoshal, S.P.: A novel IOT SRAM cell for low power circuits. 978-1-4799-3358-7114/$31.00. IEEE (2014)

3. Yan, H., Wang, D., Hou, C.: The design of low leakage SRAM cell with high SNM. 978-1-61284-193-9/11/$26.00. IEEE (2011)
4. Singh, S., Lakhmani, V.: Read and write stability of 6T SRAM. Int. J. Adv. Res. Electron. Commun. Eng. (IJARECE) 3(5) (2014)
5. Singh, P., Vishvakarma, S.K.: Ultra-low power high stability 8T SRAM for application in object tracking system. 216-3536 (2017)
6. Shiny Grace, P., Sivamangai, N.M.: Design of 10T SRAM cell for high SNM and low power. 978-1-5090-2309-7/16/$31.00. IEEE (2016)
7. Shivaprakash, G., Suresh, D.S.: Design of low power 6T-SRAM cell and analysis for high speed application. Indian J. Sci. Technol. 9(46) (2016). https://doi.org/10.17485/ijst/2016/v9i46/106144
8. Banga, H., Agarwal, D.: Single bit line 10T SRAM cell for low power and high SNM. In: Proceeding International Conference on Recent Innovations is Signal Processing and Embedded Systems (RISE - 2017), 27–29 October 2017
9. Priya, S., Gavaskar, K.: Design of efficient low power 9T SRAM cell. Int. J. Eng. Res. Technol. (IJERT) 2(1) (2013)

Low Power VLSI and Memory Design

A CMOS/MTJ Based Novel Non-volatile SRAM Cell with Asynchronous Write Termination for Normally OFF Applications

Kanika Monga[✉] and Nitin Chaturvedi

Birla Institute of Technology and Science, Pilani, India
{P20170027,nitin80}@pilani.bits-pilani.ac.in

Abstract. Non-volatile SRAM (NV-SRAM) enables normally off computing while achieving faster power off/on time by storing the state in its locally embedded non-volatile elements. Emerging magnetic memory such as spin transfer torque magnetic tunnel junction (STT-MTJ) is preferred in the NV-SRAM design because of its attractive features like unlimited endurance, high density, scalability and CMOS compatibility. However, write operation in MTJ is stochastic which means duration of MTJ write is undeterministic. As a result, it suffers from reliability issue like write errors. Existing solution to reduce the write error rate mainly consist of increased write pulse duration which leads to high power consumption. However, if write completion could be detected on fly and write current could be cut-off immediately, energy consumption can be reduced by a large extent. Therefore, this work proposes a novel non-volatile SRAM cell with asynchronous write termination scheme. In the proposed NV-SRAM cell, write operation is continuously monitored and terminated as soon as MTJ is switched to the required state. Our analysis indicates that the proposed cell achieves reduction in write power by 23% when compared with the cell without write assist. Moreover, the proposed write termination circuit achieves 2.52–14% more power saving when compared to existing write termination circuits.

Keywords: Normally OFF instantly ON · STT-MTJ · Hybrid memory · Non-volatile SRAM · Write termination

1 Introduction

With the advent of Internet of things, trillion of devices are being deployed in the environment to connect the real world with the world of computing [1]. These smart devices will transform the way we live by revolutionizing wide range of application domains such as healthcare, security & surveillance and wireless sensor network. However, all these devices have a common feature of low activity rate i.e. long idle period followed by short burst of computation which results in large standby power consumption [2]. The standby power consumption in a system is mainly dominated by the memory system. Therefore, significant efforts have been made in the past to design a low power SRAM.

© Springer Nature Singapore Pte Ltd. 2019
A. Sengupta et al. (Eds.): VDAT 2019, CCIS 1066, pp. 553–564, 2019.
https://doi.org/10.1007/978-981-32-9767-8_46

One of the possible approaches to reduce the standby power is to turn off the memory block when not in use. Consequently, state of the system must be stored and recalled before power off and after power on respectively. This have led to the development of "Normally OFF & Instant ON computing" which is a promising solution to ever increasing demand for energy efficient systems. Normally OFF systems work with full performance during active mode and are turned off during idle period to completely eliminate standby power dissipation. Emerging non-volatile memories such as MTJ (Magnetic Tunnel Junction) seems to be effective solution to realize normally off computing. It offers several advantages such as unlimited read/write cycles, low switching currents and fast switching times [3].

Therefore, MTJ based hybrid non-volatile SRAM cell has been proposed in this paper which offers faster store and restore of data bit for normally OFF applications. However, one critical issue with the MTJ is its high write energy. There are three main reasons which contributes to high write energy. First, requirement of large write current through the MTJ for a long time to switch its state. Since the write current of the MTJ is 10x higher than of traditional SRAM, it infers a high power consumption [4]. Second, asymmetric and stochastic nature of MTJ write. The write operation in MTJ is asymmetric which means writing '1' takes more time compared to writing '0'. The duration of write operation must be employed for the worst-case scenario, therefore the pulse width for write depends upon writing '1' time [5]. As a consequence, unnecessary current flows through the cell undergoing write '0' operation, even after the switching is complete. Moreover, due to random thermal fluctuation, switching time in the MTJ is inherently stochastic. The stochastic nature of MTJ write results in random switching time even with same operating conditions [6]. The variation in switching time results in increased probability of write errors. Therefore, to account for both stochastic and asymmetric behavior of MTJ, write pulse duration is enlarged at the expense of an increase in power consumption. The third reason for high write energy is redundant write operation which refers to the case in which data to be written matches the MTJ current state. While performing redundant write operation, same amount of switching current (in μA) flows through the MTJ as required to flip its state. Consequently, total power consumption of the memory increases. On an average, in a typical application 88% of the writes in L2 cache are redundant [7]. Therefore, huge power can be saved provided overwriting of same bit is avoided. Furthermore, unnecessary current flow through MTJ during redundant write imposes a severe stress on the device. As a result, MTJ resistance, switching current and switching time values are degraded over time. To address these challenges, this work also presents a novel write assist circuit which is integrated with the NV-SRAM cell. It allows bit wise monitoring and write current termination after detecting the successful switching of MTJ states. The switching of MTJ state is detected by constant monitoring of the voltage variation on its pinned layer terminal which is then used to asynchronously terminate the operation to save power.

In summary, this paper makes the following contributions:

- We propose a novel hybrid non-volatile SRAM cell with asynchronous write termination technique which can control each bit independently.

- We analyze energy consumption of our proposed cell with traditional 6T SRAM cell. The proposed write termination circuit is also compared with previously proposed write termination circuits and it is observed that the proposed design achieves greater power saving.
- Minimum write pulse width is determined by corner condition which is required for successful switching in proposed NV-SRAM cell.

The rest of this paper is organized as follows: Sect. 2 discusses the MTJ background and provide information related to the existing write termination techniques. Section 3 proposes a NV-SRAM cell augmented with write termination circuit. In Sect. 4 simulation results of proposed cell is presented. Finally, conclusion is drawn in Sect. 5.

2 Background

2.1 MTJ Characteristics

Magnetic memory based on MTJ is capable of storing binary bits in its two states antiparallel (AP) and parallel (P). Each MTJ is made up of two ferromagnetic layers (reference and free) separated by thin oxide layer such as magnesium oxide (MgO) as shown in Fig. 1. The reference layer has its magnetic orientation fixed whereas magnetic orientation of free layer can be flipped giving rise to two different states. When the magnetization of both layers are same, the MTJ is said to be in parallel state (P). On the contrary, when the magnetization of both the layers are opposite, the MTJ is said to be in anti-parallel state (AP). The resistance of the MTJ depends upon its state. The device exhibits low resistance in parallel state and high resistance in antiparallel state [8]. Unlike previous MRAM, MTJ uses STT (Spin Transfer Torque) writing mechanism. A bi-directional write current is required to reorient the magnetic direction of free layer resulting in state change from LRS to HRS or vice-versa [9].

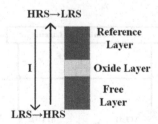

Fig. 1. Magnetic tunnel junction

2.2 Related Work

To address the challenges of high write energy various attempts have been made in the past. At the device level, Wolf et al. [10] proposed perpendicular magnetic anisotropy MTJ which had the significant lower write energy than in-plane anisotropy

MTJ. Smullen et al. [11] proposed method to improve switching efficiency by reducing retention time. However this method is suitable only for application with short idle periods. Application with long idle period requires periodic refresh which again result in higher power consumption. At circuit level, Sun et al. [12] proposed the method of 'read before write' to terminate the write operation in case of redundant write. However, read operation itself consumes energy and it also does not consider asymmetric and stochastic nature of write operation. To account for asymmetricity and stochasticity of MTJ write, Suzuki et al. [13] proposed 1T-1MTJ structure with write termination circuit. The voltage variation on node SL and BL is monitored to detect the switching and terminate the write operation. Gupta et al. [14] modified the circuit proposed by Suzuki to reduce the number of transistors. Zhang et al. [15] further reduced the number of transistors by using the feedback mechanism to terminate the write operation. This paper proposes a hybrid non-volatile SRAM cell which uses similar concept of continuous node voltage monitoring to terminate the write operation with less number of transistor. As soon as writing into the MTJ is complete, voltage on node (connected to pinned layer of MTJ) rises due to change in resistance of MTJ which serves as a detection signal for successful write operation. This detection signal is then used to disable the write path, thereby terminating the write operation.

3 Proposed Self-terminating NV-SRAM Cell

Hybrid memories combine SRAM with Non-Volatile Memories (NVM) to completely eliminate standby power in traditional on-chip cache memories. Similar to standard SRAM cell, the data bit in hybrid NV-SRAM cell is also stored in inverter pair. However, data held by the cell is written into the locally embedded non-volatile elements before power off to obtain zero static power consumption. Figure 2 illustrates the schematic diagram of proposed 8T2MTJ hybrid NV-SRAM cell. In addition to 6T SRAM core it consists of two MTJ, an isolation transistor X1 and an equalization transistor X2. The arrangement of both the MTJs (MTJ1 & MTJ2) are in such a way

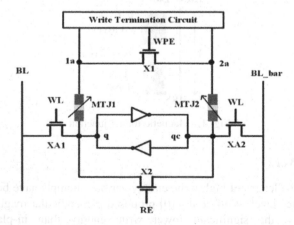

Fig. 2. Proposed 8T2MTJ hybrid NV-SRAM cell with write termination circuitry

that they hold complimentary data bit. Free layer of the MTJ1 and MTJ2 is connected to cell storage node q and qc respectively while reference layers of both MTJ are connected to write termination circuitry. The proposed write termination circuitry is augmented with every cell for independent bit control.

The proposed hybrid memory works in three different operational modes: write mode, restore mode and normal operation mode.

3.1 Write Operation

In this mode of operation, value at the nodes q and qc are stored into the MTJ1 and MTJ2 respectively. As soon as MTJs are switched to required state, write current path is disabled by the write termination circuit. The write termination circuit consist of two inverters, one AND gate and one OR gate as shown in Fig. 3.

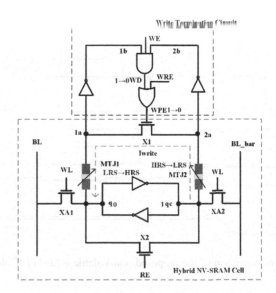

Fig. 3. Write operation of proposed 8T2MTJ hybrid NV-SRAM cell

The write detection signal (WD) used in the proposed write termination circuit is asserted low to indicate completion of switching. Whereas write path enable signal (WPE) is asserted low to terminate the write current. In Fig. 4, the first highlighted region in blue plots the write operation for proposed 8T2MTJ cell. It is assumed that the initial state of MTJ1 and MTJ2 are LRS and HRS respectively. Now, for storing q = 0/qc = 1, state of both the MTJs have to be flipped. The Write Enable (WE) signal is asserted high for the complete duration of write operation. Now, to begin the write current, a pulse of 1 ns width is applied at Write & Restore Enable (WRE) signal which turns ON the X1 transistor. As a result, I$_{write}$ flows through the MTJs whose direction is determined by the voltage present at the nodes q and qc. The current flows from qc → MTJ2 → MTJ1 → q switching MTJ1 to high resistance state (HRS) and MTJ2 to low resistance state (LRS) as shown in Fig. 3. Voltage at nodes 1a and 2a remains at lower voltage level (lower than inverters threshold) until the switching happens, therefore initial value of write detection signal (WD) is high. Due to change in resistance of MTJ, voltage at the node 1a and 2a varies. And once the switching is complete voltage at both the node 1a and 2a rises to a value higher than threshold value of the inverters. This change in voltage is amplified by a CMOS inverter. The amplified voltage now present at node 1b and 2b respectively are then ANDed together to assert WD low. With write detection signal WD low, WPE is also pulled to gnd which finally terminates the write current by turning OFF the X1 transistor. However, for the case $q = 1/qc = 0$, MTJs state are not flipped as data to be stored is same as MTJ current state. Therefore detection signal WD is low and as soon as WRE is asserted low, control signal WPE is pulled to gnd immediately terminating the write current.

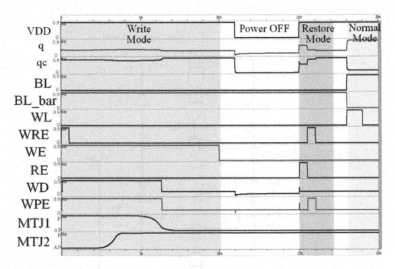

Fig. 4. Simulation waveform of the proposed non-volatile 8T2MTJ (Color figure online)

3.2   Restore Operation

In the restore mode of operation the stored values in the MTJs are written into the SRAM cell nodes q and qc. In Fig. 4, region highlighted in red plots the restore operation for the proposed 8T2MTJ cell. The application of short pulse to the restore enable signal (RE) enables equalization transistor X2 to bring the voltage at nodes q and qc to a same value. The pulse width of RE is significantly shorter compared to the restore period so as to reduce the power dissipation due to short circuit current which flows during the process of equalization of nodes. After equalization, the control signal WRE is asserted high to provide a complete path [X2 → q → MTJ1 → X1 → MTJ2 → qc] for nodes to have differential voltage. This differential voltage across nodes is translated to full voltage level as soon as WRE is asserted low by the regenerative action of two cross-coupled inverter.

3.3   Normal Operation

In normal operating mode, both the isolation (X1) and equalization transistors (X2) are OFF to disconnect the MTJs and write termination circuit from the cell. As a result, the proposed cell functions as a typical SRAM cell with similar read and write operation.

4   Simulation Methodology and Results

This section presents the HSPICE simulations results for the proposed NV-SRAM cell. The technology library used to perform the simulation are PTM 20 nm FinFET model [16] and STT-MTJ HSPICE model [17]. Depending upon magnetization anisotropy MTJ are classified into two categories: in-plane and perpendicular. In general, perpendicular MTJ have lower switching thresholds and are more scalable as compared to in-plane MTJ [18, 19]. Therefore, all the simulation in this work are performed using pMTJ. The critical parameters and their default value are tabulated in Table 1

Table 1. Critical parameters and the default value of STT-MTJ HSPICE model

Parameters	Values
Free layer volume (W * L * T) (nm^3)	20 * 20 * 1.4
Thickness of oxide layer T_{MGO} (nm)	1.14
Saturation magnetization (emu/cm^3)	700
Rp (parallel state resistance)	3.4–3.6 KΩ
Rap (anti-parallel state resistance)	7.2–9.6 KΩ
TMR ratio	>100%
α (damping factor)	0.028

Table 2 shows the performance analysis of the proposed 8T2MTJ cell with write termination. The energy consumption of proposed 8T2MTJ cell during normal read/write operation is compared with conventional 6T SRAM cell and 8T2MTJ without write termination and it is observed that adding non-volatility to 6T SRAM cell have little impact on its read and write performance. Due to introduction of write termination circuit MTJ write energy was reduced to 23% when compared with cell without write termination.

Table 2. Performance comparison of proposed 8T2MTJ NV-SRAM cell with conventional 6T SRAM cell

	Normal operation		MTJ write operation (fJ)	Restore operation (fJ)
	Write energy (fJ)	Read energy (fJ)		
6T SRAM	14	0.5	–	–
8T2MTJ without write termination	15	0.9	313	26
8T2MTJ with write termination	21.3	0.9	257	30

We also compare our write termination design with current state-of-art write termination circuits proposed by different researchers described in Sect. 2. The write energy saving obtained by different write termination circuit is tabulated in Table 3. From the obtained simulation results it is observed that proposed circuit have greater power saving of 13.75% when compared to Suzuki [13], 8.07% compared to Gupta [14] and 2.5% compared to Zhang [15], write termination circuit. Also, the area overhead is least among all which is counted in terms of number of transistors.

Table 3. Performance comparison of proposed write termination circuit with prior work

	Write '1' energy reduction	Write '0' energy reduction	No. of transistor
	0 to 1	1 to 0	
Suzuki [13]	6.80%	11.70%	40
Gupta [14]	16.66%	13.20%	38
Zhang [15]	27.77%	13.20%	20
Proposed	23%	23%	16

One of the critical design parameter of non-volatile memory cell is duration (T_w) of write operation. Due to process variation, switching time of the MTJ varies which results in increased write error rate. Therefore, in order to reduce the write error and mitigate the influence of process variation on switching time, write pulse width is determined by the worst switching time under all process corners [20]. We consider variation in oxide thickness of the MTJ (t_{MGO}), cross-sectional area of MTJ (A) and threshold voltage of NFET used in write path. These parameters are chosen because they significantly affect the switching performance of the MTJ. For our analysis, we assume $\pm 2.5\%$ for t_{MGO}, $\pm 15\%$ for A and ± 30 mV for threshold voltage of NFET [21]. Figure 5(a) and (c) shows variation of switching times with $\pm 15\%$ variation in area plotted for different values of write currents for AP to P and P to AP transition respectively. Figure 5(b) and (d) plots the process corner described as 1–8 in Table 4 for AP to P and P to AP transition respectively. In FS (Fast MTJ and Slow NFET)

Table 4. List of process variation corners [21]

	ΔA	ΔT_{MGO}	ΔV_t
N	0%	0%	0%
1	+15%	+2.5%	+30 mV
2	+15%	+2.5%	−30 mV
3	+15%	−2.5%	+30 mV
4	+15%	−2.5%	−30 mV
5	−15%	+2.5%	+30 mV
6	−15%	+2.5%	−30 mV
7	−15%	−2.5%	+30 mV
8	−15%	−2.5%	−30 mV

tabulated as 3 in Table 4, MTJ has lowest resistance (ΔA is +15% and ΔT$_{MGO}$ is −2.5%) and NFET has higher threshold value (ΔV$_t$ is +30 mV). In SF corner (Slow

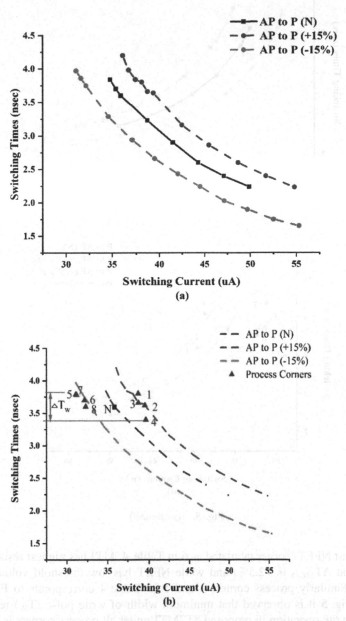

Fig. 5. (a) Switching times with variation in only area of cross-section of MTJ for AP to P transition. (b) Switching times variation at all process corners for AP to P transition. (c) Switching times with variation in only area of cross-section of MTJ for P to AP transition. (d) Switching times variation at all process corners for P to AP transition.

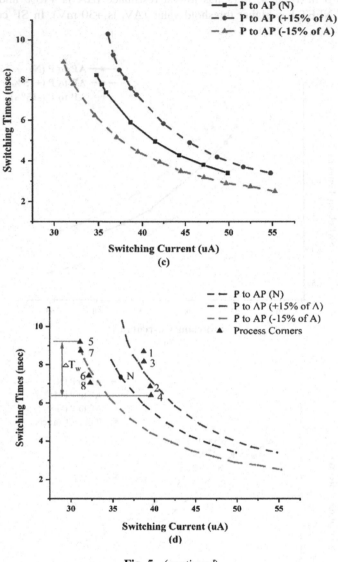

Fig. 5. (*continued*)

MTJ and Fast NFET) corner tabulated as 6 in Table 4, MTJ has highest resistance (ΔA is -15% and ΔT_{MGO} is $+2.5\%$) and while NFET has low threshold voltage (ΔV_t is -30 mV). Similarly process corners 4 and 5 in Table 4 corresponds to FF and SS. From the Fig. 5 it is observed that minimum width of write pulse (T_W) required for successful write operation in proposed 8T2MTJ under all process corners is 9.18 nsec.

5 Conclusion

In this paper, we present a hybrid non-volatile SRAM cell with write termination circuit. The proposed cell shows improved write performance by terminating the write current immediately after the MTJ switching is complete. The simulation results indicate reduction in write energy by 23% compared to NV-SRAM cell without write assist. Furthermore, 94% of write energy saving is achieved during redundant write using proposed write termination circuit. Finally, to design a process variation tolerant NV-SRAM cell worst switching time is determined at all the process corners.

References

1. Jayakumar, H., Raha, A., Raghunathan, V.: Energy-aware memory mapping for hybrid FRAM-SRAM MCUs in IoT edge devices. In: Proceedings of IEEE International Conference on VLSI Design, March 2016, pp. 264 269 (2016)
2. Alioto, M. (ed.): Enabling the Internet of Things. From Integrated Circuits to Integrated Systems. Springer, Heidelberg (2017). https://doi.org/10.1007/978-3-319-51482-6
3. Meena, J., Sze, S., Chand, U., Tseng, T.-Y.: Overview of emerging nonvolatile memory technologies. Nanoscale Res. Lett. **9**, 526 (2014)
4. Bishnoi, R., Oboril, F., Ebrahimi, M., Tahoori, M.B.: Avoiding unnecessary write operations in STT-MRAM for low power implementation. In: Proceedings of International Symposium on Quality Electronic Design (ISQED), pp. 548–553 (2014)
5. Bishnoi, R., Ebrahimi, M., Oboril, F., Tahoori, M.B.: Asynchronous Asymmetrical Write Termination (AAWT) for a low power STT-MRAM. In: Design, Automation and Test in Europe Conference & Exhibition (DATE), pp. 1–6 (2014)
6. Bishnoi, R., Ebrahimi, M., Oboril, F., Tahoori, M.B.: Improving write performance for STT-MRAM. IEEE Trans. Mag. **52**, 1–11 (2016)
7. Zhou, P., Zhao, B., Yang, J., Zhang, Y.: Energy reduction for STT-RAM using early write termination. In: IEEE/ACM International Conference on Computer-Aided Design, Technical Paper, ICCAD 2009, pp. 264–268 (2009)
8. Farkhani, H., Tohidi, M., Peiravi, A., Madsen, J.K., Moradi, F., Basics, A.S.: STT-RAM energy reduction using self-referenced differential write termination technique. IEEE Trans. Very Large Scale Integr. Syst. **25**, 476–487 (2017)
9. Ohno, H., Stiles, M.D., Dieny, B.: Spintronics [scanning the issue]. Proc. IEEE **104**, 1782–1786 (2016)
10. Wolf, S.A., Lu, J., Stan, M.R., Chen, E., Treger, D.M.: The promise of nanomagnetics and spintronics for future logic and universal memory. Proc. IEEE **98**, 2155–2168 (2010)
11. Smullen IV, C.W., Mohan, V., Nigam, A., Gurumurthi, S., Stan, M.R.: Relaxing non-volatility for fast and energy-efficient STT-RAM caches. In: Proceedings of International Symposium on High Performance Computer Architecture, pp. 50–61 (2011)
12. Sun, G., Dong, X., Xie, Y., Li, J., Chen, Y.: A novel architecture of the 3D stacked MRAM L2 cache for CMPs. In: Proceedings of International Symposium on High Performance Computer Architecture, pp. 239–249 (2009)
13. Suzuki, D., Natsui, M., Mochizuki, A., Hanyu, T.: Cost-efficient self-terminated write driver for spin-transfer-torque RAM and logic. IEEE Trans. Magn. **50**, 2–5 (2014)
14. Gupta, M.K., Hasan, M.: Self-terminated write-assist technique for STT-RAM. IEEE Trans. Magn. **52**, 1–6 (2016)

15. Zhang, D., et al.: High-speed, low-power, and error-free asynchronous write circuit for STT-MRAM and logic. IEEE Trans. Magn. **52**, 2–5 (2016)
16. PTM FINFET and MOSFET Model. http://ptm.asu.edu/
17. Fong, X., Choday, S.H., Georgios, P., Augustine, C., Roy, K.: SPICE models for magnetic tunnel junctions based on monodomain approximation (2013). https://nanohub.org/resources/19048
18. Wang, Y., et al.: Compact model of dielectric breakdown in spin-transfer torque magnetic tunnel junction. IEEE Trans. Electron Devices **63**, 1762–1767 (2016)
19. Zhang, Y.Y., et al.: Compact model of subvolume MTJ and its design application at nanoscale technology nodes. IEEE Trans. Electron Devices **62**, 2048–2055 (2015)
20. Lee, D., Gupta, S.K., Roy, K.: High-performance low-energy STT MRAM based on balanced write scheme. In: Proceedings of the 2012 ACM/IEEE International Symposium on Low Power Electronics and Design, ISLPED 2012, Redondo Beach, California, pp. 9–14 (2012)
21. Lee, D., Roy, K.: Energy-delay optimization of the STT MRAM write operation under process variations. IEEE Trans. Nanotechnol. **13**, 714–723 (2014)

Statistical Variation Aware Leakage and Total Power Estimation of 16 nm VLSI Digital Circuits Based on Regression Models

Deepthi Amuru[1]($\boxtimes$) (iD), Andleeb Zahra[2], and Zia Abbas[1]

[1] International Institute of Information Technology, Hyderabad, India
deepthi.amuru@research.iiit.ac.in,
zia.abbas@iiit.ac.in
[2] DIET, Sapienza University of Rome, Rome, Italy
andleeb.zahra@uniroma1.it

Abstract. With the technology scaling down to sub-50 nm regime, the necessity of process variation aware estimation of Leakage Power is emphasized for robust digital circuit design. Variations in Leakage power results in a large increase in the variation of total power dissipation. This paper presents a Regression based estimation of leakage powers and total power dissipation in nanoscale standard cell-based designs that show an impressive speed-up advantage with respect to analog SPICE-level simulation. We propose a statistical variation aware estimation model through a *Multivariate Linear Regression* (MLR) and *Multivariate Polynomial Regression* (MPR) techniques. Exhaustive tests report shows MPR technique outperforms MLR technique in estimating the leakage and total power for the targeted 16 nm CMOS technology with negligible error (<1%). The proposed methodology works as black box i.e. equally valid for 16 nm, 22 nm and 45 nm technology nodes.

Keywords: Machine learning (ML) · Leakage power · CMOS · VLSI

1 Introduction

Algorithm models of Integrated Circuit (IC) behavior have always been used to computationally speed up analyses and/or optimizations, by performing them on the models instead of running expensive transistor-level circuit simulations. In general, this speed-up is obtained at a penalty in accuracy, which depends on the model error [1]. Therefore, a reliable model generation, ensuring as high as possible accuracy while maintaining high computation efficiency is a challenging task, especially for models that include statistical variation effects, which significantly deviate the circuit performance from its intended behavior [2] in a complex way.

Such high sensitivity to process parameter variation translate into statistically significant higher power than the nominal value and leads to a degraded parametric yield of the chip fabrication. Ultimately, an accurate yet efficient calculation of variation-aware leakage power and total power is highly desirable before the actual fabrication of the ICs, which would allow us in tradeoffs and countermeasures.

© Springer Nature Singapore Pte Ltd. 2019
A. Sengupta et al. (Eds.): VDAT 2019, CCIS 1066, pp. 565–578, 2019.
https://doi.org/10.1007/978-981-32-9767-8_47

A Monte-Carlo is a common technique for estimating the effects of process variation on leakage power by running the randomly varying SPICE simulations, according to a specified statistical distribution. If the number of simulations is large, one can obtain a good estimate of the mean (μ) and standard deviation (σ) of the targeted performances. However, SPICE level Monte Carlo simulations are computationally very expensive and therefore cannot be considered as a feasible means for estimating leakage powers in ICs of medium and/or high complexity. However, SPICE guarantees the most accurate result and can be used as reference to compare the statistical results obtained by more computationally efficient models.

One technique to lower the huge number of circuit simulations is to create surrogate models that approximate the performance of a circuit as function of the statistical parameters. Machine learning techniques are promising approaches to generate models from a reduced number of SPICE simulations. Those models can then replace the circuit simulator in the large runs Monte Carlo analyses, thus reducing the computational time. However, the generation of such models is not trivial and requires several tasks to obtain satisfactory results. We propose a methodology based on the *Linear and polynomial regression techniques* to generate statistical variation aware models for leakage and total powers of a set of digital standard cells.

2 Simulation Setup and Related Works

2.1 Statistical Variations

Process variations have always existed in spite of designer preferences; however, their impact is gaining critical importance with progressive downsizing of MOS dimensions. Variations can be categorized broadly as global (inter-die) or local (intra-die) variations. Sometimes also refer as systematic or statistical in nature respectively. Global variations (e.g. t_{ox}) are chip-to-chip or wafer-to-wafer variations and therefore have long-range influences and affect every device of the same type in identical fashion [4]. Local process variations (e.g. V_t) characterize small-range influences. Local process variations may occur due to random dopant fluctuations (RDF), line edge roughness (LER) and other intrinsic fluctuations affecting every device in a chip individually, i.e. variability between two devices may look identical to each other.

2.2 Previous Related Work

Several techniques have been reported in literature to accurately model the leakage power in ICs. In [5], Sanyal et al. presented the STABLE methodology for the estimation of sub-threshold, gate, and junction leakage using a Newton–Raphson iteration method. In [6], dedicated abstract models based on response surface methodology have been proposed to predict leakage behavior and propagation delays of FinFET standard cells with process variations. In [7], authors have used neural network technique to model the leakage power through stack. In [8] a logic level modeling paradigm for the statistical variation aware propagation delay calculation has been proposed. Janakiraman et al. [9] proposed ANN based leakage model using the activation function that allows deriving an analytical expression for the mean and a semi-analytical expression for the variance. In [10], authors first propose a fast computation logic level (VHDL) leakage calculation model for bulk CMOS ICs based on the off-line characterization of the internal node voltages in conjunction with the off-line characterization of the currents in a single MOS device and later extended the technique for process variation aware calculation and FinFET technology [11].

The proposed leakage and power estimation model using regression techniques is computationally very efficient and models the relationship between the process parameters and leakage as well as total power with high degree of accuracy compared to the existing models.

2.3   Simulation Setup

In the proposed work, in order to generate the datasets, all the simulations and characterization are performed at SPICE level using Berkeley Short-channel IGFET Model (BSIM4) [12] with 16 nm High Performance Metal Gate/High-K models based on predictive technology model parameters (PTM) [13]. We have considered generated the training data as a vector of 50,000 random values from Gaussian distribution for each process parameter (NMOS and PMOS) in the targeted technology node considering $\pm 10\%$ variations at 3σ (reported in Table 1). Table 1 also depicts the nominal and deviated values in each process parameter. All the circuits have been simulated at 0.8 V supply voltage.

Table 1. Process variations considered.

Process parameter	Device	Lower dev.	Nominal	Higher dev.	Description
length	both	13.67 nm	16 nm	18.13 nm	Channel length
width	both	13.67 nm	16 nm	18.13 nm	Channel width
toxp	both	6.84E−10	7e−10	7.17E−10	Physical gate equivalent oxide thickness
Toxe	nMOS	9.57E−10	9.5e−10	9.04E−10	Electrical gate equivalent oxide thickness
	pMOS	1.01E−10	1e−09	9.91E−10	
toxref	nMOS	9.57E−10	9.5e−10	9.04E−10	Nominal gate oxide thickness for the gate dielectric tunneling
	pMOS	1.01E−10	1e−09	9.91E−10	
Xj	both	5.05E−09	5e−09	5.02E−09	Source/drain junction depth
ndep	nMOS	6.84E+18	7e+18	7.17E+18	Channel doping concentration at the depletion edge for the zero-body bias

We have reported the deviation in performance figures from their normal values and it is obvious from Table 2, such pronounced process variations all together can significantly deviate the circuit performance from their expected values i.e. circuit may eventually operate at lower speed and/or dissipate higher power and ultimately degrading the fabrication outcome [3].

Table 2. Impact of process variation on performances.

Circuit	Leakage power (in nano-watt)		Total power (μW)	
	Nominal	Max.	Nominal	Max.
C17	189	54748	0.63	26.16
4-bit adder	887	245307	5.35	229.9
Parity checker	878	202710	1.31	115.6
Interrupt controller	879	311217	2.01	270.9
Multiplier	3283	633345	5.61	983

3   Proposed Estimation Methodology

The simulations from SPICE have continuous data that can be suitably mined by regression techniques [14]. Regression task develops a learning model from the dataset of measured values consisting of the dependant and independent variables. In regression, important procedures are *model building, training* and *prediction*. This paper aims to perform regression analysis using multivariate linear and multivariate polynomial regression for modelling the relationship between the process variations in the targeted 16 nm CMOS technology based digital VLSI circuit and leakage powers as well as total power. Based on the analysis, an accurate estimation model is developed. The methodology can be divided broadly into the following steps.

3.1   Sensitivity Analysis

Sensitivity analysis is the method used to determine sensitivity of the 'output' of a model for changes in the value of the input parameters and in the structure of the model. An effective feature set can be determined through sensitivity analysis on the input parameters. Correctly specified regression model with the most effective feature set yields unbiased regression coefficients and unbiased predictions of the response. Over specified regression equation with the entire feature set yields correct model, however, it leads to problems such as inflated standard errors for the regression coefficients and increased computation time [17]. This multicollinearity issue occurs when two or more independent variables in a regression are highly related to one another, such that they do not provide unique or independent information to the regression. Such relationship is identified in our model with the help of Pearson correlation coefficient [16] given by Eq. 1.

$$r = \frac{\sum_{i=1}^{n}(u_i - \bar{u})(v_i - \bar{v})}{\sqrt{\sum_{i=1}^{n}(u_i - \bar{u})^2 \sum_{i=1}^{n}(v_i - \bar{v})^2}} \tag{1}$$

Where n represents the number of samples in the dataset, u_i and v_i are individual sample points of two variables and $\bar{u}$ and $\bar{v}$ are means of the sample variables respectively. The value of r represents the degree of correlation between two features.

Figure 1 shows the Pearson correlation coefficient matrix for leakage power in 16 nm *NAND2* cell when inputs = '00'. Figure 1 shows that, toxref_parn and toxref_parp are highly correlated with toxe_parn and toxe_parp respectively. They do not provide any independent information to the regression model and hence can be dropped from the feature set. The threshold for the selection of effective feature set is chosen as ±0.2. As a result, number of features (process parameters from Table 1) are reduced from 10 to 8. Reduced dimensionality reduces the complexity and computation time without effecting the prediction performance. In a Similar manner, feature selection is done for all the datasets.

In this section, missing data (if any) is also handled. Further, each attribute in the feature set is standardized by shifting its distribution to have a mean of zero and a standard deviation of one. The standardization of datasets improved the performance of the regression techniques [15].

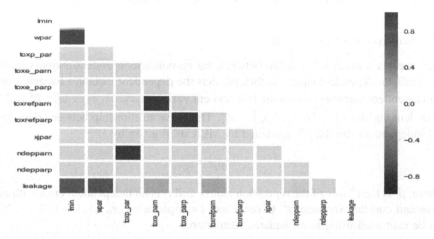

Fig. 1. Pearson correlation coefficient matrix for 16 nm high performance 2-input NAND cell with '00' input combination

3.2   Leakage Power and Total Power Transformations

The polynomial regression assumes all variables to be normally distributed and the residuals once fitted into the model follow a normal distribution. The normal distribution of data can best be examined with a histogram as shown in Fig. 2. By performing data analysis on all the datasets to check for any skewness in data, it is examined that data of response variables in all the datasets is highly skewed. Logarithmic transformation with natural log is applied on the response variables to transform the highly skewed data into moderately skewed as shown in Fig. 2(b). They transform each data point y_i of the response variable in the dataset into $z_i = \log_e (y_i)$.

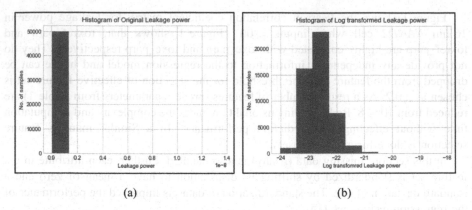

(a)   (b)

Fig. 2. Histograms for *'leakage power'* of 16 nm NAND2 cell with inputs = '00' (a) Before applying log transformation (b) After applying log transformation

3.3   Multivariate Linear Regression

MLR creates a linear relationship between the response/independent/output variables and predictor/dependent/input and then predicts the dependent variables for new values of independent variables. Given the independent variables $x = [x_1, x_2, \ldots x_k] \in R^k$ and the dependent variables $y = [y_1, y_2, \ldots y_m]^T \in R^m$. The linear relationship between dependent and independent variables is modelled by MLR as β given by

$$y_i = \beta_i x + \varepsilon_i \tag{2}$$

Where, β_i is the ith row of the regression matrix and ε_i is an independent error with zero mean and constant variance σ^2. Given a set of sample pairs $\{x_i, y_i\}$, i = 1, 2, …, N, β can be estimated using Least squares estimation.

$$min \sum\nolimits_{i=1}^{N} (y_i - \beta^T x_i)^2 \tag{3}$$

The equivalent matrix formulation is given by

$$min \left\| Y - \beta^T X \right\|^2 \tag{4}$$

where, X = [x_1, x_2, … x_N], Y = [y_1, y_2, … y_N] and $\|.\|$ represents L2 norm. β can be estimated using Eq. (5).

$$\beta = (XX^T)^{-1} XY^T \tag{5}$$

The estimated regression matrix can be used to estimate the response for new values of predictor variables.

3.4   Multivariate Polynomial Regression

Multivariate polynomial regression models the non-linear relationship between the response and predictor variables as the nth order polynomial. Second order polynomial model with one predictor or independent variable is given in Eq. 6.

$$y_i = \beta_0 + \beta_1 x_1 + \beta_{1,2} x_1 x_2 + \varepsilon_i \tag{6}$$

where, β_0, β_1, $\beta_{1,2}$ are the regression coefficients and ε_i is an independent term assumed to have a normal distribution with zero mean and constant variance σ^2. Each β coefficient represents the change in the mean response, $E(y)$ per unit increase in the associated predictor variable when all the other predictor variables are held constant. The intercept term β_0 represents $E(y)$ when all the predictors $x_1, x_2, \ldots x_k$ are held constant.

The Least squares estimate is used to estimate the non-linear relationship between dependent and independent variable.

$$Q = \sum\nolimits_{i=1}^{n} (y_i - (\beta_0 + \beta_1 x_{i1} + \beta_2 x_{i2} + \ldots + \beta_k x_{ik}))^2 \tag{7}$$

where Q is the L2 norm. With the estimated coefficients, the fitted regression equation is

$$\hat{y}_i = \hat{\beta}_0 + \hat{\beta}_1 x_{i_1} + \cdots + \hat{\beta}_k x_{ik} \quad for \quad i = 1, 2, \ldots N \tag{8}$$

where, $\hat{\beta}_0, \hat{\beta}_1, \ldots, \hat{\beta}_k$ represents the estimated coefficients. The estimated regression equation is used to estimate the target variable for a given test dataset.

The higher the degree of the polynomial, the more complex functions can be fit and therefore, greater the accuracy of the model, however, at the cost of higher complexity and chances of overfitting. The analysis is carried over for the better polynomial degree that establishes accurate relationship between response and predictor variables with the help of coefficient of determination, the R-squared value using forward selection method. The analysis showed that a polynomial degree n = 5 gives a significant reduction in error measurements with R-squared valued nearly 1 for most of the estimations without much increase in computation time as shown in Fig. 3(a). Therefore, we employed polynomial regression with degree 5 for the estimation of response variables for all the datasets. The proposed methodology in detail is explained through a flowchart in Fig. 4.

3.5   Residual Measurement

The performance evaluation has been carried out by splitting each dataset into training and test datasets with N samples and M = n − N samples respectively where n represents the total number of samples in the dataset. M is chosen to have 33% of the total number of samples. Training data set is used to train the learning model and test dataset is used to estimate the error rate of the predictive model. The predictive model is measured and compared in terms of (i) Root mean square error (RMSE) that quantifies how far away our predicted responses are from the actual responses, (ii) Mean absolute error (MAE), which describes average model performance error, and (iii) Coefficient of determination or R^2 score, a statistic measure that provides information about the goodness of fit of a model which is used as a measure of how well the regression predictions approximate the actual data points. An R^2 score of 1 indicates that the regression predictions perfectly fit the data [10].

$$RMSE = \sqrt{\frac{1}{M}\sum_{i=1}^{M}(y_i - \hat{y}_i)^2} \tag{9}$$

where, M is the number of test samples, y_i indicates the ith data point from SPICE simulation (actual value) and $\hat{y}_i$ is the predicted value for that data point.

$$MAE = \sqrt{\frac{1}{M}\sum_{i=1}^{M}|y_i - \hat{y}_i|} \tag{10}$$

$$R^2 = \frac{\left(\sum_{i=1}^{M}(y_i - \bar{y}_i)(\hat{y}_i - \bar{\hat{y}}_i)\right)^2}{\sum_{i=1}^{N}(y_i - \bar{y}_i)^2 \sum_{i=1}^{N}(\hat{y}_i - \bar{\hat{y}}_i)^2} \tag{11}$$

where, $\bar{y}_i$ and $\bar{\hat{y}}_i$ are mean of the ith data point of actual and predictor values respectively.

In this paper, we also consider the mean percentage error (MPE) between actual values and the predicted values given by Eq. 6 for performance evaluation. The value is expected to be nearly zero for the most appropriate estimation model.

$$MPE = \sum_{i=1}^{M}\frac{(y_i - \hat{y}_i)}{y_i} \times 100 \tag{12}$$

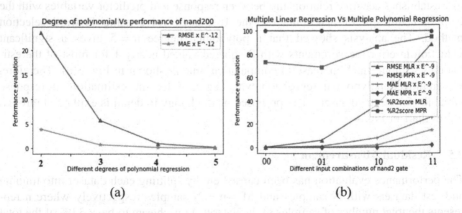

Fig. 3. (a) RMSE of different degrees of polynomial regression (b) Comparison of MLR and MPR w.r.t RMSE, MAE, R^2 score

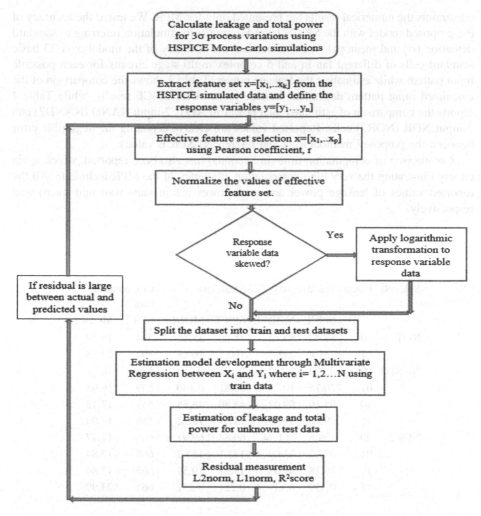

Fig. 4. Flowchart of the proposed statistical estimation model

4 Results and Performance Evaluation

As discussed in Sect. 3, the data is split into train/test datasets with 33% as test data to test the predictive capability of estimation model. The analysis is carried over MLR and MPR techniques and the accuracy of the models is compared in Fig. 3(b). Both the models take very less computation time when compared to the SPICE Monte-Carlo simulations. The performance of MPR is good for all the datasets when compared to MLR as it can model the non-linear relationship between process variations and leakage power. Figure 3(b) shows the RMSE, MAE of MPR is less when compared to MLR with R^2 score nearly 1 for all combinations of 2-input NAND gate. The efficiency of the MPR model for complex digital circuits is reported in Table 5. Due to space constraints the numerical results are presented only for MPR. We tested the accuracy of the proposed model with the SPICE level Monte-Carlo simulation referring to standard deviation (σ) and mean (μ). We also verified the accuracy of the model over 13 basic standard cells of different fan-in and 5 complex multi-stage circuits for each possible input pattern while estimating the leakage power. Table 3 shows the comparison of the calculated input pattern dependent leakage power with SPICE results, while Table 4 reports the comparison of estimated total power in NOT, 2-input NAND (NAND2) and 2-input NOR (NOR2) cells. Reported values are clearly depicting the negligible error between the proposed methodology and referenced SPICE values.

Comparison of computation time (in Seconds) has also been reported, which again clearly illustrating the very high computation efficiency of the MPR technique. All the reported values of leakage power and total power are in nano-watt and micro-watt respectively.

Table 3. Comparison of statistical variation aware leakage power (in nano-watt) and computation time (in sec)

Std. cell	Comb	Std. div. (σ)		Mean (μ)		Computation time	
		SPICE	MODEL	SPICE	MODEL	SPICE	MODEL
NOT	0	88.42	89.72	35.80	35.86	394	16.59
	1	251.4	255.7	100.5	100.8	394	19.58
NAND2	00	0.122	0.122	0.170	0.170	559	16.71
	01	10.75	10.75	6.181	6.180	559	16.93
	10	98.19	99.02	48.80	48.85	559	17.15
	11	395.0	399.9	181.9	182.2	559	17.00
NOR2	00	159.8	161.74	69.84	69.91	665	17.47
	01	333.2	334.9	185.1	185.2	665	17.84
	10	49.18	49.05	19.61	19.59	665	17.84
	11	0.339	0.339	0.251	0.251	665	23.99

Table 4. Comparison of statistical variation aware total power (in μw)

Std. cell	Std. div. (σ)		Mean (μ)		Computation time	
	SPICE	MODEL	SPICE	MODEL	SPICE	MODEL
NOT	0.219	0.229	0.194	0.195	1377	17.47
NAND2	0.272	0.280	0.345	0.345	3707	17.24
NOR2	0.161	0.164	0.365	0.366	3889	18.05

In Table 5, we have reported a subset of the input combinations carrying maximum leakage *(leak_max)* and total power *(total_pow)* in respective circuit, due to space limitation. However, we have verified the estimation accuracy and computation time on all possible combinations. The estimation efficiency of the model is also tested over several multistage complex circuits. Table 6 reports the comparison values for the combinations possessing the maximum leakage and total powers in respective complex cell.

Table 5. Comparison of statistical variation aware leakage power (max.) and total power

Std. cell	Performance	Std. div. (σ)		Mean (μ)		Computation time	
		SPICE	MODEL	SPICE	MODEL	SPICE	MODEL
AND2	leak_max	566.92	574.32	232.49	232.91	596	17.93
	total_pow	0.436	0.456	0.443	0.444	4494	23.85
XOR2	leak_max	844.67	851.46	399.82	400.34	1442	35.60
	total_pow	0.707	0.727	0.576	0.578	18541	35.48
AND3	leak_max	711.94	719.29	312.91	313.38	698	16.93
	total_pow	0.500	0.518	0.622	0.623	9582	20.39
NAND3	leak_max	520.21	526.35	257.53	258.01	695	33.86
	total_pow	0.006	0.006	0.396	0.396	9582	35.40
NOR3	leak_max	390.17	390.88	250.44	250.50	740	17.87
	total_pow	0.176	0.178	0.503	0.503	9815	20.55
MUX	leak_max	1055.9	1073.7	405.29	406.16	1027	16.54
	total_pow	0.786	0.822	0.656	0.657	10446	19.45
FA	leak_max	1560.6	1568.7	759.27	759.70	2918	19.05
	total_pow	1.499	1.532	1.137	1.139	46543	20.06
AO12	leak_max	540.91	543.80	249.32	249.57	459	17.39
	total_pow	0.365	0.376	0.619	0.619	6412	18.75
AO22	leak_max	81.782	82.735	35.286	35.321	1678	20.31
	total_pow	0.296	0.310	0.559	0.560	8101	22.49
AO31	leak_max	389.51	400.77	151.59	152.09	1865	18.84
	total_pow	0.264	0.277	0.544	0.544	8471	20.02

Table 6. Comparison of statistical variation aware leakage power (max.) and total power for respective complex circuits

Std. cell	Performance	Std. div. (σ)		Mean (μ)		Computation time (in sec)	
		SPICE	MODEL	SPICE	MODEL	SPICE	MODEL
C17	leak_max	1293.9	1304.2	574.74	575.72	1728	21.04
	total_pow	1.181	1.217	0.975	0.977	34423	17.74
4-bit adder	leak_max	6386.4	6461.4	2664.1	2667.5	4408	21.28
	total_pow	5.494	5.723	6.855	6.863	109732	18.14
Parity checker	leak_max	5576.3	5607.8	2532.4	2534.8	2144	20.96
	total_pow	5.262	5.148	2.829	2.826	73704	17.90
Interrupt controller	leak_max	7697.0	7839.2	2908.4	2914.6	4517	18.33
	total_pow	6.616	6.797	3.813	3.825	138841	20.06
Multiplier	leak_max	26796.8	27099.1	10485.3	10500.8	4861	19.67
	total_pow	20.304	20.699	11.206	11.241	161090	19.68

The performance of the proposed regression technique is also analyzed in terms of RMSE, MAE, R^2 score and MPE (discussed in Sect. 3.4). Table 7 summarizes the residual values for the input combinations obtaining maximum leakage power in multistage complex circuits. We have the similar data for all the other input combinations and for all the basic standard cells.

Table 7. Performance matrix of the proposed model (R^2 Score, RMSE, MAE, MPE): values reported for complex circuits

Standard cell	Performance	R2 Score	RMSE	MAE	MPE
C17	max_leak	0.9980	5.771e−08	6.649e−09	0.0072
	total_pow	0.9939	9.196e−08	1.444e−08	−0.0014
4-bit adder	max_leak	0.9995	1.455e−07	1.171e−08	−3.560e−5
	total_pow	0.9920	4.889e−07	8.333e−08	−0.0273
Parity checker	max_leak	0.9997	8.518e−08	1.068e−09	0.0039
	total_pow	0.9928	4.475e−07	3.316e−08	0.0076
Interrupt controller	max_leak	0.9989	2.503e−07	1.976e−08	−0.0015
	total_pow	0.9915	6.271e−13	3.385e−13	−0.0222
Multiplier	max_leak	0.9995	5.646e−07	5.114e−08	0.0004
	total_pow	0.9941	1.564e−06	1.893e−07	0.0086

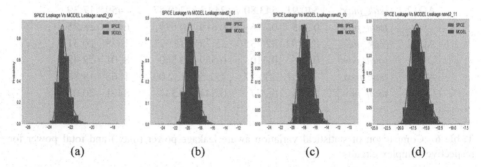

(a)   (b)   (c)   (d)

Fig. 5. Histograms of leakage power of SPICE and MODEL for 2-input NAND cell with input combinations for (a) '00' (b) '01' (c) '10' (d) '11'

The stability of the proposed model is verified using 10-fold cross validation for each combination over all the datasets. The results are averaged over all the runs and reported. The higher the performance of the model the lower the residual values. From Table 7 it is evident that the residual values of all datasets, independent of the response variable are very minimum and nearly approaching zero with R^2 score nearly 1 in all cases signifying the performance of the proposed estimation model for several multistage complex circuits.

The distribution of SPICE leakage and MODEL predicted leakage powers are shown in Fig. 5 through histograms which coincide exactly as their μ and σ are nearly same which shows that the efficiency of the proposed statistical estimation model. The accuracy of estimation is shown with the help of a scatter plot in Fig. 6 for NAND2 leakage current for all input combinations. From the figure, it is evident that the estimated leakage values from MODEL for all the test samples coincides exactly with the SPICE values. For clear visualization of data, plot is shown for only first 200 samples wherein correlation is similar for entire test samples.

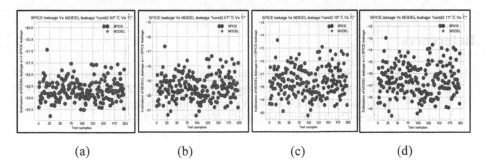

| (a) | (b) | (c) | (d) |

Fig. 6. Scatter plot of statistical estimations of leakage power from SPICE and MODEL for NAND2 test samples with input combinations (a) '00' (b) '01' (c) '10' (d) '11'.

As a final validation, we have also estimated/predicted the values of the leakage and total power of complex cells through the proposed methodology at the nominal values of process parameters (shown in Table 1, Column 4) and compare them with SPICE results. Again, the values are reported only for the combinations having max values (Table 8).

Table 8. Comparison between SPICE and MODEL at nominal values of process variations (reported for max. combinations)

Standard cell	Performance	SPICE	MODEL	Err. %
C17	*max_leak*	1.8904E−07	1.89308E−07	0.14
	total_pow	6.2783E−07	6.26068E−07	0.28
4-bit adder	*max_leak*	8.8758E−07	8.8708E−07	0.06
	total_pow	5.3415E−06	5.29769E−06	0.82
Parity checker	*max_leak*	8.7896E−07	8.79845E−07	0.10
	total_pow	1.3061E−06	1.31334E−06	0.55
Interrupt controller	*max_leak*	8.7910E−07	8.77904E−07	0.14
	total_pow	2.0111E−06	2.01222E−06	0.05
Multiplier	*max_leak*	3.2837E−06	3.28195E−07	0.05
	total_pow	5.6185E−06	5.66797E−06	0.88

5   Conclusion

In this work, we propose an efficient machine learning based estimation model for the prediction of statistical aware leakage and total powers of VLSI digital circuits using multivariate linear and polynomial regression techniques. The results obtained from the proposed estimation model using MPR show negligible error (<1%) w.r.t SPICE simulated values independent of the response variable. Moreover, it has less complexity and very less computation time when compared to SPICE simulations. Another significance of the model is that it is a black box model independent of the technology node. For future work, we aim to develop a multivariate estimation model with different dataset sizes and process parameters.

References

1. Jaffari, J., Anis, M.: Statistical thermal profile considering process variations: analysis and applications. IEEE Trans. Comput. Aided Des. Integr. Circuits Syst. **27**(6), 1027–1040 (2008)
2. Bhunia, S., Mukhopadhya, S.: Low Power Variation-Tolerant Design in Nanometer Silicon. Springer, Heidelberg (2011). https://doi.org/10.1007/978-1-4419-7418-1
3. Abbas, Z., Olivieri, M.: Impact of technology scaling on leakage power in nano-scale bulk CMOS digital standard cell library. Microelectron. J. **45**(2), 179–195 (2014)
4. Abbas, Z., Olivieri, M.: Optimal transistor sizing for maximum yield in variation aware standard cell design. Int. J. Circuit Theory Appl. **44**, 1400–1424 (2016)
5. Sanyal, A., Rastogi, A., Chen, W., Roy, K., Kundu, S.: An efficient technique for leakage current estimation in nanoscaled CMOS circuits incorporating self-loading effects. IEEE Trans. Comput. **59**(7), 922–932 (2010)
6. Chaudhuri, S., Mishra, P., Jha, N.K.: Accurate leakage estimation for FinFET standard cells using the response surface methodology. In: Proceedings of 25th International Conference on VLSI Design, pp. 238–244, January 2012
7. Viraraghavan, J., Das, B., Amrutur, B.: Voltage and temperature scalable standard cell leakage models based on stacks for statistical leakage characterization. In: 21st International Conference on VLSI Design, pp. 667–672, January 2008
8. Olivieri, M., Mastrandrea, A.: Logic drivers: a propagation delay modeling paradigm for statistical simulation of standard cell designs. IEEE Trans. Very Large Scale Integr. Syst. **22**(6), 1429–1440 (2014)
9. Janakiraman, V., Bharadwaj, A., Visvanathan, V.: Voltage and temperature aware statistical leakage analysis framework using artificial neural networks. IEEE Trans. Comput. Aided Des. Integr. Circuits Syst. **29**(7), 1056–1069 (2010)
10. Abbas, Z., Genua, V., Olivieri, M.: A novel logic level calculation model for leakage currents in digital nano-CMOS circuits. In: Proceedings of IEEE 7th Conference on PRIME, pp. 221–224, July 2011
11. Abbas, Z., Mastrandrea, A., Olivieri, M.: A voltage-based leakage current calculation scheme and its application to nanoscale MOSFET and FinFET standard-cell designs. IEEE Trans. Very Large Scale Integr. (VLSI) Syst. **22**(12), 2549–2560 (2014)
12. http://www-device.eecs.berkeley.edu/bsim/
13. Predictive Technology Model. http://ptm.asu.edu/
14. Ryan, T.P.: Modern Regression Methods, vol. 655. Wiley, Hoboken (2008)
15. Guyon, I., Elisseeffe, A.: An introduction to variable and feature selection. J. Mach. Learn. Res. **3**(6), 1157–1182 (2003)
16. Liu, R.Y.: Research and application of unsupervised feature selection algorithm with maximum correlation and minimum redundancy. Dissertation, Chinese Marine University (2010)
17. Cawley, G.C., Talbot, N.L.: On over-fitting in model selection and subsequent selection bias in performance evaluation. J. Mach. Learn. Res. **11**, 2079–2107 (2010)

A Novel Design of SRAM Using Memristors at 45 nm Technology

V. Jeffry Louis[1] and Jai Gopal Pandey[2]([envelope]) [iD]

[1] Birla Institute of Technology and Science Pilani Hyderabad Campus,
Hyderabad 500078, Telangana, India
f20160448@hyderabad.bits-pilani.ac.in
[2] CSIR- Central Electronics Engineering Research Institute (CEERI),
Pilani 333031, Rajasthan, India
jai@ceeri.res.in

Abstract. There is an ever-increasing need for low-cost, higher density, low-power and high-performance memory devices. Memristor is one of the most promising device for obtaining memories as it offers smaller area and lower consumption. In the proposed work memristor-based SRAM circuit has been designed by using 45 nm technology of Predictive Technology Model. The read time of 1-bit cell is 5 ps and the write time 7 ps. Total area of the cell is 3.861 μm^2.

Keywords: Memristors · SRAM · Memory design

1 Introduction

The semiconductor memory follows the trend of decreasing cell size and increasing density. Until now, downscaling has been yielding favorable results as per Moore's law [1]. However, replacing transistors with devices occupying lesser area would deliver results which are better than those predicted by Moore's law if not at the same level and will further improve some performance parameters.

One such device is the memristor which is being considered as the fourth element after resistor, inductor and capacitor [2]. It has been used in varied fields like signal processing, neuromorphic computing, wave-form generation, etc. [2]. Here, we designed a Static Random Access Memory (SRAM) using memristors as its 1-bit cell occupies a lot of area due to the presence of a minimum of four transistors and is also expensive due to the same reason [3].

2 Memristor Device Structure

The memristor was first materialized by Stanley Williams at HP labs in 2008 [4]. It is a two terminal device containing two rectangular electrodes which sandwich a film. It exhibits bipolar switching characteristic that is shown in Fig. 1. This film which is a transition metal oxide (TMO) can be made of Titanium dioxide (TiO_2), Zinc oxide (ZnO) or novel materials like composite ceramics, $(1 - x)\,BaTiO3\text{-}xBiFeO3$ (x = 0.725)

© Springer Nature Singapore Pte Ltd. 2019
A. Sengupta et al. (Eds.): VDAT 2019, CCIS 1066, pp. 579–589, 2019.
https://doi.org/10.1007/978-981-32-9767-8_48

(BT-BFO) [5, 6]. The extent of doping is decided by the value of voltage applied across it. This in turn decides whether the device is on or off.

2.1   An Overview of the Memristor Device Physics

Memristance (M) is the property of the memristor that connects the charge and its flux. It is given by,

$$M = \emptyset/q \tag{1}$$

Where, $\emptyset$ is the flux and q is the electric charge. By differentiating (1) w.r.t. time we arrive at,

$$M = (d\emptyset/dt)/(dq/dt) = V/I \tag{2}$$

Here, V and I are voltage and current respectively, and Memristance is equivalent to resistance.

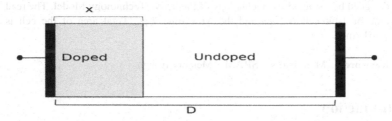

Fig. 1. A view of the memristor device structure as seen in [4].

The resistance of the memristor is dependent on the extent of doping. The resistance of the undoped region is $Roff$ while the resistance of the doped region is Ron. So, the total resistance is $Ron.w D + Roff.(1 - w D)$, where w is the length of the doped region and D is the total length of the device. The rate of change of w is given by dw $dt = \mu v Ron(t)$ and so the total memristance is given by $(q) = (1 - \mu v D2 Ronq(t))$. Hence when the range of doping is higher the resistance is lower and the device is in the on state or in the Low Resistance State (LRS).

2.2   Fabrication Advantages of the Memristor over CMOS

CMOS chips go through the following complicated steps during fabrication [7–9]. Firstly, in wafer processing, the silicon wafer must be grown as a single crystal with very high quality. There should no defect or very few defects (e.g. dislocations), must contain proper type and level of doping to attain the required resistivity. Next in photolithography, the wafer is covered with a photoresist and then a mask is aligned on the top. Subsequently, light is exposed on it and the unmasked part of the photoresist is etched. Later, in the oxidation step, silicon-dioxide is grown on the wafer by placing the exposed silicon in an oxidizing atmosphere at 1000 °C. The oxide layer serves as the gate dielectric and is also the foundation of the interconnect lines in the subsequent steps. The next step is ion implantation, where the dopant atoms are accelerated as high energy focused beam hitting the surface of the wafer and penetrating the exposed areas. This process requires annealing at 1000 °C as the dopants need to be diffused. The last stage is depositing the various materials like polysilicon, interconnects.

Chemical Vapor Deposition (CVD) wherein the wafer is placed in a gas furnace that creates the materials through various chemical reactions. The unwanted parts of the deposited materials are etched out. The whole process has to be done in a very clean and controlled environment. From the analysis, we can see that CMOS fabrication requires very high temperatures and needs to done in a very careful environment. But, the memristor's fabrication is much simpler. In a memristor, the bottom electrode is deposited by electron beam evaporation. The TMO is sputtered on the substrate which is at 250 °C. The upper electrode is deposited similar to the bottom electrode using a mask [10]. As the number of steps required is much lesser and the temperature is also not as high as the CMOS fabrication process, we deduce that it is relatively easier to fabricate memristors.

2.3   Static Random Access Memory (SRAM)

Random Access Memory (RAM) and Read Only Memory (ROM) constitute semi-conductor memories. As we know, ROMs store the boot agent of the computer while RAM is used by all the applications for storing and retrieving data. Hence the RAM is used more frequently than the ROM and so improving it is crucial for the computer. RAM is further divided into Static Random Access Memory (SRAM) and Dynamic Random Access Memory (DRAM). The SRAM is faster than DRAM but it occupies more area in comparison to the DRAM as it is usually made of six transistors per cell. Hence due to the higher speed and cost it is used for manufacturing of the cache memory while the DRAM due to its cost advantage makes up the main memory of the computer. A view of the 6 transistors (6T) SRAM circuit is shown in Fig. 2.

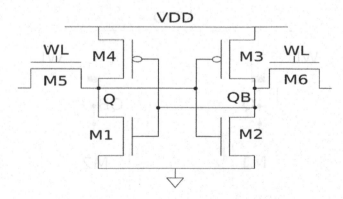

Fig. 2. The conventional 6T SRAM circuit.

In Fig. 2, M1, M2, M5 and M6 are NMOS transistors while the M3 and M4 are the PMOS transistors. M1, M2, M3 and M4 form the bi-stable latch circuitry, while M5 and M6 act as access transistors. M1 and M4 form one inverter while M2 and M3 form the other inverter. Hence the bi-stable latch is a cross coupled inverter. The access transistors are switched on by WL (Write Enable) and are connected to the bit lines (BL and BLB) [8]. While writing, the access transistors are enabled and the bitlines are charged to complementary voltages. A high '1' is stored at the node whose corresponding bitline is raised to VDD (supply voltage) and the other node's corresponding bitline is grounded. Thus, logic '1' is written at the high node while logic '0' is written at the other node.

For reading, both the bitlines are pre-charged to an equal voltage which is half of the VDD and WL is enabled. The bitlines are connected to capacitors which are the actual parts of the circuit that are charged. The bitline connected to the high node is pulled up while the other is pulled down. The capacitor connected to the bitline which is in turn connected to the low node starts discharging. This change in voltage is read by the sense amplifiers. VDD should be on for holding data otherwise the data is ambiguous as the cross coupled inverter is without power.

In this paper, we have designed the above SRAM circuit by replacing traditional transistors with memristors. Here, we have calculated area occupied by the circuit by replacing the two transistors with memristors. We have also built a 16-bit array and calculated power and delay for both single bit and the array. We have used the SPICE model of memristor given by [11] and transistors are based on the 45 nm technology PDK provided by *Predictive Technology Model* [12]. Simulations results have been obtained in *LTSpice* runs and area has been calculated in Cadence Virtuoso Layout Editor.

2.4 Proposed Design

The proposed design of the memristor based SRAM circuit is shown in Fig. 3. The design is based on the conventional 6-T SRAM cell as shown in Fig. 2.

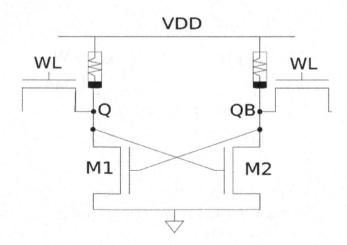

Fig. 3. Proposed memristor based SRAM.

A variant of this is made of an inverter that contains only NMOS transistors and resistors are connected as loads to the drains of the transistors. This configuration is known as the 4-T SRAM cell. The polysilicon resistor loads in the 4-T SRAM cell have been replaced by memristors. The area occupied by a memristor is only 0.000196 μm^2 calculated using the formula $4F2$ (F is the half gate width) as given in [13].

We have used the CMOS latch with the pure NMOS inverter, as PMOS occupies larger area than the memristor. We have used the designed a cell as a symbol and with the help of cells built a 4 × 4 array that is shown in Fig. 4. This has been done to test whether the bit cell could be scaled without disturbance and also to compare the performance parameters of 1-bit cell with 16-bit array as similar to [14]. A view of the 16-bit SRAM memory array using the basic cell is shown in Fig. 4.

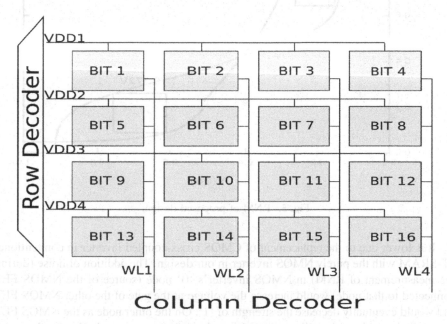

Fig. 4. 16-bit SRAM array.

3 Parameters Analysis and Comparison

In this section, parameter analysis and comparison of the proposed design is described.

3.1 Read Noise Margin (RNM)

A voltage-transfer characteristic (VTC) of the circuit is shown in Fig. 5. The RNM of the flip-flop is defined as the maximum value of noise that can be tolerated by the flip-flop before changing states in read mode [15]. A noise voltage source is introduced between the nodes and is swept to obtain the voltage transfer characteristics (VTC) when both the access transistors nodes are pulled up to VDD as given in [7].

The voltage of the $V(q)$ node is plotted against that of the $V(qb)$ node when the noise is introduced. On the same graph, the voltage swing of the $V(qb)$ node is plotted against the $V(q)$ node. The maximum square fits within the VTC and the minimum of the two squares' side is the RNM. The RNM for our design is 0.168 V, which is lower by 0.262 V than the value reported in [16].

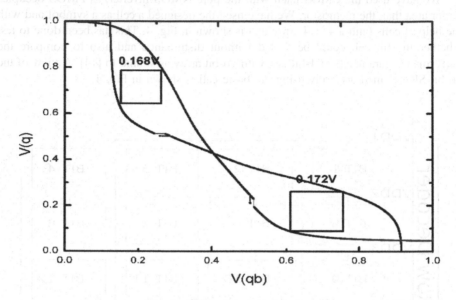

Fig. 5. RNM of proposed design.

It is lower due to the replacement of CMOS cross-coupled inverter in conventional 6T-SRAM with the purely NMOS inverter in our design. The addition of noise (during the measurement of RNM) in NMOS inverter's '0' node (source of the NMOS FET connected to that node) would increase the voltage at the gate of the other NMOS FET and would eventually decrease the strength of '1'. On the other node as the NMOS FET is attached to this node will conduct the node voltage to ground. Hence, the noise margin is lower in the design.

3.2   Write Noise Margin (WNM)

The write noise margin (WNM) is shown in Fig. 6. The WNM of the flip-flop is defined as the maximum value of noise that can be tolerated by the flip-flop before changing states in write mode. One of the access transistors is pulled up to VDD while the other is grounded. Then a noise source is introduced between the nodes of the NMOS inverters and the VTC is obtained similar to the process discussed above for RNM as given in [7]. The WNM is arrived at by marking a square for the largest possible area within the voltage transfer characteristics. In the circuit, the cell as shown in Fig. 6 has a WNM of 0.283 V. This is less by 0.98 V than the WNM reported in [16]. It is lower due to the same reason as in the case of RNM.

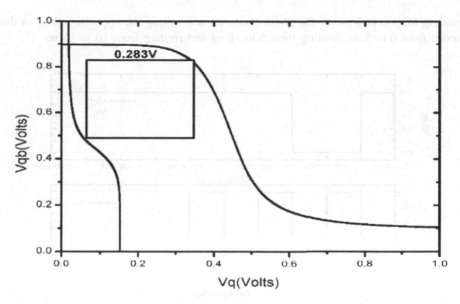

Fig. 6. WNM of the proposed design.

3.3   Static Power Consumption

Static Power is the product of voltage across a device and current through it. Our design's static power consumption during Write, Read and Hold is shown in Table 1. Due to the voltage drop across memristors the static power dissipation is very high.

Table 1. Static power consumption

Device	Write	Hold	Read
M1	328.78 nW	291.91 nW	326.98 nW
M2	2.99 µW	2.055 µW	2.96 µW
M3	465 fW	13.12 fW	35.49 fW
M4	625.71 nW	936 fW	602.71 nW
MR1	85.89 µW	85.91 µW	86.74 µW
MR2	1.20 nW	945 pW	1.18 nW
Total power consumption	2.99 µW	85.965 µW	2.96 µW

Sense amplifiers significantly increase the read delay but we have not included them in our array as the high voltage ('1') was 0.998 V and low ('0') was 0.235 V (less than Vth of 0.295 V) when the VDD is 1 V. The write delay graphs for 1-bit and 16 bits are shown in Fig. 7.

Similarly, the read delay graphs for 1-bit and 16 bits are shown in Fig. 8. Here, the WL voltage is in a separate pane in both of the figures. For the 1-bit cell, we are writing complementary voltages on each node from 2 to 4 ns, holding it from 4 to 6 ns and reading from 6 to 8 ns. In the 16-bit array, we are writing the opposite values in the nodes from 0 to 5 ns, holding from 5 to 10 ns and reading from 10 to 15 ns.

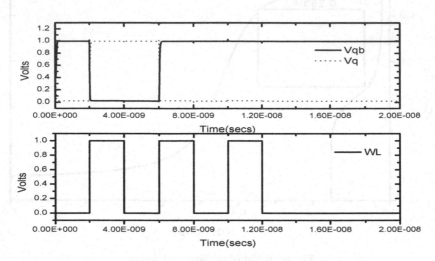

Fig. 7. Delay in 1-bit cell.

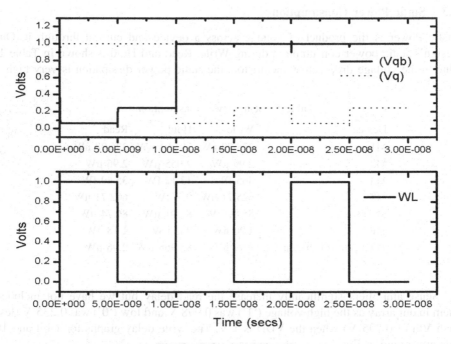

Fig. 8. Delay in 16-bit cell.

The access time is shown in Table 2. Our values for one bit read are lesser by 1 ns and it is same for the write delay too. This is similar to [17].

Table 2. Write and read delays

No. of bits	Write delay (ps)	Read delay (ps)
1	7	5
16	155	7

3.4 Area

A layout view of the design is shown in Fig. 9. The area for our one-bit cell is 3.861 μm². Each memristor occupies area of about 0.000196 μm² which is less than that of the PMOS transistors.

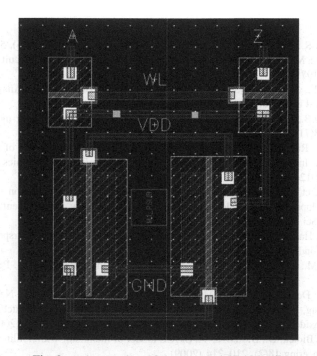

Fig. 9. A layout view of the proposed SRAM cell.

However, the NMOS inverter was not powerful enough to invert and hold the data clearly. Hence, the size of the NMOS transistors had to be increased to a width of 1000 nm and gate length of 45 nm. Thus, there is some area overhead in comparison to the conventional 6T SRAM at 45 nm [16].

4 Conclusion

In this study, we report a new design of a memristor based SRAM cell at 45 nm technology. This design performs comparably to the conventional 6T SRAM cell in all design aspects with a little area overhead. If the cross-coupled NMOS inverters could be partly or completely replaced with memristors then it would result in further reduction of area. It is to be noted that the ease of fabrication of memristors is very high when compared to CMOS and might make the process simpler.

Acknowledgement. We would like to thank Director, CSIR-CEERI Pilani, Rajasthan, India for providing access to Cadence Virtuoso and the requisite technical support through SMDP-C2SD project, sponsored by MeitY, India. We would also like to thank Dr. P. Sivaraman and Mr. Radhakrishnan of the ECE Department at PSG College of Technology for letting us to continue a part of our work in their VLSI design laboratory.

References

1. Schaller, R.R.: Moore's law: past, present and future. IEEE Spectr. **34**(6), 52–59 (1997)
2. Chua, L.O.: Memristor—the missing circuit element. IEEE Trans. Circuit Theory **18**(5), 507–519 (1971)
3. Geiger, R.L., Allen, P.E., Strader, N.R.: VLSI Design Techniques for Analog and Digital Circuits, 2nd edn. McGraw-Hill College, New York (1989)
4. Strukov, D.B., Snider, G.S., Stewart, D.R., Williams, R.S.: The missing memristor found. Nature **453**(7191), 80–83 (2008)
5. Kumar, A., Rawal, Y., Baghini, M.S.: Fabrication and characterization of the ZnO-based Memristor. In: 2012 International Conference on Emerging Electronics (ICEE 2012), pp. 4–6 (2012)
6. Kundu, S., et al.: Lead-free epitaxial ferroelectric material integration on semiconducting (100) Nb-doped SrTiO for low-power non-volatile memory and efficient ultraviolet ray detection. Sci. Rep. **5**, 12415 (2015)
7. Weste, N., Harris, D.: CMOS VLSI Design: A Circuits and Systems Perspective, 4th edn. Pearson, London (2011)
8. Rabaey, J.M., Chandrakasan, A., Nikolic, B.: Digital Integrated Circuits. Pearson, London (2003)
9. Razavi, B.: Design of Analog CMOS Integrated Circuits. Mc Graw Hill, New York (2001)
10. Joshua Yang, J., Pickett, M.D., Li, X., Ohlberg, D.A.A.: Memristive switching mechanism for metal/oxide/metal nanodevices. Nature Nanotechnol. **3**(7), 429–433 (2008)
11. Biolek, Z., Biolek, D., Biolkova, V.: SPICE model of memristor with nonlinear dopant drift. Radioengineering **18**(2), 210–214 (2009)
12. Cao, Y.: Predictive Technology Model for Robust Nanoelectronic Design. Springer, Berlin (2011). https://doi.org/10.1007/978-1-4614-0445-3
13. Eshraghian, K., Cho, K.R., Kavehei, O., Kang, S.K., Abbott, D., Kang, S.M.S.: Memristor MOS content addressable memory (MCAM): hybrid architecture for future high performance search engines. IEEE Trans. Very Large Scale Integr. Syst. **19**(8), 1407–1417 (2011)
14. Bellerimath, P.S., Banakar, R.M.: Implementation of 16 × 16 SRAM memory array using 180 nm technology. Int. J. Curr. Eng. Technol. 288–292 (2013)

15. Seevinck, E., List, F.J., Lohstroh, J.: Static-noise margin analysis of MOS SRAM cells. IEEE J. Solid-State Circuits **22**(5), 748–754 (1987)
16. Thomas, O., Vinet, M., Rozeau, O., Batude, P., Valentian, A.: Compact 6T SRAM cell with robust read/write stabilizing design in 45 nm Monolithic 3D IC technology. In: 2009 IEEE International Conference on IC Design and Technology, pp. 195–198 (2009)
17. Balobas, D., Konofaos, N.: Design and evaluation of 6T SRAM layout designs at modern nanoscale CMOS processes. In: 4th International Conference on Modelling Circuits, Systems and Technology, 7–12 January 2016 (2016)

Design and Calibration of 14-bit 10 KS/s Low Power SAR ADC for Bio-medical Applications

Yadukrishnan Mekkattillam[✉], Satyajit Mohapatra, and Nihar R. Mohapatra

Indian Institute of Technology, Gandhinagar, India
yknmekkad@gmail.com,{satyajitmohapatra,nihar}@iitgn.ac.in

Abstract. This work presents the design and calibration of an ultra-low power 14-bit 10 KS/s fully differential split SAR ADC. The integrated transient response of the ADC shows a settling accuracy of $32\,\mu V$ within $50\,\mu s$ while consuming only $19.5\,\mu W$ power. The simulated post-layout spectrum yields an SNDR of $84.5\,dB$ with an effective linearity of 13.8 bits. The ADC occupies a total area of $2.5\,mm \times 2.5\,mm$ when implemented in the SCL $0.18\,\mu m$ 2P4M CMOS processes. The implementation is shown to be highly power efficient with an energy figure of merit of $140\,fJ$/conversion step. The challenges faced during the full chip implementation of the ADC and techniques used to overcome them at various levels of design hierarchy are discussed in details.

Keywords: Differential SAR · Capacitor mismatch ·
Placement optimization · Tri-level switching · Redundancy ·
Digital correction

1 Introduction

There has been an ever-increasing demand for wireless sensing devices in portable, hand-held and implantable biomedical applications such as Pulse Oximetry, Electroencephalography (EEG), Electrocardiography (ECG) and bio-implantable devices such as pacemakers and cardiac defibrillators [1–3]. With the increasing popularity of the internet of things (IoT), most of the application are envisaged for integration into personal area networks for wireless health monitoring [3,4]. Particularly, the bio-implanted miniaturized sensing devices rely either on a small non-rechargeable batteries or intelligently harvest energy from the environment. Moreover, the lifespan of these devices is intended to be >10 years, which necessitates the inclusion of critical power management techniques at various levels of circuit design hierarchy [4].

The bio-medical signals are characterized by low bandwidth and limited dynamic range. A typical bio-medical sensor broadly consists of a band-pass filter followed by a low-noise amplifier and an Analog to Digital Converter (ADC). The ADCs consume a substantial fraction of the total power and tend to be

© Springer Nature Singapore Pte Ltd. 2019
A. Sengupta et al. (Eds.): VDAT 2019, CCIS 1066, pp. 590–604, 2019.
https://doi.org/10.1007/978-981-32-9767-8_49

the power bottleneck in such portable energy limited systems [1–4]. Hence, the energy efficiency of data converters interfacing these systems play critical role in determining the battery life of such devices [1,2]. The low power ADCs with moderate resolution (8–14 bits) and low sampling frequency (1–50 KS/s) are most suited for quantizing bio-potential signals. This makes SAR ADCs the most preferred choice for such applications [1–4]. Figure 1 shows the block diagram of a typical SAR ADC. A SAR ADC broadly consists of a comparator module, a capacitive DAC, a SAR logic circuit, the digital calibration and additional power management, timing control circuits. Note that, most of the architecture except the comparator is digital in nature and hence scale with CMOS technologies thereby leading to smaller size, improved performance and energy efficiency. This makes it highly advantageous in portable hand-held/implanted devices [1].

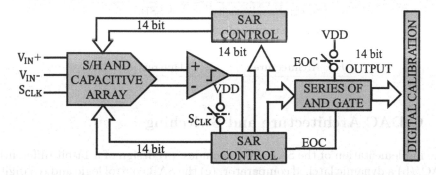

Fig. 1. The architecture of the 14 bit SAR ADC implemented in this work.

While scaling benefits the speed and power efficiency, it comes with an additional price of capacitor mismatch and reduced supply voltage headroom [3–5]. Moreover large capacitors those result in better matching, further limit the achievable bandwidth. A different way of looking at the bandwidth limitation of these designs is to look at their SNDR at frequencies beyond the 3-dB bandwidth. Amplitude lost by the limited analog bandwidth of the sampled signal can be recovered by finite impulse response filters post processing but not the noise. These trade-offs makes the design challenging than ever from a designer's perspective. Hence, certain mismatch compensation techniques [6–10] becomes necessary at various levels of the design hierarchy (from decision of circuit architecture/design to the device placement/on chip error calibration). This work discusses several critical design, layout and calibration techniques and methodologies involved in design of an ultra-low powered 14-bit 10 KS/s fully differential split SAR ADC in SCL 0.18 μm 2P4M CMOS processes. The primary design specifications of the ADC implemented in this paper is provided in Table 1.

This paper is mainly organized into five sections. A detailed analysis of the implemented C-DAC architecture is carried out in Sect. 2. A placement optimization scheme to achieve precise matching between the C-DAC capacitors is reported in Sect. 3. A digital calibration technique is discussed in Sect. 4 which addresses any further residual mismatch in the digital domain. The integrated post-layout simulation results are presented in Sect. 5 followed by the concluding remarks.

Table 1. Primary specifications of the designed SAR ADC

No.	Parameter	Specification
1	Resolution	14
2	Sampling speed	0.5–10 kS/s
3	Power dissipation	<20 μW
4	Dynamic range	±1 V
5	Differential nonlinearity	<±0.5
6	Integral nonlinearity	<1 LSB
7	Power supply voltage	1.8
8	Technology	180 nm CMOS
9	Architecture	Differential SAR

2   C-DAC Architecture and Switching

The implementation of the SAR ADC includes, (a) design of a 14-bit differential DAC, (b) a dynamic latched comparator, (c) the SAR control logic and (d) digital error correction/calibration modules. All these modules are described below.

2.1   DAC Switching Scheme and Implementation of Redundancy

The levels of segmentation of the DAC, the DAC switching scheme and the parasitic compensation plays a critical role in deciding the effective linearity and energy efficiency of the converter. In particular, the power consumption of a DAC is highly dependent on the switching strategy. Tri-Level switching have been shown to be ~94% energy efficient as compared to conventional switching schemes [4,5]. Implementation of such switching further enables bottom plate sampling which helps to reduce signal dependent charge injection and hence avoids the need for complex bootstrap switch. In addition, it is insensitive to parasitic capacitances that may arise at the DAC output node.

Various dynamic errors within the DAC arises due to momentary fluctuation of voltages or incomplete reference voltage settling. These can potentially lead to an incorrect comparison that accumulates leading to errors in bit decision. The implementation of redundancy in SAR architecture can significantly compensate for both static and dynamic errors. The redundancy implementation typically involves taking fractional capacitors which results in asymmetric window of the error correction. Here, we have considered integer sized capacitors for implementing redundancy into the DAC. A modified version of the generalized

Table 2. The multiples of unit capacitor with redundancy

Units	3072	2048	1024	896	512	256	128	128	64	32	16	8	4	2	1	1
Red.		2048	1024	1024	256	128	128	128	-	-	-	-	-	-	-	-

redundancy technique is adapted, but with integer sized capacitors that results in improved matching between the capacitor units. The development of N-bit redundant ADC requires M cycles/conversion where, M > N. A straightforward approach of defining redundancy is to take capacitor sizes as $2^k C_\mu$ or $\Sigma 2^k C_\mu$. This makes the implementation of decoding logic (M bit to N bit) at the output of ADC quite simple along with the benefits of error correction via redundancy.

Let each unit capacitor be denoted as C_μ. For the case of a 14-bit DAC with redundancy, the total sampling capacitance C_T turns out to be $2^{14}C_\mu$. A tri-level switching implementation of DAC can potentially avoid the need of the MSB capacitor thereby resulting in significant power advantages. Now for a 14 bit DAC, C_T turns out to be $2^{13}C_\mu$. The capacitor sizes with redundancy may then be derived as follows. The 2^{12} units of MSB Capacitor is split and rearranged, while still preserving the total capacitance C_T to be 2^{13}. The addition or insertion of capacitor units is illustrated for the 14 bit case as follows. $C_T = 2^{13} = (\mathbf{2^{11}} + \mathbf{2^{10}}) + 2^{11} + \mathbf{2^{10}} + (2^7 + 2^8 + 2^9) + \mathbf{2^9} + \mathbf{2^8} + \mathbf{2^7} + \mathbf{2^7} + 2^6 + 2^5 + 2^4 + 2^3 + 2^2 + 2^1 + 2^0 + 2^0$. The units represented in bold denotes the split MSB capacitors. The coefficient of capacitor with respect to C_μ is given in Table 2 with corresponding redundancy k. For the ith capacitor, k can be evaluated by expression $k_i = \Sigma_{j=1}^{i-1}C_j - C_i$. The amount of intentional redundancy, k_i decides the extent to which mismatch can be tolerated over that particular capacitor.

2.2   Choice of Unit Capacitance

The decision of the unit capacitor size typically depends on thermal noise requirements (1) and random mismatch statistics (2) specified by the foundry. The unit capacitors are selected in such a way that any non-linearity arising from these sources are significantly suppressed much below the quantization noise floor of 0.5 LSB.

$$\frac{KT}{C_T} < \frac{1}{2}(\frac{\Delta^2}{12}) \Rightarrow \frac{KT}{C_T} < \frac{1}{2}\frac{(60uV)^2}{12} \Rightarrow C_T > 13.2\,pF \tag{1}$$

$$\frac{\Delta C}{C}\alpha\frac{A_c}{\sqrt{Area}} \Rightarrow \frac{\sigma_{C\mu}}{\mu_{C\mu}} = \frac{\sigma_{DNLmax}}{\sqrt{2^N-1}} \Rightarrow \frac{0.2LSB}{\sqrt{2^N-1}} = \frac{A_c}{\sqrt{WL}} \tag{2}$$

The thermal noise (1) imposes a lower bound of $\sim$13 pF on the total sampling capacitor which is quite large. Such capacitors are susceptible to systematic effects and hence demands critical placement optimization strategies that will be discussed in Sect. 3. Additionally in presence of fabrication mismatches, the requirement of C_μ can be decided from DNL specification (2). Now, considering random mismatch coefficient of $A_C = 3.2 \times 10^{-8}$, $(3.2\mu\%)$ obtained from the SCL $0.18\,\mu$m CMOS foundry specifications, the total sampling capacitor turns out to be significantly much higher than that initially set by the thermal noise limit in (1). This is too large to implement on chip and additionally result in large power dissipation. An alternate approach to overcome this issue is to use lower capacitance values with intentional redundancy that can be calibrated out in the digital domain. These aspects will be investigated in Sect. 4.

2.3   Implementation of Split DAC Architecture

It is observed that the implementation of conventional architecture (without split) requires a total sampling capacitance of $8192 \times C_\mu$. To implement the thermal limited sampling capacitor of C_T of $13.2\,$pF, C_μ is computed to be $1.7\,$fF. But such low value of unit capacitor is susceptible to random mismatch and routing parasitic. Hence, splitting the capacitor array to Main-DAC and Sub-DAC array further help us scale a section of capacitor array (Main DAC) by a factor of k. This consequently leads to reasonable values of unit capacitors to be implemented.

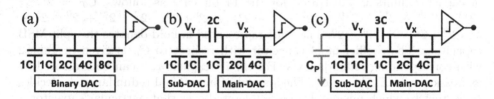

Fig. 2. 3-bit binary DAC, (a) without split and (b) with split (c) with parasitics

The splitting process for an exemplary 3-bit binary DAC is shown in Fig. 2(a) and (b). The bridge capacitor C_B is chosen in such a way that main DAC effectively senses the same capacitance after scaling (3). Here $C_{SUB(T)}$ denotes the total capacitance size of Sub-DAC array while k represent the scaling factor by which the Main DAC is intended to be scaled. For this analysis, $k = 2$ and $C_{SUB(T)} = 2 \times C_\mu$. Splitting the DAC results in an extra parasitic node V_Y. This node now additionally limits the accuracy and linearity of the conversion.

$$\frac{C_{SUB(T)}}{k} = \frac{C_B * C_{SUB(T)}}{C_B + C_{SUB(T)}} \Rightarrow C_B = \frac{C_{SUB(T)}}{k-1}, \; C_B' = \frac{C_{SUB(T)} + C_p}{k-1} \quad (3)$$

The inclusion of an extra grounding capacitor, C_P in Sub-DAC can potentially help to overcome the issue. It provides the flexibility to choose an integral bridge capacitor, that improves matching on layout. With addition of C_P, the expression for bridge capacitor is written as (3). For $C_P = C$, C_B' becomes 3C.

2.4   Dynamic Latched Comparator

The dynamic latch comparator along with the internal offset calibration scheme implemented in this design is shown in Fig. 3. During the reset phase the V_X+, V_X-, $V_{OUT}+$, $V_{OUT}-$ are pulled to VDD. When clock goes high, M_{11} turns on decreasing the voltage at nodes V_X+ and V_X-. As soon as they go below the threshold voltage of M_3 (or M_4), $V_{OUT}+$ and $V_{OUT}-$ starts to fall by a rate depending on the magnitude of differential input. As the output reaches around 0.5VDD the output nodes settle to either of the supply rails. As the comparator is idle during the sampling phase, the power gating transistor M_{12} ensure that any leakage power in the comparator is minimized. Note that M_{12} is critical to the speed performance and hence kept wide in design.

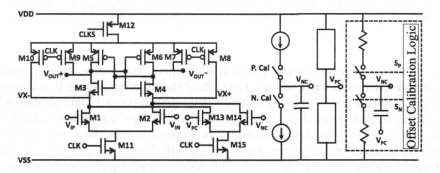

Fig. 3. The schematic of dynamic latch comparator with calibration circuitrary.

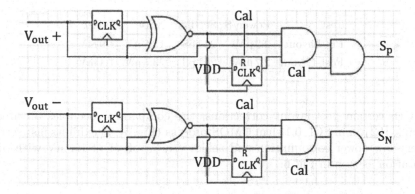

Fig. 4. The schematic of the digital control and switching logic for calibration.

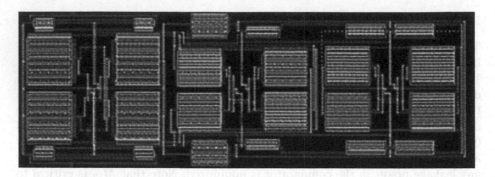

Fig. 5. Layout of the dynamic latch comparator as implemented in the SCL process.

The implemented current injection calibration technique using switched charge control is shown in Fig. 3. It compensates for lack of pre-amplifying stages without additional power. The auxiliary compensation pair $M_{13} - M_{14}$ provides current into drain nodes of input transistors. One of the compensation transistor is connected to a fixed voltage V_{CM} while the other transistor is connected to charge/discharge RC network controlled by digital control logic as shown in Fig. 4. An advantage of such calibration is that, it does not require additional calibration signals. The digital control logic is directly sensitized by outputs of the comparator. For a positive offset, the circuit charges to increase the compensation current and the vice versa. The resolution of comparator is primarily determined by the ratio of the charge added to the charge removed from the current sources generated by auxiliary transistor pair $M_{13} - M_{14}$ (Table 3).

Table 3. The performance of the designed comparator

Test	Power/S	Settling	Noise	Offset
Pre-Layout	2.2 μW	234 pS	12.8 μV	1.9 mV
Post-Layout	2.7 μW	247 pS	23.5 μV	1.4 mV

With certain post-layout corrections, the comparator occupies an area of $32\,\mu m \times 102\,\mu m$ in SCL $0.18\,\mu m$ CMOS process (Fig. 5). It exhibits fast settling at very low power consumption and achieves a 3σ offset of 1.4 mV with offset calibration as seen in Fig. 6.

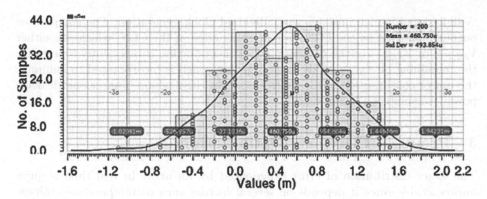

Fig. 6. Post layout Monte-Carlo simulation of comparator input referred offset.

2.5 Implementation of SAR Control Logic Circuit

The implemented SAR control logic for the tri-level switching DAC is depicted for a single bit sampling capacitor in Fig. 7. This switching requires two common mode control signals which are to be controlled by non-overlapping clocks and are connected in orthogonal clock phases. Based on the differential outputs $V_{OUT}+$ and $V_{OUT}-$ of latch comparator, an array of D flip flops are used to generate the individual clock signals CLK1, CLK2, ..., CLKM needed to connect to the M capacitor units. The asynchronous sample signal denoted by CLKS marks the initiation of the sampling process. Initially during the sampling phase, the bottom and top plate of the capacitors are connected to $V_{IN}+$ (or $V_{IN}-$) and V_{CM} respectively. As soon as the CLKS signal goes low, the top plate of the capacitor gets disconnected while the bottom plate gets connected to V_{CM}.

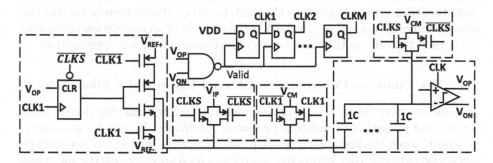

Fig. 7. The implemented SAR control logic circuit for the tri-level switching.

Subsequently the comparator is enabled by CLK, and comparison take place for MSB decision. The CLK signal operate at a frequency 16 times higher than CLKS, as the design with redundancy requires 16 cycles for a single analog sample conversion. The convergence of output from comparator is indicated by the

'Valid' signal, which initiates the individual clock generation. The comparator output is latched by the D flip-flop at rising edge of the CLK, which sets either $V_{REF}+$ or $V_{REF}-$ at the bottom plate. This operation subsequently repeats for the remaining bit cycles. A dynamic logic approach is incorporated to minimize the power consumption in the control logic. In this fashion, unnecessary leakage power consumption is minimized.

3   Proposed Placement Optimization

The exact distribution of error experienced by an array in real time is quite unpredictable since it depends on several factors such as temperature, voltage gradients, vicinity to high power modules and metal coverage. But with prior knowledge of the expected error profile, an approximate model can be developed and placement strategies to compensate them could then be formulated. In this context we briefly discuss the common centroid error model and spatial correlation model.

3.1   The Spatial Correlation Model (Random Mismatch)

Statistical fluctuations in process parameters and fabrication conditions across the die (such as random dopant fluctuations, line edge roughness and lithographic variations) cause random mismatch between identically laid out devices. Considering only random errors, increasing the size of unit capacitor by a $\sim 4\times$ effectively helps in reducing the mismatch by half. But again, the large array is susceptible to systematic effects. In reality, there exists finite statistical correlation ρ between two adjacently placed unit capacitors, as they share the same environment [6,7]. Mismatch analysis can be achieved accurately when correlation between devices is taken into account. Considering device correlation during design centring may enhance the chip yield. Based on device correlation, the correlation figure of merit F_{COR}, defined as the average of all correlation coefficients [8], is used to evaluate the effectiveness of a placement during optimization.

3.2   The Common Centroid Error Model (Systematic Mismatch)

Systematic errors can in general arise anywhere starting from chip design, fabrication, and packaging to real-time operating conditions. It includes asymmetry in layout, oxide thickness and dopant profile variation over wafer, non-uniform metal coverage and edge effects due to etching, piezo-resistive effects, die stress, voltage drop along power supply lines and vicinity to high power amplifiers. The gradient error distribution across a unary matrix can be approximated by a Taylor series expansion about its center [9]. The error ξ associated with an element located at coordinates (x, y) on the matrix is expressed as (4). It is generally assumed that linear and quadratic terms are adequate to model gradient effects in CMOS. Quadratic gradients are composed of parabolic and rotated parabolic components. The rotated parabolic components i.e the 'xy' terms arise due to angular misalignment of gradient axis [9].

$$\zeta(x,y) = \alpha_{00} + \alpha_{10}x + \alpha_{01}y + \alpha_{20}x^2 + \alpha_{02}y^2 + \alpha_{11}xy + \cdots \tag{4}$$

The mismatch caused by process gradients can be compensated to the 1st order approximation if the centroids of all capacitors coincide with the center of the array. The Euclidean distance of the centroid of ith capacitor from the center of the array gives an estimate of the common centroid error F_{CEN} [10] that can be used to estimate the effectiveness of a placement in presence of systematic errors during placement optimization.

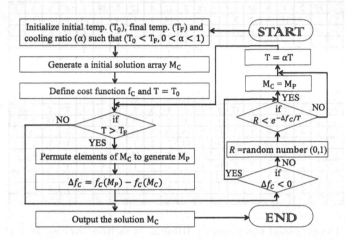

Fig. 8. The proposed placement optimization technique for DAC layout.

3.3   The Placement Optimization Technique

To implement an accurate capacitive DAC, the proposed topology requires 319 unit capacitors as shown in Fig. 12. These 319 units may be spread over an 18×18 array to compensate for the systematic effects. The placement of the capacitors must address both the systematic and random mismatch during optimization. An algorithm can be potentially useful as manual optimizations tend to be highly tedious for larger arrays. In order to search for optimal placement that performs well in presence of systematic and random error, the cost function of heuristic based simulated annealing is formulated as: $W = 0.5 \times F_{CEN} + 0.5 \times (1 - F_{COR})$. The algorithm for optimization is described in Fig. 8. It mimics the annealing process commonly used in glass manufacturing to achieve a uniform and homogeneity in material properties. Based on this optimization algorithm, the placement of 319 unit capacitors along with 4 dummy units is shown in Fig. 9. The proposed placement scheme achieves a very small common centroid error, F_{CEN} of 0.003 and a high correlation figure of merit of 0.81 considering the unit capacitor specifications obtained for 180 nm CMOS technology. The proposed

DAC layout occupies a total silicon area of $1.4 \times 1.4\,\text{mm}^2$ with unit capacitor size of $40\,fF$ in SCL 180 nm CMOS process. Dual NP guard rings are used to isolate the array from calibration switches and radiation hardening purposes. The array is shielded by intermediate metal layers (Metal-2) held at analog ground, V_{MID}. The linearity errors within the comparator and capacitive DAC is correctable in digital domain via digital error correction provided they are limited within an interval ϵ as determined by the redundancy. Further, residual mismatches if any is handled by implemented digital calibration scheme discussed in Sect. 4.

3	19	18	19	3	4	3	12	4	18	3	18	5	4	3	18	12	3
19	2	4	6	18	5	2	18	2	12	4	12	3	18	5	4	5	4
3	18	19	3	2	3	1	8	1	14	3	1	4	1	18	1	3	1
19	1	2	1	4	12	2	3	2	5	2	1	2	7	2	13	2	1
1	18	1	18	9	1	1	8	1	3	1	4	1	1	1	1	18	6
2	1	6	2	1	2	4	13	18	2	13	18	2	13	2	1	2	1
1	13	1	18	5	13	1	2	1	15	1	12	1	1	11	1	18	6
2	5	4	2	1	2	6	1	2	1	2	1	2	12	2	12	4	1
14	1	3	1	12	1	4	2	10	16	4	5	3	1	3	1	6	2
1	12	2	4	1	2	1	1	17	1	1	2	1	2	4	1	5	1
1	3	1	3	1	12	5	2	5	4	3	5	3	1	3	2	3	2
2	7	1	11	5	2	1	7	1	2	1	2	1	2	7	1	18	1
1	4	2	4	1	1	12	2	15	18	3	18	9	1	3	4	2	14
2	6	1	18	2	18	5	1	14	1	2	1	2	1	2	1	3	1
1	18	3	12	1	1	3	12	2	8	4	18	3	4	3	18	2	18
1	2	1	2	5	2	18	1	3	1	5	1	2	1	2	1	6	1
4	3	4	1	18	1	13	2	18	4	18	13	8	18	12	4	12	4
1	2	1	2	1	2	1	6	1	2	1	2	1	1	2	1	2	1

Fig. 9. The proposed placement of 319 unit capacitors over an 18 × 18 array.

4   Digital Error Correction and Calibration

Intentional redundancy described earlier along with the calibration scheme helps to remove static errors that primarily arise due to capacitor mismatch. The residual mismatch post placement optimization is addressed by the implemented digital calibration scheme. Here, we go for a one time calibration approach. A short calibration is done initially during the start-up to get an estimate of capacitor mismatch. Based on this estimate, the raw digital output codes of the ADC are modulated in the background during the normal operation. A block diagram representation of the implemented calibration is shown in Fig. 10.

The decimal equivalent of the M bit redundant digital output codes can be expressed as in (5), where, $D_M, D_{M-1}, \dots D_0$ denotes the unit capacitor multiples ranging from MSB to LSB. The bit decision in i^{th} bit cycle is represented as $b(i)$. As seen, the conversion of digital outputs depends on the capacitance sizes. The accuracy of data conversion depends on the fact, how accurately the actual step size i.e. capacitor sizes are estimated.

$$D_{OUT} = D_M + \Sigma_{i=1}^{M-1}[2b(i) - 1] \times D_i + [b(0) - 1] \times D_0 \qquad (5)$$

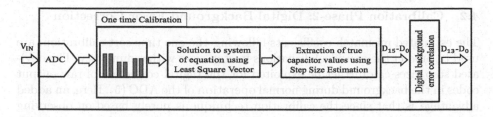

Fig. 10. The complete flow of calibration procedure implemented in this work.

4.1 Calibration Phase-1: Estimation of Capacitor Mismatch

This calibration is based on analysis of code density histogram. Initially during the calibration phase an external ramp input is used to obtain the output codes and estimate the deviated capacitor sizes. As an example, the histogram is plotted (Fig. 11) for [3 2 1 1 1] case which is 4 bit redundant, with effective number of bits as 3. The ADC is subject to ramp input ranging from 0 to 8. Now, the histogram contain bins that corresponds to 16 redundant digital levels ranging from 0 to 15. The empty bins are due to the fact that a 3-bit ADC can have only 8 digital outputs under ideal condition. For a linear ramp, the bin size represent the input voltage range while the bin edge represents comparison threshold for that digital code. The first couple of bins are found to be empty because of the aforesaid reason i.e the 3 bit ADC can have a maximum of 8 non redundant codes while the total number of codes with redundancy is 16, hence some bins are deemed to be empty. The third bin is a non-empty bin with a range [0 1]. This means any analog inputs sampled in this range is mapped to the redundant code 2 or to a final decision level 0. The final decision levels can be expressed in terms of capacitor sizes from (5) as $3 - D_3 - D_2 + D_1 - D_0 = 0$ (Fig. 11). The deviation in comparison threshold as defined by capacitor ratios was expressed earlier (5). Hence any mismatch is directly reflected in histogram bin counts. Since the linear ramp signal has uniform pdf, a unit bin width represent the same analog input range throughout the entire code range. Similarly for 5th bin, the analog input range that is mapped is [1 2], which is obtained by accumulating from previous bins. Final decision level for this range is 1 that represents the lower bound. Repeating likewise for the remaining bins, we obtain a system of equation in terms of capacitor sizes that can be solved via least square technique.

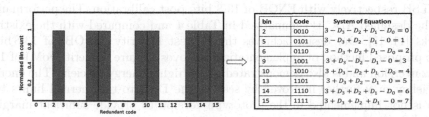

bin	Code	System of Equation
2	0010	$3 - D_3 - D_2 + D_1 - D_0 = 0$
5	0101	$3 - D_3 + D_2 - D_1 - 0 = 1$
6	0110	$3 - D_3 + D_2 + D_1 - D_0 = 2$
9	1001	$3 + D_3 - D_2 - D_1 - 0 = 3$
10	1010	$3 + D_3 - D_2 + D_1 - D_0 = 4$
13	1101	$3 + D_3 + D_2 - D_1 - 0 = 5$
14	1110	$3 + D_3 + D_2 + D_1 - D_0 = 6$
15	1111	$3 + D_3 + D_2 + D_1 - 0 = 7$

Fig. 11. The formation of system of equations based on histogram code count.

4.2   Calibration Phase-2: Digital Background Error Correction

The estimated mismatch coefficients following the one time sort calibration, are used to predict the non-ideal deviations in step sizes with redundancy. The deviated step sizes can further be exploited for the digital correction of raw output codes in the background during normal operation of the ADC (5). Here, an added advantage is that since the calibration technique is purely based on observing the output, it may be implemented off-line or on a software (for systems with signal processing capabilities).

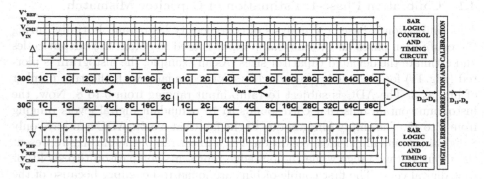

Fig. 12. The detailed implementation of the SAR ADC Architecture with split DAC topology (left) and various digital modules with calibration logic block (right).

5   Results and Discussions

The proposed ADC occupies a total silicon area of $2.5 \times 2.5 \, \text{mm}^2$ with unit capacitor size of $40 \, fF$. Any residual mismatch incorporated during routing and fabrication is further addressed by the implemented calibration scheme. From RC extraction, the maximum parasitic mismatch during the layout of the capacitor array routing is extracted to be <1% of nominal value. The design is subjected to static and dynamic linearity tests at all process corners. Figure 13 shows the post-layout spectral response of the ADC with $F_{in} = 0.1 \, \text{kHz}$ and $F_s = 10 \, \text{kHz}$ with and without calibration. The INL and DNL plots are shown in Fig. 14. As observed, the proposed design achieves an INL of 0.42 and DNL of 0.5 LSB respectively with ENOB of 13.8 bits post calibration. The performance of the designed ADC is summarized in Table 4 and compared with the existing works [11–15]. Our design achieves the highest linearity (ENOB) of 13.8 bits. The proposed method of implementation achieves a figure of merit (FoM) of 140 fJ/conversion and is also demonstrated to be highly energy efficient. The energy efficiency may further improved by scaling the DAC to the thermal limits but this is not implemented in the prototype version to provide sufficient margins for fabrication.

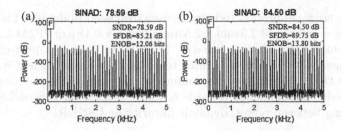

Fig. 13. FFT spectrum of ADC (a) before calibration and (b) after calibration.

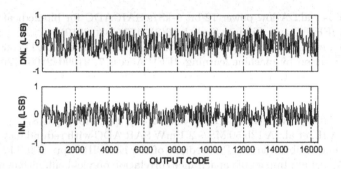

Fig. 14. DNL (top) and INL (bottom) plot obtained from integrated ramp test.

Table 4. A comparative overview of performance achieved

Parameter	Res. (bits)	Speed (Ms/S)	Power (mW)	ENOB (bits)	F.O.M (fJ/step)	Tech. (nm)
Proposed	14	0.01	0.02	13.8	139	180
Work [11]	14	35	55	12.2	330	40
Work [12]	14	30	38	12.5	218	40
Work [13]	14	0.01	0.015	13.7	113	180
Work [14]	14	40	66	13.5	142	130
Work [15]	14	80	31.1	11.6	125	65

6   Conclusion

This paper described the complete design of an energy efficient 14-bit 10 KS/s differential SAR ADC for biomedical applications. The paper brought out several challenges faced during the implementation of ADC and discussed several techniques to overcome them at various levels of design (from decision of circuit architecture and design to device placement, layout and calibration). Based on the choice of DAC architecture and switching scheme, the critical specifications for various modules, sub modules and components were derived. Certain mismatch compensation techniques included at various levels of the design hierarchy and off chip error calibration techniques were discussed in details. The designed ADC occupies an area of 2.5 mm × 2.5 mm in SCL's 0.18 μm 2P4M CMOS process and achieves an effective linearity (ENOB) of 13.8 bits post-calibration. The implementation was demonstrated to be highly energy efficient with a FoM of only 140 fJ/conversion step. In summary, this work drives the state-of-the-art ADC design methodology towards advance calibration approaches without compromising between power, dynamic linearity and SNDR.

References

1. Mao, W., et al.: A low power 12-bit 1-kS/s SAR ADC for biomedical signal processing. IEEE Trans. Circuits Syst. I **66**(2), 477–488 (2019)
2. Hirai, Y., et al.: A biomedical sensor system with stochastic A/D conversion and error correction by machine learning. IEEE Access **7**, 21990–22001 (2019)
3. Fan, H., Maloberti, F.: High-resolution SAR ADC with enhanced linearity. IEEE Trans. Circuits Syst. II Express Briefs **64**(10), 1142–1146 (2017)
4. Luo, J., et al.: A 0.9-V 12-bit 100-MS/s 14.6-fJ/Conversion-Step SAR ADC in 40-nm CMOS. IEEE Trans. VLSI Syst. **26**(10), 1980–1988 (2018)
5. Chang, A.H., et al.: A 12b 50 MS/s 2.1 mW SAR ADC with redundancy and digital background calibration. In: Proceedings of the ESSCIRC, pp. 109–112 (2013)
6. Luo, P.W., et al.: Impact of capacitance correlation on yield enhancement of mixed-signal/analog integrated circuits. IEEE Trans. Comput. Aided Des. Integr. Circuits Syst. **27**(11), 2097–2101 (2008)
7. Soares, C., et al.: Automatic placement to improve capacitance matching using a generalized common-centroid layout and spatial correlation optimization. IEEE Trans. Comput. Aided Des. Integr. Circuits Syst. **34**(10), 1691–1695 (2015)
8. Chen, J.E., Luo, P.W., Wey, C.L.: Placement optimization for yield improvement of switched-capacitor analog integrated circuits. IEEE Trans. Comput. Aided Des. Integr. Circuits Syst. **29**(2), 313–318 (2010)
9. Mohapatra, S., et al.: Mismatch resilient 3.5 bit MDAC with MCS-CFCS. In: Proceedings of IEEE Computer Society Annual Symposium on VLSI (ISVLSI), pp. 175–180 (2018)
10. Soares, C.F., Petraglia, A., de Campos, G.S.: Methodologies for evaluating and measuring capacitance mismatch in CMOS integrated circuits. IEEE Trans. Circuits Syst. II Express Briefs **64**(2), 101–105 (2017)
11. Kramer, M.J., Janssen, E., Doris, K., Murmann, B.: A 14 b 35 MS/s SAR ADC achieving 75 dB SNDR and 99 dB SFDR with loop-embedded input buffer in 40 nm CMOS. IEEE J. Solid-State Circuits **50**(12), 2891–2900 (2015)
12. Krämer, M., et al.: A 14-bit 30-MS/s 38-mW SAR ADC using noise filter gear shifting. IEEE Trans. Circuits Syst. II Express Briefs **64**(2), 116–120 (2017)
13. Yang, X., et al.: A 14.9 uW analog front-end with capacitively-coupled instrumentation amplifier and 14-bit SAR ADC for epilepsy diagnosis system. In: Proceedings of IEEE Biomedical Circuits and Systems Conference, pp. 268–271 (2016)
14. Hesener, M., et al.: A 14b 40 MS/s redundant SAR ADC with 480 MHz Clock in 0.13 pm CMOS. In: Proceedings of 2007 IEEE International Solid-State Circuits Conference, Digest of Technical Papers, pp. 248–600 (2007)
15. Kapusta, R., et al.: A 14b 80 Ms/s SAR ADC with 73.6 dB SNDR in 65 nm CMOS. IEEE J. Solid-State Circuits **48**(12), 3059–3066 (2013)

An Approach for Detection of Node Displacement Fault (NDF) in Reversible Circuit

Bappaditya Mondal[1], Anirban Bhattacharjee[1], Subham Saha[2],
Shalini Parekh[3], Chandan Bandyopadhyay[1(✉)],
and Hafizur Rahaman[1]

[1] Indian Institute of Engineering Science and Technology, Shibpur,
Howrah 711103, West Bengal, India
bappa.arya@gmail.com,
anirbanbhattacharjee330@gmail.com,
chandanb.iiest@gmail.com, rahaman_h@yahoo.co.in
[2] Indian Institute of Technology, Kharagpur, India
subhams087@gmail.com
[3] University of Ghent, St. Pietersnieuwstraat 33, 9000 Ghent, Belgium
shalini.parekh@ugent.be

Abstract. In the field of low power circuit design, reversible circuit has come out as a promising area of research. Not only making efficient design strategies has found the popularity but also developing fault detection mechanisms for such design has received high interest.

Though based on the nature of faults, there exist four different type of faults - single missing gate fault (SMGF), repeated gate fault (RGF), partial missing gate fault (PMGF) and multiple missing gate fault (MMGF), but here we introduce a new type of fault that may originates in a circuit due to the displacement of control and target nodes. This fault is termed here as node displacement fault (NDF). The generation of test vectors to track such NDF fault is also discussed here. To this extent, the way for optimizing the test set is undertaken in the work. To find the appropriateness of the developed scheme, we have tested it over several benchmark circuits and have also verified the obtained results.

Keywords: Reversible circuit · Reversible gate · Node displacement · Control node · Target node

1 Introduction

Reversible logic is used for realizing reversible operation which in turn builds the foundation for several emerging technologies that can be considered as the replacement of traditional computational logic. In this conjecture, inception of such logic found applicable for technologies like quantum computing. Introduction of such quantum technology [1, 2] is considered as the most emerging research field due to its ability in solving some intractable problems efficiently and thereby found useful for various

© Springer Nature Singapore Pte Ltd. 2019
A. Sengupta et al. (Eds.): VDAT 2019, CCIS 1066, pp. 605–616, 2019.
https://doi.org/10.1007/978-981-32-9767-8_50

technologies like nanotechnology, cryptography and bioinformatics. Moreover, advancement in the field of quantum computing has also been noted. For instance, implementation of 2-qubit quantum gate in silicon [3], physical implementation of quantum circuits [4–6], even full fledge implementation of quantum computer [7] with lower qubits has been initiated.

For the time being, the necessity for the design of quantum circuit is required and to address this issue the concept of reversible logic synthesis has been developed. There are several well-known methods available for reversible logic design such as ESOP [8], BDD [9], Reed-Muller [10].

Along with this, prevention and detection of faults [11] for the successful implementation of reversible circuits has also become significant. Some of the existing common known faults of reversible circuit are Single Missing Gate Fault (SMGF), Partial Missing Gate Fault (PMGF), Multiple Missing Gate Fault (MMGF) and Repeated Gate Fault (RGF).

As a result, some research groups are working on the field of reversible circuit testing to develop some efficient test detection algorithms. Here we are presenting some of the algorithms used for testing purposes.

The deterministic and probabilistic method of fault detection in reversible circuits and comparison of both methods is investigated in [12]. Integer linear program *(ILP)* has been implemented for the construction of efficient test sets is reported in [13]. Furthermore, an optimal test sets *(OTS)* method using a smaller number of test vectors to test a reversible circuit is introduced [14].

All the previous existing works based on fault detection in reversible circuit were not able to provide 100% fault coverage, a new testing mechanism (known as 'Ping Pong Test') with 100% fault coverage is presented in [15].

After detection of fault in reversible circuit, the detected fault needs to be corrected and theoretically it was proved in [16] that fault localization in the reversible circuits is easier than that in classical circuits.

In following years, several testing and fault detection mechanisms have also been introduced. To this end, fault detection in reversible circuit using automated test patterns [17], universal testing strategy for detection of all kinds of missing gate faults [18], fault detection using Boolean difference method [19].

The works that we have mentioned so far mainly include testing algorithms for SMGF, PMGF, MMGF and RGF type faults, but apart from the mentioned type of faults, due the displacement of control and target nodes, a circuit may incur NDF type fault. To deal with such scenario, here, in this work we have proposed a mechanism for detection of NDF fault in circuits. Along with the scheme, we also have demonstrated the way for formulating minimum size test sets for this fault.

The rest of the work is organized as follows. Preliminaries on reversible circuit and its related fault models are given in Sect. 2. The proposed technique is discussed detail in Sect. 3 followed by experimental evaluation of our work is presented in Sect. 4 and finally, the paper ends with concluding remarks in Sect. 5.

2 Preliminaries

Now, here in this section basic preliminary about the reversible logic circuit and associated fault models is discussed.

Definition 1: *A circuit is called reversible if there is one to one mapping between inputs and outputs and vice-versa. The circuit also needs to be fan out free and it must be constructed with reversible gates only.*

Some well known reversible gates are Feymen [20], Toffoli [21], Fredkin [22] and those gates are used in the design of reversible circuits.

The structure of a 2-control reversible gate (Toffoli gate) is shown in Fig. 1(a) and an example of reversible circuit is shown in Fig. 1(b). The circuit of Fig. 1(b) is constructed with 4 reversible gates over three input lines. The gate G_0 is having one control node at input line x_1, one target node at line x_3 and line x_2 is used as the through line for the gate G_0.

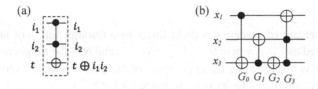

Fig. 1. (a) 2-Control Toffoli gate (b) Reversible circuit designed with 4 reversible gates

A circuit implemented with reversible gates may become faulty due to several reasons. Depending on the nature of errors in reversible circuits, faults can be classified as: Single Missing Gate Fault (*SMGF*), Partial Missing Gate Fault (*PMGF*), Multiple Missing Gate Fault (*MMGF*) and Repeated Gate Fault (*RGF*).

Definition 2: *If an entire gate completely disappears from a circuit then the fault occurred is called as Single Missing-Gate Fault (SMGF).*

Definition 3: *A repeated-gate fault (RGF) indicates an unwanted replacement of a gate by several instances of the same gate.*

Definition 4: *If more than one consecutive gate disappears from the circuit, then the fault type is termed as multiple missing-gate faults (MMGF).*

Definition 5: *If a circuit becomes faulty due to missing of any control nodes in any gate of the given circuit then such type of fault is considered as Partial missing gate fault (PMGF).*

3 Proposed Technique

Now, in this section we will discuss about a new type of fault named as 'node dis-placement fault' (NDF) that may occur in a reversible circuit. In the proposed testing technique, two different types of node displacement faults are considered and they can be: displacement of control node to a through line of the circuit while the target node is kept fixed and the displacement of target node to a through line of the circuit while keeping all the control nodes fixed. The developed testing model has two phases for each type of node displacement fault. In the first phase, the detection condition of the corresponding fault is presented and in the second phase, the test vector generation for the faults are discussed.

3.1 Detection of Control Node Displacement Fault

Definition 6: *Misplacing of a control node of a gate from its original position to a through line and thereby making the gate faulty is called as control node displacement fault (CNDF).*

The displacement of a control node at line x to a through line y of any gate G_i of circuit is denoted as $C_{G_i}^{x \to y}$, where $0 \leq i \leq (N-1)$ and N is the number of gates in the circuit. Here, it is assumed that the target node of the gate is always fixed. Test vectors needed to detect any $C_{G_i}^{x \to y}$ faults is represented as $V(C_{G_i}^{x \to y})$.

Example 1: Let's consider the gate of the circuit shown in Fig. 2(a) to describe the control node displacement fault. The gate is having two control nodes, one through line and a target node. Now, it is assumed that the control node of line b of the gate G_0 is moves to the line c (through line) from line b causing a control node displacement fault (as shown in Fig. 2(b)) and it is denoted as $C_{G_0}^{b \to c}$.

Fig. 2. (a) Toffoli gate having 2 controls and one through line (b) Displacement of control node at line b to line c of Fig. 1(a)

Phase 1: Detection Condition of CNDF
ACNDF fault in a gate of a reversible circuit can be detected by setting logic value 0 at the original position of the control node and logic value 1 both at the new position of the control node as well as for all other control nodes and applying either 0/1 to the target line and through line respectively.

Lemma 1: For any reversible circuit constructed with Toffoli gates, the above detection condition is true for any control node displacement fault in a Toffoli network.

Proof: Let us consider the Toffoli gate of Fig. 2(a) to validate the detection condition of the control node displacement fault $C_{G_0}^{b \to c}$ shown in Fig. 2(b).

As per the detection condition of the control node displacement fault, the test vector $<a, b, c, T> = <1, 0, 1, 0>$ is considered as one of the detection condition of $C_{G_0}^{b \to c}$. If the test vector $<a, b, c, T> = <1, 0, 1, 0>$ is applied at the gate of Fig. 3(a) (the fault free gate), then it is always true that $T^O = T$ as the control node of gate at line b has received the value 0.

Similarly, for vector $<a, b, c, T> = <1, 0, 1, 0>$, it is very true that $T^F = \bar{T}$ for the gate of Fig. 2(b) (the faulty gate due to node displacement fault in Fig. 2(a)) as all the control nodes of the gate has received 1. Hence, T^O cannot be made equal to T^F for the same detection condition $<1, 0, 1, 0>$ and it is also true for other detection conditions also.

So, it can be confirmed that our detection condition for the control node displacement fault is very true and applicable to any reversible circuit.

Phase 2: Test Vector Generation for CNDF
In this phase the test vector generation mechanism for CNDF would be discussed. As per the detection condition of this node displacement fault in Fig. 2(b), vectors $<a, b, c, T> = <1, 0, 1, 0>$ and $<a, b, c, T> = <1, 0, 1, 1>$ are considered for the said fault as shown in Fig. 3. Hence, $V(C_{G_0}^{b \to c}) = \{<1, 0, 1, 0>, <1, 0, 1, 1>\}$.

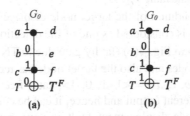

Fig. 3. Test vector generation method for $C_{G_0}^{b \to c}$ in Fig. 2(b)

3.2 Detection of Target Node Displacement Fault

Definition 7: *Misplacing of a target node of a gate from its original position to a through line and thereby making the gate faulty is called as target node displacement fault (TNDF).*

The displacement of the target node from line x to a through line y of any gate G_i is represented as $T_{G_i}^{x \to y}$, where $0 \le i \le (N - 1)$ and N represents the number of gates of the circuit. Here, it is also assumed that all the control nodes are fixed in its original position.

Test vectors needed to detect $T_{G_i}^{x \to y}$ is represented as $V(T_{G_i}^{x \to y})$.

Example 2: Let's consider the circuit depicted in Fig. 4(a) describing the target node displacement fault. Now, it is assumed that the target node located at line c of gate G_0 is displaced to the line b (through line) causing a target node displacement fault (as shown in Fig. 4(b)) and it is denoted as $T_{G_0}^{c \to b}$.

Fig. 4. (a) Toffoli gate having 2 controls and one through line (b) Displacement of target node at line c to line b in Fig. 5(a)

Phase 1: Detection Condition of TNDF
A target node displacement fault in a gate can be detected by setting logic value 1 at the new position of the target node and applying logic value 1 to all other control nodes and setting either 0/1 to through lines.

Lemma 2: For any reversible circuit constructed with Toffoli gates, the above detection condition is considered for target node displacement fault in a Toffoli network.

Proof: Let's consider the Toffoli gate of Fig. 4(a) to verify the detection condition of the target node displacement fault $T_{G_0}^{c \to b}$.

As per the detection condition of the target node displacement fault, the test vector $<a, b, c, T> = <1, 1, 0, 1>$ is considered as one of the detection condition for $T_{G_0}^{c \to b}$. For $<a, b, c, T> = <1, 1, 0, 1>$ in Fig. 4(b) (faulty gate due to TNDF), it is always true that $d = \bar{b}$, as all the control nodes and also the target node has received the value 1. So, for the same test vector $<a, b, c, T> = <1, 1, 0, 1>$, fault free circuit and faulty circuit would always produce different output and hence, it can be confirmed that our detection condition of the target node displacement fault is very true and applicable for any reversible circuit.

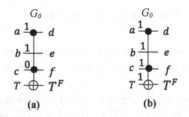

Fig. 5. Test vector generation method for $T_{G_0}^{c \to b}$ in Fig. 4(b)

Phase 2: Test Vector Generation for TNDF

Here, the test vector generation mechanism for TNDF would be discussed. As per the detection condition of the fault, vectors $<a, b, c, T> = <1, 1, 0, 1>$ and $<a, b, c, T> = <1, 1, 1, 1>$ are considered (as shown in Fig. 5(a) and (b)) for $T_{G_0}^{c \to b}$ of Fig. 4(b). So, $V(T_{G_0}^{c \to b}) = \{<1, 1, 0, 1>, <1, 1, 1, 1>\}$.

Example 3: Let's consider the circuit shown in Fig. 6 discussing about the node displacement fault (control and target node displacement fault) in reversible circuit. The circuit is having 3 inputs and containing five Toffoli gates.

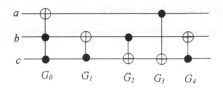

Fig. 6. Fault free reversible circuit

All possible control node displacement faults for the circuit given in Fig. 6 are $C_{G_1}^{c \to a}$, $C_{G_2}^{b \to a}$, $C_{G_3}^{a \to b}$ and $C_{G_4}^{c \to a}$.

Test vectors needed for the detection of those control node faults are $V(C_{G_1}^{c \to a}) = <1, 3, 4, 7>$, $V(C_{G_2}^{b \to a}) = <1, 2, 4, 6>$, $V(C_{G_3}^{a \to b}) = <1, 2, 4, 6>$, $V(C_{G_4}^{c \to a}) = <2, 3, 6, 7>$.

Similarly, the target node displacement faults for the given circuit are $T_{G_1}^{b \to a}$, $T_{G_2}^{c \to a}$, $T_{G_3}^{c \to b}$ and $T_{G_4}^{b \to a}$ and test vectors needed for the detection of corresponding faults are $V(T_{G_1}^{b \to a}) = <4, 5, 6, 7>$, $V(T_{G_2}^{c \to a}) = <2, 3, 4, 5>$, $V(T_{G_3}^{c \to b}) = <1, 3, 5, 6>$ and $V(T_{G_4}^{b \to a}) = <1, 2, 5, 7>$.

It can also be inferred that there is hardly any possibility of control and target node displacement faults can appear for the gate G_0 in the circuit depicted in Fig. 6.

3.3   Test Vector Minimization Algorithm

The procedure used for test set minimization for node displacement faults (control, target) in reversible circuit is stated in Algorithm 1.

ALGORITHM 1: Minimization of test vector for the detection of node displacement faults in reversible circuits

---

> **Input:** Test vectors for a type of fault in a circuit.
> **Output:** Minimum test vectors to detect the fault.
> **begin**
> | Step1: Calculate test vectors for each kind of F in a circuit,
> | where F may be a control node or target node displacement fault.
> | Step2: Find out test vector (T) of the circuit for F.
> | Step3: Calculate occurrence (O_n) of a vector n∈T in different F.
> | Step4: Test vector or set of test vectors which covers all F is the mini
> | mized test set for the circuit to detect F.

To illustrate this minimization algorithm in detail, the circuit shown in Fig. 6 is again considered.

Test Set Minimization for CNDF

According to Algorithm 1, the term F designates the control node displacement fault in this case.

In this context, different control node displacement faults are: $F = <C_{G_1}^{c \to a}, C_{G_2}^{b \to a}, C_{G_3}^{a \to b}, C_{G_4}^{c \to a}>$ for the circuit represented in Fig. 6. As per the detection condition of CNDF, the vectors for the corresponding faults are $V(C_{G_1}^{c \to a}) = <1, 3, 4, 7>$, $V(C_{G_2}^{b \to a}) = <1, 2, 4, 6>$, $V(C_{G_3}^{a \to b}) = <1, 2, 4, 6>$, $V(C_{G_4}^{c \to a}) = <2, 3, 6, 7>$.

Hence, $T = V(C_{G_1}^{c \to a}) \cup V(C_{G_2}^{b \to a}) \cup V(C_{G_3}^{a \to b}) \cup V(C_{G_4}^{c \to a}) = <1, 3, 4, 7> \cup <1, 2, 4, 6> \cup <1, 2, 4, 6> \cup <2, 3, 6, 7> = <1, 2, 3, 4, 6, 7>$.

By investigating, it can be found that the test vector n = 1 in T appears within $V(C_{G_1}^{c \to a})$, $V(C_{G_2}^{b \to a})$ and $V(C_{G_3}^{a \to b})$, so, occurrence of vector 1 is 3 i.e. $O_1 = 3$. Similarly, $O_2 = 3$, $O_3 = 2$, $O_4 = 3$, $O_6 = 3$ and $O_7 = 2$. Now, we can see that each of test vector containing in set $S_1 = \{1, 2, 4, 6\}$ covers maximum of three control displacement faults and each vector within the set $S_2 = \{3, 7\}$ covers at most two control displacement faults. So, initially the vectors in S_1 is combined to determine the test vector set covering all the possible control node displacement faults and then if required test vectors of S_1 and S_2 can be combined to realize the solution.

However, if test vectors 1 and 2 from S_1 are combined then the entire control node displacement fault F ($<C_{G_1}^{c \to a}, C_{G_2}^{b \to a}, C_{G_3}^{a \to b}, C_{G_4}^{c \to a}>$) of the given circuit can be detected. So, the test set $S_{min} = \{1, 2\}$ is considered as the minimal set containing minimum numbers of vectors required for identifying all CNDFs of the given circuit.

Test Set Minimization for TNDF

Like as in CNDF, all possible TNDF for the circuit (see Fig. 6) are: $F = <T_{G_1}^{b \to a}, T_{G_2}^{c \to a}, T_{G_3}^{c \to b}, T_{G_4}^{b \to a}>$ and test vectors required for the detection of corresponding faults are $V(T_{G_1}^{b \to a}) = <4, 5, 6, 7>$, $V(T_{G_2}^{c \to a}) = <2, 3, 4, 5>$, $V(T_{G_3}^{c \to b}) = <1, 3, 5, 6>$ and $V(T_{G_4}^{b \to a}) = <1, 2, 5, 7>$.

Now, $T = V(T_{G_1}^{b \rightarrow a}) \cup V(T_{G_2}^{c \rightarrow a}) \cup V(T_{G_3}^{c \rightarrow b}) \cup V(T_{G_4}^{b \rightarrow a}) = <4, 5, 6, 7> \cup <2, 3, 4, 5> \cup <1, 3, 5, 6> \cup <1, 2, 5, 7> = <1, 2, 3, 4, 5, 6, 7>$.

Thereby the occurrence of the vectors turned out to be as $O_1 = 2$, $O_2 = 2$, $O_3 = 2$, $O_4 = 2$, $O_5 = 4$, $O_6 = 2$ and $O_7 = 2$. So, two sets are formed as: $S_1 = \{5\}$ and $S_2 = \{1, 2, 3, 4, 6, 7\}$.

The test vector 5 contained within S_1 covers all possible target node displacement fault F and hence, $\{5\}$ is considered as the set having minimum number of vectors needed for detecting all TNDFs.

4 Experimental Results

We have tested our technique over a wide range of benchmarks [23] and the obtained results are summarized in Tables 1 and 2, respectively. In Table 1, first and second column represents benchmark name, number of gates and number of lines respectively. Test vector count needed for CNDF and its corresponding minimized test set

Table 1. Experimental results for control node displacement fault

Benchmark name	Number of gates	Number of lines	Test vectors to detect CNDF	Minimized test set by Algorithm 1	Test set reduced (%)
peres gate	2	3	(1, 4, 6, 7)	(1)	75%
nth_prime	4	3	(1, 2, 3, 4, 5, 6)	(1)	84%
ham3tc	5	3	(1, 2, 3, 4, 6, 7)	(1, 2)	67%
rd32d1	4	4	(2, 3, 5, 6, 7, 8, 9, 10, 11, 12, 13, 14, 15)	(7, 8, 10, 14)	69%
ham3	5	3	(1, 2, 3, 4, 6, 7)	(1, 2)	67%
3_17_tc	6	3	(1, 2, 3, 4, 5, 6, 7)	(4)	86%
xor5d1	4	5	(1, 2, 3, 4, 5, 6, 7, 8, 9, 10, 11, 12, 13, 14, 15, 16, 17, 18, 19, 20, 21, 22,23, 24, 25, 26, 27, 28, 29, 30, 31)	(7, 10)	94%
hwb4d3	11	4	(1, 2, 3, 5, 6, 7, 8, 9, 10, 11, 12, 13, 14, 15)	(2, 3, 4)	80%
mod5d1	8	5	(2, 3, 4, 5, 6, 7, 8, 9, 10, 11, 12, 13, 14, 15, 16, 17, 18, 19, 20, 21, 22, 23, 24, 25, 26, 27, 28, 29)	(7, 11, 12, 20, 22)	81%
mod5d2	9	5	(0, 1, 2, 3, 4, 5, 6, 7, 8, 9, 10, 11, 12, 13, 14, 15, 16, 17, 18, 19, 20, 21, 22, 23,24, 25, 26, 27, 28, 29, 30, 31)	(0, 4, 11, 15)	88%

Table 2. Experimental results for target node displacement fault

Benchmark name	Number of gates	Number of lines	Test vectors to detect TNDF	Minimized test set by Algorithm 1	Test set reduced (%)
peres gate	2	3	(1, 3, 5, 7)	(1)	75%
nth_prime	4	3	(1, 2, 3, 4, 5, 6, 7)	(7)	86%
ham3tc	5	3	(1, 2, 3, 4, 5, 6, 7)	(5)	86%
rd32d1	4	4	(4, 5, 6, 7, 8, 9, 10, 11, 12, 13, 14, 15)	(10, 12)	84%
ham3	5	3	(1, 2, 3, 4, 6, 7)	(5)	86%
3_17_tc	6	3	(0, 1, 2, 3, 4, 5, 6, 7)	(5)	88%
xor5d1	4	5	(2, 3, 4, 5, 6, 7, 8, 9, 10, 11, 12, 13, 14, 15, 16, 17, 18, 19, 20, 21, 22, 23, 24, 25, 26, 27, 28, 29, 30, 31)	(8, 16)	94%
hwb4d3	11	4	(1, 2, 3, 5, 6, 7, 8, 9, 10, 11, 12, 13, 14, 15)	(11, 12)	87%
mod5d1	8	5	(2, 3, 4, 5, 6, 7, 8, 9, 10, 11, 12, 13, 14, 15, 16, 17, 18, 19, 20, 21, 22, 23, 24, 25, 26, 27, 28, 29, 30, 31)	(21, 31)	93%
mod5d2	9	5	(0, 1, 2, 3, 4, 5, 6, 7, 8, 9, 10, 11, 12, 13, 14, 15, 16, 17, 18, 19, 20, 21, 22, 23, 24, 25, 26, 27, 28, 29, 30, 31)	(6)	97%

determined using the Algorithm 1 is shown in column 4 and column 5 respectively. Percentage improvement in the form of test vector reduction is displayed in column 6 of Table 1.

Similarly, in result Table 2, the first three columns holds identical interpretation as that of Table 1. Number of test vectors needed for detecting TNDF is recorded in column 4. The minimized test set derived for TNDF and percentage reduction obtained (using Algorithm 1) is tabulated in column 5 and column 6 respectively. As no such work exists on the area of NDF fault, we could not compare our results with related techniques' data.

5 Conclusion

The existing fault detection algorithms mainly work for detection and localization of gate faults like SMGF, PMGF, MMGF and till date no such works exist where fault incurred due to displacement of control and target nodes is considered. In way to address such type of fault, here, in this work we have come up with a strategy that not only identifies this NDF effectively but also locates the position of the fault accurately. The way for generating fault specific test vector also has been undertaken here. The developed fault detection scheme has been successfully tested over a wide spectrum of benchmarks and the obtained results have been reported along with.

References

1. Shor, P.W.: Algorithms for quantum computation: discrete logarithms and factoring. In: Foundations of Computer Science, pp. 124–134 (1994)
2. Grover, L.K.: A fast quantum mechanical algorithm for database search. In: Theory of Computing, pp. 212–219 (1996)
3. Veldhorst, M., et al.: A two qubit logic gate in silicon. Nature **526**, 410 (2015)
4. Haffner, H., et al.: Scalable multiparticle entanglement of trapped ions. Nature **438**, 643–646 (2005)
5. Laforest, M., et al.: Using error correction to determine the noise model. Phys. Rev. A **75**, 133–137 (2007)
6. Ghosh, J.J., et al.: High-fidelity CZ gate for resonator based superconducting quantum computers. Phys. Rev. A **87**, 022309 (2013)
7. Kane, B.: A silicon-based nuclear spin quantum computer. Nature **393**, 133–137 (1998)
8. Fazel, K., Thornton, M., Rice, J.E.: ESOP-based Toffoli gate cascade generation. In: IEEE Pacific Rim Conference on Communications, Computers and Signal Processing, pp. 206–209. Citeseer (2007)
9. Wille, R., Drechsler, R.: BDD-based synthesis of reversible logic for large functions. In: DAC 2009, pp. 270–275 (2009)
10. Agrawal, P.A., Jha, N.K.: An algorithm for synthesis of reversible logic circuits. IBM Res. Dev. **25**(11), 2317–2329 (2006)
11. Hayes, J.P., Polian, I., Becker, B.: Testing for missing-gate faults in reversible circuits. In: IEEE Asian Test Symposium, pp. 100–105 (2004)
12. Perkowski, M., Biamonte, J., Lukac, M.: Test generation and fault localization for quantum circuits. In: International Symposium on Multi-valued Logic, pp. 62–68 (2005)
13. Patel, K.N., Hayes, J.P., Markov, I.L.: Fault testing for reversible circuits. In: IEEE VLSI Test Symposium, pp. 410–416 (2003)
14. Kole, D.K., Rahaman, H., Das, D.K., Bhattacharya, B.B.: Derivation of optimal test set for detection of multiple missing-gate faults in reversible circuits. In: IEEE Asian Test Symposium, pp. 33–38 (2010)
15. Zamani, M., Tahoori, M.B., Chakrabarty, K.: Ping-pong test: compact test vector generation for reversible circuits. In: IEEE VLSI Test Symposium, pp. 164–169 (2012)
16. Ramasamy, K., Tagare, R., Perkins, E., Perkowski, M.: Fault localization in reversible circuits is easier than for classical circuits. In: IEEE Asian Test Symposium (2004)
17. Polian, I., Hayes, J.P., Fienn, T., Becker, B.: A family of logical fault models for reversible circuits. In: IEEE Asian Test Symposium, pp. 422–427 (2005)
18. Rahaman, H., Kole, D.K., Das, D.K., Bhattacharya, B.B.: On the detection of missing-gate faults in reversible circuits by a universal test set. In: IEEE International Conference on VLSI Design, pp. 163–168 (2008)
19. Mondal, B., Kole, D.K., Rahaman, H., Das, D.K.: Generator for test set construction of SMGF in reversible circuit by Boolean difference method. In: IEEE Asian Test Symposium, pp. 68–73 (2014)

20. Toffoli, T.: Reversible computing. MIT Lab for Computer Science, Technical memo MIT/LCS/TM-151 (1980)
21. Feynman, R.: Quantum mechanical computers. Found. Phys. **16**, 507–531 (1986)
22. Fredkin, E., Toffoli, T.: Conservative logic. Int. J. Theor. Phys. **21**, 219–253 (1982)
23. Wille, R., Grosse, D., Teuber, L., Dueck, G.W., Drechsler, R.: RevLib: an online resource for reversible functions and reversible circuits. In: 38th ISMVL, pp. 220–225 (2008)

Novel Approach for Improved Signal Integrity and Power Dissipation Using MLGNR Interconnects

Vijay Rao Kumbhare$^{(\boxtimes)}$ ⓘ, Punya Prasanna Paltani ⓘ,
and Manoj Kumar Majumder ⓘ

Dr. Shyama Prasad Mukherjee IIIT Naya Raipur,
Naya Raipur 493661, Chhattisgarh, India
{vijay,punya,manojk}@iiitnr.edu.in

Abstract. In order to reduce the crosstalk-induced delay along with the impact of peak noise on the victim line, this paper introduces a passive shielding methodology accurately using multilayer graphene nanoribbon (MLGNR) based equivalent single conductor (ESC) model at 32 nm technology. To mitigate interconnect issues, the aforementioned model is used for different interconnect spacing using coupled driver-interconnect-load (DIL) arrangement. In the proposed work, the passive shielding is used innovatively to reduce the crosstalk-induced delay and the impact of peak noise on the victim line, while maintaining the minimum interconnect pitch. For better understanding, the shielded and unshielded approaches are presented to show the significant improvement and compared with copper (*Cu*) interconnect at global length. In regard to shield approach, it is observed that the shielded interconnect lines are outperformed in terms of peak noise on the victim line and crosstalk-induced delay as compared to unshielded interconnect lines. At 32 nm technology, the impact of crosstalk-induced delay and peak voltage of shielded MLGNR are improved by 94.58% and 90.23%, respectively, as compared to shielded *Cu* line for 5 nm spacing at 1000 μm interconnect length. Additionally, the power consumption is also investigated for shielded and unshielded interconnect, wherein 51.70% improved performance has been observed for shielded MLGNR over shielded *Cu* interconnect at global length. Therefore, the MLGNR with passive shielding can be treated as the most appropriate model in order to improve the signal integrity as compared to *Cu* for future on-chip interconnects.

Keywords: Crosstalk induced delay · Passive shielding ·
Multilayer graphene nanoribbon (MLGNR) · Peak noise ·
Copper (*Cu*) interconnect

1 Introduction

With the miniaturization of feature size and operating at gigahertz frequency, interconnect plays a significant role that dominates circuit delay, logic faults, and power dissipation. The coupling capacitance can significantly affect the performance of the digital circuit that causes signal integrity problem [1]. In a high-speed digital system,

© Springer Nature Singapore Pte Ltd. 2019
A. Sengupta et al. (Eds.): VDAT 2019, CCIS 1066, pp. 617–629, 2019.
https://doi.org/10.1007/978-981-32-9767-8_51

the peak noise generated from aggressor to victim line is the major cause of logic faults and unintentional switching behavior of the system. According to Miller's effect, when both the lines (aggressor and victim lines) are switched in opposite direction, the coupling capacitance has more impact on victim line that degrades the overall signal integrity of the system [2, 3]. With shrinking technology, the coupling capacitance has major impact on crosstalk that shows three major effect on circuit performance (i) logic faults at far end of interconnect line due to peak noise induced in the victim line (ii) increased delay due to change in signal shape, and (iii) large power dissipation due to noise voltage induced in the victim line [4].

To alleviate these problems, shield insertion is a much better approach to reduce the peak noise, logic faults, and delay instead of increasing the width and separation between the coupled interconnects. However, the copper (*Cu*) interconnect has reached its limit due to electromigration, hillock and void formations [5, 6]. Therefore, the researchers are motivated to work on alternate promising material as multilayer graphene nanoribbon (MLGNR) based passive shielding approach to mitigate these problems. An MLGNR can be chosen as emerged material that provides higher electrical performance in terms of crosstalk, longer mean free path (MFP), large current density, and insignificant electromigration as compared to *Cu* interconnect.

Previously, Kose *et al.* [7] investigated the consequence of power/ground noise behavior on the crosstalk for different interconnect width and lengths. The authors observed that the shielded line degraded the performance instead of enhancing it due to increase coupling of Power/Grid noise on the victim line. Later, Majumder *et al.* [8] explored a comparative investigation of crosstalk-induced delay and area effect on MWCNT, that is compared with bundled SWCNT based on the 3-line interconnect structure. The authors have neglected the impact of peak noise and power dissipation on digital logic circuits. Afterward, Kumar *et al.* [9] analyzed and compared the performance in relation to power, bandwidth, and delay of MLGNR and *Cu* interconnect at 14 nm technology. However, the work did not consider the effect of logic fault occurs due to a higher peak voltage on the victim line. Recently, Qian *et al.* [10] demonstrated a comparative investigation between MLGNR and *Cu* based on the equivalent *RLC* model to observe the impact of crosstalk-induced delay at different technology. The authors have neglected the effect of peak voltage and power dissipation on the victim line. To the best of the author's knowledge, no investigation has been demonstrated until now for shielding in order to reduce the crosstalk-induced delay and logic faults using MLGNR interconnect.

This proposed work critically addresses the impact of crosstalk-induced delay, power consumption, and peak noise, wherein the main attention is to reduce the delay and noise voltage using the passive shielding approach for a coupled interconnect. In order to reach this goal, passive shielding is considered innovatively and proposed an accurate geometry for *Cu*/MLGNR interconnect. On the basis of interconnect geometry, an equivalent electrical model is demonstrated using driver-interconnect-load (DIL) setup for aggressor and victim lines at different spacing and lengths. Further, the proposed shielded and unshielded interconnects are analyzed for peak noise, power dissipation, and crosstalk-induced delay. Afterward, the analysis based on the aforementioned model is compared with *Cu* interconnect at 32 nm node.

The proposed work is organized as follows: Sect. 1 describes the brief overview of the research scenario and the importance of shielding approach. Section 2 presents the proposed passive shielding geometry of interconnect model and brief about accurate equivalent *RLC* model for MLGNR and *Cu* interconnect at 32 nm technology. Section 3 demonstrates the interconnect parasitics and simulation setup based on DIL for shielded *Cu*/MLGNR interconnect. Further, the performance comparison of shielded and unshielded interconnect is presented for *Cu* and MLGNR for spacing ranges from 5 to 20 nm at global interconnect length in Sect. 4. Finally, Sect. 5 summarizes the proposed work.

2   Proposed Shielded Geometry and Model

This section provides a detailed understanding of an *RLC* based ESC model of *Cu* and MLGNR interconnect. Further, it is used to determine the peak noise, power dissipation, and the crosstalk-induced delay for shielded and unshielded methodology. A multi-conductor transmission line (MTL) model is simplified to an ESC model for an *RLC* network by considering the accurate parasitics associated with the *Cu*/MLGNR interconnect.

2.1   The ESC Model of MLGNR

In this subsection, an *RLC* based ESC model is obtained by simplifying the MTL model using the structure shown in Fig. 1. The *Cu*/MLGNR is positioned over the surface plane with distance h_g, and each line is separated with spacing S. The width (*W*), height (*H*), and dielectric constant (ε_r) of interconnect lines are considered accurately using international technology roadmap for semiconductor (ITRS) 2015 benchmark [11].

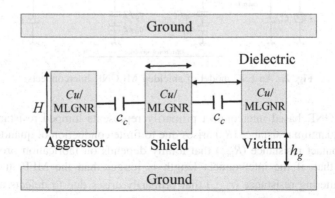

Fig. 1. The geometry of passive shielded *Cu*/MLGNR interconnect.

In case of MLGNR interconnect, each layer of GNR is sandwiched on one another with an interlayer ($\delta = 0.34$ nm) separation due to Vander wall force [12, 13] and the number of layers (N_{layer}) is obtained as

$$N_{layer} = 1 + Int \left\lfloor \frac{H}{\delta} \right\rfloor \tag{1}$$

where $int[.]$ is considered only an integer value. Figure 2 illustrates an equivalent interconnect model of shielded MLGNR that is primarily driven by a resistive driver with resistance R_{tr}, capacitance C_{tr}, and terminated by capacitive load C_L. The number of conducting channel ($N_{ch,MLGNR}$) can be determined in each layer of MLGNR as [13]

$$N_{ch,MLGNR} = \alpha_0 + \alpha_1 W + \alpha_2 W + \alpha_3 E_F + \alpha_4 W E_F + \alpha_5 E_F^2 \tag{2}$$

where $E_F = 0.6$ eV is the Fermi energy and α_0 to α_5 are the constant parameters associated with the number of conducting channel of MLGNR. The $N_{ch,MLGNR}$ dependent parasitics (*i.e.* capacitance, resistance, and inductance) associated with Fig. 2 are modeled for global interconnect length at 32 nm technology.

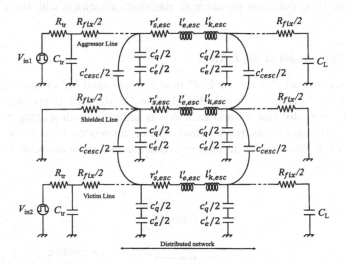

Fig. 2. An ESC model of shielded MLGNR interconnects.

The MLGNR based interconnect primarily represents lumped resistance R_{fix} that consists of quantum resistance (R_q) arises due to finite conduction of quantum wire and imperfect contact resistance (R_{imc}) that totally depends on fabrication process [9]. In addition to that, if the interconnect length is longer than the MFP, it exhibits an effective scattering resistance ($r'_{s,esc}$) that primarily arises due to defects and acoustic scattering phenomenon. The lumped resistance ($R_{fix} = R_{imc} + R_q/N_{ch,MLGNR}$) is considered accurately as a sum of imperfect contact and quantum resistance at far and near end of the wire to maintain the fabrication aspects at the metal-semiconductor interface.

Apart from $r'_{s,esc}$, the interconnect line also exhibits an effective kinetic inductance ($l'_{k,esc}$), and magnetic inductance ($l'_{e,esc}$) in per unit length (*p.u.l*) that are primarily represent the kinetic energy stored in individual single layer, and magnetic field associated with MLGNR, respectively as shown in Fig. 2 and calculated as [13, 17, 18]

$$r'_{s,esc} = \frac{h/2e^2}{N_{layer}N_{ch,MLGNR}\lambda_{eff}} \tag{3}$$

$$l'_{k,esc} = \frac{h/2e^2}{N_{layer}N_{ch,MLGNR}v_F} \tag{4}$$

$$l'_{e,esc} = \frac{\mu_0 h_g}{W} \tag{5}$$

where h, e, λ_{eff}, μ_0, and $v_F \approx 8 \times 10^5$ m/s, are referred as the Planck's constant, charge of an electron, MFP considered as 419 nm [14], the magnetic permeability of free space, and Fermi energy of MLGNR, respectively.

The equivalent capacitive parasitic of interconnect consists of electrostatic capacitance ($c'_{e,esc}$) due to the lowermost layer of MLGNR facing the surface and quantum capacitance ($c'_{q,esc}$) as a result of the charge stored in each layer of MLGNR, respectively. Thus, the total effective capacitance (c'_{esc}) in *p.u.l.* can be expressed as [13]

$$c'_{esc} = \left(1/c'_{q,esc} + 1/c'_{e,esc}\right)^{-1} \tag{6}$$

where $c'_{q,esc} = 2e^2 N_{layer}N_{ch,MLGNR}/hv_F$, $c'_{e,esc} = \varepsilon_0\varepsilon_r W/h_g$, and ε_0 denotes the electrostatic permittivity of free space.

2.2   An ESC Model of *Cu*

In order to perform comparative analysis between MLGNR and *Cu*, this subsection provides interconnect parasitics (i.e. resistance (r'_{cu}), mutual inductance ($l'_{cu,MI}$), self-inductance ($l'_{cu,SI}$), ground capacitance ($c'_{cu,g}$), and coupling capacitance (c'_c) between the lines used for *Cu* material based on Fig. 1. In *p.u.l.* the *Cu* interconnect parasitics of the rectangular cross-section can be calculated as [15, 16]

$$r'_{cu} = \rho_{cu}l/W.H \tag{7}$$

$$l'_{cu,SI} = (\mu_0 l/2\pi)[\ln(2l/(W+H)) + 0.5 + 0.22(W+H)/l] \tag{8}$$

$$l'_{cu,MI} = (\mu_0 l/2\pi)[\ln(2l/d) - 1 + d/l] \tag{9}$$

$$c'_{cu,g} = \varepsilon_r\varepsilon_0\left[\frac{W}{h_g} + 2.22\left(\frac{S}{0.70h_g+S}\right)^{3.19} + 1.17\left(\frac{H}{4.53h_g+H}\right)^{0.12}\left(\frac{S}{1.51h_g+S}\right)^{0.76}\right] \tag{10}$$

$$c'_c = \varepsilon_r \varepsilon_0 \left[\begin{array}{l} 1.14 \frac{H}{S} \left(\frac{h_g}{2.06S + h_g} \right)^{0.09} + 0.74 \left(\frac{W}{1.59S + W} \right)^{1.14} \\ + 1.16 \left(\frac{h_g}{0.98S + h_g} \right)^{1.18} \left(\frac{W}{1.87S + W} \right)^{0.16} \end{array} \right] \tag{11}$$

where l and ρ_{cu} denote the wire length and resistivity property of *Cu* material, respectively, whereas two parallel wires having the centre to centre distance referred as d.

3   Interconnect Parasitics and Simulation Setup

In this section, the physical parameter is considered based on ITRS2015 as shown in Table 1. Using expression (1) through (13), the quantitative value of wire parasitics and coupling capacitance associated with *Cu*/MLGNR are illustrated in Tables 2 and 3. Using the interconnect geometry as depicted in Fig. 1, a DIL setup for shielded *Cu*/MLGNR interconnect is shown in Fig. 3. It consists of aggressor and victim line, where the victim line experiences peak noise if the aggressor line triggered with input wave with respect to victim line as grounded *i.e.* termed as functional crosstalk. Similarly, the crosstalk-induced delay occurs due to the simultaneous triggering of both the lines either in the opposite (out-phase) or same (in-phase) direction *i.e.* termed as dynamic crosstalk. In the worst-case scenario, the victim line experiences a large crosstalk-induced delay because the coupling capacitance becomes double due to miller's effect [2, 3]. In order to reduce the impact of crosstalk-induced delay and peak noise experiences by victim line, a passive shielding approach is considered and placed between the coupled interconnect line as shown in Fig. 3.

Table 1. Interconnect physical parameters based on ITRS2015 [11].

Technology node	At global level
	32 nm
Width (W nm)	48
Height (H nm)	115.2
h_g (nm)	110.4
Dielectric constant (ε_r)	2.3
Resistivity (ρ_{cu} µΩ-cm)	3.52

The coupling capacitance in *p.u.l.* (c'_c) for MLGNR can be calculated between the interconnect lines as follows [16–18]

$$c'_c = (\varepsilon/4)M \left[\sqrt{1 - (1 + 2W/S)^{-2}} \right] \tag{12}$$

where,

$$M(x) = \begin{cases} \dfrac{2\pi}{\ln\frac{2(1+\sqrt[4]{1-x^2})}{1-\sqrt[4]{1+x^2}}}, & 0 \leq x \leq 0.7071 \\[4mm] \dfrac{2}{\pi}\ln\dfrac{2(1+\sqrt{x})}{1-\sqrt{x}}, & 0.7071 \leq x \leq 1 \end{cases} \tag{13}$$

Table 2. Summarizes the quantitative value of interconnect parasitics at 32 nm technology.

Parasitics	At 32 nm technology, the quantitative value of parasitics for interconnect material of	
	Cu	MLGNR
Driver resistance R_{tr} (kΩ)	12.13	
Driver capacitance C_{tr} (fF)	0.081	
Capacitive load C_L (fF)	0.28	
N_{layer}	–	339
$N_{ch,MLGNR}$	–	35
Resistance (Ω/μm)	$r'_{cu} = 6.3657$	$r'_{s,esc} = 2.6028$
Inductance (pH/μm)	$l'_{cu,SI} = 152$	$l'_{e,esc} = 2.8902$
		$l'_{k,esc} = 0.6816$
Capacitance (aF/μm)	$c'_{cu,g} = 10.257$	$c'_{e,esc} = 8.8541$
Quantum capacitance (fF/μm)	–	$c'_{q,esc} = 2292.05$

*The self-inductance ($l_{cu,SI}$) value is at interconnect length of 100 μm and ground capacitance ($c_{cu,g}$) value is at $S = 5$ nm for Cu material.

Table 3. Summarizes the quantitative values of coupling capacitance for Cu and MLGNR

Spacing (nm)	At 32 nm technology, the quantitative values of coupling capacitance in aF/μm for interconnect material of	
	Cu	MLGNR
5	704.4	28.455
10	363.5	24.275
15	248.4	21.928
20	190.1	20.331

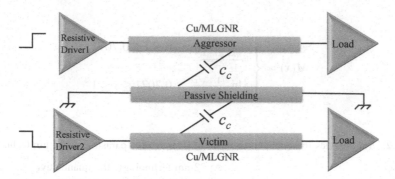

Fig. 3. A coupled DIL arrangement for shielded *Cu*/MLGNR wire with the out-of-phase signal transition.

4 Performance Comparison and Discussions

A comparative analysis for signal integrity and power dissipation is demonstrated for shielded and unshielded *Cu*/MLGNR interconnect using the dimension described in Table 1 at 32 nm technology. The crosstalk is the primary reason for degrading the performance of the coupled interconnect line that causes due to coupling capacitance. Therefore, shielded and unshielded coupled wires are analyzed to observe the impact of the crosstalk-induced delay, peak noise, and power dissipation for different interconnect spacing ranges from $S = 5$ nm to $S = 20$ nm for 100 to 1000 μm lengths.

Using Industry standard HSPICE, the performance in terms of crosstalk-induced delay is investigated based on the DIL arrangement for unshielded and shielded *Cu*/MLGNR interconnect as depicted in Figs. 4(a) and (b), respectively for different separation between the lines at 32 nm technology. For the aforementioned equivalent model, the delay and peak noise primarily depend on coupling capacitance, electrostatic capacitance, and resistance of interconnect. It is evident from the Figs. 4(a) and (b), the delay under the influence of dynamic crosstalk drastically increases in case of *Cu* and MLGNR for the longer wire. It is due to the *p.u.l.* interconnect parasitics that increases with lengths as observed in Table 2 and the crosstalk-induced delay increases substantially. However, the performance in terms of crosstalk-induced delay is improved due to the reduction in coupling capacitance that primarily depends on the separation between the lines as observed in Table 3. It is observed from Figs. 4(a) and (b) that the crosstalk-induced delay for shielded *Cu* outperformed by 48.38% and 50.57% *w.r.t.* unshielded *Cu* interconnect at 100 μm and 1000 μm length for spacing $S = 5$ nm at 32 nm, respectively. Similarly, it can also be observed from Figs. 4(a) and (b) that the performance of passive shielded MLGNR is improved in terms of crosstalk-induced delay by 32.42% and 42.87% *w.r.t.* unshielded MLGNR at 100 μm and 1000 μm length for spacing $S = 5$ nm at 32 nm technology, respectively. Moreover, from Table 4, it is evident that the proposed shielded MLGNR outperformed on an average of 94.58% and 84.64% *w.r.t.* shielded *Cu* interconnects for spacing $S = 5$ nm and $S = 20$ nm, respectively for global length at 32 nm node. Therefore, the results indicate that the proposed passive shielded MLGNR possesses an improved crosstalk-induced delay *w.r.t.* the shielded *Cu* interconnect at 32 nm technology.

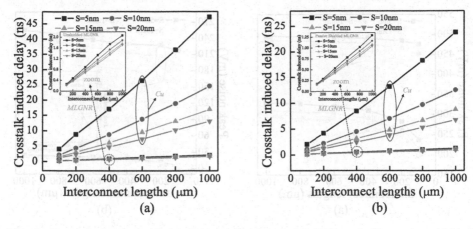

Fig. 4. Crosstalk induced delay of (a) unshielded *Cu*/MLGNR and (b) passive shielded *Cu*/MLGNR interconnect for difference spacing at different interconnect length.

Table 4. Percentage improvement of the crosstalk-induced delay for MLGNR *w.r.t. Cu* based passive shielded interconnect at 32 nm technology for different spacing

Length (μm)	% improvement of the crosstalk induced delay for MLGNR *w.r.t. Cu* based passive shielded interconnect at 32 nm technology for different spacing (nm) of			
	$S = 5$	$S = 10$	$S = 15$	$S = 20$
100	91.64	85.31	79.84	75.72
200	93.13	88.13	84	80.25
400	93.33	89.42	86.07	82.81
600	94.08	90.00	86.48	83.79
800	94.43	90.45	87.21	84.61
1000	94.58	90.72	87.66	84.64

Apart from this, the peak noise can be observed when the aggressor line is switched with pulse wave and the victim line is grounded. It is evident that unintentional peak experiences by victim line is the primary reason for logic faults in digital circuits. To alleviate these problems, passive shielding is placed between the coupled interconnect line. Consequently, Figs. 5(a) and (b) depict the observation of peak noise for unshielded and shielded *Cu*/MLGNR interconnect line for different spacing and length at 32 nm technology to minimize the impact of peak noise. Further, it can be observed that the *p.u.l.* parasitic value increases for increased interconnect length of MLGNR and *Cu*, as a result, the peak noise also increases. However, the impact of peak noise is significantly lower for MLGNR *w.r.t Cu* due to its reduce coupling capacitance as observed from Table 3. Therefore, on an average, 50.21% and 33.87% improvement

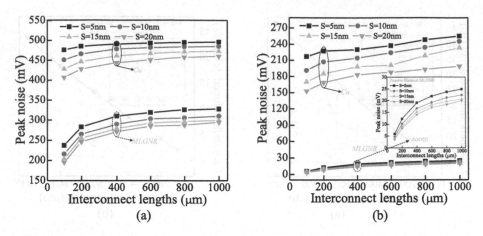

Fig. 5. Peak noise variation of (a) unshielded *Cu*/MLGNR and (b) passive shielded *Cu*/MLGNR interconnect for different spacing at difference interconnect length.

Table 5. Percentage reduction of peak noise for MLGNR *w.r.t. Cu* based passive shielded interconnect at 32 nm technology for different spacing

Length (μm)	% reduction of peak noise for MLGNR *w.r.t. Cu* based passive shielded interconnect at 32 nm technology for different spacing (nm) of			
	$S = 5$	$S = 10$	$S = 15$	$S = 20$
100	97.28	97.54	97.64	97.66
200	94.58	95.07	95.10	95.12
400	91.69	92.19	92.32	92.38
600	90.78	91.43	91.49	91.53
800	90.44	90.89	90.92	90.96
1000	90.23	90.85	90.89	90.93

on peak noise is observed from Figs. 5(a) and (b) for unshielded MLGNR *w.r.t. Cu* interconnects for $S = 5$ nm at local and global lengths, respectively. Similarly, an approximate of 97.28% and 90.23% improvement on peak noise is observed from Table 5 for shielded MLGNR *w.r.t. Cu* for $S = 5$ nm at local and global interconnect lengths, respectively.

Additionally, the load capacitor (C_L) consumes energy when an input pulse is applied to interconnect lines. The performance of the DIL system is not only dependent on delay but also depends on the power dissipation. Therefore, using different interconnect spacing, the power dissipation of unshielded and shielded *Cu*/MLGNR is also observed from Figs. 6(a) and (b). It is observed that the power dissipation of shielded and unshielded MLGNR substantially reduces in comparison to *Cu* similar to the crosstalk-induced delay. Fundamentally, the resistive and capacitive components are

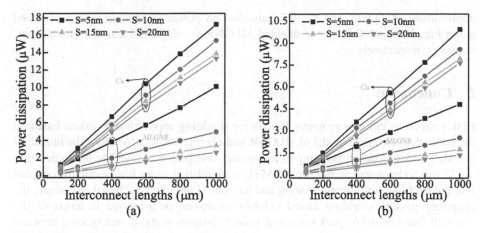

Fig. 6. Power dissipation of (a) unshielded *Cu*/MLGNR and (b) passive shielded *Cu*/MLGNR interconnect for different spacing and interconnect lengths.

Table 6. Percentage reduction of power dissipation for MLGNR *w.r.t.* *Cu* based passive shielded interconnect at 32 nm technology for different spacing

Length (μm)	% reduction of power dissipation for MLGNR *w.r.t.* *Cu* based passive shielded interconnect at 32 nm technology for different spacing (nm) of			
	$S = 5$	$S = 10$	$S = 15$	$S = 20$
100	24.99	53.38	65.16	72.29
200	38.68	61.58	71.01	76.09
400	46.50	68.39	75.31	79.60
600	48.42	69.18	76.78	80.75
800	49.89	70.10	77.84	81.70
1000	51.70	70.66	77.95	82.09

primarily responsible for the crosstalk-induced delay and power dissipation of interconnect lines. The more number of conducting channels related to the individual single layer of MLGNR primarily exhibits substantially lower line resistance than *Cu* as observed from Table 2. Although, the *p.u.l.* c_q' increases for more number of conducting channels but due to the dominating influence of $c_{e,esc}'$, the equivalent capacitance (c_{esc}') remains almost constant. Hence, the overall impact of equivalent scattering resistance and total effective capacitance expressed in (3) and (6) reduces the overall power dispassion as compared to *Cu* interconnect. The results demonstrate that the 24.86% and 45.87% reduction in power dissipation for unshielded MLGNR *w.r.t.* *Cu* as observed from Fig. 6(a) at local and global lengths, respectively. Similarly, an approximate of 24.99% and 51.70% reduction on power dissipation is also observed using Fig. 6(b) and Table 6 for shielded MLGNR *w.r.t. Cu* at local and global interconnects, respectively.

5 Conclusion

In this paper, an efficient geometry for passive shielding approach is proposed based on the equivalent electrical model of MLGNR and *Cu* interconnect to reduce the impact of crosstalk-induced delay, peak noise, and power dissipation to alleviate the logic fault. At 32 nm technology, an *RLC* based MTL is simplified as an ESC model of coupled interconnect line for different spacing and lengths. Using the ESC based DIL setup, the proposed passive shielding model exhibits improved performance in terms of the crosstalk-induced delay, peak noise, and power dissipation at different spacing between the coupled lines. It is observed that the proposed shielded MLGNR outperformed by 94.58% and 84.64% *w.r.t.* shielded *Cu* for 5 nm to 20 nm spacing, respectively at global lengths. Similarly, the improvement in peak noise is observed for shielded MLGNR *w.r.t. Cu* interconnect by 97.28% and 90.23% for 5 nm spacing at local and global lengths, respectively. In addition to that, the power dissipation is also investigated for shielded and unshielded *Cu*/MLGNR interconnect for different spacing at 32 nm technology. Consequently, it is observed that an unshielded line dissipates 48.59% and 42.39% more power as compared to shielded *Cu* and MLGNR interconnect lines, respectively for 5 nm spacing at 1000 µm length. Moreover, the results illustrate 24.99% and 51.70% reduced power dissipation using shielded MLGNR *w.r.t. Cu* for 5 nm spacing at local and global interconnects, respectively. Therefore, it can be concluded that the passive shielding approach is essential for advanced technology in order to improve signal integrity. Hence, shielded MLGNR can be treated as the most promising interconnect material for next-generation VLSI technology.

References

1. Zhang, J., Friedman, E.G.: Crosstalk noise model for shielded interconnects in VLSI-based circuits. In: Proceedings IEEE International (Systems-on-Chip) SOC Conference, Portland, OR, USA, pp. 243–244 (2003)
2. Majumder, M.K., Kaushik, B.K., Manhas, S.K.: Analysis of delay and dynamic crosstalk in bundled carbon nanotube interconnects. IEEE Trans. Electromagn. Compat. **56**(6), 1666–1673 (2014)
3. Majumder, M.K., Das, P.K., Kaushik, B.K.: Delay and crosstalk reliability issues in mixed MWCNT bundle interconnects. Microelectron. Reliab. **54**(11), 2570–2577 (2014)
4. Mehri, M., Masoumi, N.: A thorough investigation into active and passive shielding methods for nano-VLSI interconnects against EMI and crosstalk. Int. J. Electron. Commun. **69**(9), 1199–1207 (2015)
5. Rossnagel, S.M., Kaun, T.S.: Alteration of Cu conductivity in the size effect regime. J. Vac. Sci. Technol. B Microelectron. Nanometer Struct. Process. Meas. Phenom. **22**(1), 240–247 (2004)

6. Wen, W., Brongersma, S.H., Hove, M.V., Maex, K.: Influence of surface and grain-boundary scattering on the resistivity of copper in reduced dimensions. Appl. Phys. Lett. **84** (15), 2838–2840 (2004)
7. Kose, S., Salman, E., Friedman, E.G.: Shielding methodologies in the presence of power/ground noise. IEEE Trans. Very Large Scale Integr. (VLSI) Syst. **19**(8), 1458–1468 (2011)
8. Majumder, M.K., Pandya, N.D., Kaushik, B.K., Manhas, S.K.: Analysis of MWCNT and bundled SWCNT interconnects: impact on crosstalk and area. IEEE Electron Device Lett. **33** (8), 1180–1182 (2012)
9. Kumar, V.R., Majumder, M.K., Kukkam, N.R., Kaushik, B.K.: Time and frequency domain analysis of MLGNR interconnects. IEEE Trans. Nanotechnol. **14**(3), 484–492 (2015)
10. Qian, L., Xia, Y., Shi, G.: Study of crosstalk effect on the propagation characteristics of coupled MLGNR interconnects. IEEE Trans. Nanotechnol. **15**(5), 810–819 (2016)
11. International Technology Roadmap for Semiconductors (ITRS). http://www.itrs.net
12. Xu, C., Li, H., Banerjee, K.: Modeling, analysis, and design of graphene nano-ribbon interconnects. IEEE Trans. Electron Devices **56**(8), 1567–1578 (2009)
13. Majumder, M.K., Kukkam, N.R., Kaushik, B.K.: Frequency response and bandwidth analysis of multi-layer graphene nanoribbon and multi-walled carbon nanotube interconnects. IET Micro Nano Lett. **9**(9), 557–560 (2014)
14. Wong, S.C., Lee, G.Y., Ma, D.J.: Modeling of interconnect capacitance, delay, and crosstalk in VLSI. IEEE Trans. Semicond. Manuf. **13**(1), 108–111 (2000)
15. Predictive Technology Model. http://ptm.asu.edu/
16. Stellari, F., Lacaita, A.L.: New formulas of interconnect capacitances based on results of conformal mapping method. IEEE Trans. Electron Devices **47**(1), 222–231 (2000)
17. Kumbhare, V.R., Paltani, P.P., Venkataiah, C., Majumder, M.K.: Analytical study of bundled MWCNT and edged-MLGNR interconnects: impact on propagation delay and area. IEEE Trans. Nanotechnol. **18**, 606–610 (2019)
18. Kumbhare, V.R., Paltani, P.P., Majumder, M.K.: An efficient method to reduce crosstalk for multi-layered GNR interconnects at 32 nm technology. In: Proceeding the 19th IEEE International Conference on Nanotechnology, the Parisian Macao, Macao SAR, China (2019, accepted)

A Robust Low-Power Write-Assist Data-Dependent-Power-Supplied 12T SRAM Cell

Neha Gupta, Jitesh Prasad, Rana Sagar Kumar, Gunjan Rajput, and Santosh Kumar Vishvakarma[✉]

Nanoscale Devices, VLSI Circuit and System Design Lab, Discipline of Electrical Engineering, Indian Institute of Technology Indore, Indore 453552, M.P., India
{phd1701202008,mt1802102014,mt1802102019, phd1601102014,skvishvakarma}@iiti.ac.in

Abstract. This paper presents a new write assist 12T SRAM cell with data dependent power supply with read decoupled circuit to enhance the read stability and write ability at the low supply voltage. The proposed 12T cell is design to isolate the read path for enhancing the read static noise margin. Stacking effect is used to control leakage current and improved write static noise margin of the cell. As compared with the 6T SRAM cell, the proposed cell offers $8.66\times$, $3.4\times$, and $1.53\times$ higher write, read and hold stability respectively at $0.4\,V$ supply voltage. Our evaluation indicates that the leakage and write power of the proposed cell is reduced by 59% and 99.98% respectively as compared to the conventional 6T cell. For a better perspective of the proposed cell, a compound figure of merit has been introduced and it is found that the proposed cell has 38.048% higher FOM as compared to 6T SRAM cell. All the implementations have been performed using the industry standard $180\,nm$ CMOS technology.

Keywords: SRAM · Stability · Data dependent power supply · Low power · Leakage power

1 Introduction

Memory is one of the essential building blocks for VLSI system design. Recently, the demand for battery operated systems like mobile devices, biomedical implants, and wireless body sensing networks are growing relentlessly, necessitate the requirements of low power SRAMs. Therefore, a robust low power SRAM has drawn great research attention towards their power saving mode [1]. These systems face many problems related to process and performance. However, power reduction in the memory cell has been addressed by many researchers and proposed different SRAM cell architecture for low power application. The scaling of a supply voltage is one of the most effective and aggressive methods for sub-threshold regions because the active power is a quadratic relative to voltage and

© Springer Nature Singapore Pte Ltd. 2019
A. Sengupta et al. (Eds.): VDAT 2019, CCIS 1066, pp. 630–642, 2019.
https://doi.org/10.1007/978-981-32-9767-8_52

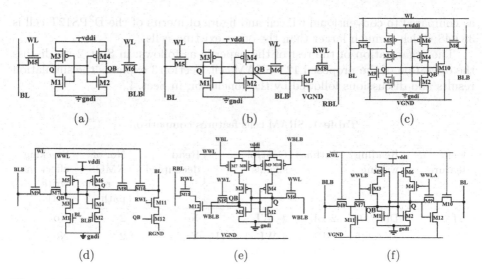

Fig. 1. Different SRAM bitcell structure: (a) Conventional 6T (b) Read Decoupled-8T [14] (c) PPN10T [10] (d) WILP12T [8] (e) Kim12T [11] (f) DAWA12T [12]

leakage power is exponentially dependence on supply voltage [2]. Therefore, the supply voltage reduction is also required for the robustness of the SRAM circuit. In the category of power dissipation, supply voltage reduction is the most challenging task for the near threshold region in deep submicron technology. Most of the time, SRAM cells stay in standby mode, hence leakage power is also one of the most important parameters for energy efficient application [3].

The conventional 6T SRAM cell is constructed using six transistors that is a very simple structure. However, it suffers from many problems like read disturb, half-select issue, read current interruption and noise margin reduction with supply voltage scaling. Moreover, the threshold voltage swings caused by variation of different local and global processes, the rapid degradation has found in the read and write stability of 6T SRAM cell with supply voltage variation. Further, it is exacerbated by conflicting the read/write storage data due to undesirable charging/discharging of node voltage [4].

To conquer these situations which were facing in the conventional 6T cell, various state of art have been proposed in the literature that introduce design techniques such as read decoupling [5,6], feedback cutting [7,8], single ended approach [9], stacking effect [10], and write assist [11,12] etc. Designers are required to use lower technology nodes, therefore the memory read and write failure probability increases [13]. Figure 1 shows different SRAM cells which have been considered in this work.

To apply all the above issues in a single topology, we propose a new write assist data dependent power supply based 12T SRAM cell. The proposed 12T cell is referred as the "D^2PS12T" hereafter. The D^2PS12T cell has not affected by the lower supply voltage and negligible leakage power consumption of 59%

as compared to conventional 6T cell and figure of merits of the D^2PS12T cell is 38.048 which is much larger than the other existing cells.

The organization of the rest of the paper is as follows: in Sect. 2 we discuss the operation of the proposed 12T SRAM cell. Section 3 explains the simulation results and discussions followed by the conclusion in Sect. 4.

Table 1. SRAM cells features comparison

Cell feature	Reading/ writing	Bitlines	Control signals	Read decoupled	No. of NMOS in read path	Stacking effect in write path
6T	Diff./Diff.	2-BL	1- WL	No	2	No
8T	SE/Diff.	2-BL, 1-RBL	1-WL, 1-RWL, 1-VGND	Yes	2	No
PPN10T	Diff./Diff.	2-BL	1-WL, 1-VGND	Yes	2	Yes
WILP12T	SE/Diff.	2-BL	2-WL, 1-RWL, 1-RGND	Yes	2	Yes
Kim12T	SE/Diff.	2-BL, 1-RBL	1-WWL, 1-RWL, 1-VGND	Yes	2	Yes
DAWA12T	Diff./Diff.	2-BL	2-WWL, 1-RWL, 1-VGND	Yes	2	Yes
D^2PS12T	SE/Diff.	2-BL, 1-RBL	2-WWL, 1-RWL, 1-VGND	Yes	2	Yes

2   Proposed 12T SRAM Cell

The cell schematic and layout design of D^2PS12T SRAM cell is shown in Fig. 2(a) and (b) respectively. The D^2PS12T cell consists of two cross-coupled inverters with additional NMOS transistors (M3 & M4), which placed in each inverter pair. The Word Line (WL) and Read Word Line (RWL) are row based connected lines, and Write Word Line A (WWLA), Write Word Line B (WWLB), and Virtual ground (VGND) are column based line. The structural comparison of the different SRAM cell is shown in Table 1 and the status of the control signals used for the D^2PS12T cell is shown in Table 2.

The salient features of the proposed D^2PS12T cell are:

– Stacked combination integrated with pull-down path of inverter pair, which supports to enhance write stability and reduce the leakage power of the cell.

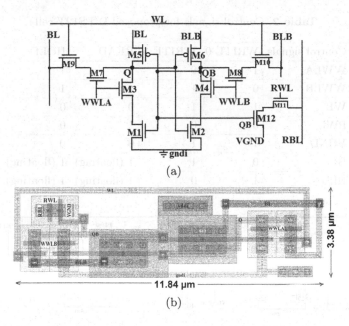

(a)

(b)

Fig. 2. (a) Schematic and (b) Layout of proposed D^2PS12T SRAM cell

- Additional NMOS transistor connected in write access path select the column-wise line which enables bit-interleaving structure and resolve the issue regarding write half select.
- Read decoupling technique is used to resolve the problem of read/write trade-off and to improve the RSNM.
- The data dependent power supply is powered by bit lines (BL and BLB), which is the analogous data of bit lines instead of giving an exclusive supply voltage and hence, it drastically reduces the dynamic power.

When to perform the read operation as shown in Fig. 3(a), two NMOS transistors M11 and M12 play an important role. Initially, all the bit lines (BL, BLB, RBL) are precharged at logic 1, read word line (RWL) is made at logic high, virtual ground (VGND) and word line (WL) are forced to logic low, while the signal WWLA and WWLB are enabled to high. During read 0 operation, when logic 0 and 1 are stored at the storage node Q and QB respectively, the NMOS transistor M12 is activated by the node QB and M11 is also turned ON by the signal RWL. This makes the direct discharging path from RBL to virtual ground node through M11 and M12 transistors. This isolate read path facilitate quick discharge RBL to 0. Similarly, for read 1 operation, the node QB is stored logic 0 which turn OFF the M12 transistor and does not allow to discharge RBL. Hence RBL preserves its precharge value and is sensed by the sense amplifier. Hence the half-select issue is resolved in the D^2PS12T cell.

During the write 0 operation in Fig. 3(b), WL, WWLA and WWLB is at logic 1, 1, and 0 respectively. BL and BLB are set to logic low and high respectively,

Table 2. Control signals for proposed D²PS12T cell

Control signals	WRITE 0	WRITE 1	READ	HOLD
WWLA	1	0	1	1
WWLB	0	1	1	1
WL	1	1	0	0
RWL	0	0	1	0
VGND	1	1	0	0
BL	0	1	1 (floating)	1 (floating)
BLB	1	0	1 (floating)	1 (floating)

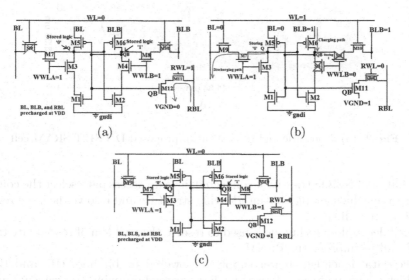

Fig. 3. (a) Read operation, (b) Write 0 operation, (c) Hold operation of D²PS12T SRAM cell

while RWL and VGND signals are connected to 0 and 1 respectively. Due to WWLB is set at logic 0, M4 is cut off and QB gets disconnect from the ground node and BLB is completely charged up the storing node QB through M6 only. This stored logic high value at node QB helps to turn off the transistor M5 and thus discharge the node Q to zero value through the path M7/M9 and M1/M3 and logic 0 is successfully write into the cell. Similarly, for write 1, the operation is same. In the standby mode of D²PS12T cell, WL is disabled, WWLA and WWLB are enabled, RWL remains disabled, VGND is high while RBL, BL, and BLB are precharged to logic 1. The hold condition is operated by assuming logic 0 and 1 at the storage node Q and QB respectively, QB still hold logic 1 through the transistor M6 and thus preserve the stored data and depicted in Fig. 3(c).

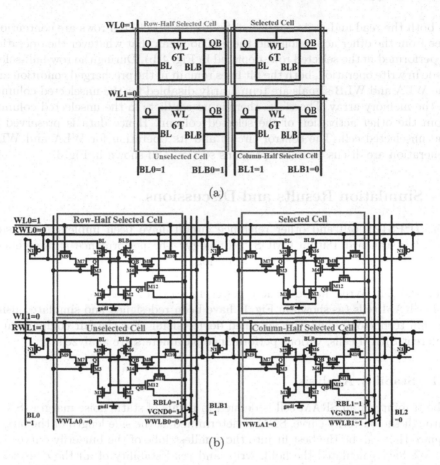

Fig. 4. 2×2 array during write operation (a) 6T cell array (b) D^{2}PS12T cell array

2.1 Half Select Disturbance

The 6T SRAM cells are arranged in the memory array to perform the successful write operation. The WL signal is made high for the selected cell using row decoder circuit and bit lines are forcing to write the corresponding data into the selected cell. However, in this structure, the unselected cells are also placed in the same column of the selected cell, which gets affected by the bit line voltages (WL is low) and thus there is a chance to invert the stored data in the storage node of these unselected cells. This issue is called a column half-select issue. In the same way, the WL signal is enabled the entire row of the selected cell. However, all the access transistors of 6T cell are activated and bit lines of unselected cell are now clamped to high. Thus the unselected cell in the row may distort the stored data. This issue is entitled as row half-select issue [15,16].

To eliminate the column half-select issue in the proposed D^{2}PS12T cell, the RWL signal (row-wise connected) is temporarily made low for all unselected row in both the read and write operation. So all the unselected rows are contention-free from the other activation and there is no mean that whatever the operation is performed in the selected row, depicted in Fig. 4(b). During the row half-select issue in write operation, both the bit lines remain in the precharged condition and the WLA and WLB signals are temporarily disabled for the unselected columns in the memory array. Therefore, there is no conflicts in the unselected columns from the other activation of the selected column. Hence data is preserved in the unselected cell. The control circuit and its operation for WLA and WLB generation are discussed in the previous section and shown in Fig. 3.

3   Simulation Results and Discussions

The D^2PS12T cell and other reference circuit have been implemented using industry standard 180 nm CMOS technology. The performance parameters of D^2PS12T cell is compared with conventional 6T and other cells such as read decoupled 8T [14], PPN10T [10], data-aware write assist (DAWA12T) [12], Kim12T [11], Write improved low power 12T (WILP12T) [8]. All the considered SRAM cells (as shown in Fig. 1) have been redesigned and simulated using 180 nm technology node with specified device sizing. For the fair comparison of different SRAM cells, various performance parameters are analyzed.

3.1   Stability Analysis

The stability of an SRAM cell is defined in terms of static noise margin (SNM) through the butterfly curve. SNM is determined as the side length of the largest square that can be the best fit into the smallest lobe of the butterfly curve [17].

We have calculated the hold, write and read stability of all the considered SRAM cells at 0.4 V supply voltage as shown in Fig. 5. It is observed from result that the WSNM of D^2PS12T cell is 8.66× higher as compared to the standard 6T cell. The increment in WSNM of D^2PS12T cell is due to the data-dependent power supply which is given by bit lines in pull up network. The RSNM of proposed D^2PS12T cell is increased by 3.4× higher as compared to conventional

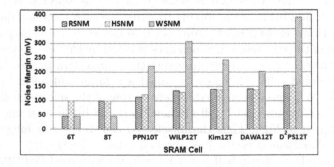

Fig. 5. Noise margin of different SRAM cells

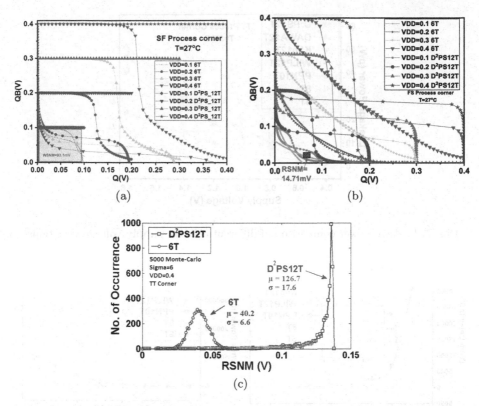

Fig. 6. Comparison of D^2PS12T cell and conventional 6T cell at different VDD (a) for WSNM (b) for RSNM (c) statistical distribution plot of RSNM

6T SRAM cell. The enhancement of RSNM for D^2PS12T cell is due to the presence of separate read decoupled path during read operation. The HSNM of proposed D^2PS12T cell is $1.53\times$ higher than the conventional 6T cell.

Figure 6(a) and (b) show the WSNM and RSNM of 6T and D^2PS12T cell for near threshold and subthreshold operations. The results show that the WSNM and RSNM of 6T cell is unstable below 0.4 V supply voltage whereas the D^2PS12T SRAM cell provides stable result even at the 0.1 V supply voltage and having WSNM of 93.1 mV at worst SF corner and RSNM of 14.71 mV at worst FS corner. Further, Fig. 6(c) shows the Monte-Carlo simulation for process variation analysis on 6T and D^2PS12T cell. From the result, it is observed that the RSNM mean (μ) of D^2PS12T cell is 68.27% higher as compared to 6T cell. Based on the above results, it is concluded that the proposed D^2PS12T cell has less effected from process variation.

3.2 Leakage Power

Leakage power is a major concern in deep submicron transistors. The leakage power of different SRAM cells for supply voltage variation is shown in Fig. 7

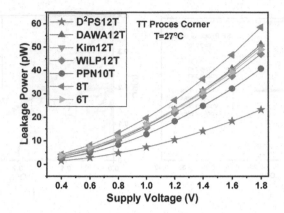

Fig. 7. Leakage power comparison of different cells for supply voltage variations

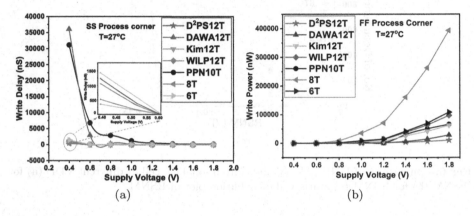

Fig. 8. (a) Write delay at SS process corner, and (b) Write power comparison at FF process corner at different supply voltages

and from result, it is observed that the D^2PS12T cell contributes an exponential reduction in sub-threshold leakage current by 59% as compared to conventional 6T. This enormous amount of reduction is because of the data-dependent power supply and the combination of stacked transistors technique, which are used in the hold state. It is also observed that the leakage power of the other considered cell increases drastically with supply voltage, whereas the D^2PS12T cell shows better resilience against supply variation at TT process corner.

3.3   Write Delay and Power

The time from triggering ON the WL, WWLB and triggering OFF the WWLA, till the storage node Q reaches 90% of maximum supply voltage, that time is known as the write '1' access time. Write '0' access time is defined as the time from triggering ON the WL, WWLA and triggering OFF the WWLB until the

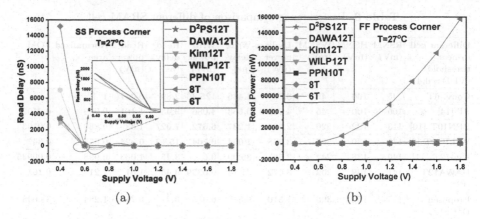

Fig. 9. (a) Read delay at SS process corner, and (b) Read power at FF corner at different supply voltages

storage node Q reaches 10% of the maximum supply voltage. Figure 8(a) shows the write '1' delay of different SRAM cells at various supply voltages. The result indicates that the D^2PS12T cell provides faster speed and 64.27% improvement in delay as compared to the 6T cell because when the write 1 operation is performed, transistors M3 and M7 is in cutoff mode. Hence, the storage node Q is directly charged through the path BL and M5, as explain previous in Sect. 2.

The analysis of write power consumption for different cells is shown in Fig. 8(b). Results show that the D^2PS12T cell consumes the least amount of write power and 99.95% improvement as compared to the 6T cell and other existing cells because of the data-dependent power supply in the circuit. Therefore, the D^2PS12T cell is more power efficient at lower supply voltages.

3.4 Read Delay and Power

Read delay can be calculated as a time difference between the activation of read word line (RWL) and discharging of read bit line by 50 mV from its initial value. Figure 9(a) shows the read speed comparison at different supply voltage for the worst process (SS) corner. From results it is observed that the D^2PS12T cell has faster read performance than that of PPN10T [10], and WILP12T [8] due to lower bit line capacitance and read delay is approximately same as Kim12T [11], read decoupled 8T [5], and DAWA12T [12].

The power analysis of different SRAM cell, during the read operation, is shown in Fig. 9(b). The result shows that the D^2PS12T emphasizes almost the same power consumption for all considered cells except the conventional 6T. The reason behind that the read path is same in all the considered and D^2PS12T cell which causes a same current flow in that path hence the read power is same.

Table 3. Performance comparison of different SRAM cell

Different cell in near threshold (VDD = 0.4)	RSNM (mV)	HSNM (mV)	WSNM (mV)	Leakage power (pW)	Write delay (µs)	Write power (nW)	Read delay (ns)	Read power (nW)	Normalized area	FOM
Conv. 6T	45	100	45	3.78	1.436	125.36	2.89	0.057	1	1
8T [14]	100	100	45	4.252	0.553	4.086	3.45	1.161	0.999	0.0103
PPN10T [10]	113	122	220	2.504	1.237	6.672	7.027	1.33	0.839	0.0103
WILP12T [8]	135	130	307	3.088	1.054	0.704	15.17	0.328	0.855	0.307
Kim12T [11]	140	138	242	3.56	36.09	0.6	3.45	1.063	0.998	0.00935
DAWA12T [12]	141	139	202	3.072	31.14	0.0339	3.45	1.01	1.212	0.161
Proposed D^{2}PS12T	153	153	390	1.516	0.513	0.055	3.4	0.713	1.284	38.048

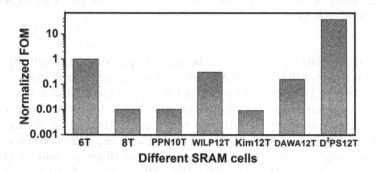

Fig. 10. Figure of merit for different SRAM at 0.4 V supply voltage

3.5   Figure of Merit (FOM)

The figure of merit (FOM) is often defined for a particular device or circuit in order to determine their relative utility and to evaluate their performance for an application. The power consumption, delay, leakage, and area are absolutely reduced and stability is increased in any circuit. Hence, the stability and area are two important parameters for any SRAM cells.

Therefore, a novel FOM is introduced by taking power, delay, leakage, area, and stability into account. For high performance, stable and low power requirement, stability should be as large as possible, and less area overhead is preferable. Here, the proposed figure of merit (FOM) is expressed as:

$$FOM = \frac{SNM_{norm}}{P_{w/r,norm} \times t_{w/r,norm} \times P_{l,norm} \times A_{norm}} \tag{1}$$

Where, SNM_{norm}, $P_{w/r,norm}$, $t_{w/r,norm}$ $P_{l,norm}$ and A_{norm} are the normalized values of stability (product of read, write and hold stability), power (product of write and read), circuit delay (product of write and read) and estimated area, respectively. Figure 10 shows the FOM for different circuits at 0.4 V supply voltage. From the results, it is also observed that the FOM of D^2PS12T cell is $38.048\times$ higher than the conventional 6T cell.

For the fair analysis, a comprehensive comparison of the D^2PS12T cell with the other state-of-art memory cell is given in Table 3. The table shows the results in the near-threshold region, where the supply voltage is 0.4 V is efficient for the low energy efficient application [18].

4 Conclusion

This paper presents a robust proposed subthreshold 12T SRAM cell which is write assist, low power and data dependent power supply. The D^2PS12T cell achieves high read and write stability of 14.71 mV and 93.1 mV respectively against the unstable read and write SNM of 6T cell at 0.1 V of the supply voltage at the respective worst process corners. The D^2PS12T circuit also offers the lowest leakage power of 1.51 pW, the smallest write delay of 513 ns, and the smallest read delay of 3.4 ns against other circuits at 0.4 V supply voltage. To put things into better outlook, we initiate the figure of merit (FOM) as compound performance merit. Our analysis indicated that the proposed cell has $38.048\times$ higher FOM as compared to the conventional 6T SRAM cell and it is high enough as compared to other considered cells. Therefore, the proposed circuit would be more suitable for stable, power efficient, and high-performance applications.

Acknowledgment. The authors would like to thank Special Manpower Development Program for Chips to System Design (SMDP-C2SD) research project of Department of Electronics and Information technology (DeitY) under Ministry of Communication and Information Technology, Government of India to provide the lab facilities.

References

1. Calhoun, B.H., Chandrakasan, A.P.: Static noise margin variation for sub-threshold SRAM in 65-nm CMOS. IEEE J. Solid-State Circuits **41**(7), 1673–1679 (2006)
2. Chuang, C.T., Mukhopadhyay, S., Kim, J.J., Kim, K., Rao, R.: High-performance SRAM in nanoscale CMOS: design challenges and techniques. In: IEEE International Workshop on Memory Technology, Design and Testing, MTDT 2007, pp. 4–12. IEEE (2007)
3. Kursun, V., Friedman, E.G.: Multi-voltage CMOS Circuit Design. Wiley, New York (2006)
4. Wen, L., Li, Z., Li, Y.: Single-ended, robust 8T SRAM cell for low-voltage operation. Microelectron. J. **44**(8), 718–728 (2013)
5. Kushwah, C., Vishvakarma, S.K.: A single-ended with dynamic feedback control 8T subthreshold SRAM cell. IEEE Trans. Very Large Scale Integr. (VLSI) Syst. **24**(1), 373–377 (2016)
6. Chang, I.J., Kim, J.J., Park, S.P., Roy, K.: A 32 kb 10T subthreshold SRAM array with bit-interleaving and differential read scheme in 90 nm CMOS. In: IEEE International Solid-State Circuits Conference, ISSCC 2008. Digest of Technical Papers, pp. 388–622. IEEE (2008)

7. Sharma, V., Gopal, M., Singh, P., Vishvakarma, S.K.: A 220 mV robust read-decoupled partial feedback cutting based low-leakage 9T SRAM for Internet of Things (IoT) applications. AEU-Int. J. Electron. Commun. **87**, 144–157 (2018)
8. Sharma, V., Vishvakarma, S.K., Chouhan, S.S., Halonen, K.: A write-improved low-power 12T SRAM cell for wearable wireless sensor nodes. Int. J. Circuit Theory Appl. **46**, 2314–2333 (2018)
9. Ahmad, S., Gupta, M.K., Alam, N., Hasan, M.: Single-ended Schmitt-trigger-based robust low-power SRAM cell. IEEE Trans. Very Large Scale Integr. (VLSI) Syst. **24**(8), 2634–2642 (2016)
10. Lo, C.H., Huang, S.Y.: PPN based 10T SRAM cell for low-leakage and resilient subthreshold operation. IEEE J. Solid-State Circuits **46**(3), 695–704 (2011)
11. Kim, J., Mazumder, P.: A robust 12T SRAM cell with improved write margin for ultra-low power applications in 40 nm CMOS. Integr. VLSI J. **57**, 1–10 (2017)
12. Chiu, Y.W., et al.: 40 nm bit-interleaving 12T subthreshold SRAM with data-aware write-assist. IEEE Trans. Circuits Syst. I Regul. Pap. **61**(9), 2578–2585 (2014)
13. Kulkarni, J.P., Roy, K.: Ultralow-voltage process-variation-tolerant schmitt-trigger-based SRAM design. IEEE Trans. VLSI Syst. **20**(2), 319–332 (2012)
14. Chang, L., et al.: Stable SRAM cell design for the 32 nm node and beyond. In: 2005 Symposium on VLSI Technology. Digest of Technical Papers, pp. 128–129. IEEE (2005)
15. Sharma, V., Gopal, M., Singh, P., Vishvakarma, S.K., Chouhan, S.S.: A robust, ultra low-power, data-dependent-power-supplied 11T SRAM cell with expanded read/write stabilities for internet-of-things applications. Analog Integr. Circuits Signal Process. **98**(2), 331–346 (2019)
16. Ahmad, S., Iqbal, B., Alam, N., Hasan, M.: Low leakage fully half-select-free robust SRAM cells with BTI reliability analysis. IEEE Trans. Device Mater. Reliab. **18**(3), 337–349 (2018)
17. Seevinck, E., List, F.J., Lohstroh, J.: Static-noise margin analysis of MOS SRAM cells. IEEE J. Solid-State Circuits **22**(5), 748–754 (1987)
18. van Santen, V.M., Martin-Martinez, J., Amrouch, H., Nafria, M.M., Henkel, J.: Reliability in super-and near-threshold computing: a unified model of rtn, bti, and pv. IEEE Trans. Circuits Syst. I Regul. Pap. **65**(1), 293–306 (2018)

Low Leakage Highly Stable Robust Ultra Low Power 8T SRAM Cell

Neha Gupta[1], Tanisha Gupta[2], Sajid Khan[1], Abhinav Vishwakarma[1], and Santosh Kumar Vishvakarma[1(✉)]

[1] Nanoscale Devices, VLSI Circuit and System Design Lab,
Discipline of Electrical Engineering, Indian Institute of Technology Indore,
Indore 453552, M.P., India
{phd1701202008,phd1601102015,abhinavvishvakarma,
skvishvakarma}@iiti.ac.in
[2] School of Electronics, Devi Ahilya Vishwavidyalaya,
Indore 452001, M.P., India
ttanisha.gupta2512@gmail.com

Abstract. This paper presents a new ultra low power 8T SRAM cell with data dependent power supply circuit with read decoupled technique to enhance the read stability and sleep transistor is used to reduce the leakage power at the low supply voltage. The data dependent circuit reduces the dynamic power and enhances the write ability drastically. The area penalty is also very less due to the absence of access transistor. As compared with the 6T SRAM cell, the proposed cell offers 3.13%, 89.56%, and 68.35% higher write, read and hold stability respectively at 0.4 V supply voltage. Our evaluation indicates that the leakage and read power of the proposed cell is reduced by 98.75% and 99.74% respectively as compared to the conventional 6T cell and read delay and write PDP is reduced by 63.41% and 88.17%, respectively as compared to 6T cell. For a better perspective of the proposed cell, a compound stability to energy ratio has been introduced and it is found that the SER of proposed cell has very high as compared to 6T SRAM cell. All the implementations have been performed using the industry standard 65 nm CMOS technology.

Keywords: SRAM · Leakage power · Data dependent circuit · Stability-energy-ratio · PDP

1 Introduction

With the ever-increasing demand of storage, the scaling of silicon technology has been carried out continuously due to which larger memory can be fabricated on a single chip so that huge amount of data can be stored and retrieved at high speed [1]. As the device density of system increases, the number of transistor also increases which results in power dissipation, so there is a need to design low power, high-performance storage unit. Semiconductor memories are the most

© Springer Nature Singapore Pte Ltd. 2019
A. Sengupta et al. (Eds.): VDAT 2019, CCIS 1066, pp. 643–654, 2019.
https://doi.org/10.1007/978-981-32-9767-8_53

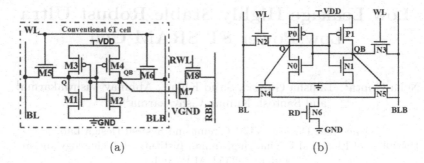

(a)   (b)

Fig. 1. Different SRAM structure: (a) Read decoupled 8T [9] (b) Differential 9T [12]

important subsystem of the modern digital system [2]. SRAM is a form of random access memory in which the data is held statically that means the data is stored in the memory without any periodic refreshment as long as power is supplied to the memory. SRAM has become the main constituent in many VLSI chips due to their large storage density, low power consumption, and high speed [3]. SRAM is widely used as a cache memory in microprocessor, digital signal processors and also used as both on-chip and off-chip memories in various handheld devices, laptops, notebooks because they are battery powered portable devices so they must consume a smallest possible amount of power. When the memory is used as an on-chip cache it must be reliable and stable. It should have high performance and low power consumption [4,5].

However, the conventional 6T SRAM cell is constructed using six transistors that is a very simple structure and it suffers from many problems like read disturb, half-select issue, read current interruption and noise margin reduction with supply voltage scaling. Moreover, the threshold voltage swings caused by variation of different local and global processes, the rapid degradation has found in the read and write stability of 6T SRAM cell with supply voltage variation. Further, it is exacerbated by conflicting the read/write storage data due to undesirable charging/discharging of node voltage [6].

To overcome the read/write conflict and enhance the read stability [7,8], a read decoupled circuit is proposed in the literature [9] as shown in Fig. 1(a), but it has some limitation in terms of leakage power and stability [10,11] which is overcome by the new architecture that is also proposed in the literature named as differential 9T cell [12], as shown in Fig. 1(b).

To apply all the above issues in a single topology, we propose a new ultra low power 8T SRAM cell. The proposed 8T cell is referred as the "ULP8T" hereafter. The ULP8T cell has not affected by the lower supply voltage and has negligible leakage power consumption of 98.75% as compared to conventional 6T cell and read power of the ULP8T cell is 98.74% which is much larger than the other existing cells.

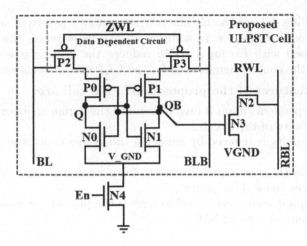

Fig. 2. Proposed ultra low power 8T (ULP8T) SRAM cell

Table 1. Control signals for proposed ULP8T cell

Control signals	WRITE 0	WRITE 1	READ	HOLD
RWL	0	0	1	0
VGND	1	1	0	1
ZWL	0	0	0	0
En	1	1	1	0
BL	0	1	1 (floating)	1 (floating)
BLB	1	0	1 (floating)	1 (floating)

The organization of the rest of the paper is as follows: in Sect. 2, we discuss the operation of the proposed 8T SRAM cell. Section 3 explains the simulation results and discussions followed by the conclusion in Sect. 4.

2   Proposed 8T SRAM Cell

The schematic architecture of proposed 8T SRAM cell is shown in Fig. 2. It consists of a latch circuit (P0-P1-N0-N1), where P0 and P1 are the pull-up PMOS transistors, N0 and N1 are the pull-down NMOS transistors, and N3 and N4 make a read decoupled circuit. The proposed cell consists of two additional data dependent PMOS switches (P2 and P3) which are placed between the bit line pair and pull up transistors, instead of using an external power supply and controlled by a ZWL control signal. The data dependent PMOS transistors is used in place of external power supply with drastically reduces the dynamic power and also enhance the write ability. These transistors also used as a access transistor which reduces the write delay and area as compared to conventional 6T cell. In this way, the data dependent power supply strategy works in which the corresponding data of the bit line pair is used as a source of supply voltage for the cross-coupled inverter. In addition of PMOS switches, one NMOS sleep transistor is used with En input which reduces the leakage power of the cell. The status of the control signals used for the ULP8T cell is shown in Table 1.

The salient features of the proposed ULP8T cell are:

- The data dependent circuit is used to reduced the dynamic power and enhance the write ability of the circuit.
- The area penalty is reduced by removing the access transistor from the proposed cell.
- Extra NMOS sleep transistor is used to form virtual ground (V_GND) node which reduces the leakage power.
- Read decoupling technique is used to resolve the problem of read/write tradeoff and to improve the RSNM.

2.1   Read Operation

When to perform the read operation, the major role played by the NMOS transistors (N2 and N3). Initially, all the bit lines (BL, BLB, RBL) are precharged at logic 1, read word line (RWL) is made at logic high, while virtual ground (VGND) are forced to logic low. During read 0 operation, when logic 0 and 1 are stored at the storage node Q and QB respectively, the NMOS transistor N3 is activated by the node QB and N2 is also turned ON by the signal RWL. This makes the direct discharging path from RBL to VGND node through N2 and N3 transistors. This make sure that the quick discharge path from RBL to 0. Similarly, for read 1 operation, the node QB is stored logic 0 which turn OFF the N3 transistor and does not allow to discharge RBL. Hence RBL preserves its precharge value and is sensed by the sense amplifier. Hence the half-select issue is resolved in the ULP8T cell.

2.2   Write Operation

During write 1 operation the BL and BLB are set to logic 1 and logic 0, the RWL and VGND are kept at 0 and 1 respectively. The PMOS transistors P2 and P3 turn on due to low ZWL. Initially, the Q and QB are at logic 0 and 1 respectively. The node voltage QB is quick discharge through P1 and P3. Similarly, write 1 operation is performed.

2.3   Hold Operation

In conventional 6T SRAM cell, the leakage power is very high due to non-availability of virtual ground. In proposed ULP8T cell, the sleep N4 transistor is used to cutoff the connection between supply to ground node and connect the circuit with virtual ground terminal which is controlled by an external signal EN during hold operation. The low EN signal turns off the N4 sleep transistor which drastically reduced the leakage power. Due to absence of access transistor, there is direct path or no chance to flip the stored data in the cell, therefore the hold stability of the proposed ULP8T is also high.

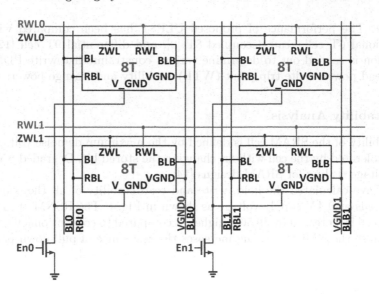

Fig. 3. Array arrangement of proposed ULP8T cell architecture

2.4 Half Select Issue

The 6T SRAM cells arranged in any memory array to perform the successful write operation. The WL signal is made high for the selected cell using row decoder circuit and bit lines are forcing to write the corresponding data into the selected cell. However, in this structure, the unselected cells are also placed in the same column of the selected cell, which gets affected by the bit line voltages (WL is low) and thus there is a chance to invert the stored data in the storage node of these unselected cells. This issue is called a column half-select issue. In the same way, the WL signal is enabled the entire row of the selected cell. However, all the access transistors of 6T cell are activated and bit lines of unselected cell are now clamped to high. Thus the unselected cell in the row may distort the stored data. This issue is entitled as row half-select issue [5,13].

To eliminate the half-select issue, Bit line sharing architecture is proposed. In this array, row wise signals are ZWL and RWL and column wise signals are VGND and En as shown in Fig. 3. In write operation, ZWL and En signal is logic 0 and 1 respectively for the selected cell in the array and reserved logic for the unselected cells. Further in the read operation, RWL and VGND signal is logic high and low, respectively for the selection of cell and disabled these signals for non-working condition. In such manner, the half select issue is completely resolved by using proposed ULP8T cell.

3 Simulation Results and Discussions

The proposed ULP8T SRAM cell and other existing cell have been redesigned and implemented using a industry standard 65 nm CMOS technology as shown in Fig. 1. The performance of proposed ULP8T has been compared with the conventional 6T cell, read decoupled 8T [9], and differential 9T cell [12]. The simulation is carried out to determine various constraints like write PDP, read delay, read power, write trip point (WTP), stability and leakage power.

3.1 Stability Analysis

The stability of the SRAM cell is defined by the maximum dc noise voltage that can be tolerated by the cell without changing the stored bit. Degraded SNM can limit voltage scaling for SRAM designs [14].

We have calculated the hold, write and read stability of all the considered SRAM cells at 0.4 V supply voltage as shown in Fig. 4. The RSNM of proposed ULP8T cell is increased by 89.56% higher as compared to conventional 6T SRAM cell because the NMOS stacking increases the resistance of pull-down path and therefore switching voltage of inverter increases which results in larger lobe formation in read butterfly curve, due to the presence of separate read decoupled path during read mode and hence read stability increases. The HSNM of proposed ULP8T cell is 68.35% higher than the conventional 6T cell due to absence of the access transistor and less chance to flip the stored data. It is observed from result that the WSNM of ULP8T cell is 3.13% higher as compared to the standard 6T cell. The proposed cell has better write ability due to the absence of an external power supply. The inverter is powered by BL and BLB with the help of P2 and P3 PMOS devices and ZWL control signal. Based on the above results, it is concluded that the proposed ULP8T cell has less effected from process variation.

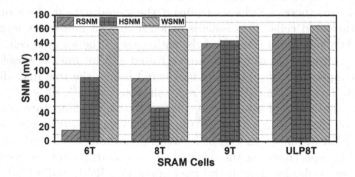

Fig. 4. Noise margin of different SRAM cells at 0.4 V supply voltage

3.2 Leakage Power

The leakage power is a major factor to concern because at most of the time the cell is in standby mode. Leakage power of different SRAM cell at various supply voltage is shown in Fig. 5(a). From result, it is observed that the ULP8T cell contributes an exponential reduction in sub-threshold leakage current by 98.75% as compared to conventional 6T cell. This enormous amount of reduction is due to the sleep N4 transistor, which is cutoff the connection between supply to ground node and connect the circuit with virtual ground terminal. Figure 5(b) shows the comparison of 6T cell with proposed ULP8T cell at various supply voltage and temperature and shows the proposed ULP8T cell has lesser than conventional 6T cell.

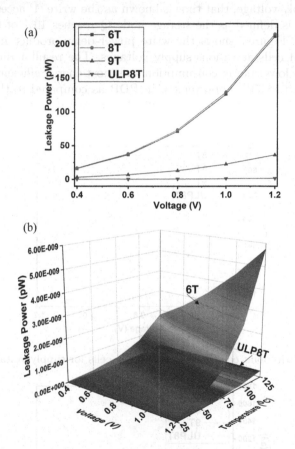

Fig. 5. Leakage power comparison (a) Different SRAM cells for supply voltage variations and (b) Comparison of conventional 6T cell and proposed ULP8T cell at different supply voltage and temperature variations

3.3   Write Trip Point

Write trip point is one more special factor to define the write ability of the SRAM cell, it is determined as the difference between supply voltage and WL values at which storage node flips its value which is to be written into the cell. Figure 6 shows the write trip point at different supply voltage variation, which exhibits that significantly higher WTP value of 21.75% as compared to 6T cell due to data dependent circuitry.

3.4   Write Power-Delay-Product

The time from triggering OFF the ZWL, till the storage node Q reaches 90% of maximum supply voltage, that time is known as the write '1' access time. Write '0' access time is defined as the storage node Q reaches 10% of the maximum supply voltage. Figure 7 shows the write power-delay-product means PDP of different SRAM cells at various supply voltages. The result indicates that the ULP8T cell has lower power consumption and most energy efficient as compared to other cell and 88.71% improvement in PDP as compared to the 6T cell due to the cause of data dependent circuit which is powered by bit lines.

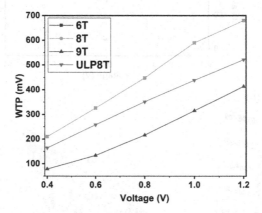

Fig. 6. Write trip point comparison of different cells for supply voltage variations

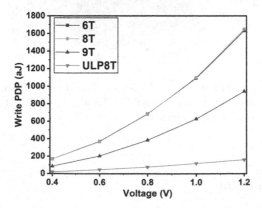

Fig. 7. Write power-delay product (PDP) at different supply voltage

3.5 Read Delay and Power

Read delay can be calculated as a time difference between the activation of read word line (RWL) and discharging of read bit line by 50 mV from its initial value. Figure 8(a) and (b) shows the read power and delay comparison of different SRAM cell at various supply voltage. From results it is observed that the ULP8T cell has the lowest power that is 98.74% and faster read performance of 63.42% as compared to 6T cell due to lower bit line capacitance and separate read path circuitry.

3.6 Stability to Energy Ratio (SER)

Stability to energy ratio (SER) is often defined for a particular device or circuit in order to determine their relative utility and to evaluate their performance for an application. The power consumption, delay, and leakage are absolutely reduced and stability is increased in any circuit. Hence, the stability and energy are two important parameters for any SRAM cells. Here, the proposed stability to energy ratio is expressed as:

$$SER = \frac{SNM_{norm}}{PDP_{write,norm} \times PDP_{read,norm} \times P_{leak,norm}} \tag{1}$$

Where, SNM_{norm}, $PDP_{write,norm}$, $PDP_{read,norm}$, and $P_{leak,norm}$ are the normalized values of stability (product of read, write and hold stability), power delay product in write case, and power delay product in read case, respectively. Figure 9 shows the SER for different circuits at 0.4 V supply voltage. From the results, it is also observed that the SER of ULP8T cell is very high as compared to other considered cell. The main factor involved is the leakage power for increasing the value of SER.

For the fair analysis, a comprehensive comparison of the ULP8T cell with the other state-of-art memory cell is given in Table 2. The table shows the results in

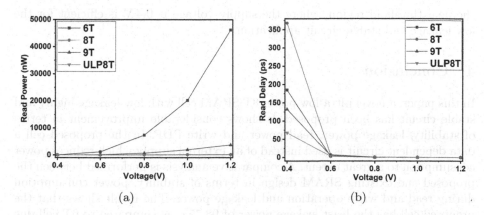

(a)   (b)

Fig. 8. (a) Read power and (b) Read delay, of different cells at different supply voltage

Table 2. Performance comparison of different SRAM cell

Different cell at near threshold (VDD = 0.4)	6T	8T [9]	9T [12]	Proposed ULP9T
Write0 PDP (aJ)	160.21	194.39	27.63	21.422
Write1 PDP (aJ)	169.12	168.43	85.78	20
Read delay (ps)	185	368	132.1	67.67
Read power (nW)	5.03	4.67	2.41	0.064
Leakage power (pW)	16.15	16.67	3.17	0.22
WTP (mV)	210	210	78.52	164.3
RSNM (mV)	16	90	139.6	153.2
WSNM (mV)	160	160	163.8	165
HSNM (mV)	91	48	143.7	153.2
Area (μm)	103.17	118	79.8	64.8
SER	1	1.56	414.84	2462171

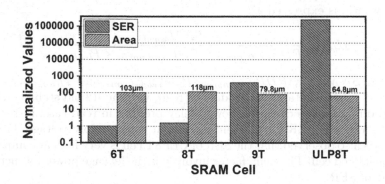

Fig. 9. Normalized value of SER and cell area for different cells

the near-threshold region, where the supply voltage is 0.4 V is efficient for the low leakage and stable circuit application.

4   Conclusion

In this paper, a novel ultra-low power 8T SRAM cell with low leakage highly and stable circuit has been proposed. It shows considerable improvement in terms of stability, leakage power, read power and write PDP. In the proposed cell a data dependent circuit is used instead of an external supply which reduces power consumption to a great extent. A comparative analysis is performed between the proposed and existing SRAM design in terms of stability, power consumption during read and write operation and leakage power. The result shows that the proposed cell has the least leakage power of 98.75% as compared to 6T cell due to the presence of stacking effect and sleep transistor connected at bottom of the cell. The proposed cell is also better in the context of SNM, therefore the cell is more stable even at the subthreshold region as compared to other cells. Further, we initiate the stability to energy ratio (SER) as new compound performance parameter, which indicate the overall performance of the proposed ULP8T cell is very high as compared to other cells. Hence, the proposed cell is significantly used in the applications where low power, low leakage, and highly stable cell is required.

Acknowledgment. The authors would like to thank Special Manpower Development Program for Chips to System Design (SMDP-C2SD) research project of Department of Electronics and Information technology (DeitY) under Ministry of Communication and Information Technology, Government of India to provide the lab facilities.

References

1. Calhoun, B.H., Chandrakasan, A.P.: Static noise margin variation for sub-threshold SRAM in 65-nm CMOS. IEEE J. Solid-State Circuits **41**(7), 1673–1679 (2006)
2. Chuang, C.T., Mukhopadhyay, S., Kim, J.J., Kim, K., Rao, R.: High-performance SRAM in nanoscale CMOS: design challenges and techniques. In: IEEE International Workshop on Memory Technology, Design and Testing, MTDT 2007, pp. 4–12. IEEE (2007)
3. Kursun, V., Friedman, E.G.: Multi-voltage CMOS Circuit Design. Wiley, New York (2006)
4. Gupta, N., Parihar, P., Neema, V.: Application of source biasing technique for energy efficient DECODER circuit design: memory array application. J. Semicond. **39**(4), 045001 (2018)
5. Ahmad, S., Iqbal, B., Alam, N., Hasan, M.: Low leakage fully half-select-free robust SRAM cells with BTI reliability analysis. IEEE Trans. Device Mater. Reliab. **18**(3), 337–349 (2018)
6. Wen, L., Li, Z., Li, Y.: Single-ended, robust 8T SRAM cell for low-voltage operation. Microelectron. J. **44**(8), 718–728 (2013)
7. Kushwah, C., Vishvakarma, S.K.: A single-ended with dynamic feedback control 8T subthreshold SRAM cell. IEEE Trans. Very Large Scale Integr. (VLSI) Syst. **24**(1), 373–377 (2016)
8. Chang, I.J., Kim, J.J., Park, S.P., Roy, K.: A 32 kb 10T subthreshold SRAM array with bit-interleaving and differential read scheme in 90 nm CMOS. In: IEEE International Solid-State Circuits Conference, ISSCC 2008. Digest of Technical Papers, pp. 388–622. IEEE (2008)
9. Chang, L., et al.: Stable SRAM cell design for the 32 nm node and beyond. In: 2005 Symposium on VLSI Technology. Digest of Technical Papers, pp. 128–129. IEEE (2005)
10. Sharma, V., Vishvakarma, S.K., Chouhan, S.S., Halonen, K.: A write-improved low-power 12T SRAM cell for wearable wireless sensor nodes. Int. J. Circuit Theory Appl. **46**, 2314–2333 (2018)
11. Sharma, V., Gopal, M., Singh, P., Vishvakarma, S.K.: A 220 mV robust read-decoupled partial feedback cutting based low-leakage 9T SRAM for Internet of Things (IoT) applications. AEU-Int. J. Electron. Commun. **87**, 144–157 (2018)

12. Liu, Z., Kursun, V.: High read stability and low leakage cache memory cell. In: 2007 IEEE International Symposium on Circuits and Systems, pp. 2774–2777. IEEE (2007)
13. Sharma, V., Gopal, M., Singh, P., Vishvakarma, S.K., Chouhan, S.S.: A robust, ultra low-power, data-dependent-power-supplied 11T SRAM cell with expanded read/write stabilities for internet-of-things applications. Analog Integr. Circuits Signal Process. **98**(2), 331–346 (2019)
14. Seevinck, E., List, F.J., Lohstroh, J.: Static-noise margin analysis of MOS SRAM cells. IEEE J. Solid-State Circuits **22**(5), 748–754 (1987)

Compact Spiking Neural Network System with SiGe Based Cylindrical Tunneling Transistor for Low Power Applications

Ankur Beohar[1], Gopal Raut[1], Gunjan Rajput[1], Abhinav Vishwakarma[1],
Ambika Prasad Shah[2], Bhupendra Singh Renewal[3],
and Santosh Kumar Vishvakarma[1(✉)]

[1] Nanoscale Devices, VLSI Circuit and System Design Lab,
Discipline of Electrical Engineering, Indian Institute of Technology Indore,
Indore 453552, M.P., India
{ankurbeohar,1701102005,1601102014,abhinavvishwakarma,
skvishwakarma}@iiti.ac.in
[2] Institute for Microelectronics, TU Wien, Vienna, Austria
ambika_shah@rediffmail.com
[3] Senior Product Development Engineer, UST Global, Bayan Lepas, Malaysia
gs.bhupendra@gmail.com

Abstract. In this paper, the spiking neural network has been implemented by using 3D tunneling device based on SiGe as a source for circuit applications. Here, Device circuit co-design investigations have been made in terms of device characteristics and circuit parameters using Synopsys 3D TCAD software and HSPICE simulation. The implemented circuit minimizes the spiking time with the help of tunneling transistors. The proposed tunneling device use the merits of low band gap material such as SiGe, used as a material in the source region with low spacer width, reduces the depletion of the fringing field over source gate edge, leads to high (I_{ON}). Whereas, drain underlap increases the drain channel resistance, and significantly reduces leakage current (I_{OFF}). The spiking neural network circuit has been simulated by applying the test signal at the excitatory input to the benchmark circuit and observe the output response at the inhibitory node, it has a quick response and efficient spiking pulse train with negligible leakage current.

Keywords: Analog integrated circuits · Annihilation ·
Action-potential · Spiking neuron network · Threshold point

1 Introduction

The conventional VLSI era applications and neural system originated from MOS transistors have faced with fundamental physical limit and reflect the degradation in terms of cost and performances. Recently in [1], a neuromorphic system inspired by the neuron system has been developed. Numerical simulation is one

A. Sengupta et al. (Eds.): VDAT 2019, CCIS 1066, pp. 655–663, 2019.
https://doi.org/10.1007/978-981-32-9767-8_54

of the vast suitable technique used for the modeling of artificial spiking neural networks (SNN). Physical model is an uncommon implementation technique, which rise to the evolution application of an analog VLSI neural network. In this model, important physiological quantities such as the membrane potential, should be assigned as an equivalent physical quantity. Presently, VLSI is one of the physical system with which it is feasible to model a neural circuit. Previously, some implementations of neurons and synapses have been reported [2,3]. In these works, speed was not a primarily motivation but the continuous-time behavior.

The technique presented in this paper focuses on an analog VLSI architecture as the starting point of a innovative fast process, continuous-time neural model that could perform digital simulations. The recent research is focusing on the various implementation of efficient SNNs development. The implementation can be classified according to the kind of synaptic devices used. In case of the MOSFET-based synapse, its multiple different terminals could be implement to emulate the behavior of neuron cell, but it has higher power dissipation and low charge transport as the technology node shrinks [4,5]. The SNN require less delay for the neural network system, so contemporary CMOS device is not that much efficient. On replacing CMOS with tunneling transistor, the efficiency in terms of power, the delay has been increased manifolds.

In particular, the Conventional MOSFET has a scaling limit [6], due to its sub-threshold slope (SS) limited to 60 mV/decade at room temperature governed by thermionic emission over a thermal barrier. With the technology scaling, speed and leakage power are the two major issues in the low power circuit applications. As an alternative to the earlier system based on conventional MOSFET, the transistors based on interband tunneling are the most demandable to achieve high speed, high density, and low power. The TFET (Tunnel field effect transistor) operation is based on BTBT (Band to Band tunneling), i.e. flow of drain current in n-channel-TFET through tunneling of electrons from valence-band of the source to the conduction band of the channel region. TFET's carrier movement owing ballistic transport because electrons travel in a well mannered without mutual scattering to each other. Therefore, it possesses the special properties of high immunity to short channel effects (SCEs), and temperature effect when compared to other conventional device [7].

The rest of the paper is organized as follows: Sect. 2 describe the device model and simulation result. Section 3 presents the neuron circuit model implementation. Section 4 describes the simulation results and discussion of proposed device based neuron circuit architecture followed by the conclusion in Sect. 5.

2   SiGe Based Synaptic Tunneling Transistor

Previously, we have proposed a 3D Cylindrical GAA Tunnel FET based on Si and Ge source with reliability concern [8–10]. However, the pure Ge on Si, the crystal relaxes immediately forming huge dislocation networks and may destroy the TFET performances. Therefore, in this work, we have proposed a circuit based on our extended work of cylindrical device with a SiGe source as a low bandgap material to support the ease of fabrication. GAA-TFET is the ideal device architecture to achieve the highest degree of electrostatic control of the gate over the channel. Here, the proposed device of low bandgap material with SiGe for the SNN. It produces the improved performances of neural circuit applications due to low fringing field effects with high BTBT rate and high drain channel resistance caused by drain underlap.

Further, the hetero-gate dielectric approach was also employed for the improved device performance, Although limited to analyze the impact of hetero-spacer on the GAA Tunnel FET. In addition to this, Anghel et al. and Chattopadhyay et al. analyzed that low-k spacer with high-k gate dielectric are significant for high ON current [11,12]. However, the work was limited in further analysis of spacer engineering. Please note that spacers are insulator required for isolation to prevent carrier leakage over the gate edge, and thus the structure based on SiGe with the placement of optimized spacer plays an essential role in high BTBT across the source-channel junction with non-depletion of the source/drain fringing field towards the edge of the gate. We know that Pure Ge on Si, the crystal relaxes immediately forming huge dislocation networks destroying the performance of the pin body of the TFET.

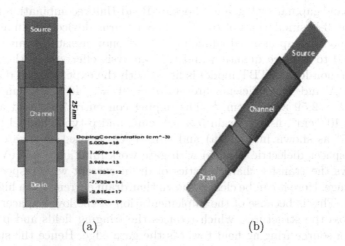

Fig. 1. Device design and 3D view of asymmetrical under-lap (AU) Cyl-GAA Tunnel FET based on SiGe-source with low spacer width (LSW). (a) Cross-sectional view, and (b) 3-D view of the proposed device along channel length direction with magnitude of electron current density and doping concentrations. The device with S-Source, D-Drain, and C-Channel having $L_D = 40$ nm, $L_S = 40$ nm, and $L_{ch} = 30$ nm represents the drain, source and channel length respectively. Here, gate length $(L_G) = 25$ nm, spacer width $(L_{sw}) = 15$ nm, Radius $(R) = 7$ nm, oxide thickness $(t_{ox}) = 2$ nm are used.

The physical models comprise the device simulation based on BTBT are Kanes model, Schenk model, HURKX BTBT model, and the dynamic non-local

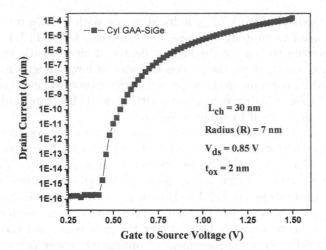

Fig. 2. Transfer characteristics of drain current with respect to gate source voltage for the proposed device.

BTBT. Here, non-local BTBT model is included combined with field-dependent mobility, band gap narrowing, and Shockley-Read-Hall recombination model [13] at 300 K via 3-D simulations of the TCAD Sentaurus device [14] In addition, e-quantum model, trap assisted tunneling and phonon assisted tunneling model are included to analyze quantum and trap analysis effects over the optimized device. The non-local BTBT model is fitted with the experimental data of [15]. The fitted A and B coefficients are $A_{path} = A = 1.46 \times 10^{17}\,\mathrm{cm^{-3}s^{-1}}$ and $B_{path} = B = 2.59 \times 10^6\,\mathrm{V\,cm^{-1}}$. The doping concentrations used are P-type source $1 \times 10^{19}\,\mathrm{cm^3}$, n-type drain $5 \times 10^{17}\,\mathrm{cm^3}$, and p-type channel region $1 \times 10^{18}\,\mathrm{V\,cm^{-1}}$ as shown in Fig. 1(a) and (b). HfO_2 is used as a gate dielectric as well as spacer dielectric (k = 25) with gate work function = 4.53 eV. Further, Fig. 2 shows the transfer characteristics of drain current with respect to gate-source voltage. Here it can be clearly shown that drain current has a high value of 1.67 A/um. This is because of the implementation of the low-k spacer and SiGe source across the structures, which reduces the fringing fields and prevent the depletion of source fringing field towards the gate edge. Hence the suppression of the depletion field results to the high band to band tunneling at the source channel region of the device surface. Consequently, it increases the drain current that flows through the device.

Here in this work, we have developed a Verilog-A device model for the proposed device. The Verilog-A model used herein is comprised of look-up tables tabulating I_{DS} (V_{GS} and V_{DS}), I_{GS} (V_{GS} and V_{DS}), C_{GS} (V_{GS} and V_{DS}), and C_{GD} (V_{GS} and V_{DS}) characteristics of the Cyl GAA-TFET based on SiGe source within the working bias range investigated in this paper. Using this custom Verilog-A model, we performed the circuit analysis using HSPICE circuit simulator.

3 Neuron Circuit Model Implementation

The neuron cell circuit inspired by the biological model as shown in Fig. 3. The biological neuron contains many functions by different cell body (soma), dendrites, synapse, and a single axon. An action (activation) potential triggers the pre-synaptic neuron to release neurotransmitters. These molecules bind to receptors on the post-synaptic cell and make it more or less likely to fire an action potential. People thought that signaling across a synapse involved the flow of sodium and potassium ions, that directly flow from one neuron into another neuron [16].

The membrane potential V is governed by the following differential equation [17]:

$$c_a \frac{dV}{dt} = g_a(V - E_l) + \sum_k p_k(t) \, g_k(V - E_{exi})$$
$$+ \sum_l p_l(t) \, g_l(V - E_{inh})$$

From the above equation right-hand term indicates the current by an individual to the total activation current, which is calculated by derivative of activation potential generated by sodium and potassium ions multiplied by a constant c_a then the contribution of ions will determine the potential E_l. The activation function gets high when no other inputs are present. The unlike reversal potentials E_{inh} and E_{exi} are used by the synapses to model inhibitory and excitatory ion channels. The first sum runs overall excitatory synapses while the index l in the second represents the inhibitory ones. The synapses controlled by the parameter $p_{k,l(t)}$ for individual activation. Although the variation in g_k and g_l will help for plasticity in membrane activation. The synaptic weight $weight_{k,l}(t)$ present the synaptic strength relatively at a given time t.

$$g_{k,l}(t) = weight_{k,l}(t) \cdot g_{max \, k,l} \tag{1}$$

The conventional transistors of the circuit is replaced by the proposed device and analysis the comparison for current driven by the simple neuron cell. Here, The circuit implementation is based on current driven simple neuron cell with the application based W/L variation. The biological neuron contains soma, which initiates the electronic reaction by an external stimulus. The circuit behavior is observed by applying the current as an external stimulus. Initially, the circuit is in steady state. In the benchmark circuit having two input node named as an excitatory and inhibitory input signal. The circuit has two capacitor C_1 and C_2. The stored charge accumulated on the capacitor corresponds to the charged ions of sodium (Na^+) & potassium (K^+) ion. The benchmark circuit having two input nodes namely excitatory or inhibitory node. The charging of capacitance C_2 depends on the switching of device M_2 and M_3, which is shown in Fig. 3. It has been found that based on the conventional MOS circuit the spiking activation time is more, which degrades the circuit performance in SNN applications.

Hereby, on replacing the conventional device by tunneling FET in order to get efficient and fast train pulse in SNN. In this benchmark circuit, after applying

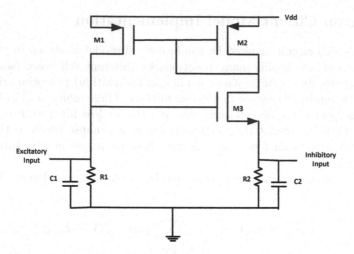

Fig. 3. Spice simulated actual circuit model of the voltage-mode neuron cell with two input nodes [18].

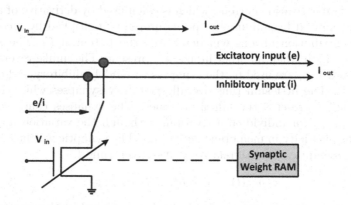

Fig. 4. Working principle of the spiking neural network have synapses and other modules with I_{out} current sensing node, moreover the signal processing have been presented for synapses, neurons, and synapse drivers [17].

the test train pulse, it activates the transistor M_3, which short the transistor M_3 to ground (0 or 1). Consequently, the transistor M_2 and M_3 turns ON through transistor M_3. In this phenomenon, the circuit starts charging the capacitor C_2 through Vdd. At the same time, the transistor M_2 and M_3 will be allowed the flow of current through them, which can be sensed at the inhibitory node. Thus, the high magnitude of current with minimum spiking time enhanced the circuit performance.

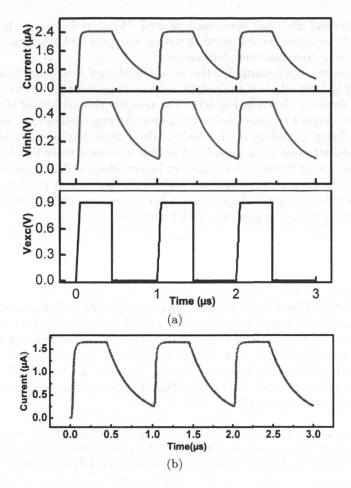

Fig. 5. Operation characteristics with transient tendency of the (a) Synapse for voltage and current response in to the synapse using proposed device. (b) Synapse for current response in to the synapse using MOSFET.

4   Results and Discussion

We have designed the neuromorphic circuit using TFET has a better response as compared with the conventional CMOS device. The spiking neural network using the novel device is shown in Fig. 3. In this circuit, we replace the CMOS device with that of the Tunneling FET. The output response is much better than the conventional MOS device. According to Moore's law, we know that the number of transistors per chip on integrated circuits had doubled every 1.8 years since the integrated circuit was invented and by device scaling short channel effects come into the picture. However, by using Tunnel FET, short channel effects have been reduced and Also at the same time, the device area has been reduced as the channel length is very small as compared with that of the CMOS. By considering these parameters SNN has been implemented. Whereas in Fig. 4, the working principle of the spiking neural network having synapses and other modules with current sensing node has been demonstrated.

The simulation waveform for the circuit with the Tunneling transistor is shown in Fig. 5(a), whereas the output current response by the circuit with a MOSFET device is shown in Fig. 5(b). The transfer characteristics of the drain current with respect to gate-source voltage for the proposed device clearly indicates the charge tunneling of the device. The circuit has been simulated the circuit model for same clock period and output waveform trace that the current spike magnitude at the inhibitory input in higher which is $2.4\,\mu A$ using the proposed device compared to $1.63\,\mu A$ for MOSFET. However, it can be concluded from the results, the speed of operation in the neuron cell chain to the axon will be increasingly using the proposed TFET module.

5   Conclusion

In this paper, we have developed a compact neuromorphic system using Cyl GAA Tunnel FET based on low band gap material of SiGe. From results, it has been found that the tunnel transistor with a low-k spacer placed over a source of SiGe reduces the fringing field and produces the high performances without the additional switch and logic operation. It successfully presents critical functions of the signal in an artificial neural network. Thus, we implemented the neural mechanism with the simple analog operation. Further, it can be implemented in pulse-coupled neural networks.

Acknowledgment. This work was supported by the "CSIR HRDG, Scientist Pool scheme No. 9010-A", Government of India and in part with the UGC, New Delhi under JRF scheme no. 22745/(NET-DEC. 2015) for funded financial support.

References

1. Schemmel, J., Meier, K., Mueller, E.: A new VLSI model of neural microcircuits including spike time dependent plasticity. In: Proceedings of the 2004 International Joint Conference on Neural Networks (IJCNN 2004), pp. 1711–1716. IEEE Press (2004)
2. Douence, V., Laflaquière, A., Le Masson, S., Bal, T., Le Masson, G.: Analog electronic system for simulating biological neurons. In: Mira, J., Sánchez-Andrés, J.V. (eds.) IWANN 1999. LNCS, vol. 1607, pp. 188–197. Springer, Heidelberg (1999). https://doi.org/10.1007/BFb0100485
3. Haflinger, P., Mahowald, M., Watts, L.: A spike based learning neuron in analog VLSI. In: Advances in Neural Information Processing Systems, vol. 9 (1996)
4. Ambrogio, S., Balatti, S., Nardi, F., Facchinetti, S., Ielmini, D.: Spike-timing dependent plasticity in a transistor-selected resistive switching memory. Nanotechnology **24**(38), 384012 (2013)
5. Asai, T., Kanazawa, Y., Amemiya, Y.: A subthreshold MOS neuron circuit based on the Volterra system. IEEE Trans. Neural Netw. **14**(5), 1308–1312 (2003)

6. Bhuwalka, K.K., Schulze, J., Eisele, I.: Scaling the vertical tunnel FET with tunnel bandgap modulation and gate workfunction engineering. IEEE Trans. Electron Devices **52**(5), 909–917 (2005)
7. Seabaugh, A.C., Zhang, Q.: Low-voltage tunnel transistors for beyond CMOS logic. Proc. IEEE **98**(12), 2095–2110 (2010)
8. Beohar, A., Vishvakarma, S.K.: Performance enhancement of asymmetrical underlap 3D-cylindrical GAA-TFET with low spacer width. IET Micro Nano Lett. **11**(8), 443 (2016)
9. Beohar, A., Yadav, N., Shah, A.P., Vishvakarma, S.K.: Analog/RF characteristics of a 3D-Cyl underlap GAA-TFET based on a Ge source using fringing-field engineering for low-power applications. J. Comput. Electron. **17**(4), 1650–1657 (2018)
10. Beohar, A., Yadav, N., Vishvakarma, S.K.: Analysis of trap-assisted tunnelling in asymmetrical underlap 3D-cylindrical GAA-TFET based on hetero-spacer engineering for improved device reliability. IET Micro Nano Lett. **12**(12), 982–986 (2017)
11. Anghel, C., Chilagani, P., Amara, A., Vladimirescu, A.: Tunnel field effect transistor with increased ON current, low-k spacer and high-k dielectric. Appl. Phys. Lett. **96**(12), 122104 (2010)
12. Chattopadhyay, A., Mallik, A.: Impact of a spacer dielectric and a gate overlap/underlap on the device performance of a tunnel field-effect transistor. IEEE Trans. Electron Devices **58**(3), 677–683 (2011)
13. Macdonald, D., Cuevas, A.: Validity of simplified Shockley-Read-Hall statistics for modeling carrier lifetimes in crystalline silicon. Phys. Rev. B **67**(7), 075203 (2003)
14. Sentaurus device manual 2017.1. https://www.synopsys.com/silicon/tcad/sentaurus-device.html
15. Kim, S.H., Agarwal, S., Jacobson, Z.A., Matheu, P., Hu, C., Liu, T.-J.K.: Tunnel field effect transistor with raised germanium source. IEEE Electron Device Lett. **31**(10), 1107–1109 (2010)
16. https://www.khanacademy.org/science/biology/human-biology/neuron-nervous-system/a/the-synapse
17. Schemmel, J., Grubl, A., Meier, K., Mueller, E.: Implementing synaptic plasticity in a VLSI spiking neural network model. In: The 2006 IEEE International Joint Conference on Neural Network Proceedings, pp. 1–6. IEEE (2006)
18. Ota, Y., Wilamowski, B.M.: Analog implementation of pulse-coupled neural networks. IEEE Trans. Neural Netw. **10**(3), 539–544 (1999)

Device Modelling

Compact Modeling of Drain-Extended MOS Transistor Using BSIM-BULK Model

Shivendra Singh Parihar(✉)🆔 and Ramchandra Gurjar🆔

Department of Electronics and Instrumentation Engineering,
Shri G. S. Institute of Technology and Science, Indore, India
pshiv.92@gmail.com

Abstract. The charge based compact model for Drain-Extended MOS (DEMOS) transistor is presented in this work. Proposed model accurately predicts the special effects of quasi-saturation, present in high voltage MOSFETs. Modeling methodology used in this paper includes the drift resistance model based on intrinsic drain current, and low voltage BSIM-BULK model. Developed model along with the BSIM-BULK compact model can be used for the modeling of low voltage bulk MOSFETs to DEMOS transistors. Proposed model results are validated with Technology Computer-Aided Design (TCAD) DEMOS data. The model is accurately capturing the impact of drift region on DC I-V characteristics and their derivatives.

Keywords: High voltage MOSFET · DEMOS · Bulk MOSFET · BSIM-BULK · Compact model · Quasi saturation

1 Introduction

Digital and Analog applications use low voltage (~1.8 V) MOSFETs. However, RF applications, such as I/O devices, power amplifiers, hybrid and electric vehicles, communication, building automations and actuators use high voltage MOS devices. Need of integration of both low and high voltage devices on a monolithic IC has dramatically increased the interest in designing and modeling the high voltage devices. High voltage (HV) circuits can be made along with low voltage circuits on a single IC by using (i) larger gate oxide thickness and lightly doped drain (LDD) implants in HV devices, (ii) circuit techniques, and (iii) Drain Extended MOS (DEMOS) transistors. Larger gate oxide thickness and cascade connection of low voltage devices increase the process and circuit complexities. However, DEMOS offers reduction in chip area and circuit complexity.

DEMOS devices use larger gate oxide thickness and extended drain region to avoid the gate dielectric breakdown and to sustain higher drain voltage [1]. Due to the extended drain region, high voltage DEMOS transistors exhibit quasi-saturation and peak in transconductance, impact ionization and self heating

© Springer Nature Singapore Pte Ltd. 2019
A. Sengupta et al. (Eds.): VDAT 2019, CCIS 1066, pp. 667–678, 2019.
https://doi.org/10.1007/978-981-32-9767-8_55

effects [2–5]. Conventional low voltage MOSFET models can't accurately predict the physical behavior of high voltage devices. Numerous analytical models, compact models and macro-models for HV transistors with acceptable accuracy are available in literature [6–14]. Out of them, analytical and compact models based on EKV and BSIM3 are main stream models for DEMOS [15–18]. However, some of these models [14] have limited scalability and slow convergence, and consider only limited number of physical effects. Hence, accurate and fast compact model for HV MOSFETs is needed for efficient circuit design. Lightly doped extended drain region, in HV MOSFETs, is modeled, using both the constant resistor and bias dependent resistor, to predict the impact of velocity saturation on drain characteristics [19].

In this work, we have developed the current dependent resistance model, considering velocity saturation in drift region for HV DEMOS transistors [20–25] and added it in the BSIM-BULK compact model. This extended BSIM-BULK model accurately captures the DEMOS DC characteristics that include terminal currents and their derivatives, for wide range of drain and gate voltages. Proposed model is also scalable with the width, length and doping of the drift region.

This paper is organised as follows: Device design for numerical simulation is described in Sect. 2. Model development incorporating the quasi saturation effect of DEMOS, is explained in Sect. 3. Validation of the model against TCAD data is presented in Sect. 4. Conclusions are given in Sect. 5.

2   DEMOS Structure

Figure 1 shows the DEMOS transistor used in this work. A lightly doped region exists between the channel and drain implant region of the MOSFET. This excess region helps in operating the transistors at high voltages, applied at drain terminal. DEMOS is a planar device and hence does not require local oxidation (LOCOS) and LDD diffusion, to prevent the dielectric and drain junction breakdown. Operating voltage of the DEMOS is constrained by the following factors: (i) gate oxide thickness, (ii) gate length of the transistor, (iii) length of the drain-gate overlap, and (iv) spacing between the drain implant and poly gate. Optimization of these parameters is necessary to achieve the operating voltage required for an application.

The n-type DEMOS device structure used in TCAD simulation is shown in Fig. 2. Drain-gate overlap is kept such that (i) it will allow alignment variation resulting from fabrication process and (ii) it does not affect the conduction between channel region and drain terminal. Gate length is chosen such that the transistor doesn't reach punch through. Total poly silicon gate length, consisting of channel length and gate-drain and gate-source overlap length, of $1\,\mu m$ is used in the simulation. Drain to poly gate spacing, decided on the basis of voltage supply and alignment tolerance requirements, is set to $0.75\,\mu m$ for our TCAD simulation. The device is designed in Sentaurus TCAD tool to obtain the electrical characteristics. Electrostatic potential distribution inside the device with $V_{ds} = 40\,V$ is shown in Fig. 2. The source implant, channel, drain extension and

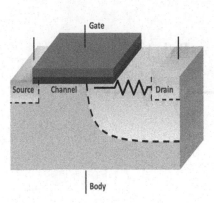

Fig. 1. DEMOS structure

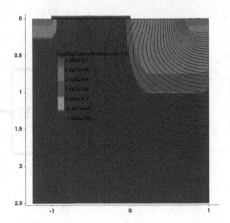

Fig. 2. Electrostatic potential contour
with $V_{ds} = 40\,V$ and $V_{gs} = 0.5\,V$ in
DEMOS structure (Color figure online)

drain implant regions are from left to right on top surface of the device. Orange
and yellow shaded regions on top surface are highly doped n-type S/D implants.
Dark blue and light green shaded regions, in between these implants, are p-type
substrate and lightly doped n-type drain extension region, respectively. Contour
lines on drain side of the device, represent the equipotential lines and these lines
show that most of the drain voltage is dropped in the extended drain region.
This allows to apply higher voltage at drain terminal and also prevents gate
dielectric breakdown.

3 Modeling of DEMOS Transistor

3.1 Quasi Saturation

Current in a high voltage MOSFET can saturate due to following effects: (i)
velocity saturation in the channel region, (ii) channel pinch-off, and (iii) saturation of the carrier velocity in extended drain region. In the case of velocity
saturation in channel, increase in the drain current becomes almost equal to
increase in gate voltage (V_g). Impact of the channel pinch-off can be observed
on the output characteristics at low V_g and high drain biases (V_d) as shown
in Fig. 4(b). Carrier velocity saturation in the intrinsic transistor is generally
noticed at medium to high V_g and high V_d. When carrier velocity is limited by
the drift region, and is not saturated in intrinsic channel region, this is called as
quasi-saturation effect [4,26] and is normally observed at high V_g. In the quasi-
saturation regime, impact of V_g is small and, hence increase in current with V_g is
not significant. The above-mentioned effects can be present in the device simultaneously and their impact on drain current cannot be distinguished. This quasi
saturation effect can be modeled by considering the carrier velocity saturation
in the drift region.

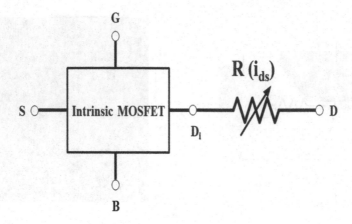

Fig. 3. Equivalent circuit representation of the modeling approach

3.2   Model Development

From Figs. 1 and 2 it is evident that extended drain region is combination of gate-drain overlap region and lightly doped drift regions. Intrinsic drain terminal voltage remains almost constant and has low value for entire applied drain biases [4]. This indicates that resistance of the extended drain region has weak dependence on V_g and is mostly controlled by V_d [26]. Based on these behaviours, for modeling purpose, we have divided the DEMOS transistor into two parts (i) Intrinsic MOSFET and (ii) Drift region. Impact of the quasi saturation in the drift region is modeled using a current dependent resistor R_{drift}. Equivalent network consisting of an n-type FET and current dependent resistor used for the modeling of DEMOS is shown in Fig. 3 [17].

Intrinsic MOSFET is modeled using the charge based symmetric BSIM-BULK compact model [27–35]. Intrinsic MOSFET is assumed to have uniform doping throughout the channel region, however, impact of non-uniform doping can also be incorporated in the model [36–40]. As shown in Fig. 4, impact of the DIBL, GIDL, DITS, mobility degradation, noise, impact ionization, self-heating etc. are modeled for the intrinsic MOSFET, using BSIM-BULK, with acceptable accuracy. Modeling of the lightly doped extended drain region, through the bias dependent resistor, provides high accuracy and fast convergence [41,42]. These models use the voltage dependent resistance model for incorporating the impact of velocity saturation. In this work, impact of the drain and gate voltages on the drift resistance is modeled using the intrinsic drain current. Impact of the velocity saturation, due to drift region, is modeled using the V_{SAT} parameter.

Resistivity of a semiconductor bar can be written as, $\rho = n \cdot q \cdot \mu$, where n is the charge density, q is the charge of carriers, and μ is the mobility of carriers. Current density in a semiconductor bar is given by, $J = n \cdot q \cdot V_{sat}$. Resistance of the semiconductor bar is defined as, $R = \rho \cdot L \cdot A^{-1}$, where, L and A are the length and cross-sectional area respectively.

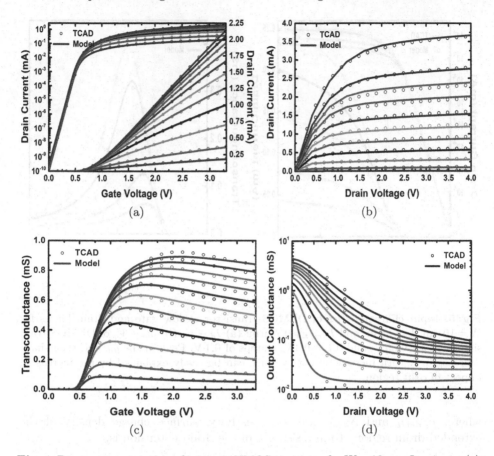

Fig. 4. Parameter extraction of intrinsic NMOS transistor for $W = 10\,\mu m$, $L = 1\,\mu m$: (a) transfer characteristics for $V_d = 0.05\,V$ and $0.1\,V$–$1.0\,V$ in steps of $100\,mV$, (b) output characteristics for $V_g = 0.5\,V$–$3.3\,V$ in steps of $300\,mV$, and $4.0\,V$, (c) transconductance, and (d) output conductance

By using these expressions, a model for current dependent drift resistance is developed [43–48]. This model of bias dependent resistor along with the intrinsic MOS model is able to predict the accurate behaviour of quasi saturation effect, occurs in HV MOSFETs. Total drift resistance of the extended drain region can be modeled as:

$$R_{drift0} = \rho_{s,drift} \cdot \frac{L_{drift}}{W} \qquad (1)$$

where,

$$\rho_{s,drift} = \frac{1}{q \cdot \mu_{drift} \cdot N_{drift}}$$

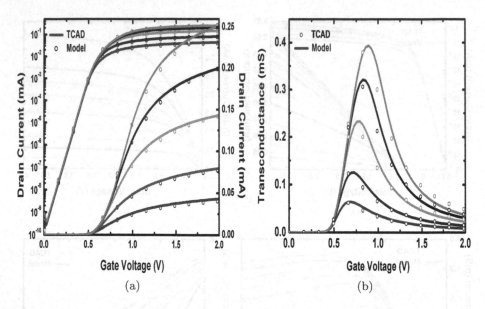

Fig. 5. Input characteristics of DEMOS transistor at low gate and drain biases for $W = 10\,\mu\mathrm{m}$, $L = 1\,\mu\mathrm{m}$, and $L_{drift} = 0.75\,\mu\mathrm{m}$: (a) $I_d - V_g$ (b) $g_m - V_g$ of DEMOS transistor at $V_d = 0.05\,\mathrm{V}$, and 0.1 V–0.4 V in steps of 0.1 V. Peak in the g_m and then sharp decrease in it with increase in gate voltage can be easily explained by the increasing impact of drift region.

where, $\rho_{s,drift}$ and N_{drift} are the resistivity, surface charge density of the extended drain region. Total resistance of the drain extension is,

$$R_{drift} = R_{drift0} \cdot \left[1 - \left(\frac{I_{drift}}{I_{dsat}} \right)^P \right]^{-\frac{1}{P}} \tag{2}$$

where,

$$I_{drift} = W \cdot q \cdot N_{drift} \cdot V_{satdrift}$$

where, I_{drift} and P are current of the extended drain region and exponent for drift region resistance. μ_{drift} and $V_{satdrift}$ are assumed to be independent of the vertical electric field.

4   Model Validation

The model is validated with the data obtained from TCAD simulations of the DEMOS transistor. We have neglected the parasitic and body bias effects, by keeping source and body terminals at ground. $I_d - V_d$ characteristics for V_d up to 40 V, for different gate biases are matching with TCAD data. Transfer characteristics and their derivatives at low and high drain biases are shown in

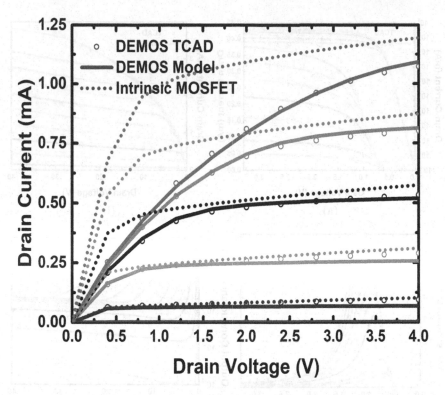

Fig. 6. Output characteristic of intrinsic and DEMOS transistor at low V_g and V_d for $W = 10\,\mu m$, $L = 1\,\mu m$. Developed model of DEMOS transistor including the velocity saturation in extended drain region gives excellent accuracy at low drain voltage.

Fig. 5. In, $I_d - V_g$ characteristics (Fig. 5(a)) of DEMOS, excellent matching at low V_d, of the simulated and modeled data of subthreshold slope and current depicts that mobility models used in this work, are accurate.

Peak transconductance (g_m) region is very important for analog circuit design, Fig. 5(b) shows that developed model is very well matching the $g_m - V_g$ characteristics obtained from TCAD data from low to medium drain biases. Output characteristics of the NMOS, with and without drift region are shown in Fig. 6. Impact of the drift region on $I_d - V_d$ curve for lower drain bias, can be easily seen from the transition regions for different V_g values.

$I_d - V_g$, $I_d - V_d$, and their derivatives, for DEMOS having drift region of $0.75\,\mu m$, for higher gate and drain biases, are shown in Fig. 7. Accurate modeling of the impact of quasi saturation at high V_g and for entire range of V_d can be observed from Fig. 7(c).

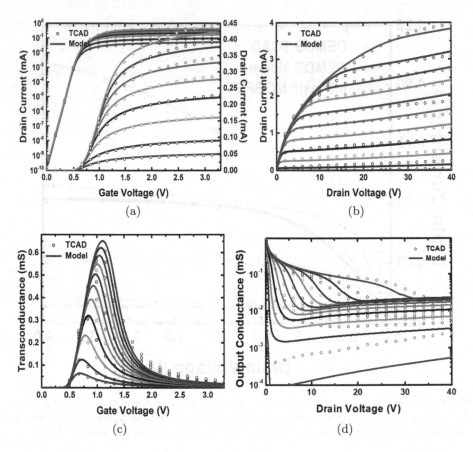

Fig. 7. DEMOS validation (a) $I_d - V_g$ characteristics at low gate and drain biases, (b) $I_d - V_d$ characteristics at different gate biases, (c) $g_m - V_g$ characteristics, (d) output conductance (g_{ds})

5   Conclusion

Compact model for the DEMOS, including the effect of quasi-saturation, is presented in this paper. BSIM-BULK model is used to model the intrinsic transistor, and current dependent drift resistance is used to model the quasi-saturation effect. Drift resistance model is based on intrinsic drain current and saturation velocity, and it is highly efficient in terms of convergence and implementation. The developed DEMOS model is highly scalable with the width, channel length, and drift region length of the transistor.

References

1. Mitros, J.C., et al.: High-voltage drain extended MOS transistors for 0.18-μm logic CMOS process. IEEE Trans. Electron Devices **48**(8), 1751–1755 (2001). https://doi.org/10.1109/16.936703
2. Chauhan, Y.S.: Compact modeling of high voltage MOSFETs, p. 136 (2007). https://doi.org/10.5075/epfl-thesis-3915. http://infoscience.epfl.ch/record/109934
3. Chauhan, Y.S., et al.: Scalable general high voltage MOSFET model including quasi-saturation and self-heating effects. Solid-State Electron. **50**(11), 1801–1813 (2006). https://doi.org/10.1016/j.sse.2006.09.002. http://www.sciencedirect.com/science/article/pii/S0038110106002966
4. Anghel, C., et al.: Physical modelling strategy for (quasi-) saturation effects in lateral DMOS transistor based on the concept of intrinsic drain voltage. In: 2001 International Semiconductor Conference. CAS 2001 Proceedings (Cat. No. 01TH8547), vol. 2, pp. 417–420, October 2001. https://doi.org/10.1109/SMICND.2001.967497
5. Chauhan, Y.S., et al.: A compact DC and AC model for circuit simulation of high voltage VDMOS transistor. In: 7th International Symposium on Quality Electronic Design (ISQED 2006), pp. 109–114, March 2006. https://doi.org/10.1109/ISQED.2006.7
6. Pawel, S., Kusano, H., Nakamura, Y., Teich, W., Terashima, T., Netzel, M.: Simulator-independent capacitance macro model for power DMOS transistors. In: Proceedings of 2003 IEEE 15th International Symposium on Power Semiconductor Devices and ICs, ISPSD 2003, pp. 287–290, April 2003. https://doi.org/10.1109/ISPSD.2003.1225284
7. Anghel, C., Chauhan, Y.S., Hefyene, N., Ionescu, A.M.: A physical analysis of HV MOSFET capacitance behaviour. In: Proceedings of the IEEE International Symposium on Industrial Electronics, ISIE 2005, vol. 2, pp. 473–477, June 2005. https://doi.org/10.1109/ISIE.2005.1528963
8. Anghel, C., et al.: New method for threshold voltage extraction of high-voltage mosfets based on gate-to-drain capacitance measurement. IEEE Electron Device Lett. **27**(7), 602–604 (2006). https://doi.org/10.1109/LED.2006.877275
9. Chauhan, Y.S., et al.: Analysis and modeling of lateral non-uniform doping in high voltage MOSFETs. In: 2006 International Electron Devices Meeting, pp. 1–4, December 2006. https://doi.org/10.1109/IEDM.2006.347000
10. Chauhan, Y.S., Krummenacher, F., Gillon, R., Bakeroot, B., Declercq, M., Ionescu, A.M.: A new charge based compact model for Lateral Asymmetric MOSFET and its application to High Voltage MOSFET modeling. In: 20th International Conference on VLSI Design Held Jointly with 6th International Conference on Embedded Systems (VLSID 2007), pp. 177–182, January 2007. https://doi.org/10.1109/VLSID.2007.15
11. Roy, A.S., Chauhan, Y.S., Sallese, J.M., Enz, C.C., Ionescu, A.M., Declercq, M.: Partitioning scheme in lateral asymmetric most. In: 2006 European Solid-State Device Research Conference, pp. 307–310, September 2006. https://doi.org/10.1109/ESSDER.2006.307699
12. Roy, A.S., Chauhan, Y.S., Enz, C.C., Sallese, J.M.: Noise modeling in lateral asymmetric MOSFET. In: 2006 International Electron Devices Meeting, pp. 1–4, December 2006. https://doi.org/10.1109/IEDM.2006.346994
13. Khandelwal, S., Sharma, S., Chauhan, Y.S., Gneiting, T., Fjeldly, T.A.: Modeling and simulation methodology for SOA-aware circuit design in DC and pulsed-mode operation of HV MOSFETs. IEEE Trans. Electron Devices **60**(2), 714–718 (2013). https://doi.org/10.1109/TED.2012.2218112

14. D'Halleweyn, N.V., Tiemeijer, L.F., Benson, J., Redman-White, W.: Charge model for SOI LDMOST with lateral doping gradient. In: Proceedings of the 13th International Symposium on Power Semiconductor Devices and ICs, ISPSD 2001, pp. 291–294 (2001). https://doi.org/10.1109/ISPSD.2001.934612
15. Level = 88 HV MOS Model. https://www.silvaco.com.cn/tech_lib_eda/kbase/ams/pdf/hvmos_jpws.pdf
16. Enz, C.C., Krummenacher, F., Vittoz, E.A.: An analytical MOS transistor model valid in all regions of operation and dedicated to low-voltage and low-current applications. Analog Integr. Circuits Signal Process. 8(1), 83–114 (1995). https://doi.org/10.1007/BF01239381
17. Chauhan, Y.S., Gillon, R., Bakeroot, B., Krummenacher, F., Declercq, M., Ionescu, A.M.: An EKV-based high voltage MOSFET model with improved mobility and drift model. Solid-State Electron. 51(11), 1581–1588 (2007). https://doi.org/10.1016/j.sse.2007.09.024. http://www.sciencedirect.com/science/article/pii/S0038110107003437. Special Issue: Papers Selected from the 36th European Solid-State Device Research Conference - ESSDERC 2006
18. Chauhan, Y.S., et al.: A highly scalable high voltage MOSFET model. In: 2006 European Solid-State Device Research Conference, pp. 270–273, September 2006. https://doi.org/10.1109/ESSDER.2006.307690
19. Subramanian, V.: High voltage MOSFET technology, models, and applications. In: 12th MOS-AK Workshop (2012)
20. Agnihotri, S., Ghosh, S., Dasgupta, A., Chauhan, Y.S., Khandelwal, S.: A surface potential based model for GaN HEMTs. In: 2013 IEEE Asia Pacific Conference on Postgraduate Research in Microelectronics and Electronics (PrimeAsia), pp. 175–179, December 2013. https://doi.org/10.1109/PrimeAsia.2013.6731200
21. Ghosh, S., et al.: Modeling of temperature effects in a surface-potential based ASM-HEMT model. In: 2014 IEEE 2nd International Conference on Emerging Electronics (ICEE), pp. 1–4, December 2014. https://doi.org/10.1109/ICEmElec.2014.7151197
22. Dasgupta, A., Khandelwal, S., Chauhan, Y.S.: Compact modeling of flicker noise in HEMTs. IEEE J. Electron Devices Soc. 2(6), 174–178 (2014). https://doi.org/10.1109/JEDS.2014.2347991
23. Dasgupta, A., Ghosh, S., Chauhan, Y.S., Khandelwal, S.: ASM-HEMT: compact model for GaN HEMTs. In: 2015 IEEE International Conference on Electron Devices and Solid-State Circuits (EDSSC), pp. 495–498, June 2015. https://doi.org/10.1109/EDSSC.2015.7285159
24. Khandelwal, S., Ghosh, S., Chauhan, Y.S., Iniguez, B., Fjeldly, T.A.: Surface-potential-based RF large signal model for GaN HEMTs. In: 2015 IEEE Compound Semiconductor Integrated Circuit Symposium (CSICS), pp. 1–4, October 2015. https://doi.org/10.1109/CSICS.2015.7314527
25. Ahsan, S.A., Ghosh, S., Khandelwal, S., Chauhan, Y.S.: Modeling of kink-effect in RF behaviour of GaN HEMTs using ASM-HEMT model. In: 2016 IEEE International Conference on Electron Devices and Solid-State Circuits (EDSSC), pp. 426–429, August 2016. https://doi.org/10.1109/EDSSC.2016.7785299
26. Aarts, A.C.T., Kloosterman, W.J.: Compact modeling of high-voltage LDMOS devices including quasi-saturation. IEEE Trans. Electron Devices 53(4), 897–902 (2006). https://doi.org/10.1109/TED.2006.870423
27. Chauhan, Y.S., et al.: BSIM6: analog and RF compact model for bulk MOSFET. IEEE Trans. Electron Devices 61(2), 234–244 (2014). https://doi.org/10.1109/TED.2013.2283084

28. Chauhan, Y.S., et al.: BSIM6: symmetric bulk MOSFET model. In: Workshop on Compact Modeling (WCM), June 2012
29. Gupta, C., et al.: BSIM-BULK 106.2.0 Technical Manual. http://bsim.berkeley.edu/models/bsimbulk/
30. Chauhan, Y.S., et al.: BSIM compact MOSFET models for spice simulation. In: Proceedings of the 20th International Conference Mixed Design of Integrated Circuits and Systems - MIXDES 2013, pp. 23–28, June 2013
31. Dutta, A., Sirohi, S., Ethirajan, T., Agarwal, H., Chauhan, Y.S., Williams, R.Q.: BSIM6 - benchmarking the next-generation MOSFET model for RF applications. In: 2014 27th International Conference on VLSI Design and 2014 13th International Conference on Embedded Systems, pp. 421–426, January 2014. https://doi.org/10.1109/VLSID.2014.79
32. Agarwal, H., et al.: Recent enhancements in BSIM6 bulk MOSFET model. In: 2013 International Conference on Simulation of Semiconductor Processes and Devices (SISPAD), pp. 53–56, September 2013. https://doi.org/10.1109/SISPAD.2013.6650572
33. Chalkiadaki, M.A., et al.: Evaluation of the BSIM6 compact MOSFET model's scalability in 40 nm CMOS technology. In: 2012 Proceedings of the European Solid-State Device Research Conference (ESSDERC), pp. 50–53, September 2012. https://doi.org/10.1109/ESSDERC.2012.6343331
34. Agarwal, H., Khandelwal, S., Dey, S., Hu, C., Chauhan, Y.S.: Analytical modeling of flicker noise in halo implanted MOSFETs. IEEE J. Electron Devices Soc. **3**(4), 355–360 (2015). https://doi.org/10.1109/JEDS.2015.2424686
35. Mohamed, N., Agarwal, H., Gupta, C., Chauhan, Y.S.: Compact modeling of nonquasi-static effect in bulk MOSFETs for RF circuit design in sub-THz regime. In: 2016 3rd International Conference on Emerging Electronics (ICEE), pp. 1–4, December 2016. https://doi.org/10.1109/ICEmElec.2016.8074573
36. Dabhi, C.K., et al.: BSIM4 User Manual. http://bsim.berkeley.edu/models/bsim4/
37. D'Halleweyn, N.V., Benson, J., Redman-White, W., Mistry, K., Swanenberg, M.: MOOSE: a physically based compact DC model of SOI LDMOSFETs for analogue circuit simulation. IEEE Trans. Comput. Aided Des. Integr. Circuits Syst. **23**(10), 1399–1410 (2004). https://doi.org/10.1109/TCAD.2004.835125
38. Chauhan, Y.S., Gillon, R., Declercq, M., Ionescu, A.M.: Impact of lateral nonuniform doping and hot carrier injection on capacitance behavior of high voltage MOSFETs. IETE Tech. Rev. **25**(5), 244–250 (2008)
39. Chauhan, Y.S., Krummenacher, F., Gillon, R., Bakeroot, B., Declercq, M.J., Ionescu, A.M.: Compact modeling of lateral nonuniform doping in high-voltage MOSFETs. IEEE Trans. Electron Devices **54**(6), 1527–1539 (2007)
40. Chauhan, Y.S., Gillon, R., Declercq, M., Ionescu, A.M.: Impact of lateral nonuniform doping and hot carrier degradation on capacitance behavior of high voltage MOSFETs. In: ESSDERC 2007 – 37th European Solid State Device Research Conference, pp. 426–429, September 2007
41. Sahoo, J.R., et al.: High voltage LDMOSFET modeling using BSIM6 as intrinsic-MOS model. In: 2013 IEEE Asia Pacific Conference on Postgraduate Research in Microelectronics and Electronics (PrimeAsia), pp. 56–61, December 2013. https://doi.org/10.1109/PrimeAsia.2013.6731178
42. Gupta, C., et al.: Modeling of high voltage LDMOSFET using industry standard BSIM6 MOS model. In: 2016 IEEE International Conference on Electron Devices and Solid-State Circuits (EDSSC), pp. 124–127, August 2016. https://doi.org/10.1109/EDSSC.2016.7785225

43. Khandelwal, S., Ghosh, S., Ahsan, S.A., Dasgupta, A., Chauhan, Y.S.: ASM-HEMT 101.0.0 Technical Manual. http://iitk.ac.in/asm/
44. Khandelwal, S., et al.: Robust surface-potential-based compact model for GaN HEMT IC design. IEEE Trans. Electron Devices **60**(10), 3216–3222 (2013). https://doi.org/10.1109/TED.2013.2265320
45. Sharma, K., Dasgupta, A., Ghosh, S., Ahsan, S.A., Khandelwal, S., Chauhan, Y.S.: Effect of access region and field plate on capacitance behavior of GaN HEMT. In: 2015 IEEE International Conference on Electron Devices and Solid-State Circuits (EDSSC), pp. 499–502, June 2015. https://doi.org/10.1109/EDSSC.2015.7285160
46. Ahsan, S.A., Ghosh, S., Sharma, K., Dasgupta, A., Khandelwal, S., Chauhan, Y.S.: Capacitance modeling in dual field-plate power GaN HEMT for accurate switching behavior. IEEE Trans. Electron Devices **63**(2), 565–572 (2016). https://doi.org/10.1109/TED.2015.2504726
47. Ahsan, S.A., Ghosh, S., Khandelwal, S., Chauhan, Y.S.: Physics-based multi-bias RF large-signal GaN HEMT modeling and parameter extraction flow. IEEE J. Electron Devices Soc. **5**(5), 310–319 (2017). https://doi.org/10.1109/JEDS.2017.2724839
48. Ahsan, S.A., Pampori, A., Ghosh, S., Khandelwal, S., Chauhan, Y.S.: A new small-signal parameter extraction technique for large gate-periphery GaN HEMTs. IEEE Microw. Wirel. Compon. Lett. **27**(10), 918–920 (2017). https://doi.org/10.1109/LMWC.2017.2746661

Technology Characterization Model and Scaling for Energy Management

Harshil Goyal(✉) ⓘ and Vishwani D. Agrawal(✉) ⓘ

Department of Electrical and Computer Engineering, Auburn University,
Auburn, AL 36849, USA
{hzg0007,agrawvd}@auburn.edu

Abstract. We present a low-cost methodology to find the highest energy
efficiency operating conditions (voltage and frequency) for a processor
with given performance requirements. Taking a black box approach,
we start with processor specifications: nominal voltage, clock frequency,
thermal design power (TDP), maximum frequency and maximum power,
and a knowledge of the device technology. To determine the behavior of
the processor, we use a small model circuit that can be economically but
accurately simulated in Spice to learn the delay and energy characteristics of the technology. We simulate the model with random vectors to
determine power consumption profiles and critical path delays at several
voltages. Comparisons between the model data and processor specifications provide scale factors for area, voltage, nominal frequency and maximum frequency. We then optimize the operating modes of the processor
for highest cycle efficiency (clock cycles per unit energy). An illustration
considers a processor with 3.3 GHz clock, 1.2 V nominal voltage, and
95 W thermal design power. Several optimization scenarios are possible.
Observing that the clock is power constrained, we reduce the voltage
to 0.92 V, keeping the clock at 3.3 GHz, which now becomes structure-
constrained. This gives a 127% higher cycle efficiency over the nominal operation. For highest performance, we set the voltage to 1.1 V and
increase the clock to 4.5 GHz while holding power unchanged at 95 W.
This gives 38% higher cycle efficiency than the nominal operation. The
highest cycle efficiency, ten times greater than the nominal, occurs for
subthreshold voltage operation at 0.35 V and 36 MHz.

Keywords: Microprocessor · Power management ·
Managing performance · Energy efficiency · Subthreshold operation

1 Introduction

Most VLSI chips, including microprocessors, come with prescribed operating
conditions, found in specifications supplied by the manufacturer. While such
specifications serve a majority of users they are not optimized for specific applications. For example, a portable application must conserve energy without compromising too much on performance. In a remote sensing system, energy, not
performance, may be paramount.

© Springer Nature Singapore Pte Ltd. 2019
A. Sengupta et al. (Eds.): VDAT 2019, CCIS 1066, pp. 679–693, 2019.
https://doi.org/10.1007/978-981-32-9767-8_56

Application-specific optimization of operation requires power-delay characterization of the chip at various supply voltages. Although this could be done through either actual hardware experiment or entire chip simulation, both options present difficulties. Experimental set up is expensive. Simulation requires a complete model of the chip, often not available from the manufacturer. Even if a simulation model is available, accurate timing and power analysis can be expensive.

This paper presents an inexpensive alternative that a user can adopt with reasonable effort and with readily available information. One needs the specifications of the processor and knowledge of its semiconductor technology. Relevant data from specifications include nominal voltage, clock frequency, thermal design power (TDP), maximum frequency (f_{max}) and peak power (P_{max}).

The *main idea* is to simulate a *model* digital circuit at the circuit-level using the technology of the target device. The model can be any circuit of convenient size. The simulator can be any efficient version of Spice with accurate technology models. In our illustration of the methodology, we use HSPICE [1] and, in the absence of actual models, employ the *predictive technology model* (PTM) [2]. The simulation is repeated at several voltages over the entire range in which the device can function. The results are then matched with the device specification data to determine suitable scale factors for size (area), voltage and frequency. In a typical example discussed in the paper the area factor is 7.34×10^5, which results in tremendous savings in computation costs over those of full device simulation.

Section 2 examines relevant papers on power and performance, highlighting the principal differences in the work presented in this paper. Section 3 outlines relevant definitions. Section 4 describes modeling and simulation used in this low-cost learning methodology applied to the processor black box. Section 5 continues with an example of the Intel Sandy Bridge processor, deriving five (both static and dynamic) power management scenarios. Section 6 provides a study of processors in 45 nm, 32 nm and 22 nm *bulk* and *high*-K CMOS technologies. Results in Sects. 4 and 6 are based on a predictive technology model (PTM) [2] only to illustrate the methodology and allow a preview of the type of results expected if real models were available. Section 7 summarizes the main ideas. Section 8 outlines proposals for future research.

2   Background and Experimental Methods

With consumption of desktop microprocessors reaching 130 W, power has emerged as a major challenge facing microprocessor designers [4,9]. A microprocessor must deliver the highest possible performance while keeping power consumption within reasonable limits. Recent theoretical and experimental investigations aim at managing the power (energy and temperature) and delay (speed) of CMOS circuits. In this section, we discuss some recent work.

Wong *et al.* [21] examine changes when moving from Intel's 32 nm planar (32 nm Sandy Bridge processor: Core i5-2500K) to 22 nm Tri-Gate (22 nm Ivy

Bridge processor: i5-3570K) process by comparing their power, voltage, temperature, and frequency. Power consumption is measured using a multimeter on the 1.2 V power connector to record current and voltage. Biostar TZ77MXE motherboard allows adjustment of processor frequency and voltage. The processor's operating voltage is measured by the on-board IT8728F chip. Temperature is measured using core-temp (CPU on-die temperature sensors), reporting the temperature of the hottest core. The results from this experiment indicate that the 22 nm Ivy Bridge has significantly lower static (leakage) power consumption over 32 nm Sandy Bridge, but only shows a small reduction in dynamic power. Ivy Bridge requires higher voltage increase for the same frequency increase, leading to more difficult overclocking but saves power at lower (standard) speeds. In addition to the CMOS process changes, the thermal resistance of Ivy Bridge increased over Sandy Bridge, perhaps due to the change from solder to polymer thermal interface material between the die and the heat spreader.

Sankari [13] developed two proactive thermal aware approaches, PTAS (Proactive Thermal Aware Scheduler) and PTFM (Proactive Thermal aware scheduling with Floating point and Memory access rates), which reduce CPU temperature by predicting the temperature gradient from the rate of change in the CPU temperature, floating point access rate and memory access rate. Their experiments were conducted on desktop and laptop machines with the Ubuntu operating system. They ran eight SciMark benchmarks: Fast Fourier Transform (FFT), Jacobi Successive Over-Relaxation (SOR), Dense Unit Factorization (LU), Sparse Matrix Multiplication (Sparse), FFT-Large, SOR-Large, LU-Large, and SparseLarge. For PTAS, the reductions in peak temperature were 2 °C to 4 °C. The reduction in peak/average temperatures on a laptop were 3 °C to 5 °C/5 °C. Corresponding penalties in the schedule length were between 15% and 30%. For PTFM, there was a decrease in peak/average CPU temperatures: 3 °C to 6 °C/6 °C for small benchmarks and 3 °C to 6 °C/5 °C for large benchmarks. The schedule length penalties were less than 2% to 10%. The corresponding results in peak/average temperature on a laptop were 3 °C to 6 °C/6 °C.

Travers [16] reduces power usage by splitting tasks between several cores. Energy reduced to half with performance greater than that of a single core. Ye et al. [22] introduce learning-based dynamic power management (DPM) for multicore processors. Using task allocation they manipulate idle periods on processor cores to achieve a better trade-off between power consumption and system performance. Ghasemazer et al. [7] minimize total power consumption of a chip multiprocessor (CMP) while maintaining a target average throughput. They use coarse-grain dynamic voltage and frequency scaling (DVFS), task assignment at the CMP level, and fine-grain DVFS based on closed-loop feedback control at the core level.

Cited here are just a few examples. In contrast, our approach relies on electrical (non-functional) characteristics of the processor. This makes the power-performance management independent of any specific application. We could term it *macro-management*, as opposed to micro-management that involves internal hardware details of the processor, as well as, is dependent on the specific soft-

ware being run. Benefits and weaknesses of the present approach are brought
out in Sects. 4 through 8.

3   Energy Metrics

Although power-delay product (PDP) [10] has been a popular metric for energy,
we use cycle efficiency [15], which is a meaningful measure of computation per
unit of energy.

3.1   Cycle Efficiency

We consider clock cycle as a unit of computational work. It has two dimensions,
time and energy, and is characterized by the time per cycle (TPC) often referred
to as clock period and the energy per cycle (EPC). Inverses of these parameters
are frequency, $f = 1/TPC$, and *cycle efficiency*, $\eta = 1/EPC$ [15]. Clearly, f and
η are numbers of cycles per unit of time and energy, respectively.

To make the operation fast we increase f, thereby reducing the time to
execute a clock cycle, and to make the operation efficient we increase η by
reducing the energy used in a cycle. Suppose, a program running on a processor
takes c clock cycles to execute. Then we have,

$$\text{Execution time} = \frac{c}{f} \tag{1}$$

$$\text{Energy consumed} = \frac{c}{\eta} \tag{2}$$

where, η is cycle efficiency of the processor in cycles per joule. Equation 1 gives
the performance in time as,

$$\text{Performance in time} = \frac{1}{\text{Execution time}} = \frac{f}{c} \tag{3}$$

Similarly, Eq. 2 gives the energy performance as,

$$\text{Performance in energy} = \frac{1}{\text{Energy consumed}} = \frac{c}{\eta} \tag{4}$$

Clearly, cycle efficiency (η) characterizes the energy performance in a similar
way as frequency (f) characterizes the time performance. These two performance
parameters are related to each other by the power being consumed, as follows:

$$\text{Power} = \frac{f}{\eta} \tag{5}$$

For a computing task, f is the rate of execution in time and η is the rate of
execution in energy. Taking the automobile analogy, f is analogous to speed in
miles per hour (mph) and η is analogous to miles per gallon (mpg).

Table 1. Intel i5 Sandy Bridge 2500 K processor specifications [11].

Technology node	32 nm
Voltage range, V_{dd}	1.2–1.5 V
Nominal base frequency, f_{TDP}	3.3 GHz
Overclock frequency, f_{max}	5.01 GHz
Thermal design power, TDP	95 W
Peak power, P_{Peak}	132 W

3.2 Two Power Limits: Thermal and Peak

- *Thermal design power* (TDP) is the maximum average power in watts the processor dissipates when operating at base (nominal) frequency under a manufacturer defined, high complexity workload.
- *Peak power* is the maximum power dissipated by the processor under the worst case conditions - at the maximum core voltage, maximum temperature and maximum signal loading conditions.

4   Technology Characterization and Scaling

Technology characterization describes the electrical behavior of a circuit in terms of voltage, power, frequency, energy and time (performance). For a processor, such characterization allows one to estimate its frequency and cycle efficiency as functions of the supply voltage. These data are then used to manage the operation of the processor.

We use a ripple carry adder (RCA) circuit as a model for technology characterization. In general, any circuit of reasonable size can be used for this purpose. Simulation of the RCA is carried out using HSPICE [1], with suitably selected input vectors to determine the critical path delay, power consumption and a minimum energy point. This approach differs from that of the co-called "canary software" [14] or "canary circuit" [20], which predict an impending failure of the full scale system. However, a similarity is the predictive behavior of our model circuit, whose analysis characterizes the full-scale processor, sometimes even for future technologies.

To illustrate the proposed methodology, we use the Intel i5-2500K processor [3]. A full scale gate or transistor-level circuit model was not available to us. Even otherwise, it would be too complex for detailed simulation at various voltages. We will only use the operational data, such as, voltage, maximum clock frequency and power consumption, available from the published specification datasheet of the processor. These are extracted in Table 1, where the technology of the device is specified as well.

The main idea in the presented low-cost methodology is to first learn the voltage-power-speed behavior of the technology by simulating a reasonably small model circuit and, then, derive scale factors to scale up the model data to represent the actual device (such as a processor) in terms of voltage, size, nominal frequency and maximum frequency. Finally, the scaled data allows energy and speed trade-offs, both in static and dynamic operation scenarios.

We define four scale factors to scale the model circuit data up to the processor [8]:

1. Voltage Scale Factor (σ): It accounts for the difference between the voltage at which adder (RCA) is simulated and the processor supply voltage,

$$\sigma = \frac{V_{dd}^2 \, (Processor)}{v_{dd}^2 \, (Adder)} \qquad (6)$$

2. Area Scale Factor (β): It represents the relative size of processor to that of the adder (RCA),

$$\beta = \frac{TDP}{\sigma[(e_{dyn} \times f_{TDP}) + p_{stat}]} \qquad (7)$$

where e_{dyn} and p_{stat} are dynamic energy and static power of the model. Since e_{dyn} is a function of signal activity in the model, the difference in activities of the model circuit and the processor is implicit in the area scale factor. We have, therefore, not used a separate scale factor for activity.

3. Nominal Frequency Scale Factor (δ): It is the ratio of processor's nominal frequency to adder's maximum frequency at rated voltage, e.g., $V_{dd} = 1.2 \, V$, and is used to find suitable frequency for processor at any supply voltage,

$$\delta = \frac{f_{nomVdd}(Processor)}{f_{maxVdd}(Adder)} \qquad (8)$$

4. Maximum Frequency Scale Factor (γ): It is the ratio of processor's maximum frequency to adder's maximum frequency at rated voltage, e.g., $V_{dd} = 1.2 \, V$, and is used to find the maximum (structural or critical path) frequency for processor at any supply voltage,

$$\gamma = \frac{f_{maxVdd} \, (Processor)}{f_{maxVdd} \, (Adder)} \qquad (9)$$

4.1   Nominal, Structure-Constrained and Power-Constrained Frequencies

Three frequencies, f_{nom} (nominal or base frequency), f_{max} (maximum, structure-constrained or critical path frequency) and f_{TDP} (power constrained frequency), are determined by scaling adder data. This also results in energy per cycle (EPC) and cycle efficiency (η) for each frequency. We will express frequencies in gigahertz (GHz), or billion cycles per second.

Processor's *base* or *nominal* clock frequency is specified in manufacturer's datasheet. It is the frequency at which TDP is defined. We calculate the nominal frequency, f_{nom} as:

$$f_{nom} = \delta \times f_{max}(Adder) \tag{10}$$

In a structure constrained system, f_{max} is limited by the critical path delay of the circuit. Therefore,

$$f_{max} = \gamma \times f_{max}(Adder) \tag{11}$$

In a power constrained system [17,18], the frequency f_{TDP} is limited by the maximum allowable power for the circuit [8]

$$f_{TDP} = \frac{TDP - \sigma\beta p_{stat}}{\sigma\beta e_{dyn}} \tag{12}$$

where TDP is thermal design power of processor at given f_{TDP} and rated voltage, σ is voltage scale factor, β is adder to processor area scale factor, p_{stat} is the static power of the adder, and e_{dyn} is the dynamic energy of the adder.

At any voltage, the highest clock frequency is [8],

$$f_{opt} = min(f_{TDP}, f_{max}) \tag{13}$$

4.2   Energy per Cycle and Cycle Efficiency for Processor

The energy per cycle for the processor for the nominal frequency and over-clock/maximum frequency for a any given V_{dd} is defined by:

$$EPC_{nom} = \frac{TDP}{f_{nom}} \tag{14}$$

$$EPC_{F_0} = \frac{P_{dyn}}{f_{nom}} + \frac{P_{static}}{F_0} \tag{15}$$

Equation 15 defines the energy per cycle EPC_{F_0} for any given frequency F_0 of processor where F_0 lies in the range, $f_{nom} \leq F_0 \leq f_{max}$. In this case, $F_0 = f_{max} = 5.01$ GHz. Therefore, we call EPC_{F_0} as EPC_{fmax}, i.e., energy per cycle for maximum frequency allowed to run the system at a given voltage. As we know, cycle efficiency $\eta = 1/EPC$, therefore, from Eqs. 14 and 15 we can define cycle efficiency for the processor as:

$$\eta = \frac{1}{EPC_{nom}} \tag{16}$$

$$\eta_0 = \frac{1}{EPC_{F_0}} \tag{17}$$

where η is defined as nominal cycle efficiency and η_0 as cycle efficiency for any given frequency F_0 in the range, $f_{nom} \leq F_0 \leq f_{max}$. Here, $EPC_{F_0} = EPC_{f_{max}}$, therefore, we call η_0 as peak cycle efficiency.

All parameters defined above are used in the next section that illustrates the proposed power management method. We show how one can optimize time and energy of a processor based on the performance and efficiency requirements of the user.

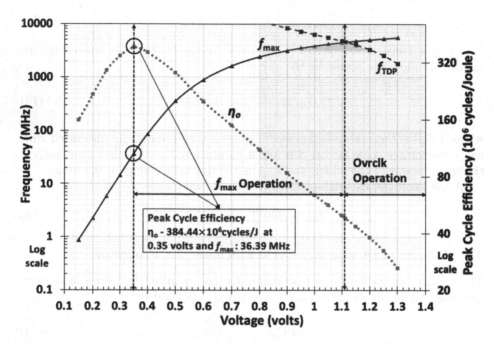

Fig. 1. Plot showing highest performance with respect to clock f_{max} at 1.1 V, highest efficiency at 0.35 V, and overclock operation (1.1 V–1.4 V) for Intel i5 Sandy Bridge 2500K processor. At the nominal voltage 1.2 V, the two frequencies f_{TDP} and f_{max} match the processor specifications of Table 1.

5   Power Management

Power management provides a system solution to boost the processor frequency to values higher than the nominal value, whenever required as per performance criteria. For workloads that are not operating at the cooling/power supply limits this can often result in real performance increase. The focus of this experiment is to evaluate the benefits of the proposed methodology and not necessarily assess the capability of any particular device.

We consider all aspects necessary for time and energy optimization, such as: (a) What will be the most energy-efficient point for the processors that requires low power, ruling out high performance as a main criteria explained through Fig. 1 (b) When is it possible to operate a processor at a higher clock speed

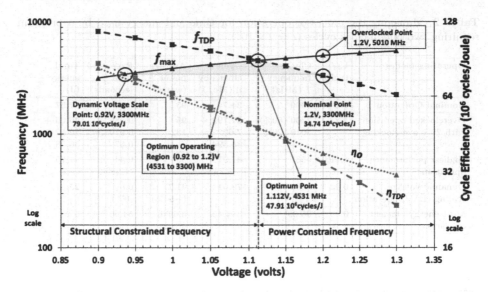

Fig. 2. Scaled version of Fig. 1 from 0.85 V to 1.4 V showing Intel i5 Sandy Bridge 2500K processor's calculated scaled curves of f_{max} and f_{TDP} at various voltages. At the nominal voltage 1.2 V, the two frequencies f_{TDP} and f_{max} match the processor specifications of Table 1.

without exceeding the power limits explained through Fig. 2 And (c) the value of doing so explained with five scenarios in Table 2. Using the processor performance counters to measure execution events of applications, we identify the characteristics that determine the extent of performance benefits in terms of time and energy from higher as well as lower clock frequencies and those characteristics that cause the application to become power-limited. Consider a program that executes in two billion clock cycles ($c = 2 \times 10^9$). Five scenarios of Table 2 are:

Nominal Operation: For nominal conditions, $V_{dd} = 1.2$ V and clock frequency $f = 3.3$ GHz, Figs. 1 and 2 indicate that operation is power-constrained. Cycle efficiency $\eta_{TDP} = 34.74 \times 10^6$ cycles/J. Power consumption = 95 W, which agrees with the processor specification shown in Table 1 and can also be calculated from Eq. 5. The execution time of the two billion clock cycle program is 0.61 s from Eq. 1 and the total energy consumed by the program is 57.57 J from Eq. 2.

Overclock Operation: Overclocking a microprocessor refers to faster than the nominal clock speed, prescribed for sustained operation. Overclocking is a popular technique for getting a performance boost from the system, without acquiring faster hardware. Overclocking can be sustained only for short bursts because CPU will have increased heating. One may also employ additional cooling. This scenario also uses 1.2 V and 80% of the program is executed at 3.3 GHz clock, but the remaining 20% of the program is executed at an overclock frequency of 5.0 GHz, which is the highest frequency the critical path will allow at 1.2 V (Fig. 2). Thus, the power exceeds TDP for 20% of time. Note

Table 2. Managing the processor operation for time and energy used by a program requiring two billion clock cycles ($c = 2 \times 10^9$).

Operating modes	V_{dd} (volts)	Clock frequency f (MHz)	Cycle efficiency η (Mc/J)	Average power $\frac{f}{\eta}$ (watts)	Execution time $\frac{c}{f}$ (seconds)	Total energy $\frac{c}{\eta}$ (J)
Nominal Operation	1.2	3300	34.74	95	0.61	57.57
Overclocked operation with 20% overclocking	1.2	3300 (80%) 5010 (20%)	27.792 + 7.602 = 35.394	95 132	0.485 + 0.0798 = 0.57	46.06 + 10.52 = 56.58
Highest performance operation	1.112	4531	47.91	95	0.44 (−28%)	41.75 (−28%)
Dynamic voltage scaling (DVS) operation	0.92	3300	79.01	41.77 (−56%)	0.61 (0%)	25.31 (−56%)
Most energy efficient operation	0.35	36.39	384.45	0.0946	54.96	5.20

that power increase from 95 W to 132 W is not proportional to the frequency ratio, because only dynamic power increases, leaving static power unchanged. Cycle efficiency η_{TDP} at 3.3 GHz is 34.74×10^6 cycles/J and η_0 at 5010 MHz is 38.01×10^6 cycles/J. The execution time is reduced to 0.57 s and total energy consumption is slightly lower at 56.58 J. We do not observe a significant reduction in execution time or total energy in this scenario despite higher power consumption. To illustrate this, let f_1 and f_2 be two frequencies such that:

$$f_1 \leq f_{max}; \quad \text{at } V_1 \text{ (Rated voltage)}$$

$$f_2 \leq f_{max}; \quad \text{at } V_2 \, (V_2 \leq V_1)$$

Let x be the fraction of time f_1 is used, where $0 \leq x \leq 1$. Therefore, to maximize average performance, we *maximize* $\{xf_1 + (1-x)f_2\}$ under the following constraint:

$$x(E_{dyn}f_1 + P_{stat}) + (1-x)\frac{V_2^2}{V_1^2}(E_{dyn}f_2 + P_{stat}) \leq TDP \qquad (18)$$

where, E_{dyn} and P_{stat} are dynamic energy per cycle and static power for processor at rated voltage. The voltage ratio V_2/V_1 will be denoted by σ; this is unlike the scale factor of Eq. 6 since no model circuit is involved. Now, TDP for the processor is expressed as:

$$TDP = E_{dyn} \cdot f_{TDP} + P_{stat} \qquad (19)$$

Solving Eq. 19 for f_{TDP}, we get:

$$f_{TDP} = \frac{TDP - P_{stat}}{E_{dyn}} \qquad (20)$$

Therefore, from relations 18 and 20, we derive an upper bound for $\{xf_1 + (1 - x)f_2\}$ as follows:

$$xf_1 + \sigma^2(1 - x)f_2 \leq f_{TDP} + \frac{(1 - \sigma^2)(1 - x)P_{stat}}{E_{dyn}} \qquad (21)$$

Here, f_1 and f_2 have an upper bound of f_{max}, the critical path frequency, which is generally higher than f_{TDP} at the rated voltage (Fig. 2). However, an overall performance higher than f_{TDP} would be possible only when the last term on the right hand side is positive, requiring $\sigma < 1$, which implies dual voltage operation. One the other hand, if $\sigma = 1$ the average performance does not exceed the performance at a single frequency f_{TDP}, because inequality 21 reduces to:

$$xf_1 + (1 - x)f_2 \leq f_{TDP} \qquad (22)$$

Performance optimization with single frequency is discussed next.

Highest Performance Operation: If we let $x = 1$ in inequality 22, then $f_1 < f_{TDP}$ and its optimum value is $f_1 = f_{opt} = f_{TDP}$. The only way to increase f_{TDP} is to reduce voltage. However, f_{opt} must not exceed the critical path frequency f_{max}. In this scenario we find optimum voltage, frequency and cycle efficiency ($V_{ddopt}, f_{opt}, \eta_{opt}$). From Fig. 2 we determine $V_{dd} = 1.112\,V$ and clock frequency $f = 4.531\,GHz$, which give cycle efficiency $\eta_{opt} = 47.91 \times 10^6$ cycles/J. This is a single clock operation where the processor is operated at maximum frequency (f_{max}) giving the highest performance. The power consumption is no more than 95 W (TDP) and the program execution time reduces to 0.44 s and total energy consumed is 41.75 J. Thus, we observe 28% reduction in both energy consumption and execution time.

Dynamic Voltage Scaling (DVS) Operation: There have been a number of efforts over the years examining the implementation and effectiveness of dynamic voltage and frequency scaling for saving power in embedded systems [12]. Performance-oriented explorations include attempts to quantify and/or reduce the performance loss encountered in an energy-saving adoption of DVS. In contrast, our fourth scenario targets performance increase from DVS in a power-constrained environment. Here the program can execute at the rated frequency, which is 3300 MHz, by decreasing the voltage to 0.92 V. Now, $\eta_0 = 79.01 \times 10^6$ cycles/J as obtained from Fig. 2. The power consumption is 41.77 W, but the program execution time is 0.61 s, the same as that obtained at the rated voltage. However, total energy consumed is reduced to 25.31 J. Here, we see performance enhancement in terms of energy and not time, therefore, when the criterion is lower energy and not higher speed, this type of operation is appropriate.

Highest Energy Efficiency Operation: The fifth scenario is derived for highest cycle efficiency. Figure 1 shows minimum energy operation at $V_{dd} = 0.35\,V$ and frequency 36.39 MHz. This is subthreshold voltage operation [19]. When a program executes at this low voltage, it gives cycle efficiency $\eta_0 = 384.45 \times 10^6$ cycles/J, which is the peak cycle efficiency for this processor. The power consumption for this type of execution is 0.0946 W, or 94.6 mW, but the program execution time is increased to 54.96 s and the energy consumption is the lowest at 5.20 J.

Table 3. Specified (nominal) operation and optimized high efficiency mode at the specified performance for Intel processors characterized using a predictive technology model (PTM [2]).

CMOS technology	Intel microprocessor	Manufacturer's specification				
		Nominal operation		High efficiency		
		f_{TDP} MHz	V_{dd} V	η_{TDP} Mc/J	V_{dd} V	η_0 Mc/J
45 nm *Bulk*	Core2 Duo T9500	2600	1.25	74.29	1.07	108.58
45 nm *High*-K	Core2 Duo T9500	2600	1.25	74.29	0.79	350.91
32 nm *Bulk*	Core i5 2500K	3300	1.20	34.74	0.92	79.01
32 nm *High*-K	Core i5 2500K	3300	1.20	34.74	0.67	267.57
22 nm *Bulk*	Core i7 3820QM	2700	0.80	60.00	0.70	96.22
22 nm *High*-K	Core i7 3820QM	2700	0.80	60.00	0.61	137.65

Table 4. Maximum performance (highest frequency) and minimum energy (highest efficiency) modes for Intel processors characterized using a predictive technology model (PTM [2]).

CMOS technology	Intel microprocessor	Optimized operation					
		Maximum speed			Minimum energy		
		V_{ddopt} V	f_{opt} MHz	η_{opt} Mc/J	V_{dd} V	f_{η_0} MHz	η_0 Mc/J
45 nm *Bulk*	Core2 Duo T9500	1.200	2920	82.28	0.35	33.51	829.29
45 nm *High*-K	Core2 Duo T9500	1.226	3120	89.08	0.30	304.48	1795.00
32 nm *Bulk*	Core i5 2500K	1.112	4531	47.91	0.35	36.39	384.45
32 nm *High*-K	Core i5 2500K	1.155	4940	51.77	0.30	414.2	953.81
22 nm *Bulk*	Core i7 3820QM	0.771	3494	75.46	0.38	177.3	213.99
22 nm *High*-K	Core i7 3820QM	0.760	3626	80.38	0.30	332.6	375.76

6 Summary

Performance and energy optimization data for processors in *bulk* and *high*-K technologies using 45 nm, 32 nm and 22 nm transistor sizes, respectively, are given in Tables 3 and 4 [8]. We make following observations:

Optimizing Nominal Operation (Table 3, columns 5 and 7): For nominal clock frequency, optimized efficiency is always higher than the efficiency for the specified operation. This is accomplished by lowering the supply voltage.

***Bulk* vs. *High*-K:** *High*-K consistently has higher frequency (Table 4), as well as higher cycle efficiency (Table 4 and high efficiency mode in Table 3), perhaps due to the reduced leakage.

Performance Optimization (Table 4, columns 3–5): Clock rate can be increased by suitably lowering the voltage, but the efficiency (Table 4, column 5) drops below the maximum achievable at the nominal clock rate (Table 3, columns 7). Still, this efficiency is superior to the rated specification (Table 3, columns 5).

Energy Optimization (Table 4, columns 6–8): Highest efficiency is achieved in the subthreshold voltage range, and is almost an order of magnitude higher than that for the rated specification (Table 3, column 5 or 7), even though the performance in the sub-threshold voltage region (Table 4, columns 7) is reduced almost by an order of magnitude compared to all other operating modes.

In interpreting the available information on the specifications and structure of these processors, we made several assumptions. Hence the data and observations presented here may not exactly represent the behavior of Intel processors. Notably, the outcome of this investigation is a *methodology* for performance and energy optimization.

7   Conclusion

We explored how power management affects the energy and performance of a processor. The proposed method is entirely a simulation based evaluation that accomplishes the goal of performance and energy optimization. Some observations are:

1. Highest performance mode has a superior sustained clock rate than the rated (nominal or specified) clock rate.
2. Highest efficiency at rated clock needs voltage lowering.
3. Performance is enhanced by overclocking, which may require raising voltage whenever frequency is increased.
4. Highest efficiency operation without performance bound uses subthreshold voltage and clock in megahertz range.

Strengths of our methodology are low-cost, simplicity and generality. The black box approach works with minimal details from the datasheet of the processor. The result serves a wide variety of applications. It also allows us to evaluate technologies before a processor chip becomes available. Technology evaluation is through circuit level (Spice) simulation and is more accurate than a coarse evaluation normally done when whole processor is simulated.

Some results on the Sandy Bridge processor have been verified against those obtained in experiments [21]. Still a weakness of the method is lack of application-specific customization where other methods may work better.

8   Future Work

Energy efficiency continues to be a major issue [5]. The present work creates an optimization framework. The simplicity of our *black box macro-modeling approach* makes it useful to many users. However, we must acknowledge areas where work still needs to be done. Besides giving solutions to existing problems, it opens the door for other research venues:

1. Analysis and simulation in this work ignored process variability that is important in nanometer technologies.
2. Although thermal design power (TDP) and peak power may take some heating effects into account, certain applications can produce severe hot spots on the chip. Fine grain thermal management is an area for research.
3. We notice that energy efficiency increases as voltage drops. For given performance, operating voltage should be the lowest to allow that frequency. This suggests further exploration of the near (but above) threshold range of V_{dd} where increased energy efficiency may be possible with only minor loss of performance [6].
4. Operation in the sub-threshold voltage region [19] may be sensitive to the thermal as well as other types of noises. Reliability of such operation requires study.
5. Signal activity of the ripple carry adder (RCA) need not be the same as in the processor. Any difference in the activity is implicitly compensated for by adjustment of the area scale factor. Alternatively, a separate scale factor can account for different activities in the two circuits.

References

1. HSPICE Signal Integrity User Guide: Synopsys Inc., 700 East Middlefield Road, Mountain View, CA 94043 (2010)
2. Predictive Technology Model. Nanoscale Simulation and Modeling (NIMO) Group, Arizona State University (2012). http://ptm.asu.edu/
3. Intel core i5–2500k processor specifications (2016). http://ark.intel.com/products/52210/Intel-Core-i5-2500K-Processor-6M-Cache-up-to-3_70-GHz. Accessed 20 Feb 2016
4. Annavaram, M., Grochowski, E., Shen, J.: Mitigating Amdahl's law through EPI throttling. In: Proceedings of 32nd IEEE International Symposium on Computer Architecture (ISCA), pp. 298–309 (2005)
5. Borkar, S., Chien, A.A.: The future of microprocessors. Commun. ACM **54**(5), 67–77 (2011)
6. Dreslinski, R.G., Wieckowski, M., Blaauw, D., Sylvester, D., Mudge, T.: Near-threshold computing: reclaiming Moore's law through energy efficient integrated circuits. Proc. IEEE **98**(2), 253–266 (2010)
7. Ghasemazar, M., Pakbaznia, E., Pedram, M.: Minimizing the power consumption of a chip multiprocessor under an average throughput constraint. In: Proceedings of 11th International Symposium on Quality Electronic Design (ISQED), pp. 362–371, March 2010
8. Goyal, H.: Characterizing processors for time and energy optimization. Master's thesis, Auburn University, Auburn, Alabama, USA, August 2016
9. Grochowski, E., Ronen, R., Shen, J., Wang, H.: Best of both latency and throughput. In: Proceedings of the International Conference on Computer Design, pp. 236–243 (2004)
10. Rabaey, J.M., Chandrakasan, A.P., Nikolic, B.: Digital Integrated Circuits, vol. 2. Prentice-Hall, Englewood Cliffs (2002)
11. Rotem, E., Naveh, A., Rajwan, D., Ananthakrishnan, A., Weissmann, E.: Power-management architecture of the Intel micoarchitecture code-names Sandy Bridge. IEEE Micro **32**, 20–27 (2012)

12. Rubio, J., Rajamani, K., Rawson, F., Hanson, H., Ghiasi, S., Keller, T.: Dynamic processor over-clocking for improving performance of power-constrained systems. Technical Report RC23666 (W0507-124), IBM Research Division, Austin Research Laboratory, Texas, USA, July 2005
13. Sankari, A.: Proactive thermal-aware scheduling. Ph.D. thesis, Auburn University, Auburn, Alabama, USA, December 2014
14. Sartori, J., Kumar, R.: Software canaries: software-based path delay fault testing for variation-aware energy-efficient design. In: Proceedings of International Symposium on Low Power Electronics and Design, pp. 159–164 (2014)
15. Shinde, A.: Managing performance and efficiency of a processor. Master's thesis, Auburn University, Auburn, Alabama, USA, December 2012
16. Travers, M.: CPU power consumption experiments and results analysis of Intel i7-4820K. Technical Report NCL-EEE-MICRO-TR-2015-19, Newcastle University, Newcastle-upon-Tyne, NE17RU, UK, June 2015
17. Venkataramani, P.: Reducing ATE test time by voltage and frequency scaling. Ph.D. thesis, Auburn University, Auburn, Alabama, USA, May 2014
18. Venkataramani, P., Sindia, S., Agrawal, V.D.: A test time theorem and its applications. J. Electron. Test.: Theory Appl. $30(2)$, 229–236 (2014)
19. Wang, A., Calhoun, B.H., Chandrakasan, A.P.: Sub-Threshold Design for Ultra Low-Power Systems. ICIR. Springer, Boston (2006). https://doi.org/10.1007/978-0-387-34501-7
20. Wang, J., Calhoun, B.H.: Techniques to extend canary-based standby V_{DD} scaling for SRAMs to 45 nm and beyond. IEEE Jour. Solid-State Circ. $43(11)$, 2514–2523 (2008)
21. Wong, H.: A comparison of Intel's 32nm and 22nm core i5 CPUs: power, voltage, temperature, and frequency (2012). http://blog.stuffedcow.net/2012/10/intel32nm-22nm-core-i5-comparison. Accessed 13 Nov 2015
22. Ye, R., Xu, Q.: Learning-based power management for multicore processors via idle period manipulation. IEEE Trans. Comput. Aided Des. $33(7)$, 1043–1055 (2014)

GaAs-SiGe Based Novel Device Structure of Doping Less Tunnel FET

Shivendra Yadav[1]([✉])[iD], Chithraja Rajan[2][iD], Dheeraj Sharma[2],
and Sanjay Balotiya[2]

[1] RGM College of Engineering and Technology, Nandyal, Kurnool, A.P., India
shivendra1307@gmail.com
[2] PDPM IIITDM, Jabalpur, M.P., India
rajan.chithraja@gmail.com, dheeraj24482@gmail.com,
sanjaybalotiya1996@gmail.com

Abstract. Tunnel field effect transistors (TFETs) are a new approaching transistors with similarities of MOSFET. Tunnel FET (TFET) has believable usage in the forward generation ultra-low power applications as an alternative of the conventional FETs. In this paper, we have designed a state of the art device structure of hetero material based electrically doped TFET (EDTFET) for raising the DC/RF performance and reducing the ambipolarity. In this concern, high band gap material(GaAs) is used instead of silicon in drain-channel region and low band gap material (SiGe) in source region for reducing ambipolarity and improving RF performance which is not much significant. Therefore, for further betterment in device performance a live metal film is installed in source-channel interface with gate-underlapping as a proposed structure.

Keywords: GaAs · SiGe · LMF · EDTFET

1 Introduction

In recent years, the consecutive down scaling of conventional MOSFET gives betterment in the form of higher speed, high frequency FOMs, compactness of equipment, improved functionality, low power consumption, and high packing density [1–3]. Although, MOSFET shows sensitivity for short channel effects (SCEs) such as threshold roll-off, leakage current, high static power dissipation and sub-threshold swing (SS) limited to 60 mV/decade in the sub micron scale [4,5]. For resolving these problems a new device tunnel field effect transistor (TFET) is introduced [6]. The structure of the TFET is almost similar to the MOSFET but, different in carrier transport mechanism. The switching mechanism of TFET is performed by modulating quantum tunneling barrier through gate voltage whereas, in traditional MOSFETs it is done by modulating thermionic

Supported by organization x.

A. Sengupta et al. (Eds.): VDAT 2019, CCIS 1066, pp. 694–701, 2019.
https://doi.org/10.1007/978-981-32-9767-8_57

emission (over the barrier) [5]. TFET offers many advantages over the MOSFET: it can have sub-threshold swing (SS) lower than 60 mV/dec., has capability to work at very low supply voltage [7]. But, despite having these benefits conventional TFET has some disadvantage also like precise control on the doping concentration at three different type of doping regions (P+, I, N+) on single wafer leads to random dopant fluctuations (RDFs) [8]. Non-ideal doping profile because of movement of dopant atoms about the junction due to processes variability causes degradation in tunneling probability. To get rid-off this problem a work-function based charge plasma TFET (CP-TFET) is introduced [9,10]. In which, N+ and P+ regions are induced by metal contact with work-function 3.9 and 5.93 eV respectively over a lightly doped silicon film. CP-TFET has cost efficiency in terms of thermal annealing budget and less RDFs problem, but at the same time it has also poor ON-state current. In the similar fashion, electrical doping is reported for resolving the RDFs issues and forming the P+ I N+ structure of TFET [11,12]. But the major issue with doping less TFETs is that they undergo poor DC/RF performance and inherent nature of negative conduction. So, in this pursuit, the article first time put-forward a novel device structure, which employs a higher band gap hetero-material (GaAs) in drain/channel region and gate underlapping for reducing ambipolar current and low band gap material (SiGe) at source side with live metal film at source/channel junction in proposed structure as advanced version of conventional EDTFET. In the manuscript, a sequence of ideas are implemented for visualizing the effect of individual modifications.

2   Description of Structural Parameters and Models

The cross sectional view of conventional EDTFET and other three devices has shown in the Fig. 1(a–d) respectively. To design a P-I-N type structure, N+ and P+ regions are constructed by applying +1.2 V and −1.2 V respectively at the source and drain electrodes over intrinsic silicon. All the four devices having 1×10^{15} cm^{-3} net absolute substrate doping and lateral length of source and drain regions with DE and DS is 50 nm. Control gate length is 50 nm accept GU-LMF-HM-EDTFET, it is of 30 nm. Workfunction of DE, SE and GE is considered 4.5 eV; Si and oxide (SiO2 and HfO2) thickness is 10 and 3 nm respectively. Total device length is 160 nm by choosing 5 nm spacer length between DE/SE and GE. The HM-EDTFET have same structural parameters except channel-drain (GaAs) and source (SiGe) material. The device structure of LMF-HM-EDTFET is same as HM-EDTFET but additionally a live metal film is used at source-channel interface. Thickness of LMF (including vertical and horizontal) is 2 nm. In device GU-LMF-HM-EDTFET gate underlapping is executed from DE side. Device simulation is performed using the 2-D device simulator ATLAS Silvaco TCAD V5.19.20 [13]. There are several models used in simulation like Band to band tunneling (BTBT) model [13,14], Fermi–Dirac statistical model, Shockley Read Hall (SRH) recombination model and Auger recombination model and Schottky tunneling model for drain/channel contacts. NiSi is used as drain source contacts with barrier height 0.45 eV.

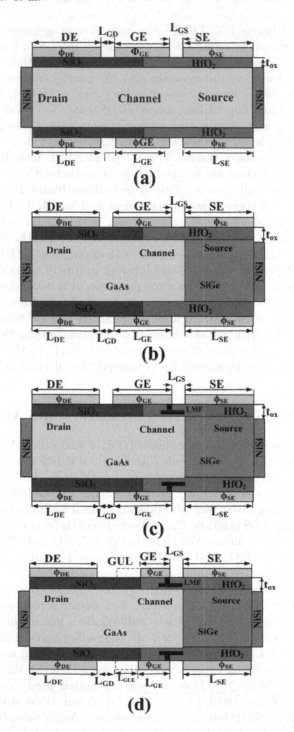

Fig. 1. Device view of (a) EDTFET, (b) hetero material-EDTFET (HM-EDTFET), (c) live metal film hetero material-EDTFET (LMF-HM-EDTFET) and (d) gate under-lapping LMF-HM-EDTFET (GU-LMF-HM-EDTFET)

3   Elaborative Discussion About the Results

3.1   DC Figures of Merit

In this section, we observe a relative analysis of DC characteristics of proposed device (GU-LMF-HM-EDTFET) with other three structures. Electron and hole concentration for all four structures in thermal equilibrium condition is shown Fig. 2(a). The figure clearly indicating the difference in the band gap among EDTFET and other three structures. The larger band gap and gate electrode underlapping provides largest tunneling width in ambipolar state as presented in Fig. 2(b). Larger the tunneling width, higher the tunneling barrier which is illustrated by Fig. 3(b), which notifies the lowest hole tunneling rate for GU-LMF-HM-EDTFET as compared other devices. This significantly reduces ambipolar current for GU-LMF-HM-EDTFET given in transfer characteristic (Fig. 4(a)). Figure says that larger band gap material reduces the negative conduction up to some extend, not completely, but gate underlapping used in proposed device is significant approach for suppressing ambipolar current. Further, energy band distribution in Fig. 2(c) comprises the effect of LMF at source/channel junction in terns of reduced tunneling width as compared to other structures as can be seen. Reduction in tunneling width increases the tunneling probability which is supported by higher electric field at source/channel interface a depicted in the Fig. 2(d). GU-LMF-HM-EDTFET and LMF-HM-EDTFET have almost same electric field due to presence of LMF, this leads to higher electron tunneling rate at source/channel junction by the Fig. 3(a) in ON-state. Figure illustrating that lower band gap material at source side improving tunneling in HM-EDTFET and it is more significant in LMF-HM-EDTFET. Further, output characteristic investigation reveals lower out put resistance by offering higher drain current in case of GU-LMF-HM-EDTFET and LMF-HM-EDTFET through Fig. 4(b) due to presence of LMF. All the DC parameters are concluded in the Table 1, which clearly mentions the utility of proposed modifications in terms of threshold voltage (V_{th}), I_{on}, OFF-state (I_{off}), ambipolar current (I_{ambi}) and subthreshold swing (SS).

Table 1. Comparison of DC parameters for all the four devices

Parameter/Unit	EDTFET	HM-EDTFET	LMF-HM-EDTFET	GU-LMF-HM-EDTFET
V_{th} (V)	0.85	0.71	0.51	0.51
I_{on} (A/μm)	3.17×10^{-7}	1.06×10^{-6}	7.27×10^{-6}	7.27×10^{-6}
I_{off} (A/μm)	5.58×10^{-18}	1.02×10^{-20}	6.36×10^{-21}	5.59×10^{-21}
I_{ambi} (A/μm)	9.31×10^{-12}	9.07×10^{-14}	9.69×10^{-16}	4.05×10^{-21}
SS (mV/dec)	27.05	13.12	6.5	6.5

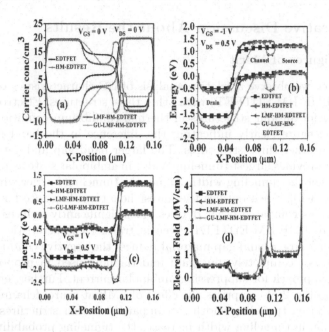

Fig. 2. (a) Carrier concentration (thermal state), (b) energy band diagram (ambipolar state), (c) ON-state and (d) electric field (thermal equilibrium state)

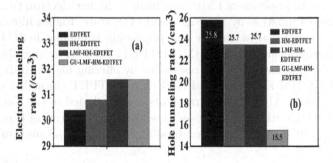

Fig. 3. (a) Electron tunneling in ON-state and (b)holes tunneling in ambipolar state.

3.2 High Frequency Analysis

Transconductance is the relating parameter of output current to the voltage across the input of a device, which mostly shows the strength of a device to switch gate-to-source voltage into drain current. It defined as $g_m = \partial I_{ds}/\partial V_{gs}$. Higher g_m can be visualised by the Fig. 4(c) for proposed designed device compared to others. This indicates that the device LMF-HM-EDTFET has improved sensitivity for converting gate voltage into drain current and serves the higher efficiency. Figure 4(d) demonstrates C_{gd} with respect to (V_{gs}). It seen that HM-EDTFET have lower C_{gd} as compared to EDTFET due to presence of hetero material at source region; LMF-HM-EDTFET have slightly high C_{gd} with respect to HM-EDTFET due to existence of live metal film at channel region. But, finally the gate underlapping in GU-LMF-HM-EDTFET results in suppression in parasitic as well as inversion capacitance [15].

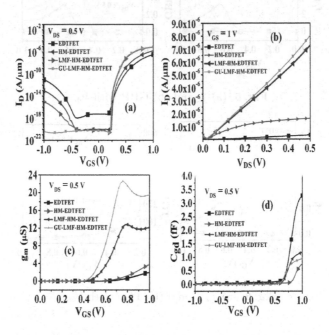

Fig. 4. (a)Transfer curve (b) I_D-V_D characteristics (c)g_m and (d) C_{gd}

Figure 5(a) depicts the changes of cut-off frequency f_t as a function of (V_{gs}). The cut-off frequency is depend on both parameters (g_m) and C_{gd}. Dominating factor among them has ability to influence f_t; in case of GU-LMF-HM-EDTFET both parameters are in four thats why it has highest cut-off frequency. From the figure it can also be seen that HM-EDTFET has better (g_m) but poor C_{gd}; whereas, LMF-HM-EDTFET has lower (g_m) and higher C_{gd} rather than GU-LMF-HM-EDTFET. Another crucial parameter which affect RF performance and offers trade off between gain and bandwidth is gain bandwidth product (GBP), which depicts same trend as f_t. Figure 5(b) show changes of GBP for LMF-HM-EDTFET, HM-EDTFET and EDTFET with respect to gate voltage. The proposed device has higher GBP due to presence of low band gap material and live metal at source channel junction.

Others high frequency parameter (f_{max}) and TGF are shown in Fig. 6(a) and (b) respectively. Maximum oscillation frequency(f_{max}) is frequency where power gain of circuit is unity. Initially f_{max} increases with V_{gs} and than falls after achieving peak value. GU-LMF-HM-EDTFET obtains f_{max} higher than others as shown in the same. For high frequency applications it is appropriated

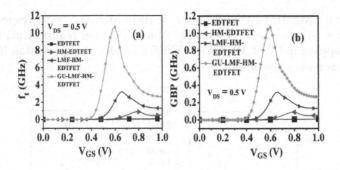

Fig. 5. (a) f_t and (b) GBP with V_{gs}

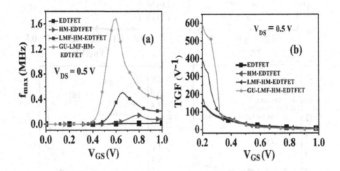

Fig. 6. (a) f_{max} and (b) TGF with V_{GS}

because of higher g_m and lower parasitic capacitance. In addition to this, TGF is ratio of g_m and I_{ds} as shown in Fig. 6(b) which decides device efficiency in terms of DC to AC conversion [16]. GU-LMF-HM-EDTFET shows highest TGF with respect to other devices. Near threshold voltage TGF is maximum for all, but it falls with increment in V_{gs} because drain current increases expeditiously with V_{gs}.

4   Conclusion

After analysis of all four structures through various characteristic following points can be concluded: hetero material (GaAs-SiGe) is use full to reduce ambipolar current up to some extend, whereas gate underlapping is more significant. SiGe at source side contributes for increasing the tunneling probability, however, deposition of LMF gives drastic rise in DC as well as RF parameters (g_m, f_f, GBP, f_{max}, and TGF). Further, it is seen that gate underlapping does not have any adverse effect on device performance, but significantly suppresses negative conduction in TFET.

References

1. Lundstrom, M.: Moore's law forever? Science **299**(5604), 210–211 (2003)
2. Mohankumar, N., Syamal, B., Sarkar, C.K.: Influence of channel and gate engineering on the analog and RF performance of DG MOSFETs. IEEE Trans. Electron Devices **57**(4), 820–826 (2010)
3. Kilchytska, V., et al.: Influence of device engineering on the analog and RF performances of SOI MOSFETs. IEEE Trans. Electron Devices **50**(3), 577–588 (2003)
4. Bangsaruntip, S., Cohen, G.M., Majumdar, A., Sleight, J.W.: Universality of short-channel effects in undoped-body silicon nanowire MOSFETs. IEEE Electron Devices Lett. **31**(9), 903–905 (2010)
5. Koswatta, S.O., Lundstrom, M.S., Nikonov, D.E.: Performance comparison between p-i-n tunneling transistors and conventional MOSFETs. IEEE Trans. Electron Devices **56**(3), 456–465 (2009)
6. Ionescu, A.M., Riel, H.: Tunnel field-effect transistors as energy-efficient electronic switches. Nature **479**(7373), 329–337 (2011)
7. Zhang, Q., Zhao, W., Seabaugh, A.: Low-subthreshold-swing tunnel transistors IEEE Electron Device Lett. **27**(4), 297–300 (2006)
8. Damrongplasit, N., Shin, C., Kim, S.H., Vega, R.A., Liu, T.J.K.: Study of random dopant fluctuation effects in germanium-source tunnel FETs. IEEE Trans. Electron Devices **58**(10), 3541–3548 (2011)
9. Kumar, M.J., Janardhanan, S.: Doping-less tunnel field effect transistor: design and investigation. IEEE Trans. Electron Devices **60**(10), 3285–3290 (2013)
10. Kumar, M., Jit, S.: Effects of electrostatically doped source/drain and ferroelectric gate oxide on subthreshold swing and impact ionization rate of strained-Si-on-insulator tunnel field-effect transistors. IEEE Trans. Nanotechnol. **14**(4), 597–599 (2015)
11. Lahgere, A., Sahu, C., Singh, J.: Electrically doped dynamically configurable field-effect transistor for low-power and high-performance applications. Electron. Lett. **51**(16), 1284–1286 (2015)
12. Lahgere, A., Sahu, C., Singh, J.: PVT-aware design of dopingless dynamically configurable tunnel FET. IEEE Trans. Electron Devices **62**(8), 2404–2409 (2015)
13. ATLAS Device Simulation Software, Silvaco Int., Santa Clara, CA, USA (2014)
14. Schenk, A.: A model for the field and temperature dependence of SRH lifetimes in silicon. Solid State Electron. **35**(11), 1585–1596 (1992)
15. Yang, Y., Tong, X., Yang, L.-T., Guo, P.-F., Fan, L., Yeo, Y.-C.: Tunneling field-effect transistor: capacitance components and modeling. IEEE Electron Device Letter **31**(7), 752–754 (2010)
16. Madan, J., Chaujar, R.: Interfacial charge analysis of heterogeneous gate dielectric-gate all around-tunnel FET for improved device reliability. IEEE Trans. Device Mater. Reliab. **16**(2), 227–234 (2016)

Performance Modelling and Dynamic Scheduling on Heterogeneous-ISA Multi-core Architectures

Nirmal Kumar Boran[✉], Dinesh Kumar Yadav, and Rishabh Iyer

Computer Architecture and Dependable Systems Lab (CADSL), IIT Bombay, Mumbai, India
nirmalkboran@gmail.com, dineshyadav1652@gmail.com, rishabh246@gmail.com
https://www.ee.iitb.ac.in/student/~cadsl

Abstract. Heterogeneous-ISA multi-core architectures have emerged as a promising design paradigm given the ever-increasing demands on single threaded performance. Such architectures comprise multiple cores that differ not just in micro-architectural parameters (e.g., fetch width, ROB size) but also in their Instruction Set Architectures (ISAs). These architectures extract previously latent performance gains by executing different phases of the program on the core (and ISA) best suited to it, as opposed to executing the entire program on a single ISA. In such a computing paradigm, maximum performance is only extracted when we ensure that at every point in the program's execution, the program runs on the core best suited to it. In this work, we propose a migration framework that practically and accurately decides when to migrate the program across different cores (and ISAs) to extract maximum performance gains. Under the covers, this framework combines a regression based performance modelling technique with a greedy scheduling algorithm. Our performance modelling technique leverages hardware performance counters prevalent in all major processors today to accurately estimate the performance of the program on different ISAs to within an error of 6%. Putting it together with our greedy scheduler enables our framework to achieve single thread performance speedups of 29.6% with respect to a baseline single ISA heterogeneous architecture.

Keywords: Heterogeneous ISA multi-core chip ·
Single thread performance · Regression techniques ·
Execution migration

1 Introduction

A look at the history of microprocessor evolution throws light on the fact that the performance of single-threaded programs has always of prime importance. During the last century, researchers were successful in improving single threaded performance until saturation of the frequency scaling. Further performance enhancement required the addition of resources like increasing the size of the register

© Springer Nature Singapore Pte Ltd. 2019
A. Sengupta et al. (Eds.): VDAT 2019, CCIS 1066, pp. 702–715, 2019.
https://doi.org/10.1007/978-981-32-9767-8_58

file, ROB and instruction window which led to an increase in the processor's power dissipation. However, designers eventually hit the power wall [10], which led to a marked shift from single-core to multi-core architectures.

Multi-core architectures can be classified into three types: (1) Homogeneous, (2) Heterogeneous and (3) Dynamic. Homogeneous multi-core (HoMC) architectures [13] consist of several identical cores (both ISA & micro-architecture) and focus on extracting Thread Level Parallelism (TLP). Heterogeneous multi-core (HeMC) [6] architectures, on the other hand, improve the energy efficiency of the processor by leveraging variation in micro-architectural parameters (not ISA) across cores. They typically contain a combination of several small and a few aggressive cores and allowing them to exploit both TLP and Instruction Level Parallelism (ILP). Finally, to increase the energy efficiency further, Dynamic Core (DC) architectures [5] attempt to modify the micro-architectural parameters of cores on-the-fly, morphing from a single big core into many small cores (or vice-versa) depending upon the program.

Venkat et al. [3,15] introduced the notion of Heterogeneous ISA multi-core (HeIMC) architectures. Unlike the previous designs, in which all the cores of the processor had the same ISA, different cores in the processor were now built using different ISAs (e.g., x86, ARM, MIPS). The insight behind this work is that ISA diversity can play a vital role in improving both performance and energy efficiency for single threaded programs. The authors show that different phases of the same program can display an affinity for different ISAs. This affinity arises due to a number of factors namely *code density, dynamic instruction count, register pressure* etc. of the program phase. Hence, if the program is migrated across cores with different ISAs, such that each phase is executed on the ISA it is most affine to, previously latent gains in single threaded performance can be achieved. The authors also describe compiler modifications [3] that make this migration practical.

However, Venkat et al. [3,15] focus only on the prospective gains of HeIMC architectures and NOT on how to achieve them. To extract maximum performance gain, HeIMC architectures require that the program be migrated correctly, ensuring that each phase of the program is executed on the core (and ISA) it is most suited to. In fact, as we show in Sect. 2, incorrect decisions can lead to deterioration in single-threaded performance. Venkat et al. do not address this issue at all, assuming the existence of a prediction oracle which makes perfect decisions. This is naturally infeasible in practice.

To address this gap and close the loop on HeIMC architectures, we propose a framework that practically and accurately decides when to migrates the program across different cores (and ISAs) to extract maximum performance gain. Under the covers, this system combines a regression-based performance modelling technique with a greedy scheduling algorithm. The performance modelling technique practically estimates the performance of the current phase of the program by leveraging micro-architectural parameters obtained from hardware performance counters present in every major processor today [12]. By making accurate predictions and scheduling decisions, our system achieves single thread performance speedups of 29.6% with respect to a baseline single ISA HeMC architecture.

The remainder of the paper is organized as follows: Sect. 2 motivates the need for a novel performance modelling technique for HeIMC architectures. Section 3 explains the proposed method of performance modelling with the required details. Section 4 explains our scheduling mechanism and the trade-offs involved. Section 5 presents the results of our evaluation and finally, Sect. 6 concludes, with certain directions for future research.

2 Motivation and State-of-the-Art

In this section, we show the proposed performance benefits of HeIMC architectures and then describe why we need a novel performance modelling technique.

To demonstrate the ISA affinity exhibited by programs and the proposed benefits in single threaded performance, we divide the *'astar'* benchmark from SPEC CPU2006 [4] into 15 phases and execute it on ARM (RISC) and x86 (CISC) cores. The configurations used for both the cores is mentioned in Table 1. Apart from the number of General Purpose Registers (GPRs) which is an intrinsic property of the ISA, all micro-architecture parameters are identical across the two cores.

Figure 1 shows the execution time of each phase on both cores. The results show that by only changing the ISA, there is sufficient variability across the execution time of each phase. Further, neither core is dominant throughout, with x86 performing considerably better on phases 1, 7–14 and ARM performing considerably better on phases 2–6 and 15. Clearly, running the entire program solely on any one of these cores does not lead to optimal performance.

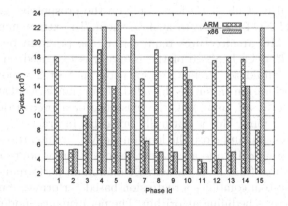

Fig. 1. Execution time of different phases of benchmark astar

Figure 2 shows the latent performance benefits that can be extracted by HeIMC architectures (accurate-migrations). When running each phase of the program on the core (and ISA) it is most suited to, the performance of the program can increase by up to 39% (This is an upper bound because it ignores migration overhead). On the other hand, if the performance modelling is flawed, and mispredicts where to execute each phase of the program, it can lead to unacceptable performance deterioration of up to 26.4%.

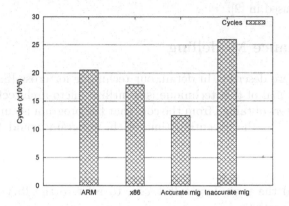

Fig. 2. Execution time when the program is run on ARM, x86 and execution time when each phase is run on the core most suited to it ("Accurate mig") and least suited to it ("Inaccurate mig")

Clearly, maximum performance benefits are only achieved when the program is migrated across the cores at the right time. Naturally, this requires a prediction and scheduling mechanism, which dictates when this migration is supposed to take place. Given this need for an accurate cross-ISA performance modelling technique, we now explain why prior work on the subject is inadequate.

The first work on performance modelling in multi-core architectures was by Kumar et al. [6] who used a sampling-based technique to predict migration of programs on different cores. In this approach, they would run a small section of the code on all available cores and run the remainder of the code on the core that performed best for the small section. This leads to poor resource utilization and does not scale with increasing core counts. Hence, researchers made attempts to use analytical models to model CPI of various programs on single ISA heterogeneous architectures. Van Craeynest et al. [14] introduced a regression-based performance impact estimator that used ILP and MLP (Memory level parallelism) as parameters to predict migration. This was taken further by Lukefahr et al. [9] and Pricopi et al. [11].

While techniques work well for HeMc architectures, they do not make accurate predictions for HeIMC architectures. This is because they are simply not designed to take into account factors that determine performance variation across ISAs, such as code density, register pressure and instruction mix since these factors are identical across cores of the same ISA. Boran et al. [2] demonstrate this by attempting to predict execution time across ISAs using a regression model which takes into account only micro-architectural parameters. *However, their approach leads to unacceptably high prediction errors which motivated us to build a better model that takes into account inter-ISA heterogeneity.* Thus, in this work, in addition to incorporating features that take into account inter-ISA heterogeneity, we also change our machine learning model, using linear regression which is more accurate than the General regression neural network(GRNN) and the model used in [2].

3   Performance Modelling

In this section, we describe, in detail, our technique for cross-ISA performance modelling. The goal of this technique is to utilize micro-architectural and ISA-specific parameters obtained from the core that the program is currently running on, to predict what the execution time of the program would be if run on a different core (and ISA). This prediction will then be fed to the scheduler which dictates when the migration should take place. From here-on, we will use the term *source ISA/core* to refer to the ISA/core that the program is currently running on, and the term *target ISA/core* to refer to the ISA/cores that the program can migrate to.

The work most closely related to ours [2] proposed a two-phased approach for performance modelling wherein they used the micro-architectural parameters from the source ISA to predict the same parameters on the target ISA. Then, using these predicted target ISA parameters, they predicted the execution time on the target ISA. Their approach has two main shortcomings:

- The decoupling of execution time prediction into two independent phases compounds prediction errors. In their work, Boran et al. [2] show that execution time predictions can be off by up to 54%.
- They do not take into account any parameters that characterize the inter-ISA heterogeneity, such as code density, register pressure or instruction mix, leading to high prediction errors.

We improve upon their model in the following ways:

- We eliminate the artificially enforced decoupling in the prediction of execution time. Consequently, we directly predict the execution time on the target ISAs using the parameters of the source ISA.
- We specifically introduce parameters that quantify the inter-ISA heterogeneity, specifically the instruction mix, dynamic instruction count and parallelism (ILP, MLP)
- We replace their regression model with a linear regression model, which performs better for single-level predictions.

3.1   Extracting Relevant Parameters

We now describe the list of parameters we use to predict the execution time on the target ISA and how we extract them. In this work, we use a total of thirteen parameters to predict execution time (number of execution cycles). The parameters include branch miss-predictions, L1-I-cache misses, L1-D-cache misses, L2 cache misses, Reorder Buffer full events, Instruction Queue full events, Store Queue full events, ILP, MLP, MSHR (Miss Status Handling Register) full events, instruction mix (Number of load instructions, Number of floating point instructions) and the dynamic instruction count.

L1-I-cache, L1-D-cache, and L2 cache misses capture the effects of the cache hierarchy on the execution time. Information regarding data-dependency induced stalls has been extracted by the occurrences of the ROB, Instruction Queue and Store Queue being full. ILP and MLP have been considered for determining the available parallelism given the specific ISA and core that the program is running on. Instruction mix and dynamic instruction count are chosen to quantify ISA specificity and finally, the behaviour of the branch predictor is captured using the branch misprediction parameter.

A common feature of all of these parameters is that their extraction is simple and practical. All parameters except ILP and MLP can be directly obtained from hardware performance counters prevalent in every major processor variant today. To calculate ILP and MLP we rely on schemes proposed by previous work [9]. ILP is estimated by using a hardware counter which maintains a running sum of the instructions in the issue stage whose execution requires the data from the other instructions currently under execution. This counter captures all the instructions which are stalled due to dependencies, thus providing us with an inverse measure. For MLP, we leverage a hardware counter that maintains a running sum of the number of MSHR entries at every cache miss. This gives us an estimate of MLP because during a cache miss, all misses currently being handled in parallel will have an entry in the MSHR. We take individual averages of the running sums maintained by both counters ($running\_sum/total\_instructions$) to estimate the ILP and MLP respectively.

3.2   Linear Regression Model

Given those parameters, we now describe our linear regression based performance model. In our evaluation Sect. 5, we show that it outperforms the GRNN model proposed in previous work. Given a source ISA in execution (ISA_A) and a target ISA (ISA_B), our linear regression model for estimation of the number of cycles is given by:

$$
\begin{aligned}
Cycle_B =\ &K + a_1.(L1DcacheMiss_A) + a_2.(L1IcacheMiss_A)\\
&+ a_3.(L2cacheMiss_A) + a_4.(IQFullEvents_A)\\
&+ a_5.(SQFullEvents_A) + a_6.(ROBFullEvents_A)\\
&+ a_7.(BranchMissPrediction_A) + a_8.(MLP_A)\\
&+ a_9.(MSHRFullEvents_A) + a_{10}.(ILP_A)\\
&+ a_{11}.(LoadCount_A) + a_{12}.(FloatInstruction_A)\\
&+ a_{13}.(DynamicInstructionCount_A)
\end{aligned}
\tag{1}
$$

where a_1 to a_{13} are regression coefficients, $Cycle_B$ is number of cycles for ISA_B and K is a constant.

In this work, we consider three ISAs namely x86, ARM and Alpha. We build a total of 6 regression models: for each of the three ISAs, we predict the performance of the other 2. The idea here is that these models are built offline and incorporated into the processor with the coefficients of the model stored in special registers. Then, when programs are executed, these models continuously predict the performance on the other two ISAs and pass these predictions to the scheduler.

4   Scheduling

In this section, we describe the design of our scheduler. We first provide necessary background on how a cross-ISA compiled program looks like, before detailing our scheduling algorithm and the tradeoffs involved.

De Vuyst et al. [3] describes compiler modifications that allow a program to efficiently migrate across cores. The generated binary possesses a number of *equivalence points* at which the memory state of the binary is consistent across different ISAs. This identical memory state allows for low-overhead migration of the program at one of these equivalence points. Note, migrating at any other point is expensive and requires dynamic binary translation on the target ISA till the next equivalence point is reached. Given the overhead of migration, these equivalence points are typically kept around 100M instructions apart. We call each such division of 100M instructions a *phase*. Figure 3 further illustrates equivalence points and phases.

This division of the program into phases poses a significant challenge for the scheduler. Ideally, we would like to use the first few (10–20M) instructions of the phase to predict which ISA it is suited to, much like [6]. Unfortunately, this is infeasible since migration can only occur at the equivalence points. Consequently, all scheduling decisions must be made before the phase begins to execute.

We extract the parameters mentioned in Sect. 3.1 for only the final 10M instructions of a phase and feed it into our regression-based performance model which predicts the performance on the target ISAs. Using the final 10M instructions leads to accurate predictions because it is a small yet significant number of instructions closest to the next phase and variations will be few, but meaningful predictions can be made.

Once we have the predictions for execution time for all the target ISAs, we simply employ greedy scheduling, i.e., at the next equivalence point, the scheduler migrates the program to the ISA with least predicted execution time. Naturally, for all the target ISAs we include the migration overhead into the estimation.

5   Evaluation

In this section, we describe the results from our evaluation, which answer 2 primary questions: (1) Does the regression-based performance model predict per-

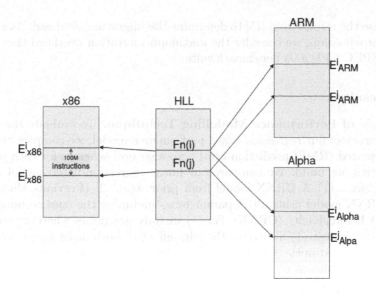

Fig. 3. Equivalence points are chosen at function call sites in the compiler IR. They are typically around 100M instructions apart

formance accurately across ISAs and (2) Does the scheduling algorithm correctly migrate the program to deliver overall speedups in single-threaded performance?

5.1   Methodology

As mentioned previously, we consider 3 ISAs in this work - x86, ARM and Alpha. Since the focus is on inter-ISA heterogeneity, we keep the configuration for all 3 ISAs identical (Number of GPRs is a property of the ISA). The configuration for all the cores is shown in Table 1. The clock speed for all three cores is 2 GHz. We use the gem5 simulator [1] to simulate performance and SPEC CPU2006 [4] benchmark suite as our target programs.

Table 1. Core configurations

Design Parameter	ARM	Alpha	x86
Architectural Registers	32 GPR	64GPR	16 GPR
Cache line size (bytes)	64	64	64
LSQ size (bytes)	32	32	32
Fetch width	4	4	4
Instruction Queue entries	64	64	64
ROB entries	192	192	192
DCache,ICache size	32 KB	32 KB	32 KB
L2 Cache size	256 KB	256 KB	256 KB

We use the results from [15] to determine the migration overhead. As a simple over-approximation, we consider the maximum migration overhead they report for the SPEC CPU2006 benchmark suite.

5.2 Results

Accuracy of Performance Modelling Technique. To evaluate the prediction accuracy of our regression-based performance model, we compare the Root Mean Squared (RMS) prediction error across several schemes for each of the 6 models that we build. We compare our linear regression-based model against two schemes - (1) A GRNN model from prior work [2] (Previous Model) and (2) A GRNN model using all 13 parameters - including the ones accounting for inter-ISA heterogeneity (GRNN). For (1) we only use values wherever provided. Comparing against (1) illustrates the joint effect of both using linear regression and including parameters that capture the inter-ISA heterogeneity. Comparing against (2) enables us to quantify the improvements due to using linear regression since the parameter set is identical for both schemes.

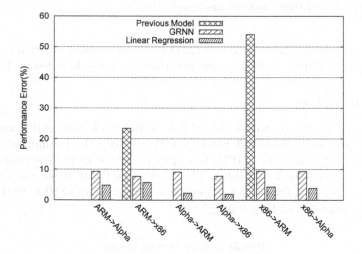

Fig. 4. Root mean squared error of performance modelling of Previous Model [2], GRNN and Linear Regression. $ISA_1 \longrightarrow ISA_2$ denotes estimation of performance for the core with ISA_2 while running the program on the core with ISA_1

Figure 4 compares the RMS prediction error for all three schemes across predictions for all phases of all the benchmarks in the SPEC CPU2006 benchmark suite. The phase length taken for performance modelling is 10M.

Two clear trends emerge:

- Irrespective of the model, linear regression always outperforms the GRNN. The linear regression based model leads to errors ranging from 1.7% to 5.7%, while the GRNN leads to errors ranging from 7.5% to 9.4%.
- Both schemes outperform prior work considerably. This is due to two factors - (1) The introduction of additional parameters that capture inter-ISA heterogeneity such as the dynamic instruction count and the instruction mix and (2) Replacing the two-phase prediction which compounds prediction errors with a simple one-phase prediction scheme.

We also compare the standard deviation of the RMS error for both the GRNN and Linear regression-based models. Linear regression has a 26% lower standard deviation than the GRNN model making it lesser uncertain and more reliable.

Dynamic Scheduling. To evaluate whether our scheduling algorithm migrates the program correctly, we compare the speedup obtained in the HeIMC architecture as opposed to the base case of a single ISA architecture. Figure 5 illustrates the result. Our regression based scheduler shows a 29.6% increase in mean performance when compared to the x86 baseline and a 19.5% increase in performance on the best performing architecture. Additionally, the regression-based predictor is only 12.2% off the oracle. Please note that the *oracle is a hypothetical case in which each phase runs on the core it is most suited to. Hence the Oracle case represents the maximum possible speedup.* The phase length for dynamic scheduling is taken as 100M. The models were trained using data from all of the SPEC CPU2006 benchmarks (70% training data, 30% testing data).

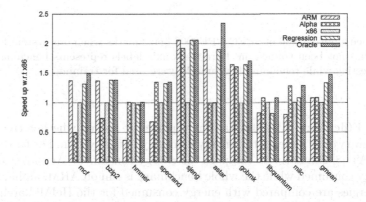

Fig. 5. Average speedup of different benchmarks when entire program is scheduled on ARM, Alpha or x86 and compared with HeIMC architecture with regression and oracle based scheduling

In the previous experiment, the model was only evaluated on programs it had already been exposed to. When deployed, however, our framework must run accurately even for programs it has not been trained on. To evaluate this generality and resilience of our migration framework, we trained the model using only a subset of the SPEC CPU2006 benchmark suite and tested it on others. Then we measured how accurately the scheduler migrates the program and the speedups achieved on these unseen programs. Figure 6 illustrates the results. We see that on average, our system works even for programs it has not seen before, producing an average speedup of 24.4% over x86 and only 16% less than the oracle. Additionally, our system migrates the program to the core it is most suited 82.94% of the time. Given that the SPEC CPU2006 benchmark suite consists of programs that are inherently very different from one another, these results show that our model is resilient and can be deployed without having to be re-trained frequently.

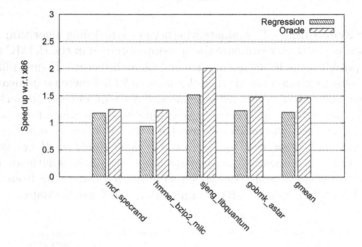

Fig. 6. Speedup w.r.t x86 of SPEC CPU2006 benchmarks when our system faces programs it has not been trained on. Here the x-axis labels represents benchmarks used only for testing while remaining benchmarks were used for training.

Energy Efficiency. We also ran an experiment to see whether the HeIMC architecture would increase the energy efficiency of the system. For this, we used the McPAT [8] simulator to compare the energy consumed. We have calculated the energy consumed while the whole benchmark is run on ARM, alpha, x86 and these energies are compared with energy consumed for the HeIMC architecture which uses our performance model and scheduling algorithm (Fig. 7). In our experiments, we find that there is very little change in energy consumption. This is likely because all three cores in our system had an identical configuration the ISA which displays the maximum performance also consumes the maximum power. Additionally, our scheduler is only designed for optimizing performance. In future work, we plan to incorporate the energy consumption also into the decision making process.

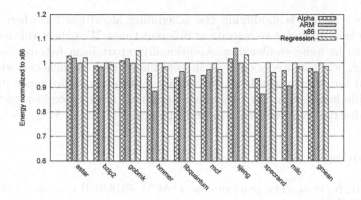

Fig. 7. Energy comparison

Hardware Overhead. The proposed modelling method and scheduling algorithm have minimal hardware overhead. Since we are doing the training offline in software, we only require 14 registers to store the weights for performance modelling using the linear regression method. The compute scheduler requires thirty-nine 8-bit multipliers for applying weights to the input parameters along with three 32-bit adders. Please note that a GRNN based model has more hardware overhead when compared to a linear regression based one.

6 Conclusion and Future Work

In this work, we have shown that it is feasible to extract performance benefits from HeIMC architectures by utilizing lightweight and practical techniques for performance modelling and dynamic scheduling. Our framework combines a regression-based performance model with a greedy scheduling algorithm. Our performance model estimates the performance of a program across ISAs within 6% error-limit and our scheduler migrates the program to the core it is most suited to 83% of the time for program types it has never seen before. Together, these techniques achieve an average increase of 29.6% in single-threaded performance on the SPEC CPU2006 benchmark suite.

We see several interesting avenues for future work. First and foremost, we plan to introduce energy efficiency into the scheduling decisions which will allow HeIMC architectures to save considerable energy as opposed to HeMC ones. For instance, introducing a specifically energy-efficient ISA such as thumb and only migrating when the ILP of the program is very low can lead to an energy efficient system with minimal degradation in performance. In such energy efficient systems, we would also like to focus on the idea proposed by Lee et al. [7] which shows that reducing the instructions in the ARM ISA has shown to greatly reduce the logical complexity of hardware, such ISA diversity enables further energy efficiency.

Another avenue is modifying the scheduling algorithm for when multiple programs exist and want to migrate at different times. We expect this co-located scenario to be quite challenging. Additionally, apart from heterogeneous ISA scheduling, performance modelling can have many other applications which may be helpful for other researchers. For instance, accurate performance modelling can provide information w.r.t to which workloads must be co-located together to avoid destructive interference in performance.

References

1. Binkert, N., et al.: The gem5 simulator. ACM SIGARCH Comput. Archit. News **39**, 1–7 (2011)
2. Boran, N.K., Meghwal, R.P., Sharma, K., Kumar, B., Singh, V.: Performance modelling of heterogeneous ISA multicore architectures. In: 2016 IEEE East-West Design & Test Symposium (EWDTS), pp. 1–4. IEEE (2016)
3. DeVuyst, M., Venkat, A., Tullsen, D.M.: Execution migration in a heterogeneous-ISA chip multiprocessor. ACM SIGARCH Comput. Archit. News **40**(1), 261–272 (2012)
4. Henning, J.L.: SPEC CPU2006 benchmark descriptions. SIGARCH Comput. Archit. News (2006). https://doi.org/10.1145/1186736.1186737
5. Ipek, E., Kirman, M., Kirman, N., Martinez, J.F.: Core fusion: accommodating software diversity in chip multiprocessors. ACM SIGARCH Comput. Archit. News **35**(2), 186–197 (2007)
6. Kumar, R., Farkas, K.I., Jouppi, N.P., Ranganathan, P., Tullsen, D.M.: Single-ISA heterogeneous multi-core architectures: the potential for processor power reduction. In: Proceedings of 36th Annual IEEE/ACM International Symposium on Microarchitecture. MICRO-36, pp. 81–92. IEEE (2003)
7. Lee, W., Sunwoo, D., Emmons, C.D., Gerstlauer, A., John, L.: Exploring opportunities for heterogeneous-ISA core architectures in high-performance mobile SoCs. Technical Report UT-CERC-17-01, The University of Texas At Austin (2017)
8. Li, S., Ahn, J.H., Strong, R.D., Brockman, J.B., Tullsen, D.M., Jouppi, N.P.: McPat: an integrated power, area, and timing modeling framework for multicore and manycore architectures. In: Proceedings of 42nd Annual IEEE/ACM International Symposium on Microarchitecture. MICRO-42, pp. 469–480. IEEE (2009)
9. Lukefahr, A., et al.: Composite cores: pushing heterogeneity into a core. In: MICRO-45. IEEE Computer Society, Washington, DC (2012). https://doi.org/10.1109/MICRO.2012.37
10. Patterson, D.: The trouble with multicore. IEEE Spectr. **47**, 28–32, 53 (2010). https://doi.org/10.1109/MSPEC.2010.5491011
11. Pricopi, M., Muthukaruppan, T.S., Venkataramani, V., Mitra, T., Vishin, S.: Power-performance modeling on asymmetric multi-cores. In: 2013 International Conference on Compilers, Architecture and Synthesis for Embedded Systems (CASES), pp. 1–10. IEEE (2013)
12. Sprunt, B.: The basics of performance-monitoring hardware. IEEE Micro **22**(4), 64–71 (2002)
13. Taylor, M.B., et al.: Evaluation of the raw microprocessor: an exposed-wire-delay architecture for ILP and streams. In: 31st International Symposium on Computer Architecture (ISCA 2004), 19–23 June 2004, Munich, Germany (2004)

14. Van Craeynest, K., Jaleel, A., Eeckhout, L., Narvaez, P., Emer, J.: Scheduling heterogeneous multi-cores through performance impact estimation (PIE). ACM SIGARCH Comput. Archit. News **40**(3), 213–224 (2012)
15. Venkat, A., Tullsen, D.M.: Harnessing ISA diversity: design of a heterogeneous-ISA chip multiprocessor. In: 2014 ACM/IEEE 41st International Symposium on Computer Architecture (ISCA), pp. 121–132. IEEE (2014)

Simulation Study of III-V Lateral Tunnel FETs with Gate-Drain Underlap

Venkata Appa Rao Yempada$^{(\boxtimes)}$ and Srivatsava Jandhyala

IIIT Hyderabad, Hyderabad 500032, Telangana, India
venkat.yempada@research.iiit.ac.in,
srivatsava.jandhyala@iiit.ac.in

Abstract. Design of TFETs, with gate-drain underlap (L_{un}), exhibit suppressed off-state leakage and ambipolar conduction, thereby achieving larger on-to-off current ratio. In this work, through TCAD simulation study, we proposed an optimum value for gate-drain underlap length (L_{un}), and highlighted the advantages of designing TFETs with gate-drain underlap. Simulation framework was developed for both homojunction and heterojunction TFETs. The device design for both types of TFETs, considered similar doping profiles. The optimum value for L_{un} was determined to be half the gate length (L_g) from the DC characteristics, with little dependence of off-state leakage on the drain voltage. In the simulation study we also focused on the effect of the drain doping, and the gate length (L_g) on the performance of drain underlapped TFETs. The simulation study has been extensively performed on Ultra-Thin Body (UTB) III-V homojunction TFET and Ultra-Thin Body-Silicon On insulator (UTBSOI) Staggered gap (SG) III-V heterojunction TFET.

Keywords: Ambipolarity · Gate-drain underlap · Homojunction · Heterojunction · Tunneling · Subthreshold swing

1 Introduction

Tunnel FETs are promising candidates for low voltage applications, due to the steepness they exhibit in switching from subthreshold region to super threshold region. However, their on-currents are limited, due to their low tunneling probability. Bandgap engineering making use of III-V (compound semiconductors) TFETs is a practical solution to this. III-V Heterojunction TFETs, meet the demands of higher on-state performance, due to their band alignment that offers lower barrier width for band-to-band tunneling and also thanks to larger mobility and narrower bandgap of III-V materials. In this paper we explore Indium Arsenide (InAs), a binary compound, and Indium Gallium Arsenide (InxGa1-xAs), a ternary compound, as source injectors for the design of TFETs. Based on the nature of band alignment, Heterojunction TFETs can be designed as straddling (Type-I), staggered, and broken gap (Type-II) TFETs. Among these, the staggered and broken or nearly broken gap heterojunction TFETs, have higher tunneling probability, due their lower effective bandgap for tunneling of charge carriers [1]. TFETs with staggered heterojunction have demonstrated the best combination of currents and subthreshold swing [2]. New approaches were developed

© Springer Nature Singapore Pte Ltd. 2019
A. Sengupta et al. (Eds.): VDAT 2019, CCIS 1066, pp. 716–726, 2019.
https://doi.org/10.1007/978-981-32-9767-8_59

to integrate InAs-Si material system, using selective epitaxy in nanotube templates, template nanowire growth [11]. In this work, we explored InAs/Si staggered gap lateral heterojunction TFET with UTBSOI device architecture, and InAs (III-V) based lateral homojunction TFET with double gate UTB geometry, with the drain underlap and the optimum drain underlap for suppressing the ambipolar leakage is determined and validated with the help of TCAD simulations.

The signature behavior of TFETs, ambipolar conduction, which allows TFET to conduct for either polarity of gate voltage, is not desirable for low power VLSI applications. To overcome this limitation, gate-drain underlap or drain offset can be introduced into the device structure. This approach can reduce the ambipolar behavior by reducing the electric field at the drain end (in underlap region) [3]. The influence of the drain underlap on the DC performance of TFETs is evident, and observed in the enhancement of the on-current to off-current ratio (I_{on}/I_{off}), and the enhancement is significant for optimum values of gate-drain underlap. It is determined, from the simulation results, for larger values of drain underlap; the ambipolar conduction is suppressed. With the InAs-Si material system, Heterojunction TFET achieves very high on-to-off current ratio I_{on}/I_{off}, by the larger bandgap of Si, and seems promising for high on-current, I_{on}, due to the narrower bandgap of InAs [4, 5], instead devices based on all III-V compounds, both homojunction and heterojunction TFETs achieve high currents, but with very low I_{on}/I_{off} ratio.

2 Device Design and DC Characteristics of Drain Underlapped Homojunction TFET

2.1 Device Design

Materials with lower Density of states (DOS) and bandgap, such as InAs decrease the gate capacitance and improve I_{on}. With this consideration, in this section, we have presented the device design and simulation study of the InAs based homojunction TFETs, most importantly the effect of drain underlap or offset on its DC performance. The material characteristics that favor InAs for high performance TFET design are: (I) Due to their narrower bandgap, they are capable of delivering larger on currents. (II) Due to their lower DOS, they have less charge screening effect, and their channel potential is more sensitive to gate voltage, and so the tunneling barrier, that leads to steeper subthreshold swing (SS). (III) Due to their lower effective masses, they can deliver larger on-currents. To perform two-dimensional simulations, Sentaurus TCAD [7] is used. Figure 1 shows the simulated device structure of InAs based DG UTB homojunction TFET. The corresponding device and material parameters are listed in Tables 1 and 2. The study has mainly explored UTB geometry for better electrostatic control, and the ratio of the gate length, L_G to the body thickness, t_{body}, (L_G/t_{body}) can be designed, in order to achieve steeper SS [6]. However, this results in lower on-state current, I_{on}.

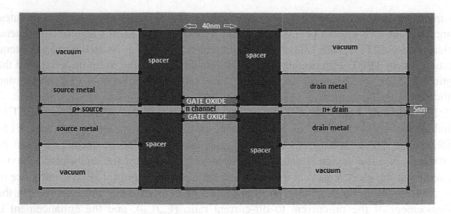

Fig. 1. Simulated device structure of DG UTB InAs based homojunction n-TFET.

Table 1. Material parameters

	Material parameters				
	Electron affinity (eV)	m_{lh}/m_0	m_e/m_0	Lattice constant (A^0)	Eg (eV)
InAs	4.9	0.026	0.023	6.05	0.354
Si	4.01	0.98	0.98	5.43	1.12

Table 2. Device doping concentrations

TFET type	Source doping	Channel doping	Drain doping
InAs homojunction	2×10^{20}	10^{17}	10^{20}
Si-based homo junction	2×10^{20}	10^{17}	2×10^{18}
InAs/Si hetero junction	10^{20}	10^{17}	10^{19}
$Al_{0.8}Ga_{0.2}Sb$/InAs-staggered gap heterojunction	3.5×10^{19}	10^{16}	10^{17}
InAs/Si heterojunction (P-type)	10^{19}	10^{15}	10^{17}

So, we explored, an optimum operating voltage for the TFET, for achieving larger I_{on} and I_{on}/I_{off}. However, this results in an increase in dynamic power consumption. The gate-drain underlap structure is used in the device design, to suppress the ambipolar leakage, and there is a little degree of freedom, for designing the ratio, channel length to body thickness L_G/t_{body} (Fig. 2). One of the design parameter here, the drain underlap length, L_{un} varied over a wider range for determining the optimum value for I_{on}/I_{off}, for a given TFET geometry. In the following section, the effect of gate-drain underlap on the DC characteristics of InAs based Homojunction TFETs is discussed.

2.2 Effect of Gate-Drain Underlap on DC Characteristics of InAs Based Homojunction TFET

To ensure higher accuracy, 2-dimensional device simulations have been done by incorporating, Auger recombination, dynamic nonlocal Band-to-Band tunneling (BTBT) model, SRH recombination and Bandgap narrowing (BGN) models. Figure 2 emphasizes the need for scaling the device geometry, both vertical and lateral dimensions in proportionate with the L_{un}. To study the effect of drain underlap on ambipolar conduction in TFETs, device simulations were carried out for negative gate voltages, for various values of drain underlap, L_{un} (Fig. 3). It is observed from the Fig. 3, that the ambipolar conduction is significantly suppressed, for L_{un} of 20 nm, for the TFET with channel length, L_G of 40 nm. The ambipolar leakage for the optimum value of L_{un} is degraded by more than 5 decades, and this is due to increased depletion region near the drain-channel junction. The larger the underlap, the more sensitive the TFET's electrostatics to the applied drain voltage. To understand more clearly, electrostatics of TFET with an optimum L_{un}, the tunneling path behavior must be clearly analyzed. The series resistance of a TFET, is attributed to tunneling barrier resistance and channel resistance [8]. It is observed from the transfer characteristics (Fig. 3), the drain underlap has little influence on the on current (I_{on}), as the variation of channel resistance has negligible influence on I_{on}, and the tunneling barrier resistance is the dominating component that determines the I_{on} [12]. This is due to the reduced impact of the electric field by the gate voltage over the channel region (underlap region) near the drain [8], and this lower electric field results in smaller band bending between the channel and the drain interface. So, in our design the optimum value for drain underlap

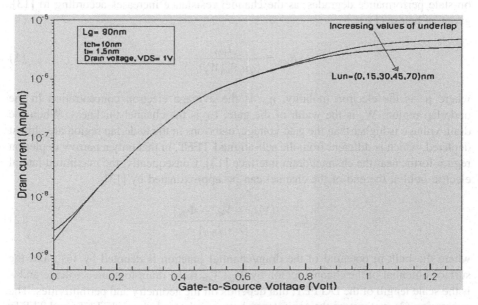

Fig. 2. On-state performance of InAs based homojunction N-TFET, for underlap length, L_{un} ranging from 0 nm to 70 nm. TFET geometry: gate length L_g = 90 nm, channel thickness, t_{ch} = 10 nm, and gate oxide thickness, t_i = 1.5 nm. Drain-to-Source voltage V_{DS} = 1 V.

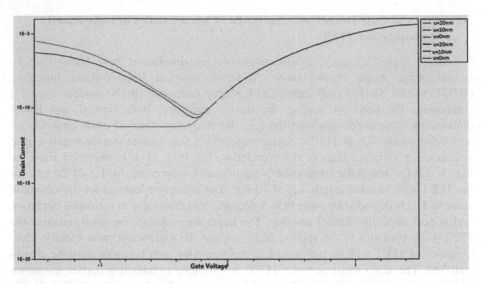

Fig. 3. Simulated Transfer characteristics of InAs based homojunction N-TFET (L_g = 40 nm), at V_{ds} = 1 V for different gate-drain underlap lengths, L_{un} of 0 nm, 10 nm, 20 nm. The gate voltage V_{gs} is swept from −1.5 V to 1.5 V. The negative values of V_{gs} cause ambipolar conduction.

is determined to be 20 nm (L_{un} = $L_G/2$), that suppresses the ambipolar leakage without affecting the on-state performance. However, for larger values of drain underlap, the on-state performance degrades, as the channel resistance increases according to [13], given as below (1).

$$R_{un} = \frac{L_{un}}{\left(q\mu_e n_{un} W_g t_{ch}\right)} \tag{1}$$

where μ_e is the electron mobility, n_{un} is the average electron concentration in the underlap region; W_g is the width of the gate, t_{ch} is the channel thickness. When the drain voltage is higher than the gate voltage, electrons in the underlap region are almost depleted, which is different from the self-aligned TFET, in that only a narrow depletion region forms near the channel/drain interface [13]. Consequently, the maximum lateral electric field at the end of the channel can be approximated by [13]

$$E_m = \frac{\left(V_{bi,d} + V_{ds} - \Phi_{dg}\right)}{\left(\lambda + L_{un}\right)} \tag{2}$$

where the built-in potential of the drain/channel junction is denoted by $V_{bi,d}$ and the surface potential of the channel region by Φ_{dg}, V_{ds} is the drain-to-source voltage and λ is the scale length of the DG FET, that depends on the geometry and permittivities. The expression (2), guarantees the consistency between the underlapped TFETs and TFETs with symmetric junctions [13]. When the underlap region L_{un} increases, leading to larger tunneling distance, that results in a reduction in the maximum electric field, E_m

near the drain side. So, it is clear from the study of homojunction TFETs with drain underlap, that under negative bias the tunneling probability and the carrier tunneling rate through the channel/drain barrier decreases [13]. To validate the same, and for cross technology comparison, simulated energy band diagram of Si N-TFETs with drain underlap, shown in the Fig. 4, by using Bandprofiler, a 1-D Poisson-Schrodinger solver [9]. From the energy band diagram (Fig. 4), it is clear that the tunneling barrier width between the channel and drain is significant with drain underlapped structure, and thus the source-drain direct tunneling leakage and the ambipolar behavior are suppressed.

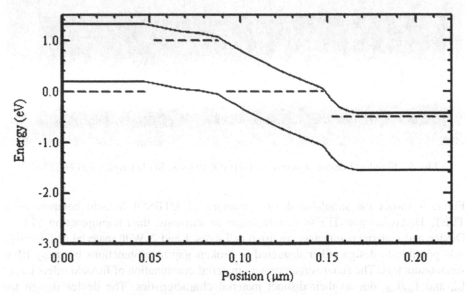

Fig. 4. Energy band diagram along the channel of Si based homojunction N-TFET, simulated in Bandprofiler (1D Poisson-Schrödinger solver), with $V_{gs} = -1$ V, $V_{ds} = 0.5$ V and gate-drain underlap length, L_{un} of 20 nm. Dashed lines represent Fermi level.

From the Fig. 2, transfer characteristics of InAs based homojunction TFETs with optimum drain underlap, I_{on} and I_{on}/I_{off} measured: They were found to be 10 µA/µm and 10^5, respectively, for $V_{gs} = V_{ds} = 1$ V, and so the ambipolar leakage is suppressed by a factor of 10^5, with an underlap length of 20 nm. Larger underlap values cause drain voltage to have dominant influence on the channel, leading to current saturation due to drain voltage, rather than gate voltage, i.e., when the channel length becomes comparable to the L_{un}, the on-state performance is more sensitive to the drain voltage. Apart from larger I_{on}/I_{off}, the homo junction TFET also delivers steeper subthreshold slope, due to their energy filtering behavior. In the following section, the device design and the effect of gate-drain underlap for heterojunction TFETs is discussed.

3 Device Design and DC Characteristics of Drain Underlapped Heterojunction TFET

3.1 Device Design

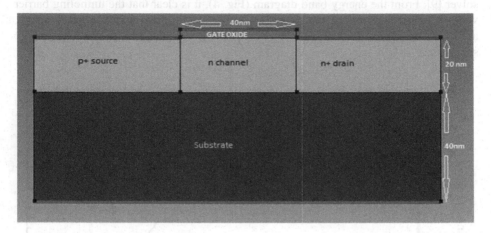

Fig. 5. Simulated device structure of UTBSOI InAs/Si SG heterojunction N-TFET.

Figure 5 shows the simulated device structure of UTBSOI InAs/Si heterojunction TFET. Heterojunction TFETs deliver larger on currents, than homojunction TFETs. Device and material parameters are listed in Tables 1 and 2. With material engineering, it is possible to design either staggered or broken gap heterojunctions by using III-V semiconductors. The Heterostructure with material combination of InAs/Si offers larger I_{on} and I_{on}/I_{off}, due to their distinct material characteristics. The device design for improved electrostatics, considers UTB geometry thickness and thereby to improve the steepness of the SS.

3.2 Effect of Gate-Drain Underlap on DC Characteristics of InAs/Si SG Heterojunction TFET

Figure 6 shows transfer characteristics of the heterojunction TFET, demonstrating the influence of drain underlap on the I_{on} and I_{on}/I_{off}. The optimum underlap for the TFET with gate length of 40 nm, is observed to be 20 nm, i.e., optimum value of $L_{un} = L_g/2$. The device is simulated with the same simulation framework, as that of homojunction TFETs. So, the ambipolar leakage current estimation is not accurate, as quantization effects have not been included for simulation [10], it is over estimated. While, the on-state performance is not degraded by the increase in the drain underlap, the ambipolar conduction is significantly suppressed. Figure 7 shows the dependence of the I_{on} on gate length for the same Heterostructure, with an L_{un} of 10 nm. From the channel length scaling study done, the screening effect of the underlap region decreases when the channel length decreases, leading to degradation of the on-state performance, with little influence on the off-state performance (Fig. 7). From the transfer characteristics of the InAs/Si heterojunction TFET with the optimum drain underlap (Fig. 6), I_{on} and I_{on}/I_{off} measured: They were found to be 1.4 mA/μm and 10^6, respectively, for $V_{gs} = V_{ds} = 1$ V, and so the ambipolar leakage is suppressed significantly, dropped to few Pico amperes, with an optimum L_{un} of 20 nm. This scenario explains the importance of fabricating hetero junction TFETs with gate-drain underlap.

To analyze the impact of the drain underlap on the ambipolar behavior, energy band diagrams of heterojunction TFETs were simulated by the Bandprofiler tool [9]. From the energy band diagram of the lateral InAs/Si heterojunction n-TFET shown in the Fig. 8, it is clear that the electric field inside the drain underlap region is lower. So, the ambipolar conduction is suppressed for the design with the optimum value for L_{un} of 20 nm. With lightly doped drain ($10^{17}/Cm^3$) the ambipolar conduction is suppressed further. Doping conditions are given in Table 2. To emphasize the importance of band gap engineering in III-V Heterojunction TFETs, the $Al_{0.8}Ga_{0.2}Sb/InAs$ material system is used for designing staggered gap heterojunction p-TFET with optimum drain underlap. From the energy band diagram of the $Al_{0.8}Ga_{0.2}Sb/InAs$ hetero TFET, shown in Fig. 9, the drain underlap increases the tunneling distance between channel and drain, thereby suppressing the ambipolar leakage.

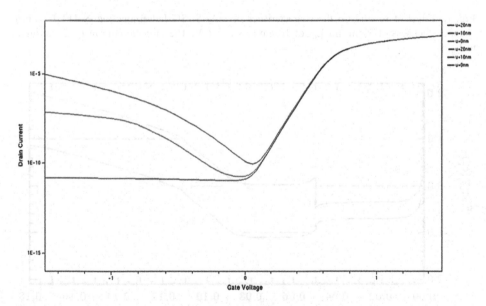

Fig. 6. Transfer characteristics of InAs/Si SG heterojunction N-TFET at $V_{ds} = 1$ V for different values of gate-drain underlap lengths, of 0 nm, 10 nm, 20 nm.

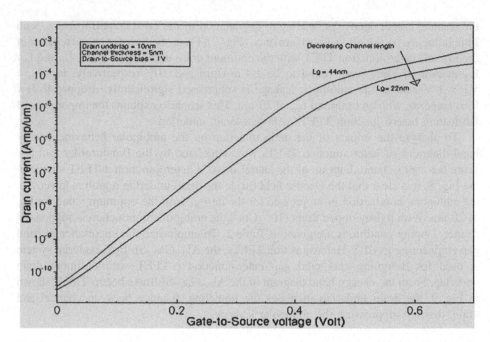

Fig. 7. Effect of scaling on the characteristics of InAs/Si SG heterojunction N-TFET with a channel thickness of 5 nm, for L_{un} of 10 nm at $V_{ds} = 1$ V. The on-state current I_{on} is sensitive to L_g.

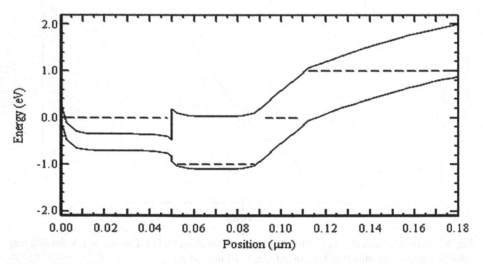

Fig. 8. Energy band diagram along the channel, of p-type (InAs/Si) SG Heterojunction TFET simulated in Bandprofiler (1-D solver), with lightly doped drain diffusion.

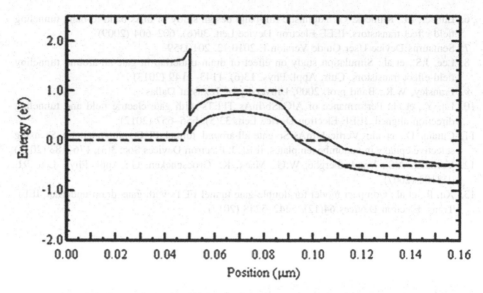

Fig. 9. Energy band diagram along the channel, of SG (Al$_{0.8}$Ga$_{0.2}$Sb/InAs) III-V Heterojunction N-TFET simulated in Bandprofiler (Doping concentrations of the simulated device structures are shown in Table 2), with lightly doped drain diffusion.

4   Conclusions

In this paper, we present TFET design with drain underlap to suppress the ambipolar conduction and for optimizing the on-state performance. From TCAD simulations, it is predicted that the InAs based homojunction TFET delivers an on-current of 10 μA/μm and the heterojunction TFET delivers an on-current of 1.4 mA/μm. We also demonstrate the influence of gate-drain underlap on the device DC characteristics of both the types of TFETs, with the help of Bandprofiler, a 1-dimensional Poisson-Schrodinger solver. The optimum value for L$_{un}$ determined from TCAD simulations, to be around half of the gate length, L$_G$. This definition considered both the on and off currents, as well as on-to-off current ratio of TFETs.

References

1. Mayer, T.S., Datta, S., Narayanan, V.K.: Very low energy dissipation computing using tunneling injected nonequillibrium ballistic carriers. SRC, P061953, November 2011
2. Memisic, E.: Vertical III-V Nanowire Tunnel Field-Effect Transistor. https://lup.lub.lu.se/search/publication/c40eab84-1f8f-469b-bc64-889e9514f4d0
3. Krishna Mohan, T., Kim, D., Raghunathan, S., Saraswat, K.: IEDM Tech. Digest 947 (2008)
4. Riel, H., et al.: InAs-Si heterojunction nanowire tunnel diodes and tunnel FETs. In: IEDM (2012). (13384078)
5. Moselund, K.E., et al.: InAs-Si nanowire heterojunction tunnel FETs. IEEE Electron Device Lett. **33**(10), 1453–1455 (2012)

6. Luisier, M., Klimeck, G.: Atomistic full-band design study of InAs band-to-band tunneling field-effect transistors. IEEE Electron Device Lett. **30**(6), 602–604 (2009)
7. Sentaurus Device User Guide Version E-2010.12, 2010359
8. Lee, J.S., et al.: Simulation study on effect of drain underlap in gate-all-around tunneling field-effect transistors. Curr. Appl. Phys. **13**(6), 1143–1149 (2013)
9. Fransley, W.R.: Band prof, 2009, University of Texas at Dallas
10. Lu, Y., et al.: Performance of AlGaSb/InAs TFETs with gate electric field and tunneling direction aligned. IEEE Electron Device Lett. **33**(5), 655–657 (2012)
11. Cutaia, D., et al.: Vertical InAs-Si gate-all-around tunnel FETs integrated on Si using selective epitaxy in nanotube templates. IEEE J. Electron Devices Soc. **3**(3), 176–183 (2015)
12. Verhulst, A.S., Vandenberghe, W.G., Maex, K., Groeseneken, G.: Appl. Phys. Lett. **91**, 053102 (2007)
13. Xu, P., et al.: Compact model for double-gate tunnel FETs with gate–drain underlap. IEEE Trans. Electron Devices **64**(12), 5242–5248 (2017)

Low-Voltage Dual-Gate Organic Thin Film Transistors with Distinctly Placed Source and Drain

Shagun Pal$^{(\boxtimes)}$ (iD) and Brijesh Kumar

Department of Electronics and Communication,
Madan Mohan Malaviya University of Technology, Gorakhpur, India
pshagun.pal@gmail.com, bkece@mmmut.ac.in

Abstract. Dual Gate Organic Thin Film Transistor (DG-OTFT) preferred device because of significantly higher performance in comparison to Single Gate Organic Thin Film Transistor (SG-OTFT). This paper presents the behavior analysis of proposed novel structures of DG-OTFT in terms of electrical parameters such as on-current, subthreshold slope, and threshold voltage. Subsequently, this research paper analyzes the impact on these performance parameters of the asymmetrically placed source and drain in DG-OTFTs. The two dimensional (2D) numerical device simulator is used to investigate the behavioral changes of three (3) different structures based on the distinct arrangements of contacts either at the top or bottom/asymmetric on active layer. High-voltage (>10 V) based DG-OTFTs have been thoroughly discussed in the recent research phase: yet a very less work has been reported on the low-voltage DG-OTFTs (<10 V) due to the fabrication challenges. Consequently, this paper also presents the low-voltage DG-OTFTs based on the fabricated devices for the three different proposed devices by using parylene film as the gate dielectric to meet the fabrication challenge. Simulation results show that the distinct placements of contacts may result in different device speed that leads to better switching speed for organic digital circuit applications.

Keywords: Organic thin film transistor (OTFT) · Parylene ·
Low voltage · Bottom source top drain dual gate OTFT ·
Top source bottom drain dual gate OTFT ·
Asymmetric source and drain dual gate OTFT

1 Introduction

Organic thin film transistor (OTFT) have been actively served as the fundamentals for applications in the flexible electronics because of their proficiency in terms of low cost, large area fabrication techniques [1]. These features have enabled OTFTs to be extensively utilized in as the backplane of flat-panel displays [2], sensors [3], organic light emitting diode, RFID system, organic SRAM and various flexible circuits [1–3]. These implementations need high carrier mobility, low operating voltage and low processing technique for the improvements in device [4].

© Springer Nature Singapore Pte Ltd. 2019
A. Sengupta et al. (Eds.): VDAT 2019, CCIS 1066, pp. 727–738, 2019.
https://doi.org/10.1007/978-981-32-9767-8_60

The Threshold voltage (V_{TH}) of the OTFTs is defined as the gate voltage at which the transistors swing between the depletion mode to the accumulation mode. Hence, the control of threshold voltage requires several engineering process [5]. Unlike in a CMOS technology, where the threshold voltage is controlled by the doping applied by the ion implantation, the OTFTs make use of dual gate transistors with different conventional device structures as depicted in Fig. 1. DG-OTFTs structures consist of bottom gate and its dielectric followed by organic semiconductor, source and drain and lastly the top gate and its dielectric. This second gate electrostatically control the flow of charge accumulated by the first gate thereby externally setting the threshold voltage.

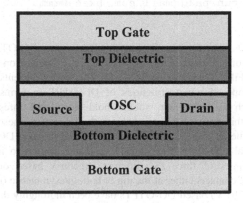

Fig. 1. Conventional structure of dual gate based organic thin film transistors (DG-OTFTs).

Cui and Liang was the first to report the DG-OTFT in 2005 [6]. In the same year, Gelinck et al. [7], Iba et al. [8], Morana et al. [9], Chua et al. [10] published their work on dual gate OTFTs. Later on, numerous research has been done in the field of DG-Organic Thin Film Transistors. Behavioral analysis of low voltage DG-OTFTs are important as its signifies various issues of which contact resistance is the most essential to study. The operation of low voltage OTFTs is not quite feasible due to its fabrication challenges however, Shiwaku et al. [11] has first reported the fabricated low voltage (<5 V) by making use of thin parylene film as the gate dielectric. This study subsequently makes use of the fabricated device of Shiwaku to analyze the behavioral response of the proposed device structures.

The improvement in the device parameters can also be achieved by variations in the structural placements. For example, the conventional device structures with the placements of gate either at top, bottom or using dual gate or by either placements of contacts at the bottom or top contacts briefly known as Bottom contact organic thin film transistors (BC-OTFTs) and Top contacts organic thin film transistors (TC-OTFTs). These structures have its own merits and demerits depending upon various parameters. The placements of contacts have impacts on gate to drain capacitances which offers several device improvements. Islam et al. [12], was the first to report this analysis of impact of placements of contact on single gate OTFTs in the year 2013. This work henceforth addresses the impact on Dual gate organic thin film transistors (DG-OTFTs) with the distinctly placed source and drain of the proposed Bottom source top drain dual gate organic thin film transistors (BSTD-DG-OTFTs), Top source bottom drain dual gate organic thin film transistors (TSBD-DG-OTFTs) and asymmetric source and drain dual gate based OTFTs (A-DG-OTFTs). We demonstrate the device speed characteristics for better switching response for these proposed device improvement characteristics in the field of organic Flextronics.

Table 1. State of art for dual gate based organic thin film transistors (DG-OTFTs)

Organic semiconductor	Device architecture	Contacts	Dielectric	Year	References
Pentacene	DG-BC	Al	SA-SiO$_2$	2005	[7]
Pentacene	DG-TC	Au	Parylene Polymide	2005	[8]
PTAA	DG-BC	Au	PIBMA/Teflon/SiO$_2$	2010	[16]
F8T2	DG-BC	Au	Polystyrene/cPVP	2010	[17]
PDPPTPT	DG-New Architecture	–	–	2010	[18]
Pentacene	DG-BC	Au/Ti	Al$_2$O$_3$	2015	[19]
PDPPTPT	DG-BC	Au	CYTOP/SiO$_2$	2016	[15]
P3HT	DG-BC	–	Parylene/SiO$_2$	2016	[20]
p-type Polymer	DG-BC	Ag	Parylene	2018	[11]
Pentacene	Three-proposed structures	Ag	Parylene	This work	

A thorough research has been made in the conventional Dual gate based organic thin film transistors (DG-OTFTs) and its state of art is shown in Table 1. The fabrication flow process for the Dual gate organic thin film transistors is shown in Fig. 2. The first processing step is the selection of substrate depending upon the application needed for the thin film transistor as for flexible applications substrate like paper, foil, plastic etc. is used. Thereafter, the bottom gate is deposited followed by the gate dielectric. The gate dielectric can either be organic like parylene, CYTOP etc. or Inorganic such as silicon di-oxide (SiO$_2$), Aluminum oxide (Al$_2$O$_3$) or Hafnium oxide (HfO$_2$) which can be formed either by oxidation or vacuum evaporation Technique. The contacts are deposited by the patterned lithography. The contacts with work function close to the HOMO (Highest occupied molecular orbital) and LOMO (Lowest occupied molecular orbital) of organic film are so chosen in order to minimize the contact resistance which is the main drawback in the organic thin film transistors. The most commonly used contact is Gold (Au), Silver (Ag) etc. By the process of spin coating, solution processing or vacuum technique, the organic active layer can be deposited at low temperature which is the next process in the fabrication flow. Several organic materials have been reported which work as a p- or n-type channel for TFTs. The last step is the deposition of top dielectric like sputtering (for inorganic) or spin coating (for organic) followed by Top gate at low processing temperature which does not damage the active layer.

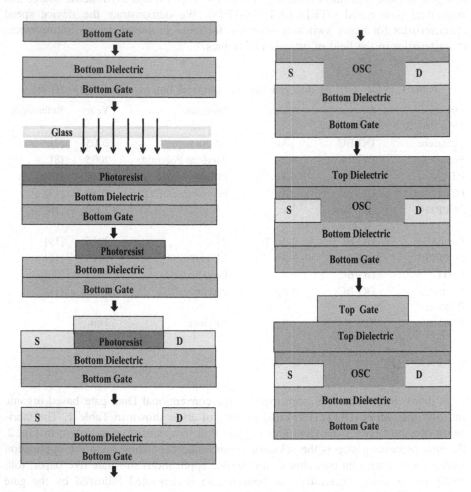

Fig. 2. Fabrication process steps for conventional dual gate based organic thin film transistors (DG-OTFTs).

2 Simulation Setup

The Dual gate organic thin film transistor (DG-OTFTs) is analyzed using 2-D mathematical device simulator (ATLAS Silvaco). This tool enables to define any material for the devices and hence material with the known properties can be implemented for the device simulation. It is generally used for silicon based devices but can be used for organic devices also by using Poole-Frenkel (PF) mobility model as given by Eq. 1 [21].

$$\mu(E) = \mu_0 \exp\left[-\frac{\Delta}{kT} + \left(\frac{\beta}{kT} - \gamma\right)\right] \tag{1}$$

where $\mu(E)$, E and μ_0 is field dependent mobility, electric field and zero field mobility. Activation energy is Δ (1.792×10^{-2} eV) and Hole Poole-Frenkel constant is β (7.758×10^{-5} eV $(cm/V)^{0.5}$), T is the temperature and γ is fitting parameters. The Device used in this work is of Shiwaku et al. [11] whose dimension is given in Table 2.

Table 2. Parameters used in 2D device simulator

S. No.	Name of device parameters	Parameter values
1	Top Gate electrode (Ag)	50 nm
2	Top Gate dielectric (Parylene)	140 nm
3	OSC (Pentacene)	10 nm
4	Bottom Gate dielectric (Parylene)	140 nm
5	Bottom Gate electrode (Ag)	50 nm
6	Source, S/Drain D contacts (Ag)	50 nm
7	Channel width, W	800 μm
8	Channel length, L	5 μm

2.1 Device Parameter Extraction for Dual Gate Organic Thin Film Transistors (DG-OTFTs)

Generally, Dual gate organic thin film transistors operates in two modes: common mode where both the top and bottom gate are tied to common biasing and the other is mixed mode where the top and bottom gate are differently biased and respective contact resistance are analyzed. Here, in this work we have analyzed all proposed device structure using common mode analysis. Thus, the total contribution of the charge is mainly given as [13] in Eq. 2

$$Q_t = C_{tg}V_{tg} + C_{bg}V_{bg} \tag{2}$$

where C_{tg}, V_{tg} represents the top gate capacitance and voltage respectively and C_{bg}, V_{bg} represents the bottom gate capacitance and voltage respectively. The value of trans conductance g_m [14] is defined from the slope of $I_{DS} - V_{GS}$ curve and is given as

$$g_m = \frac{\partial I_{DS}}{\partial V_{GS}} \tag{3}$$

Further, making use of Eq. 3 the mobility for dual gate organic thin film transistors [13] is evaluated as given in Eq. 4

$$\mu = \frac{\partial I_{DS}}{\partial V_{GS}} \frac{L}{WC_{ox}V_{DS}} \tag{4}$$

where C_{ox}, L is oxide capacitance and channel length respectively. The threshold voltage [13] based on concentration is shown Eq. 5 as

$$V_{TH} = \frac{q t_{OSC} N_A}{C_{ox}} \qquad (5)$$

where q is the charge and t_{OSC} is the active layer thickness. The subthreshold slope SS [13] can be defined as the ratio of gate voltage to the logarithmic change of the drain current as in Eq. 6

$$SS = \frac{\partial V_{GS}}{\partial \log_{10} I_{DS}} \qquad (6)$$

3 Result and Discussions

Figures 3(a), 4(a), 5(a) and 6(a) shows the all four possible configuration of Dual Gate Organic thin film transistors (DG-OTFTs). Unlike conventional placements of source and drain at either top or bottom, this work introduces three new proposed structures: Bottom source top drain dual gate organic thin film transistors (BSTD-DG-OTFTs), Top source bottom drain dual gate organic thin film transistors (TSBD-DG-OTFTs) and asymmetric source and drain dual gate based OTFTs (A-DG-OTFTs) respectively. An additional processing steps is required for the distinct placement of source and drain but can be advantageous if there is a device improvement. The BSBD-DG-OTFT was simulated and verified with the experimental work which is shown in Table 3. Figure 3 (b, c) represents the output and transfer characteristics respectively. The variation in the experimental and simulated results is due to several consideration of parameters fittings in the device simulator.

Table 3. Comparison of experimental results with the simulated data

Parameters	Experimental values [11]	Simulated values
	$V_{DS} = -5$ V, $V_{GS} > -5$ V	
μ (cm²/Vs)	0.050	0.61
Ion (μA)	1.9	2.9
Subthreshold slope (mV/dec.)	0.3	0.67
V_{TH} (V)	0.42	0.73

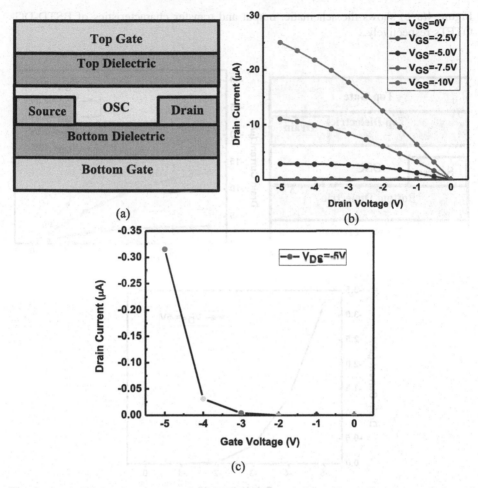

Fig. 3. (a–c) Schematic representation, output characteristics and transfer characteristics of conventional bottom source bottom drain (BSBD-DG-OTFTs).

3.1   Bottom Source Top Drain Dual Gate Organic Thin Film Transistor (BSTD-DG-OTFTs)

In BSTD-DG-OTFTs, it can be seen that there is improvement in the ON current and is found to 3.2 μA which is much higher than the conventional BSBD-DG-OTFTs having ON current value of 0.32 μA. The trans conductance value is also much higher which suggests that it does not have the channel resistance as the source is in active layer and drain at the top 12. This modulates the charge carrier in the channel thereby increasing the trans conductance. These simulation results are considered on the facts that worth the advancements in the technology the barrier height injection is not considered and that is readily determined by the bulk transport in the active layer.

Figure 4(a–c) shows the schematic, output and transfer characteristics of BSTD-DG-OTFTs respectively.

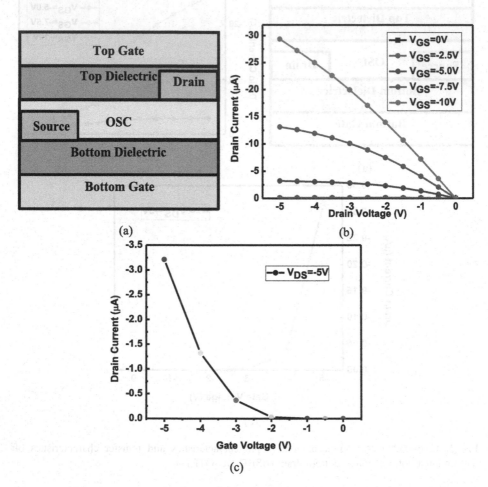

(a)   (b)

(c)

Fig. 4. (a–c) Basic diagram, output characteristics and transfer characteristics of bottom source top drain (BSTD-DG-OTFTs).

3.2 Top Source Bottom Drain Dual Gate Organic Thin Film Transistors (TSBD-DG-OTFTs)

In TSBD-DG-OTFTs, the drain is placed at the bottom and its variations mainly effect the drain – gate capacitance. Figure 5(a–c) represents the schematic, output and transfer characteristics of TSBD-DG-OTFTs respectively. The output current shown in the output characteristics is almost same as that of BSTD-DG-OTFTs however there is some variation of electrical parameters.

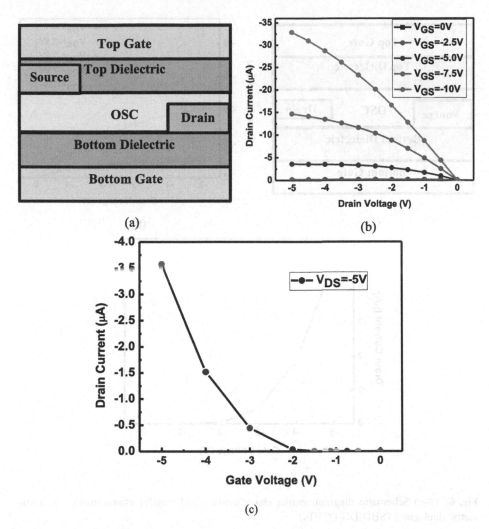

Fig. 5. (a–c) Basic diagram, output characteristics and transfer characteristics of top source bottom drain (TSBD-DG-OTFTs).

3.3   Asymmetric Based Dual Gate Organic Thin Film Transistors (A-DG-OTFTs)

In this the dimensions of source and drain are not equal and hence the name asymmetric based dual gate organic thin film transistors. In this the width of Source is taken as 40 nm and that of drain is considered as 30 nm. The drain is placed within the active layer in center of it. Figure 6(a–c) shows the schematic, output and transfer characteristics respectively. The output characteristics shows the highest improvement in the drain current of 5 µA. Several other electrical parameters are compared in Table 4 with other proposed structure.

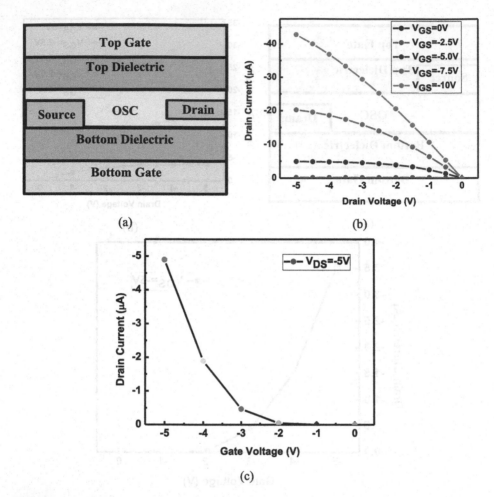

Fig. 6. (a–c) Schematic diagram, output characteristics and transfer characteristics of asymmetric dual gate (TSBD-DG-OTFTs).

Table 4. Electrical performance parameters comparison for different proposed structures

Parameters	μ (cm^2/Vs)	Ion (μA)	Subthreshold slope (V/dec.)	g_m (μS)
BSBD-DG-OTFT	0.61	0.32	0.67	0.16
BSTD-DG-OTFT	0.74	3.2	0.61	1.88
TSBD-DG-OTFT	0.78	3.5	0.50	2.06
A-DG-OTFT	1.27	4.9	0.68	3.00

4 Conclusion

The proposed device structures using dual gate organic thin film transistors are analyzed and the simulation results shows that they exhibit much better performance parameters when compared to the conventional BSBD-DG-OTFTs. The other proposed structures are Bottom source top drain dual gate organic thin film transistors (BSTD-DG-OTFTs), Top source bottom drain dual gate organic thin film transistors (TSBD-DG-OTFTs) and asymmetric source and drain dual gate based OTFTs (A-DG-OTFTs) and Table 5 shows the percentage improvements in the device parameters. Among all three the A-DG-OTFT shows the maximum variations which suggests that drain can be considered as small as possible for the applications in the sensing applications in order to improve the switching capability.

Table 5. Percentage improvement in the performance parameters for different proposed structures

Device structures	μ (cm^2/Vs)	Ion (μA)	g_m (μS)
BSTD-DG-OTFT	0.21	9.00	10.75
TSBD-DG-OTFT	0.27	9.93	11.88
A-DG-OTFT	1.82	14.31	17.75

References

1. Kumar, B., Kaushik, B.K., Negi, Y.S.: Static and dynamic characteristics of dual gate organic TFT based NAND and NOR circuits. J. Comput. Electron. **13**(3), 627–638 (2014)
2. Kumar, B., Kaushik, B.K., Negi, Y.: Perspectives and challenges for organic thin film transistors: materials, devices, processes and applications. J. Mater. Sci.: Mater. Electron. **25** (1), 1–30 (2014)
3. Kumar, B., Kaushik, B., Negi, Y., Mittal, P., Mandal, A.: Organic thin film transistors characteristics parameters, structures and their applications. In: 2011 IEEE Recent Advances in Intelligent Computational Systems, pp. 706–711. IEEE (2011)
4. Negi, S., Rana, A., Baliga, A., Mittal, P., Kumar, B.: Performance analysis of dual gate organic thin film transistor and organic SR latch application. In: International Conference on Computing, Communication & Automation, pp. 1427–1432. IEEE (2015)
5. Horowitz, G., Hajlaoui, R., Bouchriha, H., Bourguiga, R., Hajlaoui, M.: The concept of "threshold voltage" in organic field-effect transistors. Adv. Mater. **10**(12), 923–927 (1998)
6. Cui, T., Liang, G.: Dual-gate pentacene organic field-effect transistors based on a nanoassembled SiO$_2$ nanoparticle thin film as the gate dielectric layer. Appl. Phys. Lett. **86**(6), 064102 (2005)
7. Gelinck, G., Van Veenendaal, E., Coehoorn, R.: Dual-gate organic thin-film transistors. Appl. Phys. Lett. **87**(7), 073508 (2005)
8. Iba, S., et al.: Control of threshold voltage of organic field-effect transistors with double-gate structures. Appl. Phys. Lett. **87**(2), 023509 (2005)
9. Morana, M., Bret, G., Brabec, C.: Double-gate organic field-effect transistor. Appl. Phys. Lett. **87**(15), 153511 (2005)
10. Chua, L.-L., Friend, R.H., Ho, P.K.: Organic double-gate field-effect transistors: logic-AND operation. Appl. Phys. Lett. **87**(25), 253512 (2005)

11. Shiwaku, R., Tamura, M., Matsui, H., Takeda, Y., Murase, T., Tokito, S.: Charge carrier distribution in low-voltage dual-gate organic thin-film transistors. Appl. Sci. **8**(8), 1341 (2018)
12. Islam, M.N., Mazhari, B.: Organic thin film transistors with asymmetrically placed source and drain contact. Org. Electron. **14**(3), 862–867 (2013)
13. Gupta, D., Katiyar, M., Gupta, D.: An analysis of the difference in behavior of top and bottom contact organic thin film transistors using device simulation. Org. Electron. **10**(5), 775–784 (2009)
14. Gupta, D., Hong, Y.: Understanding the effect of semiconductor thickness on device characteristics in organic thin film transistors by way of two-dimensional simulations. Org. Electron. **11**(1), 127–136 (2010)
15. Lee, J., Roelofs, W.C., Janssen, R.A., Gelinck, G.H.: Dielectric interface-dependent spatial charge distribution in ambipolar polymer semiconductors embedded in dual-gate field-effect transistors. Appl. Phys. Lett. **109**(4), 043301 (2016)
16. Spijkman, M.J., et al.: Dual-gate organic field-effect transistors as potentiometric sensors in aqueous solution. Adv. Func. Mater. **20**(6), 898–905 (2010)
17. Baeg, K.J., Noh, Y.Y., Sirringhaus, H., Kim, D.Y.: Controllable shifts in threshold voltage of top-gate polymer field-effect transistors for applications in organic nano floating gate memory. Adv. Func. Mater. **20**(2), 224–230 (2010)
18. Colalongo, L., Torricelli, F., Kovacs-Vajna, Z.M.: A new electroluminescent organic dual-gate field-effect transistor. IEEE Electron Device Lett. **36**(7), 717–719 (2015)
19. Saini, D., Kaushik, B.K.: Unipolar organic ring oscillator using dual gate organic thin film transistor. In: 2015 National Conference on Recent Advances in Electronics & Computer Engineering (RAECE), pp. 196–201. IEEE (2015)
20. Fu, L.-N., Leng, B., Li, Y.-S., Gao, X.-K.: Photoresponsive organic field-effect transistors involving photochromic molecules. Chin. Chem. Lett. **27**(8), 1319–1329 (2016)
21. ATLAS User's manual, SILVACO, Santa Clara, CA, USA (2014)

Hardware Implementation

A Latency and Throughput Efficient Successive Cancellation Decoding of Polar Codes

Sistla Lakshmi Manasa$^{(\boxtimes)}$ ⓘ and G. Lakshmi Narayanan

Department of Electronics and Communication Engineering,
National Institute of Technology, Tiruchirappalli, India
lakshmimanasa.manasa1@gmail.com, laksh@nitt.edu

Abstract. By their capacity achieving property, Polar codes have emerged as the most prevailing error correcting codes. Successive Cancellation (SC) Decoding follows a greedy search algorithm that decodes each bit successively thereby increasing the latency of the decoding process which is the major bottleneck of the decoding in polar codes and this leads to the necessity of designing a low latency Successive Cancellation decoder. In this paper, a stage merged decoder along with the pre-computation technique is proposed which reduces the overall latency of the decoder by more than 72% compared to some of the existing decoders and by 82% with the conventional Successive Cancellation decoder.

Keywords: Successive Cancellation · Precomputation · Stage merge · Low latency

1 Introduction

Polar Codes has an immense growth in coding theory since their discovery in 2009 by Arikan [1]. Polar codes possess many attractive features practically such as lack of error floors, fixed low encoding and decoding complexity, ease of implementation due to its deterministic structure, area efficiency due to component sharing and utilizing the limited sources efficiently. For the application of 5G in the enhanced mobile broadband (eMBB), polar codes were selected as the coding scheme. However, the sequential nature of Successive Cancellation Decoding used in polar decoders accompany to a long decoding latency which is one of the major problems of SC decoding.

Several researchers attempted to reduce the latency of the SC decoder. The conventional SC decoder that was initially proposed by Arikan [1] utilized 2N-2 clock cycles to complete the whole decoding process which is one less than double the code length. One of the problems first addressed in literature was to improve the code construction [8]. Also, an attempt was made to use alternatives for the original 2x2 kernel [1] and interestingly there are many capacity achieving kernels with higher dimensions but they have higher error exponent [9]. The high latency of conventional architecture doesn't lead to a high throughput SC decoder. For longer code lengths the decoding latency increases drastically thereby making the polar codes unsuitable for high speed real time applications. The butterfly-based, pipeline tree and the line architectures were proposed later. The butterfly-based architecture is similar to a Fast Fourier Transform

© Springer Nature Singapore Pte Ltd. 2019
A. Sengupta et al. (Eds.): VDAT 2019, CCIS 1066, pp. 741–748, 2019.
https://doi.org/10.1007/978-981-32-9767-8_61

(FFT) except the fact that it is decoded sequentially. The tree and line architectures [7] focused mainly on the reduction of hardware complexity. Later, to reduce the latency bottleneck, f and g nodes are merged into a single Merged Processing Element (MPE) and a precomputation technique for the g node was applied. This resulted in a reduction of latency from 2N-2 to N-1 which means nearly by 50%. The number of MPE's required in this tree architecture are N-1. It can be observed that only one stage is activated at a time in the decoding process. The maximum number of MPE's are present in stage 1 i.e. N/2 which operates in parallel. So, the number of MPE's are reduced to N/2 in the line architecture without any penalty in the latency. In [2], a novel 2-bit decoding SC pre computation (2b-SC) was proposed. The last stage of the decoder was modified and look-ahead technique was performed in the last stage through which the latency gets reduced to 0.75N-1. Many attempts have been made to reduce the latency but the long latency issue of SC Decoder is still an open problem despite the studies that are made on polar codes.

This paper presents a latency efficient architecture of an SC Decoder by further reducing the number of clock cycles with a stage merging. This leads to a huge reduction in latency by nearly 50% and precomputation technique combined with it leads to an overall reduction of latency by 72% compared to the existing architectures. Also comparison with some of the existing decoders has been made and this proposed decoder has lower latency and higher throughput compared to many of the existing architectures.

The design of rest of the paper is as follows: From the basic conventional SC decoder and the existing architectures in Sect. 2, a latency and throughput efficient SC decoder has been proposed in Sect. 3. Section 4 draws various conclusions of the proposed architecture with those existing already. Section 5 concludes the proposed architecture.

2 Review of Polar Codes

Channel polarization is the major phenomenon underlying the polar codes. Any given Binary input discrete memoryless channel is polarized, and a set of N new channels are obtained out of which k are considered good as they are completely noiseless, and information can be transmitted through these channels and N-k are frozen because of their lower capacity comparatively as they are completely noisy through which no information can be transmitted. An (N, k) SC decoder contains k information bits and N-k frozen bits. Here N is the length of the code word. Initially the input bit vector U is transformed to a code word X using the following transformation

$$X^N = U^N F^{\otimes^n} \tag{1}$$

Polar Transform is given by Arikan in [1], $F2 = \begin{bmatrix} 1 & 0 \\ 1 & 1 \end{bmatrix}$ and the nth kroneckor of F is given by $F^{\otimes^n} = \begin{bmatrix} F^{\otimes^{n-1}} & 0 \\ F^{\otimes^{n-1}} & F^{\otimes^{n-1}} \end{bmatrix}$. The code word, X thus obtained is transmitted through the channel. The code word that is received at the receiver end after getting corrupted by the transmission noise will no longer be same as the transmitted code word. The new code word can be represented by Y and the information bits have to be estimated from this code word which is the main challenge to the decoder. As proposed by Arikan [1], this code word can be recovered by the Successive Cancellation (SC) algorithm.

Successive Cancellation (SC) decoder is a structure which resembles the Fast Fourier Transform (FFT) except the fact that the output is decoded sequentially in an SC decoder. This means the bits that are to be decoded next depends on the bits already decoded. Conventional SC Decoder architecture utilized $Nlog_2N$ Processing Elements (PE) which is hardware inefficient and not practical. The basic low complexity SC Decoder is shown in Fig. 1. Likelihood ratios from the previous stage were used to calculate the likelihood of the present stage initially. Each processing Element have two inputs and three outputs in the pre computation technique. There are two different functions f and g in each processing element and these two functions can be defined using the following equations

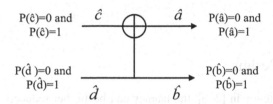

Fig. 1. Basic low complexity SC decoder module

$$f(c, d) = \frac{1 + cd}{c + d} \tag{2}$$

$$g(c, d, \hat{u}_{sum}) = c^{1-2\hat{u}_{sum}}d \tag{3}$$

Due to the presence of multiplications and divisions, the complexity of the Processing Element is more. So, a min-sum algorithm was proposed in [7] to reduce the multiplications and divisions to addition and subtraction. The new transformed equations are given by the following

$$f(a, b) = sign(a) \, sign(b) \, min(|a|, |b|) \tag{4}$$

$$g(a, b) = a(-1)^{\hat{u}_{sum}} + b \tag{5}$$

Later, to reduce the complexity of the Merged PE further, Log Likelihood ratios were proposed. After the last stage of SC decoder is processed, there is a decision unit to decode the bits. The SC decoding follows a binary tree, the levels of the binary tree are indicated by the bits and the nodes by the path metrics. Each node has two leaf nodes out of which only one is selected based on the likelihood metrics of those two nodes. In this way out of all the 2^n paths only one path is traversed which means a hard decision is made. Later, Successive Cancellation List (SCL) decoding [10–12] was proposed and used but the hardware complexity of list decoder is very high.

Table 1 shows the latency analysis of initial clock cycles of a 1024-bit SC 2-bit decoder in [2]. From the Table 1, it can be inferred that only one stage is activated in one clock cycle. One more inference from the Table 1 is stage 8 is activated in a separate clock cycle. The first 4 bits are decoded at the clock cycle 10.

Table 1. Decoding schedule for initial clock cycles of 2-bit SC decoder for N = 1024, k = 512 in [2]

Clock cycles	1	2	3	4	5	6	7	8	9	10	11	12	...
Stages activated	1	2	3	4	5	6	7	8	9	10	9	10	...
Bits decoded										$\hat{u}_1,$ $\hat{u}_2,$ $\hat{u}_3,$ $\hat{u}_4$		$\hat{u}_5,$ $\hat{u}_6,$ $\hat{u}_7,$ $\hat{u}_8$	...

3 Proposed Design

Despite the low latency in [2–6], the latency can be further reduced. It can be noticed that each stage of the SC decoder is pipelined to reduce the critical path which leads to a longer latency. So, if two stages can be activated in one clock cycle the number of clock cycles can be reduced by 50%. The proposed design merges the f nodes of two stages together through which the latency reduces to a larger extent. Besides reducing the latency, there is a reduction in the number of registers between the merged stages. As we are merging two stages the critical path may be lengthened by the delay of a Merged Processing Element (MPE). The delay can be reduced by employing efficient adder instead of conventional 2's complement scheme. The MPE used in this architecture is shown in Fig. 2 which is of sign magnitude form. In sign magnitude form the critical path of the MPE takes the Type-I PE path of the g-node. So, a very low delay adder like Radix addition reduces the critical path to a greater extent.

Table 2 shows the number of times each stage gets activated and number of MPE's for N = 1024, k = 512. The number of active times of the design increases with the stage index which implies the stages that are latter in the design are activated a greater number of times than the former stages and thus causing more latency in the whole decoding process. The other improvement in this architecture is the usage of pre-computation in one of the last stages, as they are having a smaller number of MPE's, to further reduce the latency which leads to a major reduction in the latency.

Table 2. Number of active times and number of MPE's of each stage for N = 1024, k = 512

Stage index	Number of active times	Number of MPE's
1	1	512
2	2	256
3	4	128
4	8	64
5	16	32
6	32	16
7	64	8
8	128	4
9	256	2
10	512	1

All the possible LLR's are precomputed in stage N-2 and they have to be selected when necessary thereby reducing the latency. For example, if we check Table 1 stage 8 for N = 1024 is activated in a separate clock cycle and thus taking N/16 clock cycles which can be reduced if we precompute those values in the previous clocks.

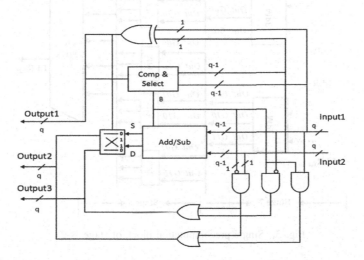

Fig. 2. Merged Processing Element (MPE)

The precomputed block in the stage N-2 in an N-stage decoder is shown in Fig. 3. As the stage N-3 has N/128 MPE's, each pair of MPE's require one precomputation block in stage N-2. So, four such blocks are operated in parallel in stage N-2. For N = 1024, an additional 16 MPE's are required. The outputs of these blocks are fed to the stage N-1 using a feedback logic. The proposed architecture for N = 1024, K = 512 is shown in Fig. 4. However, there is an additional delay of an MPE of the stage N-1 to the critical path. This delay can be reduced by using redundant arithmetic which takes less delay comparatively. As we can see in Fig. 4, the eight stage for N = 1024 has been precomputed for all the LLR outputs from the seventh stage which reduces the activation of that stage by N/16 times. There is a slight increase in the number of MPE's which can be reduced by reusing the MPE's in the previous stages using MUX based architecture.

Table 3. Decoding schedule for initial clock cycles of proposed SC decoder for N = 1024

Clock cycles	1	2	3	4	5	6	7	8	9	...
Stages activated	1,2	3,4	5,6	7,8	9,10	9,10	9,10	9,10	7,8	...
Proposed design stages	I	II	III	IV	V	V	V	V	IV	
Bits decoded					$\hat{u}1$, $\hat{u}2$, $\hat{u}3$, $\hat{u}4$	$\hat{u}1$, $\hat{u}2$, $\hat{u}3$, $\hat{u}4$				

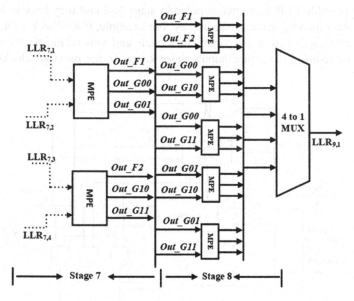

Fig. 3. Single precomputation block of stage N-2

As shown in Fig. 4, the registers for f node are at every alternate stage as its metrics are necessary at that instant and not required later in the design. It can be observed that if we combine more than two stages for processing i.e. three or four stages, then the critical path will be increased to a larger extent thereby reducing the frequency of operation. Table 3 shows the decoding schedule for initial few clock cycles of the proposed architecture. 1, 2 indicate the stage 1 and stage 2 in the original SC 2-bit decoder which is merged into a single Stage I for f node in the proposed architecture. Similarly, the remaining stages are merged. It can be observed that stage 8 activation after clock 6 for g-node calculation can be avoided by pre-computation scheme. So, stage N-2 activation can be reduced by N/16 clock cycles with affordable hardware.

This can be observed from Table 3 that stage 8 for N = 1024 is not activated in a separate clock cycle as it was the case in 2-bit SC decoder shown in Table 2. The memories used for g node are kept intact even if the memories for f node are removed in the alternate stages and this is because the g node values are required to be selected whenever they are necessary in the latter clock cycles. Besides reduction in the number of registers there is a considerable reduction in the area and power by using this architecture. PSG at the last stage is the Partial Sum Generation unit.

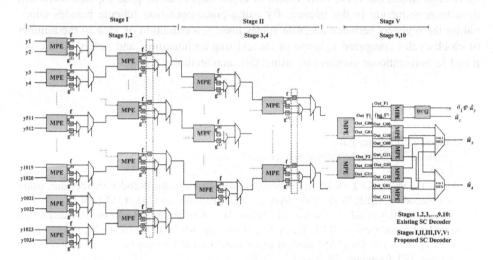

Fig. 4. Proposed architecture of SC decoder for code length N = 1024, K = 512

4 Implementation Results

An SC decoder for a code length of N = 1024 and K = 512 which means R = 1/2 with 5-bit quantization has been synthesized using cadence Genus in 180 nm technology with a sign magnitude MPE. A comparison has been made in Table 4 with the conventional and the already existing architectures. Synthesis results project that there is a reduction in the latency by 76.7% compared to the architecture in [5] and by 82.5% compared to the conventional architecture when it is also implemented in 180 nm. There is a reduction in the number of registers by nearly 33% due to removal of registers for f node. The layout of the proposed architecture has been obtained using cadence innovus. The latency has been reduced to almost N/3 which shows a huge reduction.

Table 4. Comparison of the proposed design with existing architectures for N = 1024

Design	[2]	[3]	[4]	[5]	[6]	Proposed design
CMOS technology	45 nm	65 nm	65 nm	180 nm	40 nm	180 nm
Frequency (MHz)	750	500	670	150	1000	500
Decoding latency (clocks)	767	2080	1023	1560	1023	362
Throughput (Mbps)	500	123	335	49	500	707

5 Conclusion

The inference that has been made from the above proposed architecture is only one stage computations are performed in a single clock cycle. Instead of pipelining every stage if we use registers at alternate stages latency can be reduced through which registers can also be reduced thereby reducing the power and area to some extent. Also, it can be observed that the stages present latter in the design are activated a greater number of times. So, if the LLR values of those stages can be precomputed there will be a huge reduction in the latency. By using precomputation scheme besides eliminating the registers between alternate stages there is a reduction of 75% in the number of clock cycles compared to some of the existing architectures and nearly 82% compared to conventional architecture using this architecture.

References

1. Arikan, E.: Channel polarization: a method for constructing capacity achieving codes for symmetric binary-input memoryless channels. IEEE Trans. Inf. Theory **55**(7), 3051–3073 (2009)
2. Yuan, B., Parhi, K.: Low-latency successive-cancellation polar decoder architectures using 2-bit decoding. IEEE Trans. Circ. Syst. I: Regul. Pap. **61**(4), 1241–1254 (2014)
3. Leroux, C., Raymond, A., Sarkis, G., Gross, W.: A semi-parallel successive-cancellation decoder for polar codes. IEEE Trans. Signal Process. **61**(2), 1241–1254 (2013)
4. Yun, H., Lee, H.: Simplified merged processing element for successive cancellation polar decoder. IET Commun. **52**, 270–272 (2016)
5. Mishra, A., et al.: A successive cancellation decoder ASIC for a 1024-bit polar code in 180 nm CMOS. In: IEEE Asian Solid-State Circuits Conference (A-SSCC) (2012)
6. Kim, C., Yun, H., Ajaz, S., Lee, H.: High-throughput low complexity successive-cancellation polar decoder architecture. J. Semicond. Technol. Sci. (JSTS) **13**(3), 427–435 (2015)
7. Leroux, C., Tal, I., Vardy, A., Gross, W.J.: Hardware architectures for successive cancellation decoding of polar codes. In: Proceedings of IEEE International Conference on Acoustics, Speech, Signal Processing (ICASSP) Conference, pp. 1665–1668 (2011)
8. Tal, I., Vardy, A.: How to construct polar codes. IEEE Trans. Inf. Theory **59**(10), 6562–6582 (2013). (On pg: 3, 17, 64, 65, 68, 82, 92, and 139)
9. Lin, H.P., Lin, S., Abdel-Ghaffar, K.A.S.: Linear and nonlinear binary kernels of polar codes of small dimensions with maximum exponents. IEEE Trans. Inf. Theory **61**(10), 5253–5270 (2015). (On pg: 3)
10. Chen, K., Niu, K., Lin, J.R.: Improved successive cancellation decoding of polar codes. IEEE Trans. Commun. **61**(8), 3100–3107 (2013)
11. Yuan, B., Parhi, K.K.: Low-latency successive-cancellation list decoders for polar codes with multibit decision. IEEE Trans. VLSI Syst. **23**(10), 2268–2280 (2015)
12. Zhang, C., You, X., Jin, S.: Hardware architecture for list successive cancellation polar decoder. In: Proceedings of IEEE International Symposium on Circuits and Systems (ISCAS), pp. 209–212 (2014)

All-Digital CMOS On-Chip Temperature Sensor with Time-Assisted Analytical Model

Ankur Pokhara[1]📷, Biswajit Mishra[2](✉)📷, and Purvi Patel[2]📷

[1] Government Women Engineering College, Ajmer 305002, India
ankur@gweca.ac.in
[2] Dhirubhai Ambani Institute of Information and Communication Technology,
Gandhinagar 382007, India
{biswajit_mishra,201521008}@daiict.ac.in

Abstract. This paper proposes a Time-to-Digital Converter (TDC) as an on-chip temperature sensor. An all-digital TDC, with 12-bit coarse and 5-bit fine output bits, has been implemented in $0.18\,\mu$m CMOS with a time-resolution of 92.71 ps, time range upto 12.151 μs and power consumption of 353.8 μW. The temperature dependence of the clock period, of ring oscillator in the TDC, has been carried out to develop an analytical model. The proposed analytical model is used to estimate the temperature directly from the digital counts obtained from the TDC. The time to digital conversion achieves a temperature resolution $<0.01\,°$C and temperature range $(-55 \sim 125)\,°$C, sampled at 125 KHz frequency. The results of the temperature sensor are first validated with temperature independent inputs to the TDC. Further, a Proportional To Absolute Temperature (PTAT) current reference circuit for time inputs is integrated with the TDC. The PTAT current reference circuit has a 12.21 ppm/$°$C drift in time input with the temperature. The proposed TDC based temperature sensor with current reference circuit restricts the error within $-0.4\,°$C $\sim 1.24\,°$C and compares favourably with the reported literature.

Keywords: All-digital · On-chip temperature sensor · PTAT circuit · TDC · Time-assisted circuit · Time-to-Digital Converter · 0.18 μm CMOS

1 Introduction

On-chip temperature sensing finds applications in monitoring high-performance power efficient processors and is gaining interest. The current research is driven

The authors would like to thank Space Application Centre (ISRO), Ahmedabad for the financial support through RESPOND programme under the grant reference ISRO/RES/3/717/2016-17 and SCL, Chandigarh for the ASIC fabrication support.

© Springer Nature Singapore Pte Ltd. 2019
A. Sengupta et al. (Eds.): VDAT 2019, CCIS 1066, pp. 749–763, 2019.
https://doi.org/10.1007/978-981-32-9767-8_62

towards finding alternate designs based on the traditional Analog-to-Digital Converter (ADC) with time-domain digital circuits. This is because, digital circuits have smaller chip area, lower power consumption and robustness against noise [1–5]. To address the problems associated with traditional sensors, the time domain circuits take advantage of digital circuits and compare the time delays instead of the voltage levels [1].

The performance of digital circuits, such as the ring oscillator, an important component of Time-to-Digital Converter (TDC) [2,6], depends upon the temperature. Since mobility decreases and propagation time of the delay cells increase with the temperature, it is observed that the output clock of ring oscillator is proportional to temperature [1,7,8]. This dependence of the clock period with temperature in a ring oscillator can be used to develop on-chip temperature sensor and extend it with an analytical models to support the behaviour.

Authors in [1,3,4] present a time-domain temperature sensor based on TDC which uses an external clock reference signal to quantify the temperature. With Proportional To Absolute Temperature (PTAT) current reference circuits, it is possible to achieve lesser drift in time signals with temperature [9,10]. Fully-integrated temperature sensors, with the PTAT current reference circuit, are presented in [8,11].

In this work, we discuss the temperature sensor in a phased manner. Firstly, the temperature sensor with external time inputs is discussed. The time inputs (Start and Stop) to the TDC are required to be temperature independent for accurate temperature sensing and is a major challenge. Later, we introduce the temperature independent current reference circuit integrated with the proposed TDC for fully-integrated on-chip time inputs. Furthermore, TDC with on-chip implementation of temperature independent time inputs is presented and has several challenges in achieving minimal time variability with temperature variations.

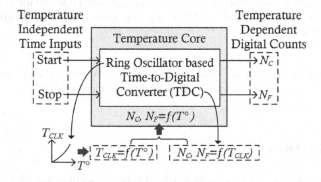

Fig. 1. Concept of temperature sensor

Temperature sensing with ring oscillator based TDC is shown in Fig. 1. The TDC consists of a ring oscillator block generating clock period (T_{CLK}) which depends upon temperature (T°) as $T_{CLK} = f(T^\circ)$. The counts obtained from the TDC based on coarse and fine count $(N_C$ and N_F respectively) are dependent upon T_{CLK} for a fixed known pulse $i.e.$ $N_C, N_F = f(T_{CLK})$. Therefore, the digital outputs $(N_C$ and $N_F)$ are also dependent on temperature $i.e.$ $N_C, N_F = f(T^\circ, T_{CLK})$. This dependence on temperature is used to interpret the TDC as a Temperature sensor. With the observations on temperature variation, we have developed an analytical model. The novelty of this work lies in the analytical model, which will help in directly converting the digital count of TDC to the corresponding temperature value.

This paper is organised as follows: Sect. 2 discusses the proposed TDC architecture. The operating principle of the TDC as temperature sensor is explained in Sect. 3. Further, the analytical model for temperature sensing is proposed in Sect. 3. In Sect. 4, the temperature sensor is characterized in terms of resolution and power consumption. In Sect. 5, the details of on-chip temperature independent time input signal to the sensor is discussed. Sect. 6 concludes the paper with discussion on future work.

2   Time-to-Digital Converter

The TDC architecture is shown in Fig. 2. The TDC quantifies the time input based on Start and Stop signal to digital outputs in the form of coarse count (N_C) and fine count (N_F). It consists of a 16-stage ring oscillator (15 buffers and 1 inverter), a 12-bit counter for coarse counting, 16-latches and a 5-bit encoder for fine counting. The edge detector is employed to generate a Latch Enable (LE) signal, which helps in reducing switching power [12]. The MUX network, with 3-bit select line (S), is designed to reduce the 17-bit output lines for N_C and N_F to 3-bit output lines, outputting data in a serial manner.

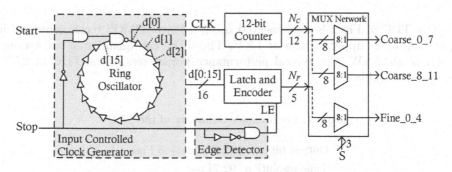

Fig. 2. Block diagram of TDC

The working of the TDC is explained with the timing diagram shown in Fig. 3. Initially, when Start pulse is '1', the NAND gate in clock generator configures the circuit as a ring oscillator. In the absence of this, TDC isn't switching and can be utilized for power saving state of the TDC. The clock output (CLK) of clock generator (when Start = '1') is further fed to the 12-bit counter for generating coarse count (N_C) that defines the time range of the TDC. By increasing the coarse count, higher time range can be measured with the TDC with an increase in the power. Further, the outputs of 16 delay units is forwarded to the 16 latches, where the edge detector circuit enables Latch when Stop goes '1' and data is sampled and encoded to obtain the fine count (N_F). Since, 16 latches are used to obtain fine count from 15 buffers and 1 inverter, it introduces non-linearity in the TDC [6]. From the obtained values of N_C and N_F, the measurement time (T_M) is given by:

$$T_M = N_C T_{CLK} + N_F T_{LSB} \tag{1}$$

where, T_{CLK} is the time period of the ring oscillator. N_D is the number of delay units and is equal to 16. The resolution of the TDC (T_{LSB}) is defined as:

$$T_{LSB} = \frac{T_{CLK}}{2N_D} = \frac{T_{CLK}}{32} \tag{2}$$

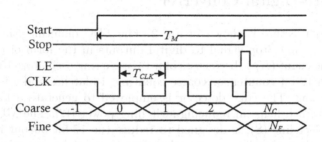

Fig. 3. Timing diagram of the TDC

The TDC in Fig. 2 is implemented using 0.18 μm CMOS technology and is operating at a supply voltage of 1.8 V. The TDC can quantize at an average power of 353.8 μW. The typical performance parameters of the TDC at 27 °C are given in Table 1.

Table 1. Performance Summary of the TDC

Output bits	12 Coarse + 5 Fine
Time resolution	92.71 ps
Time range	92.71 ps − 12.151 μs
Supply voltage	1.8 V
Power	353.8 μW
Process	0.18 μm CMOS

The time range of the TDC is dependent on the coarse bits. The time range can further be increased by increasing coarse bits. To design the TDC with better resolution, more number of fine bits is necessary. Furthermore, in Sect. 4, we discuss additional sampling method, where we target to operate it with sampling frequency of 125 KHz for better temperature resolution. To measure this particular time input, a minimum 12-bit coarse count is required and is set as the standard width for the TDC. The implementation details of the TDC is discussed in [6].

3 TDC as Temperature Sensor

To interpret the TDC as temperature sensor, it is supplied with a temperature independent fixed time input, where output digital counts seem to vary with temperature (Fig. 1). The variation in temperature, causes deviation in the clock period (T_{CLK}) of the ring oscillator and successively in digital counts (N_C and N_F). We have analysed the behavior of T_{CLK} with temperature (T°) to understand the functioning of the TDC as temperature sensor. The obtained samples of T_{CLK} for every $10\,^\circ$C is shown in Fig. 4.

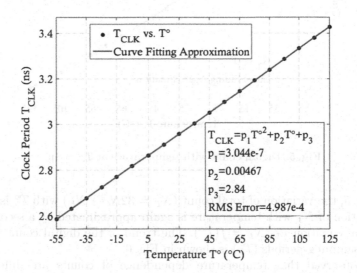

Fig. 4. Clock period of the TDC with temperature

As can be seen in Fig. 4, the plot of T_{CLK} vs. T° shows the change in time period, a second order function given by $T_{CLK} = f(T^\circ) = p_1 T^{\circ 2} + p_2 T^\circ + p_3$ where, $p_1 = 3.044e{-}7$, $p_2 = 0.00467$ and $p_3 = 2.84$ is obtained from a curve fitting approximation of second order polynomial. It should be noted that the RMS error is minimal in the curve fitting is $\sim$0.49 ps, and can be used as a standard equation to estimate the temperature. The analytical model, for temperature sensing, developed from this dependence of T_{CLK} with T° is discussed in Sect. 3.2. The analytical model will help in converting the digital count to the respective temperature.

3.1   Analytical Model of Temperature from Counts

For a fixed time input, the N_C and N_F varies with temperature. As can be seen, the plot in Fig. 5 shows the total count as $N_T = 32N_C + N_F$ with temperature varying from $-55\,°C$ to $125\,°C$ at a fixed sampling period (T_S) of $8\,\mu s$ $(f_S = 125\,KHz)$. This T_S is the input to the TDC.

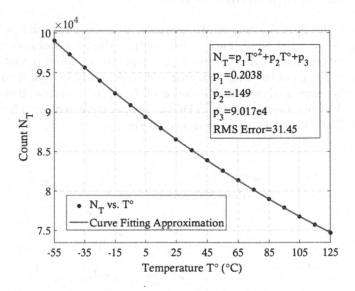

Fig. 5. Digital count with temperature at $T_S = 8\,\mu s$

In Fig. 5, the variation of total count $(N_T = 32N_C + N_F)$ with $T°$ is plotted. The variation of N_T with temperature is again approximated by a second order polynomial equation *i.e.* $N_T = f(T°)$. The trend of the digital count (N_T) for different sampling periods (T_S) is shown in Fig. 6.

It is observed that temperature dependence of counts are different for sampling periods (T_S). The analytical model with a second order polynomial $(N_T = p_1 T°^2 + p_2 T° + p_3)$ is developed for different T_s, and polynomial coefficients are summarized in Table 2.

Knowing the relationship of $N_T = f(T°)$ at different sampling periods, helps the derivation of temperature from an analytical model described as $T° = f(N_T) = q_1 N_T^2 + q_2 N_T + q_3$. For deriving the coefficients at different T_S, Table 3 data is being used.

From Table 3, it can be observed that the RMS error is slightly higher in the curve approximation, therefore, not a suitable model for temperature sensing. Also, this model will have potential challenges post ASIC fabrication, since it is

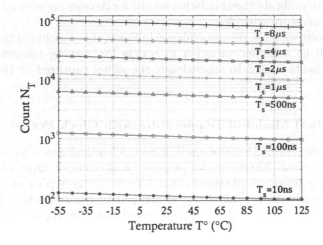

Fig. 6. Digital count with temperature at different T_S

Table 2. Polynomial coefficients of $N_T = f(T^\circ) = p_1 T^{\circ 2} + p_2 T^\circ + p_3$

T_S	p_1	p_2	p_3	RMS error
10 ns	2.808e-4	-0.1907	112.9	0.3681
100 ns	2.506e-3	-1.862	1128	0.6954
500 ns	0.01209	-9.244	5636	2.049
1 μs	0.02538	-18.59	1.127e4	9.748
2 μs	0.04745	-36.87	2.254e4	12.74
4 μs	0.1018	-74.49	4.509e4	16.3
8 μs	0.2038	-149	9.017e4	31.45

Table 3. Polynomial coefficients of $T^\circ = f(N_T) = q_1 N_T^2 + q_2 N_T + q_3$

T_S	q_1	q_2	q_3	RMS error ($^\circ$C)
10 ns	0.05223	-17.12	1267	2.848
100 ns	0.5152e-3	-1.705	1267	0.4463
500 ns	2.02e-5	-0.337	1257	0.5666
1 μs	5.273e-6	-0.1732	1282	0.4764
2 μs	1.247e-6	-0.08358	1250	0.6397
4 μs	3.286e-7	-0.0432	1279	0.4347
8 μs	8.223e-8	-0.02162	1280	0.4162

cumbersome to calibrate the simulation results for developing accurate analytical model of temperature with N_T.

Furthermore, with the results achieved in Fig. 6, it is concluded that at higher T_s, there will be a higher variation in counts for varying temperature. This variation in counts is used to approximate the values captured by the analytical model.

3.2   Analytical Model of Temperature with Clock Period

The temperature estimation discussed in Sect. 3.1 introduces a relatively higher approximation error. Therefore, we propose an alternative approach, where we calculate T_{CLK} from the obtained count ($N_T = 32N_C + N_F$) at a known T_S using Eq. 3. Furthermore, this T_{CLK} is mapped to the respective T° with the second order polynomial of T_{CLK}, and is calculated with Eq. 4.

$$T_{CLK} = \frac{32T_S}{N_T} \tag{3}$$

$$T^\circ = f(T_{CLK}) = p_1 T_{CLK}^2 + p_2 T_{CLK} + p_3 \tag{4}$$

The coefficients in Eq. 4 are obtained from the inverse function of that obtained from Fig. 4. Coefficients p_1, p_2 and p_3 are calculated as -2.95, 230.9 and -632. This analytical model introduces an RMS error of $\sim 0.1071\,^\circ$C in temperature estimation and is less than the previously stated method. Therefore, we use this analytical model (Eqs. 3 and 4) for the proposed temperature sensor.

4   Analysis of Temperature Sensor

The proposed temperature sensor (Sect. 3.2) is analysed at different sampling frequencies for temperature resolution and power consumption.

4.1   Resolution of the Temperature Sensor

From Fig. 6, it can be seen that $T^\circ = f(N_T)$ is a non-linear second order function, where the resolution (T_Δ°) of the temperature sensor can be obtained by differentiating T° with respect to the counts and given as $T_\Delta^\circ = \frac{dT^\circ}{dN_T}$. The plots of N_T with respect to T° (see Fig. 6) is used to obtain the temperature resolution. This resolution of temperature sensor is a linear function with total count (N_T). The continuous plot of temperature resolution at sampling frequency of 125 KHz is shown in Fig. 7. For the rest of sampling periods, the temperature resolution is given in Table 4.

In Table 4, it is observed that a slightly better resolution is achieved at lower sampling frequency. Resolution of the temperature sensor compared to the similar research work discussed in [1,4] can be achieved at 125 KHz sampling frequency. For the rest of the paper, we consider 8 μs as a standard sampling period

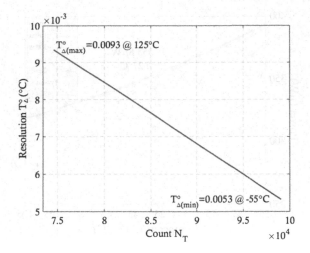

Fig. 7. Resolution of the temperature sensor at 125 KHz

Table 4. Temperature resolution at different T_S

T_S	$T^\circ_{\Delta(min)}$ (°C)	$T^\circ_{\Delta(max)}$ (°C)
10 ns	4.167	7.3
100 ns	0.4283	0.7436
500 ns	0.0875	0.1484
1 μs	0.0426	0.0748
2 μs	0.022	0.037
4 μs	0.0107	0.0187
8 μs	0.0053	0.0093

as at this T_S, the temperature sensor has a better resolution. To accommodate the increase in T_s, counter size may have to be increased. However, it is not feasible to design the sensor with $\sim ms$ sampling period, since it will increase the TDC complexity and subsequently increase in switching power consumption. During application development, with the introduction of sleep cycle, sampling of sensor can be modified according to the application constraints.

4.2 Power Consumption of the Temperature Sensor

The power consumption of the temperature sensor with temperature at different T_S is investigated and shown in Fig. 8. It can be seen that power is nearly independent of T_S, except for the outliers at a relatively higher sampling frequency (100 MHz). The power consumption of the temperature sensor varies with temperature and is 353.8 μW at 27 °C. In the sensor systems, this power consumption can be effectively reduced by sleep cycle *i.e.* take 1 sample of tem-

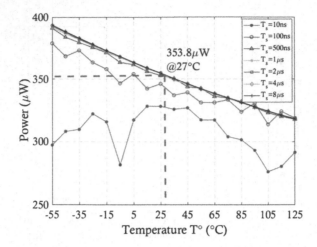

Fig. 8. Power consumption of the temperature sensor

perature sensor in ~8 μs and power-disable the sensor during sleep phase of the system. However, it should be noted that there are outliers in power consumption at $T_S = 10$ ns, since frequency of operation in this case is significantly high.

5   PTAT Based Current Reference Circuit

Till this point, we have assumed that the TDC has a time input that is independent of the temperature and is supplied from an external source. For an internally generated signal, a PTAT based current controlled clock generator is designed [9,10]. In such a case, the variation in time trigger signals (Start and Stop) is required to be minimal with temperature to restrict error well below the resolution of the TDC.

The PTAT current reference circuit, shown in Fig. 9, provides a temperature independent time input trigger (Start and Stop) to the temperature sensor. The variation of the current output is proportional to the absolute temperature and the threshold voltage of MOS transistor is complementary to the absolute temperature in the current source. Therefore, a PTAT current reference [10] is designed to counter the effect of temperature.

The current output of the PTAT (I_{PTAT}) is used to drive the trigger generation block (highlighted in Fig. 9) and is proportional to the absolute temperature (Fig. 10). Therefore, it can be used to generate the temperature independent time triggers (≥ 8 μs). As stated earlier in Sect. 4.1, temperature resolution at 8 μs is better and is observed to be as (<0.01 °C) compared to other sampling rates. The output of the circuit at every 10 °C is observed, shown in Fig. 11. These data points have a drift of 12.21 ppm/°C. Therefore, this time trigger is approximated as ~8.183 μs with an RMS error of ~5.01 ns. The temperature sensor with PTAT current reference considers ~8.183 μs as a fixed time trigger to the TDC for temperature sensing.

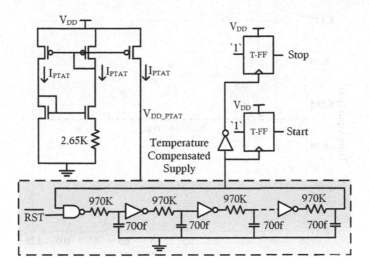

Fig. 9. PTAT current reference circuit

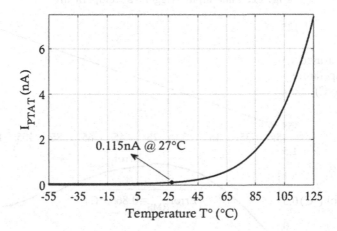

Fig. 10. I_{PTAT} vs. temperature

Further, this time trigger is provided to the TDC and the analytical model proposed in Sect. 3.2 is used to estimate the temperature for various digital counts obtained. The error at various temperature observed in temperature sensing is shown in Fig. 12, and the maximum error is found to be $-0.4\,°\mathrm{C} \sim 1.24\,°\mathrm{C}$ (RMS error $= 0.8663\,°\mathrm{C}$), which is comparable with similar research discussed in [1,4,8,11], where on-chip PTAT based circuit have been used to implement temperature sensor. Also it is noted that the approximation of time-trigger for temperature variation (Fig. 11) leads to error in the measurement of temperature. Therefore, an improved design of PTAT circuit with lesser $ppm/°C$ will have additional advantage of accuracy, and is challenging. Power consumption

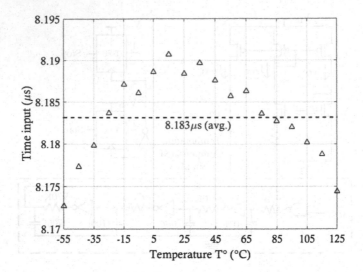

Fig. 11. Time-input trigger vs. temperature

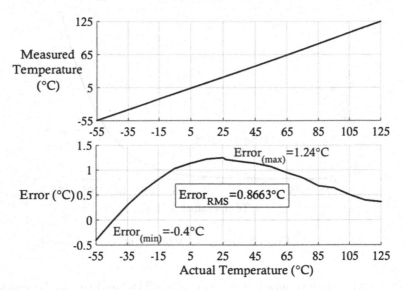

Fig. 12. Performance of the temperature sensor

of this PTAT current reference circuit for temperature independent time inputs is $46.92\,\mu$W at $27\,^{\circ}$C in addition to the power consumed by the TDC unit.

5.1   Future Scope of Work

We have designed a PTAT current reference circuit for temperature independent time inputs to the TDC, to replace the external time inputs ((a) in Fig. 13).

Table 5. Performance comparison of temperature sensors with existing works

Parameter	This work*	This work#	[1]	[3]	[4]	[8]	[11]
Technology	0.18 μm	0.18 μm	0.18 μm	FPGA	0.35 μm	65 nm	0.18 μm
Resolution	<0.01 °C	<0.01 °C	0.09 °C	0.133 °C	0.0918 °C	0.94 °C	0.3 °C
Sampling period	8 μs	8.183 μs	800 ms	22.72 ms	500 ms	2.13 μs	30 ms
Temperature range	$(-55 \sim 125)\,°C$	$(-55 \sim 125)\,°C$	$(-20 \sim 80)\,°C$	$(0 \sim 100)\,°C$	$(0 \sim 90)\,°C$	$(0 \sim 110)\,°C$	$(0 \sim 100)\,°C$
Error	0.1071 °C@	$(-0.4 \sim 1.24)\,°C/0.8663\,°C@$	±0.99 °C@	$(-0.7 \sim 1.6)\,°C$	$(-0.25 \sim 0.35)\,°C$	$(-1.4 \sim 1.5)\,°C$	$(-1.4 \sim 1.5)\,°C$
Fully integrated	No	Yes	No	No	No	Yes	Yes
Energy/conversion	2.83 nJ	3.28 nJ	656 nJ	–	18.1 μJ	1.1 nJ	2.2 nJ
FOM$ (nJ°C²)	0.283e − 3	0.328e − 3	5.3136	–	0.152	0.94	0.19

*With off-chip time input signal

#With on-chip time input signal; PTAT circuit

$ FOM (nJ°C²) = Energy/conversion × (Resolution)² [13]

@RMS Error

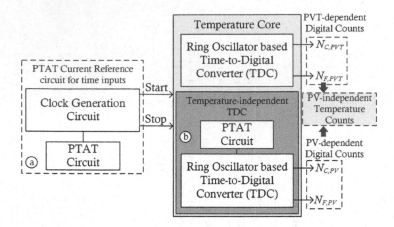

Fig. 13. Proposed architecture of the PV-independent temperature sensor

Further, it should be noted that the process variations may affect the performance of the sensor itself. To eliminate the variations, the ring oscillator within the TDC ⓑ should be designed in temperature-independent mode (see Fig. 13). Since, designing TDC circuit with minimal temperature variation is potentially challenging, it is not within the scope of this paper.

6   Conclusion

The temperature sensor using TDC has been designed and analysed in this work. An all-digital CMOS based TDC with 92.71 ps time resolution and time range upto 12.151 µs is presented. The 0.18 µm CMOS based TDC consumes 353.8 µW power at 1.8 V supply voltage at room temperature. The analytical model for on-chip temperature sensing is proposed, with changes in T_{CLK} with temperature. The model assumes a temperature independent time input signal. The temperature sensor achieves temperature resolution <0.01 °C at a sampling period of 8 µs. With the introduction of a PTAT current reference circuit (12.21 ppm/°C deviation with temperature), we restrict the error in measurement in temperature sensor within −0.4 °C ∼ 1.24 °C and RMS error of 0.8663 °C. The results of both the models (with external inputs and on-chip time inputs) of temperature sensors are compared with the existing research shown in Table 5. As can be seen, the proposed temperature sensor achieves a better Figure of Merit (FOM) [13] compared to existing works. The design presented in this work for on-chip temperature sensing can be extended to ambient temperature sensing, with calibration model considering thermal gradient of packaging, and is left as future work. The higher sampling frequency (∼125 KHz) of the design has additional advantages in temperature sensing systems with sleep phase, leading to the energy autonomous sensing applications.

References

1. Song, W., Lee, J., Cho, N., Burm, J.: An ultralow power time-domain temperature sensor with time-domain delta-sigma TDC. IEEE Trans. Circ. Syst. II Express Briefs **64**(10), 1117–1121 (2017)
2. Watanabe, T., Isomura, H.: All-digital ADC/TDC using TAD architecture for highly-durable time-measurement ASIC. In: 2014 IEEE International Symposium on Circuits and Systems (ISCAS), pp. 674–677. IEEE (2014)
3. Chen, P., Chen, S.C., Shen, Y.S., Peng, Y.J.: All-digital time-domain smart temperature sensor with an inter-batch inaccuracy of $-0.7°C \sim +0.6°C$ after one-point calibration. IEEE Trans. Circ. Syst.-I-Regul. Pap. **58**(5), 913 (2011)
4. Chen, P., Chen, C.C., Peng, Y.H., Wang, K.M., Wang, Y.S.: A time-domain SAR smart temperature sensor with curvature compensation and a 3σ inaccuracy of $-0.4°C \sim +0.6°C$ over a $0°C$ to $90°C$ range. IEEE J. Solid-State Circ. **45**(3), 600–609 (2010)
5. Savaliya, A., Mishra, B.: A 0.3 V, 12 nW, 47fJ/conv, fully digital capacitive sensor interface in 0.18 μm CMOS. In: 2015 International Conference on VLSI Systems, Architecture, Technology and Applications (VLSI-SATA), pp. 1–6. IEEE (2015)
6. Pokhara, A., Agrawal, J., Mishra, B.: Design of an all-digital, low power time-to-digital converter in 0.18 μm CMOS. In: 2017 7th International Symposium on Embedded Computing and System Design (ISED), pp. 1–5. IEEE (2017)
7. Mishra, B., Al-Hashimi, B.M., Zwolinski, M.: Variation resilient adaptive controller for subthreshold circuits. In: Proceedings of the Conference on Design, Automation and Test in Europe, pp. 142–147. European Design and Automation Association (2009)
8. Hwang, S., Koo, J., Kim, K., Lee, H., Kim, C.: A $0.008mm^2$ $500\mu W$ $469kS/s$ frequency-to-digital converter based CMOS temperature sensor with process variation compensation. IEEE Trans. Circ. Syst. I: Reg. Pap. **60**(9), 2241–2248 (2013)
9. Kamakshi, D.A., Shrivastava, A., Calhoun, B.H.: A $0.2V$, $23nW$ CMOS temperature sensor for ultra-low-power IoT applications. J. Low Power Electron. Appl. **6**(2), 10 (2016)
10. Oporta, H.I.: An ultra low power frequency reference for timekeeping applications. Ph.D. thesis, Oregon State University (2008)
11. Jeong, S., Foo, Z., Lee, Y., Sim, J.Y., Blaauw, D., Sylvester, D.: A fully-integrated $71nW$ CMOS temperature sensor for low power wireless sensor nodes. IEEE J. Solid-State Circ. **49**(8), 1682–1693 (2014)
12. Mishra, B., Al-Hashimi, B.M.: Subthreshold FIR filter architecture for ultra low power applications. In: Svensson, L., Monteiro, J. (eds.) PATMOS 2008. LNCS, vol. 5349, pp. 1–10. Springer, Heidelberg (2009). https://doi.org/10.1007/978-3-540-95948-9_1
13. Makinwa, K.A.A.: Smart Temperature Sensor Performance Survey. http://ei.ewi.tudelft.nl/docs/TSensor_survey.xls. Accessed 03 June 2019

Intelligent Traffic Light Controller: A Solution for Smart City Traffic Problem

Anam Sabir(✉), Anushree Jain, Yashwini Nathwani,
and Vaibhav Neema

Institute of Engineering and Technology, Devi Ahilya University,
Indore 452017, India
anamsabir1331@gmail.com, anushree.vandana@gmail.com,
yashwini.n@gmail.com, vaibhav.neema@gmail.com

Abstract. Traffic congestion has been causing many setbacks and challenges in the major developing and developed smart cities in India and all over the world. The typical traffic light sequence works on the specific switching of Red, Green and Yellow lights in a particular way with stipulated time irrespective of peak traffic hour and situation, this makes typical traffic light sequence method inefficient for present situation where density of traffic is exponentially increasing over the time. In this work, we propose and develop a design of Intelligent Traffic Light Control System to manage the road traffic according to the real time traffic situation. This work is intended to propose methods of dynamic time allocation for traffic lights according to traffic density and situation. In this paper, we acquired real time traffic density using image sensors and obstacle detector, where according to the traffic density, traffic controller dynamically generates "ON" and "OFF" time of traffic light sequence. The EDGE Spartan 6 FPGA (Field Programmable Gate Array) development board is programmed as controller to implement the proposed work and MATLAB programming in used to capture real time traffic image and generate dynamic time for the traffic light sequence to control the traffic situation in real time.

Keywords: Traffic light controller · Image sensor · FPGA controller

1 Introduction

India has the second largest road network in the world with over 3 million km of roads of which 60% are paved. These roads make a vital contribution to the India's economy. On the whole, the safety facilities for the road users are not up to the mark, leading to a high toll of the death victims. According to the Ministry of Road Transport and Highways, in 2018 around 1,46,133 people were killed and 5,00,279 were injured in road accidents in India [1]. This number is not only the highest that India has ever recorded in history, but it also represents a 53.9% increase over the last decade, and nearly a tenfold increase since 1970 [2]. The major cause of the increase in the rate of accident is due to increased vehicle density and developed infrastructure for smart cities. The type of accidents occurring on road traffic is majorly divided in two types: accidents at highways and inside the city. In city roads, accidents are majorly observed

© Springer Nature Singapore Pte Ltd. 2019
A. Sengupta et al. (Eds.): VDAT 2019, CCIS 1066, pp. 764–772, 2019.
https://doi.org/10.1007/978-981-32-9767-8_63

due to vehicles crossing without caring for the light. The main motive behind Red light jumping is saving time. The common conception is that stopping at red signal is wastage of time and fuel due to present static traffic signal controlling.

In this work, we propose the intelligent solution of present static traffic light problem, the use of technology defiantly improve quality of life and safety which is one major goal of future smart cities. Typical traffic light controllers are based on fixed-time method assigning each lane equal passing time regardless of current traffic density. Due to even passing time allocation for lanes having uneven vehicular queuing, people face many problems like loss of time, energy resources and money because of unnecessary waiting. One of the solutions to this problem is to sense real time traffic and hence calculate passing time for each lane. This can be achieved using sensor arrays, image processing, etc. [3, 4].

The rest of the paper is organized as follows: Sect. 2 presents the proposed design solution for the static traffic problem. Section 3 presents development of proposed solution using image sensors, FPGA board controller and MATLAB Programming, Sect. 4 shows the results, conclusion and future aspects for the propose work.

2 System Design

The block diagram of the proposed design is presented in Fig. 1.

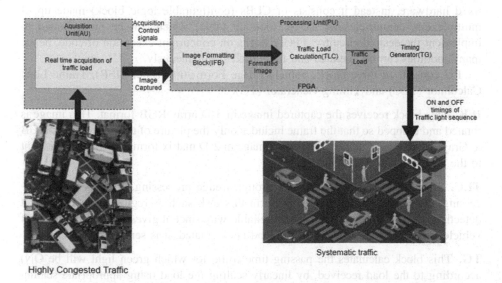

Fig. 1. Block diagram of the proposed design

To overcome the disadvantage of conventional static traffic light controller system currently deployed all over the country, the proposed solution i.e. Intelligent Traffic Light Controller is based on the idea of allocation of passing time to each lane depending on the instantaneous traffic at that lane. This method aims at removing the traffic congestion arising due to inefficient control.

The design consists of two main units namely Acquisition Unit (AU) and Processing Unit (PU). AU does real time acquisition of current traffic. There are various ways of acquiring real time data such as deploying sensors, camera, etc. The proposed model works on camera interface due to obvious advantages of image processing. PU processes the captured image to calculate traffic load. Further linear scaling of traffic load is done to generate passing time accordingly.

2.1   Acquisition Unit (AU)

The task of AU is to acquire real time image using camera. The camera is deployed such that it captures the top view of the intersection. It is configured such that it captures image only when it receives appropriate control signal from the Processing Unit. Once the image is captured, it is transmitted to the Processing Unit in a 3-D matrix RGB format.

2.2   Processing Unit (PU)

All the functions of PU are carried out by the FPGA Controller. FPGA is chosen as the central processor of the system as it has many advantages over microcontroller such as availability of large number of I/O ports and faster operation; also, it doesn't have any fixed hardware, instead it consists of CLBs (configurable logic block) made up of multiplexers, demultiplexers, LUTs (look up table) which can be programmed to implement the desired circuitry. FPGA works on concurrent execution of code, hence many modules can be operated and monitored simultaneously.

PU consists of three blocks namely Image Formatting Block (IFB), Traffic Load Calculator (TLC) and Timing Generator (TG).

IFB. This block receives the captured image in 3-D array RGB format. This image is rotated and cropped so that the frame includes only the picture of the desired lane. RGB to Gray conversion is done to obtain the image in 2-D matrix format. This matrix is sent to the TLC for further processing.

TLC. This block calculates the load through image processing. Various image processing algorithms can be used to perform this task such as region detection, object detection, etc. Object detection is more reliable way since it gives the exact number of vehicles waiting in the lane. Once the load is calculated, it is sent to TG block.

TG. This block calculates the passing time (time for which green light will be ON) according to the load received, by linearly scaling the load using appropriate scaling factor. Finally, the traffic lights are operated according to the timing generated.

As a result of this design, the congested traffic intersection is now systematic and efficient. Also, the probability of occurrence of traffic congestion reduces drastically.

3 Prototype Design and Overview

We designed two prototypes of ITLC to test the core idea and operate the system in a realistic setting. The first prototype is a sensor-based model and the other is based on Image Processing. Both the prototypes consist of Acquisition Unit (AU) and Processing Unit (PU). The only manner in which they differ is traffic sensing method.

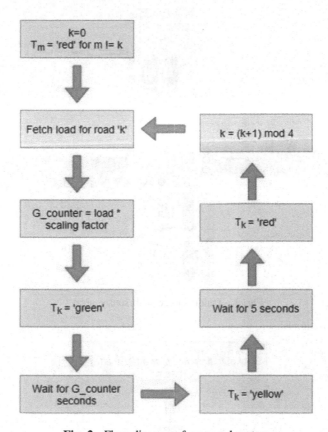

Fig. 2. Flow diagram of proposed system

Figure 2 shows the flow of control among four traffic lights of an intersection. Four traffic lights T0, T1, T2 and T3 for four lanes of an intersection is considered as shown in the flow chart. We have assumed that the execution starts from traffic light T0. The green signal for T0 is ON, while all other traffic lights are red. T0's green light remains ON based on the timing generated with the help of the load calculated, followed by yellow for 5 s. Then T0 turns red, and T1 turns green and so on. This continues in circular fashion as T0–T1–T2–T3–T0. This is followed by both the prototypes.

3.1 Obstacle Detector Based Traffic Controller

In this design, obstacle detector sensors are deployed along the lane to find out the current traffic density on the lane shown in Fig. 3. Edge Spartan 6 Development Board is used as the central controller. It provides 50 MHz clock that is generated by the on-board crystal oscillator. It requires 5 V DC for operation while FPGA works on 3.3 V.

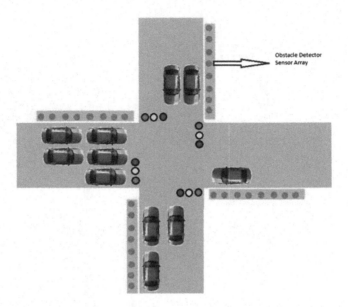

Fig. 3. Traffic square with sensor array

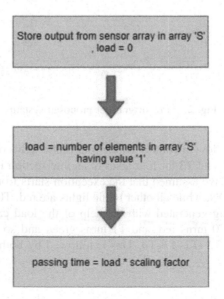

Fig. 4. Timing generation through object detector

The number of sensors blocked by cars is directly proportional to the traffic density; this gives the traffic load on the lane. This load is appropriately scaled to generate the passing time (the time for which Green light will be ON for this lane) shown in Fig. 4.

3.2   Image Processing Based Controller

Image processing is a method to convert an image into digital form and perform some operations on it, in order to get an enhanced image or to extract some useful information from it. It is a type of signal dispensation in which input is image, like video frame or photograph and output may be image or characteristics associated with that image [5]. The hardware setup for proposed work is presented in Fig. 5.

Fig. 5. Hardware setup of prototype-1

In context of this project, input is an image of the lane for which we want to find out density of traffic and output is the passing time duration calculated on basis of traffic load. Density of traffic can be estimated by observing and analyzing pixels of image of road to find out how much region of road is covered by vehicles. There are some popular algorithms for detection of common objects like cars in an image. In this project, instead of deploying any such algorithm, we designed our own algorithm which works with the assumption that vehicles waiting in a queue in a lane of an intersection divide the lane into two regions: one region without any vehicles and the other mostly covered with vehicles is shown in Fig. 6.

The analysis of differences between strips of pixels starts from empty region (opposite side of intersection). In this region, differences between pixels will be much less than the differences between pixels near separation of two regions. Therefore, whenever difference between strips under consideration is large, separation is reached. Once we get the separation point, we can calculate fraction of lane filled by vehicles which can be taken as density of traffic.

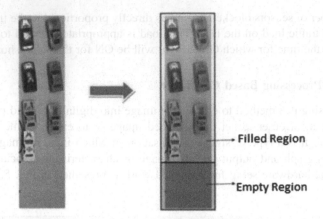

Fig. 6. Region distinction in a traffic lane

Finally, product of traffic load and maximum allowed passing time gives appropriate passing time for that lane.

3.3 MATLAB GUI

A GUI demonstrating the above approach was developed using GUIDE (graphical user interface development environment) feature of MATLAB [6]. Using GUIDE, front end of the GUI was designed followed by back end programming which included following steps:

- Acquisition of image using webcam connected to system.
- Processing the image so that it is appropriate for applying algorithm to find density of traffic: rotation, cropping and conversion to gray scale.
- Applying the algorithm to find duration for passing of vehicles.

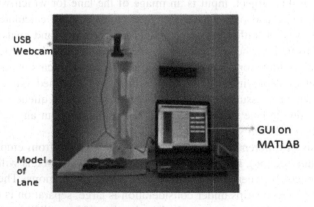

Fig. 7. MATLAB based GUI for image processing

MATLAB support package for USB webcam was installed to interface GUI and webcam. Logitech's C110 webcam. Figure 8 shows the flow diagram for the image processing algorithm and Fig. 7 shows the MATLAB based GUI for image processing.

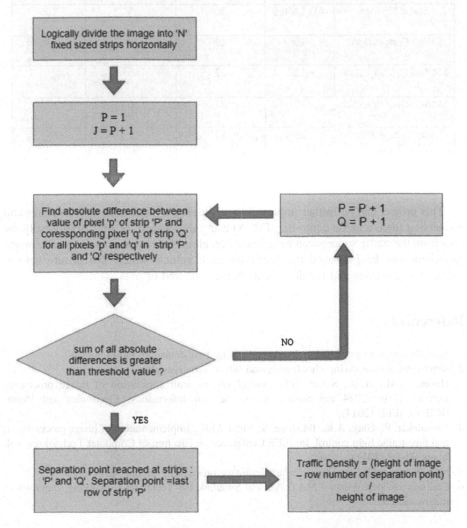

Fig. 8. Flow diagram for image processing algorithm.

4 Result, Conclusion and Future Work

As it can be observed from the obtained results shown in the Table 1 that system becomes efficient on using dynamic traffic control system. The image processing makes the implementation even more reliable reducing the hardware and maintenance up to a large extent and increasing the life of the system.

Table 1. Output results obtained for the design.

Traffic Density	Lane	Green (secs)	Yellow (secs)	Red (secs)
Static Timings	ALL LANES	30	5	105
High Congestion	L0	42	5	-
Moderate Congestion	L1	27	5	-
Moderate Congestion	L2	22	5	-
Low Congestion	L3	13	2	-

This project can be further improved by deploying a number of traffic squares and connecting them and the controller (FPGA) using the concept of IoT. Additionally the data from the traffic squares can be uploaded on cloud for required analysis. The image processing can be improved by identifying each vehicle which will in turn help in checking if the rules and regulations are being followed or not.

References

1. https://www.india.gov.in/official-website-ministry-road-transport-and-highways
2. http://www.indiandrivingschools.com/road-safety-initiatives.php
3. Hasan, M.M., et al.: Smart traffic control system with application of image processing techniques. In: 2014 International Conference on Informatics, Electronics and Vision (ICIEV). IEEE (2014)
4. Choudekar, P., Garg, A.K., Banerjee, S., Muju, M.K.: Implementation of image processing in real time traffic light control. In: IEEE Conference on Electronics Computer Technology, vol. 2, pp. 94–98 (2011)
5. https://www.engineersgarage.com/articles/image-processing-tutorial-applications
6. Courtesy of MathWorks - MATLAB and Simulink for Technical Computing. http://www.mathworks.com

Author Index